Modeling and Tools for Network Simulation

Klaus Wehrle
Mesut Güneş
James Gross

Editors

Modeling and Tools for Network Simulation

Springer

Volume Editors

Klaus Wehrle
RWTH Aachen University
Aachen, Germany
E-mail: klaus.wehrle@rwth-aachen.de

Mesut Güneş
FU Berlin
Institut für Informatik
Berlin, Germany
E-mail: guenes@inf.fu-berlin.de

James Gross
RWTH Aachen University
Aachen, Germany
E-mail: gross@umic.rwth-aachen.de

ISBN 978-3-662-50624-0   ISBN 978-3-642-12331-3 (eBook)
DOI 10.1007/978-3-642-12331-3
Springer Heidelberg Dordrecht London New York

ACM Computing Classification (1998): I.6, C.2, C.2.5, D.2.8, C.2.1, I.6.8, C.4, G.1.6

Typesetting: Camera-ready by author, data conversion by Scientific Publishing Services, Chennai, India

Printed on acid-free paper   219/3180

Springer is part of Springer Science+Business Media (www.springer.com)

In Favour of Network Simulation

A lot of research in computer science and electrical engineering is being carried out in the field of distributed systems and computer networks. Topics being addressed include the development of new and improved protocols, applications, architectures, security and quality-of-service techniques, just to name a few. A crucial step during the design and engineering of communication systems, respectively protocols, algorithms and architectures, is the estimation of their performance, and the understanding and visualization of the micro and macro behavior of the systems and their components. Typically, this can be (more or less) realized by applying three different methodologies: (1) experiments with real systems and prototypes, (2) mathematical analysis, and (3) simulation.

In research and development of communication systems the latter two methodologies are most important during the conceptual phase, since prototyping such systems is mostly infeasible due to financial and technical constraints. Simulation is particularly used for systems which are highly dynamic and whose properties are difficult to capture in a mathematical way. Often, analytical methods show the borderline behavior of system characteristics or offer upper and lower bounds for specific research questions. However, more fine grained analysis often leads to an unacceptable complexity of the analytical models. In contrast, simulation offers scientists and researchers a controlled environment in which a system can be investigated in more detail. Different parameter sets and scenarios can be analyzed with comparably little effort. Thus, simulation is a powerful and versatile methodology to analyze and visualize the behavior and performance of communication systems and networks.

Considering simulation as the methodology to analyze a communication system (which may not even exist), one has to consider a very important fact: All simulations are carried out on models of the system under investigation and not on the system itself. All models have to be created in advance. Since analyzing a system without prior modeling is not possible, and as all inferred knowledge is deducted from the model itself, the process of modeling is crucial for the overall process of simulation-based evaluation. Considering the importance of the modeling process for the quality of the observed results, it is very surprising and disappointing, which techniques are known and applied to guarantee high-quality simulation models. Typically, next to some very generic guidelines – like the following – there exist no further rules, methods, techniques or just a simple cookbook to create and assure adequate simulation models:

"All actions, events and properties have to be modeled as accurately and with as much detail as possible." But on the other hand: *"... only as accurately and with as much detail as actually needed and required."* Another important aspect of simulation-based evaluation is the comparison of approaches, such as protocols and algorithms. Up to now, this has rarely been possible in the

area of communication systems, since most models are highly specialized for the respective investigation. Often, models are made for a distinct context of investigation, and hence, they are neither compatible nor comparable to other competing models or approaches. This means that a reasonable comparison between research carried out by different parties is practically impossible.

In our opinion, these problems are fundamental facts about network simulations. While it appears as if an unified modeling methodology is missing, there is no such method that suites all considered systems in networking research. In contrast, especially over the last few years, the networking community has developed a set of "best-practice" approaches for different problems at different layers. In addition, a large set of tools have evolved that support the modeling, the programming and the execution of simulation code for the evaluation of networks at all layers. However, common text books do not address these topics, and furthermore, typical simulation courses only focus on the fundamentals of simulation, but not on best practice or on tools for network simulations. This was the motivation for this book.

This book is the result of a workshop to which PhD students from all over Germany were invited to present and discuss their experiences. The intended audience of this book are graduate students, PhD students, researchers, and professionals with interest in computer networks, wireless networks, and performance evaluation of networks by means of simulation. The book is organized in three parts. Part I contains material about tools and methods for network simulations. In this part two famous and widely used network simulators and two special simulators are described. Furthermore, the usage of parallel simulation, the simulation of hardware aspects considering the simulation of networks, and the integration of simulators with real systems are addressed. The focus of Part II is on models for simulation of the lower layers of the network protocol stack, particularly the lower layers of wireless networks. The topics covered span the modeling of the physical layer, link layers, communication channels, mobility, and handover. Part III contains models for the simulation of higher layers of the protocol stack. Most of the models discussed in this part can be used for wired networks as well as for wireless networks.

Finally, this book would not have been finalized without the help and support of many people. Primarily, we thank all authors for their valuable contributions. Furthermore, we are grateful for the support of:

- Research Cluster UMIC (Ultra High-Speed Mobile Information and Communication) and RWTH Aachen University
- DFG Research Training Group GK 643: "Software for Mobile Communication Systems"

- Chair of Communication Networks (ComNets, Prof. Dr.-Ing. Bernhard Walke), RWTH Aachen University
- Gesellschaft für Informatik

More information on the book and slides on selected topics of the book can be found on this website: `www.network-simulation.info`.

February 2010

Klaus Wehrle
Mesut Güneş
James Gross

Address by the UMIC Cluster

Simulation is an inevitable methodology for specification, design and analysis of computer and communication networks. It is extensively used at all levels ranging from hardware to network. However, to obtain valid results that properly predict the behavior of a real system, all relevant effects must be captured in the simulation model. This task has become very challenging today, since one can rarely model and simulate the different levels in isolation. Rather, advanced system optimization causes dependencies in the behavior across all layers. Further, systems have become extremely complex and so have the simulation models. To get relevant statistical results and to cover critical corner cases the simulated time (i.e., the time elapsed in the simulated system) has to be sufficiently long. To avoid excessive simulation time even on high-performance computers, modeling not only has to be proper but also efficient.

Abstraction of lower layer effects in higher layer simulation models always has been a formidable task. Because of the increasing cross layer optimization, however, this task has become significantly more challenging. Finding the right way of combining the simulation models of different layers is a key issue. While plain co-simulation of layers yields the highest precision, it usually results in low simulation speed. Abstraction of effects in other layers and efficient modeling are a key to higher simulation speed but require a lot of care to capture all relevant behavior.

Therefore, it has become essential for engineers and computer scientists to understand the modeling and simulation concepts applied to different layers of a network. As this book addresses both modeling and simulation techniques at all levels, it is extremely useful and very timely. It should become a handbook for all engineers involved in computer and communication system simulation.

Finally, a short word of advice: To understand the behavior of a particular system it is not sufficient to perform a huge amount of simulations. Simulations must be set up to address the right questions and the results must be analyzed thoroughly and be interpreted properly. Simulation does not replace the use of the brain. But when used right, it is an extremely powerful tool.

February 2010

Gerd Ascheid
Coordinator of the UMIC Research Center
RWTH Aachen University
www.umic.rwth-aachen.de

Table of Contents

1. Introduction

James Gross (RWTH Aachen University)
Mesut Güneş (Freie Universität Berlin)

In general there are three different techniques for performance evaluation of systems and networks: mathematical analysis, measurements, and computer simulation. All these techniques have their strength and weaknesses. In the literature there are plenty of discussions about *when* to use which technique, *how* to apply it, and which pitfalls are related to which evaluation technique.

One major question in performance evaluation is whether to use the actual *system* or a *model*. As measurements require an implementation of the system to be available, often either analysis or computer simulation must be applied due to cost and effort reasons. Both evaluation techniques are based on a model which represents the system with respect to the goal of the study as accurate as possible. As mathematical analysis can often only provide a limited insight for system design (as detailed mathematical models often get intractable), in fact computer simulation is very often applied either for comparing different design alternatives or for optimizing a certain design.

In a computer simulation a real-world process or system is "imitated" over time [48, 277]. Computer simulations are actually applied in many different fields and there are several different types of computer simulations, like discrete-event simulation, continuous simulation, Monte Carlo simulation, spreadsheet simulation, trace-driven simulation etc. In the field of computer networks the dominant simulation technique is *discrete-event simulation*. The key property of discrete-event simulations is that the state of the simulation model can only change at discrete points in time which are referred to as *events* [48].

To date, discrete-event simulation is used to do research on all layers of computer networks, including signal processing issues in the physical layer, medium access in the link layer, routing in the network layer, protocol issues in the transport layer, and finally design questions of the application layer. The reason behind the success of discrete-event based simulation in computer networking is on the one hand that the simulation paradigm fits very well to the considered systems while on the other hand discrete-event based simulation is easily applied. Hence, discrete-event simulation provides a simple and flexible way to evaluate their approaches and study their behavior under different conditions. A further important aspect of computer simulations is repeatability, i.e. different designs can be evaluated under exactly the same (random) environment parameters.

In the remainder of this chapter we provide a brief introduction to discrete-event simulation in Section 1.1 and a discussion about modeling for network simulations in Section 1.2. Readers familiar with the principle of discrete-event simulations and with the modeling process can thus skip this chapter.

1.1 Discrete-event Simulation

In this section we give a brief introduction into discrete-event simulation. For this, we introduce the basic terminology used in literature and describe their relationship. Furthermore, we present the core algorithm for a discrete-event simulator, i.e., the time-advance event-scheduling algorithm. For an in-depth introduction the reader is referred to [48, 277].

1.1.1 Terminology and Components of Discrete-event Simulation

In this section we introduce some terminology and components that are common to all discrete-event simulation systems. Unfortunately, there is no standardized set of terms and the naming may vary in literature. We loosely adapt the definitions in [48, 277].

An *entity* is an abstraction of a particular subject of interest. An entity is described by its attributes, e.g., an entity packet could have attributes length, source address, and destination address. The term *object* is often used as synonymous.

A *system* is defined by a set of entities and their relationship. The set of entities and their relationships fulfill a certain purpose, i.e., the system has a certain goal that it tries to achieve. For example, a network may be defined by the entities hosts, routers, and links while its goal is to provide end-to-end connectivity.

A *discrete system* is a system whose state, defined by the state of all entities of the system, changes only at discrete points in time. The change of the state is triggered by the occurrence of an *event*. What an event exactly is, depends mainly on the system and on the goal of the study, examples are the sending of a packet, reception of a packet, or the selection of a hyperlink on a web page.

Usually, the system of interest is quite complex. In order to evaluate its performance by means of computer simulation a *model* is built. The model is an abstraction of the system, hence it consists of selected entities of the system of interest and selected relationships between the entities. By definition, the model is a system itself, however, in the following we will refer to the abstracted system as the model for clarity. In computer simulations it is always the model that is considered, mainly to reduce the involved complexity and the associated cost and effort.

1.1.2   The Principle of Discrete-event Simulation

The idea of a discrete-event simulator is to jump from one event to the next, whereby the occurrence of an event may trigger changes in the system state as well as the generation of new, so called event notices in future. The events are recorded as *event notices* in the *future event list* (FEL), which is an appropriate data structure to manage all the events in the discrete-event simulation. An event notice is composed at least out of two data *(time, type)* where *time* specifies the time when the event will occur and *type* gives the kind of the event. The future event list should implement efficient functions to insert, to find, and to remove event notices, which are placed in the future event list. Figure 1.1 shows the evolution of a discrete-event simulation over time. Events occur at time t_i and may change the system state. With every discrete event time t_i a snapshot of the system is created in the computer memory that contains all required data to progress the simulation. In general

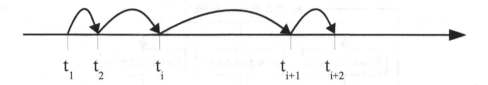

$$t_1 \quad t_2 \qquad t_i \qquad\qquad t_{i+1} \quad t_{i+2}$$

Fig. 1.1: Principle of discrete-event simulation. During the simulation the system state changes only at discrete points t_i in time.

all discrete-event simulators share the following components:

- System state: A set of variables that describe the state of the system.
- Clock: The clock gives the current time during the simulation.
- Future event list: A data structure appropriate to manage the events.
- Statistical counters: A set of variables that contain statistical information about the performance of the system.
- Initialization routine: A routine that initializes the simulation model and sets the clock to 0.
- Timing routine: A routine that retrieves the next event from the future event list and advances the clock to the occurrence time of the event.
- Event routine: A routine that is called when a particular event occurs during the simulation. Usually, for each event type an event routine is defined. In literature the term *handler* is often used synonymously.

1.1.3   The Event-scheduling Time-advance Algorithm

In this section we describe the core algorithm of a discrete-event simulator. During the simulation the system state evolves over time, thus there is a clock which gives the current time during the simulation. The future event list contains all event notifications which are ordered according their occurrence time, i.e., $fel = [t_1, t_2, \ldots, t_k]$ where $t_1 \leq t_2 \leq \ldots \leq t_k$. In this case t_1 is the next point in time where an event occurs.

The flow diagram of the event-scheduling time-advance algorithm is depicted in Figure 1.2. It consists of three parts: initialization, event processing loop, and output.

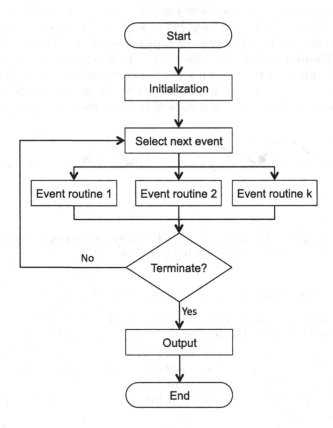

Fig. 1.2: Flow diagram of the core of a discrete-event simulator, i.e., the event-scheduling time-advance algorithm

In the initialization part the clock, entities, and state variables are initialized. Subsequently, the simulator enters the second part. In a loop the events are processed. For this, the next event is retrieved from the future event list and depending on its type a particular event routine (the handler) is called. The event routine may change the state variables, entities, update statistics, and generate new event notices. When the termination condition of the loop is valid the simulation enters the last part. In the output part statistics are finally computed and if necessary written into files.

1.1.4 Starting and Stopping of Simulations

In the previous section we did not describe how a simulation *starts* and *terminates*. The termination condition for the event processing loop is particularly important.

Since the future event list is empty at the beginning of the simulation it is required that somehow the simulation is impinged. Typically, this is done in the initialization part of the simulation. Here initial event notices are generated and put into the future event list, e.g., the first packet in a network.

The termination of a simulation is typically based on:

− Special termination event, e.g., until a packet delay larger than 500 ms, 1000 bytes are transmitted, or 50 dropped packets.
− Specified simulation time, e.g., simulation for 1000 sec.
− Until the future event list gets empty.

In the first and last case the simulation run time is not known a-priori and may vary from a simulation run to other.

1.1.5 Types of Simulation Runs

Simulation runs can be classified into *transient* and *steady state* simulations. The selection of a simulation type is particularly important for the output analysis of simulations. A transient simulation is also referred as *terminating* simulation, because in this case the simulation runs for a defined simulation time. The simulation run time may be given by a special termination event or a specific time.

A *steady state* simulation is also referred as *non-terminating* simulation. The goal in this kind of simulation is to study the long-term behavior of the system. Thus, the simulation run time in this case has to be set so that initial conditions do not have influence on the simulation results anymore. A critical issue is to figure out suitable simulation run times.

1.2 Modeling for Computer Simulation

As mentioned previously, the model of the system under study is an *abstraction*, meaning that it only represents selected features and characteristics while usually not considering a much larger set of features and characteristics of the system. Hence, the obtained model is a reduced representation of the considered system based on simplifications and assumptions. *Modeling* is the process of identifying and abstracting the relevant entities and relationships from the system under study. From the fact that any model is an abstraction two important questions arise for any researcher or engineer dealing with performance evaluation:

1. What is a good model?
2. How do I obtain a good model?

If computer simulation is chosen as evaluation method, two further issues need to be taken care of. (i) Once a performance model is built, it has to be implemented in software. Hence, the implementation needs to represent the performance model as good as possible. (ii) Therefore, an appropriate tool needs to be chosen that suites the evaluation process well.

All together, these are the four cornerstones of modeling for computer simulations. This section addresses all of them. Unfortunately, the issues are quite complex and usually require some experience with modeling and simulation. Still, there are many issues for which recipes are available that lead to better models and implementations in general.

1.2.1 Good Performance Models and Good Simulation Models

A basic fact about performance models is that "Essentially, all models are wrong, but some are useful" [75]. Having this in mind, a good performance model (either for analysis or for simulation) has the following characteristics:

– **Simplicity**: Good performance models are as simple as possible. This does not mean that a performance model should not be detailed or should not try to take complex relationships into account. However, a good performance model only spends complexity when it serves the purpose of the evaluation (also referred to as goal of the study). This is an important point as simulation models are often criticized for their lack of accuracy in comparison to reality. However, this is exactly the nature of computer simulations. If it is to be avoided, there is no alternative to building the system of interest. This also has some consequences for the reusability of performance models. As evaluation studies usually have different goals (especially if they are going to be published in the scientific community), the used performance models are likely to differ. To some extent this explains the vast number of open-source simulation models for networks and the absence of dominant or standard simulation models for wide-spread networking systems. There is no simulation model that serves all purposes. Any simulation model that is available has been designed with a specific evaluation goal in mind. If one wants to reuse such a simulation model, one should better first check the original evaluation purpose that the model served.

– **Credibility**: A very important feature of performance models is their credibility. Essentially, a performance model is credible if it is validated and design decisions can be based on it. Alternatively to making decisions, there are models which are common ground in research and engineering communities. For example, there exist IEEE 802.11 simulation models which are accepted within the IEEE regarding the standardization efforts going on in the various task groups. However, by far not every IEEE 802.11 simulation model is accepted. Establishing credibility of new performance models requires at least their validation (see Section 1.2.3).

– **Documentation**: A good performance model is the result of a thorough modeling process. At the beginning of this modeling process the purpose of the evaluation study needs to be defined (among other issues, see Section 1.2.3). Next, the assumptions and simplifications of a model need to be documented as well as its evolution (which changes have been made due to which reasons etc.). From the documentation it should also be clear what is not considered in the model, hence, for which purposes the model is not useful.

Modeling for computer simulation is more specific as the built performance model has to be implemented in software. This might lead to additional modeling assumptions and is a significant source of error. While in common practice there is often no difference between the performance model and its implementation (in fact, modeling is interpreted by some as programming the model), it is useful to differentiate between these throughout the evaluation process. In addition to the characteristics of a good performance model, a good simulation model should have the following ones:

– **Efficiency**: With respect to the performance model, it should be implemented efficiently. Therefore, run times of the simulation model are moderate (in relationship to the model complexity) and allow a thorough investigation campaign.

– **Verified**: The implemented simulation model should be verified, i.e. the match between the performance model and the simulation model must have been checked by various methods. Note that this step is different from validating a performance or simulation model (see Section 1.2.3).

– **Code Quality**: Depending on the used simulation tool, the implementation should maintain a certain coding style and should make use of object-orientation in combination with a sufficient documentation.

– **Availability**: The simulation model should be accessible such that other groups can verify and validate the model themselves.

As stated above, a performance model is not required to be as detailed as possible. In fact, finding the right level of accuracy for a performance model is quite difficult. A common mistake in modeling is to put too much detail into a model due to a lack either of experience in performance evaluation or of background knowledge about the system under study. However, too much modeling depth makes a model more complex and introduces more parameters on which performance depends on. This slows down the entire evaluation project and increases the potential sources of an error (either in the modeling or in the implementation). Finally, a good performance model does not have to be universal nor generally reusable.

1.2.2   Good Modeling Practice for Computer Simulation

One of the most difficult steps in computer simulations is to build a good model. In fact, there is no general recipe for coming up with a good model. The major problem here is that experience in modeling and a deep knowledge of the system under study is required to come up with a good model. Bot requirements take time to build up, however, even if both requirements are fulfilled the resulting model can still be of low quality.

Hence, as computer simulation is always embedded in a *performance evaluation* study, good modeling practice for simulations also depends on good evaluation practice. This is the best way to ensure that performance and simulation models are inline with the overall goals of the performance evaluation and have a good quality. A thorough performance evaluation study based on simulations contains the following steps [235, 277]:

1. **Problem Formulation and Definition of the System/Model**: Fundamental to any performance evaluation is the definition of the goals of the study. Typically, an evaluation is either performed to compare several system designs or to optimize parameters of a specific design. Goals of an evaluation always need to be unbiased, i.e., the outcome of the evaluation must be unknown (also with respect to related work) and there must not be a *preferred* outcome of the evaluation study. Once the goals of the study have been specified, the system/model boundaries must be defined.

2. **Choice of Metrics, Factors, and Levels**: The second step in an evaluation study is the choice of metrics, factors and levels. The choice of these three issues basically defines the way the evaluation is conducted and has a significant impact on the performance model. Factors are parameters of a system or of a model that are varied during the evaluation study. Their numerical values that are considered during the evaluation are called levels.

3. **Data Collection and Modeling**: Before a performance model can be built, knowledge about the system under study has to be obtained. Apart

from gaining insight of the system under study, during this phase also input-output relationships should be identified by which the performance model can be validated later on. In other words, data characterizing the performance of the system under study has to be collected. Once the system and its operational procedure have been studied, the modeling process can be started. It is preceded by creating a document on the assumptions about the system and its operation that the model is based on. Then the performance modeling is conducted. Based on the definition of the model boundaries, the single elements of the system are described in detail as well as defining their quantitative and qualitative interactions. Usually, this is an iterative process which starts with rather simple elements and interactions. Later on, the model is refined as needed. During this process it is very important to track the level of detail that is put into the model. Is it really required with respect to the goal of the study? Does it make a difference for the considered performance results? Finally, the obtained performance model should be documented.

4. **Choice of Simulation Environment, Model Implementation, and Verification**: Once the performance model is completed, it has to be implemented for computer simulations. This requires first a decision about the simulation framework to be used. In the networking context, there are several open-source simulation tools which provide specific model libraries for different layers of the protocol stack. Availability of certain libraries for example for traffic or for lower layer protocols can be factors that determine the choice. Other factors are the programming language that the simulation tool is based on, its debugging features, its built-in functions for statistical analysis, its graphical user interface as well as its performance. Based on this decision, the performance model is to be implemented. Different simulation tools offer different support for modular and structured implementation of performance models. This should be considered during the decision phase for a simulation environment as well. Finally, the implemented performance model should be verified. *Verification* ensures that the simulation model is implemented right, i.e., it is a correct representation of the performance model. Different methods for verification exist, a thorough discussion is presented in [277].

5. **Validation and Sensitivity Analysis**: The next step in the evaluation requires the validation of the performance model. *Validation* ensures that the performance model is a correct representation of the system with respect to the chosen metrics, factors and levels. Validation can be performed by comparing the output of the performance model with the output of the real system. However, usually the real system is not available. In those cases, a validation can be done by considering performance results obtained by mathematical analysis based on the same performance model. Alternatively, often there are already published performance results either obtained by analysis or by simulations which can be used

for validation. After the model has been validated, a sensitivity analysis can be performed in order to determine the factors that have a strong impact on performance. Those factors are the ones to spend more detail on during a further iteration step (if this is of interest).

6. **Experimentation, Analysis and Presentation**: Based on a verified and validated simulation model, the performance evaluation can be conducted. Hence, the production runs of the simulation are started, the data is collected, analyzed and finally graphically represented.

Obviously, the entire evaluation method is an iterative process due to mistakes in the single steps but also due to unexpected behavior of the model or problems with the complexity. Still, following these guidelines supports the development of good simulation models. The simplicity of the model is supported on the one hand by the strict orientation of the performance model according to the goal of the study. This is a key paradigm: It is the model that depends on the goal of the study (not vice versa). On the other hand, modeling should be done iteratively. Each iteration step should contain a verification and validation. Then a sensitivity analysis is performed which indicates candidate factors for adding more accuracy. If further elements are added instead, the next sensitivity analysis quantifies the impact of the additional elements on the performance model. Thereby, model complexity is spent where it pays off in terms of the evaluation study. Next, the credibility of the model is supported by the methodology as simulation models should be verified and validated. Ideally, validation can be done based on external data or on a different evaluation technique (like analysis or experimentation). This increases the credibility of the model. Finally, the methodology also ensures a sufficient documentation. Contrarily, the methodology supports neither the efficiency nor the code quality of the simulation model explicitly. Here, the experience of the programmer has to ensure these two points.

1.2.3 Common Modeling Practice

The biggest difference between the above mentioned methodology and common practice is that the implemented simulation model *is* the performance model, i.e. performance evaluation studies do not come up with a performance model from which an implementation is built. In the consequence, there is no need for verification as the simulation model only needs to be validated (which in this case also verifies it). While this common practice can save time, it makes the validation process more difficult as a mismatch between the true system behavior and the model behavior can be either due to a bug or due to a modeling mistake. Nevertheless, the complexity of the used simulation models today has lead to skipping the explicit development of a performance model.

A further difference of the above mentioned methodology and common practice is that it is often difficult to validate a simulation model at all. Often, computer simulation is applied at a stage when the future system design is open and there is no data available from real systems to validate the simulation models. In this case, one can try to obtain results from mathematical analysis, however, for many cases this does not lead to a sufficient level of validity at a reasonable effort. These difficulties of validating simulation models is one of the most important reasons why simulation results are less trustworthy than results achieved either by analysis or (of course) by measurements.

Finally, in many cases today computational power is a minor concern for an evaluation by simulations. Hence, simulation models are often reused. While this can save again much time and effort, it is clear that it can lead to severe problems during the validation process. Unless the reused simulation models are checked and understood carefully, there is always the danger that the reused simulation model is based on insufficient assumptions and functional relationships. As simulation models are usually not accompanied by a performance model, the programmer has to "read" the source code to understand the exact scope of the simulation model to be reused. This can be a demanding task and adds to the potential source of errors during the evaluation process.

Part I

Tools and Methods for Network Simulation

2. The *ns-3* Network Simulator

George F. Riley (Georgia Tech)
Thomas R. Henderson (University of Washington, and Boeing Research & Technology)

2.1 Introduction

As networks of computing devices grow larger and more complex, the need for highly accurate and scalable network simulation technologies becomes critical. Despite the emergence of large-scale testbeds for network research, simulation still plays a vital role in terms of *scalability* (both in size and in experimental speed), *reproducibility, rapid prototyping,* and *education*. With simulation based studies, the approach can be studied in detail at varying scales, with varying data applications, varying field conditions, and will result in reproducible and analyzable results.

For many years, the venerable *ns-2* network simulation tool[81] was the de-facto standard for academic research into networking protocols and communications methods. Countless research papers were written reporting results obtained using *ns-2*, and hundreds of new models were written and contributed to the *ns-2* code base. Despite this popularity, and despite the large number of alternative network simulators documented later in this book and elsewhere, the authors and other researchers undertook a project in 2005 to design a new network simulator to replace *ns-2* for networking research. Why create a new tool? As the Introduction to this book states, this book is about *how to model* network stacks, and the decision to develop a new tool was motivated by a particular view of how to model networks in a manner that best suits network research, and by the authors' collective experiences in using and maintaining predecessor tools. As this tool was designed to replace *ns-2*, the name chosen for this tool was *ns-3* (http://www.nsnam.org).

One of the fundamental goals in the *ns-3* design was to improve the *realism* of the models; i.e., to make the models closer in implementation to the actual software implementations that they represent. Different simulation tools have taken different approaches to modeling, including the use of modeling-specific languages and code generation tools, and the use of component-based programming paradigms. While high-level modeling languages and simulation-specific programming paradigms have certain advantages, modeling actual implementations is not typically one of their strengths. In the authors' experience, the higher level of abstraction can cause simulation results to diverge too much from experimental results, and therefore an emphasis was placed on realism. For example, *ns-3* chose C++ as the programming language in part because it better facilitated the inclusion of C-based implementation code. *ns-3* also is architected similar to Linux computers, with internal interfaces (network to device driver) and application interfaces (sockets) that map well to how computers are built today. As we describe later, *ns-3* also emphasizes emulation capabilities that allow *ns-3* to be used on testbeds and with real devices and applications, again with the goal of reducing the possible discontinuities when moving from simulation to experiment.

Another benefit of realism is *reuse*. *ns-3* is not purely a new simulator but a synthesis of several predecessor tools, including *ns-2* itself (random number generators, selected wireless and error models, routing protocols), the Georgia Tech Network Simulator (GTNetS)[393], and the YANS simulator[271]. The software that automates the construction of network routing tables for static topologies was ported from the quagga routing suite. *ns-3* also prioritizes the use of standard input and output file formats so that external tools (such as packet trace analyzers) can be used. Users are also able to link external libraries such as the GNU Scientific Library or IT++.

A third emphasis has been on *ease of debugging* and better alignment with current languages. Architecturally, this led the *ns-3* team away from *ns-2*'s mixture of object-oriented Tcl and C++, which was hard to debug and was unfamiliar (Tcl) to most students. Instead, the design chosen was to emphasize purely C++-based models for performance and ease of debugging, and to provide a Python-based scripting API that allows *ns-3* to be integrated with other Python-based environments or programming models. Users of *ns-3* are free to write their simulations as either C++ main() programs or Python programs. *ns-3*'s low-level API is oriented towards the power-user but more accessible "helper" APIs are overlaid on top of the low-level API.

Finally, *ns-3* is not a commercially-supported tool, and there are limited resources to perform long-term maintenance of an ever-growing codebase. Therefore, software *maintenance* was a key design issue. Two problems with *ns-2* led the *ns-3* team, after careful consideration, to abandon the goal of backward compatibility with or extension of *ns-2*. First, *ns-2* did not enforce a coding standard, and accepted models with inconsistent software testing and model verification, as well as a lack of overall system design considerations. This policy allowed the tool to grow considerably over time but ultimately led users to lose confidence in the results, made the software less flexible to reconfiguration, and created challenges and disincentives for maintainers to maintain software once the personnel maintaining the simulator changed. *ns-3* elected to prioritize the use of a single programming language while exporting bindings to Python and potentially other scripting languages in the future. A more rigorous coding standard, code review process, and test infrastructure has been put into place. It would have been possible to build *ns-3* with full backward compatibility at the Tcl scripting level, but the *ns-3* project does not have the resources to maintain such a backward-compatibility layer. Therefore, the decision was made to create a new simulator by porting the pieces of *ns–2* that could be reused without compromising the long-term maintainability of *ns–3*.

With significant backing from the U.S. National Science Foundation, IN-RIA and the French government, the Georgia Institute of Technology, the University of Washington, and Google's Summer of Code program, *ns–3* has also been operated as a free, open source software project from the onset, and has accepted contributions from over forty contributors at the time of this writing. The remainder of this chapter will further describe a number of the design decisions that were incorporated into *ns–3*, and gives some simple examples of actual simulations created using *ns–3*.

2.2 Modeling the Network Elements in *ns–3*

As in virtually all network simulation tools, the *ns–3* simulator has models for all of the various network elements that comprise a computer network. In particular there are models for:

1. Network *nodes*, which represent both end–systems such as desktop computers and laptops, as well as network routers, hubs and switches.
2. Network *devices* which represent the physical device that connects a node to communications channel. This might be a simple Ethernet network interface card, or a more complex wireless IEEE 802.11 device.
3. Communications *channels* which represent the medium used to send the information between network devices. These might be fiber–optic point–to–point links, shared broadcast–based media such as Ethernet, or the wireless spectrum used for wireless communications.
4. Communications *protocols*, which model the implementation of protocol descriptions found in the various Internet *Request for Comments* documents, as well as newer experimental protocols not yet standardized. These protocol objects typically are organized into a *protocol stack* where each *layer* in the stack performs some specific and limited function on network packets, and then passes the packet to another layer for additional processing.
5. Protocol *headers* which are subsets of the data found in network packets, and have specific formats for each of the protocol objects they are associated with. For example, the IPv4 protocol described in RFC760 has a specified layout for the protocol header associated with IPv4. Most protocols have a well-defined format for storing the information related to that protocol in network packets.
6. Network *packets* are the fundamental unit of information exchange in computer networks. Nearly always a network packet contains one or more protocol headers describing the information needed by the protocol implementation at the endpoints and various hops along the way. Further,

the packets typically contain *payload* which represents the actual data (such as the web page being retrieved) being sent between end systems. It is not uncommon for packets to have no payload however, such as packets containing only header information about sequence numbers and window sizes for reliable transport protocols.

In addition to the models for the network elements mentioned above, *ns-3* has a number of helper objects that assist in the execution and analysis of the simulation, but are not directly modeled in the simulation. These are:

1. Random variables can be created and sampled to add the necessary randomness in the simulation. For example, the behavior of a web browser model is controlled by a number of random variables specifying distributions for think time, request object size, response object size, and objects per web page. Further, various well–known distributions are provided, including uniform, normal, exponential, Pareto, and Weibull.

2. Trace objects facilitate the logging of performance data during the execution of the simulation, that can be used for later performance analysis. Trace objects can be connect to nearly any of the other network element models, and can create the trace information in several different formats. A popular trace format in *ns-3* is the well known *packet capture* log, known as *pcap*. These *pcap* traces can then be visualized and analyzed using one of several analysis tools designed for analyzing actual network traces, such as *WireShark*. Alternately, a simple text–based format can be used that writes in human readable format the various information about the flow of packets in the simulated network.

3. Helper objects are designed to assist with and hide some of the details for various actions needed to create and execute an *ns-3* simulation. For example, the *Point to Point Helper* (described later in this chapter) provides an easy method to create a point–to–point network.

4. Attributes are used to configure most of the network element models with a reasonable set of default values (such as the initial time–to–live TTL value specified when a new IPv4 packet is created). These default values are easily changed either by specifying new values on the command line when running the *ns-3* simulation, or by calling specific API functions in the default value objects.

2.3   Simulating a Computer Network in *ns-3*

The *ns-3* simulator is developed and distributed completely in the *C++ +* programming language.[1] To construct a simulation using *ns-3*, the user writes a *C++* main program that constructs the various elements needed to describe

---

[1] The distribution does include some *Python bindings* for most of the publicly available API.

thc communication network being simulated and the network activity desired for that network. The program is then compiled, and linked with the library of network models distributed with *ns-3*.

In writing the *C++* simulation program, there are four basic steps to perform:

1. Create the *network topology*. This consists of instantiating *C++* objects for the nodes, devices, channels, and network protocols that are being modeled in the simulation.
2. Create the *data demand* on the network. This consist of creating simulation models of various network applications that send and receive information from a network, and cause packets to be either created or accepted and processed.
3. Execute the simulation. Typically, this results in the simulator entering the *main event loop*, which reads and removes events in timestamp order from the sorted event data structure described earlier. This process repeats continually until either the event list becomes empty, or a predetermined *stop time* has been reached.
4. Analyze the results. This is typically done by post-analysis of the trace information produced by the *ns-3* program execution. The trace files will usually have enough information to compute average link utilization on the communication channels in the simulation, average queue sizes at the various queue, and drop rate in the queues, just to name a few. Using the optional *pcap* trace format, any of the various publicly available tool for analyzing *pcap* traces can be used.

To illustrate these steps in the context of *ns-3*, we next discuss an actual, albeit quite simple, *ns-3* simulation program in detail. The script in question is a simple two–node point–to–point network that sends one packet from node zero to node one. The *C++* program is shown in listing 2-1.

1. The use of a `NodeContainer` helper is shown in lines 5 – 6. The `Create` method for the `NodeContainer` object is used to construct exactly two network nodes. In this particular example, the two nodes both represent end systems, with one creating and transmitting a packet and the second receiving the packet.
2. The use of a `PointToPointHelper` is shown in lines 8 – 10. The `SetDeviceAttribute` method in the helper illustrates the use of the attribute system, and the ability to override the default values for most configuration items with the values desired for the particular simulation execution. Then the `Install` method is called at line 12, passing in the `NodeContainer` object, and returning a new `NetDeviceContainer` which contains the network devices that were created when installing the point–to–point network connecting the two nodes.
3. The use of the `InternetStackHelper` is shown in lines 14 – 15. The `Install` method in the `InternetStackHelper` is called at line 15, which

```
1    // Simple ns3 simulation with two node point to point network
2
3    int main (int argc, char** argv)
4    {
5      NodeContainer nodes;
6      nodes.Create (2);
7
8      PointToPointHelper pointToPoint;
9      pointToPoint.SetDeviceAttribute ("DataRate", StringValue ("5Mbps"));
10     pointToPoint.SetChannelAttribute ("Delay", StringValue ("2ms"));
11
12     NetDeviceContainer devices = pointToPoint.Install (nodes);
13
14     InternetStackHelper stack;
15     stack.Install (nodes);
16
17     Ipv4AddressHelper address;
18     address.SetBase ("10.1.1.0", "255.255.255.0");
19
20     Ipv4InterfaceContainer interfaces = address.Assign (devices);
21
22     UdpEchoServerHelper echoServer (9);
23
24     ApplicationContainer serverApps = echoServer.Install (nodes.Get (1));
25     serverApps.Start (Seconds (1.0));
26     serverApps.Stop (Seconds (10.0));
27
28     UdpEchoClientHelper echoClient (interfaces.GetAddress (1), 9);
29     echoClient.SetAttribute ("MaxPackets", UintegerValue (1));
30     echoClient.SetAttribute ("Interval", TimeValue (Seconds (1.)));
31     echoClient.SetAttribute ("PacketSize", UintegerValue (1024));
32
33     ApplicationContainer clientApps = echoClient.Install (nodes.Get (0));
34     clientApps.Start (Seconds (2.0));
35     clientApps.Stop (Seconds (10.0));
36
37     Simulator::Run ();
38     Simulator::Destroy ();
39   }
```

Program 2-1 first.cc

adds the protocol objects normally associated with a typical Internet protocol stack, including Address Resolution Protocol (ARP), Internet Protocol (IPv4), User Datagram Protocol (UDP), and Transmission Control Protocol (TCP).

4. Next, the use of the `Ipv4AddressHelper` is shown in lines 17 – 20. The `SetBase` call at line 18 specifies the network address and the network mask for the sequential *IPv4* addresses to be assigned. The `Assign` call at line 20 assigns sequential addresses to each of the network devices in the `devices` container, and returns a new `Ipv4InterfaceContainer` which holds all of the *IPv4* software interfaces created by the address assignment. Note that in *ns-3*, as in actual networks, Internet addresses are assigned to network layer interface instances, rather than to network nodes.

5. Lines 22 – 35 illustrate the use of several application helper objects. The `UdpEchoServerHelper` constructor at line 22 creates the helper and specifies the port number on which the *UDP Echo* application will listen for packets (9 in this case). Next, the `Install` method is called on the `UdpEchoServerHelper` object, which creates an instance of the *UDP Echo Server* on the specified node. Note the use of the call to the `Get` method on the `NodeContainer`. This returns a pointer to the node at index one in the node container object. The `Install` method returns a container of echo server applications. In this particular example, there is only one application in the container since we only passed a single node object pointer to the `Install` method. Had we passed a container object, the echo server application would have been installed on every node in the container, and the returned `ApplicationContainer` would contain a pointer to the application at each node.

6. The use of the `Start` and `Stop` calls in the `ApplicationContainer` object is illustrated in lines 25 and 26. The times specified represent the time the application is to begin processing (the *Start time*) and when it is to stop processing (the *Stop* time).

7. Lines 28 – 35 illustrate several more features of the application helpers, including the constructor at line 28 that initializes the destination address and port for the echo data, and the `SetAttribute` methods that again override default values as we saw above.

8. The echo client application is finally installed on a single node (node zero in the `NodeContainer object`), and start/stop times are specified in lines 33 – 35.

9. Lastly, the `Simulator` method `Run` is called at line 37, which causes the simulation be start executing simulated events. In this particular example, the echo client only sends one packet and receives one reply, after which there are no more pending events and the simulation terminates and the `Run` method returns to the caller.

10. The **Destroy** method is called explicitly to allow all objects in the *ns-3* environment to exit cleanly and return all allocated memory. This call is not strictly necessary in order to obtain correct simulation results, but does allow thorough memory leak checking to be done.

2.4   Smart Pointers in *ns-3*

```
1    // Code snippet from the ns-3 OnOff application
2    void OnOffApplication::SendPacket()
3    {
4      NS_LOG_FUNCTION_NOARGS ();
5      NS_LOG_LOGIC ("sending packet at " << Simulator::Now());
6      NS_ASSERT (m_sendEvent.IsExpired ());
7      Ptr<Packet> packet = Create<Packet> (m_pktSize);
8      m_txTrace (packet);
9      m_socket->Send (packet);
10     m_totBytes += m_pktSize;
11     m_lastStartTime = Simulator::Now();
12     m_residualBits = 0;
13     ScheduleNextTx();
14   }
```

Program 2-2 onoff-app.cc

All network simulation tools written in the *C++* programming languages make extensive use of *dynamic memory*, utilizing the built-in **new** and **delete** operators to allocate and free memory as needed by the application. However, when allocating memory in this way, a common occurrence is a *memory leak*. A leak results when some memory is allocated with the **new** operator, but due to a programming mistake the memory is never returned. Memory leaks are prevalent in *C++* programs, and sometimes result in long–running programs aborting due to apparent memory exhaustion. Additionally, memory mismanagement by referring to memory that has already been freed often results in erroneous behavior or fatal crashes in program execution.

The *ns-3* simulator makes extensive use of *smart pointers* to help alleviate these concerns. When using smart pointers, the simulation models do not call **new** and **delete** directly. Rather, they call a special templated **Create** method that both allocates the requested memory and increments a special *reference count* value associated with the allocated memory. Whenever a smart pointer is copied (for example when passing the pointer to another function by value), the associated reference counter is incremented, indicating there are additional pointer variables pointing to the underlying memory region. Whenever an instance of the smart pointer goes out of scope (resulting in a call to the destructor for the smart pointer object), the reference count is decremented. If the value decrements to zero, then all outstanding references to the memory have been destroyed, and at that time the underlying memory will be returned with the `delete` operator. This approach greatly eases the programming of handling dynamic memory, at the expense of some minor overhead during object creation, copying, and deletion, and the avoidance of reference cycles among the pointers.

The code snippet in listing 2-2 illustrates the use of a smart pointer to manage an *ns–3* `Packet` object. At line 7 an object of type `Ptr<Packet>` is defined and created by a call to the global static function `Create`. The type `Ptr<Packet>` is an object with several member variables, but primarily consists of the pointer to the actual memory of the `Packet` object, and a pointer to a shared reference counter. The `Ptr` objects have all of the semantics of pointer variables, and for all intents and purposes can be considered to be pointers. Also in this example, note that the `Create` function has an argument `m_pktSize`. During the `Packet` object creation, the argument is passed to the constructor for the `Packet` object. This allows large packet payloads to be modeled without actually requiring that memory be allocated for the simulated payload. In *ns–3*, Packet objects may also carry real data buffers if the application requires them to do so.

Later, at line 9, the packet smart pointer object "`packet`" is passed as a parameter to the `Send` method for the associated socket. It is likely that the packet will eventually be forwarded to another *ns–3* `Node` object by scheduling a future event. However, since the smart pointer was passed by *value* to the `Send` method, the reference counter has been incremented to two, indicating that two different packet pointers to the same packet are in existence. When the `SendPacket` function exits at line 14, the reference counter is decremented to one. Since it is still non–zero, the underlying packet data is not freed. When the packet eventually reaches the final destination, the reference count will then become zero and the packet data will be freed and returned to the available pool.

Readers familiar with the sockets application programming interface (API) may be surprised to see packets being passed at the application/socket boundary. However, the *ns–3* Packet object at this layer of the simulation can be simply considered to be a fancy byte buffer. *ns–3* also supports a variant of the Send method that takes a traditional byte buffer as an argument.

2.5   Representing Packets in *ns–3*

A fundamental requirement for all network simulation tools is the ability to represent network packets, including both the packet payload and the set of protocol headers associated with the packet. Further, it is important to allow for actual payload data in the packets in the case where the payload is meaningful (such as routing table updates in routing protocols), or to simply represent the existence of the payload but not actual contents (such as when measuring the behavior of a transport protocol that is data agnostic). Further, the design must support the presence of any number of protocol headers of any sizes. Finally, the design should support fragmentation and reassembly by network or link layer protocol models.

The design of *ns-3* allows for all of these capabilities. The size of the so–called *dummy payload* can be specified on the object constructor for the `Packet` object. If so, the payload size is simply stored as an integer, but no actual payload is represented.

Then, any object that is a subclass of the class `Header` can be added to the packet using the `AddHeader` method for packets, and any object that is a subclass of the class `Trailer` can be added at the end of the packet data using the `AddTrailer` method. Removing headers or trailers can easily be accomplished using the defined `RemoveHeader` and `RemoveTrailer` functions.

Another feature of *ns-3* packets is the inclusion of *copy on write* semantics for packet pointers. Consider the simple example discussed earlier in listing 2-2. At line 9 the newly created packet is passed as a parameter to the socket `Send` function. This will undoubtedly result in the addition of several protocol headers to the packet as it progresses down the protocol stack. However, semantically, passing an object by value, as is done here, should not result in any changes to the objects passed as arguments. In the *ns-3* design this is accomplished by the implementation of *copy on write*. In this design, the actual packet data and all protocol headers are stored in a separate helper object called a `Buffer`. Any time a `Buffer` associated with a packet is modified and holders of pointers to the packet need to access the different views of the buffer contents, the original buffer is replicated and the original packet buffer pointer points to the original buffer. The replicated packet pointer object gets pointed to the newly revised buffer, so that two packet pointers for the same logical packet in fact see two different representation of the packet data. This is implemented in an efficient manner that avoids actual data copying as much as possible.

2.6 Object Aggregation in *ns-3*

In a program design intended to be continually modified and enhanced by a number of users over a long period of time, it becomes important to allow flexibility in design, while at the same time having efficiency in memory usage and simplicity in object class implementation. For example, *ns-3* defines a `Node` object to that is a model of a network end system or router. However, not all `Node` objects have the same requirements. For example, some may want an implementation of IP version 6 (IPv6) and others may not. Some may need an indication of physical location while others may not. Some may need instances of specialized routing protocols, but others may not. Clearly, the notion of a *one size fits all* design for Node objects is not appropriate.

The *ns-3* design solves this problem by using a methodology loosely modeled after the Microsoft *Component Object Model (COM)* design approach[73]. In this approach, objects deriving from a special base class can be aggregated (associated with) other such objects. After the objects have been aggregated, later queries to the objects can determine if an object of a specified type has been previously aggregated, and if so, a pointer to the associated object is returned. In the example cited above, the model developer might create an object representing a three–dimensional location value that should be associated with a given Node object. To achieve this, the Location object is created, given a value, and then aggregated to the specific Node object. Later, the model can query each Node and retrieve a pointer to the Location object associated with each node.

```
1   // Revised Code snippet from the Dumbbell topology object
2   // Add a node location object to the left side router
3
4   // Get a pointer to the left side router node
5   Ptr<Node> lr = GetLeft();
6   // See if a node location object is already present on this node
7   Ptr<NodeLocation> loc = lr->GetObject<NodeLocation>();
8   if (loc == 0)
9     { // If not, create one and aggregate it to the node.
10       loc = CreateObject<NodeLocation>();
11       lr->AggregateObject(loc);
12     }
13   // Set the associated position for the left side router
14   Vector lrl(leftX, leftY, leftZ);
15   loc->SetLocation(lrl);
```

Program 2-3 aggregation.cc

This approach is illustrated in the code snippet shown in listing 2-3. The code snippet is a slightly simplified excerpt from the dumbbell topology helper object. This illustrates the creation of an object of class NodeLocation and subsequent aggregation of that object to a specified Node object.

First, line 5 simply obtains a smart pointer to a particular node, the left side dumbbell router in this case. Line 7 starts by querying if an object of type NodeLocation is already aggregated to the node by calling the GetObject method. The returned value is a smart pointer to a NodeLocation object if one is found, or a null pointer if not. Line 10 creates the new NodeLocation object (if one was not found), and then line 11 aggregates the location object with the node by calling the AggregateObject method. Finally, the desired location information is specified for the NodeLocation object starting at line 14.

2.7   Events in *ns–3*

In discrete event simulations the engine maintains a sorted list of future events (sorted in ascending order of event timestamp), and then simply removes the earliest event, advances simulation time to the time for that event, and then calls the appropriate event handler for the event. Earlier network simulators written in *C++*, notably *ns–2* and *GTNetS*, accomplish this design by defining a base class called `Handler` that include a pure virtual function called `Handle`. The argument to this `Handle` function is simply a pointer to any object that subclasses from a base class `Event`. Then, each object in the simulation that is designed to handle events (such as the network device to handle packet reception events) simply subclasses from the base class `Handler` and implements the `Handle` function.

This approach is simple, easy to understand, and easy to implement. However, it is cumbersome when a given model must process several different types of events. For example, a network device is likely required to process packet reception events, transmission complete events, and link up or down events, just to name a few. This requires somewhat tedious type casting and definition of a number of different event objects to represent the necessary data for each different event.

The *ns–3* simulator takes a different approach that results in considerably more flexibility for the model developer, at the expense of substantial complexity in the design and implementation of the event scheduler and simulator main loop. In *ns–3*, any static function, or any public member function for any object can be an event handler. Rather than defining new event subclasses for each event type, the *ns–3* approach simply specifies the required information as arguments to the function that creates and schedules new events. This is implemented by a complex set of templated functions in the simulator object.

A simple example illustrating this approach to event scheduling and event handling is shown in listing 2-4. This code snippet is excerpted from the `mac-low.cc` implementation of the IEEE 802.11 protocol in *ns–3*.

Line 4 demonstrates creating and scheduling a new event. The first three arguments are common to all member function event scheduling calls, and specify the amount of time in the future the event occurs, the address of the member function to call, and the object pointer for the event handler object. In this example, the future time is `GetSifs()`, the member function is `MacLow::SendCtsAfterRts`, and the object pointer is `this`. The next four parameters are those specifically required by the event handler function. In this case those are a 48–bit address of type `Mac48Address`, a duration of type `Time`, an enumeration value of type `WifiMode`, and a signal to noise ratio of type `double`.

Line 13 shows the specified handler function `SendCtsAfterRts`. Note that the parameter list expect four arguments, and types of those arguments match

```
 1   // Code snippet from mac-low.cc, ilustrating event scheduling
 2
 3   // Excerpt from function MacLow::ReceiveOk
 4   m_sendCtsEvent = Simulator::Schedule (
 5                             GetSifs (),
 6                             MacLow::SendCtsAfterRts, this,
 7                             hdr.GetAddr2 (),
 8                             hdr.GetDuration (),
 9                             txMode,
10                             rxSnr);
11
12   // Excerpt from function MacLow::SendCtsAfterRts
13   void MacLow::SendCtsAfterRts (
14                             Mac48Address source,
15                             Time duration,
16                             WifiMode rtsTxMode,
17                             double rtsSnr)
18   {
19     NS_LOG_FUNCTION (this << source << duration
20                           << rtsTxMode << rtsSnr);
21     // Remainder of code removed for brevity.
```

Program 2-4 schedule.cc

those specified earlier during the event scheduling. Should any of the argument types not match, a compile–time error occurs.

The end result of the call to the Schedule function is that the specified member function will be called at the appropriate time in the future (GetSifs() seconds in this case), and the parameters specified on the Schedule call will be passed to the event handler. It is easy to see that such an approach avoids the need to introduce an intermediate, generic event handler object that later dispatches events to specific model functions; instead, the functions themselves can be the event handlers.

2.8 Compiling and Running the Simulation

As discussed above, *ns-3* programs are typically *C++* programs that link against a library providing the *ns-3* core and simulation models. The project uses the Waf build system to configure and manage the build of the simulator and its documentation. Waf is a Python-based framework supporting configuration, build, installation, packaging, and testing. Once a simulation program is built, the final executable will be placed in a build/ directory, where it can be run from a shell like any other program. Waf also provides a custom shell, which features integration of dynamic library path discovery and support for debugging tools and memory checkers, that can be used to run programs such as typing ./waf -run my-program for a program my-program.cc.

Because the *ns–3* API is also exported as Python bindings, users can also write Python programs instead of *C++* programs, such as in listing 2-5 that corresponds to listing 2-1 above.

```
1   import ns3
2   def main(argv):
3       nodes = ns3.NodeContainer()
4       nodes.Create(2)
5
6       pointToPoint = ns3.PointToPointHelper()
7       ...
```

Program 2-5 first.py

2.9   Animating the Simulation

The *ns–3* tool has the ability to create a trace file specifically designed to facilitate the animation of the flow of packets through the simulation, allowing visual confirmation that the packets are indeed flowing through the simulated network as desired. The addition of the animation trace file output is quite simple, and is illustrated in listing 2-6. This particular example is a snippet from the `test-dumbbell.cc` example program. Presently, the animation interface supports only the *point–to–point* network devices and channels, with support of other device types planned.

To facilitate the animation, the only requirement is to specify a *location* for each node object in the simulation, and to create and configure an object of class `AnimationInterface`. In the example, line 11 simply creates a dumbbell topology with the specified number of leaf nodes on the left and right side, and the specified helper objects to connect the nodes together. The majority of the animation work is done by the call to `BoundingBox` at line 23. This specifies the upper left X and Y coordinates and the lower right X and Y coordinates that will contain the nodes in the dumbbell. They are dimensionless units, and the nodes in the dumbbell are positioned in this box in such a way to result in a symmetric and visually pleasing animation.

The `AnimationInterface` object is created at line 26. Then a file name specified on the command line argument is assigned as the name of the output trace file. Once all nodes are created and given node locations, the `StartAnimation` function is called, which results in the complete list of nodes, locations, and connectivity being written to the specified trace file. During the simulation execution initiated by the `Run` call at line 38, all packet transmission events are written to the trace file, along with sufficient information to later animate the path of that packet during the animation. Finally, the

`StopAnimation` function at line 40 causes the output file to be closed and all remaining trace data to be flushed to the trace file.

A sample animation visualization for the `test-dumbbell` program is shown in Figure 2.1.

2.10   Scalability with Distributed Simulation

In order to achieve scalability to a very large number of simulated network elements, the *ns–3* simulation tools supports *distributed simulation*. Rather than running a single simulation instance that must handle all events and all network object models, the distributed simulation approach allows the execution of the simulation on multiple, independent computing platforms. By doing this, the overall scalability of the simulated networks can increase considerably.

The approach to supporting distributed simulation in *ns–3* is derived from prior work designing distributed simulation for the Georgia Tech Network Simulator (*GTNetS*). Consider the simple topology shown in Figure 2.2. To execute an *ns–3* simulation using distributed simulation, one approach would be to use four separate simulation processes, each maintaining its own timestamp–ordered event list, and each modeling a subset of the overall topology. For example, simulator 0 would model all of the network elements in subnet 0, simulator 1 would model subnet 1, and so on. However, if this approach is used, then the complete global topology is not known by any one simulator instance. Lacking the global topology picture, the simulators cannot easily make routing decisions globally, and must resort to models for routing protocols and the corresponding overhead for maintaining routing tables.

An alternative approach is shown in Figure 2.3. Here, each simulator instantiates *ns–3* objects for *every* network element in the complete topology. However, each instance only maintains the state (and processes events) for the topology subset assigned to it, as described above. For the remaining network elements (those assigned to other simulator instances) the only state created is the existence of the node, device, and link objects. This is called a *Ghost Node* in simulation parlance. In the figure below, simulator 0 is responsible for all elements in subnet 0 (as described above), and additionally creates ghost nodes for the remaining three subnets. However, no events are scheduled or processed for ghost nodes. Rather, the responsible simulator for those nodes handle those events. In this example, simulator 1 would create complete model elements for the subnet1 objects, and create ghost objects for subnets 0, 2, and 3.

The *ns–3* simulator provides an easy way to create the ghost elements, by assigning a global *simulator id* to the simulator instance, and individual *node id* values to each network element. If the node id does not match the

```
1    // Excerpt from the test-dumbbell.cc illustrating the animation interface
2
3    // Create the point-to-point link helpers
4    PointToPointHelper pointToPointRouter;
5    pointToPointRouter.SetDeviceAttribute  ("DataRate", StringValue ("10Mbps"));
6    pointToPointRouter.SetChannelAttribute ("Delay", StringValue ("1ms"));
7    PointToPointHelper pointToPointLeaf;
8    pointToPointLeaf.SetDeviceAttribute    ("DataRate", StringValue ("10Mbps"));
9    pointToPointLeaf.SetChannelAttribute   ("Delay", StringValue ("1ms"));
10
11   Dumbbell d(nLeftLeaf, pointToPointLeaf,
12             nRightLeaf, pointToPointLeaf,
13             pointToPointRouter);
14
15   // Assign IP Addresses
16   d.AssignAddresses(Ipv4AddressHelper("10.1.1.0", "255.255.255.0"),
17                     Ipv4AddressHelper("10.2.1.0", "255.255.255.0"),
18                     Ipv4AddressHelper("10.3.1.0", "255.255.255.0"));
19   // Install on/off app on all right side nodes
20   // Omitted for brevity
21
22   // Set the bounding box for animation
23   d.BoundingBox(1, 1, 10, 10);
24
25   // Create the animation object and configure for specified output
26   AnimationInterface anim;
27   // Check if a file name specified on command line, and set it if so
28   (!animFile.empty())
29     {
30       anim.SetOutputFile(animFile);
31     }
32   anim.StartAnimation();
33
34   // Set up the acutal simulation
35   Ipv4GlobalRoutingHelper::PopulateRoutingTables();
36
37   // Run the simulation
38   Simulator::Run();
39   Simulator::Destroy();
40   anim.StopAnimation();
41   return 0;
```

Program 2-6 anim.cc

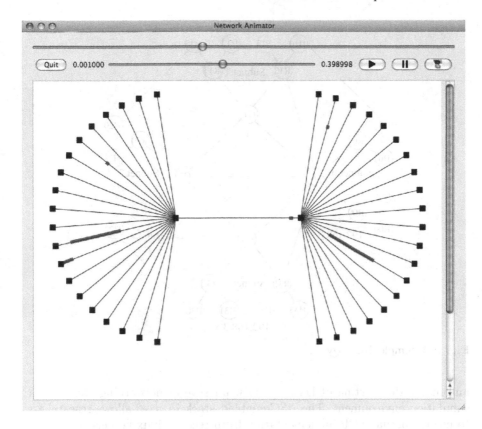

Fig. 2.1: Sample *ns-3* Animation

simulator id, then a ghost node is created. No applications or protocol stacks should be created for the ghost nodes.

2.11   Emulation Capabilities

In the past decade, experimental research in networking has migrated towards testbeds and virtualization environments, in large part because of the realism that such environments provide compared to simulation abstractions, and also because real implementation code can be reused. A design goal in *ns-3* has been to offer several options for the support for emulation, virtualization, and the running of real implementation code, to minimize the experimental discontinuities when moving between simulation, emulation, and live experiments, and to enable experiments that may want to combine the techniques.

   The first emulation capability that was integrated to *ns-3* was the Network Simulation Cradle (NSC)[240]. NSC is a framework that largely

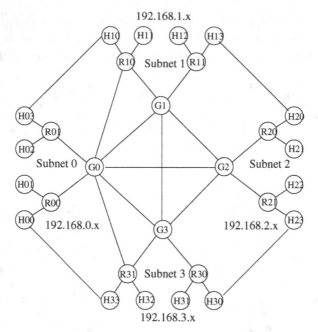

Fig. 2.2: Simple Topology

automates the porting of kernel code from several networking stacks to a simulation environment. The NSC-enabled stack in *ns–3* allows researchers to use the actual TCP implementation from recent Linux kernels.

Another emulation capability that has been used to integrate *ns–3* with experimental wireless testbeds is the emulation NetDevice, which allows an *ns–3* process on a physical computer to bind a simulation-based network interface to a physical interface on the host machine. This capability also requires the use of a real-time scheduler in *ns–3* that aligns the simulation clock with the host machine clock. One testbed in which this has been used is the ORBIT testbed at Rutgers University[385]. ORBIT consists of a deployment of a two dimensional grid of four hundred computers in a large arena, on which various radios (802.11, Bluetooth, and others) are deployed. *ns–3* has been integrated with ORBIT by using their imaging process to load and run ns-3 simulations on the ORBIT array. The technique uses an emulation NetDevice to drive the hardware in the testbed, and results are gathered either using the ns-3 tracing and logging functions or the native ORBIT data management framework.

The inverse of the above capability is also an important use case. Rather than run *ns–3* protocol stacks over real network interfaces, one can run real systems over an *ns–3*-provided emulation of a (typically wireless) network. For example, lightweight virtual machines have been developed that provide varying degrees of system isolation between instances. Specially tailored

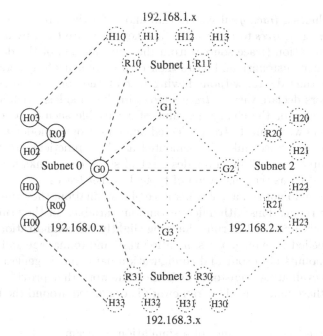

Fig. 2.3: Distributed Topology

machines can be used to virtualize instances of the network stack and provide partly shared and partly private file systems and access to system resources. The term "slicing" has often been used to describe this type of virtualization, such as in PlanetLab[366]. While slices on an experimental testbed run over real (distributed) network segments, by using *ns-3* as an underlay, they can also be run over simulated networks. This hybrid of emulation and (real-time) simulation is particularly useful for wireless networking, which is not always provided or is provided only in a limited fashion on virtualized testbeds.

As the maturity and cost-effectiveness of virtualization software continues to increase, the authors foresee that blending the use of *ns-3* with lightweight virtual machines will become a very useful research capability. The project is also exploring new techniques to run multiple instances of unmodified application processes in simulations on a single host.

2.12 Analyzing the Results

The design goal for *ns-3* has been to equip the core of the simulator with tools that allow for highly customizable extraction of event logs and output statistics, to provide a framework for managing large numbers of simulation runs and output data, and to allow third-party analysis tools to be used where possible.

ns–3 includes a *tracing* subsystem that allows for the export of simulation data from *trace sources* to *trace sinks*. The key ideas are that, by decoupling the data generation (trace source) from the consumption of the data (trace sink), users can customize and write their own trace sinks to generate whatever output they desire, without having to edit the core of the simulator. Model authors declare various *trace sources* in their models, such as the arrival of a packet or the change in value of a variable such as a congestion window. Users who want to trace selected behavior from a model will simply attach their own trace sinks (implemented as C++ functions) to the trace sources of interest. *ns–3* also provides a set of stock trace sinks for common trace events such as the generation of typical packet traces.

Users often do not run a single instance of a simulation; they run multiple independent replications with different random variables, or they run a set of simulations with each set of runs changing slightly the configuration. Frameworks are needed to manage the simulation runs and to manage and organize the large amounts of output and configuration data that is generated. *ns–3* is presently evaluating a custom statistics framework that provides support for each of these functions. The framework is organized around the following principles:

– Define a *trial* as one instance of a simulation program;
– Provide a control script to execute instances of the simulation, varying parameters as necessary;
– Collect data and marshal into persistent storage for plotting and analysis using external scripts and tools;
– Provide a basic statistical framework for core statistics as well as to perform simulation run-length control based on observed data; and
– Use the *ns–3* tracing framework to instrument custom code.

This framework defines metadata to collect run information, and provides support to dump simulation configuration and output data to a relational database or to other existing output formats.

ns–3 also supports standardized output formats for trace data, such as the `pcap` format used by network packet analysis tools such as `tcpdump`, and supports standardized input formats such as importing mobility trace files from *ns-2*. By aligning to existing data standards, *ns–3* allows users to reuse a wide range of existing analysis tools. Likewise, the project makes use of existing support libraries such as the GNU Scientific Library (GSL) to avoid reinventing statistical and analysis tools.

3. OMNeT++

Andras Varga (Opensim Ltd.)

3.1 Introduction

3.1.1 Overview

OMNeT++ (www.omnetpp.org) is an extensible, modular, component-based C++ simulation library and framework which also includes an integrated development and a graphical runtime environment. Domain-specific functionality (support for simulation of communication networks, queuing networks, performance evaluation, etc.) is provided by model frameworks, developed as independent projects. There are extensions for real-time simulation, network emulation, support for alternative programming languages (Java, C#), database integration, SystemC integration, HLA and several other functions.

OMNeT++ has been created with the simulation of communication networks and other distributed systems in mind as application area, but instead of building a specialized simulator, it was designed to be as general as possible. Since then, the idea has proven to work, and OMNeT++ has been used in numerous domains from queuing network simulations to wireless and ad-hoc network simulations, from business process simulation to peer-to-peer network, optical switch and storage area network simulations.

OMNeT++ is often quoted as a network simulator, when in fact it is not. It includes the basic machinery and tools to write simulations, but itself it does not provide any components specifically for computer networks, queueing networks or any other domain. Instead, these application areas are supported by various simulation models and frameworks such as the INET Framework or Castalia. Model frameworks are developed completely independently of the simulation framework, and follow their own release cycles.

3.1.2 The OMNeT++ Approach for Modeling

Many network simulators have a more-or-less fixed way of representing network elements in the model. In contrast, OMNeT++ provides a generic *component architecture*, and it is up to the model designer to map concepts such as network devices, protocols or the wireless channel into model components. Model components are termed *modules*, and, if well designed, modules can be used in a variety of different environments and can be combined in various ways like LEGO blocks. Modules primarily communicate via message passing, either directly or via predefined connections. Messages may represent events, packets, commands, jobs or other entities depending on the model domain.

The facilities provided by OMNeT++ include a C++ kernel and class library for building simulation components (modules); infrastructure to assemble simulations from these components and to configure them (NED language, ini files); graphical and batch mode simulation runtime interfaces; a simulation IDE for designing, running and evaluating simulations; extension interfaces for real-time simulation, emulation, MRIP, parallel distributed simulation, database connectivity and so on.

The simulation library provides a message and event handling mechanism (scheduling events, sending and receiving messages), support for configuring and assembling modules, a random number architecture with various distributions, a publish-subscribe style signal mechanism, and utility classes for queues, statistics collection, topology discovery and routing, and other tasks.

3.1.3   The Simulation IDE

An important part of OMNeT++ is the Eclipse-based Simulation IDE, cf. Figure 3.1. Although Eclipse (eclipse.org) is best known as a Java IDE, it is really an integration platform for all sorts of developer-oriented applications. Core Eclipse projects offer C++ development, web development and other capabilities, and web sites like the Eclipse Marketplace (marketplace.eclipse.org) and Eclipse Plugins (eclipse-plugins.2y.net) host literally thousands of Eclipse plug-ins for a wide spectrum of purposes, from UML designers to database browsers and language IDEs.

The Simulation IDE is a customized Eclipse instance, which extends the IDE with a graphical-and-text round-trip editor for designing simulation models, a simulation configuration editor, C++ build support, a simulation launcher also capable of running simulation batches, a result plotting and analysis tool, a trace analyzer tool that visualizes simulation execution on a sequence chart, and other smaller tools like documentation generator. C++ source editing is provided by the Eclipse CDT project, and the IDE also includes version control system integration, currently subversion and git. Additional features can be installed from the Eclipse Marketplace and other plug-in sites.

In the spirit of Eclipse, the OMNeT++ team intends the Simulation IDE to become a host and integration platform for various 3rd party simulation utilities and tools. At the time of writing, there are various UI and command-line tools for topology generation, network scenario generation, batch launching, etc, using a variety of languages and widget toolkits. It is our intention to attract researchers to implement their future tools as Eclipse plug-ins, and port existing ones into Eclipse. For this reason the OMNeT++ Eclipse plugins are well documented, provide public API, and expose several extension points where new functionality can be plugged in or existing ones can be customized.

To simplify deployment of plug-ins further, the Simulation IDE loads plug-ins from user projects as well, not only from the installation directory. This makes it possible to bundle simulation framework specific plug-ins (such as INET Framework or MiXiM tools) with the simulation frameworks, so when a user imports the simulation framework into the IDE, the framework-specific UI contributions will immediately appear in the IDE.

The IDE also makes it possible to write wizards without any Java or C++ programming, using an XML-based UI description language and a template language for content generation. This feature offers a relatively quick and painless way to bring topology generators and file importers into the IDE.

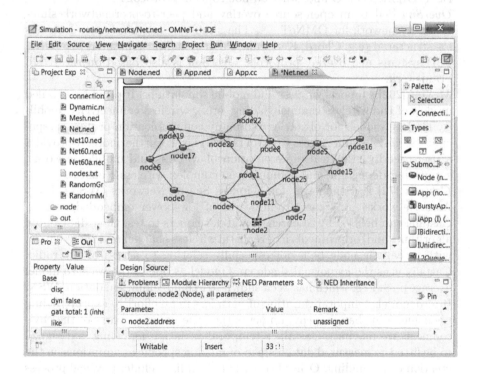

Fig. 3.1: The Simulation IDE

3.1.4   Network Simulation Frameworks

The following major network simulation frameworks have been developed for OMNeT++ and are in common use:

- *INET Framework* (inet.omnetpp.org) is an open-source communication networks simulation package, which contains models for several Internet protocols: UDP, TCP, SCTP, IP, IPv6, Ethernet, PPP, IEEE 802.11, MPLS, OSPF, and others. The INET Framework also contains emulation capabilities. Extensions include the INET port of the Quagga routing daemon (quagga.net), and that of the Network Simulation Cradle (NSC) [239] package. An alternative to NSC is the OppBSD [61] model.
- *INETMANET* [378] is a fork of the INET Framework, and extends INET with support for mobile ad-hoc networks. INETMANET supports AODV, DSR, OLSR, DYMO and other ad-hoc routing protocols.
- *OverSim* [54] is an open-source overlay and peer-to-peer network simulation framework for OMNeT++. The simulator contains several models for structured (e.g. Chord, Kademlia, Pastry) and unstructured (e.g. GIA) P2P systems and overlay protocols. OverSim is also based on the INET Framework.
- *MiXiM* [262] supports wireless and mobile simulations. It provides detailed models of the wireless channel (fading, etc.), wireless connectivity, mobility models, models for obstacles and many communication protocols especially at the Medium Access Control (MAC) level. Furthermore, it provides a user-friendly graphical representation of wireless and mobile networks, supporting debugging and defining even complex wireless scenarios.
- *Castalia* [72] is a simulator for Wireless Sensor Networks (WSN), Body Area Networks and generally networks of low-power embedded devices. Castalia can be used by researchers and developers to test their distributed algorithms and/or protocols in a realistic wireless channel and radio model, with a realistic node behavior especially relating to access of the radio. Castalia uses the lognormal shadowing model as one of the ways to model average path loss, which has been shown to explain empirical data in WSN. It also models temporal variation of path loss in an effort to capture fading phenomena in changing environments (i.e., the nodes or parts of the environment are moving). Castalia's temporal variation modeling is designed to be fitted to measured data instead of making specific assumptions on the creation of fast fading. Other features of Castalia include: physical process modeling, sensing device bias and noise, node clock drift, and several MAC and routing protocols implemented.

3.2 The Component Model

3.2.1 Overview

It has been mentioned that an OMNeT++ model consists of modules that communicate with message passing. The active modules are termed *simple modules*; they are implemented in C++, using the simulation class library. Groups of modules can be encapsulated into *compound modules*; the number of hierarchy levels is not limited.

In network simulations, simple modules may represent user agents, traffic sources and sinks, protocol entities like TCP, network devices like a 802.11 interface card, data structures like routing tables, or user agents that generate traffic. Simulation-related functions such as controlling the movement of mobile nodes or auto-assigning IP addresses in a network are also often cast as simple modules. Network nodes such as hosts and routers are typically compound modules assembled from simple modules. Additional hierarchy levels are occasionally used above node level (to represent subnetworks) or within nodes (i.e. to group simple modules representing individual protocols of the IPv6 family into IPv6 compound module).

Both simple and compound modules are instances of *module types*. While describing the model, the user defines module types; instances of these module types serve as components for more complex module types. The network to be simulated is an instance of a module type. When a module type is used as a building block, there is no distinction whether it is a simple or a compound module. This allows the user to transparently split a module into several simple modules within a compound module, or do the opposite, re-implement the functionality of a compound module in one simple module, without affecting existing users of the module type. The feasibility of model reuse is proven by model frameworks like the INET Framework or Mobility Framework, and their extensions.

Modules communicate with messages, which, in addition to predefined attributes such as a timestamp, may contain arbitrary data. Simple modules typically send messages via *gates*, but it is also possible to send them directly to their destination modules. There are input, output and inout gates. An input and an output gate or two inout gates may be linked with a *connection*. Connections are defined as part of a compound module, and may connect two submodules, a submodule with the parent, or two gates of the parent module. Connections spanning across hierarchy levels are not permitted, as it would hinder model reuse. Due to the hierarchical structure of the model, messages typically travel through a chain of connections, to start and arrive in simple modules. Compound modules act as "cardboard boxes" in the model, transparently relaying messages between their inside and the outside world. Properties such as propagation delay, data rate and bit error rate, can be assigned to connections. One can also define connection types with specific properties (termed *channels*) and reuse them in several places.

Modules can have *parameters*. Parameters are mainly used to pass configuration data to simple modules, and to help defining the model topology. Supported parameter types are string, integer, double, boolean, and XML element tree, the latter being used for accessing XML-based custom configuration files. Parameters may have default values, units of measurement and other attributes attached to them. An interesting concept is *volatile parameters*. They are re-evaluated every time the simulation code reads their value, thus, when they are assigned an expression like `exponential(2.0)`, the simulation code will get a different random number each time. Volatile parameters are commonly used to pass stochastic input to modules.

3.2.2   The NED Language

OMNeT++ has its own DSL (Domain Specific Language) called *NED* for describing the above component model. XML has been considered but discarded as being too verbose and generally unsuitable for human consumption.[1] The idea of using a general-purpose programming language such as Tcl, Python, Ruby or Lua has been discarded as well, because models written that way cannot be supported with a graphical editor in a round-trip manner. (When the user hand-modifies the code, there would be no guarantee that the graphical editor can parse and meaningfully display it).

Typical ingredients of a NED description are simple module declarations, compound module definitions and network definitions. Simple module declarations describe the interface of the module: gates and parameters. Compound module definitions consist of the declaration of the module's external interface (gates and parameters), and the definition of submodules and their interconnection. Network definitions are compound modules that qualify as self-contained simulation models. Limited programming constructs (loop, conditional) allow for parametric topologies, such as a router with an unbound number of ports, or a hexagonal mesh with parametric dimensions.

In order to be prepared for unforeseen use cases, the NED language supports adding metadata annotations to types, parameters, submodules, connections and other items. So far, metadata annotations have been used to store graphics attributes (position, icon, etc.); to override the default choice of the underlying C++ class name for simple modules and channels; to denote the C++ namespace; to mark gates that are expected to remain unconnected; to declare measurement units and the prompt text for parameters; to label gates for automatic matching by the graphical editor's *connect* tool; to

---

[1] The NED language has a one-to-one XML binding though, and there are tools for (lossless) conversion in both directions. This feature is useful for machine processing of NED sources. The XML format is virtually the abstract syntax tree (AST) of the NED code, but includes source code comments as well.

denote compound modules that represent physical network nodes in the INET Framework; and for other purposes.

To support simulation in-the-large (the INET Framework contains well over 150 module types), the NED language has a Java-style package system, and supports inner types, component inheritance and dependency injection via parametric submodule types and interfaces.

To give you a feel of the NED language, here is some sample code that defines a compound module (the code should be mostly self-explanatory):

```
//
// A "Node" consists of a Routing module, an App module,
// and one L2Queue per port.
//
module Node
{
    parameters:
        int address;
        string appType;
        @display("i=misc/node_vs,gold");
    gates:
        inout port[];
    submodules:
        app: <appType> like IApp {
                address = address;
                @display("p=140,60");
        }
        routing: Routing {
                @display("p=140,130");
            gates:
                in[sizeof(port)];
                out[sizeof(port)];
        }
        queue[sizeof(port)]: L2Queue {
                @display("p=80,200,row");
        }
    connections:
        routing.localOut --> app.in;
        routing.localIn <-- app.out;
        for i=0..sizeof(port)-1 {
            routing.out[i] --> queue[i].in;
            routing.in[i] <-- queue[i].out;
            queue[i].line <--> port[i];
        }
}
```

Normally all modules of a simulation are instantiated as descendants of the system module, but the simulation library provides support for dynamic instantiation as well. Both simple and compound modules may be created at runtime, the latter will have its internal structure (submodules, connections) built automatically as well. Examples when dynamic instantiation can be useful include loading of the network topology at runtime, and having a dynamically changing network (for example, mobile devices arriving to or leaving from the playground, or network links being cut or added).

3.2.3   IDE Support for NED

The Simulation IDE provides a dual-mode (graphical and source) round-trip editor for NED files. Graphics attributes are stored in *display strings*, which are part of the NED source as metadata annotations. The source editor provides content assist, on-the-fly validation, navigate-to-declaration, and other features in addition to basic editing and syntax highlighting.

The IDE also provides programmatic access to the ASTs of all NED files and the details of NED types defined in them, via a public Java API. This API is helpful for the authors of Eclipse plug-ins who want to extend the IDE with NED-related functionality.

One example that uses the above API is the NED Documentation Generator plug-in, which is part of the IDE. The plug-in produces browsable, fully hyperlinked HTML documentation from NED sources and Javadoc-style comments in them. The resulting documentation contains network graphics, usage and inheritance diagrams, and can also hyperlink to Doxygen documentation generated from C++ sources that implement simulation components.

3.3   Programming

3.3.1   Modules, messages and events

Simple modules are implemented as C++ classes, derived from the cSimple Module library class. Message sending and receiving are the most frequent tasks in simple modules. Messages are represented with the cMessage class, and can be sent either via output gates, or directly to other modules.

The simulation kernel delivers messages to the handleMessage(cMessage*) method of the module; module authors primarily need to override this method to add functionality. The alternative to handleMessage() is a process-style description, where users have to override the activity() method, and messages can be obtained via blocking *receive* calls. In general, using activity() is not recommended because it does not scale due to the underlying coroutine stacks, but there are situations when it is extremely useful, such as when porting a process-based program into simulation.

Timers and timeouts are implemented with normal messages that the module sends to itself. These self-messages are sent with a *schedule* call, and are delivered back to the module in the same way as messages arriving from other modules. Self-messages can also be canceled. Note that there is no separate event class, its role is fulfilled by cMessage.

The programmer can provide code to execute on module initialization and finalization by overriding corresponding methods of the module class. OMNeT++ also supports multi-stage initialization, and it has proven essential for large models like the INET Framework. Finalization takes place on successful simulation termination only, and its code is most commonly used to record summary simulation results.

Some other simulators implement timers as arbitrary functions or function objects that are called back from the simulation kernel. OMNeT++ prefers the *handleMessage* approach, because we have found *handleMessage*-based code to be easier to understand than callback-based, and code readability is very important for model verification. The reason for greater readability is that with *handleMessage*, there is a single place in the component's code where a newcomer can start reading. By looking at *handleMessage*, it is immediately clear to the reader what inputs (packets, timers, timeouts) the module is prepared to handle, and all there is left to do for understanding dynamic behavior is to go into the various *if* branches and see how each message or timer type is handled. With the callback approach, there is no such central place, and with the scheduled code blocks being scattered around in the code, it is significantly harder for a reader to hunt down the pieces and assemble the puzzle.

3.3.2   Simulation Time

OMNeT++ represents simulation time with a 64-bit fixed-point number with a base-10 exponent, wrapped into the SimTime class.[2] The exponent is stored in a global variable to eliminate the need for normalization, and to conserve memory. We have found that the range provided by 64 bits is more than enough for practical simulations (approx. ± 292 years with nanosecond precision, or ± 107 days with picosecond precision).

---

[2] OMNeT++ versions prior to 4.0 have used double-precision floating-point numbers, but precision problems with floating point operations (non-associativity, diminishing precision as simulation time advances, etc.) have caused problems in simulations from time to time.

3.3.3   Library Classes

Most classes in the OMNeT++ simulation library represent various parts of the component model: modules, channels, gates, module parameters, objects and so on. Messages and packets are represented by the cMessage class and its subclass, cPacket. A frequently used container class is cQueue, which can also be set up to operate as priority queue.

The library contains a *topology discovery* class, which can extract the network topology from a model according to the user's specification, make it available as a graph, and supports algorithms such as Dijkstra's shortest path.

Random number generation is available via streams provided by the simulation framework's random number architecture (see 3.3.11). Several distributions are available. Continuous ones include uniform, exponential, normal, truncated normal, gamma, beta, Erlang, chi-square, Student-t, Cauchy, triangular, lognormal, Weibull, and Pareto; discrete ones include uniform, Bernoulli, binomial, geometric, negative binomial, and Poisson. It is possible to add new distributions programmed by the user, and make them available in the NED language and in the configuration (see 3.4.3). It is also possible to dynamically load distributions defined as histograms.

There are several statistical classes, from simple ones which collect the mean and the standard deviation of the samples to a number of distribution estimation classes. The latter include three highly configurable histogram classes and the implementations of the P^2 [236] and the k-split [472] algorithms. It is also supported to write time series result data into an output file during simulation execution.

3.3.4   Ownership Tracking

Instances of several classes in the OMNeT++ class library, most notably cMessage, maintain pointers back to their owners. The owner is usually the module which has created or received the given message, a queue or other container object in a module, or the simulation kernel (more precisely, the future events list). The owner pointer allows the simulation kernel to catch common mistakes such as sending the same message object twice, sending out a message while it is sitting in a queue, or accessing a message which is being held by another module.

Ownership management is transparent for most of the time. The most frequent case when it needs manual help is when a module passes a message object to another module by means of a C++ method call; then the target module explicitly needs to *take* the object from its current owner. Modules are *soft owners* and will yield to such requests, but if the owner is a queue for example, it is a *hard owner* and will raise an error instead.

Since modules maintain a list of owned objects, it is possible to recursively enumerate all objects in the simulation in a generic way, that is, without using pointer fields declared in simple module subclasses. This mechanism makes it possible for the user to inspect the simulation in the graphical runtime environment on object level, and to find leaked objects.

3.3.5   Representing Network Packets

An important aspect of network simulation is representing network packets. In OMNeT++, packets are C++ classes derived from cPacket, which is in turn a subclass of cMessage. cPacket's fields include the length of the packet, an error flag used to signal a corrupted packet, and a pointer to the encapsulated packet. The latter is used by the packet's encapsulate() and decapsulate() methods that are used when a message is passed up or down between protocol layers. These methods automatically update the length of the outer packet. The *encapsulated packet* pointer also gives an opportunity to OMNeT++ to reduce the number of packet object duplications by performing reference counting and copy-on-access on the encapsulated packet.

3.3.6   The Message Compiler

In OMNeT++, messages and network packets are represented with C++ classes. With getter and setter methods for each field, a copy constructor, assignment operator, and a virtual dup() function (network packets are often copied or duplicated during simulation), plus hand-written reflection information needed for displaying packet contents in the graphical runtime Tkenv, it would be a time-consuming and tedious task to implement packet classes in plain C++. OMNeT++ takes the burden off the programmers by providing a simple language (not unlike C structs with metadata annotation support) for describing messages, and the build system automatically generates C++ classes from them during the build process. Generic classes and structs may also be generated this way, not only packets and messages. If customizations are needed, the message compiler can be asked (via metadata annotations) to generate an intermediate base class only, from which the programmer can derive the final packet class with the necessary customizations. The success of the concept is proven by the fact that in modern OMNeT++ models practically all packet classes are generated.

An example message description:

```
//
// Represents a packet in the network.
//
packet SamplePacket
```

```
{
    int srcAddr;
    int destAddr;
    int hopLimit = 32;
}
```

3.3.7   Control Info

In OMNeT++, protocol layers are usually implemented as modules that exchange packets. However, communication between protocol layers often requires sending additional information to be attached to packets. For example, when a TCP implementation sends down a TCP packet to IP, it needs to specify the destination IP address and possibly other parameters. When IP passes up a packet to TCP after decapsulating from an IP datagram, it will want to let TCP know at least the source and the destination IP addresses. This additional information is represented by *control info* objects in OMNeT++. Control info objects are attached to packets.

3.3.8   Wired Packet Transmission

When modeling wired connections, packets are sent from the transmitter (e.g. the MAC module) of one network node to the receiver of another node, via a connection path that contains exactly one channel object. Like modules, channels are programmable in C++ as well, and they are responsible for modeling propagation delay, calculating and modeling transmission duration, and performing error modeling. The default channel model, `DatarateChannel`, performs simple BER and/or PER-based error modeling. Error modeling sets a flag in the packet, and it is the responsibility of the receiver module to check this flag and act accordingly.

Normally, the packet object gets delivered to the receiver module at the simulation time that corresponds to the end of the reception of the packet. However, the receiver module may request that packets are delivered to it at the beginning of their reception, by "reprogramming" the receiver gate with an appropriate API call. The last transmission duration is available in a field of the packet object, and may be used by the receiver to determine how long the channel is to be considered busy.

3.3.9   Wireless Packet Transmission

Wireless transmission is based on directly sending the packet to the wireless nodes within range. Usually there is a separate dedicated module (the *channel controller*) for keeping track which nodes are within range of others, and which frequency they occupy. The packet (frame) may be encapsulated into a conceptual *air frame* which contains the physical properties of the radio transmission. The (air) frame object needs to be duplicated for each receiving node.[3]

Modeling of the wireless channel and the radio reception is done in the destination node(s), possibly with help from the channel controller. It is up to the individual model frameworks (MiXiM, INET Framework, Castalia, etc.) how accurate a propagation, interference and reception model they choose to implement.

3.3.10 Signals

The OMNeT++ simulation library contains a built-in notification mechanism, which allows for publish-subscribe style communication between simulation components, and has many other uses.[4]

Signals are emitted by components (modules and channels), and propagate on the module hierarchy up to the root. At any level, one can register listeners (callback objects); these listeners will get notified (called back) whenever a signal is emitted.

The significance of upwards propagation is that listeners registered at a certain module will receive signals from all components in that submodule tree. Listeners registered at the top level will receive signals from the whole simulation. Since a module can register listeners at any other module, it can get notified about events anywhere it wishes. For example, a simple module representing a routing protocol may register a listener for the hypothetical *INTERFACE_UP* and *INTERFACE_DOWN* signals at the parent compound module that represents the router, and initiate actions to update the routing tables accordingly.

Signals are identified by names, but for efficiency, calls use dynamically assigned numeric signal identifiers. Names and identifiers are globally valid in the whole simulation.

When a signal is emitted, it can carry a value with it. The value can be of a basic type (long, double, string, etc.), or a pointer to an arbitrary object. Objects can be already existing objects, or ones specially crafted for the purpose of emitting the signal. Computing the signal value or propagating the signal may cost valuable CPU cycles, so the signal mechanism was

---

[3] Duplicating all protocol layers encapsulated in the frame would be a waste of CPU cycles because in a wireless network, most frames are immediately discarded by the receiver due to incorrect reception or wrong destination MAC address. Hence, OMNeT++ uses reference counting on encapsulated packets, and only duplicates them if needed, that is, when they actually get decapsulated in a higher layer protocol module.

[4] The notification mechanism appeared in version 4.1.

implemented in a way that helps avoid emitting or further propagating signals for which there are no listeners.

Simulation signals can be used for several purposes:

- for implementing publish-subscribe style communication among modules; it is advantageous when the producer and consumer of the information do not know about each other, and possibly there is many-to-one or many-to-many relationship among them;
- when some module needs to get notified about simulation model changes such as module creation and deletion, connection creation and deletion, parameter changes and so on. Such signals, both pre- and post-change ones, are emitted by the OMNeT++ simulation kernel, with attached objects that contain the details of the change;
- for emitting variables to be recorded as simulation results, for example queue lengths, packet drops, or end-to-end delays. Then it is up the simulation framework to add listeners which record the selected data in some form;
- for emitting animation primitives or auxiliary information that can be used by an animation engine;
- for emitting *pcap* traces that can be captured and written to file by (a) dedicated module(s) or the simulation framework

A historical note: OMNeT++ models written before the introduction of signals used specialized modules, such as `Blackboard` that was introduced as part of the Mobility Framework, and the `Blackboard`-inspired `NotificationBoard` in the INET Framework.

3.3.11   Random Number Architecture

OMNeT++ primarily uses Mersenne Twister [308] for random number generation.[5] A configurable number of global random number streams are provided to the simulation. Global random number streams are mapped to module-local ones; module parameters and module code consume random numbers from these module-local streams. The mapping from global streams to module-local ones can be configured in a flexible way, allowing the use of variance reduction techniques and other "tricks" without the need to change anything in the simulation model.

Seeding is automatic (seeds are auto-assigned using the run number, as described later), but it is also possible to use manually selected seeds in the configuration. The simulation requires as many seeds as the number of

---

[5] Mersenne Twister is the RNG class selected by default, but two others are provided (the LCG-32, a.k.a. "default standard" RNG, and one wrapping random numbers from the Akaroa library). It is also possible to write others and select them from the ini file, without changing anything in the simulation framework.

global RNG streams configured. Due to the practically infinite cycle length of Mersenne-Twister, overlapping RNG streams is not an issue.

3.3.12   Emulation, Distributed Simulation, Co-simulation

OMNeT++ provides a facility to replace the event scheduler class with a custom one, which is the key for many features including co-simulation, real-time simulation, network or device emulation, and distributed simulation.

The job of the event scheduler is to always return the next event to be processed by the simulator. The default implementation returns the first event in the future events list. For real-time simulation, this scheduler is replaced with one augmented with *wait* calls (e.g. `usleep`) that synchronize the simulation time to the system clock. There are several options on what should happen if the simulation time has already fallen behind: one may re-adjust the reference time, leave it unchanged in the hope of catching up later, or stop with an error message.

For *emulation*, the real-time scheduler is augmented with code that captures packets from real network devices, and inserts them into the simulation. The INET Framework contains an emulation scheduler, and uses *pcap* to capture packets, and raw sockets to send packets to the real network device. Emulation in INET also relies on *header serializer* classes that convert between protocol headers and their C++ object representations used within the simulation. The emulation feature has been successfully used to test the interoperability of INET's SCTP model with real-life SCTP implementations [470].

For parallel simulation (OMNeT++ contains support for conservative parallel simulation via the Null Message Algorithm [108]), the scheduler is modified to listen for messages arriving from other LPs, and inserts them into the simulation. The scheduler also blocks the simulation when it is not safe to execute the next event due to a potential causality violation, until clearance arrives from other LPs to continue in the form of a null message. Parallel simulation is covered in detail in Chapter 8.

OMNeT++ supports distributed simulation using HLA (IEEE 1516)[6] as well. The OMNeT++ scheduler also plays the role of the HLA Federate Ambassador, is responsible for exchanging messages (interactions, change notifications, etc.) with other federates, and performs time regulation.

OMNeT++ also supports mixing SystemC (IEEE 1666-2005) modules with OMNeT++ modules in the simulation. When this feature is enabled, there are two future event lists in the simulation, OMNeT++'s and SystemC's, and a special scheduler takes care that events are consumed from both lists in increasing timestamp order. This method of performing mixed

---

[6] The source code for the HLA and SystemC integration features are not open source, but they are available to researchers on request free of charge.

simulations is orders of magnitude faster and also more flexible than letting the two simulators execute in separate processes and communicate over a pipe or socket connection.

3.4 Running Simulations

3.4.1 Building Simulation Models

OMNeT++ uses *make* to build simulation models. To simplify things for model developers, OMNeT++ provides a tool named `opp_makemake` for generating makefiles. `opp_makemake` takes into account the source files found in a given directory, handles translating message files into C++ sources, and has options to generate a standalone simulation program, a shared library or a static library. The generated makefile can be customized via further command-line options, and/or by providing a `makefrag` file which gets textually included into the makefile.

A unique feature of the OMNeT++ build system is accessible with the `-deep` option. Building deep source directory trees that have complex inter-dependencies often poses a challenge to C++ developers. The usual approach to multi-directory builds is recursive make, which, however, tends to lead to a complicated, fragmented system of makefiles. In order to avoid having a complicated build system, projects often resort to artificial limitations like limiting the number of directory levels, mandating that "public" header files are put into designated `include/` directories, and so on.

The authors of OMNeT++ are of the opinion that there is no reason why the build system for a multi-directory project should be that complicated. The OMNeT++ approach is to cover the whole source tree with a single makefile, generated with the `opp_makemake -deep` command. The problem of include path is solved in the following way: simply *all* directories are put on the include path (`-I`). As most header files have unique names, this usually causes no problem at all. In the case of conflicting header files, names in the `#include` directive can be qualified with the partial or full path of the header file. For example, if there is both a `base/Util.h` and a `network/ipv6/Util.h` in the source tree, the former can be included as `"base/Util.h"` and the latter as `"ipv6/Util.h"` or `"network/ipv6/Util.h"`. Paranoid users can always fully qualify their includes, which essentially leads to something similar to Java imports.

If there are directories in the tree where the generated makefile is not suitable for some reason, it is possible to exclude that directory from the scope of `-deep`, and let *make* recurse into it and call a custom makefile.

Large model frameworks, for example the INET Framework which had about 70 deeply nested directories in its source tree at the time of writing, are being built using `opp_makemake -deep`, without the need for custom makefiles or large makefile fragments.

3.4.2   Simulation Programs

OMNeT++ simulations are ordinary programs. Usually simple modules are
linked into an executable which links against the simulation kernel, but it
is also possible to build shared libraries from the sources and load them
dynamically into other simulation executables or into the standalone opp_run
program.

Simulation programs are also linked against one or more *user interface
libraries*. Currently there are two user interfaces: *Cmdenv* is a console-based
one optimized for batch execution, and *Tkenv* is a GUI-based user interface
which is most useful during the development, testing, and model validation
phases of the project. One can also write new user interfaces and dynamically
register them without requiring modification to existing OMNeT++ sources;
for example, a Java and SWT-based GUI interface with sophisticated animation capabilities is currently under development. If a simulation program has
been linked with more than one user interfaces, a command-line option can
be used to select the desired one.

3.4.3   Configuration

The configuration for running the simulation comes from ini files. An ini file
defines the NED type to be instantiated as network; provides values for model
parameters that do not have default values or the default is not suitable; and
contains simulation options such as simulation time limit, RNG configuration, names of output files, or the set of statistics to be recorded to files. At
the time of writing, there are over 80 configuration options; many of them
define executable extensions to the simulation kernel, for example a custom
scheduler class, custom result file writer class, custom synchronizer class for
parallel simulation, or custom random number generator.

Ini files may contain multiple named configurations. Configurations can
build upon each other, adding new settings or overriding existing ones. This
feature practically implements single inheritance among configurations.

The Simulation IDE has a dual-mode (form and text) editor and several
associated views for setting up and editing simulation options, parameter settings and other configuration information. The editor provides wizards, syntax highlighting, content assist, on-the-fly validation and other convenience
features.

3.4.4   Parameter Studies

Ini files may also define *parameter studies*. A configuration may contain one
or more iteration variables in the syntax ${numHosts=1..5,10,20,50}; the

simulation runtime will take the Cartesian product of the sequences, and generates simulation runs for each. For example, the above `numHosts` iteration variable together with a `${pkLen=100,200,500}` variable will generate 8x3=24 simulation runs. Of course, not all combinations may make sense, so the user than specify additional constraints to filter out the unwanted ones. For example, the constraint `numHosts>10 || pkLen==500` would mean that for 10 or fewer hosts, the user is only interested in testing with $pkLen = 500$.

One can also specify that each run has to be repeated 10 times with different random number generator seeds, which will yield 24x10=240 runs. They are numbered from 0 through 239, and the user can tell the simulation program (via command-line options) to execute, say, run #146 of configuration `ThroughputTest` in the specified ini file. The seeds for these runs are generated automatically (but in a configurable way) from the run number and/or the repetition counter. It is also possible to specify seeds manually, but this is rarely needed or desired.

Experiment, measurement and replication labels are generated automatically from the configuration name, iteration variables and repetition counter, respectively; these labels are saved into the result files, and can be used to organize the data during result analysis. It is not mandatory to use machinery described above (named configurations, iteration variables, constraint, repeat count) to organize parameter studies: the user can set up configurations or runs manually as well, and if he or she explicitly sets the experiment-measurement-replication labels in the ini files in the correct way, result analysis tools will see those runs as part of the same parameter study.

3.4.5   Running Batches

As outlined in the previous section, running parameter studies with OMNeT++ usually boils down to running a simulation program several times with an ini file, a configuration name and a 0..n run number as command-line arguments.

There are various ways to execute such batches. The simplest way is perhaps to write a 3-line *bash* script with a `for ((i=0;i<$n;i++))` loop that launches the simulations one by one. A somewhat more sophisticated way is to employ GNU Make's `-j` n option, which instructs *make* to launch multiple processes to keep n (usually 2 or 4) processor cores busy. The `opp_runall` program is a simple OMNeT++ utility that supports exactly that: it generates a makefile with a target for each simulation run, and launches *gmake* with the user-specified `-j` option.

Smaller simulation batches that are expected to finish within minutes are most conveniently launched from the OMNeT++ Simulation IDE. The IDE also supports a *number of concurrent processes* option similar to GNU Make's `-j`.

To execute larger simulation batches, one may utilize computing clusters. One of the most user-friendly faces of *cluster computing* is Apple's *Xgrid*, which has also been successfully used with OMNeT++ [413]. Unfortunately, Xgrid is only available on Mac OS X computers. *RSerPool* [282] is another lightweight solution for distributing jobs to cluster nodes, and has also been successfully used with OMNeT++, as part of the *SimProcTC* toolkit [124]. Further potential candidates for running simulation batches are clusters running SUN Grid Engine (gridengine.sunsource.net), Condor (cs.wisc.edu/condor) or other grid middleware.

A more specialized way to make use of clusters is Akaroa [166, 437]. Akaroa is an implementation of the MRIP (Multiple Replications In Parallel) principle, which can be used to speed up steady-state simulations. Akaroa runs multiple instances of the same simulation program (but with different seeds) simultaneously on different processors, e.g. on nodes of a computing cluster, and a central process monitors certain output variables of the simulation. When Akaroa decides that it has enough observations to form an estimate of the required accuracy of all variables, it halts the simulation. When using n processors, simulations need to run only roughly $1/n$ times the required sequential execution time. Support for Akaroa is integrated into OMNeT++.

A related project is oProbe [56]. oProbe aims at providing an instrument that helps OMNeT++ simulation models produce statistically sound results at known quality. oProbe adds a probe component which applies a controlled stochastic sampling technique in the simulation model, and provides a graphical user interface for configuring and running simulations with it. Unfortunately, oProbe has not yet been ported to OMNeT++ 4.x, and remains available for OMNeT++ 3.x only.

There have also been attempts to utilize large-scale distributed grid systems like EGEE (eu-egee.org) with OMNeT++ [265]. However, the main problem on those grids is the lack of support for proper sandboxing (i.e. enforcing resource and access limits on submitted jobs), which makes it necessary for the operators of those grids to set up administrative and technical procedures that make getting access and submitting simulation jobs a lengthy and complicated procedure. For this reason, running discrete event simulations on large-scale grid systems has not really taken off yet.

3.4.6   Animation

Network animation is provided by the graphical runtime interface *Tkenv*, cf. Figure 3.2. Animation is automatic, that is, the simulation code does not need to be instrumented with animation requests. The animation is also generic, that is, not specific for network simulation: it works equally well for queueing network simulations, process chain simulations and other simulations. Tkenv lets the user open a graphical inspector (animation canvas) for any compound module or several compound modules. The canvas shows the submodules (network nodes, protocols, etc.) and their interconnections. Positions, icons, background image and other graphics attributes come from module (or channel) display strings. On startup, Tkenv automatically opens a canvas for the toplevel compound module which represents the network.

During simulation, Tkenv animates as messages or packets travel between modules, and animates method calls between modules as well. The simulation author can affect the animation by manipulating display strings (for example, updating coordinates of a mobile node, or changing the coloring of a protocol module depending on its state) during simulation.

Tkenv provides *live* animation, as opposed to *playback* provided by ns-2's *nam* tool. Compared to playback, live animation has its advantages (all objects can be examined in detail at any time, see next section; can be combined with C++ debugging) and disadvantages (it is not possible to play backwards or to re-play parts of the history) as well.

Limitations of Tkenv have been well understood, and it is planned to have a better animation framework, with support for custom animation effects, and the possibility to go back and re-play past events.

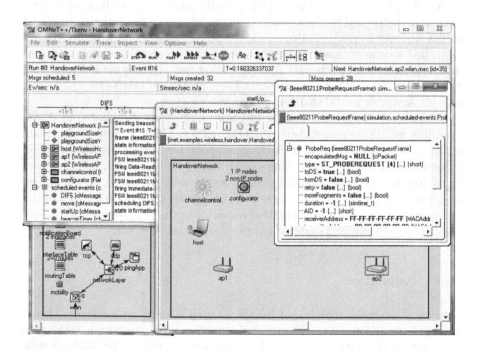

Fig. 3.2: The Tkenv Graphical Runtime Environment

3.4.7   Debugging and Visualization

Inspectors

In addition to animation, Tkenv also displays debug log output of modules, and lets the user inspect the model on object and field level. For example, it is possible to examine the contents of queues, or peek into network packets. The contents of the future event list is also visualized on a log-scale time strip. The simulation runtime knows about all objects in the model, and it is possible to search, for example, for all IP datagrams in the network.

Event Logs and Sequence Diagrams

OMNeT++ simulations can optionally create an event log file, which records simulation events such as message creations and deletions, event scheduling and cancellation; message sends and packet transmissions; model topology changes; display string changes; debug log messages from simple modules; and other information. Message and packet fields may also be captured in the event log file at a configurable level of detail; this feature relies on reflection information generated by the message compiler. Overall, event log files may be meaningfully compared to ns-2/ns-3 network animation files.

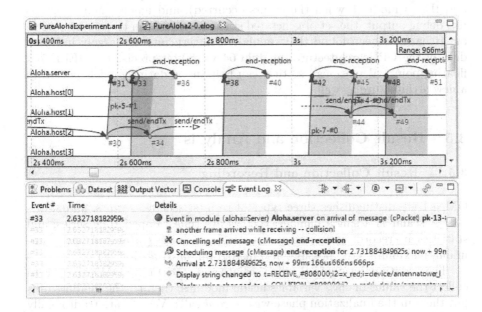

Fig. 3.3: Sequence Diagram

The Simulation IDE can visualize the log using an interactive sequence diagram, which significantly facilitates the verification of protocol models, cf. Figure 3.3. The chart can be panned and zoomed, there are several ways (linear, nonlinear, step, etc.) to map simulation time and events to the x axis, and the chart can be filtered by modules and by various other criteria. Tooltips show the properties of events and messages/packets in detail, and it is also possible to browse the detailed log of actions by simulation event. The sequence chart can also be exported in the SVG format. During operation, the tool only keeps parts of the file in memory, so it is feasible to view event log files of several gigabytes in size.

Simulation Fingerprint

An interesting OMNeT++ concept is the *simulation fingerprint*. This is practically a hash code calculated with a simple algorithm during the runtime of a simulation. The fingerprint can be used as a simple regression testing tool: very often the development of a new feature or a refactoring on the C++ code (for example adding or removing statistics, or rewriting informal code to a state machine pattern) is not supposed to change the operation of a simulation model, and the fingerprint before and after the code change should be the same. The fingerprint algorithm takes into account variables that are very likely to differ if the model diverges to another trajectory (event timestamps and IDs of modules when the events occurred), and ignores non-essentials like debug output, the set of generated statistics, names in the model, and so on. It has also been found that simulation fingerprints are largely independent of the CPU architecture (modulo 64 vs. 80-bit precision of IEEE 754 floating-point calculations), so they can help in validating models ported to a new architecture as well.

3.5   Result Collection and Analysis

3.5.1   Result Collection and Recording

OMNeT++ distinguishes three types of results: *scalars*, *vectors*, and *statistics*. A scalar is a single number; vectors are timestamped time series; and statistics are records composed of statistical properties (mean, variance, minimum, maximum, etc.; possibly also histogram data) of time series.

The traditional way of recording scalars and statistics in OMNeT++ is to collect the values in class variables inside modules, then let the modules output them in the finalization phase with *record* calls. Vectors are traditionally recorded via *output vector* objects. Recording of individual vectors, scalars and statistics can be enabled or disabled via the configuration (ini file), and it is also the place to set up recording intervals for vectors. The problem with this approach is that the result types are hardcoded in the simple modules' code, whereas different experiments (validation run vs. parameter study) often require one to record the same variable at different detail levels (i.e. all values as a vector, or only the mean as a scalar).

With the introduction of the signals mechanism, result recording is being transitioned to use signals for greater flexibility. Modules would act as signal sources, and the user would be able to decide whether to record a particular variable as a vector, as a statistic (mean, variance, histogram data, etc.), or to record only a single property of the variable (mean, time average, count, maximum value, etc.) as a scalar. The simulation framework would implement result recording by registering listeners on the modules. The signal framework would also allow for implementing aggregate statistics (such as the total number of packet drops in the network) and warmup periods (ignoring an initial time interval when computing scalars or statistics) as well. It would also allow the user to employ dedicated statistics collection and aggregation modules in the simulation, without the need to change existing modules.

3.5.2   Result Files

Simulation results are recorded into textual, line-oriented *scalar files* (which actually hold statistics results as well) and *vector files*.[7] The file format is well specified, extensible, and open for other simulators to adapt. There are standalone implementations (Java) for recording files in this format, and experimental support for the format is included in the *ns-3* simulator as well. The advantage of a text-based format is that it is very accessible with a wide range of tools and languages including Matlab, GNU R, Python or Ruby.

Vectors are recorded into a separate file for practical reasons: vector data usually consume several magnitudes more disk space than others. Vector files are self-describing: they contain many attributes of the simulation run: the network, experiment-measurement-replication labels; iteration variables; time/date, host, process id of the simulation, etc. By default, each file contains data from one run only. The vector file contains data clustered by vectors, and indexed for efficient access. This allows for extracting certain vectors from the file, and even near random access within vectors, without having to read the full contents of the vector file even once.

---

[7] Recording is actually configurable. Users can provide their own plug-in output vector manager and output scalar manager classes, and activate them in the configuration. Implementations that write into a MySQL database are provided as examples.

3.5.3   Visualization using the Simulation IDE

The OMNeT++ Simulation IDE provides an integrated result analysis tool. The tool intends to combine the ease of use of graphical user interfaces with the power of scripting. One of the design goals of the tool was to eliminate repetitive work: the user does not want to re-do all charts after re-running simulations due to some change in the code or in the configuration.

The tool lets the user specify a set of result files to work with, and lets the user browse the data in them. For browsing, data can be displayed in tables, in a tree organized by experiment-measurement-replication labels or various other ways, and it can also be filtered.

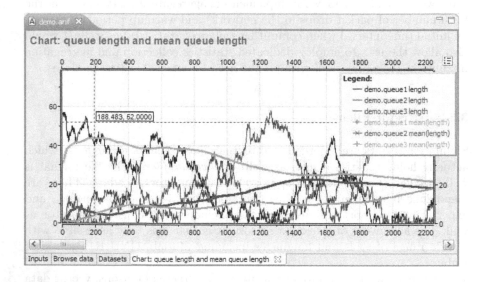

Fig. 3.4: Line Chart in the Result Analysis Tool

The tool also lets the user create various charts from simulation results: line charts from vectors, cf. Figure 3.4; bar charts and scatter plots from scalars; histogram charts, and other charts. These charts can be exported in various raster and vector image formats. Data for the charts are the result of filtering operations on the result files (*"select all vectors named end-to-end delay"*), possibly followed by other operations (*"apply moving average"*). The set of files to operate on can be specified using wildcards; if new matching files are created or existing files are replaced, charts and data tables in the UI get updated automatically.

There are several built-in operations. Extensibility is provided via GNU R (r-project.org), an open-source statistical computing and graphics language. In the IDE, users can create custom charts and custom processing nodes as GNU R scripts.

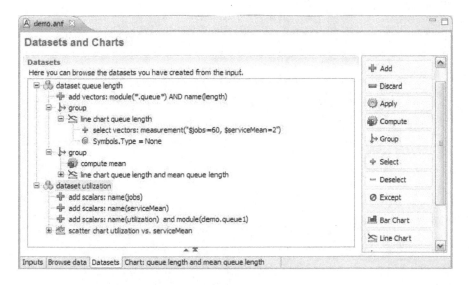

Fig. 3.5: Datasets in the Result Analysis Tool

The analysis tool is actually an editor for an *analysis file*. The analysis file contains the file names or wildcard patterns for the input files, and various *dataset* items that describe the steps of selecting data from the inputs, the operations to apply, and the charts to draw from them, cf. Figure 3.5. Datasets serve as "recipes" for drawing the desired charts from raw data, and can be thought of as a GUI-based script language.

An alternative to the Simulation IDE's analysis tool is to use the visualization part of SimProcTC [124], a GNU R-based toolset and script library which also covers the parametrization of OMNeT++ simulation runs and distributed batch processing.

4. IKR Simulation Library

Jörg Sommer (University of Stuttgart, Institute of Communication Networks and Computer Engineering)
Joachim Scharf (University of Stuttgart, Institute of Communication Networks and Computer Engineering)

4.1 Introduction

The *Simulation Library* (SimLib) of the Institute of Communication Networks and Computer Engineering (IKR) [216] at the University of Stuttgart is a tool for *event-driven simulation* of complex systems in the area of communications engineering. The first version of the *IKR SimLib* was implemented in Pascal in the 1980s. Later in 1993, during his dissertation [256] Hartmut Kocher redesigned the Pascal simulation library and developed an object-oriented class library of the IKR SimLib in C++. Since that time, we have enhanced and improved the library continuously. Driver for this development is the wide usage at the IKR as well as the involvement of many programmers. In 2008, we translated the IKR SimLib to Java while keeping all concepts and mechanisms of the existing C++ class library. Today, two editions of the IKR SimLib are available: The C++ edition and the Java edition. Each edition comes as a separate class library. The IKR SimLib is publicly available under the GNU Lesser General Public License (LGPL) and thus allows changes within the libraries itself as well as proprietary programs to use it.

The design objectives of the IKR SimLib were manifold. The IKR SimLib is problem-oriented in a sense that it supports an effective implementation of an abstract communication system model. Each *simulation* model component can consist of submodels and components. This leads to a hierarchical modeling approach. The components are encapsulated and communicate with each other by exchanging messages using ports. This offers a high reuse and an evolutionary redefining of new components by modifying existing ones.

The IKR SimLib includes all components that are necessary to control and execute an event-driven simulation. Examples for such components are a global *calendar* and *events*. Besides, the library supports a modular I/O concept. During a simulation run, the IKR SimLib computes statistical data, e.g., confidence intervals. Therefore, a complex post-processing step is unnecessary. In order to reduce large simulation execution times, the IKR SimLib supports distributed simulation on different CPUs and/or cores in a computing cluster.

The continuous enhancements and improvements lead to a wide field of application, also outside of the institute. The IKR SimLib was used and is still used for several publicly and privately funded research projects. Simulations based on this library are also performed in student projects. Up to now, more than one hundred of these student projects have been finished. Furthermore, IKR's industrial partners use this library for complex simulations.

Since its launch, the IKR SimLib has proved its applicability for performance evaluation in a multitude of communication areas, e.g., for IP, photonic, mobile, signaling, in-vehicle, and P2P networks. For getting the latest version of the IKR SimLib, a more detailed list of examples, and getting selected publications, please visit the website *http://www.ikr.uni-stuttgart.de/IKRSimLib*.

4.2   Architecture and Conceptual Structure

The IKR SimLib is structured into three main parts as shown in Figure 4.1. The *basic concepts* include simulation support mechanisms as well as I/O concepts. Besides, the modeling concepts support a hierarchical modeling approach to create individual components that communicate with each other by exchanging messages. The *standard components* are composed entities like a traffic generator, which provide a simple model implementation. In the following sections, we describe each part in more detail.

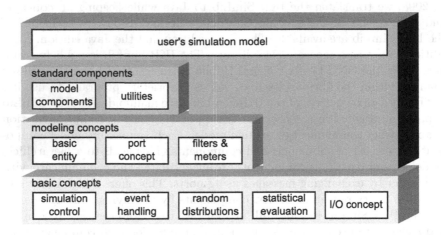

Fig. 4.1: Basic structure of the IKR SimLib

4.2.1   Basic Concepts

The *basic concepts* support mechanisms and components for an event-driven simulation. One of these mechanisms is the *simulation control* that handles the initialization, e.g., when to stop the transient phase and begin with the actual performance evaluation phase and finally when to stop the simulation *batches*. The control also signals the according changes to all objects needing this information. Furthermore, the basic concepts offer inherent support for event handling, e.g., by providing a calendar. While processing an event, it is possible to post new events, which are entered into the calendar. After processing of an event is finished, the next event in the calendar is processed.

The IKR SimLib supports *stochastic processes* and *on-the-fly statistical evaluation*. One important aspect is the distribution-oriented *random number* generation. The IKR SimLib implements many continuous and discrete *random distributions*. *Statistical evaluation* is supported by many different statistics, too. Examples are the sample, counter, conditional mean, and correlation statistic. One distinguishing feature from many other *simulation tools* is the provisioning of metrics dealing with the statistical significance, which is in case of the IKR SimLib a student t-test based confidence interval. In addition, the library includes a flexible *I/O concept* which consists of a file parser for reading parameters and an XML-based output concept for printing results.

4.2.2   Modeling Concepts

The next main part of the IKR SimLib provides modeling concepts. In general, a model has a hierarchical structure and consists of several components and entities that communicate with each other. Entities are able to post and handle events. Each entity is derived from the base class *Entity* and has a unique local name which is chosen arbitrarily. This name helps to identify the entity and to locate it via a central component manager. This base class defines the common properties of all entities and methods for dealing with ports and events.

The hierarchical decomposition of an entity into a hierarchy of components or entities decreases the complexity. In other words, the division into components brakes down the complexity. It enables a separate handling and treatment of each entity. This principle corresponds to the *divide-and-conquer* approach and leads to a tree structure of entities and components with the model itself as the root entity [257]. All entities are strictly encapsulated and communicate with each other by exchanging messages. This message exchange works by using so-called ports, which define a generic external interface of an entity. This *port concept* enables the interconnection of entities in a plug-n-play manner.

Furthermore, *filters* and *meters* are connected to ports. Filters inspect and may change messages based on certain rules, e.g., changing specific fields within the message. In contrast to this, meters primarily update statistics with values derived from the messages, e.g., the message length or time of arrival.

4.2.3   Standard Components

The *standard components* are the third part. *Model components* like *traffic generators, queues, servers, multiplexers, traffic sinks* etc. are provided to ease model implementation. They have also a hierarchical structure. This offers a reuse of submodels and components that can be further redefined. Together with further utilities, they allow a simple model generation, especially for queuing networks.

4.2.4   Simple Simulation Model

For illustrating the concepts of the IKR SimLib, Figure 4.2 depicts a model of a simple single-server *queuing network* which comprises the network model, a traffic generator, and a traffic sink. The port concept and a message transfer protocol enable that the simulation messages are passed from component to component. After a component recognizes a new message at the output port, this port notifies the corresponding input port. For example, in Figure 4.2 each time when the traffic generator generates a new message, its output port informs the input port of the queue. Then, the receiving component decides if the message will be accepted.

Because of the flexible port concept, the integration of filters and meters into the model is easy. They read and evaluate the flow of messages at various points within the model. In Figure 4.2 the integrated *Time Meter* measures the processing time in the network model including the waiting time in the queue and the holding time in the server. For this purpose, the time meter adds a time stamp to the message when it passes the output port of the traffic generator. When the message passes the input port of the traffic sink, the time meter reads and removes the time stamp. In this figure, we have also two filters. They observe the messages that are passing the input port of the queue. For example, one of these filters might record a trace of messages of a defined traffic class.

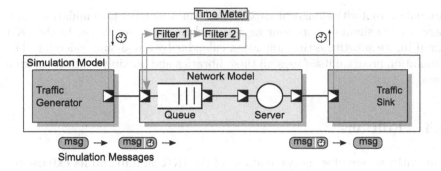

Fig. 4.2: Message-based simulation

4.3 Extensions

We build two additional libraries on top of the IKR SimLib: The IKR TCP Library [64] and the IKR Emulation Library [330, 329]. The usage of both libraries is optional.

4.3.1 TCP Library

The IKR TCP Library (*IKR TCPLib*) offers a basic implementation with all important *TCP* mechanisms (e.g., flow and congestion control). This library allows simulation of elastic applications and elastic traffic flows. The TCP components, which are included in this library, enable to model unidirectional TCP connections. This means components on the sender side create TCP data messages, which they transfer over the network. Components on the receiver side collect the data messages and send back ACK messages to the sender components. Sender and receiver side may be represented either by separate collection entities or by a single collection entity integrating both parts. A further constraint concerns connection control. We model the connection setup and release in a simplistic manner by providing *Setup* and *Release* methods which have to be called separately on sender and receiver side. The simulations results of the IKR TCPLib are comparable to other simulation environments, such as ns-2 (UC Berkeley, LBL, USC/ISI, and Xerox PARC).

4.3.2 Emulation Library

The second extension library is the IKR Emulation Library (*IKR EmuLib*). This library can emulate a system that is specified as a simulation model, i.e., we can use the same model in simulation and *emulation* in an efficient and lightweight manner. Additionally, the effort for enhancing an existing simulation tool with emulation capabilities is minimal. For the emulation, messages in the simulator are sent as real packets, and vice versa. In the IKR EmuLib, we substitute the simulation calendar by a real-time calendar. The simulation program itself uses all these libraries and possibly further external ones.

4.4   Editions

Currently, we are offering two editions of the IKR SimLib and its extensions: The C++ edition and the Java edition. Each edition comes as a separate class library that consists of more than 400 classes and tens of thousands lines of pure code. We developed both editions in consideration of modern object-oriented design principles and clean software architecture. As the libraries have almost no platform dependent code, they run under the most common operation systems (Linux and MS Windows) without any problems. Although both editions use the same concepts and mechanisms, there exist differences concerning base libraries and extensions. In this section, we describe both editions and their differences.

4.4.1   C++ Edition

The C++ edition utilizes two other libraries, namely the IKR Component Library [63] and the IKR Utility Library [62] as shown in Figure 4.3 on the left side. These two libraries provide amongst others simple to use strings, memory management, an argument parser, as well as data structures like dynamic lists, arrays, and matrices. With respect to these data structures, the IKR Component Library is comparable to the C++ Standard Template Library (STL).

As shown in Figure 4.3, the above mentioned extension libraries are available for the C++ edition.

4.4.2   Java Edition

As depicted in Figure 4.3 on the right side, the Java edition of the IKR SimLib does not utilize any other libraries, beside Java's Base Libraries, which are part of the *Java Standard Edition Runtime Environment* (JRE). It takes advantage of the additions to the Java language. The Java Base Libraries like the *lang* and *util* libraries provide all fundamental data structures, functions, and a rich set of APIs for managing I/O.

To the best of our knowledge, the Java edition is one of the first network simulators implemented in Java. As shown in Figure 4.3, currently only the IKR EmuLib is available for the Java edition.

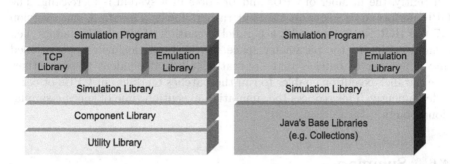

Fig. 4.3: Simulation program in practical usage (C++ and Java edition)

4.5 Application

Writing a simulation program based on the IKR SimLib requires a basic understanding of the library. The simulation libraries come along with extensive documentation, comprehensible tutorials, and examples. These help to get a fast understanding of the library. The philosophy of the IKR SimLib is that the challenge lies in the appropriate modeling. The model has to reflect the object of investigation in an abstract, but specialized manner. Therefore, the library does not include ready-to-use implementations such as a HTTP/TCP/IP protocol stack or a WDM network. The library offers basic components such as queues, statistics, and generators that enables an easy and fast implementation of a pre-designed model.

The implementation complexity of the simulation program depends on the complexity of the model, but also on the extent of already existing components. As already mentioned, a model of a queuing network can profit significantly from the standard components. In contrast to this, complex components and all kind of algorithms have to be implemented by hand. This step can be rather straightforward or very complex, depending on the problem. There is no simple rule of thumb to quantify the effort.

After finishing the implementation of the model, the execution of simulations is the next step. An extra tool called SimTree supports a user-friendly definition of simulation parameters. The defined simulation parameters span a parameter tree. SimTree generates this parameter tree automatically and controls the simulations runs. The results are written to an XML log file. SimTree also supports the collection of the results from independent simulation runs and the evaluation of a simulation study. Again, this extra tool is well documented.

Today's research problems get more and more complex, which leads to higher model complexity and consequently to longer duration of simulations. Currently, the number of CPUs and/or cores in a system is increasing. The CPU performance increases also, but rather slowly. Therefore, since version 2.7 the IKR SimLib provides a parallel execution of simulation points, i.e., a single point in the parameter space. Each simulation run is partitioned into a number of batches that are statistically independent to each other. The parallel execution enables to run the batches on different CPUs or cores independently. This reduces the simulation execution time of specific simulations points.

4.6 Summary

The IKR SimLib is well suited for event-driven simulations but can also be used for other kinds of simulations, e.g., Monte-Carlo [276] simulation. It is publicly available and continuously improved. Its key advantages are the clear design, the number of included components, and the powerful statistical evaluation support. The IKR SimLib provides a hierarchical modeling concept. This enables the decomposition of complex models and the implementation of reusable submodels and components.

The library showed its applicability and flexibility in many projects. Thereby, it is not only usable for experts in the field of simulation, but also for beginners due to the documentation and tutorials.

5. openWNS

Daniel Bültmann (RWTH Aachen University)
Maciej Mühleisen (RWTH Aachen University)
Sebastian Max (RWTH Aachen University)

5.1 Introduction

Performance evaluation by means of simulation is an integral part of any standardization, system development or research activity. It allows for conducting repeatable experiments in a controllable low-cost environment. Typically such activities involve multiple parties, which pursue different interests. This usually leads to a situation where results of own evaluations need to be defended and evaluation results of other parties need to be reviewed. In such situations a common simulation platform has a significant potential for reduction of cost and effort, quality increase and process speed-up. This was one of the reasons for the decision to release the simulation platform used and developed at ComNets to the open source community. For additional information on *openWNS* see [6].

Whereas most other open source simulation tools are released under the GNU General Public License (GPL) for openWNS the Lesser General Public License (LGPL) license was chosen. Compared to the GPL the LGPL additionally allows for closed source simulation modules if you only use (link against) openWNS, but still all modifications to the openWNS libraries themselves must be made open source. This relaxation was accepted to alleviate the adoption of openWNS within the industry.

The presented simulation tool is highly modular and allows users to select an extension point, which fits best to their needs. However, most of the protocol models that were released are based on an implementation of the Functional Unit Networks (FUNs) [402, 403]. Modularization is consequently applied even to protocol building blocks, such that new protocols can be easily built by selecting appropriate blocks from the Layer Development Kit (LDK) - a toolbox of protocol building blocks such as Automatic Repeat Request (ARQ), Segmentation And Reassembly (SAR), buffers, schedulers, etc.

openWNS has built-in support for simulation and compilation clusters. Simulation campaigns can be easily managed by users and results of parallel simulation runs can be browsed with a graphical front-end. The backend is built by a relational database and a grid engine such as SUN's SGE.

5.2   The Simulation Platform

This section introduces the simulation platform of openWNS, which includes the core components of an event-driven stochastic simulation tool and is the basis for the simulation framework and simulation modules (cmp. Figure 5.1). It is written in C++ and is heavily based on the Boost libraries [1] which provide already many features of the upcoming C++ standard [10], today.

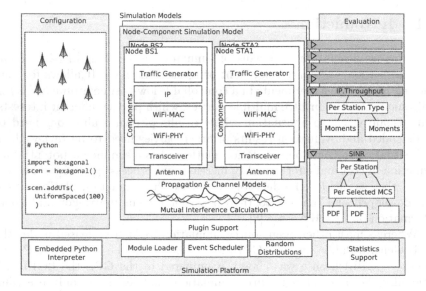

Fig. 5.1: openWNS Structure

5.2.1   Event Scheduler

The event schedulers used in openWNS can be used to directly schedule C++ functions. The event schedulers are designed to be used with the Boost C++ library. With the help of Boost's function and bind library you can simply make a complex function call in your code and tell the event scheduler to actually perform that call at a later point in time. There is no need to implement special Event classes that can be scheduled. Just write down the call and perform it later. The simulation platform also provides a flavor of the event scheduler that runs in real time (as long as your CPU is fast enough).

5.2.2   Random Distributions

The *random number generator* is based on the Mersenne Twister algorithm
[308]. The implementation that is used is the one provided by the Boost
random library (i.e. mt19937). The algorithm provides a period of of $2^{19937} - 1$
and passed a number of stringent statistical tests.

The available random number distributions include Uniform, Normal,
Exponential, Poisson, Ricean, Pareto, Erlang, and Binomial. Furthermore,
the random number distributions provided by the boost random library are
available.

For debugging purposes it is possible to use multiple base generators.
In this way one could use a fixed seed for the mobility components but use
random seeds within the link to system level interface to conduct packet error
rate experiments.

5.2.3   Configuration

The *Python* language is used for configuration of simulation scenarios (cmp.
Figure 5.1). The most important advantage to choose a programming language instead of a data representation language such as XML is its scalability. To be useful for a wide range of users the configuration mechanism must
be capable to scale with the scenario size and also scale with increasing complexity of simulation models. With an object oriented programming language
the first scale-up can be achieved by functional decomposition of the scenario
setup task, while the second can be achieved through sub-classing or structural composition of class hierarchies. Python was chosen for its syntactical
clarity and its wide support within the open source community.

5.2.4   Evaluation

The evaluation subsystem of openWNS provides means to sort measurements
according to a measurement context and compress the data by statistically
processing the measurements during the runtime of the simulator. This is
illustrated on the right hand side of Figure 5.1.

At compile time the developer defines measurement sources within the
model and also defines context information that accompanies each measurement (i.e. the node position, the base station to which it is associated, the
used modulation and coding scheme, etc.).

At configuration time the user of the model can decide on the kind of evaluation that suits his investigation best. For instance, the user could configure
an evaluation for a Signal-to-Interference-plus-Noise-Ratio (SINR) measurement source. The Probability Density Function (PDF) for each station and

for each modulation coding scheme can be gathered to determine the number of false scheduling decisions.

The major advantage of this approach over post-mortem measurement evaluation is the support for longer simulation runs. When running large simulation campaigns storage capacity is soon a problem. For example, consider a simulation campaign which collects the mean SINR for 100 user terminals within a cell. Assuming that a double precision float value (8 bytes) is used for the value and that every frame (2ms) a new measurement is generated, the data rate for this scenario would be 800 bytes per frame. With 100 drops (terminal positions are fixed but chosen randomly) and 100 seconds simulation time for each drop the necessary storage capacity would be 4GB - only for the SINR values.

The online statistical evaluation saves space. Furthermore, the clear distinction between the measurement source and the sorting stages makes it easy for users to quickly implement their desired evaluation. No changes to the original models have to be made.

5.3   Simulation Framework

The development of a simulator often requires the implementation of recurring software patterns. The openWNS provides a framework that makes developing of protocols easy. The goal of the simulation framework is to make development of simulation models and often used parts of protocol stacks easy to implement and to configure. This is achieved through well-defined clear interfaces, a rich set of predefined protocol building blocks and a high degree of code reuse, which is achieved by a component-based development approach.

5.3.1   Simulation Model

There is an indispensable need to simulate both, simple queueing systems as well as complex simulation scenarios with an entirely equipped protocol stack. The openWNS provides a software architecture that supports both. Each simulation is defined through the simulation model which specifies two basic methods: start() and shutdown(). These methods define the entry point of the simulation model and a point of notification about the end of the simulation.

5.3.2   Node-Component Model

As stated above the simulation is based on a simulation model which can be a simple queueing system or a more complex scenario with several stations.

The Node-Component model allows for the flexible specification of protocol stacks. Therefore, each station is represented by a `Node` class. Each Node contains a set of components which represent the protocol layers, equivalent to protocol layers of the *ISO/OSI* reference model [218]. Figure 5.1 shows the structure of the Node-Component Simulation Model. Usually each simulator module defines a specific component type, that can be instantiated inside a node, see also Section 5.4.

5.3.3   Layer Development Kit

Protocol layer development is often the fundamental step of developing an openWNS module. Protocol layers in openWNS correspond to ISO/OSI layers and are subdivided into Functional Units (FUs). There is a simple mechanism to connect FUs. These connected FUs form a Functional Unit Network (FUN) and represent the central packet processor of the openWNS layer, see Figure 5.2.

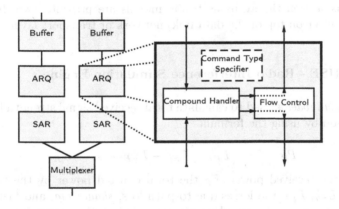

Fig. 5.2: Functional Unit Network

Messages between and inside layers are transmitted through compounds of commands, which is similar to the blackboard software pattern [83]. Each FU defines a unique command type. Each compound contains a single instance of the specific command, that is defined by the command type specifier and which can only be accessed by the FU.

The compound handler is the central element of the FU. It defines the actions that are performed for incoming and outgoing compounds. Often, the developer has only to define the function of the compound handler. Other elements of the FU can easily be aggregated by predefined components of the LDK toolbox.

Another important aspect of the LDK is flow control. FUs provide flow control for outgoing packets. Each FU provides an interface that gives information, whether a compound would be accepted. Hence upper FUs ask lower FUs before they send outgoing compounds. For incoming compounds, flow control in terms of blocking is not necessary.

New protocols can be easily built by selecting appropriate blocks from the LDK, that contains a predefined toolbox of protocol building blocks such as ARQ, SAR, buffers, schedulers, multiplexers, de-multiplexers, etc. A detailed description of the FU concept can be found in [403].

5.4 Simulation Modules

This section presents the simulation modules included in openWNS. Starting with the channel and interference modeling, the WiMAX and WiFi data link layer modules are presented. openWNS allows for simulations that include multi-standard nodes that may operate concurrently below the IP network layer. The transport layer modules for TCP and UDP are introduced. At the end of this section the available traffic models are presented which can be operated either on top of the data link, network or transport layer.

5.4.1 RISE - Radio Interference Simulation Engine

The *channel model* is used to calculate total received signal strength for every transmission by using the formula

$$P_R = P_T - L_{PL} - L_{Sh} - L_{FF} + G_T + G_R \tag{5.1}$$

P_R is the received power, P_T the total emitted power by the transmitter, L_{PL}, L_{Sh}, L_{FF} the losses due to path-loss, *shadowing*, and fast fading, and $G_T(\phi, \theta)$, $G_R(\phi, \theta)$ are the antenna gains at the transmitter and receiver. The radio propagation model can be independently chosen for each transceiver type pair. This can be used for example to have different models for different moving speeds or to define Line-of-Sight (LOS) and Non-Line-of-Sight (NLOS) connections.

It is possible to include directive antenna models which depend on ϕ and θ. Two antenna types are distinguished. The static antenna is described by its gain in all directions. The *beamforming* antenna allows to dynamically adjust its directivity. The algorithm used to calculate the gain is the optimal beamformer algorithm described in [177].

Several models to calculate the path loss between transmitter and receiver are available. Those are:

– Constant (distance independent)

- Free space
- Single slope
- Multi slope

Distance ranges can be defined and a model applied for each range. The single slope model is described by the equation $L_{PL} = (\frac{\lambda}{4\pi d})^\gamma$. d is the distance between transmitter and receiver, λ the electromagnetic wavelength and γ the propagation coefficient. In a logarithmic notation γ becomes the slope. Free space propagation is a special case of the single slope model with $\gamma = 2$.

The multi slope model is created by defining multiple distance ranges using single slope propagations with different propagation factors. Constant, distance independent path loss is usually applied for very short or very long distances. The pathloss models for the IMT-Advanced evaluation have already been partly included [228].

Different shadowing models to describe the scenario are available. These models describe the influence of solid obstacles on radio wave propagation. Three different models are available:

- Map based
- Scenery object based
- Spatially correlated log-Normal

The map based model assumes fixed base station positions. The shadowing is pre-calculated for each base station by a map of the signal degradation due to shadowing at several sampling points on the scenario. The signal strength between sampling points is interpolated.

The scenery object based model includes geometric obstructions with a fixed penetration loss. The total shadowing is defined by the total penetration loss of all penetrated walls assuming LOS propagation. This is typically used to create indoor scenarios with walls or outdoor scenarios with whole buildings. In contrast to the map based model this model does not require fixed base stations to be one communication end point. It can therefore be used for mobile-to-mobile station communication.

Spatially correlated log-Normal shadowing is modeled stochastically. A description of the model can be found in [486]. It is based on a sequence of correlated, log-Normal distributed random values.

Additionally to shadowing and path-loss, a fast fading model can be enabled. Currently, rician fading [484] as well as time correlated and frequency selective models are available. Time correlation is modeled according to the *Jakes model* [238]. The frequency selective fading process is modeled according to [426].

5.4.2   IEEE 802.11 WLAN

The IEEE 802.11 MAC procedure, based on Carrier Sense Multiple Access with Collision Avoidance (CSMA-CA), is well known; hence, it is used as an example how a protocol is implemented using the tools available from the openWNS. Figure 5.3 shows the data flow graph of the implementation. Each box in the figure represents a FU which is able to process outgoing and incoming packets in a certain way. As their interfaces are standardized, these FUs can be aligned and re-used as required by the protocol. The figure does not show the additional non-standard interface part which is required by some components, e. g., to get receive of the current channel state (busy/idle) from the physical layer below.

The implementation in each FU contains both the functionality of a transmitter and a receiver of a packet. In the figure, outgoing packets flow from top to bottom, incoming packets the other way around. Depending on the characteristics of a packet (e. g. size, type), outgoing packets can take different paths; at the receiver side the corresponding incoming packet takes automatically the same path (in reversed direction, of course). FUs are able to differentiate between incoming- and outgoing packets via their interface.

The implementation can be divided into two parts. The top part, from the "Overhead" to the first "Packet Switch" FU, is responsible for the non-timing relevant parts of the protocol:

- The "Overhead" FU adds a fixed-size header to every outgoing data packet.
- The "Buffer" stores a limited number of outgoing packets if immediate transmission is not possible (e. g. if the channel is busy); the buffer is configured as a dropping First-In/First-Out (FIFO) queue.
- The "Stop-And-Wait ARQ" is responsible for the transmission of an Acknowledgment (ACK) packet for every correctly received data packet; Furthermore, it stores every outgoing data packet and repeats the transmission until an ACK packet is received or the maximum number of transmission attempts is reached.
- Finally, the "Rate Adaptation" uses information about average number of required tries of past transmission to select a Modulation- and Coding Scheme (MCS) which assures efficient operation.

At the end of the non-timing relevant part, the "Packet Switch" FU determines the further processing of outgoing packets.

- ACK frames are transmitted after a constant delay, which is defined by the IEEE 802.11 standard as the Short Inter Frame Space (SIFS).
- Non-ACK frames with a size less than a (configurable) threshold are transmitted using the Distributed Coordination Function (DCF), i. e. CSMA-CA with a contention window that grows for retransmissions.
- Non-ACK frames with a size greater or equal than the threshold are preceded by an exchange of small Ready to Send (RTS) and Clear to

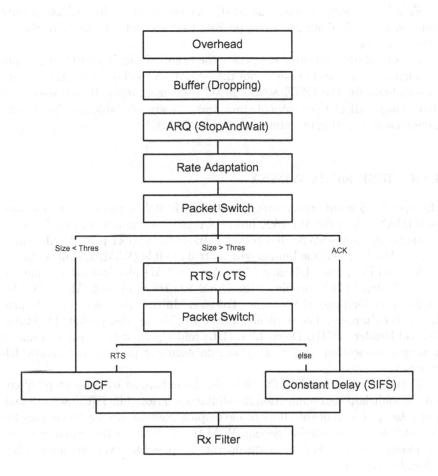

Fig. 5.3: The IEEE 802.11 MAC in the openWNS.

Send (CTS) packets that reserve the channel for the successive longer transmission. The RTS packet uses same DCF as data packets; all further packets of the exchange can be transmitted with a SIFS delay only. Additionally, the FU stores the outgoing data packet until the CTS is received or a timeout occurs. In the later case, the failure is reported to the ARQ.

Finally, all packets leave the MAC via the receive filter which is only responsible to filter out incoming packets that are not addressed to the receiver's address.

Figure 5.3 also indicates with color the origin of each FU: FUs in red are all-purpose components taken from the openWNS toolbox, FUs in black are custom-build for the IEEE 802.11 MAC implementation. It becomes clear that nearly half of the protocol stack was already available, neither implementation nor testing or debugging was necessary.

5.4.3   IEEE 802.16 WiMAX

The openWNS additionally supports the IEEE 802.16 protocol, also known as WiMAX. Since the WiMAX protocol realizes a frame based medium access scheme, the openWNS has been enhanced to support periodically timed frames. The WiMAX medium access control module (WiMAC) supports the Orthogonal Frequency Division Multiplex (OFDM) physical layer Time Division Duplex (TDD) profile of the IEEE 802.16e standard. Also, WiMAC supports the Orthogonal Frequency Division Multiple Access (OFDMA) profile for flat channels. The implementation provides special packets for Frame Control Header (FCH), Down Link (DL) and Up Link (UL) maps, ranging messages, association and connection establishment packets and bandwidth requests.

In the recent years, WiMAC has also be enhanced to support relay enhanced multihop communication in cellular scenarios. The IEEE 802.16j task group has put significant effort in developing medium access techniques for the relay enhanced cellular system. WiMAC implements the transparent relay mode, which makes multihop operations possible, even for unmodified subscriber stations.

5.4.4   TCP/IP Module

The Internet Protocol (IP) module included in openWNS implements a subset of IP version 4. Within each simulation node an unlimited number of data link layers may be included. Each is handled similar to a device node in a real computer system. This allows for simulation of hybrid multi-technology nodes. *Virtual* services for ARP, Domain Name System (DNS) and Dynamic

Host Configuration Protocol (DHCP) have been implemented, whereby *virtual* denotes that there are no Protocol Data Units (PDUs) actually transmitted, but the service is realized transparently within the simulation tool. It is possible to include delay models for each of these services.

By now, only static routing tables with Time To Live (TTL) support have been implemented, but the flexible architecture allows for extension of routing protocols. Furthermore, the module implements IP Tables and provides internal tunnel devices (similar to Linux's tunnel device) to support IP in IP encapsulation. There is no Internet Control Message Protocol (ICMP) implemented.

The support of DNS and DHCP has been added to make the scenario configuration as easy as possible. Higher layers address their traffic streams by using domain names. Tedious IP address mangling is not needed. The DHCP sub-module takes care of address allocation and also automatically updates lookup tables within the DNS service.

UDP and TCP models with accurate UDP and TCP headers are available. The congestion avoidance and slow start algorithms have been implemented as strategies and can be exchanged by configuration. Currently Tahoe and Reno are available.

One very beneficial feature of the TCP/IP modules is their capability to write *Wireshark* [11] compatible trace files. In this way the powerful network analysis tool can be used to visualize protocol behavior. There is also a TUN device available that actually connects the simulator to the operating system, allowing for live captures during the simulation run.

5.4.5   Traffic Models

The openWNS load generator is named *Constanze*. Basically, it consists of *traffic generators* and *bindings*. Traffic generators create packets while the binding ties the generator to a specific lower layer. Within openWNS it is possible to connect the traffic generator either to the data link layer, network layer or transport layer depending on the scenario. The traffic models you can choose from are:

– Simplistic Point Process (PP) models including Constant Bitrate, Poisson distributed traffic or the more generic version that allow for arbitrary random distributions for both packet inter-arrival time and packet size.
– *Markov-Modulated Poisson Process* (MMPP) models. The *IMT-Advanced VoIP* model [228] or variable bit-rate models like MPEG2.
– *Autoregressive Moving Average* (ARMA) models. These are typically used to model variable bit rate video or ATM traffic but have also been applied to model online game traffic.

Constanze's traffic generator bindings take care of adapting the traffic source and sink to the desired protocol layer. Traffic sinks record throughput and delay statistics and are called *listener bindings*. Generators can be bound to the

– Data Link Layer (DLL). In this case the binding is aware of the MAC address of source and sink and it injects the generated packets accordingly into the protocol stack.
– Network Layer (IP). openWNS uses IP as its network layer. The IP binding is similar to the DLL binding but uses IP-Addresses instead of MAC addresses.
– Transport Layer (TCP, UDP). The UDP binding additionally is aware of the destination port. The TCP binding is responsible to open and close a connection before transmitting any packets.

This structure of the traffic generator module makes its usage very simple. The traffic source characteristics are configured completely separate from the deployment within the simulation scenario. Sources can be plugged on any layer and traffic routing can be decided individually per generator instance.

5.5   Cluster Computing Support

One of the most advanced features of the openWNS simulation platform is its support for cluster computing. During the *development phase,* compilation cycles can be significantly accelerated by employing a compile cluster. openWNS supports *icecc* out of the box.

Even more important is the support during the *simulation phase,* parallelizing whole simulation campaigns, which consists of multiple simulation runs, each simulation run with different parameter sets is performed on a single processor. Many simulation tools do not offer support for this and leave the implementation of collecting results, extraction of measurements and parameter plots to the user. openWNS offers the Wrowser (an acronym for *W*ireless network simulator *R*esult B*rowser*) which solves this problem and lets users focus on the research rather than on the scripts that collect their measurements.

The approach taken by *Wrowser* is illustrated in Figure 5.4. *Wrowser* supports *Sun Grid Engine* and Postgresql databases as cluster and database backends. The starting point for running a simulation campaign (i.e. parameter sweeps) and analyzing the results is a scenario configuration file. This file is augmented by the user with definitions of the parameters that should be altered between different parallel simulation runs on the cluster, e.g. one could define to increase the offered traffic from 0 to 30 Mbit/s in steps of 1 Mbit/s and for all of these load settings set the packet sizes to 80 byte and 1480 byte.

Once this is done these settings are written to the database and the simulation directories are prepared. The user queues all simulation runs and waits for the simulations to finish. Once a job executes on a cluster node it

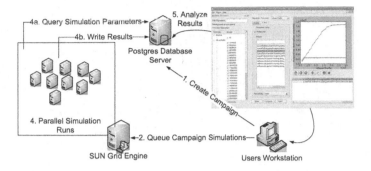

Fig. 5.4: Wrowser

first retrieves its simulation parameters from the database and then starts the simulation run. After the job has finished, all results are written to the database for further study. All these steps are highly automated and require no user interaction.

As soon as the first results have been written to the database the graphical frontend of Wrowser can be used to access the results. Wrowser is aware of all the simulation parameters and parameter plots can be generated within a few steps. Figure 5.4 shows a plot of the carried traffic over the offered traffic for different packet sizes within a WiFi system.

6. From Simulations to Deployments

Georg Kunz (RWTH Aachen University)
Olaf Landsiedel (RWTH Aachen University)
Georg Wittenburg (Freie Universität Berlin)

6.1 Introduction

Ever since network simulation was established the community is holding a never ending discussion on its credibility and degree of realism [35, 146, 148, 149, 270, 359]. Hence, network researchers and developers feel an increasing pressure to deliver experimentation results next to simulation such as from testbed and real-world settings for a credible and realistic evaluation of protocols and distributed systems.

In this chapter, we discuss evaluation tools beyond network simulation and put a special focus on frameworks that enable a seamless transition back and forth between different evaluation tools such as network simulators and operation systems to limit the need for protocol reimplementation.

6.1.1 A Protocol or Distributed System Coming to Life

The road that a protocol or distributed system takes from an initial idea to a deployable version is long and bumpy (see Fig. 6.1). Commonly, after a design phase, often including mathematical analysis, a distributed system or protocol is implemented in a network simulator. Its abstraction from real systems provides invaluable evaluation features such as controllability, repeatability and observability which allow to gain an insight and understanding of complex communication systems.

Next, *testbeds* employ real hardware, and thus promise a protocol evaluation under real-world conditions. This increases *accuracy* and *credibility* of the evaluation results significantly, especially regarding those properties that are typically hard to model in simulations such as radio propagation, system artifacts, realistic Internet traffic and topologies. The final step of the protocol development process is an initial *deployment* in kernel or user-space of an *operating system*, allowing an exact evaluation in terms of performance under high system load. Finally, a protocol awaits *standardization* and inclusion into major operating systems or applications.

Optionally, *network emulation* and *full-system emulation* complete the journey of a protocol from concept to deployment. Network emulation aims at combining the advantages of simulation, e.g. controllability and observability,

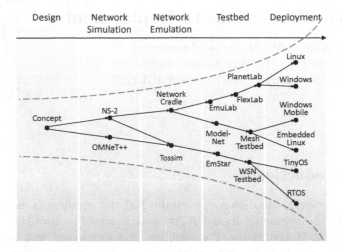

Fig. 6.1: During their evolution, communication protocols and distributed systems pass through a heterogeneous set of evaluation tools, requiring multiple re-implementations.

with real-world runtime behavior and code compatibility by executing real-world network stacks or operating systems in simulation environments. Full-system emulation models the hardware of a target platform and executes its operating system and application. Figure 6.2 lists the specific advantages and disadvantages of each of the classes of tools discussed.

During its evolution, a protocol is re-implemented or ported frequently to match the different APIs and programming languages of the tools required for its evaluation, resulting in additional implementation and testing effort. This effect is further amplified by the need for feedback between the individual steps in the *development cycle*. Thus, results from testbed based evaluation are fed back into the design and simulation processes and require multiple implementations to be maintained in parallel. Overall, we note that network simulation is only a single step in the process of a protocol coming to life.

6.1.2   Bridging the Gap between Simulation and Deployment

Aiming to ease protocol development and to reduce the need for re-implementation, a number of tools have emerged to bridge between network simulation and deployment. Their design bases on the observation that in the domain of communication protocols simulation models often resemble complete and fully functional protocol implementations. Hence, these tools provide an *abstraction layer* between a protocol implementation (or even the complete system) and the evaluation tools. Thus, such an abstraction layer allows a

Simulation		Emulation		Testbed
– Model based		– Model based		+ Real system
– Algorithm		+ Real code		+ Real code
– Simplified		+ Accurate		+ Accurate
+ Insight		+ Insight		– Black box
+ High Scalability		– Low scalability		– Low scalability
+ Fast		– Slow		– Slow
+ High flexibility		– Low flexibility		– Low flexibility
+ Easy to repeat		+ Easy to repeat		– Difficult to repeat
+ Cheap		+ Cheap		– Expensive
+ Manageable		+ Manageable		– Not manageable
+ No deployment		+ No deployment		– Deployment

Fig. 6.2: Each class of tools for protocol evaluation provides its own, specific advantages and disadvantages.

protocol or distributed system to be directly executed and evaluated on a large number of platforms and evaluation tools without the need for reimplementation. Typically, their benefits are (1) simulator interoperability, (2) co-simulation, (3) testing of OS user space or kernel code in network simulators and – vice versa – testing of simulation models in the real-world. We briefly discuss each benefit in the following:

Simulator Interoperability. Commonly, network simulators focus on selected domains of communication systems in terms of available models and visualization capabilities, such as wireless networks, Internet communication or wireless sensor networks. Thus, an abstraction layer offers a common API and programming paradigm to a protocol implementation. It allows to move a protocol seamlessly back and forth between network simulators taking benefits of their individual strength such as the models of underlying network layers.

Co-Simulation. Co-simulation combines different network simulators, testbeds and real-world deployments to provide more realistic results while keeping the scale of an experiment manageable. However, these tools typically have independent network models – each with its own level of abstraction and packet representation, limiting the interoperability of the implementations.

Using the same protocol implementation on different systems via an abstraction layer inherently ensures interoperability. Thus, we can connect network simulation and testbed or real-world deployments to achieve advantages in terms of realism and scalability and gain insight and controllability.

Testing of Simulation Models in Real-World *and Vice Versa.* Finally, platform abstraction allows to move protocols and distributed systems from network simulators to operating systems and vice versa. Hence, it allows testing of simulation based implementations in testbeds and also enables model calibration. Furthermore, it allows to move kernel and user-space protocol stacks to the simulator for large scale evaluation [239, 61, 284] and testing [240].

6.1.3   Chapter Overview

The remainder of this chapter is structured as follows: Section 6.2 discusses design concepts for abstraction layers to enable the integration of a single implementation into multiple evaluation tools. We introduce widespread integration frameworks in Section 6.3. Section 6.4 briefly discusses use cases and Section 6.5 concludes this chapter.

6.2   Design Concepts

In this section, we address the fundamental design concepts that lay the ground for the tools discussed above and in Section 6.3. We specifically focus on the design of their abstraction layers and present design challenges and trade-offs.

The primary task of an abstraction layer is to enable the execution of one system or program (guest) on top of another system (host) which is not its natural execution environment. This is achieved by mimicing the guest's execution environment while utilizing the interfaces and properties of the host execution environment.

At the very core of the design process is the quest for a lightweight abstraction layer. This quest is motivated by the desire to reduce the impact on system properties such as performance, maintainability, and portability, typically caused by a complex abstraction layer: First, a complex abstraction layer degrades system performance due to a significant amount of additional operations that need to be performed within the layer. Second, it reduces maintainability because changes to the underlying systems may demand time consuming modifications of the abstraction layer. Finally, a complex abstraction layer hinders portability since it may require considerable programming effort to support new platforms.

However, the complexity of the abstraction layer heavily depends on the properties of the systems involved. In the following, we discuss selected properties and their influence on the system architecture.

6.2.1   Interfaces to System Resources

Network protocols, just as any other program executed on a computer, require a distinct and clearly defined set of *system resources*: i) memory, ii) timer and obviously iii) network access. In the following, we review these resources in more detail. Furthermore, we discuss how the complexity of their platform specific interfaces influences the abstraction layer design.

Memory. Network protocols need to be able to dynamically manage system memory in order to maintain state information such as routing table entries.

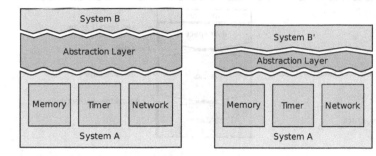

Fig. 6.3: Mapping two rich interfaces (left) increases the complexity of the abstraction layer in comparison to slim interfaces (right).

Across most systems, the memory management interface is very similar and typically provides functions for allocating and freeing memory at runtime. Differences arise when a platform offers multiple functions for managing memory with different specific properties as it is often the case in operating system kernels. Furthermore, embedded operating systems, which are used on sensor nodes for example (*TinyOS*, *Contiki*, etc.), may not support dynamic memory allocation, but memory usage is often statically determined at compile time.

Timer. Time-outs are an essential mechanism in network protocols to avoid deadlocks caused by infinitely waiting for a remote host. Thus, network protocols make use of timers in order to be notified of time-outs. In accordance with the event-based runtime execution model, a timer interface usually allows to define a handler function that is executed when the timer duration expires. Furthermore, protocols need to query the current system time in order to measure connection properties such as round-trip-times.

Network Access. The ability to send and receive network packets is a basic requirement for network protocols. While a packet is generally sent by calling a specific function, receiving is handled using either a synchronous (user-space sockets) or asynchronous (network simulators and operating system kernels) mechanism depending on the execution environment.

These resources are available on every operating system and network simulator, but can only be accessed via system specific and thereby incompatible *interfaces*. Hence, a program that has been implemented for one specific system cannot generally be executed on another system. Consequently, the abstraction layer has to map one set of interfaces to another set.

Network protocols generally require only narrow interfaces to the three different types of system resources. However, many systems provide a rich set of interfaces for either convenience or access to platform specific functionality. For instance, instead of one, the Linux kernel offers several different timers

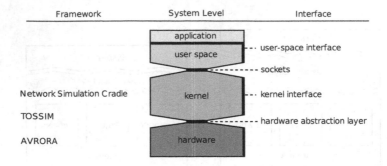

Fig. 6.4: The interfaces of a typical operating system differ in complexity.

with varying granularity. As a result, mapping those rich interfaces increases the complexity of the abstraction layer in comparison to systems with simpler interfaces.

Figure 6.3 further illustrates this fact. In this example. the underlying system A provides a rich set of interfaces to its resources – indicated by the sinuous line. The abstraction layer on the left side of the figure intends to offer a similarly rich interface to system B – indicated by the zigzag line. In contrast, the abstraction layer on the right side restricts its interfaces to a minimum as illustrated by a smoothed zigzag line. As a result, the right abstraction layer is of significantly lower complexity (height) then the abstraction layer on the left side.

Independently from particular systems, the complexity of resource interfaces varies depending on their position in the system architecture. A typical operating system provides two sets of exceptionally slim interfaces: the *socket interface* and the *hardware abstraction layer (HAL)*. Those interfaces form a "narrow waist" and are hence well suited for platform abstraction. In contrast, operating system kernel-space and user-space offer rich sets of interfaces requiring a considerable amount of glue code in order to map the available functionality (see Fig. 6.4).

6.2.2   Runtime Execution Model

The runtime execution model defines how the program flow is driven forward and how the processing of inputs is conducted at runtime. In the *event-based programming model*, a program continuously awaits external and internal inputs, i.e., events, upon whose occurrence it processes the associated input data. In terms of communication protocols, sending and receiving of packets as well as time-outs naturally resemble events. Hence, the event-based programming model forms the substrate for implementing communication protocols across all platforms considered in this chapter.

Within the event-based programming model, we distinguish between two different execution paradigms: i) synchronous and ii) asynchronous execution. In the synchronous execution model, the program continuously awaits input data at certain synchronization points. This data is then subsequently processed. In contrast, in the asynchronous execution model the runtime system executes a specific handler function upon the occurrence of an event.

The abstraction layer is responsible for transparently translating between different execution models. Fortunately, most of the target systems considered here such as common network simulators and the network stack of operating systems employ the asynchronous execution model. The central scheduler of a discrete event simulator consumes events from an event queue and executes the associated event handler function. Similarly, the scheduler in an operating system calls the appropriate handler function when a hardware or software interrupt is fired, e.g., upon arrival of a network packet. Consequently, frameworks that focus on bridging these asynchronous systems (e.g., [61, 239]) do not require a translation between different execution models, but interrupt and event handling can directly be mapped to the according set of functions. However, there are exceptions to this observation such as the well-known *socket interface* and simulators like SimPy [307] which employ a synchronous execution model. Thus, when connecting a user application, which typically communicates via sockets, to a discrete event simulator, an execution model translation is essential.

6.2.3   Programming Language Adaptation

The third major area that needs to be addressed by the abstraction layer is *programming language adaptation* that comprises of two sub-tasks: i) interfacing between different programming languages and ii) state isolation of the systems to be bridged. We discuss both tasks in the following.

Interfacing Programming Languages. Interfacing different programming languages is not a design issue that first arose in the context of abstraction frameworks, but it has already been widely used before. Hence, all major programming languages such as C/C++, Java, and even scripting languages like Python and Tcl provide libraries for executing code in any of the other languages. In particular, the network simulators ns-2 and OMNeT++ employ a bi-language programming approach in which the simulation model core is defined in C++ and network topology as well as visualization is realized in Tcl. Especially the OMNeT++ community has recently developed projects like JSimpleModule [473] and CSharpModule [272] that allow to program the core functionality in Java and C# respectively instead of C++. Since these languages provide advanced features such as automatic memory management, those projects offer easier access to network simulation for beginners.

In general, the most commonly used programming language today is still C as it is supported on all operating system platforms which themselves, especially the kernel and thus the network stack, are implemented in C. Since C is basically a sub-language of C++ and many network simulators are based on C++ (OMNeT++, ns-2/3, SSFNet), those systems can easily be combined. Hence despite its age, C is still the programming language of choice when designing an abstraction layer.

State Isolation. Typically, a simulation model consists of multiple instances of the system under investigation, e.g., a simulated network contains several nodes that each run an instance of a new network protocol. Hence, being able to create and maintain multiple instances with isolated state spaces in parallel is essential. Achieving state isolation is trivial if the model to be instantiated is implemented in an object oriented language because the runtime system takes care of separating state variables. If this is not the case or if the system makes use of global variables, new means of state isolation need to be enforced by the abstraction layer. We discuss two very different approaches to this problem in the following.

The first approach to eliminate global variables, taken by the Network Simulation Cradle [239] (see Sec. 6.3.2), bases on an automatic source code transformation. The basic idea is to replace all global variables with an array of variables. Consequently, each instance is assigned one particular array index. In the second approach, implemented by COOJA [342] (see Sec. 6.3.2), the simulation framework keeps record of the memory blocks which contain the states of all instances. At runtime, the framework dynamically swaps the memory region of one particular instance in place before executing the event handler and saving the potentially updated memory block again. The latter does not require changes to the source code, but causes a relatively high runtime overhead due to extensive memory copy operations.

In conclusion, we observed that i) network protocols require only a well defined set of system resources and ii) many systems provide very similar interfaces and execution models. Thus, the design and development of an abstraction layer is in general feasible with reasonable effort. Furthermore, the introduction of an additional abstraction layer is achievable with acceptable performance overhead.

6.3   Integration Frameworks

After introducing the fundamental design concepts in the previous section, we now present a selection of *representative implementations* of these concepts. We start by introducing a set of criteria and requirements to highlight advantages and disadvantages of each implementation and then continue with a more in-depth discussion of each of them. Finally, we proceed to classify the approaches based on the previously established criteria.

6.3.1 Classification Criteria

In order to classify existing approaches to software integration, it makes sense to focus on the user perspective on the framework. The major concerns fall into three categories: *(i) usability*, i.e. how difficult is it to work with a given integration framework, *(ii) correctness*, i.e. in how far are the results trustworthy, and *(iii) performance*, i.e. what is the overhead imposed by the framework. These concerns can be further subdivided as follows:

- **Usability:** The usability aspects describe how difficult a framework is to use, in particular for new developers. This includes the initial learning curve as well as the repetitive work required for running simulations.
  - **Complexity:** The complexity of the API may range between the very narrow interface of plain packet and timer handlers and an entire kernel or firmware API. The more complex the API is, the harder it is for new developers to port their system or protocol in reasonable time. This effect may be mitigated by reusing a well-known API in the glue code (see below).
  - **Familiarity:** Reimplementing a well-established API in the glue code is preferable to starting from scratch. The drawback is, however, that established APIs are commonly platform-specific and tend to be rather complex (see above).
  - **Integration:** If an existing codebase is to be integrated into a simulator, two problems arise: First, in most cases a number of initial changes need to be applied to the codebase, and second, an ongoing effort may be required while continuing work on the project. Some frameworks include special-purpose tools to help the developer with these issues.
- **Correctness:** The correctness of a framework depends on in how far the API has the very same functional properties on all supported platforms and in how far the lower level components, i.e. those below the API, are modeled correctly.
  - **Consistency:** The semantics of the API provided by the glue code on the simulator should be as close as possible to those of the real platform. Consequently, any code running on top of the API should be completely agnostic about whether running as part of a simulation or on a real system.
  - **Accuracy:** Depending on the focus of the simulation, it may be desirable to evaluate low-level metrics, e.g. the radio signal strength or the number

of bytes transmitted. Especially for high-level APIs, this requires the framework to properly model and implement all underlying components. Alternatively, frameworks may also decide against providing low-level metrics for the sake of speed and simplicity.

– **Performance:** The performance of a framework relates to how efficient in term of runtime overhead the integration into the simulator is handled.

  – **Overhead:** Integrating the codebase of a system or protocol into a simulator usually imposes a runtime overhead over a native implementation in the simulator. This is due to only part of the simulator API being indirectly exposed to the codebase via the glue code. Additionally, running several instances of a non-native system or protocol within the simulator requires explicit memory management.

The key aspect that influences all of these criteria is the level of abstraction provided by the integration framework, i.e. at which layer in the network stack is the glue code inserted to translate between different platforms. Obviously, if a rather high level of abstraction is chosen, e.g. the UNIX socket API, then it is more challenging for the framework to guarantee correctness and accuracy of the simulation. In contrast, if a low level of abstraction is chosen, e.g. DLL frames, then inaccuracies induced by the simulated routing and transport layers become a non-issue. The choice of which layer of abstraction (and consequently which framework) to use depends on the focus of the system or protocol under development.

6.3.2   Exemplary Frameworks

In the following, we will describe four software integration frameworks and sketch their focus and internal design. Three of these exemplary frameworks have their background in the simulation of wireless sensor networks (WSNs) and are suitable to discuss design alternatives due to the lack of established software interfaces in this particular field.

Network Simulation Cradle

The aim of the *Network Simulation Cradle* (NSC) [239] is to integrate existing kernel-space implementations of networking stacks into the ns-2 network simulator. The approach is to parse the C code of the network stack, replace the declarations of global variables with per-node instance variables and compile the code as a shared library. As part of this library, kernel-level interfaces are mapped to ns-2 via a layer of architecture-specific glue code. The library can then be linked against ns-2 and run simulations of the kernel-space protocol implementations.

The network stacks of both Linux, FreeBSD and OpenBSD have been successfully integrated into ns-2. Integration is supported in part by the parser that semi-automatically handles global symbols. However, exactly which symbols need to be adapted needs to be set manually for each stack. The evaluation shows that there is a runtime overhead of running integrated code, but it is linear in both number of nodes and simulation time and hence large simulations are still feasible. Further, a comparison of packet traces shows that real and simulated network stacks generally behave quite similarly, with the main source of differences being the granularity of timing information.

TOSSIM

TOSSIM [284] is a simulator with the specific goal of transparently running *TinyOS*[1]applications. It does not follow the approach of integrating existing code into a simulator via glue code, but rather implements a new simulator from scratch. The component-oriented software architecture of TinyOS greatly supports integration into a simulator: Hardware abstraction is provided by software components with specific interfaces which are enforced at compile time. For the simulation, these components are replaced with pure software counterparts that model the behavior of the real hardware. In the code that is to be simulated, the compiler is used to replace global variables with arrays indexed by the node ID. The simulation is event-driven and radio communication is modeled with bit error rates for each uni-directional link.

The key advantage of TOSSIM is its seamless integration with TinyOS and the nesC programming language. As TinyOS applications are already inherently structured into components, it is relatively easy to replace the hardware abstraction layer, i.e. the components that interact with the hardware, with a different, simulated one. On the other hand, the radio model is quite simplistic, e.g. it does not accurately describe interference caused by simultaneous transmissions. The simulator is also missing some other features, e.g. mobility models are not part of TOSSIM.

Avrora

Avrora [465] is a full-system emulator and models widespread sensor nodes. As full-system emulator it models the hardware of a sensor node, including micro-controller, radio chips and sensors, representing typical sensor nodes such as *Mica2, Mica2dot and MicaZ*. Thus, it is binary compatible to these platforms and executes a sensor node operating system including its device drivers and applications without the need for cross-compilation. Avrora

---

[1] TinyOS is a special-purpose operating system for wireless sensor networks developed at UCLA. It is implemented in the nesC programming language.

provides highly realistic results in terms of timing and memory usage, as it executes the binary compiled for the sensor node itself. Overall, full-system emulation provides a very detailed insight into a communication system, operating system, and application. For more details on emulation, please see Chapter 7.

COOJA

While the previous integration frameworks were always tied to one particular level of abstraction, *COOJA* [342] explicitly supports simulation at different levels and even combining multiple levels in the same simulation. More precisely, COOJA supports systems or protocols implemented in Java specifically for the simulation, code written for *Contiki*[2] and machine code compiled for the *ScatterWeb ESB*[3] sensor node. The simulator core is a in-house development and supports simple unit-disc models for radio propagation as well as ray tracing. The method used for integration depends on the level of abstraction, however, in contrast to other approaches, it does not require changes to the source code. Instead, COOJA swaps the content of the memory region in which the global variables are located based on which node is currently active.

By supporting simulations across several levels of abstraction, COOJA allows for more flexibility during the design process of a new system or protocol. Essentially, it is up to the user to decide which part of the system should be evaluated at which level of abstraction. An additional bonus is the fact that no changes to the codebase are required. However, the way global state is handled in COOJA incurs some additional runtime overhead as compared to the other frameworks.

Other Approaches

As part of the ActComm project, Liu et al. [293] integrate several user-space routing protocols into their simulator by redirecting calls to the socket API into the simulator. Their goal is to compare routing metrics across different simulators and validate the results using data from a testbed deployment.

The OppBSD project [61] developed an abstraction layer that enables the integration of the FreeBSD network stack in the OMNeT++ network simulator. Thereby, it allows a detailed analysis of full-featured Internet protocol implementations such as TCP, IPv4, ARP and ICMP.

---

[2] Contiki, like TinyOS, is an operating system for wireless sensor nodes developed at the Swedish Institute of Computer Science (SICS).

[3] The ScatterWeb ESB sensor node is based on the TI MSP430 micro-controller and the TR-1001 radio transceiver and was developed at Freie Universität Berlin.

Criteria \ Framework	NSC	TOSSIM	Avrora	COOJA*
Level of Abstraction	NET	PHY	HW	variable
Usability	0	+	+	+
Complexity	-	0	-	-/0/+
Familiarity	+	+	0	0/+/-
Integration	0	++	++	++/+/++
Correctness	+	0	++	+
Consistency	++	+	++	+/+/+
Accuracy	0	-	++	+/0/-
Performance / Overhead	+	+	-	--/0/++
Supported Platforms	Linux	TinyOS	Mica2	ESB
	FreeBSD	own sim.	Mica2dot	Contiki
	OpenBSD		MicaZ	own sim.
	ns-2			
Maintenance	-	0	-	-

* By level of abstraction (hardware/operating system/network) where applicable.

Table 6.1: Comparison of Integration Frameworks

6.3.3 Comparison of Approaches

There is no single framework that is equally suitable for all use cases. In fact, the choice of framework will in most cases be dictated by which platforms need to be supported. However, for projects in their very early stages, it may well pay off to choose a platform based on the availability of tools for software integration.

Table 6.1 summarizes the comparison of the frameworks presented in the previous section. Of all four frameworks, NSC focuses most on the correctness and that at a comparatively high level of abstraction. This is more challenging to achieve as compared to frameworks that provide an abstraction closer to the hardware. Furthermore, it is the only one to build upon a well established simulator as opposed to implementing the simulator and low-level components from scratch. The main goal of TOSSIM is to provide a development sandbox for TinyOS applications. As a hardware emulator, it is comparatively easy for Avrora to achieve very trustworthy results, however, this comes at the price of a significant runtime overhead. Finally, COOJA combines the advantages of TOSSIM and Avrora for the Contiki and Scatter-Web ESB platforms and leaves it up to the user to fine-tune the simulation.

Looking at the internals, NSC and TOSSIM are alike in that they pre-process the codebase in order to integrate it into the simulator, while this is not required for Avrora and COOJA. Only the approach taken by TOSSIM results in a comparatively low maintenance burden on the framework developer, because the other three approaches have to ensure consistency and accuracy for more complex interfaces.

6.4   Use Case Examples

Software integration frameworks can be used to validate the simulation core and the implementation of low-level components. The following exemplary use cases run simulated and real systems based on the same software stack and evaluate the differences in the traces in order to judge the validity of the simulation.

In [240], the authors of NSC use their framework to generate traces of the network stacks of Linux, FreeBSD and OpenBSD and compare these traces to those gathered from an emulation testbed running the same stacks natively. Generally, the traces are very similar. However, looking at the details of the traces, e.g. for the Linux stack, there are subtle and yet noteworthy differences. First, the TCP PUSH flag is set differently on the simulator because of the way the simulated application interacts with the integrated network stack. Second, the TCP window size is dependent on the memory allocation strategy in the network card driver. This behavior needs to be considered in the simulation glue code in order to achieve a matching progression of window sizes. The things to be learned from this use case are twofold: On the one hand, the similarity between the traces supports the validity of simulation-based results using this stack. And on the other hand, the work on subtle differences points at shortcomings of the simulation architecture which one may consider to address in future version of the simulator.

In the domain of wireless sensor networks, energy and consequently execution time are crucial when developing applications that are to sustain multiple years of deployment without support. As a result, it is necessary to evaluate new protocols and applications in terms of energy consumption. We need to measure the number of processor cycles that were consumed by a certain protocol or application and the duration that individual device parts, such as the radio, sensors, etc., were active. As full-system emulator, Avrora provides extensions for energy models [274] and allows detailed traces of energy consumption. Furthermore, PowerTOSSIM [422] and TimeTOSSIM [275] provide timing and energy extensions for TOSSIM (see Sec. 6.3.2). As TOSSIM is a simulator instead of a full-system emulator, these extensions are slightly less accurate and detailed than the Avrora extensions, but benefit from the high scalability of simulation and allowing their usage even in large scale scenarios.

In [501], the authors use software integration to evaluate the accuracy of the radio propagation models as implemented in the ns-2 network simulator. The experimental setup consists of two *ScatterWeb ESB* sensor nodes which are placed at various distances from each other and from these positions send a fixed number of packets at various transmission power settings. The same experimental setup is replicated in the simulator and simulations are run with different parameter sets for the radio model according to several sources from the literature. The comparison between the packet delivery rates as measured in the real experiment and gathered from the simulations shows average differences between 8% and 12%, but for some combinations of inter-node distance and transmission power settings the data differed by up to 50%. Software integration was used in this experiment in order to avoid having to re-implement the required code on multiple platforms. It also turned out that the API of the glue code had to be extended, as it did not provide hooks for changing the transmission power at runtime. This underlines that there is no one-size-fits-all API for software integration, and that adaptations may be required for experiments that require more fine-grained control over the simulated system.

6.5 Conclusion

In this chapter we discussed software integration frameworks that enable a seamless transition of network protocols between different evaluation tools. These frameworks broaden the evaluation basis available to protocol developers while at the same time keeping the programming effort low.

The central component of all integration frameworks is an abstraction layer that transparently translates between two or more systems. We briefly presented the central design concepts and challenges that require consideration during the development of an abstraction layer.

A set of classification criteria was introduced and discussed. Based on those criteria, a selection of frameworks was presented and evaluated. Finally, three use cases showed in detail the benefits of integration frameworks.

7. Tools and Modeling Approaches for Simulating Hardware and Systems

Muhammad Hamad Alizai (RWTH Aachen University)
Lei Gao (RWTH Aachen University)
Torsten Kempf, Olaf Landsiedel (RWTH Aachen University)

7.1 Introduction

Due to its high level of *abstraction*, *flexibility* and *scalability* network simulation is the standard means for the evaluation of distributed systems. Its abstraction from implementation details such as target platforms, operating systems and devices limits the impact of system artifacts and allows a researcher to solely focus on algorithmic challenges.

However, abstraction can lead to unexpected side effects and make the implementation of detailed and accurate simulation models challenging [35, 146, 148, 149, 270, 359]. Furthermore, abstraction from system properties in network simulation makes it prohibitively complex to model properties such as system load, operating system effects or memory usage.

7.1.1 Need for System Models

In the following we discuss selected use cases to underline the need for modeling *system details* at a level of detail that is typically not covered by network simulation: (1) timing, deadlines and system load (2) energy consumption, (3) memory usage, and (4) task placement at design and run-time.

Timing, Deadlines and System Load

For delay sensitive applications such as interactive ones the duration that operations as voice and video coding or cryptography take on a specific hardware platform are of high interest during system and application design. During system design a developer has to ensure that time-critical operations, for example on a cell phone, will meet application and system specific deadlines. On systems with severely limited resources such as wireless sensor-nodes with some 10 KByte of RAM and about 10 MHz CPUs these challenges are further aggravated, as the choice of algorithms is strongly influenced by these limited resources. As network simulation abstracts from target systems and their properties, it inherently cannot model such details.

Energy Consumption

We expect the batteries of cell phones to last longer than just a couple of days and hope to deploy wireless sensor networks with a life-time in the order of multiple years. In both cases, we need to include energy considerations during hardware and software development. While estimates on bandwidth usage and the number of transmitted and received packets can be derived from detailed simulation models, an energy model that includes the effects of CPU, radio and I/O on energy consumption requires a full system model. Such models include detailed CPU models and a platform specific implementation of the algorithm to be evaluated. This may either be an implementation for a general purpose CPU and includes an operating system to evaluate effects such as scheduling, memory management, interrupt handling and device drivers or a target-application specific processor such as a DSP or a custom chip.

Memory Consumption

Next to the resource consumption in terms of computing cycles on a generic purpose or specialized processor the memory consumption of tasks is an issue. Especially in the domain of embedded systems it is a goal to equip processors with the amount of memory required to fulfill its tasks, but not more than that. This reduces costs and energy usage. However, even when an implementation of an algorithm is available for a specific platform its memory consumption cannot be derived easily. First off all, load factors such as queued packets, or stack depth depend on dynamic runtime properties that are determined not only by the system itself but also by the environment which causes for example - in case of interference - retransmissions and thereby impacts queue length.

Task Placement at Design and Run-Time

In addition to the utilization of individual resources such as CPU cycles or memory, the placement of functionality on dedicated hardware is a key challenge during the design phase. Developers have to choose from a combination of generic purpose processors, DSPs and custom chips while trying to keep costs, overall complexity and energy consumption low. Thus, during the development and design phases one needs to decide where to place which functionality of a system. This decision can either be done statically at design time or dynamically changed at run-time.

7.2   Approaches for System Modeling next to Simulation

From the electrical engineering perspective low level simulation techniques like those based on the Register Transfer Level (RTL) are an essential part of system development. However, those simulation techniques typically provide simulation speeds in the range of approximately 10-100 Kcycles per second. For fine-grained hardware simulation those speeds might be acceptable, but for software development where millions of cycles have to be simulated those simulation techniques do not scale.

To cope with the demands of software development and debugging the technique of Instruction Set Simulation (ISS) has been introduced in the past. Such simulations achieve sufficiently high simulation speeds for up to a small number of processor cores. For example, the simulation of platforms like TI OMAP[1] achieve simulation speeds close to real-time. Because the simulation speed of such ISS based simulators behaves anti-proportional to the number of simulated processor cores, the advent of future Multi-Processor System-on-Chips puts a particular pressure on the development of such simulators. A promising alternative technique is based on the principle of timing annotations. Frameworks like the ones in [404], and [171] increase the abstraction level to achieve higher simulation speeds, whereas the framework in [252] makes use of this technique to allow design space exploration for hardware/software co-design.

In the remainder or this chapter, we introduce both classes of simulation techniques in detail:

- *Instruction Set Simulation* (ISS) based techniques (Section 7.3). The technique of Instruction Set Simulation allows to imitate the behavior of an Instruction Set Architecture (ISA), e.g., a processor core. This technique can be further subdivided:
  - *Cycle accurate ISS.* Cycle accurate ISS operates on the granularity of processor core cycles.
  - *Instruction accurate ISS.* Instruction accurate ISS operates on the granularity of instructions.
- *Time based annotation of simulation models* (Section 7.4). Simulation models are instrumented with system properties like processing time.

Each (sub-)technique is evaluated and rated in terms of four criteria: hardware modeling complexity, software modeling complexity, accuracy of the provided hardware performance metrics, and speed. Finally, we conclude the chapter by comparing the presented techniques in Section 7.5.

---

[1] TI OMAP platforms are one of the most prominent platforms for wireless handsets like NOKIA's N- and E-series.

7.3   ISS based Techniques

The technique of Instruction Set Simulation allows to imitate the behavior of an Instruction Set Architecture (ISA) that may differ from the one the host machine. Apart from the traditional intention of debugging, testing and optimizing an application on a different ISA, Instruction Set Simulation (ISS) can be used to analyze the performance of a given hardware platform during the design of new processor architectures or embedded systems.

The general *principle of ISS* is as follows: A given executable is initially loaded into the memory of the Instruction Set Simulator. During simulation the simulator sequentially fetches an instruction from memory, decodes it for the targeted ISA and mimics the behavior of the target processor core by executing the instruction on the host machine. Figure 7.1 depicts the basic principle of ISS by means of a simplified example.

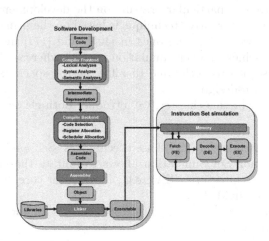

Fig. 7.1: ISS Principle

Since the simulated ISA typically differs from the ISA of the host machine, the software executable has to be compiled by a so called cross-compiler. The emitted executable is based on the machine code of the targeted ISA. Typically such cross-compilers are built upon a front- and backend while optimizations operate on an Intermediate Representation (IR). Examples for such cross-compilers are manifold. Probably the most prominent ones are based on the GNU GCC compiler for ARM and MIPS processor cores. The advantage of such a compiler structure is that re-targeting the compiler to a different ISA requires merely the replacement of the backend while the frontend and the optimization engines can remain unchanged. [28] discusses the frontend-design in detail, whereas [325] focuses on optimization techniques and the backend.

The technique of Instruction Set Simulation (ISS) can be further subclassified into the two classes of cycle and instruction accurate simulation[2]. While both techniques operate on the previously illustrated principle which ensures the correct execution of the given application. However, in comparison to instruction accurate simulation, cycle accurate models additionally incorporate detailed modeling of the timing effects of a hardware platform. These timing effects are mostly caused by the pipeline structure of today's modern processor cores. After introducing the basic pipeline principle the techniques of cycle and instruction accurate ISS will be discussed.

7.3.1 Pipeline Principle

The concept of pipelining can be found in nearly all modern processor cores and is a common principle to increase the overall throughput. We explain the principle of pipelining on the basis of an aircraft assembly line. Assume that a single aircraft is assembled out of three pieces A, B, and C. The respective time for adding piece A is 20 time units (tu), whereas for B 5tu and for C 10tu are needed. To assemble the complete aircraft in one stage $(20 + 5 + 10)$tu $= 35$tu are necessary with each new aircraft finishing after 35tu. When applying a 3-staged pipeline, in each stage one piece is added and then the aircraft is passed on to the next stage. Thus in the first stage piece A is added to the aircraft and in the latter two stages the other two pieces B and C. Starting with an initially empty pipeline the first aircraft is ready after 35tu the second one after 55tu and the third one after 75tu. Further aircraft are leaving the pipeline every 20tu. Please note that a balanced pipeline is highly desired to achieve maximum throughput. For example, when assuming an assembling time of 15tu for piece A and B, a new aircraft would be completed every 15tu.

As previously mentioned, computer architectures make heavily use of such pipelines. Common processor architectures such as the Cortex-R4 ARM processor have an 8-stage pipeline whereas general purpose processors from Intel and AMD contain 10 to 20 pipeline stages. Figure 7.2 illustrates a 5-stage pipeline and its execution characteristic. The example execution does not include *hazards*, such as pipeline stalls and flushes. Such hazards can be classified as *control hazards* and *data hazards* – especially read-after-write (RAW), write-after-write (WAW), and write-after-read (WAR) hazards. In [201] those issues are discussed in detail.

---

[2] Some technical domains use the term "emulation" for instruction accurate simulation.

Since the pipeline is key to differentiate cycle and instruction accurate ISS, its concept should be kept in mind for the following discussion of both techniques.

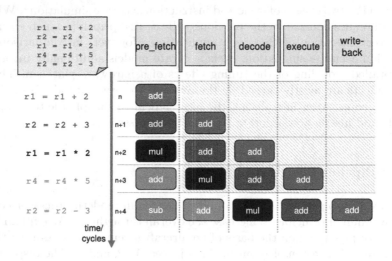

Fig. 7.2: Pipeline Principle

7.3.2   Cycle Accurate ISS

Figure 7.2 illustrates a pipeline architecture that executes in regular operation mode (no occurrence of pipeline stalls or flushes [201]). Here each instruction is processed within its current pipeline stage and passed to the next stage in the following cycle. This repeats till the instruction has completely propagated through the pipeline. Following this concept, a cycle accurate ISS models the complete pipeline in full detail. Being sensitive to the clock of the processor, each pipeline stage is executed based on the current instruction. The results of each pipeline stage are – just like in real hardware – passed to the next pipeline stage and processing starts for each pipeline stage with the next clock cycle.

In addition to the modeled pipeline, other effects occurring on the real hardware like memory accesses are modeled accurately on the level of the processor clock. Please note however, that despite being called "cycle accurate", timing differences might occur in comparison to real hardware due to abstractions. Those timing differences are typically in the range of a few processor clock cycles. However, final verification and measurements for highly critical real-time constraints should be performed in an RTL simulation or even on the real hardware.

In today's markets, processor-core vendors follow two different business models. Whereas the more general purpose domain processor core vendors like AMD and Intel sell fabricated IP cores (intellectual property cores), other vendors like ARM, Tensilica and MIPS are fabless and sell their processor cores on IP basis. Especially companies selling IP cores require well suited simulators to provide other partners the possibility to include the processor IP into their systems. Therefore, cycle accurate as well as instruction accurate simulation models are mostly provided by the vendors themselves. Examples for such simulators are the Realview [39] processor models of ARM. Electronic Design Automation (EDA) companies developing system-level design tools such as CoWare and Synopsys sell within their portfolio simulators for different processor models. Open-source approaches are mostly build upon the GNU project debugger (GDB).

Concluding, Figure 7.3 shows the rating for cycle accurate simulation models. Since cycle accurate models have to capture all hardware effects, the hardware modeling complexity is rather high (5 points). Additionally, the complete software has to be developed and compiled for the targeted processor core, causing the highest software complexity (5 points). Please note that this effort is not dissipated since the software executable can be directly copied to the final real hardware. Due to this detailed modeling and the required modeling effort, highly accurate performance metrics, which are close to the real hardware, can be extracted from cycle accurate models (5 points). However, those models suffer from the high level of detail in terms of simulation speed (0 points) and should therefore only be used for fine-grained investigations of timing effects and performance issues.

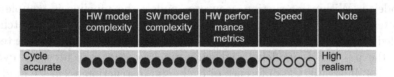

	HW model complexity	SW model complexity	HW performance metrics	Speed	Note
Cycle accurate	●●●●●●	●●●●●●	●●●●● ○○○○○		High realism

Fig. 7.3: Rating and use-case for cycle accurate Instruction Set Simulation

7.3.3 Instruction Accurate ISS

In today's embedded systems more and more processor cores are applied. Likewise the amount of software increases steadily [466] and is key for future systems. Since for software development and debugging a fast exploration cycle is needed, simulators of the targeted system have to achieve high simulation speeds, which run at real-time or at least close to that. Therefore, research and industry have recently focused on increasing the speed of such simulators. Results are ISSs achieving high simulation speeds which can be combined to so called Virtual Platforms (VPs). Such VPs model complete System-on-Chips (SoCs) including processor cores along with the system's peripherals such as USB, Ethernet and VGA-output devices. Prominent EDA vendors providing such VPs are Synopsys, CoWare, Vast and Virtutech. Development of such VPs is based on the SystemC language on top of C++. Recently SystemC has become a IEEE Standard 1666™-2005 [214] and the so called Transaction Level Modeling (TLM) standard 2.0 [214] has been announced. Both standards have made a significant impact on the modeling efficiency and acceptance of SystemC as the Electronic System Level (ESL) [45] modeling language.

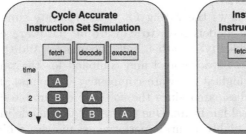 

Fig. 7.4: Cycle versus Instruction Accurate ISS model

A key differentiator of instruction accurate models compared to cycle accurate ones is the abstraction level in which the underlying HW architecture is modeled. Within instruction accurate models the pipeline is completely neglected in terms of timing. At each clock cycle the instruction is fetched, decoded and executed in one clock cycle, whereas in the cycle accurate technique the pipeline is modeled and each pipeline stage executes per cycle. Figure 7.4 illustrates the difference of cycle and instruction accurate models. Since effects like pipeline stalling or flushing have a significant impact on the real execution time, instruction accurate models that do not include such effects might be inaccurate in their timing. By simplifying the modeling of the processor core a much higher simulation speed can be achieved. Since it is essential that the functionality behaves equally to the real hardware and cycle accurate model, effects caused by e.g., pipeline interlocking, bypassing, stalling and flushing have to be captured by the model. [201] discusses those hardware issues in detail. Today, instruction accurate ISSs include further enhancements such as just-in-time (JIT) compilation [337] and binary-to-binary translation to achieve simulation speeds close to real-time. Based on such ISSs complete platforms like TI's OMAP platform including two processor cores and several peripherals such as video accelerators can be simulated close to real-time. Hence, instruction accurate models allow for software development and debugging.

Figure 7.5 presents the rating for instruction accurate simulation. Due to the increased abstraction the HW model complexity is reduced to 4 points. The software executed in ISS is equal to the software executed on a cycle accurate one or the real hardware. Thus software modeling complexity remains at 5 points. To accent the simulation speed-up compared to cycle accurate models, two points have been selected for simulation speed, which come with only a minor reduction of HW performance characteristics (4 points).

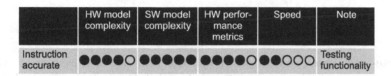

	HW model complexity	SW model complexity	HW performance metrics	Speed	Note
Instruction accurate	●●●●○	●●●●●	●●●●○	●●○○○	Testing functionality

Fig. 7.5: Rating and use-case for instruction accurate Instruction Set Simulation

7.4   Time Based Annotations

ISS based techniques, as discussed in the previous sections, are designed to imitate a specific hardware platform. They provide a software based implementation of all the platform components and executes the binary compiled for the specific platform and is therefore of high use for a detailed evaluation of applications, operating systems and the hardware platform. Despite several advancements in the field of cycle accurate ISS, it is heavyweight when compared to more abstract simulation techniques and strongly limits performance and scalability. Hence, for network evaluation, which is typically carried out on a scale of hundreds and thousands of network nodes, ISS is not a viable choice.

Next to ISS, test-beds are also used for a detailed evaluation of protocols and applications. Obviously, test-bed results are highly realistic. However, commonly test-beds contain some tens of nodes and therefore the scalability of a proposed design and operations with a large number of interactions are hard to evaluate. Furthermore, repeatability, controllability and system insight are limited and test-beds are quite cost and space intensive. Concluding, test-beds are unable to replace simulation as a principle mean for analyzing, evaluating and validating system design.

In this section, we discuss time annotation based techniques developed to enable detailed system evaluation while minimizing the need to use expensive ISS. The idea is to simulate hardware specific behavior but deliver better speed and scalability, the goal, which instruction set simulators have so far failed to achieve. Section 7.4.1 presents simulation instrumentation based techniques, which instrument network simulations - based on the discrete-event paradigm - with essential hardware properties, like timing and power. The Hybrid Simulation Framework (HySim) is presented in Section 7.4.2, which enables switching between native execution of application source code and instruction set simulation. Finally, Virtual Processing Units (VPU), as discussed in Section 7.4.3, investigate the mapping of application tasks with respect to space and time.

7.4.1   Simulation Instrumentation

Discrete-event based simulations model the behavior of a system at event granularity. Thus, time in simulation is handled discretely, i.e. at the beginning of an event the simulation time is set to the execution time of the event and remains unadjusted throughout the event execution, resulting in each event taking zero execution time. As a result, discrete-event based simulations are unable to model the time dependent behavior of the real hardware, limiting its contribution only to testify the functional correctness of protocols and applications.

Simulation instrumentation is a technique developed to incorporate essential hardware properties, like timing and power, into the simulation. The idea is to calibrate the simulation models with timing information obtained from the platform dependent code to enable time-accurate simulation. This technique nearly provides the accuracy of ISS while perpetuating the key properties of simulation, such as speed, scalability and easy adaptation to new hardware platforms and operating systems. Hence, eliminating the need to use expensive cycle and instruction accurate ISS.

Instrumenting the simulation with timing properties is possible when nearly identical application and operating system code is executed in simulation and on the hardware platform, which is typically the case in sensor network operating systems - such as TinyOS [285]. This technique, even though it introduces instrumentation overhead, outperforms instruction set simulators in terms of speed and scalability. Currently, TimeTOSSIM [275] and PowerTOSSIM [422] - simulation platforms for sensor networks - employ such instrumentation techniques to achieve accurate timing and energy modeling in simulation, respectively.

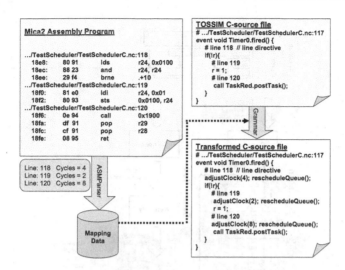

Fig. 7.6: Source-code line mapping between the mica2 sensor-node platform and TOSSIM simulation source-code

Code Mapping and Clock Advancement

The timing discrepancy of simulation is resolved by enabling it to track the system time during event execution. Like many other simulation environments for sensor networks, TOSSIM compiles directly from the platform dependent source code to the host ISA. Therefore, it is possible to determine the execution time (clock-cycles) of each source-code line being executed inside a simulator-event and then increment the simulation clock accordingly (see figure 7.6). The underlying technique is to automate the mapping between simulation source-code and the platform specific executable. This is only possible when nearly identical application and operating system code is executed in simulation and on the hardware platform, which is typically the case in sensor network operating systems. Such a mapping enables to identify the processor instructions corresponding to a source-code line. The number of cycles consumed by each instruction can easily be determined from the respective processor data-sheets. Therefore, we can compute the time to execute each source code line on the sensor-node platform.

The code mapping technique is particularly suited for embedded CPUs (such as in sensor-nodes) employing sequential instruction execution without any pipelining and caching strategies. For such platforms, the execution time of a binary instruction is static and can be modeled without interpreting each individual instruction.

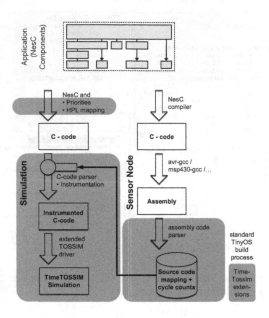

Fig. 7.7: Integration of TimeTOSSIM into TinyOS build process

Event-queue Adaptation

Instrumenting each source code line with the corresponding execution time results in overlapping events. Thus, events in the simulation queue shall be delayed until the execution of the current event is finished. This overlapping between events can be removed by assigning a priority to every event and delaying its execution. In the case of TOSSIM, events in the simulation queue represent hardware interrupts, hence, it is possible to determine the type of an event and its execution priority. This technique enables rescheduling of the event-queue and intensifies the simulation models even further to exhibit timing as well as interrupting behavior of a hardware platform. Correct ordering of events can be achieved by visiting the event queue at the start of every source-code line after incrementing the simulation clock. The idea is to reschedule events with lower priority, execute events with higher priority immediately, and thereby delay or interrupt the execution of currently active events.

Static Code Mapping

For compiling the source code to the host ISA, TOSSIM replaces low-level platform specific device drivers with simulation wrappers. Therefore, simulation and platform specific code differ at this level and the code mapping technique is of limited use for low-level device drivers. However, code at this level provides direct hardware access and usually does not contain loops and conditional statements and therefore executes in a constant number of cycles. By profiling different hardware components of a sensor-node platform, it is possible to determine the number of cycles consumed by different operations performed by these components. This cycle count information is used to statically map the simulation-wrappers to reinforce time accuracy when simulation enters their execution. Although this process does not introduce inaccuracies in terms of cycles, it is not as fine granular as the commonly used source line granularity. Thus, interrupts may get delayed by a number of cycles. However, code sections that provide hardware access are usually 10 to 100 cycles and therefore executed in a couple of micro seconds. Overall, TimeTOSSIM achieves beyond 99% accuracy when compared to ISS. Figure 7.7 shows the complete process and integration of TimeTOSSIM into TinyOS.

PowerTOSSIM is another tool that employs simulation instrumentation to model the energy consumption of sensor network applications. It extends TOSSIM by adding a new *PowerState* module that records energy-state transitions of each hardware component. Similarly, for the CPU, a mapping technique is used at the basic-block granularity to determine the number of clock-cycles for which the CPU remained in its active state. PowerTOSSIM obtains power-models for each hardware device (e.g. LEDs, sensors, ADC, radio, CPU) of a sensor-node platform by profiling its components independently and in different modes. For example, the energy consumed by the radio chip in transmitting and receiving modes, LEDs when on and off, and CPU in active and idle modes. The TOSSIM simulation is instrumented to record traces of the usage of each hardware component. Later, i.e. after the simulation run, these traces are combined with the power consumption profiles of each component to compute the overall energy consumed by the whole simulated network.

	HW model complexity	SW model complexity	HW performance metrics	Speed	Note
Simulation Instrumentation	●OOOO	●●●●O	●●OOO	●●●●O	Timing

Fig. 7.8: Rating and use-case for Simulation Instrumentation

Simulation instrumentation based techniques are focusing on modeling execution time and power consumption. As shown in Figure 7.8, the HW modeling complexity is limited to high level simulation wrappers and their instrumentation with timing information. Therefore, it has been assigned one point. Existing simulation instrumentation based techniques execute the complete OS in simulation. As a result, the SW model complexity is higher and is assigned with four points. Moreover, only the timing and power related behavior of the hardware can be traced during simulation (2 points). However, this technique achieves a very high simulation speed when compared to cycle and instruction accurate ISS and is therefore assigned with 4 points.

7.4.2   HySim

The previously discussed time based annotation technique delivers an approximate estimation of the clock advancement, whereas an extremely high execution speed is provided by compiling the software to the host ISA. However, some compatibility is lost due to the lack of support of several widely used programming approaches – e.g., using closed source libraries or inline assembly. Noticing that the limitations of time based annotation are offered by the aforementioned instruction set simulators, a hybrid approach is proposed.

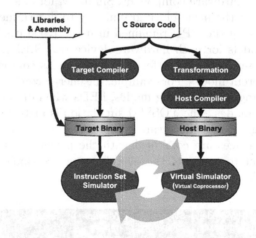

Fig. 7.9: HySim Infrastructure

HySim [171, 266, 170] is a versatile hybrid simulation framework for early software performance estimation. It is capable of dynamically switching between two simulation levels – using a slow ISS or a fast but less accurate *Virtual Simulator* (VS, also known as virtual coprocessor). Unlike an ISS, the VS utilizes the application's C source code directly to achieve high simulation speed. The entire execution sequence is *temporally* partitioned and mapped to the two execution engines. The partitioning is based on a source code analysis that detects the target dependent code that cannot be supported by the VS. In turn, the target dependent code is mapped to the

ISS to permit the rest of the code to be natively executed after proper transformation.

C Virtualization

To preserve the functional correctness, a unique global execution context that resides in the ISS is maintained, and the VS refers to it as its virtual resource. This is implemented by transforming the C source code with redirected global value accesses before it is compiled by the host compiler [171], as shown in Figure 7.9. This transformation is called *C Virtualization* since it virtualizes the resource accessing of C code.

As an example, a piece of C code and its virtualized form are given in Figure 7.10. The global variable g is located in memory at a specific memory address. Using this address, the virtualized code can access the variable located at the ISS through some helper function.

```
int g;
void foo()
{
    g = 1;
}
```
a) Original C code

```
int * _g = MEMORY_ADDRESS_OF_G;
void foo()
{
    WriteInt(_g, 1);
}
```
b) Virtualized form

Fig. 7.10: Example of C Virtualization

Switching Between VS and ISS

For a C application, it is impossible to stop at an arbitrary *statement*, where 1) every statement preceding this statement in the source code is already executed, and 2) any statement succeeding this statement is not yet executed. This is due to the side effect of compiler scheduling [325], out-of-order execution [201] and instruction pipelining [201]. Moreover, the *de facto* debug information [3, 4] is inadequate for indicating the location (memory address or register index) of every local variable at an arbitrary point of execution. Therefore, the only possible switching points are the function boundaries (i.e., function calling and returning), which are natural scheduling barriers if the functions are not inlined. At these points, the usage of registers and the stack is clearly specified by the calling conventions, and the values of the global variables are accessible.

Performance Estimation

Time based annotation is performed by the VS to provide cycle advancement estimation. Apart from that, dynamic events are also simulated. For example, data cache simulation is enabled by instrumenting memory referencing operations into the source code, and these operations can be simulated at runtime to provide the statistics of the application's cache behavior. Moreover, a profiling based approach [170] is also introduced, in which HySim can use ISS as a profiler to obtain the accurate timing information in order to further improve the precision of performance estimation.

7.4.3 VPU

Compared to the previously discussed technique of timing annotated models, other frameworks such as [404],[71],[175] and [252] utilize this technique for design space exploration in the process of building embedded systems, e.g., the TI DaVinci and OMAP platforms.

In comparison to general purpose processors and platforms like a personal computer (PC) embedded systems especially in the domain of mobile devices have much tighter energy and real-time constraints. For example, execution of general purpose applications like Internet browsing and office applications have no tight timing constraints, while voice communication over a wireless communication device has significant real-time constraints. Additionally, energy efficiency is highly mandatory for battery driven devices. In [433] an experiment is considered, where a general purpose processor is performing the baseband computation of 20 GOPS with a state of the art battery device of 1400mAh capacity. The resulting active time would be 40 seconds and the standby time 30 minutes. In comparison, the latest generation of mobile devices achieve a 100-1000 times higher energy efficiency.

Due to those demands, embedded systems are typically tailored for a particular application such as wireless communication. To determine the structure and components of such systems, design space exploration is a key technique. In the following the technique of timing annotation for design space exploration is discussed based on the framework introduced in [252]. Central component of this framework is the so called Virtual Processing Unit (VPU) which can be configured to imitate the behavior of arbitrary processor cores within a system level simulation. Compared to ISSs the simulation is based on timing annotation which allows modeling of software execution exclusively on the basis of timing annotations. During early design phases no functionally correct software implementation needs to be available that must be cross-compiled for the anticipated processor core. In a later refinement stages, functionality, e.g., in terms of C-based software, can be included

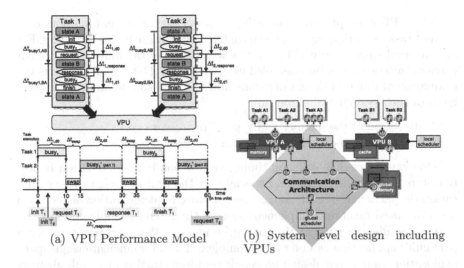

(a) VPU Performance Model   (b) System level design including VPUs

Fig. 7.11: Principle and use case of the Virtual Processing Unit

until the final implementation is available. In the following the concept and principle of such timing annotation will be sketched exemplary on the basis of the VPU.

The example depicted in Figure 7.11(a) illustrates the timing annotation and VPU mapping mechanisms. The upper part of the figure illustrates two tasks with their individual timing characteristics which are mapped to a single VPU instance. The lower part of Figure 7.11(a) shows the resulting behavior of the VPU according to an assumed scenario, which will be discussed in the following:

First task 1 is activated by the external $init\,T_1$ event and executes the first portion of the task. The simulated execution time directly corresponds to the annotated time $\Delta t_{1,d0}$. Before entering state B, task 1 initiates an external data transfer request. Waiting for the response of this request, task 2 can execute in the meantime. First a task swap e.g., initiated by an Operating System (OS), is performed which requires 5 time units for the given example such that task 2 can start execution after 15 time units. The VPU takes care that this swapping time is taken into account and shields the tasks from external events. In the given scenario execution of task 2 requires more time then the response of the data transfer of task 1. Assuming task 1 has higher priority than task 2, a task preemption occurs and task 2 cannot be resumed before the second portion of task 1 has completed its functionality. The request generated by task 2 is delayed by the VPU till the correct point in time is due. Thus, from the perspective of external system components the external events are visible at the corresponding time of concurrent task execution.

The VPU concept allows modeling of processor cores that support concurrent task execution, e.g., by means of OS or hardware multi-threading. For system level simulation multiple VPUs which mimic the different processor cores of the system can be assembled like in Figure 7.11(b). This supports the evaluation of different design decisions in a fast and simple manner. Typical goals of such system evaluations are:

– Identification of the number and type of processor cores.
– Identification of the application to architecture mapping.

One key issue while utilizing timing annotation based simulation is how to obtain those timing budgets. Especially at the time of design space exploration (in particular at early stages) no software implementation or merely a non-optimized functional implementation of the intended application exists. Hence, the identification of the timing budgets or the execution time for a particular application can be rather complex. Thus, for efficient design space exploration an iterative design process is required starting at a high abstraction level with only rough estimates. In a subsequent refinement loop those estimates are continuously improved till finally the complete implementation is available. To allow for such an iterative design process, the VPU supports different levels of software modeling and timing annotation. The supported ones are illustrated in Figure 7.12.

At the highest level of abstraction, the timing information is extracted based on statistical functions. In later stages, when at least a rough understanding of the algorithm exists, developers can annotate the simulation models on more fine grained levels. In the first case annotations are based on complete tasks whereas in later stages annotations can be added within tasks in the software implementation. Please note that those abstraction levels on top of the VPU support simulation without having any software implementation at hand. More fine-grained timing annotation based on the μProfiler [249] or trace-based instrumentation require naturally a software implementation. When more detailed information about a task and its execution characteristic exist, higher abstraction levels can be skipped and the refinement loop can be entered according to the available knowledge.

Concluding, Figure 7.13 summarizes the rating for the VPU technology. This technique focuses on efficient design space exploration. The HW modeling complexity is less in comparison to instruction accurate modeling. As a result it has been assigned 3 points. Considering the SW modeling complexity, the method of timing annotation has a special status since different complexities are supported. When utilizing trace based simulation, SW complexity is as high as in cycle and instruction accurate ISS (5 points) while at high levels of abstraction only the timing characteristic has to be extracted which requires only minor modeling (1 point). HW performance metrics like resource utilization, timing, or the communication on the system buses can easily be traced in simulation; therefore 3 points are given. Compared to ISS

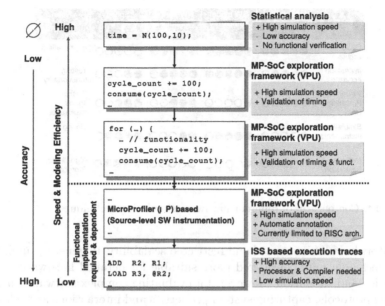

Fig. 7.12: Support timing annotation models of the VPU

this technique achieves higher simulation speeds, but less then pure simulation instrumentation. Therefore it has been assigned 3 points.

	HW model complexity	SW model complexity	HW perfor-mance metrics	Speed	Note
Virtual Processing Units	●●●○○	●○○○○	●●●○○	●●●○○	Design space exploration

Fig. 7.13: Rating and use-case for Virtual Processing Unit

7.5 Comparison

After discussing different techniques for modeling hardware systems, we now provide a comparison between these techniques taking into account different modeling issues like the level of detail, complexity, and performance.

ISS delivers highly accurate performance metrics of a system since it executes platform dependent binary code at a cycle or instruction accurate level. Providing such a level of detail requires complete implementations of complex models of the underlying hardware. As a result, instruction set

	HW model complexity	SW model complexity	HW performance metrics	Speed	Note
Cycle accurate	●●●●●	●●●●●	●●●●●	○○○○○	High realism
Instruction accurate	●●●●○	●●●●●	●●●●○	●●○○○	Testing functionality
Virtual Processing Units	●●●○○	●○○○○	●●●○○	●●●○○	Design space exploration
Simulation Instrumentation	●○○○○	●●●●○	●●○○○	●●●●○	Timing
Network Simulation	○○○○○	●○○○○	○○○○○	●●●●●	Algorithms, Protocols

Fig. 7.14: Comparison of different hardware simulation techniques

simulators have limited speed and restricted scalability. In general, emulation based techniques are considered more suitable for detailed hardware design evaluation and validation. However, for evaluating complex software, such as network protocols, capturing system properties and interactions at cycle and instruction accurate level is exceedingly heavy and may not be a suitable choice for software developers.

Next to ISS are time annotation based techniques that try to bridge the gap between emulation and high speed but abstracting simulation. These techniques aim at modeling essential hardware properties, timing in particular, while minimizing the need for using expensive emulation for software evaluation. In terms of performance and scalability, these techniques outperform emulation but are still much slower than the original uninstrumented discrete-event based simulations. Overall, these techniques are more suitable for evaluating time critical applications that heavily depend on the behavior of the underlying hardware.

Finally, discrete-event based simulations offer much higher speed and scalability than emulation as well as simulation instrumentation. Nonetheless, it completely leaves out the modeling of hardware dependent behavior of the system. Thus, it only contributes to testing the functionality and algorithmic properties of a software. Figure 7.14 summarizes and rates all the techniques that we have discussed in this chapter.

Concluding, it is important to model the hardware dependent behavior of the system where the underlying platform is limited in resources like energy, computation power, and communication bandwidth. Typical examples of such systems include embedded systems and battery driven mobile and wireless systems. A wide variety of techniques and tools exist to model hardware in simulation. These tools provide different levels of detail, complexity and use cases. Hence, choosing the right simulation technique depends on the purpose and the focus of the particular investigation at hand. For example, for typical hardware evaluation, instruction set simulation is still the

most viable choice. But for more accurate software evaluation, time annotation based techniques are more suitable than ISS or simulation. Similarly,
discrete-event based simulations remain an automatic choice when it comes
to testifying the functionality of a software.

8. Parallel Discrete Event Simulation

Georg Kunz (RWTH Aachen University)

8.1 Introduction

Ever since discrete event simulation has been adopted by a large research community, simulation developers have attempted to draw benefits from executing a simulation on multiple processing units in parallel. Hence, a wide range of research has been conducted on Parallel Discrete Event Simulation (PDES). In this chapter we give an overview of the challenges and approaches of *parallel simulation*. Furthermore, we present a survey of the parallelization capabilities of the network simulators OMNeT++, ns-2, DSIM and JiST.

8.1.1 Why do we need Parallel Discrete Event Simulation?

Communication systems are becoming increasingly complex – and so do the corresponding evaluation tools. In general, two orthogonal trends in terms of complexity can be identified: an increase in structural complexity on the one hand and in computational complexity on the other. Both impose high demands on the simulation architecture and the hardware executing the simulations.

We denote the size of a simulated network as an indicator of the structural complexity of a simulation model. Recent developments in the Internet, in particular fast growing systems like peer-to-peer networks, caused an enormous increase in the size of communication systems. Such large systems typically posses complex behavioral characteristics which cannot be observed in networks of smaller size (e.g., testbeds) or captured by analytical models. Thus, in order to study those characteristics, simulation models comprise huge numbers of simulated network nodes. Since every network node is represented in memory and triggers events in the simulation model, memory consumption and computation time increase significantly.

Even if the investigated network is relatively small, computational complexity becomes an important factor if the simulation model is highly detailed and involves extensive calculations. In particular wireless networks which make use of advanced radio technologies such as OFDM(A) [258] and Turbo Codes [58] fall in this category. Sophisticated radio propagation models, interference modeling, and signal coding models further escalate the overall complexity.

Simulation frameworks aim to compensate these issues by enabling simulations to be executed in parallel on multiple processing units. By combining memory and computation resources of multiple processing units, simulation time can be restricted to a reasonable amount while at the same time extremely high memory requirements can be met. Although this approach is known for more than two decades [161, 163, 365], recent technological advances greatly reduce prices for parallel computing hardware – thus making such hardware available to a large research community and moving back into the focus of simulation developers.

8.1.2   Challenges of Parallel Discrete Event Simulation

The approach taken by PDES is to divide a simulation model in multiple parts which execute on independent processing units in parallel. The central challenge of PDES is thereby to maintain the correctness of the simulation results as we will see in the following.

We first briefly recapitulate the concept of discrete event simulation. Any discrete event simulation, i.e., the simulation framework and a particular simulation model, exhibits three central data structures: i) state variables of the simulation model, ii) a timestamped list of events, and iii) a global clock. During a simulation run, the scheduler continuously removes the event with the smallest timestamp

$$e_{min} = \min\{T(e)|\forall e \in E\}$$

from the event list and executes the associated handler function. T denotes the timestamp function which assigns a time value to each event and E is the set of all events in the event list. While the handler function is running, events may be added to or removed from the event list. Choosing e_{min} is crucial as otherwise the handler function of an event e_x with $T(e_{min}) < T(e_x)$ could change state variables which are later accessed when e_{min} is handled. In this case the future (e_x) would have changed the past (e_{min}) which we call a *causal violation*.

By complying with this execution model, a sequential network simulator prevents causal violations. However, this model cannot easily be extended to support parallel execution since causal violations may occur frequently. The following example presents a naive approach and illustrates its flaws.

Assume that n processing units, e.g., CPUs, can be utilized by a parallel simulation framework. In order to keep all available CPUs busy, the central scheduler continuously removes as many events in timestamp order from the event queue as there are idle CPUs. Hence, at any time, n events are being processed concurrently. Now consider two events e_1 and e_2 with $T(e_1) < T(e_2)$ that have been assigned to different CPUs in timestamp order. The processing of e_1 creates a new event e_3 with $T(e_1) < T(e_3)$ and $T(e_3) < T(e_2)$.

Since e_2 has already been scheduled and may have changed variables that e_3 depends on, a causal violation has occurred.

Thus, we formulate the central challenge of PDES as follows:

Given two events e_1 and e_2, decide if both events do not interfere, hence allowing a concurrent execution, or not, hence requiring a sequential execution.

Parallel simulation frameworks employ a wide variety of synchronization algorithms to decide this question. The next section presents a selection of fundamental algorithms and discusses their properties.

8.2 Parallel Simulation Architecture

In this section, we introduce the general architecture of parallel discrete event simulation. This architecture forms the substrate for algorithms and methodologies to achieve high simulation performance while maintaining correctness of the simulation results.

A parallel simulation model is composed of a finite number of partitions which are created in accordance to a specific partitioning scheme. Three exemplary partitioning schemes are i) space parallel partitioning scheme, ii) channel parallel partitioning, and iii) time parallel partitioning.

The *space parallel partitioning* scheme divides the simulation model along the connections between simulated nodes. Hence, the resulting partitions constitute clusters of nodes. The *channel parallel partitioning* scheme bases on the assumption that transmissions that utilize different (radio) channels, mediums, codings etc. do not interfere. Thus, events on non-interfering nodes are considered independent. As a result, the simulation model is decomposed in groups of non-interfering nodes. However, channel parallel partitioning is not generally applicable to every simulation model, thus leaving it for specialized simulation scenarios [288]. Finally, *time parallel partitioning* schemes [290] subdivide the simulation time of a simulation run in time-intervals of equal size. The simulation of each interval is considered independent from the others under the premise that the state of the simulation model is known at the beginning of each interval. However, the state of a network simulation usually comprises a significant complexity and is not known in advance. Thus, this partitioning scheme is also not applicable to network simulation in general. Consequently, the remainder of this chapter focuses on space parallel partitioning.

A *Logical Process (LP)* constitutes the run-time component which handles the simulation of partitions. In this context, each partition is typically mapped to exactly one LP. Furthermore, every LP resembles a normal sequential simulation as each LP maintains state variables, a timestamped list of events and a local clock. Additionally, inter-LP communication is conducted by sending timestamped messages via *FIFO channels* which preserve

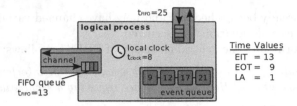

Fig. 8.1: A logical process (LP) maintains a local clock, an event queue and is connected to other LPs via FIFO channels.

a local FIFO characteristic. This means that all messages arrive at the receiving LP in exactly the same order as they were send in. Based on the notion of LPs, the *local causality constraint* defines an execution model for LPs that prevents causal violation:

Local Causality Constraint. A discrete-event simulation, consisting of logical processes that interact exclusively by exchanging time stamped messages obeys the local causality constraint if and only if each LP processes events in non-decreasing time stamp order.

In practice, the number or LPs (i.e., partitions) is equal to the number of CPUs provided by the simulation hardware. Consequently LPs directly map to physical processes. Furthermore, the timestamped and message-based communication scheme constitutes two important properties. First, they allow a transparent execution of LPs either locally on a multi-CPU computer or distributed on a cluster of independent computers. Second, and more importantly, timestamps provide the fundamental information used by synchronization algorithms to decide which events to execute and to detect causal violations. We now present two classes of synchronization algorithms: conservative and optimistic algorithms. While conservative algorithms aim to strictly avoid any causal violation at time of the simulation run, optimistic algorithms allow causal violations to occur, but provide means for recovering.

8.2.1   Conservative Synchronization Algorithms

Conservative synchronization algorithms strive to strictly avoid causal violations during a simulation run. Hence, their central task is to determine the set of events which are *safe* for execution. In order to decide on this question, conservative algorithms rely on a set of simulation properties [43].

The *Lookahead* of a LP is the difference between the current simulation time and the timestamp of the earliest event it will cause at any other LP. The *Earliest Input Time (EIT)* denotes the smallest timestamp of all messages that will arrive at a given LP via any channel in the future. Accordingly, the

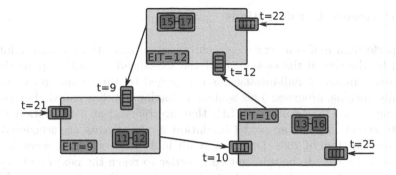

Fig. 8.2: Three LPs are deadlocked in a circular dependency: Every LP waits for its neighbor to send a message in order to increase the EIT.

Earliest Output Time (EOT) denotes the smallest timestamp of all messages that a given LP will send in the future to any other LP.

Based on these definitions, a LP can safely execute all events which have a smaller timestamp than its current EIT since it is guaranteed that no messages with a smaller timestamp will arrive later. Figure 8.1 shows an exemplary LP and the corresponding time values.

Null-Message Algorithm

The simple approach presented above does not solve the synchronization problem entirely as it can cause the simulation to deadlock. Figure 8.2 illustrates this behavior. The LPs can neither execute an event from their local event queue nor any incoming message since the local EIT is too small. Hence, each LP waits for a message from its direct neighbor in order to increase the EIT thereby creating a circular dependency.

This problem is addressed by the *Null-Message Algorithm (NMA)* which was first introduced by Misra and Chandra [317]. The algorithm uses null-messages, i.e., messages which do not contain simulation model related information, to continuously increase the EIT of all neighboring LPs. For this purpose, null-messages carry the LP's current EOT timestamp, which is determined by adding the lookahead to its current local time. Hence, null-messages can be considered as a promise of an LP not to send any message with a smaller timestamp than EOT in the future. Upon receiving a null-message, each LP updates its EIT to a potentially greater value. If the updated EIT has advanced beyond events in the event queue, those are now considered safe for execution. This algorithm guarantees to prevent deadlocks if the simulation model does not contain zero-lookahead cycles.

Performance Considerations

The performance of conservative synchronization algorithms is highly influenced by the size of the lookahead. If the lookahead is small, a potentially excessive number of null-messages is exchanged by the simulation without actually making progress. This system behavior is often called the "time-creeping" problem: Assume two LPs that are blocked at a simulation time of 100 seconds and whose next (simulation model) events are scheduled at a simulation time of 200s. Due to a small lookahead of only 1 second, 100 null-messages have to be transmitted in order to reach the next event.

However, the actual size of the lookahead is an inherent property of the simulation model – not of the synchronization algorithm. In network simulations the lookahead is usually determined by the link delay between the nodes. This works well for simulation models of fixed and wired networks such as the Internet by considering long distance backbone links. Unfortunately, link delays are extremely small in wireless networks, thus decreasing the lookahead significantly. As a result, extensive research work has been conducted on the development of techniques to extract the maximum lookahead from a simulation model [291, 315]. The general idea of these approaches is to exploit standardized protocol-specific properties such as timeouts or waiting periods (e.g., SIFS and DIFS in IEEE 802.11) to increase the available lookahead.

In consideration of these facts, it is important to determine the potential of a simulation model for achieving a satisfactory parallel performance. Given a specific simulation model and particular simulation hardware, Inequality (8.1) allows for roughly answering this question for the Null-Message Algorithm:

$$E_{seq} \geq \frac{n\tau P\lambda}{L} \qquad (8.1)$$

If (8.1) holds, then the model is expected to perform well under NMA. E_{seq} denotes the event density of the simulation model under sequential execution, i.e., the number of events per simulated second, and n is the number of LPs under parallel execution. Furthermore, τ measures the messaging latency of the physical simulation hardware, while P characterizes its computing power in processed events per second. λ represents the coupling factor of the LPs, describing how fluctuations of E and P effect blocking of LPs, and finally, L denotes the lookahead. An in-depth discussion of these approximations can be found in [476].

Ideal-Simulation-Protocol

Researchers have proposed a wide range of synchronization algorithms providing different properties and characteristics. The *Ideal Simulation Protocol*

(ISP) [43] is a means for determining the overhead of any conservative synchronization algorithm, thereby allowing an objective performance comparison.

ISP bases on the observation that each synchronization algorithm imposes two types of overhead: messaging overhead which is caused by sending (simulation model) messages to LPs on remote machines and the actual synchronization overhead which is caused by blocking and additional (synchronization) messages that are only used by the algorithm (e.g., null-messages). While messaging overhead is a property of the simulation model, the synchronization overhead is a property of a particular algorithm. The idea of ISP is to eliminate the synchronization overhead while preserving the messaging overhead, hence achieving an optimal simulation performance which acts as a baseline for any other synchronization algorithm.

ISP is a two-phase synchronization protocol: in the first phase, ISP employs an arbitrary conservative algorithm for the parallel simulation of a simulation model of choice. During this phase it collects meta information about all messages and events that occurred in the simulation run and writes those to a trace file. In the second phase the simulation is re-run with respect to the information from the trace file. By utilizing this information, an optimal synchronization is achieved without the need for inter-LP synchronization. Thus the efficiency of an algorithm S with respect to a specific simulation architecture A is given by

$$\text{Efficiency}(S, A) = \frac{\text{Execution time using ISP on } A}{\text{Execution time using } S \text{ on } A}$$

8.2.2 Optimistic Synchronization Algorithms

In contrast to conservative algorithms, *optimistic synchronization algorithms* allow LPs to simply execute all events (in time stamp order) as they come in, but without ensuring that causal violations will not occur. This probably counter-intuitive behavior is motivated by the observation that conservative algorithms sometimes block LPs unnecessarily: Often not enough information is available to mark a certain event safe, although it actually is. Hence, the simulation performance is reduced significantly.

Thus, optimistic algorithms assume that an event will not cause a causal violation. This approach has two primary advantages: First, it allows exploiting a higher degree of parallelism of a simulation model. If a simulation model contains two largely independent partitions, which interact only seldom, only infrequent synchronization is actually needed. Second, the overall performance of the parallel simulation depends less on the lookahead. Thus making it attractive to models with small lookahead such as in wireless networks.

Clearly, the downside is that a causal violation leaves the simulation in an incorrect state. As a result, optimistic algorithms provide recovery mechanisms: during a simulation run, the PDES engine continuously stores the simulation state. Upon a causal violation, the simulation is rolled-back to the last state known to be correct.

Time-Warp Algorithm

The *Time-Warp Algorithm* [241] is a well-known optimistic algorithm. A causal violation is detected when an LP lp_i receives a message m with a smaller time stamp than its own local clock: $T(m) < T(LP)$. As a result, lp_i restores the latest checkpoint known to be valid. Since the incorrect simulation state not only affects lp_i, but also any other LP that recently received a message from lp_i, the subsequent roll-back must also include those LPs. Hence, lp_i initiates the roll-back by sending an *anti-message* to all neighboring LPs for every message sent since the restored checkpoint. If an anti-message is enqueued in a channel queue together with the corresponding original message, i.e., this message was not yet processed by the receiving LP, both annihilate each other. If, however, the original message was processed, the receiving LP also initiates a roll-back. By using this process, the algorithm recursively drives all incorrect messages and states out of the system.

Performance Considerations

A major drawback of this class of algorithm is the significant amount of hardware resources needed for storing the simulation state checkpoints. Additionally, I/O operations pose a special problem as they cannot be rolled-back in general.

One approach to these challenges bases on the notion of *Global Virtual Time (GVT)* which is given by the smallest time stamp of all unprocessed messages in the simulation. Since GVT denotes the oldest message in the system, it is guaranteed not to be rolled-back. A garbage collector subsequently reclaims all resources occupied by older events and commits pending I/O operations.

Another performance issue of optimistic algorithms is thrashing: a significant decrease in simulation performance caused by frequent roll-backs. This behavior is often triggered by fast LPs that rush ahead and induce roll-backs in the majority of slower LPs. To counteract this behavior, a time window W is introduced which limits the amount of optimism. LPs may then only execute events within $GVT+W$, thus restricting fast LPs from rushing ahead.

8.3   Parallelization in Practice

In this section we analyze a selection of contemporary network simulators in terms of their PDES capabilities.

8.3.1   OMNeT++

OMNeT++ natively supports PDES by implementing the conservative Null-Message Algorithm and the Ideal-Simulation-Protocol [108]. By utilizing different communication libraries, a parallel simulation can furthermore make use of multi-CPU machines as well as a distributed setup.

In order to distribute a simulation model to a set of LPs, OMNeT++ employs a placeholder approach: A simple placeholder module is automatically created for each module which is assigned to a remote LP. When a message arrives at a placeholder module, it transparently marshals the message and sends it to the real module in the particular LP, which unmarshals and processes it.

Due to this (almost) transparent integration of PDES into the simulator architecture, OMNeT++ imposes only very few restrictions on the design of a simulation model for parallel execution. According to the definition of the LP-based architecture of PDES (c.f. Section 8.2), parallel OMNeT++ models must not use global variables or direct method calls to other modules. However, since the lookahead is given by the link delays, currently only static topologies are supported, making it difficult to parallelize mobile scenarios.

The properties of a parallel simulation setup are entirely specified in the global omnet.ini configuration file. This file defines the partitioning, which assigns every module and compound to a specific LP, as well as the synchronization and communication algorithms to use.

8.3.2   ns-2

PDNS [394] constitutes the parallel simulation architecture of ns-2. It is based on a conservative synchronization algorithm, which coordinates distributed instances of ns-2 which execute the partitions of the parallel simulation model. In PDNS terminology these instances are called federates.

PDNS was designed to integrate seamlessly into ns-2 without effecting existing simulation models. However, parallelization is not transparent to the simulation models. Instead, the parallelization process requires modifications of the simulation models in order to make use of the functionality provided by PDNS. In particular, links between nodes in different federates have to be replaced by dedicated "remote links", which implement PDES functionality. For the actual inter-federate communication, PDNS itself builds upon two communication libraries (libSynk and RTIKIT), which provide a variety of communication substrates such as TCP/IP, Myrinet and shared memory for testing and debugging.

8.3.3   DSIM

DSIM [96] is a parallel simulator which relies on optimistic synchronization. It is designed to run on large-scale simulation clusters comprised of hundreds to thousands of independent CPUs.

The core of DSIM is formed by a modified optimistic time warp synchronization algorithm carefully designed for scalability. For instance, the obligatory calculation of the GVT does not require message acknowledgments and utilizes short messages of constant length in order to reduce latency and messaging overhead. Furthermore, resource management is performed by a local fossil collection algorithm (garbage collection), which intends to increase locality by immediately reusing freed memory regions.

A performance evaluation using the synthetic PHOLD benchmark [162] indicates that DSIM achieves a linear speedup with an increasing number of CPUs. However, no evaluations using detailed network simulations are known to the author.

8.3.4   JiST

JiST [52, 51] is a general purpose discrete-event simulation engine that employs a virtual machine-based simulation approach. Implemented in Java, it executes discrete event simulations by embedding simulation time semantics directly into the execution model of the Java virtual machine. Simulation models are programmed using standard object-oriented language constructs. The JiST system then transparently encapsulates each object within a JiST entity, which forms the basic building block of a simulation model. While program execution within an entity follows the normal Java semantics, method invocations across entities act as synchronization points and are hence handled by the JiST run-time system. Invocations are queued in simulation time order and delivered to the entity when its internal clock has progressed to the correct point in time.

By utilizing this approach, entities can independently progress though simulation time between interactions - thus natively allowing a concurrent execution. Furthermore, an optimistic execution model can be supported via check-pointing.

8.3.5   IKR SimLib

The IKR SimLib [216] (see Chapter 4) is a simulation library that uses the common *batch means* method. This method seeks to obtain sufficient exactness and small confidence intervals [278]. For this purpose, a simulation run is divided over time into batches that are statistically independent. The results of each batch are interpreted as samples and are used to compute mean values and confidence intervals. The IKR SimLib provides support to execute these independent batches on multiple CPUs in parallel. Moreover, as soon as all batches are finished, the library supports aggregation of the statistical data calculated in each batch. Consequently, the parallel execution of batches efficiently reduces the time in comparison of sequential batch execution.

Thanks to the assumption of independent batches and their parallel execution, the IKR SimLib does not need to employ synchronization algorithms. This avoids the overhead typically imposed by synchronization and increases the simulation speed. Furthermore, it allows good scalability in terms of processing units. However, this approach is less suited for running extremely complex simulations, which impose huge demands on the hardware as within one batch the complete model needs to be simulated on one machine. As a result, very large simulations may not fit in the memory of a single machine or may take longer in comparison to other parallelization approaches.

8.4   Conclusion

Parallel discrete event simulation has been the field of intensive research in the last two to three decades. As a result, a plethora of different algorithms, frameworks and approaches exist today. We could hence sketch selected approaches only briefly in this chapter.

We first introduced the primary challenges that PDES faces: given a simulation model, a partitioning of the model needs to be found and distributed among the parallel simulation hardware. Next, an efficient synchronization algorithm is needed to maintain the correctness of the distributed simulation and to avoid causal violations. We presented two major classes of synchronization algorithms: conservative and optimistic synchronization. Along their discussion, performance considerations were presented. Finally, a selection of contemporary parallel simulation frameworks was introduced.

Although a wide range of simulation frameworks natively support PDES today, PDES still hasn't achieved a final breakthrough in network simulation due to a lack of performance and challenging programming models. Instead, often multiple sequential simulations are run on multi-core hardware in parallel. Hence, PDES remains a hard problem today. However, due to the ongoing development in the hardware sector, which favors an increasing number of processing units over an increasing speed of a single unit, PDES will remain an important and active field of research.

Part II

Lower Layer Wireless Modeling

9. Physical Layer Modeling

A. de Baynast (European Microsoft Innovation Center)
M. Bohge, D. Willkomm (Technische Universität Berlin)
J. Gross (RWTH Aachen University)

The Physical Layer (PHY) is serving as the interface between the Data Link Layer (DLL) and the environment. Accordingly, it defines the relation between the device and the physical medium. In wireless systems, the general task of the PHY is to convert bit streams into radio waves and vice versa. Though the transmitter and the receiver are dual, they are comprised of different components in the physical layer. The transmitter takes digital input in form of (payload) bits and converts them into an analog signal, generally around a given carrier frequency which is then radiated via the antenna. At the receiver, this analog signal which has been distorted during the propagation is then converted back into a (payload) bit stream. The general goal of the PHY is to ensure that the bit stream at the transmitter and at the receiver are identical. This is a very challenging task as the wireless channel (see Section 11) can distort and corrupt the analog signal in many different, random ways. In the following, we first provide an overview of the different functionalities of the PHY at the transmitter and receiver as applied in most common standards today like for cellular networks (such as Global System for Mobile Communications (GSM), Universal Mobile Telecommunications System (UMTS), Long Term Evolution (LTE)) or local/metropolitan area networks (e.g. IEEE 802.11, IEEE 802.16) as well as for broadcast networks (Digital Audio Broadcasting (DAB), Digital Video Broadcasting (DVB)). Then we discuss common simulation approaches used in the PHY and their shortcomings for network simulation. Finally, we comment on ways to include selected aspects of the PHY in network simulation models.

9.1 Overview of the PHY Layer

In wireless systems the PHY layer can be subdivided into four domains as depicted in Figure 9.1: the **bit domain**, the **symbol domain**, the **sample domain** and the **waveform/analog domain**. Note that any layer above the PHY can be considered to be part of a fifth domain referred to as the "packet domain", as indicated for the DLL in Figure 9.1. Data through the PHY layer is sequentially represented in each of these domains, i.e., by packets, bits, symbols, samples and finally by waveforms.

There are historical reasons behind this decomposition. Until the emergence of powerful processors in embedded communication devices during the last two decades, the bit stream was directly transformed into waveforms, representing the information either by amplitude levels referred to as Amplitude Modulation (AM) [375, Chap. 4, p.169], or by frequencies referred to as Frequency Modulation (FM) [395]. The corresponding waveform was directly modulated by an oscillator set to a specific carrier frequency. At the receiver, the analog signal was filtered by a matched filter in order to reduce the noise power outside the bandwidth of interest. In the particular case of FM receiver [395], a simple Phase-Locked Loop (PLL) could be used to lock to the current frequency of the signal. Whereas the hardware implementation of such a receiver was extremely cheap, the spectral efficiency (i.e. the ratio of throughput over the required system bandwidth) remained low.

As the demand for higher data rates increased dramatically over the last two decades, designs of transmission systems with higher spectral efficiency over broadband channels were required. Higher spectral efficiency has been achieved by using more sophisticated transmission schemes, which in turn require more complex algorithms especially at the receiver. In order to support complex algorithms, the devices nowadays comprise of one or several digital signal processors [442] that support a significant number of the operations represented in Figure 9.1. Besides the historical aspect, this decomposition into different domains is also fundamental in the comprehension of the results and the limitations of any wireless network simulator since some of these domains correspond to the different abstraction levels used by simulation tools as shown later. In this subsection, we first give a functional overview of the four different domains of the PHY before we discuss single, functional elements in the next subsection as second step.

Bit Domain. At the transmitter, a packet coming from the DLL enters the *bit domain* of the PHY. Three main functions are performed here: Cyclic Redundancy Check (CRC) coding, Forward Error Correction (FEC) coding and interleaving. Firstly, CRC bits are added to the packet bits. The main purpose of CRC code is to detect at the receiver if an error occurred during a transmission. Note that a CRC code only allows usually the detection of errors, it does not allow the correction. In order to correct eventual transmission errors, FEC coding schemes are used. Many different codes with different characteristics are known today: for correcting only few errors (less than 1 erroneous bit for 1000 bits transmitted) without penalizing the transmission rate too much, Reed-Solomon (RS) codes are good candidates. If the transmission channel introduces more errors (like typical GSM channels do), convolutional codes can be used. Even more efficient error correction codes are Turbo-codes [58] or Low-Density-Parity-Check (LDPC) codes [169, 300]. While they are more efficient than convolutional codes, their decoding algorithms are more complex as they require several decoding iterations. However, most of the current communication standards support them at least as option

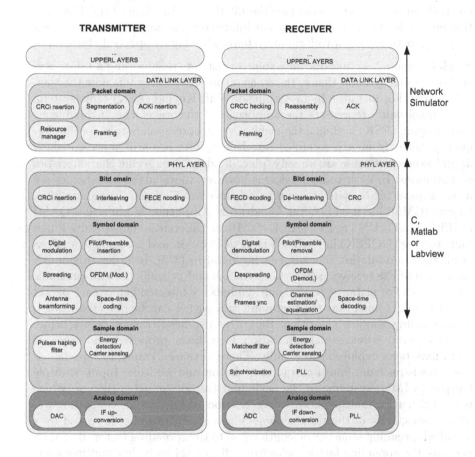

Fig. 9.1: Decomposition of the MAC and PHY layer into 5 domains for wireless transmission systems: the packet domain (MAC), the bit domain, the symbol domain, the sample domain and the analog domain. A tentative list (non exhaustive) of operations that enable reliable transmission between the transmitter and the receiver in current transmission systems is also represented in the figure. The operations are listed by domain which corresponds to the abstraction level in network simulators.

(like in UMTS, LTE, DVB or IEEE 802.11n). As the transmission errors often happen in bursts [38], the coded bit stream is interleaved before transmission so that the corresponding de-interleaver at the receiver will spread the bit errors uniformly within the received coded bit stream. All these operations are realized on the bit stream (see the bit domain in Figure 9.1). However, this binary description of the transmit information is not sufficient for direct mapping to an analog waveform in systems with higher spectral efficiency.

Symbol Domain. An intermediate step consists of transforming a bit or several bits into a symbol. Hence, the transmit information enters now the *symbol domain*. For instance, in an Amplitude Shift Keying (ASK) radio system, the symbol value represents the amplitude of the waveform. In Frequency Shift Keying (FSK) systems, the symbol value corresponds to a specific frequency taken from a pre-defined set. Hence, bits are still represented by digital values but these are already "place-holders" for specific characteristics of waveforms. In most today's systems however, more advanced schemes are used. Typical bit-to-symbol mapping schemes are Gaussian Minimum Shift Keying (GMSK) as used in GSM, Quadrature Amplitude Modulation (QAM) in IEEE 802.11, UMTS, LTE, IEEE 802.16, or Differential Quadrature Phase Shift Keying (DQPSK) in DAB/DVB. A description and a complete analysis of all these modulation schemes can be found in [375]. In order to simplify the design of the receiver, some pilot symbols and preamble or end-preamble are inserted. For instance, several null symbols are inserted before each packet in IEEE 802.11 such that the beginning of a packet can be detected using a double sliding window algorithm. Recently, advanced transmission schemes for broadband wireless communication have been proposed and some of them have been deployed successfully. These advanced transmission schemes are spread-spectrum, multi-carrier modulation and Multiple Input Multiple Output (MIMO) systems. In the particular case of spread-spectrum (which is used either for multiple access – see Section 10.1.4 – or for combating frequency selectivity of the transmission channels) each symbol is spread by a so-called spreading sequence of length equal to the spreading factor. In UMTS systems, the spreading factor varies from 16 to 1024 such that multiple users can simultaneously transmit in the same band without interfering with each other since the spreading sequences are mutually orthogonal. Hence, the bit-to-symbol mapping leads to a few bits mapped to many modulation symbols (i.e. "spreading" the information over many symbols). This leads to a better performance in channels with inter-symbol interference. A further advanced transmission scheme are multi-carrier modulation systems; the most successful example of such schemes is Orthogonal Frequency Division Multiplex (OFDM). An OFDM system combats efficiently the inter-symbol interference occurring in frequency selective propagation channels [375, Chap.12, p.718] by applying the Digital Fourier Transform (DFT) at the receiver and its inverse at the transmitter. This technique considerably simplifies the receiver implementation in case of frequency-selective channels since it is much easier to invert the channel effect in the frequency domain, i.e. after taking the DFT operation as long as it is done at the correct time lag (and assuming that the inverse of the coherence bandwidth of the channel does not exceed the guard interval of the system). Finally, a third advanced transmission scheme consists of utilizing antenna arrays at the transmitter or at the receiver or at both sides. The main advantage of MIMO systems is to considerably increase the spectral efficiency of the system by exploiting the spatial diversity, as demonstrated in [157]. Three techniques for MIMO systems are generally used. Firstly, beamforming consists of steering the energy of the signal towards the receiving antenna(s) by adjusting the weights of the phase array of the antennas [477]. The second technique is called space-time coding [457] which in contrary consists of spreading the energy spatially into all directions in an uniform way such that all potential receivers can receive the signal. Finally, the third technique consists of spatially multiplexing the emitted signal over all transmit antennas. Whereas considerable gains in terms of throughput and reliability are achieved, the drawback of these techniques is their computational complexity since matrix inversion of the channel coefficients is often required at the receiver side.

Sample and Waveform Domain. The description of the transmit information in terms of symbols is still not enough since it corresponds to a stream of consecutive discrete values. However, there are several different ways to map the symbols into waveforms, especially regarding the transition from one symbol to the next one. Most importantly, these different ways end up in different bandwidths that the signal consumes in the frequency domain. The exact transition from one symbol to the next one is governed by the so-called pulse shaping filters which limit the signal to the required bandwidth. Most of the current systems are using a square-root raised cosine filter at the transmitter and receiver. This filter reduces the required bandwidth to a minimum while no symbol interference occurs (theory of the eye pattern [375, Chap. 9]). As digital signal processors have become more and more powerful, the pulse shaping filtering is nowadays realized digitally. We refer to this level as *sample domain* since the output of the filter are sampled at much higher rate than the incoming symbols. The samples are then converted into an analog signal by a Digital-to-Analog Converter (DAC) which is finally modulated to the respective carrier frequency (for instance 2.4 GHz for 802.11, 1.6 GHz for LTE, 900 MHz or 1800 MHz for GSM, 400-700 MHz for DVB).

It has to be mentioned that the whole process is performed by quite specialized hardware. In order to support a transmission rate of 10 or 20 megabit per second, the digital sequence representing the same information at the sample domain can easily consume a bit rate of several hundred megabit per second. These information flows are processed by digital signal processing units which realize all functions on dedicated hardware as ASIC or DSPs. This obviously also applies to the analog part (D/A conversion, mixing, amplification) which is performed by a radio.

Compared to the transmitter, the receiver is far more complex in its functionality. This is mainly due to the processing steps of the sample domain since the receiver needs to be synchronized in time and frequency (and possibly space for systems with multiple antennas) in order to accurately retrieve the symbols. In fact, a wireless receiver is usually able to detect and decode transmit signals which are only a few decibel above the noise power of the system (every electromagnetic system features some form of noise which interferes with very weak signals arriving from some transmitter – see Section 11.10). This requires quite sophisticated and specialized processing operations to be performed which relies on digital signal processors. After synchronization the received signal basically works its way through the transmitter components in an opposite way.

In the next section, we detail each operation at the transmitter and the receiver into independent paragraphs with special emphasize on the computational complexity. When the description of the operation at the receiver is dual of the operation at the transmitter, we describe the operation of the transmitter and its counterpart function at the receiver within the same paragraph. We would like to insist that the list is not exhaustive. It provides an overview of the main functions implemented in current wireless transmission standards. The purpose of the list is to give an overview of the operations commonly utilized in current wireless transmission standards.

9.2   Description of the Main Components of the PHY Layer

In this section, a brief description of the aforementioned components at the transmitter and at the receiver is given. A complete list and explanation of all techniques used in the PHY layer is beyond the scope of this book. Furthermore, whereas the transmitter steps are clearly described in the standards, the implementation of the receiver is left free for manufacturers and therefore the exact operations at the receiver are generally not documented in details. The following descriptions are intended only to give an overview of the functional blocks present at a transmitter and receiver to the reader. For more details, the reader is asked to refer to the citations and references therein.

9.2.1   Components of the Bit Domain

Cyclic Redundancy Check Codes. CRC codes are hash functions designed to detect transmission errors. A CRC-enabled device calculates a short, fixed-length binary sequence, known as the CRC code, for each block of data (i.e. usually a frame, a header or a packet) and sends them both together. Generally, the CRC bits are padded at the end of the block. When a block is read or received, the device repeats the calculation. If the new CRC does not match the one calculated earlier, then the block contains a data error and the device may take some action such as discarding the block (DAB, DVB, GSM, UMTS) or requesting the block to be sent again (WLAN). The term CRC code originates from the fact that the check code is redundant (it adds zero information) and the algorithm is based on cyclic codes. CRC codes are popular because they are simple to implement, and are particularly effective at detecting common errors caused by noise in transmission channels.

All popular wireless systems are using CRC codes at the PHY (mostly for header protection) and at the MAC layer (header protection as well as payload protection). CRC codes are quite efficient at detecting the accidental alteration of data. Typically, an n-bit CRC, applied to a data block of arbitrary length, will detect any single error burst not longer than n bits and will detect a fraction $1 - 2^{-n}$ of all longer error bursts. As errors in wireless channels tend to be distributed non-randomly, i.e. they are "bursty", CRC codes' properties are more useful than any alternative schemes.

Forward Error Correction Codes. Encoding and decoding information via FEC codes is a system of error control for data transmission, whereby the sender adds redundancy to the transmitted information using a predetermined algorithm, also known as an error-correction code. Each redundant bit is invariably a complex function of many original information bits. The original information may or may not appear in the encoded output; codes that include the unmodified input in the output are called systematic, while those that do not are non-systematic. Contrary to CRC, FEC coding schemes allow the receiver to correct errors (within some upper bound). The advantages of FEC codes are that a feedback-channel is not required (as in GSM, UMTS systems and broadcasting systems) or that retransmissions of data are dramatically reduced in presence of a feedback-channel (as in IEEE 802.11 or LTE). This advantage comes at the cost of a lower throughput as redundancy is added to the bit stream. Given a FEC code of rate $1/3$ generates 2 bits of redundancy per information bit, which triples the bandwidth needed for the transmission or equivalently reduces the effective throughput of the system by a factor of three. The maximum fraction of errors that can be corrected is determined in advance by the design of the code, so different FEC codes are suitable for different transmission conditions.

There are two main categories of FEC codes: Convolutional codes and block codes [375, Chapter 8]. Convolutional codes work on bit or symbol streams of arbitrary length. They are most often decoded with the Viterbi algorithm [165]. Viterbi decoding allows asymptotically optimal decoding efficiency with increasing constraint length of the convolutional code, but at the expense of exponentially increasing complexity with respect to the constrained length. Most of the current wireless transmission standards (GSM, UMTS, LTE, IEEE 802.11, DAB, DVB) are using convolutional codes. The corresponding coding rate and constrained lengths are shown in Table 9.1.

	GSM	UMTS	LTE	IEEE 802.11	DVB-T
Coding rate	1/2	1/2-1/3	1/3-7/8	1/3-5/6	1/2-3/4
Constrained length	7	7 (9)	7-9	7	8

Table 9.1: Coding rate of convolutional codes as used in the wireless transmission standards GSM, UMTS, LTE, IEEE 802.11, and DVB-T.

Block codes work on fixed-size blocks of bits or symbols of predetermined size. Practical block codes can generally be decoded fast due to their block length. There are many types of block codes, but among the classical ones the most notable is Reed-Solomon (RS) coding. In current systems, block codes and convolutional codes are frequently combined in concatenated coding schemes. A short constraint-length convolutional code with low coding rate does most of the work and a Reed-Solomon code with larger symbol size and block length corrects the few errors left by convolutional decoder. Due to their order in the transmission chain, the Reed-Solomon and the convolutional codes are usually referred as outer and inner codes, respectively.

Whereas the convolutional codes provide a good trade off between the computational complexity and error-correction capability, there are other FEC coding schemes whose performance is within few tenths of decibels of the maximal theoretical rate. The maximal theoretical rate is referred as the *Shannon limit* in information theory [106]. The best known of these codes are the Turbo-codes [58] and the LDPC codes [169]. Although the complexity of the decoding is higher than for convolutional codes, their performance is such that they are proposed in most of the current standards as optional schemes (for example turbo-code of coding 1/3 in UMTS and LDPC in IEEE 802.11n). The Turbo-codes and LDPC codes share the same decoding algorithm referred to as belief propagation, sum-product or sigma-pi [111, 268]. This is an iterative algorithm for performing inference on graphical models, such as factor graphs that can be used to represent Turbo-codes and LDPC codes. Several iterations are required before convergence as illustrated in Figure 9.2.

FEC codes have often an all-or-nothing tendency, i.e. they can perfectly extract the transmitted message if the Signal-to-Noise-Ratio (SNR) of the transmission channel is large enough and cannot correct any error if the SNR of the transmission channel is too small. Therefore, digital communication systems that use FEC coding tend to work well above a certain minimum SNR and not at all below. Typical values are 8 decibels in GSM and 10 decibels for UMTS. This all-or-nothing tendency becomes more pronounced the more efficient the code works, i.e. the closer the FEC code approaches the theoretical limit imposed by the Shannon capacity [106]. This is particularly true for the Turbo-codes, the LDPC codes and the concatenated schemes with convolutional code as inner code and RS code as outer code.

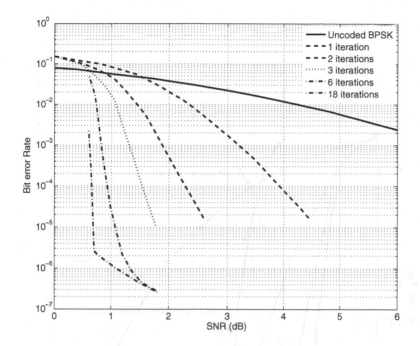

Fig. 9.2: Probability of bit error as a function of the signal-to-noise ratio of the transmission channel and the number of iterations of the decoding algorithm. For Turbo-codes, 5 iterations are usually sufficient. The computational complexity of the decoding algorithm is linear with respect to the number of iterations (data taken from [289]).

The performance gain of coded transmission compared to an uncoded transmission is illustrated in Figure 9.3 and is referred as the *coding gain*.

Finally, FEC coding schemes are often combined with puncturing (IEEE 802.11, LTE, DVB). Puncturing is a technique used to make the rate of a code slightly higher than the basic rate of the code [193]. It is reached by deletion of some bits in the encoder output. Bits are deleted according to a puncturing matrix. Punctured convolutional codes are also called "perforated".

Bit Interleaving/De-Interleaving. Data is often transmitted with FEC coding that enables the receiver to correct a certain number of errors which occur during transmission. If a burst of bit-error occurs, the number of bit-errors within the same code word may exceed the threshold under which a correction would have been possible. In order to reduce the effect of such error bursts, the bits of a number of consecutive codewords are interleaved before being transmitted [390]. This way, the wrong bits of an error burst are spread over several code words, which makes the error correction of the overall bit stream easier to be accomplished.

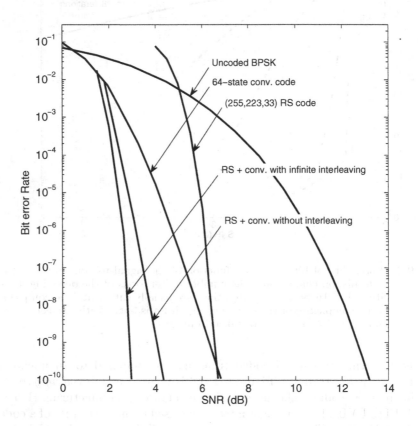

Fig. 9.3: Probability of bit error as a function of the signal-to-noise ratio of the transmission channel for several schemes: uncoded antipodal signal (uncoded BPSK), stand-alone convolutional code, stand-alone RS, concatenated scheme (convolutional code + RS) with and without interleaving. For the same spectral efficiency, the performance of concatenated schemes is superior to the performance of uncoded scheme or standalone FEC schemes especially for lower probability of bit error (data taken from [375]).

9.2.2   Components of the Symbol Domain

Digital Modulation/Demodulation.   Digital modulation and demodulation is the process of transforming a chunk of consecutive bits into one or several parameters of a sine wave (at the transmitter) and back (at the receiver). Note that digital modulation does not generate the waveform yet but it produces a stream of waveform parameters which are turned at a later stage to an analog waveform. Modulating information onto a waveform usually involves varying one sine waveform in relation to another sine waveform. The three key parameters of a sine wave that can therefore carry information are its amplitude, its phase and its frequency. Digital modulation is sometimes referred to as constellation mapping. The most common digital modulation techniques are listed in Table. 9.2.

GSM	UMTS	LTE (IEEE 802.16)	IEEE 802.11
GMSK	QPSK	4/16/64-QAM	BPSK-4/16/64-QAM
4 bits/symb	2 bits/symb	2-8 bits/symb	1-8 bits/symb

Table 9.2: Types of modulation techniques used in wireless transmission standards GSM, UMTS, LTE, IEEE 802.16, and IEEE 802.11.

In GSM systems, the GMSK modulation technique is employed. GMSK is a continuous-phase frequency-shift keying modulation scheme. It is similar to standard Minimum Shift Keying (MSK) modulation [375, Chapter 5], however the digital data stream is first shaped with a Gaussian filter before being applied to a frequency modulator. This has the advantage of reducing sideband power, which in turn reduces out-of-band interference between signal carriers in adjacent frequency channels. However, the Gaussian filter increases the modulation memory in the system and causes inter-symbol interference, making it more difficult to discriminate between different transmitted data values and requiring more complex channel equalization algorithms such as an adaptive equalizer at the receiver.

In UMTS, LTE, IEEE 802.16 and IEEE 802.11 systems, QAM is utilized. It conveys two digital bit streams by modulating the amplitudes of two carrier waves, using the ASK modulation scheme. These two waves, usually sinusoids, are out of phase with each other by 90 degrees and are thus called quadrature carriers or quadrature components – hence the name of the scheme. The modulated waves are summed, and the resulting waveform is a combination of both Phase Shift Keying (PSK) and ASK. In the digital QAM case, a finite number of at least two phases, and at least two amplitudes are used (4-QAM). However, Binary Phase Shift Keying (BPSK) and Quadrature Phase Shift Keying (QPSK) modulations can be viewed as special cases of QAM modulation. QPSK is equivalent to 4-QAM and BPSK has two amplitudes but a single phase. The operation which consists of mapping bit(s) to a symbol is illustrated in Figure 9.4 in the case of QAM modulation.

Constellation 4–QAM

```
  •          •
  00         10


  •          •
  01         11
```

Constellation 16–QAM

```
  •       •       •       •
 0000    0100    1100    1000

  •       •       •       •
 0001    0101    1101    1001

  •       •       •       •
 0011    0111    1111    1011

  •       •       •       •
 0010    0110    1110    1010
```

Constellation 32–QAM

```
        •       •       •       •
       00000   00001   10001   10000

  •       •       •       •       •       •
 00100   01100   01000   11000   11100   10100

  •       •       •       •       •       •
 00101   01101   01001   11001   11101   10101

  •       •       •       •       •       •
 00111   01111   01011   11011   11111   10111

  •       •       •       •       •       •
 00110   01110   01010   11010   11110   10110

        •       •       •       •
       00010   00011   10011   10010
```

Constellation 64–QAM

```
 •      •      •      •      •      •      •      •
000000 001000 011000 010000 110000 111000 101000 100000

 •      •      •      •      •      •      •      •
000001 001001 011001 010001 110001 111001 101001 100001

 •      •      •      •      •      •      •      •
000011 001011 011011 010011 110011 111011 101011 100011

 •      •      •      •      •      •      •      •
000010 001010 011010 010010 110010 111010 101010 100010

 •      •      •      •      •      •      •      •
000110 001110 011110 010110 110110 111110 101110 100110

 •      •      •      •      •      •      •      •
000111 001111 011111 010111 110111 111111 101111 100111

 •      •      •      •      •      •      •      •
000101 001101 011101 010101 110101 111101 101101 100101

 •      •      •      •      •      •      •      •
000100 001100 011100 010100 110100 111100 101100 100100
```

Fig. 9.4: Constellation of QAM signaling. Several bits are gathered to form one QAM symbol. The higher the modulation order the more efficient is the transmission. However, the distance between symbols becomes smaller as the number of symbols increase and is more subject to errors in presence of the transmission noise. In practice, 256 is the maximum supported order in wireless transmissions.

Pilot/Preamble Insertion and Removal. All digital wireless communication systems use pilot symbols in order to simplify the design of the receiver. Pilots are used to transmit data known in advance by the receiver. It uses them to perform synchronization and channel estimation. There are several types of pilots: preamble within the packet, few tones for OFDM systems, preamble for packet detection and null symbols for energy detection. The

type of pilots used in current wireless transmission standards arc listed in
Table 9.3.

GSM	UMTS	LTE, IEEE 802.16
Training seq	Training seq (Q)	Preamble + Pilot Tones
25% of the resources	50%	30%

IEEE 802.11	DAB	DVB-T
Preamble + Pilot tones	Preamble	Preamble + Pilot Tones
30% of the resources	5%	10%

Table 9.3: Types of pilot techniques used in wireless transmission standards.

Spreading/De-spreading. Spreading is an advanced transmission scheme used
for broadband wireless channels. It is in a sense the simplest FEC coding
technique em- ployed in the symbol domain. In spread-spectrum a signal
is generated which has a much larger bandwidth than would be required
for conveying the pure stream of information. There are three basic techniques employed to spread the information signal: direct sequence, frequency
hopping, or a hybrid of these. Spread spectrum makes use of a sequential
noise-like signal structure to spread the information signal over a much wider
band of frequencies. In direct sequence spread-spectrum, for example, each
bit of the information stream is mapped to a sequence of bits (where typical
ratios – the spreading factor – between input bit to output bits are $1/16$ or
$1/32$ in UMTS, $1/11$ in IEEE 802.11b). This sequence of bits is well-known in
advance and is referred to as spreading code. Then, the resulting "spreaded"
bit stream is fed to a modulator which generates now many more modulation
symbols than would be required for the information stream. At the receiver
the incoming signal is correlated with the spreading code to retrieve the original information signal referred to as de-spreading. Clearly, for de-spreading
to work correctly, the transmit and receive spreading sequences must be the
same and they must be synchronized. This requires the receiver to synchronize its sequence with the transmitter's sequence by taking the maximum of
the cross-correlation function between the spreading code and received data.
Good spreading codes are designed to appear as random sequences, i.e. not
having long trails of 1's or 0's and overall almost the same number of 1's and
0's. Due to the pseudo-randomness of the spreading sequence, the resulting
signal resembles white noise. Spreading by frequency hopping works in a similar manner. Here, a single bit is converted to one or several "hops" in frequency
according to a predetermined sequence. Spread-spectrum has several advantages. First of all, it decreases the potential interference to other receivers
as the transmit power of the spreaded signal is quite low. This does not
harm the reception of the signal as the receiver – which knows the spreading

sequence – sums up the transmit energy over 16 symbols in case of a spreading factor of $1/16$ and can therefore tolerate a transmit power which is lower by a factor of 16 (equaling 12 dB). Furthermore, spread-spectrum signals mitigate inter-symbol interference caused by frequency-selective fading channels as a single bit is converted – in direct sequence spread spectrum with a factor of $1/16$ – into 16 channel bits which achieves quite a coding gain. This effect even can be enhanced to resolve dominant paths of a multipath propagation environment known as RAKE receiver [446]. It is implemented in most of the UMTS receivers today. Furthermore, spread-spectrum enhances privacy as the spreading code has to be known to successfully decode the signal. Without knowing the spreading code, it is even hard to only detect the signal as the required transmit power for a large spreading factor is quite low. Due to these reasons, spread-spectrum systems were first developed by the military and are still widely applied there. Finally, spread-spectrum systems enable multiple access by assigning different data transmissions different spreading codes (in case of direct sequence spread-spectrum the corresponding multiple access schemes is referred to as Code Division Multiple Access (CDMA), see Section 10.1.4).

In current wireless standards, the two main spread-spectrum techniques are frequency hopping spread-spectrum (Bluetooth) and direct-sequence spread-spectrum (Global Positioning System (GPS), UMTS, IEEE 802.11b). In UMTS (and IS-95, CDMA2000) direct-sequence spread-spectrum is also applied for multiple-access. Its principle is illustrated in Figure 9.5.

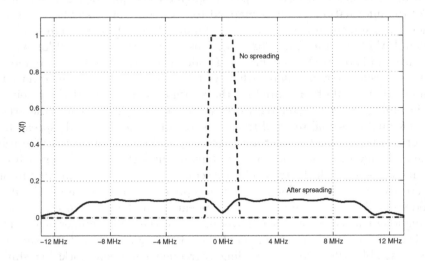

Fig. 9.5: Illustration of the spread spectrum technique. It consists of spreading spectrally the transmitted signal such that the signal is less sensitive to the frequency selectivity of the propagation channel or the interference of the other users in case of multiple-access scenario. As spreading sequence the one of IEEE 802.11b is considered: $1, -1, 1, 1, -1, 1, 1, 1, -1, -1, -1$.

Orthogonal Frequency Division Multiplexing. is an advanced Frequency Division Multiplex (FDM) transmission scheme for broadband wireless communication channels. A large number of closely-spaced orthogonal subcarriers are used to carry data. The payload data is divided into several parallel data streams or channels, one for each subcarrier. Each subcarrier is modulated with a conventional modulation scheme (such as QAM, see the description above on "Digital Modulation") at a low symbol rate, maintaining total data rates similar to conventional single-carrier modulation schemes in the same bandwidth. This is achieved by taking the inverse DFT of the set of modulation symbols (one for each subcarrier) and processing afterwards the stream of samples representing the time domain signal. At the receiver, the time domain samples are then transformed back by a DFT to the frequency domain to retrieve the modulation symbols per subcarrier. OFDM has developed into a popular scheme in modems for wired transmission over phone lines applied in Digital Subscriber Line (DSL) systems as discrete multi-tone modulation, providing quite large rates for data communications. However, today it is also applied in wireless digital systems such as DVB, DAB and wireless local/cellular systems (IEEE 802.11a/g/n, LTE, IEEE 802.16). The primary advantage of OFDM over single-carrier schemes is its ability to cope with severe channel conditions - for example, narrow-band interference or frequency-selective fading due to multipath - without complex equalization filters. Channel equalization is simplified because OFDM may be viewed as using many slowly-modulated narrow-band signals rather than one rapidly-modulated wide-band signal. The low symbol rate makes the use of a guard interval between symbols affordable, making it possible to eliminate Inter-symbol Interference (ISI). Although OFDM has been successfully deployed, it has still some disadvantages compared to single carrier systems: sensitivity to Doppler shift, sensitivity to frequency synchronization problems which requires generally a complex synchronization unit at the receiver as well as a high peak-to-average-power ratio, i.e. large power difference between the weakest and the strongest amplitudes on subcarriers. Finally, the loss of spectral efficiency caused by cyclic prefix/guard interval might not be negligible. For instance, the loss is about 20% in IEEE 802.11 a/g/n systems.

OFDM in its primary form is considered as a digital modulation technique since it is utilized for conveying one bit stream over one communication channel using one sequence of OFDM symbols. However, OFDM can be combined with multiple access using time, frequency or coding separation of the users. One particular important multiple access combination with OFDM is the frequency separation referred to as OFDMA, see Section 10.1.2. It is applied today in LTE and IEEE 802.16e systems.

The next two paragraphs discuss three techniques for transmission systems with multiple inputs or/and multiple outputs (in general summarized under the acronym MIMO). Interest for MIMO systems has considerably increased over the last decade for two main reasons: the throughput increases linearly with the number of inputs and the probability of transmission errors decreases linearly with the number of receive antennas for basic scheme. The second reason is that current powerful processors can support such techniques in wireless standards (UMTS, LTE, IEEE 802.16).

Antenna Beamforming. Beamforming is a signal processing technique used in wireless transmission systems for directional signal transmission or reception. It exploits "spatial selectivity" among a single signal transmitted from multiple antennas, or received by multiple antennas, or both. If beamforming is applied at the transmitter, the same transmit signal is sent from each antenna. However, a beamformer controls the phase and relative amplitude of the signal at each antenna in order to create a pattern of constructive and destructive interference in the wavefront. Effectively, this gives the signal a preferred direction such that the SNR at the receiver is strongly increased. However, the transmitter must know the position of the receiver (or even better, its channel characteristics with respect to each transmit antenna). When applied for receiving, the incoming signal from different antennas is combined in such a way by delaying some signals and multiplying with adequate complex coefficients (phase and amplitude). As a result, the received signal's SNR is strongly increased (but again the receiver has to know the direction from which the transmitted signal is received or even better the exact channel characteristic). If both transmitter and receiver have multiple antennas, beamforming may also be applied both at the transmitter and the receiver which leads to an even better SNR. However, beamforming can be computationally expensive if applied for several antennas at the transmitter or receiver (while also requiring control overhead). Hence, only basic beamforming techniques are being used in wireless standards today: Transmit antenna selection in GSM and UMTS which consists of selecting the transmit antenna that provides the best SNR for the considered terminal. For LTE, a pre-coding based beamforming with partial Space Division Multiple Access (SDMA) can be used optionally if the system supports MIMO techniques. A flexible system is IEEE 802.11n, which permits the application of beamforming simultaneously at the transmitter and receiver, based on the channel state information sent from the receiver to the transmitter by control frames. This technique is sometimes referred to as closed loop beamforming.

Space-time Coding/Decoding. Also in case of wireless systems with multiple transmit antenna, Space Time Coding (STC) is another method employed to improve the reliability of data transmission. Space-time coding relies on transmitting multiple, redundant copies of a data stream to the receiver in the hope that at least some of them may "survive" the physical path between transmission and reception in a good enough state to allow reliable decoding. Space time codes may be split into two categories:

1. Space-time trellis codes [458] distribute a trellis code over multiple antennas and multiple time-slots and provide both coding gain and diversity gain.
2. Space-time block codes [427],[456] act on a block of data at once (similarly to block codes) and provide only diversity gain, but are much less complex in implementation terms than space-time trellis codes.

UMTS, LTE and IEEE 802.11n support the basic Alamouti scheme [427]. Alamouti invented the simplest of all the STBCs in 1998 [427]. It was designed for a two-transmit antenna system and one receive antenna. It takes two time-slots to transmit two symbols such that it can achieve its full diversity gain without needing to sacrifice its data rate. The significance of Alamouti's proposal in 1998 is that it was the first demonstration of a method of encoding which enables full diversity with linear processing at the receiver. Earlier proposals for transmit diversity required processing schemes which scaled exponentially with the number of transmit antennas [156]. Furthermore, it was the first open-loop transmit diversity technique which had this capability. Subsequent generalizations of Alamouti's concept have led to a tremendous impact on the wireless communications industry.

Spatial Multiplexing. If a transmitter has data to be sent to multiple receivers and if it has multiple transmit antennas, it can actually transmit the information to all terminals simultaneously. This is referred to as spatial multiplexing [468]. In spatial multiplexing the transmit signal of the data for each receiver is concentrated by beamforming on the location of the receiver. However, this concentration in some preferred direction leads to a strongly attenuated signal transmitted into several other directions. These directions are the ones where further receivers can be served without having them suffer from interference of a simultaneous packet transmission. Hence, not all receiver distributions can be supported in a similar manner by spatial multiplexing. Spatial multiplexing is furthermore limited by the number of antennas the transmitter has, i.e. for n antennas up to n terminals can be served at the same point in time. In a similar manner a receiver with n antennas can receive up to n packets simultaneously by applying a beamformer. This is referred to as *space division multiple access* (see Section 10.1.3). As with spatial multiplexing, this works well for some transmitter position combinations while other combinations can not be resolved by the beamformer efficiently. Furthermore, if the receiver has multiple antennas then the constraint on the positions of the transmitters becomes less significant by the application of interference cancellation algorithms. In fact, the application of interference cancellation allows even for several, different packets transmitted over different antennas to the same receiver (if the receiver has multiple antennas as well). This is the most prominent MIMO scheme which is often characterized by a linear increase of the system capacity with the (minimal) number of antennas at the transmitter and receiver side. However, the complexity of especially the receiver is currently a strong limitation factor. Still, it is expected that this MIMO technique will be strongly used in future wireless standards.

Symbol Interleaving/De-Interleaving.   Symbol interleaving is used in digital data transmission technology to protect the data against burst errors occurring during the propagation. As with bit interleaving, if a burst error occurs, too many errors can be made within one code word, and that code word cannot be correctly decoded. To reduce the effect of such burst errors, the symbols of a number of frames are interleaved before being transmitted. This way, a burst error affects only a correctable number of symbols in each frame, and the decoder can decode the frame correctly. LTE and DVB systems are using symbol interleaving.

9.2.3   Components of the Sample and Waveform Domain

Frame/Packet Synchronization.   Once a digital train of samples is obtained, the receiving circuits (in the digital domain) first have to synchronize to the transmitter. This refers to fine tuning to the exact timing with which the modulation symbols are transmitted and to the exact carrier frequency used by the transmitter (there is always some frequency shift between any two oscillators, hence, requiring the receiver to identify the shift and correct it). Special training sequences (also referred to as preambles) are added by the transmitter to any data transmission which the receiver can use to easily acquire a precise enough synchronization. However, if the transmission occurs over a quite bad communication channel, already the step of synchronization can become very difficult and requires special design [406].

Channel Estimation and Equalization.   After obtaining synchronization, the receiver has to identify the possible random distortions that the wireless channel causes to the signal (like phase shifts and attenuations/gains). This is known as channel estimation. For this, so called pilot signals are added to the transmit signal which are transmitted with a known strength and with a known phase. After the channel has been estimated, the distortions of the channel are compensated which is known as equalization. The proper estimation and equalization of the channel is a prerequisite for decoding the payload signal (as synchronization is a prerequisite as well). As an alternate solution, *differential modulation* (DAB) can be utilized. Since the data information is contained in the phase difference between two consecutive symbols, the data can be retrieved if the phase shift occurring during the transmission is equal for both symbols.

Pulse Shaping Filter/Matched Filter.   In digital telecommunication, pulse shaping is the process of changing the waveform of transmitted pulses. Its purpose is to make the transmitted signal suit better to the communication channel by limiting the effective bandwidth of the transmission. By filtering the transmitted pulses this way, ISI caused by the channel can be reduced. Also, pulse shaping is essential for making the signal fit in its frequency band. Typically, pulse shaping is nowadays implemented in the digital domain before the digital-to-analog conversion. Two main pulse-shaping filters are used today in wireless communication systems: Either a Gaussian filter (like in GSM) or a raised-cosine filter [375, Chapter 9] (UMTS, LTE, IEEE 802.16, IEEE 802.11, DAB, DVB). The impulse response and the spectrum of the raised-cosine filter are plotted in Figure 9.6 for several values of roll-off factor β ranging from 0 to 1. The bandwidth occupied by the signal beyond the sampling frequency $1/2T$ is called the excess bandwidth and is usually expressed as a percentage of the sampling frequency. For example, when $\beta = 0.22$ as in UMTS standard, the excess bandwidth is 22%. The overall raised cosine spectral characteristic is usually split evenly between the transmitting pulse shaping filter and the receiving filter.

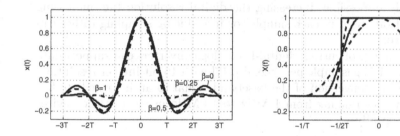

Fig. 9.6: Impulse response (left) and spectrum (right) of the raised cosine filter for several values of roll-off factor β. Most of the current standards are using raised cosine filter as pulse evenly split between the transmitter and the receiver (GSM: 0.2, UMTS: 0.22, DAB: 0.3).

Carrier Sensing/Energy Detection. Carrier sensing is usually employed by Carrier Sense Multiple Access (CSMA) protocols, as employed for example in the MAC of IEEE 802.11 systems. Through carrier sensing the transmitter evaluates the current state of the channel to determine whether the channel is idle or if it is currently busy with other data transmissions. There are different possibilities how to implement a carrier sensing algorithm. On the one hand there is energy detection which is purely checking for the current channel Received Signal Strength Indication (RSSI). If the RSSI is above a certain threshold – the so called Clear Channel Assessment (CCA) threshold – the channel is declared busy. Alternatively, a wireless device might try to sense a decodable signal on the channel, for example a header of a certain wireless system. Only if this header is decoded correctly, the channel is declared busy. The difference between this feature detection and pure energy detection is that in the first case all devices operating in the corresponding bandwidth can block the channel (by emitting energy) while in the second case only specific devices can block the channel. Carrier sensing is also used during the association process in all cellular networks (GSM, UMTS, LTE) that comprise multiple channels operating on orthogonal carrier frequencies. In these cases, the SINR of each channel is evaluated by sensing a beacon on each carrier.

DA/AD Conversion and IF Up/Down Conversion. In digital communication digital-to-analog conversion is used to convert the pulse shaping filtered output into an analog voltage which will be sent to the radio front-end of the transmitter. At the receiver, the reverse operation is known as analog-to-digital conversion. By the Nyquist-Shannon sampling theorem, a sampled signal can be reconstructed perfectly provided that the sampling frequency is at least twice as big as the Nyquist frequency of the transmitted signal in absence of noise [106]. However, even with an ideal reconstruction filter, digital sampling introduces quantization errors that make perfect reconstruction practically impossible. Increasing the digital resolution (i.e. increasing the number of bits used in each sample) or introducing sampling dither can reduce this error.

The performance of current digital-to-analog converters can support data rates as high as 1 Gigasample per second [217] with 16 bit integer resolution. Therefore, the up-conversion of the baseband signal to an intermediate frequency with values ranging from 1 MHz to 10 MHz in most of the devices can be done digitally.

9.3   Accurate Simulation of Physical Layers

With wireless transmission systems becoming more and more complex while the time-to-market is always decreasing, accurate simulations of upcoming standards are essential. Wireless communication standards become so involved due to the complexity of the system that the design and elaboration of the upcoming standards are done by means of using a simulator (and later in the process a hardware prototype).

Since most of the elementary operations in the components of the PHY layer are done on vectors of bits or symbols or samples, natural candidates are scientific programming languages, such as Matlab. As a point-to-point communication can be modeled as a chain of elementary matrix or vector operations, it is also natural to consider in addition block diagrams as in Matlab Simulink or Labview. The simulations consist usually of evaluating the symbol-, bit-, or packet-error rate of the transmitted PHY frames that have been corrupted by the modeled transmission channel. In order to take the randomness of the transmission system into account (randomness of the propagation medium, randomness of the transmitted data), a simulation provides the average performance for thousands of packet transmissions

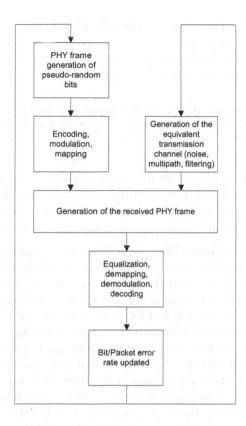

Fig. 9.7: Typical flow graph used for simulating performance of PHY layer transmission (Matlab, Labview, or C). The new algorithm(s) is (are) implemented either in the transmitter side (encoding, modulation) or on the receiver side (equalization which includes interference canceler, decoding,...).

with different transmission channel coefficients and different data to transmit. The simulation flow graph is illustrated in Figure 9.7. Most of these Matlab implementations consider equivalent symbol timing and bypass network aspects beside interference within PHY frames. Queuing, network topology, network protocols (TCP, IPv6) are rarely considered for complexity issues since the computational complexity is increasing at least linearly each time a new random parameter is introduced (depth of the queue, location of the transmitter/receiver). Moreover, the computational complexity of the simulations increases polynomially (or even exponentially) with respect to the number of users so that the computational complexity of a simulation for a full cell is prohibitive and requires a higher level of abstraction as in the network simulators. However, this is basically not the main focus of Matlab or

Domains	Bit rate (Mbits/s)
Bit domain	22.8 Mbits/s
Symbol domain	28.5 Mbits/s
Sample domain	> 914 Mbits/s

Table 9.4: Bit rate in the bit, symbol, and sample domains of the PHY layer for IEEE 802.11 system assuming a raw data rate of 10 Mbits/s at the MAC layer.

similar tools and there is no built-in libraries that allow networking considerations. Whereas their proposed environment allows fast development and design of advanced wireless techniques at the PHY layer, the next paragraphs discuss their main limitations. In the following we focus on three of them:

1. **Slow execution speed:** Whereas the Matlab environment is very convenient for developers, the fact that it is an interpreted language – especially when loops cannot be avoided – makes the simulations extremely slow. To have a better understanding of the computational complexity, the bit rate in the different domains of the PHY layer is calculated in Tab. 9.4 for IEEE 802.11 system with data rate of 10 megabits per second. From this example, it is clear that scientific programming languages as Matlab can deal well with the bit and symbol domains, but not with the sample domains (the computational complexity is 2 orders of magnitude more). One way to bypass this problem is to determine an equivalent transmission model in the symbol domain. This is very commonly done. However, there is a risk that the equivalent model does not capture accurately some effect as sample synchronization or collision at the sample level. It is also possible to use C for accelerating some functions that are not vectorial and require large *sequential* loops as in the Viterbi decoder. Matlab allows easily the integration of C functions (known as mex files).

2. **No discrete-event support:** While the sample or symbol processing at a transmitter or receiver imply a pseudo-continuous model of time, the processing steps of the higher layers of a wireless network happen much more asynchronous. In order to simulate this, discrete-event support is required, which is usually not provided. Furthermore, there is no library support for functions of the higher layers, meaning that all functionality needs to be implemented from scratch.

3. **Lack of interaction with network simulators:** While Matlab can be used via an interface for example from C code, the interfacing is not particularly easy to handle nor is it quite fast.

9.4   Physical Layer Modeling for Network Simulations

From the previous sections it is clear that physical layer simulations are quite demanding with respect to computational complexity and the required background knowledge. Hence, the question arises how physical layer behavior can and should be modeled in the context of network simulation, i.e. the typical simulation approach which only considers the packet domain.

A brute force method interfaces between a network simulator and simulator for the physical layer (like Matlab). While this provides a very detailed model, for larger deployments the approach does not scale with respect to complexity. Run times of simulations become so long, even for moderately complex topologies, that there is no benefit left from the detailed simulation model. Furthermore, analyzing simulation results becomes much more difficult as many more parameters have now an influence on the performance. Finally, as there is also a wide background knowledge required to design, execute and analyze such simulations, implementing the considered approach on a wireless prototyping platform might be a better choice. However, there is still tool support for fully detailed simulation models of wireless systems. A particular tool that can combine the different "simulation worlds" of higher layers (i.e. the simulators of the packet domain) and of the physical layer (among many other simulation domains) is Ptolemy from UC Berkeley [8]. Still, the above mentioned complexity problems remain.

Due to these reasons the common approach in wireless network simulation is to abstract from the many details of the physical layer. More precisely, almost all physical layer models in network simulators aim at capturing the physical layer impact on the transmission of frames or packets in terms of throughput, error probability and delay under the assumption of perfect synchronization. These models belong to the packet domain from Figure 9.1 and only take the following functions into account: FEC coding, digital modulation, advanced transmission schemes (like OFDM, spread-spectrum, antenna beamforming and space-time coding) and carrier sensing. All the other functions are assumed to work perfectly without any performance degradation (which is a very strong assumption compared to reality). Thus, only the packet error process (along with throughput and delay) can be taken into account. These models can not provide a "bit-true" characterization of the PHY, where the impact of the PHY layer on the transmission of each bit is modeled accurately. The difference between these two approaches leads to the important consequence that for packet-domain models only a statement can be derived if a packet/frame is received incorrectly but not which bits are wrong (which can be obtained from a bit-true model). Knowing the position of a bit error has some relevance for higher layers. If a header is corrupted the packet is most likely discarded. On the other hand, if payload bits are corrupted this may have quite different consequences for multimedia applications like video or voice, which can tolerate some bit errors. The quality degradation depends on the exact position of the bit error. However, bit-true physical layer simulation models are much more complex regarding their implementation.

Apart from other issues, two components are essential for all packet-domain models. On the one hand, most packet-domain models determine the channel quality between a transmitter and the corresponding receiver. Aspects of this step relate to considering path loss, shadowing, fading, noise and interference in combination with the used antenna and possibly advanced transmission schemes (like OFDM, spreading or MIMO systems). Another aspect of this step involves the question if the channel quality is accounted for on the average or if an instantaneous channel quality is considered, i.e. one value or even multiple values per transmitted packet. On the other hand, most packet-domain models translate the channel quality into an error rate (mostly a bit-error rate). This mapping can be quite complex and involves the modeling of the digital modulation as well as the FEC scheme. In the following, we give an overview of both modeling steps. Note that there are further aspects to be considered for a PHY layer packet-domain model, as discussed in Section 9.5.

9.4.1   Link-to-System Interface

In the following, we first discuss the mapping of the channel state to a bit-error probability for narrow-band, single-carrier transmission systems, i.e. for systems without advanced transmission schemes assuming that the channel gain is flat (see Section 11.7). For this we make in this section initially the assumption that the channel quality is fixed. This type of model is also referred to as static channel (see Section 11.12). In this case we can find a mapping of the channel state and the chosen transmission parameters (modulation type, transmit power, coding scheme, etc.) into a resulting physical layer behavior on the packet domain in terms of packet throughput, delay and bit-error rate. This mapping is referred to as *link-to-system interface*. In its simplest form, it is based on the fact that for a certain received channel quality, as measured by the SNR, the bit error rate can be derived depending on the chosen modulation type and transmit power. Once the bit error rate is determined, the corresponding packet error rate can be obtained as explained in Section 10.2. The SNR is given by

$$\gamma = \frac{P_{\text{tx}} \cdot h^2}{\sigma^2} \tag{9.1}$$

where P_{tx} is the transmit power, h^2 is the channel gain (see Chapter 11) and σ^2 is the equivalent background noise power of the transmission. The transmit power P_{tx} is usually well known during network simulation, even if it is adapted by the transmit node. Therefore, it is readily available for the computation of the SNR. This is also true for the noise power which depends on specific PHY parameters of the receiver (see Section 11.10). Furthermore, h^2 denotes the channel gain between the transmitter and the receiver, which we assume to be constant initially. In this case the computation of the resulting bit error rate from a given SNR is rather easy and is also quite close to the real system behavior. Either exact or approximate formulas are used, as derived in [100] for QAM systems. If no formulas exist, the considered modulation system might still have been investigated by related work providing a SNR-to-BER curve. This curve can then be converted into a look-up table to be used in the simulation. Finally, if no data on the modulation system exists, the only way to obtain an SNR-to-BER curve is to perform extensive and accurate PHY simulations, for example using Matlab. Then, the obtained curve can be be mapped into a look-up table as shown in Table 9.5 for the four different modulation types of the IEEE 802.11b standard as taken from [355]. Given the bit-error rate, the next step is to determine the

SNR (dB)	BPSK (1Mbps)	QPSK (2Mbps)	CCK5.5 (5.5Mbps)	CCK11 (11Mbps)
...	...	...	...	...
-5	6e-2	0.5e0	0.5e0	0.5e0
-4	2e-2	0.5e0	0.5e0	0.5e0
-3	8e-3	0.5e0	0.5e0	0.5e0
-2	4e-3	1e-1	0.5e0	0.5e0
-1	1e-4	8e-2	0.5e0	0.5e0
0	3e-5	2e-2	0.5e0	0.5e0
1	1e-5	5e-3	8e-2	0.5e0
2	1e-6	1.2e-3	4e-2	0.5e0
...	...	...	...	...

Table 9.5: An example Bit-Error Rate (BER) lookup table for the four different (uncoded) modulation types of the IEEE 802.11b Wireless Local Area Network (WLAN) standard.

packet error rate. This step is described in detail in Section 10.2. Once the packet error probability is obtained, for each transmitted packet a random decision is performed according to the packet error rate threshold and the corresponding packet is then marked to be either erroneous or not.

So far we have considered a static channel quality with a single modulation type and a simple (single-carrier) transmission system. The mapping from SNR to bit-error rate gets already more complicated if a FEC coding scheme is assumed. To account for FEC coding, two general approaches exist. Either the coding effect is taken into account by modifying the SNR. In this case, coding simply "increases" the SNR leading to a better bit error rate. However, this assumes a constant coding gain between the coded and uncoded system which is usually not the case at high or low SNRs. Hence, one has to obtain a detailed look-up table for the coded bit error rate of the FEC codes in combination with the modulation scheme depending on the SNR. If such tables are not provided by books and research papers, they have to be obtained from extensive physical layer simulations (usually performed in the symbol- or sample domain of Figure 9.1). There are also limited ways to capture the coded system behavior by formulas, see Section 12.1.2 for an example mapping for convolutional coding. Still, ultimately a packet error rate is obtained and for each transmitted packet a binary decision is performed if the packet is erroneous or not.

Next, let us consider a varying channel gain. In wireless systems a varying channel gain is almost always encountered in reality. Hence, it is likely to be included in a simulation study. The channel gain depends in general on the distance between transmitter and receiver (therefore, the chosen mobility model – see Section 14 – has an impact on the channel gain), but there are also additional time-varying, random components to the channel gain referred to as shadowing (see Section 11.6) and fading (see Section 11.7). All these effects ultimately lead to a varying h^2 in Equation 9.1 and thus the SNR γ varies over time. A quite common assumption for such cases is that the channel gain h^2 is constant during a single packet transmission but varies in between. Such channel models are also referred to as block-fading channels (see Section 11.12). This leads to determining an instantaneous SNR at the time a packet is transmitted. From this instantaneous SNR an instantaneous bit-error rate is determined using the same method as above (formulas or look-up tables for the modulation and coding scheme considered). Finally, a packet-error rate is determined and a random decision is performed if the packet is received correctly or not. Depending on the considered distribution of the channel gain, this method can lead to a very different average packet error rate behavior than considering a static channel quality. This is important to note if one is only interested in the average PHY layer behavior but fading or shadowing is to be taken into account.

9.4.2   Equivalent Channel Quality Models

The modeling of the channel quality and the corresponding PHY layer performance becomes more complicated if the channel quality is assumed to be variable during a packet transmission. This can happen due to fading, as explained in Section 11. However, interference can also contribute to a varying channel quality during a packet transmission. If interference is present, the channel quality is measured by the SINR as given below:

$$\gamma = \frac{P_{\text{tx}} \cdot h^2}{\sum_{\forall j} P_j^I \cdot h_j^2 + \sigma^2} \tag{9.2}$$

In this case, the received power in the numerator is divided by the noise power, denoted by σ^2, as well as the sum over all interfering signals multiplied by the respective channel gains between the interference sources and the considered receiver. Note that these channel gains might all be subject to stochastic variations which makes the analysis of such scenarios quite complicated.

If either fading or interference are time varying within the packet transmission, the common approach is to consider an *equivalent SINR*, meaning that a constant substitute SINR has to be found which results in the same packet error rate as the varying channel has. In general this is quite difficult and has to be redone every time a new PHY architecture or a new channel behavior is considered. For example, if three levels of channel quality are assumed to occur during a packet reception, the equivalent channel quality can be computed by the average of these three levels (weighted by their durations). However, as the mapping from channel quality to bit error rate is usually non-linear, a better approach is to average the corresponding bit error rates of the three levels weighted by the durations. Note that the correctness of this averaging for an equivalent model depends on the modulation, FEC coding and interleaving scheme used. Still, it is the best that can be done for packet-domain models. If more accurate models are to be considered, a bit-true model must be employed.

9.4.3 Modeling Advanced Transmission Systems

An accurate modeling of the PHY layer for network simulation becomes more complicated if advanced transmission systems are considered even if the transmitter/receiver pair is assumed to be perfectly synchronized (and hence the components involved in synchronization are not considered). The main reasons for the modeling difficulties are the following:

1. **Interaction between the channel and advanced transmission schemes:** Most current and upcoming standards for wireless systems employ a system bandwidth which is much larger than 500 kHz. For such bandwidth the channel becomes frequency-selective (see Section 11.7). Even for simple transmission schemes the performance on top of a frequency-selective channel is not easy to characterize. This becomes much harder if advanced schemes are employed. Even worse, if mobility is assumed, the channel might become time-selective, which adds to the modeling complexity. Finally, all these arguments also apply to interfering signals, which interact with the advanced transmission system as well. Especially if many possible transmitter/receiver/interferer constellations are considered in a large-scale simulation, the scalability of the simulation model becomes crucial [392].

2. **Multi-parameter dependency:** Any model of advanced transmission schemes such as OFDM, MIMO or spread-spectrum requires a lot of parameters to characterize the input/output behavior. It is difficult to plug a statistical characterization to each parameter, especially when they are

not mutually independent. This applies for instance to the fading gain coefficients between the antennas in MIMO systems and/or the fading gain coefficients between subcarriers in OFDM systems. Some interesting solution based on the principle of maximum entropy has been presented recently for MIMO systems [115]. Furthermore, models for so called "outage analysis" have been derived recently. The outage probability has been first considered by Shamai [345] in the context of vehicular networks for simple transmission systems. Later, this approach has been extended to more advanced schemes like MIMO [287], OFDM [114], and spread spectrum [478]. The analysis of the outage probability however has several drawbacks. Most importantly, all mentioned work consider Gaussian signaling instead of discrete constellation settings (i.e. Shannon capacity versus real modulation schemes) and the outage probability can be determined only for specific channel behaviors like the Rayleigh fading distribution.

3. **Advanced coding schemes on top of advanced transmission schemes**: For advanced FEC coding schemes– especially the decoding algorithms invoked at the receiver– there is often no analytical relationship between the input(s) and the output(s) even if simple transmission schemes are considered. Notable examples are Turbo-codes for which the algorithm was found before any analytical framework was proposed. Hence, the performance gain stemming from these advanced FEC schemes is difficult to quantify. Several new methods addressing this problem have been proposed recently [461, 389]. However, they require large computational power and can only model basic schemes.

4. **Adaptation and channel feedback**: Finally, many advanced transmission schemes are applied in an adaptive manner, i.e. there is a feedback loop from the receiver to the transmitter with channel state information and the transmitter modifies its behavior depending on this feedback. In fact, most of the current standards support feedback channels for transmitting periodically some channel state information such as acknowledgment frames (IEEE 802.11, IEEE 802.16 and LTE) or even channel state information (IEEE 802.16, LTE). Modeling of the behavior of such systems is generally difficult since it can require for example application of control system theory (complex Markov process) or some notion of the transformed channel behavior. Notable works in this field are [326, 178].

Due to these many difficulties, accurate performance models of advanced transmission schemes in the PHY layer are a challenging and still open research field today while they are essential for network simulation in the future. In the next paragraph, we illustrate the problems of modeling an OFDM system accurately in the context of IEEE 802.11 WLAN

In addition to the time-varying channel behavior, the modeling of the performance of an OFDM system requires some assumption about the frequency-varying channel behavior. Let us consider a block-fading channel behavior in the time-domain. The simplest assumption for the frequency domain is to model it static. In this case, the channel quality, varying from packet to packet transmission due to the block-fading assumption, is the same for all subcarriers. We further assume that the same modulation type is used per subcarrier. Hence, all subcarriers have the same SNR and bit-error rate. Based on the bit error rate, a packet error process can be obtained in a similar way as discussed above. Even if FEC coding is applied, the coding scheme can be taken into account by either shifting the SNR (which yields a better bit error rate) or by considering a direct mapping between input bit error rate and output bit error rate for the specific code considered.

The modeling already gets much more complicated if no static channel behavior in frequency can be assumed. In reality, this is the usual case in broadband OFDM systems, especially in indoor communication scenarios with multiple reflections recombining at the receiver. A suitable assumption in this case is to assume a narrow-band flat fading channel attenuation for the whole subcarrier spacing, but this attenuation varies in general from subcarrier to subcarrier, potentially in a correlated manner (see Section 11.7). Hence, per subcarrier we obtain a different SNR and therefore a different bit error rate. Mapping this bit error rate to a packet error probability is only possible without further assumptions if neither coding nor interleaving is applied. In this case, one simply determines the probability that all bits have been transmitted correctly (based on the recombination pattern of forming the payload packets from the parallel subcarrier bits). However, if coding and interleaving are applied, further simplifying assumptions are required. In particular, one can assume "perfect" interleaving in frequency. This allows then to average the bit error rate per subcarrier yielding a joint channel bit error rate of the system. Next, if coding is applied the joint bit-error rate might be mapped by an input-output bit-error rate characterization into a joint coded bit-error rate from which the packet-error probability can be derived. However, this method is based on a large set of assumptions. It is discussed in detail in Section 12.1.2 and in [42] for convolutional coding. This method can also be applied if different modulation types are employed per subcarrier.

From the above discussion it is clear that the probability of error of a point-to-point transmission in advanced transmission schemes is generally unknown due to the randomness of the transmission medium and the complexity of the input-output relationship of each component at the receiver. This also applies to spread spectrum systems and to MIMO systems (and more generally to any multiple access system with random interference). Even if sophisticated modeling techniques based on the statistics of the random variables of the transmission system have been developed in the past years [115], there is no general technique available. Hence, the only alternative today is to use look-up tables that can accurately predict the end-to-end performance of a PHY layer as soon as advanced techniques are used and combined.

9.5   An Example Packet Domain Physical Layer Simulation Model

In addition to the general considerations of modeling the PHY for network simulations, in the following we present an exemplary packet domain PHY simulation model that explicitly formulates the PHY functionalities required in most network simulations. The described model particularly provides the PHY functionality necessary to support DLL modeling as described in Chapter 10. Figure 9.8 shows the general structure of the presented PHY model and its interface to the DLL. It generally consists of two units: a *radio unit* that models actual radio hardware component functionality, and an *evaluation unit* that includes all functionality that is necessary for simulation but has no counterpart in real hardware, including the link-to-system model described above. Note that we do not rely on a specific link-to-system model, but keep the model open for using an arbitrary one. An exemplary implementation of the model can be found in the *MiXiM framework* [319, 262, 493] for *OMNeT++* [475].

9.5.1   Radio Unit

In general, each communication entity can act as a transmitter or receiver. Whether the entity acts as a receiver or transmitter is usually determined by the state of its radio. In principle, radios can be categorized according to their dialog modes into simplex, half-duplex, and full-duplex radios. While full-duplex radios are capable of sending and receiving simultaneously at all times (e.g. by using different frequency bands), half-duplex radios can perform one task at a time only. Moreover, in energy aware networks, devices might support sleeping modes, in which the radio is powered down and, thus, not able to send or receive frames. In the following, we focus on half-duplex operation featuring sleeping modes as the most general case. All other cases can be derived from that by setting parameters accordingly.

A half-duplex radio has three states: *send, receive,* and *sleep.* The radio state is controlled by the DLL, i.e. switching information is passed as *PHY control info* via the DLL-PHY interface. Note that it takes time to switch the radio from one state to another. Depending on the investigation, these *Radio Switching Times* might need to be modeled as well.

Transmitting Frames. For an entity to act as a transmitter, its radio has to be in the send state. Additionally, it has to be ensured that no other frame is currently being sent from the same node at the same time using the same resources. Normally, the DLL layer should only pass a message to the PHY if both conditions are fulfilled. In order to ensure the correct interaction between DLL and PHY and catch potential errors at an early point, both conditions should be checked and violations be reported (see Figure 9.9).

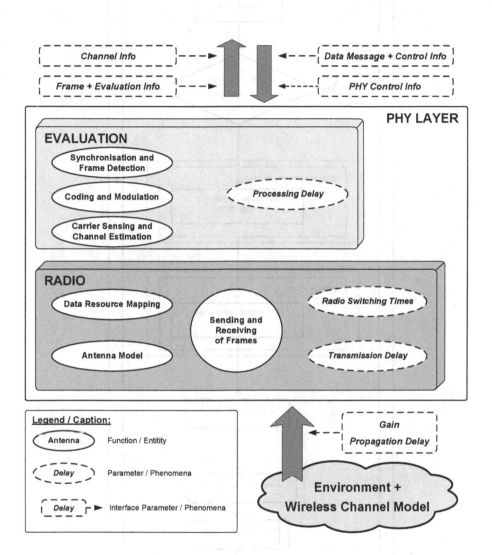

Fig. 9.8: Functional blocks of the presented PHY model including the interfaces to the environment/channel and the DLL.

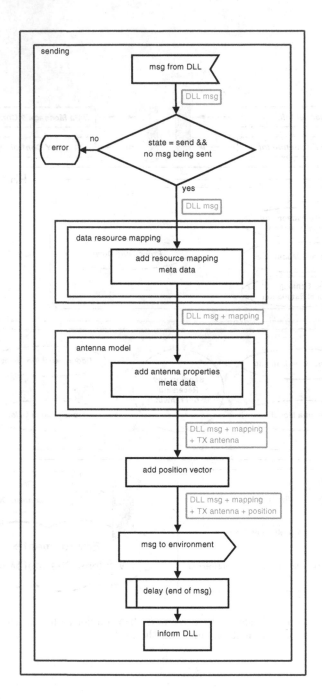

Fig. 9.9: Sending process

As mentioned earlier, the detailed effects of FEC coding and interleaving are modeled by bit-true simulation models on the bit-, symbol-, or sample domain (see Section 9.2 & 9.3). For packet domain simulations, the impact of coding and interleaving are not considered per bit, but evaluated in combination with the chosen modulation scheme as well as other transmission parameters (cf. Section 9.4.1). As all this information has to be processed at the receiver, meta data is added to the transmitted frame which contains all information that the receiver needs to accurately determine the reception of the frame. Appending all information regarding the transmission parameters is done in the *Data Resource Mapping* block. In addition to typical transmitter settings (like modulation and coding type or transmit power), also further scheduling decisions regarding the used resources have to be appended like the used sub channels in OFDMA systems or the used spatial streams in multiple antenna systems, see Section 10.1.5. Finally, information is added regarding the used antenna type and its impact on the transmit power, see Section 11.11.

The frame with its meta data is then passed to the environment (which models the channel including interference effects among other elements, cf. Chapter 11). The environment is responsible for delivering the frame to the appropriate receiving entities. Since the wireless medium is a broadcast channel, there might be more entities than the specified receiver of the frame. In order to correctly calculate the channel gain at the moment of the frame arrival at the receiver, the transmitter additionally needs to provide its momentary position, speed and direction of movement (referred to as a *position vector*) to the environment. Before passing the frame to the environment, the sending and receiving block thus attaches the position vector as meta data to the frame.

Since in simulation the whole frame is "sent" at once, the *Transmission Delay* has to be modeled explicitly, i.e. the time between sending of the first and the last bit of the frame. This is usually done by some delay process. Once the last bit of the frame is sent, the PHY has to inform the DLL, so that it can take appropriate actions (e.g. sending the next message or switching the radio back into the receive or sleep state). A state diagram for the whole sending process is shown in Figure 9.9.

Data Resource Mapping. The task of this functional block is to map the data for transmission on the system resources as determined by a resource manager (see Section 10.1.5). However, since we do not consider a bit-true model, only PHY frames with an attachment of meta data are considered. The meta data is necessary for the receiving entity to be able to process the transmitted frame. It comprises the transmission power that is reflected by the RSSI in a real system. In adaptive modulation and coding systems, the selected parameters for modulation and coding need also be attached in order to enable the receiver to correctly evaluate the transmitted data. In multi-carrier and/or multi-antenna systems, this information is necessary per carrier/antenna.

The decision on these transmission parameters is made at the transmitter by the DLL and then passed as *control info* to the PHY layer via the DLL-PHY interface. An example for a complete set of parameters in a MIMO multi-carrier transmission system can be the following: "use sub-bands 4, 6, and 8 for transmission on antenna 2: use QPSK and 100 mW on sub-band 4, QPSK and 50 mW on sub-band 6, and 64-QAM and 200 mW on sub-band 8."

Receiving Frames. The received analog signal is attenuated and distorted by the environment it traveled through on its way from the transmitter to the receiver. Depending on the modeled system, the distortion has to be calculated for different subcarriers, antennas, and once or multiple times per frame in the time domain. These effects are described in detail in Chapter 11. In order to calculate the distortions, the position vector of the receiver (as well as of the transmitter) is required. All this information is appended to the frame's meta data before it is delivered to the receiver's PHY. The details of the receiving process are shown in Figure 9.10 and described in the following.

The decision whether an entity is able to receive a frame or not depends on several parameters. First, its radio has to be in receive mode. Second, only one frame can be received at a time. Thus, if the PHY is currently in the process of receiving a frame, all other frames arriving at that time will be treated as noise (and added to the "noise messages" as shown in Figure 9.10). Alternatively, the receiver might also lock to the strongest signal received, even if it arrives later than some other frame (capturing effect). Which frame to receive and which to treat as noise is determined by the synchronization and frame detection block. Once the frame is received, bit errors have to be calculated according to some link-to-system interface.

9.5.2   Evaluation Unit

Synchronization and Frame Detection. For each frame arriving at the PHY layer, the receiver has to decide whether to receive it or treat it as noise. The point in time for the decision (denoted as t_1 in Figure 9.10) depends on the chosen model. One possibility is to make the decision immediately after the packet's arrival ($t_1 = 0$). This is useful if only a single channel gain value is present for the whole frame. Another possibility is to decide at a later time, e.g. after the preamble or header is received and there is at least one channel gain value corresponding to the preamble transmission. The decision whether to receive the frame or treat it as noise is based on the channel gain and other transmissions currently ongoing on the medium. The PHY has to derive the SINR values for the frame or the part of the frame it has already received. If desired, this is also the place to model capturing effects, as mentioned above.

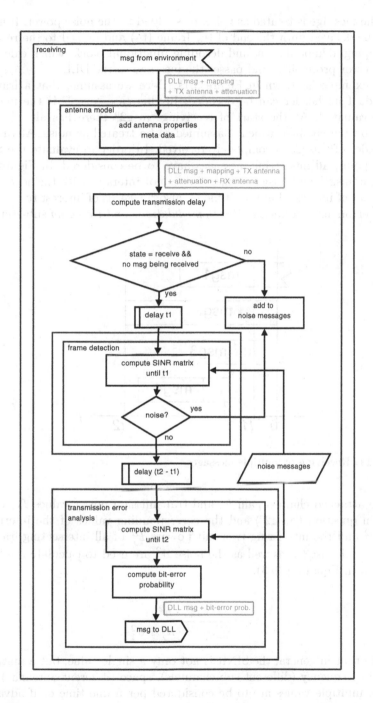

Fig. 9.10: Receiving process

If the message is treated as noise, it is added to the noise power. If not, it has to be delayed until the end of the frame (t_2) and passed to the resource de-mapping, demodulation, and decoding functional block, which calculates the bit-error probability and passes the message to the DLL.

An example is shown in Figure 9.11. Here we assume, that a frame is received, if its header can be decoded. In this case "msg2" is the message being evaluated. At the start of receiving "msg2" there has already been "msg1" on the channel, which is assumed to be treated as noise. At time t_1, the header of "msg2" is completely received. In order to evaluate the SINR at this point, all interfering messages have to be considered. In Figure 9.11 these are "msg1" and "msg3" – "msg4" does not intersect with the header and thus is not of interest. Later, at time t_2, also "msg4" is of interest to calculate the bit errors as described in the *Demodulation, and Decoding* sub-section.

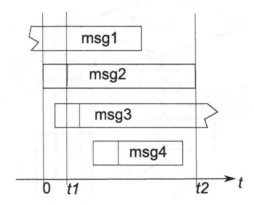

Fig. 9.11: Receiving of multiple messages

The attached channel gain h^2 and transmission power values P_{tx} of the frame in question ("msg2") and the corresponding values of the interfering gains h_j^2 and the interfering transmit powers P_j^I of all intersecting frames i ("msg1" and "msg3"), as well as the noise σ^2 are used to calculate the SINR as shown in Equation (9.3).

$$\gamma = \frac{P_{tx} \cdot h^2}{\sum_{\forall j} P_j^I \cdot h_j^2 + \sigma^2} \tag{9.3}$$

Note that in general the SINR is not only a single value, but a matrix of values in frequency (different sub-channels), space (different antennas), and time (if multiple values are to be considered per frame time or if advanced transmission schemes are employed).

Channel Estimation. As mentioned above, channel estimation is performed on the one hand at the receiver to better decode the modulation symbols. For a packet domain simulation model, this type of channel estimation is not considered but is assumed to function perfectly. On the other hand, channel estimation is required such that the transmitter can adapt transmission parameters by resource management to the channel state. This type of channel estimation is often considered by packet domain PHY simulation models. One way to model this is to let the environment determine the channel state at frame transmission analytically, according to the estimation algorithm applied. The resulting channel gains are attached to the frame as meta data (see Figure 9.10). The channel estimation part is modeled by passing the received channel attenuation values on to the DLL that saves it together with a time stamp and transmitter information for future use. In a Time Division Duplex (TDD) system, if channel reciprocity can be assumed, the stored channel state information can be used for transmission parameter adaptation (e.g. power, modulation, coding), once the receiver in turn wants to transmit something to the former transmitter. Whenever channel reciprocity cannot be assumed, e.g. in a Frequency Division Duplex (FDD) system, the receiver's DLL needs to signal the channel information back to the transmitter in order to enable it to adapt the transmission parameters in the upcoming slots. For signaling the channel state information back to the transmitter an additional signaling channel is needed.

Carrier Sensing. Carrier sensing at the transmitter is necessary for particular MAC protocols such as CSMA (like in 802.11, see Section 12.1). Carrier sensing is a service provided by the PHY to the DLL. Whenever the MAC wants to access the channel, it requests the carrier sensing information from the PHY. The carrier sensing functional block then has to provide the channel status information and pass this information via the PHY DLL interface. Based on this information, the MAC decides whether the channel is busy or idle. Possibilities to model carrier sensing range from simply introducing a random delay (done at the DLL) to explicitly modeling the carrier sensing process as described above in Section 9.2.

Depending on the type of carrier sensing, feature detection versus energy measurement, the PHY either has to calculate the RSSI or evaluate the SINR to determine whether the signal is decodable or not. One option to decide on the decodability of a frame is to consider either the SINR or the corresponding BER. The calculated value (RSSI, SINR or BER) is then compared to some threshold in order to decide whether the channel is busy or idle. In addition, the DLL has to specify how long the carrier sensing needs to be performed. In simulation, it is often assumed that carrier sensing can be done in zero time. In this case the PHY would just evaluate the most recent SINR available. For more accurate simulations however, the delay for the carrier sensing should be simulated.

Demodulation and Decoding. Coding and modulation have a major impact on the transmission quality of a frame. At the packet domain, this impact can be accounted for by a link-to-system interface (as explained above) which takes the SINR as input and determines an instantaneous BER as output. If no detailed description of the coding impact is at hand, a simple coding gain can be assumed which is added to the SINR of the frame. The calculation of transmission errors is usually done once the frame is completely received (t_2). The receiver has to calculate the SINR as described above and shown in Equation (9.3) and Figure 9.11. The SINR is used together with the BER curves or tables to get the bit-error probabilities for the message: the combination of SINR and indicated modulation/coding choice is taken as an input for the table or curve look-up, the error probability is the output (as shown in Table 9.5). The level of detail of the bit-error calculation mainly depends on the number of SINR values available. The simplest model is to only have one SINR value per frame. More detailed models have multiple values to evaluate multiple sections of the frame. One example is to have one value for the PHY header which are usually transmitted at a lower modulation to ensure the correct frame detection, and the payload, respectively. Furthermore, there might be another value to distinguish between the MAC header and the MAC payload in order to be able to evaluate both of them individually. The PHY payload is passed to the DLL layer via the PHY-DLL interface accompanied by the bit-error probability meta data.

10. Link Layer Modeling

M. Mühleisen (RWTH Aachen University)
D. Bültmann (RWTH Aachen University)
K. Klagges, M. Schinnenburg (RWTH Aachen University)

The Data Link Layer (DLL) is located above the PHY layer described in the previous chapter and below the network layer described in Chapter 16. All data received from these layers is digital. Today most parts of the DLL are implemented in software, either as device drivers running on general purpose Central Processing Units (CPUs) or as firmware running on dedicated network interface hardware.

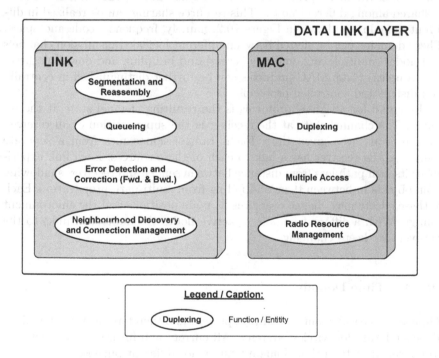

Fig. 10.1: Data Link Layer Reference Model

Figure 10.1 schematically shows the different functions of the DLL. Often, especially in Institute of Electrical and Electronics Engineers (IEEE) standards, the term MAC layer is used as a synonym for the DLL while the ISO/OSI reference model [218] does not even define medium access as a DLL task. Accessing the wireless channel, which is a broadcast medium, is one of the most challenging tasks in a wireless network. Therefore we dedicate Section 10.1 of this Chapter to MAC protocols.

In the Section 10.2, we discuss the other functions of the DLL, summarized under the term *Logical Link Control (LLC)*. The functions *Queuing*, and *Segmentation and Reassembly* are typical for both, wireless and wired communication systems. The very special topic of *Neighborhood Discovery and Connection Management* is only briefly discussed in this section and described in detail in Chapter 15. Since the wireless channel is very error prone, we discuss *Backward and Forward Error Detection and Correction* in detail. The main focus lies on backward error correction, namely ARQ.

10.1   Medium Access Control (MAC) Protocols

The task of the *MAC* protocol is to define rules on how the wireless medium is shared among different nodes. This resource sharing can be realized in different domains as shown in Figure 10.2, namely, frequency, code and space. These domains can be shared between different logical transmission channels and nodes (multiplexing, multiple access) and in uplink and downlink direction (duplex) [425]. MAC protocols can be further distinguished in centrally and distributed controlled protocols.

Essential for all MAC protocols is the resulting channel state at the receiver. The channel state at the receiver is the superposition of all received transmissions at a given time. Each transmission comes from a separate source, so the receiver has a link to each of these sources. Each link experiences its own path loss from distance between sender and receiver, shadowing from objects in between them and fading from multi-path propagation. Each of these effects may change over time as node positions and the environment change. With a different number of active nodes the number of links to the receiver also keeps changing.

10.1.1   Time Domain

Time as a physical quantity is always present and therefore the time domain is always relevant for wireless systems. All current and future wireless network standards operate in time domain using it for different purposes.

The time domain can be used for division multiplex, multiple access and duplex. One essential effect when simulating MAC protocols in time domain is propagation delay. Radio waves propagate at speed of light which is approximately 300 m in 1 μs. Depending on the possible transmission range of a communication system, propagation time can therefore become a significant factor. Since the time a transmission arrives at a receiver can be long,

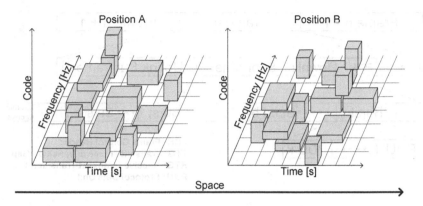

Fig. 10.2: Medium Access in Time, Frequency, Code and Space Domain.

transmissions from further away stations need to start in advance to compensate propagation delay. One commonly used communication standard affected by propagation delay is *GSM*. Here the base station provides a so called *timing advance* value to each served mobile terminal to assure transmissions traveling different distances do not overlap in time.

For simulation of such systems, it might be an advantage to not model propagation delay and therefore not to implement any timing advance protocols. This saves complexity and implementation effort.

Another aspect in time domain is synchronization of the nodes. In a centrally controlled MAC protocol this is usually done by regular transmissions like beacons. Distributed MAC protocols can synchronize by common channel state sensed by all nodes. The clocks of the nodes could for example be synchronized when the channel is sensed idle. Real system clocks would then start to drift until they are synchronized again. In a network simulator precise simulation time is always known by every node. *Synchronization* is therefore not an issue. Still the effect of missing a synchronization event like a beacon could be accounted for, if required. On the one hand beacons are usually transmitted with high power and robust modulation and coding scheme and therefore are rarely lost. On the other hand in some systems a missed beacon could prohibit a node from any transmissions until it synchronizes again successfully. Therefore, the effect of not modeling synchronization messages has to be verified.

In the following we pick the *IEEE 802.16* (Worldwide Interoperability for Microwave Access (WiMAX)) metropolitan area network standard to point out some aspects of MAC modeling in time domain. More details on the standard are described in Section 12.2. Figure 10.3 shows the timing of a WiMAX system only operating in time domain (Time Division Multiple Access (TDMA)/TDD). WiMAX is a centrally controlled, cellular network system, having a central controller in each cell called Base Station (BS) and

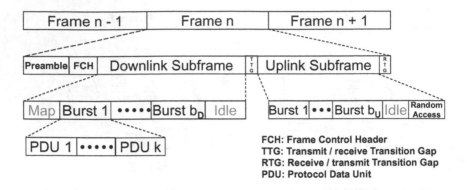

Fig. 10.3: IEEE 802.16 TDMA/TDD frame structure.

one or more Subscriber Stations (SSs) associated to it. The BS decides the periodic frame structure by periodically transmitting a preamble and FCH marking the start of a new frame. The SSs try to synchronize to this period. This is a synchronization on MAC frame time scale which should not be confused with symbol level synchronization done in the PHY layer. The PHY layer informs the DLL after the preamble has been received completely. Since the length in bit and the bit rate of the preamble are known, the transmission start of the preamble and therefore the frame start time can be calculated. What is not directly known is the propagation delay $t_{prop} = d/c$ caused by the distance d between BS and SS and the limited radio wave propagation speed c which is the speed of light. In a simulator, global simulator time is available in every node and can be used for synchronization. As stated before, propagation delay causes a delay of approximately $1\mu s$ for $300m$ distance. This has no impact on the DL since all transmissions originate from the BS. If no action is taken, UL transmissions from different SSs traveling different distances would overlap and interfere at the BS. To avoid this interference, the BS measures the propagation delay to each SS and provides the *timing advance* information to each SS, assuring that transmissions do not overlap at the BS. If propagation delay is not modeled in the channel model, *timing advance* is not needed and implementation effort is saved without much loss of accuracy. For long distances (e.g. satellite links) propagation delay might form a significant part of total delay and should therefore not be neglected. Turnaround guard times called Transmit / receive Transition Gap (TTG) and Receive / transmit Transition Gap (RTG) are also required to protect against the effects of propagation delay. They should be modeled in a simulator, even if propagation delay is not, since no data can be transmitted during that time.

In most cases, simulations are used to evaluate user data traffic. It is therefore not necessary to model control and management traffic in detail. Still the impact of those traffics, in the following called non-user data traffic,

on user data traffic needs to be modeled. Figure 10.3 shows that certain parts
of the MAC frame are not available to user data traffic. Only the UL and DL
superframes transmit user data. The portion of the frame transmitting the
preamble, FCH, map, and Random Access Slots could be simply modeled as
periods where no transmissions are active. In this case no interference is emitted, the information transmitted during these periods has to be distributed
differently. It is therefore not influenced by the channel model and does not
experience packet loss. The impact of this is discussed in more detail when the
according management and control functions are discussed (Sections 10.2.2,
10.1.5 and 10.1.5).

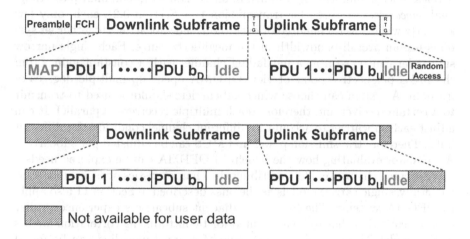

Fig. 10.4: Model of IEEE 802.16 TDMA/TDD frame structure using idle periods.

Figure 10.4 shows a possible frame setup modeling non-user data periods
as idle periods. There can also be non-user data traffic transmitted in the
DL and UL subframes. The duration and amount of those transmissions can
vary from frame to frame and can therefore not be simply modeled as an idle
period of constant duration. An example of this data is the Map. The size of
the Map depends on the number of scheduled users in the frame. Still it can
be modeled as a fixed idle period having the duration of the average Map
length.

Most digital wireless communication systems have a time unit called symbol (see Section 9.1). For a given MCS and, if OFDM is used, with a fixed
number of subcarriers, a fixed amount of bit can be transmitted in one symbol. If the PDU length in bit is not a multiple of the number of bit per
symbol, *padding* has to be used to fill the gap to the next symbol boundary. In reality, zero bits are inserted. This can be modeled by rounding the
transmission end time to the next symbol boundary rather than just dividing
the PDU length in bit by the data rate to obtain the transmission duration.

This way all transmissions start and end at a symbol boundary. If padding is not modeled, capacity, due to fragmentation effects, could be severely over-estimated if high MCSs are used. Also PDU size and *SAR* segment size (see Section 10.2.2) influence the impact of padding.

10.1.2   Frequency Domain

The frequency domain has recently become more relevant for MAC protocol development. The reason is that *OFDMA* technology is used in many modern wireless telecommunication systems. In an OFDMA system, multiple orthogonal *subcarriers* are used for transmission (see Section 9.2), each, only few kilohertz wide. Several hundred or even thousand subcarriers together let systems use an overall bandwidth in the megahertz range. Each single narrow subcarrier can be seen as a flat-fading channel with a constant gain. From the MAC perspective point of view OFDMA opens up multiple degrees of freedom. A system can choose which subcarriers should be used to transmit to a certain receiver and therefore reach multiple receivers in parallel. It can adjust each subcarrier to account for different channel conditions for different links. Therefore transmission power and MCS can be adjusted per subcarrier. A simulator evaluating how the benefit of OFDMA can be explored needs a sophisticated channel model describing the characteristics of each subcarrier. Generally, single carrier models as the ones described in Section 11 also apply to OFDMA systems. The fact that adjacent subcarriers experience similar channel conditions has to be accounted for by introducing correlation factors in the model. More details on this issue of channel modeling can be found in [102].

If wireless systems would allow any possible amount and combination of subcarriers to be used for a transmission, signalling overhead would be enormous. Therefore subcarriers are logically grouped to *subchannels*. Subchannels are the smallest unit which can be addressed in frequency domain. Complexity and simulation runtime can then be reduced by just evaluating the channel state per subchannel rather than per subcarrier. All other properties like MCS and transmission power are then adjusted per subchannel.

Figure 10.5 shows a possibility to model OFDMA in time domain. Rather than transmitting on four subchannels in parallel, data is transmitted sequentially but with four times higher rate. The model is inaccurate when measuring delays, since data transmitted earlier in the sequence experiences lower delay. This impact might be insignificant compared to the total delay. By rotating the sequence of users the data is addressed to, the error gets independent of the evaluated user.

As done in time domain (see Section 10.1.1), subchannels which are never used for user data can be modeled as not being available or even not being present. For example, in OFDM systems the total number of available

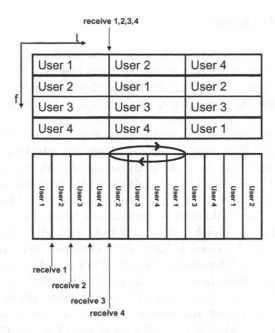

Fig. 10.5: Modeling OFDMA in time domain.

subcarriers could be reduced by the number of subcarriers which are used for pilot symbols.

OFDMA opens new Radio Resource Management (RRM) possibilities. So called *soft frequency reuse* becomes possible in centrally controlled systems where users at the cell edge are served at different frequencies and powers than users closer to the center of the cell. This requires knowledge about user positions which can be obtained through methods described in Section 10.1.3. Algorithms exploring all degrees of freedom can become very complex and require high runtime. If processing delay is not modeled in a simulator, algorithm runtime has to be evaluated separately. By reducing the degrees of freedom and using heuristics, algorithms with applicable runtime can be developed as presented in [65].

Finally, when modeling OFDMA systems in the uplink, further restrictions apply. In the downlink, a single transmitter, i.e. a base station, emits all subcarriers in parallel. In the uplink, each node transmits on the subcarriers assigned to it and transmissions from several sources are received at the base station with possible impairments in time and frequency. A link level evaluation of this effect can be found in [352].

10.1.3   Space Domain

The position of every node and therefore the space domain always implicitly plays a role. Distant nodes can suffer from the hidden node problem in CSMA-CA as described in Section 12.1. Cellular systems are deployed in a manner to allow to reuse the same frequency from a certain distance, called *reuse distance*, on.

The space domain can also explicitly be explored in a MAC protocol. If position information is present, links that are not interfering because they are far enough apart can be active simultaneously. This can be used in Mesh WLAN deployments. Another example for MAC protocol enhancements is *beamforming*. While the PHY layer forms the beam the MAC layer has to decide which nodes should receive simultaneous beams. It therefore relies on position information to pick nodes apart from each other keeping intra cell interference low as described in [206]. Both examples have in common that they rely on position information. The simulator can obtain this information from the scenario setup. In a real deployment either *GPS* or power measurements have to be used to estimate positions. Key properties of these methods are their update frequency and accuracy. GPS has an update frequency of approximately one second. It also comes with an inaccuracy of up to $100m$. Also it might be required to transmit the position data to a central controller like a base station. In this case data can become outdated if the node moves away from the reported position. A multi-antenna array can also be used to estimate the position of a transmitting node. In this case, the update frequency depends on how often transmissions take place. The accuracy depends on the channel between the nodes and the antenna array properties as described in [206]. The inaccuracy of position data can be modeled by adding a normally distributed, zero mean error on each Cartesian coordinate. The variance can be used as a simulation parameter. This allows to evaluate how sensible a protocol reacts to inaccurate position data. The update frequency, which is only required if mobility (see Chapter 14) is used, can be either modeled by periodically updating position data using the simulation environment or by really sending packets over the channel.

10.1.4   Code Domain

In the code domain *Code Division Multiple Access (CDMA)* can be used to allow multiple simultaneous transmissions. Here each bit of the signal is binary added to a pseudo random chipping sequence as shown in Figure 10.6. This is described in more detail in Section 9.2. CDMA is usually used in centrally controlled systems like UMTS [483], where each logical channel

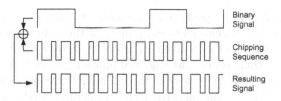

Fig. 10.6: Spreading a Binary Signal with a Chipping Sequence.

between the central controller and the user nodes has an own chipping sequence. Since the length of the chips is shorter than the length of the bits, the chip frequency is higher than the bit frequency. It therefore requires a higher transmission bandwidth. The transmission is spread in spectrum. By using codes of different bit to chip length ratio, different transmission rates can be achieved. A receiver knowing the chipping sequence of an intended transmission can decode it. All other simultaneous transmissions add to the interference power at the receiver. Therefore system capacity is still limited by the number of allowed simultaneous transmissions to assure the required SINR.

For CDMA to work, all received powers need to be almost equal at the receiver. This is challenging since the different channels between transmitters and receiver experience different attenuation. Transmission Power Control (TPC) has to be used to adjust transmission power accordingly. Accuracy and update frequency of channel state measurement and TPC therefore have an impact on performance and should be modeled in a simulator. Also an appropriate shadowing model (see Chapter 11.6) providing a varying channel needs to be used. Otherwise, the impact of changing channel conditions on the power control algorithm can not be evaluated.

10.1.5   Resource Management

Power Management. Power management serves two purposes. It saves energy for battery powered devices and limits interference to other nodes.

Wireless communication nodes consume energy when transmitting as well as when receiving in order to amplify the received signal. The PHY layer can not know if a received transmission is intended for a given node or not. If possible, it will decode it and pass it to the DLL. If the transmission was not intended for the node the whole PDU is dropped. The MAC layer can prevent this by deactivating the transceiver of the PHY layer (go to sleep mode) whenever it is not expecting any incoming transmissions. In a centrally controlled system, nodes can go to sleep mode if they know there will not be any transmission for them for a given duration. In distributed MAC protocols, nodes can inform their peers that they are planning to switch to sleep mode for a certain duration. Peer nodes can then delay PDU delivery until the node is awake again. This can increase the PDU transmission delay.

Energy consumption and interference to other nodes can be decreased by reducing transmission power. This, as mentioned earlier, is called *Transmission Power Control (TPC)*. For this to work nodes need to know how much power is required for a peer node to successfully receive a transmission. They therefore rely on information about received power and transmission success probability at the peer node. Assuming a symmetric channel, transmissions from the peer node can be used to estimate channel attenuation between the two nodes. Alternatively or additionally explicit protocol signalling can be used to inform a node about the received power strength. When using an ARQ protocol (see 10.2.2) the error rate between two nodes can be estimated and used as input for a TPC algorithm. Systems using link adaptation (see 10.1.5) experience a trade-off between transmission rate and emitted power. Using less power reduces SINR and therefore only allows the use of lower transmission rates. When transmission power is too low to provide required SINR for error free reception, the transmission can be lost and needs to be retransmitted which uses up even more energy. On the other hand, a higher transmission rate reduces the duration of the transmission and therefore the time in which power is emitted. An example on how power consumption can be simulated and evaluated can be found in [422].

The following list summarizes effects that should be considered when modeling power management:

- Channel model and channel coherence time: Estimating an invariant channel is easy. The channel model needs to capture how the channel changes over time and for how long channel state can be assumed constant when evaluating TPC.
- How much energy is consumed when transmitting / receiving? When evaluating battery lifetime improvements from TPC, accurate data about power consumption is required. Especially the knowledge of the share of power in the overall system which the radio transmission system has, is required. If the share is not significant proposed and evaluated TPC algorithms are useless in context of power management.
- How accurate is the estimation of the required power level? Every data fed back to the sender comes with a certain delay, quantization and measurement error. Trying to improve those may come at the cost of significant performance losses through control traffic overhead.

– Trade-off between link adaptation and TPC: Selecting a MCS and transmission power of own and other nodes is not independent and has influence
on each other. An overview on the topic can be found in [283].
– Higher delays and lower transmission rates due to lower duty cycles: If we
keep the radio turned off, incoming and outgoing data has to wait until the
next duty cycle. Each algorithm therefore needs to be evaluated to check if
it can meet the Quality of Service (QoS) demands of a desired application.
– Quantization when selecting power levels for transmission: Actual hardware
may only allow certain discrete power levels. Algorithms requiring a very
fine resolution are therefore not feasible on such hardware. Quantization
levels therefore need to be implemented in a simulator.

Link Adaptation. Link Adaptation (LA) refers to dynamically choosing an
appropriate Modulation- and Coding Scheme (MCS) for a transmission. Appropriate means that the MCS must assure a targeted packet error rate (PER)
when received at a certain SINR at the receiver. The received SINR depends
on the channel between transmitter and receiver, and the interference situation at the receiver. Therefore the transmitter needs information about SINR
at the receiver, which in turn either requires an explicit feedback channel or
information from ARQ. LA usually uses an information base with SINR estimations for each receiver node. This estimations can become inaccurate
because of changing channel state (shadowing, mobility) and changing interference conditions.

A multi-cell example: Cell A is very busy, there is almost always an ongoing transmission. Cell B has less ongoing transmissions, it is idle 50% of the
time. The estimated SINR for a node at the cell edge could lead to a MCS
that can be successfully received when cell B is idle but is almost always lost
when cell B transmits. This would cause an unacceptable PER of 0.5. Taking
information from ARQ into account for LA could help in this situation.

When modeling LA the following has to be considered:

– Transmitting with MCSs allowing a higher bit rate occupies the channel
for less time
– MCS with higher bit rates require a higher SINR for successful reception
– The channel and PHY layer model need to accurately calculate SINR to
model the effect (see Chapter 9)
– MCS decision relies on channel state information and can therefore be
inaccurate
– An explicit feedback channel can only periodically provide SINR estima-
tions
– Estimated SINR can only be transmitted with finite quantization

Scheduler. Several different possibilities to share the wireless medium were presented in previous sections. The task of actually assigning these resources (time, frequency, code, space) with given properties (MCS, transmission power) to communicating nodes is called *scheduling*. Goals of scheduling are to maximize throughput, minimize delays and assure fairness between nodes. These goals can be concurrent.

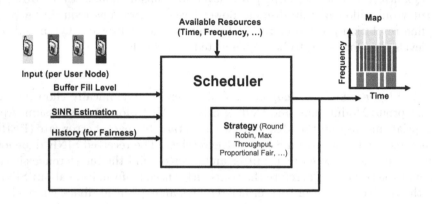

Fig. 10.7: Input, Output, and Logical Structure of a Resource Scheduler.

If link adaptation is used, nodes closer to the central controller can use higher transmission rates. A scheduler would therefore maximize system throughput by granting all resources to those stations. This *Maximal Throughput* scheduling strategy is of course not fair. With a *Round Robin* scheduling strategy each node receives the same amount of resources such as time and frequency bandwidth. Still each node experiences a different QoS since closer nodes can transmit more data by using higher transmission rates.

Figure 10.7 shows the possible structure of a scheduler in a simulator. As input, it takes the number and size of buffered PDUs, the estimated SINR at the receiver and the transmission history of each node. The output is the schedule. The scheduling strategy decides how the schedule is formed from the input. An overview of different scheduling strategies can be found in [110] and [299].

The estimated SINR has to be mapped to a transmission rate R deciding how much resources the scheduled PDU needs. Different mappings exist: most systems have a finite set of MCS, each requiring a certain minimal SINR. A simpler implementation might use the Shannon capacity

$R = Blog_2(1 + SINR)$. Here B is the used frequency bandwidth in MHz. Since the Shannon capacity is only a theoretical upper bound, the formula can be shifted to match the data rates of the MCSs used by the system. Therefore the *modified Shannon limit* model from [53] can be used, in which the formula $R = Blog_2(1 + \alpha SNR)$ is used to calculate the possible data rate for a given SINR estimation. The parameter α is system dependant and needs to be determined or looked up. It has to be chosen so that the formula matches the data rates of the finite MCS set of the system.

Scheduling history can be used to achieve fairness. Another approach is to just use buffer fill levels as input. A high buffer fill level indicates high traffic demands as well as the fact that the node was not able to empty its buffer in the past. Buffer fill levels therefore help to establish fairness.

Resource Signaling. Resource signalling describes both, distributing the schedule to each node and collecting required information to form the schedule. The schedule can be transmitted as a broadcast to all nodes simultaneously. Some technology standards refer to this schedule as the *map*. For each scheduled resource, the schedule contains a unique identifier of the node it is scheduled to, the MCS to be used and, if not fixed, some or all of the following: frequency channel(s), time and duration, and chipping sequence. The interval between the transmission of schedules has a high impact on protocol performance. The shorter the interval, the better can the system react to changes in channel state, but shorter frame durations introduce higher signalling overhead.

For the downlink direction the scheduler has almost all required information. It knows the traffic requirements for each station by observing queued PDUs in the buffers. It only requires information which MCS to use. This information can be gained as described earlier in this section. In uplink direction, the central controller needs information from the nodes about their traffic requirements. The central controller could reserve some resources for a node permanently, for a certain duration, or on a per PDU basis. Resource requests can be transmitted as control traffic, piggy-backed attached to normal user data transmissions or even in a random access channel.

As with many other control signalling, resource signalling is often transmitted using the most robust MCS which is unlikely to be lost. The whole information could therefore be obtained using the simulator environment. Still in a real system a node not receiving a schedule would not be able to send or receive until it is scheduled next time. Resource signalling overhead can be modeled by assuming a fixed amount of resources to not be available for user data.

10.2 Logical Link Control

10.2.1 Forward Error Detection and Correction

As discussed in Section 9.2, detecting and correcting errors is mainly a task of the PHY layer. Still different possibilities exist on what is carried out by the DLL depending on the link-to-system interface. One possibility is that the PHY layer decides which PDU was received successfully dropping all other PDUs without informing the DLL. This is especially true for transmissions that could not be received because PHY layer synchronization or equalization failed. If the PHY layer model allows to derive error probabilities for different parts of a PDU, it could do a CRC on the PHY header dropping any PDU not passing it. PDUs passing the PHY header CRC are passed to the DLL, which has to take the decision if the DLL-PDU was received successfully. The PHY layer model presented in Section 9.5 attaches the BER of the DLL-PDU as additional information for the DLL.

A model is required to map the BER to a *Packet Error Rate (PER)*. Assuming an independent bit error distribution, the probability of successful reception $(1 - PER)$ can be calculated using a Bernoulli distribution as given by Equation (10.1). n is the PDU size in bit and k is the maximal number of errors that can be corrected. Assuming the DLL cannot correct errors, $k = 0$ is set. Equation (10.1) can then be simplified to $1 - PER = (1 - BER)^n$. Some DLLs might implement simple error correction schemes like horizontal and vertical parity checking. In this case, the value of k has to be adjusted accordingly.

$$1 - PER(n, k) = \sum_{i=0}^{k} \binom{n}{i} (BER)^i (1 - BER)^{n-i} \qquad (10.1)$$

After calculating the PER, a Random Number Generator (RNG) can be used to draw a standard uniformly distributed random number. If the random number is less than the determined PER the PDU is dropped.

Often standard committees provide a detailed description on how the PER should be determined. Therefore the openWNS simulator described in Section 5.1 uses a common PHY layer model delivering each PDU together with the average SINR it experienced to the technology standard specific DLL. Here more advanced methods like for example using so called *Mutual Information (MI)* to directly map SINR to PER (see [435]) can be applied if required by the evaluation methodology of a standard.

In some systems even PDUs containing errors are used to obtain information. If the sender is known, a dropped PDU can help to estimate the transmission success probability of a link. This is true in point-to-multipoint systems like cellular networks or in IEEE 802.11 systems operating in Infrastructure Mode. Here the DLL can use the unsuccessfully decoded PDU to obtain new information about the link quality. Systems that have to rely on address fields to determine the sender cannot gather any additional information since bit errors could have altered the address field.

10.2.2   Backward Error Detection and Correction

The term backward error detection and correction refers to Error Detection and Correction (EDC) done with help from the sender. The sender therefore needs to detect that the receiver was not able to correctly receive a transmission. A common way to assure that is *Automatic Repeat Request (ARQ)*.

ARQ uses a back-channel between receiver and sender to inform the sender whether the transmission was successful or not. Usually this is done by sending an Acknowledgment (ACK) to confirm successful reception. Sequence numbers are used to distinguish which previous transmission is being acknowledged by an incoming ACK. A missing ACK can therefore indicate two things: Either the ACK or the data transmission could not be received successfully. In both cases the PDU is retransmitted. If a PDU is retransmitted due to a lost ACK and the transmission succeeds the receiver will receive a second copy of a previously received PDU. In this case duplicate detection by sequence numbers can be used to delete the PDU. An overview of the different kinds of ARQ protocols can be found in [451].

When modeling ARQ in a network simulator, different levels of detail are possible. On the one hand, the protocol can be fully implemented having data transmissions and ACK transmissions on the channel and being influenced by the channel model. In this case, data and ACK transmissions can be lost. A simpler simulator with a simple channel model could model ARQ as additional delay caused by retransmissions. In this case, a stochastic model for retransmission probability is used and the total transmission delay is calculated based on it. The accuracy of this model highly depends on the stochastic retransmission count model. Also the effect of lost ACKs is not accounted for. Still the loss of ACKs is less likely than the loss of a data transmission. This is because ACK transmissions are usually short and often use a more robust MCS than user data transmissions. An even simpler approach just calculates the overhead introduced by retransmissions by calculating the mean required number of transmissions until successful reception $\bar{n}$. For a Stop-and-Wait ARQ with given PER p_{PER}, the following formula is used: $\bar{n} = \sum_{i=1}^{\infty} p_{PER}^{(i-1)}(1-p_{PER}) = \frac{1}{1-p_{PER}}$. Channel capacity must therefore be scaled by $1 - p_{PER}$. This can be either achieved by reducing data rate accordingly or by reducing the amount of available resources. This model can not be used if transmission delays are evaluated.

If a sliding window ARQ is used, the window size has to be chosen appropriately. For a simple full-duplex communication system the window size W in PDUs needs to be $W = 2a + 1$ where a is the number of PDUs the sender has fully transmitted before the receiver has received the first one. For a single-hop link, a can be calculated as the ratio of propagation delay t_{prop} and transmission time for a PDU t_{trans}. In modern communication systems, even with full-duplex, other considerations are important when choosing W. Since PDU size can vary, windows size should be set in bit. For a TDD system, which is not full-duplex, W needs to be set to the maximal amount of bit that can be transmitted in one direction, since no ACK can be received before transmission direction is switched. If LA is used, the maximal amount of bit needs to be calculated using the highest possible data rate. The fact that no ACK can be received before the scheduler grants resources for the back-channel also needs to be considered.

Often *Hybrid ARQ (HARQ)* is used in modern communication systems. Hybrid means that forward- and backward error correction are done together. If forward error correction is not possible in the decoder, it informs the transmitter using an ARQ protocol. The PDU is then retransmitted. The decoder will then again try to decode the data using information from the first transmission and the retransmission. If an identical retransmission is sent using same MCS as the first transmission *Chase Combining (CC)* is used. If the retransmission is transmitted using a more robust MCS to increase success probability *Incremental Redundancy (IR)* is applied. While to the best knowledge of the author no system level models for IR exists, CC can be modeled in the following way as described in [435]: When calculating resulting SINR for a received PDU sum up the SINR of the current PDU with SINR values of all previously received copies of this PDU, in linear scale (not dB).

Segmentation and Reassembly

The DLL has to provide a common interface for the transmission of data units to the higher layers. As PHY layers differ in the amount of data that might be transmitted within a single frame transmission, the DLL may provide functionality to allow a mapping between the data units delivered from higher layers and the ones transmitted over the physical link. Segmentation And Reassembly (SAR) performs this task: if a data unit to be transmitted is larger than the maximum allowed size, it splits the data unit into several pieces of acceptable size and defines rules on how to transmit them. Depending on the PHY, several of such fragments may be transmitted right after each other, or the fragments have to be regarded as completely separate data frames. In any case, reassembly has to collect the fragments and may only deliver them to the higher layer as one reassembled data unit. In a model,

SAR can impact delays and resource utilization through fragmentation. Error models depending on PDU length are also influenced by SAR.

10.2.3   Queueing and Processing Delay

Queueing. A wireless medium is always restricted in the amount of data it might process within a specific interval of time. Clearly, if more data is provided than can be transmitted, it has to be either discarded or queued. Typical lower layers provide one or several interface queues in which data that should be transmitted is stored until it can finally be handled. Models that describe queueing behavior are often used and widely known. In case queues have specific characteristics their behavior can be described in an analytical way. Sometimes it is of interest to analyze the statistics of a queue. The *queueing delay* is defined as the difference between the time a PDU enters it and the time it finally leaves the queue. It is more difficult to obtain the statistics of the queue size. In most cases the time average of the queue size is of interest. In general, if queue size is evaluated whenever a PDU enters or leaves the queue, the results do not represent the average queue size over time. In some cases a periodic probing with fixed period could produce wrong results. If the system uses a periodic MAC frame, probing time could be correlated with MAC frame period. If the system starts emptying its queues at the beginning of each frame, queue sizes decrease as the time offset from the frame start increases. Queue sizes therefore are correlated with the periodic MAC frame and cannot be probed periodically. The solution is periodic probing with variable period length. As stated by the *Poisson Arrivals see Time Averages (PASTA) theorem* [502], period length should follow an exponential distribution. In this way, the average queue size over time is obtained.

Processing delay. This type of delay occurs due to the necessity of analyzing, handling and creating data packets and their corresponding information, e.g. packet headers. Typically, the delay introduced by a certain module can be modeled by a mathematical function that provides the amount of time which has passed until processing a packet is finished. The most simple model for processing delay is a constant one or a delay depending on the size of data units. Most simulators do not model processing delay at all. Still any implemented algorithm, for example scheduling algorithms as described in Section 10.1.5 must be verified if they can produce results within given time constraints.

10.3 Summary

Previous sections presented different functionalities of a Data Link Layer (DLL). Some possibilities on how to model the effects and impacts of those functionalities were presented. Most of these models focus on not explicitly modeling signalling traffic on the wireless channel, but just obtaining the knowledge from the simulator environment. While in the physical layer and the channel, abstract models mostly serve the purpose to reduce computational efforts, two other purposes are essential when simplified DLL models are used: For one, implementation efforts can be reduced by not implementing certain parts of a protocol. Additionally, by using perfect knowledge from the simulator environment, the optimal case can be evaluated. Each proposed solution can then be quantified by how close it comes to this optimal solution.

Any research results drawn from a simulator should include the simplifications made and an estimation of their impact.

11. Channel Modeling

Arne Schmitz, Marc Schinnenburg, James Gross (RWTH Aachen University)
Ana Aguiar (Faculty of Engineering, University of Porto)

For any communication system the *Signal-to-Interference-plus-Noise-Ratio* of the link is a fundamental metric. Recall (cf. Chapter 9) that the SINR is defined as the ratio between the received power of the signal of interest and the sum of all "disturbing" power sources (i.e. *interference* and *noise*). From information theory it is known that a higher SINR increases the maximum possible error-free transmission rate (referred to as Shannon capacity [417] of any communication system and vice versa[1]). Conversely, the higher the SINR, the lower will be the bit error rate in practical systems. While one aspect of the SINR is the sum of all distracting power sources, another issue is the received power. This depends on the transmitted power, the used antennas, possibly on signal processing techniques and ultimately on the channel gain between transmitter and receiver.

Hence, given a transmitter/receiver pair, the SINR is influenced by factors internal to the system, like the used antennas and available signal processing techniques, as well as by three "external" factors: The gain between transmitter and receiver, the sum of received interference power and the noise power. These three factors are, in general, time-varying and are denoted in the following by $h^2(t)$ for the gain, $\sum_{\forall j} P_j^I(t) \cdot h_j^2(t)$ for the sum of the interference power, and $n^2(t)$ for the noise power. Given a transmit power of P_{tx}, the SINR is defined as:

$$\text{SINR}(t) := \frac{P_{tx} \cdot h^2(t)}{\sum_{\forall j} P_j^I(t) \cdot h_j^2(t) + n^2(t)} \tag{11.1}$$

The gain depends strongly on the medium between transmitter and receiver. This medium, for example an optical fiber or an infrared link, is referred to as *communication channel*. *Wireless channels* differ a lot from wired channels because their gain varies with time in a way that is not deterministic. Alternatively, it can also be said that they are time-selective. In contrast to wired channels, the gain between two transceivers may change randomly by magnitudes within a couple of milliseconds. Therefore, performance models

---

[1] This result only holds precisely for Gaussian sources of noise and interference. However, it is often used as approximation especially for non-Gaussian sources of interference.

for wireless networks have to deal with this impact by the channel, and use models for the different effects that can be observed.

Focusing on the channel gain, the results of extensive measurement campaigns [439] allow to distinguish three different components contributing to the overall gain $h^2(t)$. First of all, if the *distance* between transmitter and receiver is kept constant and multiple samples of the gain are recorded for different placements, these samples vary significantly. However, the average gain over all placements and over time depends only on the distance from transmitter and frequency. Models have been developed which reliably predict this average gain depending on the particular propagation environment [384]. This component of the gain is termed *path loss* and we will denote it by h_{pl}^2. From here on we drop the time index for simplicity reasons, as we are primarily interested in the decomposition of the total gain in this section. Note that the designation "loss" comes from the fact that the received signal has lower power than the transmitted signal.

For a given placement of transmitter and receiver, a path loss model predicts a certain gain. However, the actually measured gain varies constantly over time on a time-scale of milliseconds. Even if the average of the gain is taken over multiple seconds, it is likely to differ from the predicted gain[2] [439]. These deviations are due to the surroundings of the transmitter/receiver and of the path between them. They are modeled stochastically and termed *shadowing*. Shadowing actually models the deviations from the predicted path loss gain in the range of seconds. We will denote this component of the channel gain by h_{sh}^2. As with the path loss, shadowing models have to be parameterized according to the particular propagation environment, being different for rural and urban areas.

Finally, the short-term variations (in the range of milliseconds) of the gain result from multipath propagation, i. e. the fact that the signal at the receiver is actually the result of a sum of several components that followed different propagation paths and suffered different reflection, diffraction and other propagation phenomena that will be revisited in Section 11.1.2. These short-term fluctuations are termed *fading* and are found to follow certain first- and second-order statistics. They depend on various environmental parameters such as a possible line-of-sight between transmitter and receiver, the center frequency etc., and are modeled by distinct stochastic processes accordingly. This (random) component is denoted in the following by h_{fad}^2.

Combining all three effects yields the overall gain of the wireless channel. The corresponding model, which is used commonly [93], is given in Equation 11.2.

$$h^2 = h_{\mathrm{pl}}^2 \cdot h_{\mathrm{sh}}^2 \cdot h_{\mathrm{fad}}^2 \tag{11.2}$$

---

[2] Recall that the path loss model only predicts an average gain for all placements with a certain distance, not for a particular placement.

The aforementioned variations of the wireless channel gain over time result basically from changes within the propagation environment of transmitter and receiver. First of all, the propagation environment of the transmitter and receiver might change due to objects moving around, doors or windows being opened and closed etc. This might affect the shadowing component and/or the fading component, such that the resulting gain changes over time. Alternatively (or in combination with moving objects) the propagation environment might change due to mobility of the transmitter and/or the receiver. This usually results in a change of the path loss, the shadowing and the fading component. However, it is important to note that the fading component is affected on a much smaller time scale than shadowing and path loss. Note that in addition to the time-selective nature of the wireless channel, there might also be a frequency-selective behavior of the gain, i. e. the gain can vary with frequency. This is due to the fading component and multipath, as will be discussed in detail in Section 11.7 below.

This chapter focuses on models for wireless channel behavior and other factors that influence the SINR. First, we summarize the basic physical phenomena that are fundamental to the time- and frequency-selective nature of the channel gain. Then, we describe various common models which capture essential aspects of the wireless channel gain with respect to path loss, shadowing and fading. Then, we briefly introduce the effect of antennas on the channel gain between a transmitter and a receiver. Finally, we describe how the different models can be combined to simulate the variable gain of the wireless channel in an example.

11.1   The Physics of Radiation

Radio communication works by using electromagnetic radiation, which is one of the four fundamental forces: strong nuclear, weak nuclear, gravitational, and electromagnetic force. In the following sections we give a rough overview of the physical concepts that are needed to understand, correctly model and simulate the SINR at the receiver end of a wireless communication channel as a function of the transmitted signal. For a more thorough understanding and details, we recommend a specialized textbook, like the one by Hecht [199] or Tse [468].

11.1.1   The Nature of Electromagnetic Radiation

The basic interaction that describes all electromagnetic effects is the electromagnetic force. It is the force that keeps electrons and protons together in the nuclei of an atom, and it also holds the atoms in a molecule together. In classical particle physics the electromagnetic force is propagated by particles called photons.

Some of the very basic incarnations of these photons are light and radio waves. As the last sentence suggests, these photons do not only have a particle nature, but also the properties of a wave. All observable instances of photons have a certain wavelength λ and energy $E = \frac{hc}{\lambda}$, where h and c are the Planck constant and the speed of light respectively. Both are not of great interest in the following anymore, but the last expression states that the energy of photons is only dependent of their wavelength. This wavelength can be expressed as a frequency $\nu = \frac{c}{\lambda}$.

This frequency is what discerns light from radio waves. In the modeling of wireless networks one mostly wants to deal with the latter. Although current work also deals with the spectrum in the Terahertz range and there are also standards for infrared wireless communication. Figure 11.1 shows an intuitive scale of the observable electromagnetic spectrum. The usable *radio spectrum* is to the left, in the order of some Kilohertz to some Gigahertz. For instance the well known 802.11 networks use frequencies of 2.4, 3.7 or 5 Gigahertz, depending on the standard used. In general, the radio spectrum consists of the frequencies ranging up to 300 GHz (or wavelengths larger than 1 mm).

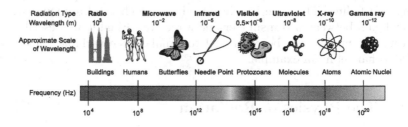

Fig. 11.1: The spectrum of electromagnetic radiation, ranging from radio to gamma rays.

The area of study that is related to the measuring of electromagnetic radiation is called radiometry. Its most basic quantity is radiant power, or flux, also denoted as Φ, it is defined as radiated energy per second and is measured in Joules per second, or Watts:

$$\Phi = \left[\frac{J}{s}\right] = [W] \tag{11.3}$$

The second most basic quantities are irradiance (E - not to be mistaken with the electric field E considered further down) and radiant exitance (B - not to be mistaken with the magnetic flux B further down), both of which describe the incoming or outgoing radiation on a surface:

$$E = B = \frac{d\Phi}{dA} = \left[\frac{W}{m^2}\right] \tag{11.4}$$

The last important quantity is dependent on a direction and is called the radiance. It is the flux over a surface per solid angle.

$$L = \frac{d^2\Phi}{dA^\perp d\omega} = \left[\frac{W}{m^2 \cdot sr} \right] \tag{11.5}$$

Also note that the surface is now called $A^\perp$, since radiance depends on the angle at which the radiation hits a surface.

As an example for the specific case of electromagnetic radiation, the radiant power or flux is the total power radiated from an antenna. It is given in Watt, or alternatively in *decibel milliwatt* (dBm) or *decibel watt* (dbW), although the latter (dBW) is less common. The decibel is a dimensionless unit and defined as:

$$L_{dB} = 10 \log_{10} \left(\frac{P_1}{P_0} \right) \tag{11.6}$$

Usually the *decibel* notation will be sufficient to describe the propagation phenomena in a model. However, it is important to keep the underlying physical phenomena and quantities in mind, for example for dealing with antenna design or for calculating specific absorption rate values (SAR) of bodies, a measure of the rate at which a body absorbs energy when exposed to an electromagnetic field.

The Wave Model

Some aspects of electromagnetic radiation can be best explained by seeing the radiation as being carried by a wave—the wave model for electromagnetic radiation. The frequency that can be measured, the destructive interference of signals and phenomena like scattering or diffraction are all best explained by using a wave model. Electromagnetic radiation behaves like a combination of orthogonal oscillating components: the electric field $\vec{E}$ and the magnetic field $\vec{H}$, as pictured in Figure 11.2.

Thus, radiation can be viewed as a vector field consisting of both $\vec{E}$ and $\vec{H}$ parts which form a traveling wave. The relationship between the electric and magnetic fields and their causes (electric charge and electric current) was first done by James Clerk Maxwell, who formulated three of the four now famous *Maxwell equations* in the mid 19th century. The four equations in their differential form are as follows:

$$\operatorname{div}\vec{D} = \nabla \cdot \vec{D} = \rho \tag{11.7}$$

$$\operatorname{div}\vec{B} = \nabla \cdot \vec{B} = 0 \tag{11.8}$$

$$\operatorname{rot}\vec{E} = \nabla \times \vec{E} = -\frac{\partial \vec{B}}{\partial t} \tag{11.9}$$

$$\operatorname{rot}\vec{H} = \nabla \times \vec{H} = \vec{J} + \frac{\partial \vec{D}}{\partial t} \tag{11.10}$$

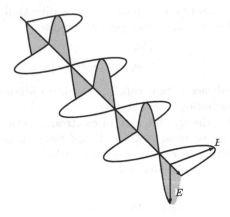

Fig. 11.2: A linearly polarized transversal electromagnetic wave. The two components are the electric field E and the magnetic field B, which oscillate
orthogonally to each other.

where $\overrightarrow{D}$ is the electric flux density, $\overrightarrow{B}$ the magnetic flux density, $\overrightarrow{E}$ the
electric field, $\overrightarrow{H}$ the magnetic field, $\overrightarrow{J}$ the current density, ρ the electric
charge density at a point, and $\mathrm{div}\overrightarrow{X}$, $\mathrm{rot}\overrightarrow{X}$, and $\nabla\overrightarrow{X}$ are the divergence,
curl and gradient operators for vector fields [369]. For a linear, isotropic and
homogeneous medium, the constitutive relationships that define the equations
above are :

$$\overrightarrow{D} = \varepsilon_r \varepsilon_0 \overrightarrow{E} \tag{11.11}$$

$$\overrightarrow{H} = \frac{\overrightarrow{B}}{\mu_r \mu_0} \tag{11.12}$$

where $\varepsilon_0 = \frac{1}{c^2 \mu_0}$ is the permittivity of free space, $\mu_0 = 4\pi \times 10^{-7}\frac{N}{A}$ is the
vacuum permeability; ε, μ and σ are the medium's characteristic constants
permittivity (also called dielectric constant), permeability and conductivity.
Further interpretations and the integral forms of the equations can be found
in specialized books on Physics or Electromagnetism, as for example in Hecht
[199] or [369]. A good introduction for the understanding and application of
these equations can be found in the introductory course by Fleisch [144].

These equations allow us to model the radio wave propagation problem
as a problem of a vector field and a set of differential equations. The main
application of this model is in antenna design. From these equations, the
equations of the electromagnetic field radiated by an antenna of a specific
shape can be derived. That field can be divided in three regions depending
on the distance from the antenna: the reactive near field, the radiating near
field (also called Fresnel region) and the far field (also Fraunhofer region) [46].

- The *reactive near field* lies in the immediate proximity of the antenna, for distances from the antenna up to $0.62\sqrt{\frac{l^3}{\lambda}}$, where l is the largest dimension of the antenna, the $\overrightarrow{E}$ and $\overrightarrow{H}$ fields are predominantly reactive.
- In the *radiating near field* or Fresnel region, for distances from the antenna between $0.62\sqrt{\frac{l^3}{\lambda}}$ and $2\frac{l^2}{\lambda}$, the $\overrightarrow{E}$ and $\overrightarrow{H}$ start being predominantly radiating, but the variations of radiated power as a function of the direction varies with the distance from the antenna.
- In the *far field* of the antenna or Fraunhofer region, for distances from the antenna larger than $2\frac{l^2}{\lambda}$, the variations of radiated power as a function of the direction—the antenna pattern—remain constant with the distance from the antenna.

The latter is the main application of Maxwell's equations: the calculation of the antenna pattern of an antenna of a certain shape at a certain frequency. Details on the calculation of antenna patterns can be found in classical books on antenna theory and design, like the ones by Elliot [130] or Balanis [46]. Due to the involved computational and spatial complexity, Maxwell's equations are not used for propagation simulation. The latter rather use models based on the particle model, like ray-tracing, or empirical and hybrid models, as we shall see later on.

The Particle Model

The second interpretation of electromagnetic radiation is that it comes in small packets or quantums that are called photons. They behave similarly to ordinary particles, like electrons, protons or neutrons. Photons are stable particles without mass that have an energy of $\mathcal{E} = h\nu$, where h is again Planck's constant. A simplified model of the photon, without many of the quantum-effects, will later be used to derive algorithms based on ray optics.

The photoelectric effect states that when metal is hit by electromagnetic radiation, it emits electrons. This can be explained by the photon model: Photons get absorbed by atoms, which results in certain electrons in the atom to be put into a higher energetic state. On the other hand, when an electron goes from a higher energetic state into its default state, it will emit a photon with a particular energy and wavelength. Viewed on a macroscopic scale this effect produces scattering, reflection and refraction of electromagnetic radiation.

11.1.2 Propagation Phenomena

The Maxwell equations from the previous section enable the deterministic calculation of the received signal at a certain distance from the antenna in

free space, the free-space loss or path loss. However, on the surface of the
Earth, there are objects in and around the propagation path and a radio
wave is subject to several phenomena like reflection, scattering, refraction
and diffraction, which are illustrated in Figure 11.3 and we briefly introduce
below. For more details on propagation phenomena, refer to specialized books
on radio propagation, like the one from Parsons [353].

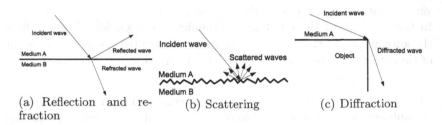

(a) Reflection and re-   (b) Scattering   (c) Diffraction
fraction

Fig. 11.3: Illustration of the basic propagation phenomena affecting a radio wave.

Path Loss. The propagation of radio waves is governed by the *free-space path
loss*, which can be calculated from the Maxwell equations 11.10. This value
is valid for a receiver that would be located is the space and for which there
are no objects in or surrounding the direct, or line-of-sight (Line-of-Sight),
propagation path. It expresses the fact that EM waves expand spherically
from their point of origin. The surface of a sphere scales as $A_S = 4\pi r^2$, so the
power received at a point at distance r from the transmitter scales with the
inverse of $4\pi r^2$. Additionally, the path loss depends on the frequency of the
radio wave. The free space path loss is the relation between received power
at a distance r from the transmitter, for an EM wave of wavelength λ, for
unit gain antennas on both sides, and is given by:

$$\left(\frac{\lambda}{4\pi r}\right)^2 \tag{11.13}$$

Reflection and Scattering. When a radio wave hits a border between two
media of different conductivity σ and dielectric constant ε (or of different
optical density), it will be *scattered* or *reflected*. In the simplest case this will
be vacuum on one side and some other, dense material on the other side,
like the Earth, a building or a tree. Scattering and reflection are basically
the same effect. Atoms scatter EM radiation, and if those atoms are aligned
in a smooth, possibly even regular grid that is much smaller than the EM
wavelength, the reflection is specular, or mirror-like (Figure 11.3-a). If the
size of the roughnesses of the surface that the wave encounters is not much
smaller than the wavelength, diffuse reflection occurs, more commonly known
as scattering. In this case, an incident wave will lead to several waves of much
less energy scattered in different directions (Figure 11.3-b).

Refraction. The effect of *refraction* can be observed at the same time reflection happens (Figure 11.3-a). In fact it is also due to the same physical processes, since EM radiation gets scattered or reflected into the new medium although with a different, refracted direction.

Diffraction. Any form of wave is subject to the propagation effect of *diffraction*. It describes the behavior of waves that bend around a corner (Figure 11.3-c). It is implicitly modeled by all approaches that build on the Maxwell equations (refer to [353] for more details of diffraction for radio waves), or for particle and ray-tracing based approaches by the geometrical theory of diffraction [311].

11.2   Classification of Propagation Models

Existing *propagation models* can be classified mainly into two categories: deterministic and empirical approaches. The first group contains the algorithms based on field and wave theory, as well as ray-tracing algorithms. Whereas the empirical methods use simpler models that are based on statistics from large scale propagation measurement and have to be chosen accordingly to the scenario they will be applied to, like indoor or outdoor or according to the terrain occupation (urban, suburban, rural). There are also some hybrid models which combine deterministic ray-tracing with empirical models. This is usually done to speed up the time consuming ray-tracing process.

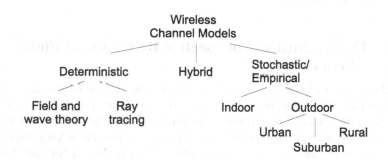

Fig. 11.4: Categories of wireless channel models.

Figure 11.4 summarizes this categorization and serves as a guide to the next sections which will describe with more detail relevant channel models in each category.

Recall from the beginning of the chapter that the goal of channel models is to calculate the received signal power at a point considering the transmitted power, and that this is achieved by calculating the channel gain $h^2(t)$.

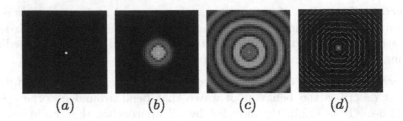

(a)   (b)   (c)   (d)

Fig. 11.5: A radio wave propagation computed according to the Maxwell equations. The E field is color coded with red and green. (a) The initial configuration with a point-like oscillator in the middle. (b) The EM field after a few iterations of solving the equations. (c) After several hundred iterations. (d) An excerpt showing only the B field as vectors orthogonal to the E field. The images were computed with software courtesy of Paul Falstad.

The previous sections briefly described the physical meaning of the gain and the phenomena affecting it and the next sections give an overview of how the effects of those phenomena on the gain can be modeled, which is ultimately the wireless channel model. First, Sections 11.3 and 11.4 describe deterministic channel models based on field theory and geometrical optics, respectively. Then, Sections 11.5, 11.6 and 11.7 describe stochastic channel models for path loss, shadowing and fast fading gains while Section 11.8 introduces fading models for systems with multiple antennas. Finally, Section 11.9 presents hybrid channel models.

11.3   Deterministic Approaches by Classical Field Theory

The classic view of the electromagnetic radiation as a wave was introduced in Section 11.1.1. It can be used to compute the wave propagation only by using the four Maxwell equations, as is done to calculate the free-space loss, for example. As explained in that section, this approach is very expensive in terms of time and memory consumption. This is due to the fact that it needs the simulation domain do be discretized into a grid, or for boundary element methods [176], to discretize the surface of the modeled objects [194]. Either solution leads to very high memory consumption or high computational complexity. Thus it is only useful in small simulation domains, e.g. when computing the radiation pattern of an antenna (see Section 11.1.1) or to calculate indoor coverage.

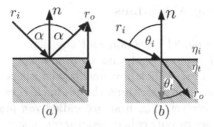

Fig. 11.6: (a) Reflection. (b) Refraction.

11.4 Deterministic Geometric Optical Approaches

Geometric optics describes the behavior of light and EM radiation through the use of geometrical concepts, such as rays. A ray is a straight line segment with a starting point and a direction along which radiation travels:

$$r(t) = o + t \cdot d \tag{11.14}$$

11.4.1 Modeling Phenomena with Geometrical Optics

Ray optics often match phenomena that are observed with high frequency radiation. A ray can be thought of as a point on an expanding spherical wave, as in the wave based model. Effects such as reflection and refraction are well-modeled by a ray based approach, as is explained in the following.

Specular Reflection. The reflected ray after a specular reflection can easily be described as:

$$r_o - 2(n \cdot r_i)n - r_i \tag{11.15}$$

An example configuration for a reflected ray can be seen in Figure 11.6.

Refraction. For the case of refraction Snell formulated the following equation:

$$\frac{\sin \theta_i}{\sin \theta_t} = \frac{\eta_t}{\eta_i} \tag{11.16}$$

Where η_t and η_i are the indices of refraction for the different materials, and the θ_t and θ_i are the angles of the inbound and transmitted ray respectively, relative to the boundary normal. See Figure 11.6 for a visualization.

The amount of radiation that is reflected, compared to the one that is refracted is described by Fresnel's equation. It depends on the polarization of the irradiance and the angle with which it hits the medium boundary. The different forms of Fresnel's equation can be found in Hecht and other textbooks. [199]

11.4.2   Ray Tracing Algorithms

Having the ability to model reflection and the like, we can now formulate algorithms that work on rays and that compute the field strength of EM radiation with some or all of the above mentioned phenomena.

We distinguish between algorithms that launch rays from the radiation source, or from the receiver. The first are called *ray launching algorithms*, while the other ones are usually called *ray tracing algorithms*. There are also approaches that compute the whole field for a general setting, which usually launch the rays from the radiation source.

The basic ray launching or tracing algorithm is of a recursive nature. A number of rays are launched from either source or receiver, and tested for intersections with the scene. Upon intersection all of the above mentioned events like reflection, refraction or diffraction may happen. Then the ray will be recursively traced further, until some criterion is met. In the following we will give a short overview of some of the most important algorithms that were developed.

In general it is advisable to speed up the ray-tracing process. The most costly operation for ray-tracing is the intersection of rays with the scene geometry. In a naive approach this takes $O(n)$ intersections for each ray. Using spatial subdivision, e.g. by using kd-trees or Octrees, this can be sped up to $O(\log n)$ tests per ray. Also ray-tracing is highly parallelizable, so that the utilization of multi-core CPUs and also of GPUs can be used to do many intersection tests in parallel.

Cube-Oriented Ray-Launching. Instead of tracing rays by intersecting them with objects in the scene, this approach uses a uniform 3D grid. The rays are traced in a manner similar to discrete line drawing using the Bresenham algorithm. The algorithm is especially suited for urban scenarios [305].

Diffraction along horizontal or vertical edges is considered by the algorithm as well as reflection. As with other methods using geometrical optics, careful optimization of the material parameters is needed to get good results. This is usually done by taking sparse test samples in the scenario in question and using some optimization algorithm or simply good guesses to fit the simulation result to the measured values.

The Photon Path Map. The algorithm is based on the photon mapping approach from computer graphics. It is a ray launching approach that computes the EM field with reflections, refractions and diffraction for a truly three-dimensional scene. The algorithm is usable for both indoor and outdoor or urban scenarios. One advantage is that it can also compute the delay spread of a signal. [409]

The method differs from other ray launching techniques in that it lends many ideas from classical Monte Carlo path tracing techniques which were developed for the simulation of visible light. The advantage of such algorithms is that they model the propagation in a more natural fashion by giving priority to the paths light really takes. This method does not need to trace propagation paths between each point in the scene and the sending antenna. Instead it uses a two pass approach.

In the first pass, rays are launched from the sender. They may intersect the geometry, where they will be reflected, refracted or diffracted. Rays also may be absorbed, according to a strategy called Russian roulette. This process randomly chooses if a ray survives the interaction with a material, or if it will be absorbed. For more detailed information, a good understanding of Monte Carlo integration and the solving of the Rendering or Heat Transfer Equation is necessary, which describe the transfer of light or heat radiation. A good primer on this subject is for example given by Dutre [128].

Diffraction of rays is modeled stochastically as well, so that an explicit diffraction path construction based on the geometrical theory of diffraction is not necessary. At the end of the first pass all the computed propagation paths form the photon path map, which implicitly describes the flux at each point of the scene.

The second pass now extracts the irradiant energy for each point in the scene from the photon path map. This is done by computing the flux density, i.e. by counting how many photons traveled through each point in space. In practice a kernel density estimator is used for this purpose, to get a continuous radiance estimate.

11.5   Empirical Path Loss Approaches

This section addresses the first set of empirical models for wireless channels and focuses on path loss. As said before, one has to choose one *empirical model* suited for the scenario in question. Both the frequency used, as well as the geometrical and physical shape of the scenario in question have to be considered. A good overview of different models is given by Rappaport [383]. The most widely used models for urban outdoor environments will be sketched here.

Okumura Model. This model is used for frequencies in the range from 150 MHz to 3 GHz and is applicable for urban scenarios at distances between 1 km and 100 km from the transmitting antenna. The model is described by Rappaport [383] as

$$h_{\text{pl}}^2[dB] = h_{\text{pl,free}}^2 + A_{mu}(f, d) - G(h_{te}) - G(h_{re}) - G_{\text{Area}} \qquad (11.17)$$

Here $h_{\text{pl,free}}^2$ denotes free space propagation loss, A_{mu} is the median attenuation relative to free space, $G(h_{te})$ is the base station antenna gain, $G(h_{re})$ is the mobile antenna gain and G_{Area} describes a gain due to the type of the terrain. Okumura described different functions for urban, semi-open or open areas. All the parameters of the model were recorded by extensive measurements, and provided as graphical plots, which is not very useful for implementation in a simulation. Therefore, Hata provided numerical values for the Okumura model.

Hata Model. As said above, this model represents an empirical formulation of the Okumura model. Rappaport again describes the model as follows:

$$
\begin{aligned}
h_{\text{pl}}^2[\text{dB}] \quad = \quad & 69.65 + 26.16 \log f_c - 13.82 \log h_{te} \\
& -a(h_{re}) + ((44.9 - 6.55) \cdot \log h_{te}) \log d
\end{aligned}
\tag{11.18}
$$

where f_c is the frequency, h_{te} and h_{re} are the base station and receiver antenna heights respectively. Furthermore $a(h_{re})$ is a correction factor for the effective mobile antenna height and d is the distance of the receiver from the base station.

Walfisch-Ikegami Model. The Okumura-Hata models do not explicitly model rooftop diffraction effects which are important in urban scenarios, where the base station is located on rooftops and the mobile receiver usually is on street level, without a line of sight to the transmitter. The methods proposed by Walfisch and Ikegami incorporate these effects [482, 210]. The model for the non-liner-of-sight case is described as follows:

$$
h_{\text{pl}}^2[\text{dB}] = h_{\text{pl,free}}^2 + L_{rts} + L_{ms}
\tag{11.19}
$$

where $h_{\text{pl,free}}^2$ represents free space path loss and L_{rts} is the rooftop to street diffraction term:

$$
L_{rts}[\text{dB}] = -16.9 - 10 \log \frac{w}{\text{m}} + 10 \log \frac{f}{\text{Hz}} + 20 \log \frac{\Delta h_{\text{Mobile}}}{\text{m}} + L_{\text{Ori}}
\tag{11.20}
$$

where w is the average width of roads, f is the frequency, Δh_{Mobile} is the height difference between sender and receiver and L_{Ori} describes the street's orientation.

Finally, Equation 11.19 also takes the multi-screen diffraction loss into account via parameter L_{ms}. It is defined by a set of equations with multiple different input parameters. Details can be found in [482, 210] or in the definition of COST 231 channel models.

11.6   Stochastic Shadowing Models

The empirical path loss models presented above provide an average gain which can be expected at a certain distance between transmitter and receiver. However, it is known from measurements [237, 439] that for a fixed distance the average gain (over time) varies significantly for several different positions of the receiver, as objects such as buildings or trees might obstruct the transmission paths. These stochastic, location-dependent variations are referred to as *shadowing*. Shadowing is modeled as a stochastic process with an average of 1, as the average over many different location dependent variations yields exactly the predicted value of the path loss model. Note that shadowing is an abstraction which represents the result of a sum of several propagation phenomena which occur when an electromagnetic wave propagates in an environment.

Since shadowing is due to the obstruction by larger objects, it has a high correlation in space. For example, if the distance between transmitter and receiver is kept constant and the receiver moves along a circle around the transmitter, the gain due to shadowing stays constant over several meters, as a large building obstructs the area around a certain position. Therefore, shadowing varies rather over longer time scales such as seconds if the transmitter and/or receiver are mobile.

From measurements of the gain for a variety of environments and distances, the variation of the measured signal level relative to the average predicted path loss can be calculated (see Figures 2.37 to 2.41 from [439]). Its distribution is normal with 0 mean (in dB), which implies a log-normal distribution of the received power around the mean value corresponding to the path loss. This hypothesis has been verified with the χ^2 and Kolmogrov-Smirnov test with a high confidence interval. Thus, the shadowing process can be modeled by a first-order distribution given by

$$p\left(h_{\text{sh}}^2\right)[\text{dB}] = \frac{1}{\sqrt{2 \cdot \pi \cdot \sigma_{\text{sh}}^2}} \cdot e^{-\frac{\left(h_{\text{sh}}^2\right)^2}{2\sigma_{\text{sh}}^2}}, \tag{11.21}$$

where σ_{sh}^2 is the variation and all variables are expressed in dB. The standard deviation $\sqrt{\sigma_{\text{sh}}^2}$ of the shadowing process has been found to take values between 5 dB and 12 dB [509, 280, 504], depending on the considered environment and system.

According to the reasoning above, the values of the shadowing gain at nearby locations are correlated. Measurements suggest an exponential model for the shadowing auto-correlation at two points separated by distance r:

$$\rho(r) = \frac{1}{\sigma^2} e^{\frac{r}{r_C}} \tag{11.22}$$

r_C is the correlation distance which, according to measurements, varies between 25 m and 100 m at 1900 MHz [490] and between a few and a few dozen meters for 900 MHz [183, 269].

To simulate the shadowing gain $h_{\text{sh},b}^2$ at location b which is r meters separated from location a for which a shadowing gain of $h_{\text{sh},a}^2$ is known, a random sample X should be generated from a Gaussian random variable $N(0, \sigma)$ and used in the expression [499]:

$$h_{\mathrm{sh},b}^2[\mathrm{dB}] = \rho(r)h_{\mathrm{sh},a}^2 + \sqrt{1-\rho^2(r)}X \tag{11.23}$$

11.7 Stochastic Fading Models

Fading is the interference of many scattered signals arriving at an antenna [93]. It is responsible for the most rapid and violent changes of the signal strength itself as well as its phase. These signal variations are experienced on a small time scale, mostly a fraction of a second or shorter, depending on the velocity of the receiver (or transmitter or any object that reflects the signal). The following discussion is based on [93].

11.7.1 Physics of Fading

The physical basis of fading is given by the reception of multiple copies of the transmitted signal, each one stemming from a different propagation path. Depending on the environment of transmitter and receiver, there can be many or only few objects reflecting the transmitted radio signal. In general these objects lead to a situation shown in Figure 11.7, which is called a *multi-path signal propagation environment*.

In such a typical environment, each path i has a different length l_i. Due to this difference, each signal traveling along a path arrives with a different *delay* $\tau_i = \frac{l_i}{c}$, where c is the speed of light. Some signal copies traveling along short paths will arrive faster than other copies traveling along longer paths. Physically, this situation is comparable to an acoustic echo. In communications, the channel is said to have a memory, since it is able to store signal copies for a certain time span. The difference between "earliest" and "latest" received signal copy is often referred to as *delay spread* $\Delta\sigma$. Apart from the delay spread, each signal copy is attenuated differently, since the signal paths have to pass different obstacles like windows, walls of different materials, trees of different sizes and so on. Also, each signal traveling along its path might reach the receiver by a different angle. If the receiver or the transmitter is moving, this leads to different Doppler shifts of all signals, according to their angle of arrival. This results in a *Doppler spread* Δf_d.

Taking all this into account, the multi-path propagation of a transmitted radio wave results in a specific self-interference pattern for each propagation environment, where at certain places the waves interfere constructively while at other places they interfere destructively. If all elements within the propagation environment (transmitter, receiver etc.) do not move, the received signal will only by distorted by the delay spread and the corresponding variable gain per path. In this case, the interference situation of the channel stays constant over time and therefore the channel is said to be *time invariant*. In contrast,

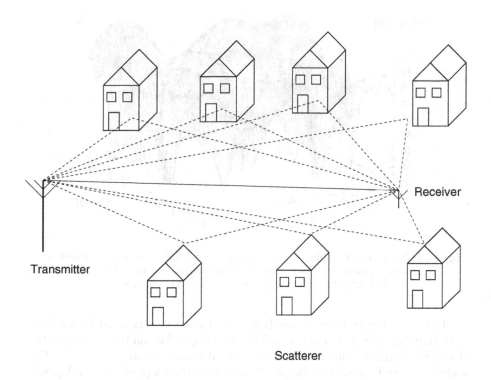

Transmitter

Receiver

Scatterer

Fig. 11.7: Multi-path propagation scenario.

if any kind of movement is encountered in the propagation environment, all or some paths change in time. As a consequence the wireless channel becomes *time variant* (see Figure 11.8). Correspondingly, if the delay spread $\Delta\sigma$ of the channel is zero, the channel is said to be *frequency invariant*. Otherwise, the channel's gain varies for different frequencies and therefore the channel is said to be *frequency variant* (see Figure 11.8). In contrast to the Doppler spread, the delay spread is almost always non zero. Thus, almost always a wireless channel is frequency variant.

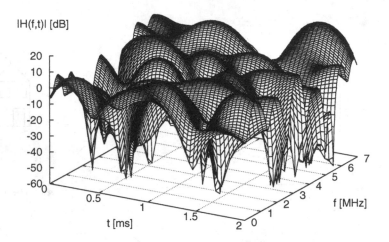

Fig. 11.8: Time and frequency variant gain due to fading of a broadband wireless channel. Depending on the observed bandwidth and duration, the channel might be time and frequency selective or not.

The frequency or time variant behavior of a wireless channel do not have to be harmful as such. Channels are classified depending on the severity of the channel's variance compared to fundamental transmission parameters. The severity of the time variant behavior caused by the Doppler spread depends on the time span the receiver processes the incoming communication signal. If coherent detection[3] is assumed, this processing time is the symbol length T_s. In general, $n \cdot T_s$ represents the processing time span (as differential detection or an equalization process cause $n > 1$). If the fade rate of the time selective process, given by the Doppler spread Δf_d, is larger than the processing rate (given by $\frac{1}{n \cdot T_s}$), then the *fading* is called *time selective* [93]. In contrast, if the fade rate is much lower than the processing rate, therefore if $\Delta f_d \cdot n \cdot T_s \ll 1$, then the fading is not time selective.

Correspondingly, the severity of the frequency variant behavior can be estimated by the product of the required baseband bandwidth of the signal

---

[3] This refers to perfectly synchronized transmitters and receivers as is often assumed for the PHY layer in network simulation.

(denoted by B) and the delay spread. If the delay spread is very small compared to the reciprocal of the bandwidth[4], then it has almost no impact on the reception of the signal ($\Delta\sigma \cdot B \ll 1$). In this case the transfer function (gain function) of the channel has no variations within the signal's bandwidth. The *fading* is called to be *flat or frequency non selective*. On the other hand, if the delay spread is significant compared to the reciprocal of the bandwidth, then the channel has a *frequency selective* behavior. That is, at certain frequency ranges of the baseband signal the received signal is significantly more attenuated than at other ranges. In this case the receiver observes *ISI* (see Figure 11.9), as the time-domain manifestation of the frequency selective behavior. If the delay spread is for example half of the symbol time, then signal copies of two consecutively sent symbols interfere at the receiver, such that the 'fast' signal copy of the latter sent symbol interferes with the 'slow' signal copy of the previous sent symbol.

In Figure 11.9 the effect of ISI is illustrated. A wireless channel with three paths is assumed and a delay spread of $\Delta\sigma = 90$ time units (channel impulse response with three major propagation paths at the top of the picture). On the left side, the symbol time is $T_s = 400$ time units, which is much bigger than the delay spread. Therefore, symbols (shown here as 'high' or 'low' values) transmitted are only marginally influenced by ISI. The received signal $eN(t)$ is almost not corrupted. In contrast, on the right side of the picture, the resulting signal is shown for a symbol duration of $T_s = 100$ time units. Thus, the symbol rate is four times higher. Hence, the delay spread of the channel is almost identical to the symbol duration. As a consequence, the transmitted symbols are severely corrupted.

In practice, most of the time both Doppler and delay spread are present. However, both effects can be of harm or not, depending on the ratio between the symbol time (baseband bandwidth) and the characteristic values of the effects Δf_d and $\Delta\sigma$. Therefore, a channel might be categorized as one of four different types, listed in Table 11.1.

Criteria	Fading Category
$\Delta\sigma \cdot B \ll 1$, $\Delta f_d \cdot n \cdot T_s \ll 1$	flat and slow
$\neg(\Delta\sigma \cdot B \ll 1)$, $\Delta f_d \cdot n \cdot T_s \ll 1$	frequency selective and slow
$\Delta\sigma \cdot B \ll 1$, $\neg(\Delta f_d \cdot n \cdot T_s \ll 1)$	flat and fast
$\neg(\Delta\sigma \cdot B \ll 1)$, $\neg(\Delta f_d \cdot n \cdot T_s \ll 1)$	frequency selective and fast

Table 11.1: Categories in order to characterize the fading of a wireless channel depending on the Doppler and delay spread

---

[4] The baseband bandwidth requirement of any communication system is strongly related to the rate of digital symbols transmitted. Thus, the delay spread might also be compared to the symbol duration T_s

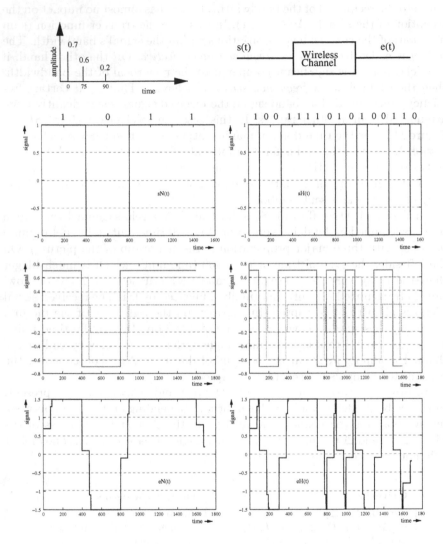

Fig. 11.9: Example illustration of the impact of ISI. Top: Channel impulse response with a delay spread of $\Delta\sigma = 90$ time units. Left three pictures below: Transmit signal, propagation path copies of the transmit signal and resulting interference signal for a symbol duration of $T_s = 400$ time units. The received signal is almost not affected. Right three pictures: Corresponding conditions for a symbol duration of $T_s = 100$ time units. The data rate is four times larger, but the received signal is significantly distorted.

11.7.2   Stochastic Models for Fading

Mathematically, fading can be modeled as a stochastic process in time and frequency. It is common to characterize this process by its first- and second-order statistics. Regarding the first-order statistics it has been shown that the so called envelope of the signal can be modeled as *Rayleigh* distributed under certain circumstances, as given in Equation 11.24[5].

$$p\left(h_{\text{fad}}\right) = h_{\text{fad}} \cdot e^{\frac{-h_{\text{fad}}^2}{2}} \tag{11.24}$$

Assuming the envelope of the channel response to be Rayleigh-distributed is a rather pessimistic model, as this assumes no dominating path to be present among all paths of the propagation environment between transmitter and receiver. A plot of the distribution is given in Figure 11.10.

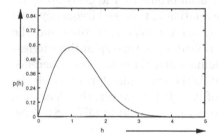
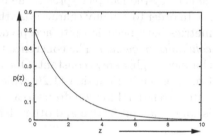

Fig. 11.10: Probability density functions related to fading: Rayleigh probability density of the signal magnitude (left) and the resulting exponential probability density of the instantaneous power (right).

For determining the actual SNR at the receiver, the instantaneous power has to be obtained rather than the instantaneous envelope. This is given by the squared envelope $z = h_{\text{fad}}^2$ and the distribution of z is given in Equation 11.25. In fact, z is exponentially distributed with mean $\bar{z}$ (If we only focus on the fading process *alone* the mean $\bar{z}$ equals 1. However, if we combine the fading model with a shadowing and path loss model, the mean $\bar{z}$ equals the current gain resulting from shadowing and path loss). A plot of the distribution is given in Figure 11.10.

$$p\left(z\right) = \frac{1}{\bar{z}} \cdot e^{\frac{-z}{\bar{z}}} \tag{11.25}$$

As mentioned, the Rayleigh distribution corresponds to a propagation environment with a NLOS setting, which is encountered for example in indoor

---

[5] Modeling the fading process requires a complex random process. In the following, h_{fad} denotes the magnitude of this complex process which is called the envelope. For a detailed discussion refer to [27, 93].

scenarios, as well as in macrocells of urban areas. Other scenarios require a different distribution (for example the *Rice* distribution for LOS settings [93]).

As with the first-order statistics of the fading process, models have also been developed for the second-order statistics. A very common model for these statistics is the *wide-sense stationary uncorrelated scatterer* (WSSUS) model [93, 375]. This model assumes the fading process to be stationary in time and frequency. Hence, the autocorrelation in time and frequency depends only on the time or frequency shift, not on the absolute time or frequency. Therefore, in an WSSUS model the autocorrelation can be easily expressed given the power delay profile and the power spectrum of the process. One popular setting for a WSSUS model is to assume the time correlation to be characterized by a *Jakes power spectral density*, while the frequency correlation is characterized by an *truncated exponential power delay profile*. Both densities are parameterized solely by their corresponding spreads – the Jakes density by the Doppler spread, the exponential profile by the delay spread.

In order to roughly characterize the correlation in time and frequency, two metrics have become quite accepted. They are the *coherence time* and the *coherence frequency*. The coherence time indicates the time span the wireless channel roughly stays constant. One mathematical definition of the coherence time is given in Equation 11.26, which equals the time shift during which the autocorrelation function drops to a value of 0.98 [93]. However, this definition is somewhat subjective and other definitions can be found in [375, 384, 438].

$$T_c = \frac{1}{2\pi\Delta f_d} \qquad (11.26)$$

The coherence bandwidth measures roughly the frequency spacing for which the channel does not change significantly. Again the exact mathematical definition is to some extend subjective. One definition of the coherence bandwidth is given by Equation 11.27, following [93]. Other definition might be found in [375, 384, 438].

$$W_c = \frac{1}{2\pi\Delta\sigma} \qquad (11.27)$$

11.8   MIMO Channel Models

So far, it has been assumed that the systems under consideration use a single antenna at the transmitter and a single antenna at the receiver. However, performance gains can be obtained from the use of multiple antennas on either side. This section briefly introduces the uses of multiple antennas in wireless communications and then explains how to model multiple-input, multiple-output (MIMO) wireless channels.

11.8.1 Multiple Antennas for Wireless Systems

Antenna diversity consists of using more than one transmit or receive antenna for the same signal. As long as the antennas are physically separated by more than half a wavelength, the receiver can choose the best among the different received signals, improving the reliability of the wireless link in the presence of fast fading.

Multiple transmit antennas can be used for beamforming (see Section 9.2). This consists in dynamically changing the phase of the signal transmitted on each antenna so that the signals from the different antennas add up coherently (in-phase) at the receiver and allocating the highest transmit power to the antenna that corresponds to the best propagation path, thus compensating for the multipath fading of the channel. This is possible only if the wireless channel gains between each transmit antenna and the receiver are known at the transmitter at the time of transmission. Inaccuracies in this information can lead to strong performance degradation [468].

For antenna diversity and beamforming, the same signal is transmitted on the different antennas as in the case of a single antenna. However, the most efficient way to use MIMO channels is to transmit different data streams simultaneously on different antennas, a technique know as spatial multiplexing [468].

The set of multiple antennas jointly used is often called an antenna array. In any case mentioned, the antenna arrays on either side of the channel should have a minimum antenna separation (D_r or D_t in Figure 11.11) of $\lambda/2$ for obtaining the desired performance gains. Hence, $\lambda/2$ is called the critical spacing and sparsely spaced antenna arrays have antenna separations larger than $\lambda/2$. Antenna arrays with equally spaced antennas along a line are called *uniform linear arrays*, and these will be assumed here henceforth. For detailed analysis of multiple antenna techniques for wireless communications, refer to specialized books like the one from Tse [468].

11.8.2 MIMO Fading Channel Models

In all situations described above, the advantages of using multiple antennas are obtained by signal processing techniques used before the transmitter and/or after the receiver antennas. Figure 11.11 illustrates the *MIMO channel*. Modeling the MIMO channel is about describing the signals received at the receiving antenna array as a function of the signals transmitted on the transmitted antenna array. As long as the dimension of the antenna arrays is much smaller than the distance between them, the path loss and shadowing components of the channel gain are the same for all antennas on each side and are modeled as described in sections 11.5 and 11.6 for a single antenna case. The rest of this section is concerned only with modeling fading for MIMO channels.

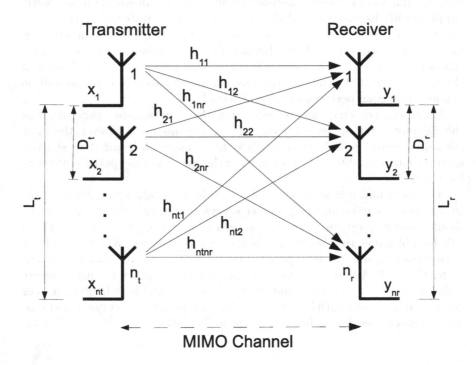

Fig. 11.11: MIMO wireless channel.

A linear, narrowband, time-invariant MIMO channel is described by:

$$\mathbf{y} = \mathbf{H}\mathbf{x} + \mathbf{n} \qquad (11.28)$$

where $\mathbf{y}$ and $\mathbf{x}$ are the signal vectors at the output of the receiver and transmitter antenna array, respectively, $\mathbf{H}$ is the channel matrix, and $\mathbf{n}$ is AWGN noise. The element h_{ij} of the channel matrix is the complex channel gain between transmit antenna j and receive antenna i, and the matrix $\mathbf{H}$ actually models the narrowband, time-invariant wireless MIMO channel (i.e. channels which are neither frequency- nor time-selective). For time-variant channels, when significant Doppler spreads are present (see Table 11.1), the channel matrix is time-dependent $\mathbf{H}(t)$ and so are its elements $h_{ij}(t)$. For wideband channels, when significant delay spreads are present (see Table 11.1), the channel is frequency-selective and the channel matrix is dependent on the delay $\mathbf{H}(\tau)$, as are its elements $h_{ij}(\tau)$. For details on wideband MIMO channel models, please refer e. g. to Yu [508] or Paetzold [350].

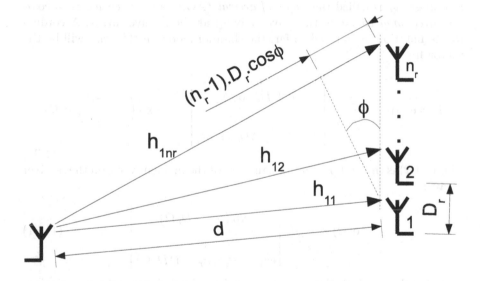

Fig. 11.12: MIMO wireless channel.

A few concepts that will be helpful in understanding the MIMO fading model are introduced here with the help of Figure 11.12. This figure shows the simplified case of a single transmitter antenna and several receiver antennas within Line-of-Sight. The channel gain between the single transmitter antenna and antenna j at the receiver is

$$h_{j1} = a_j \exp\left(-\frac{j 2\pi d_j}{\lambda}\right) \qquad (11.29)$$

where a_j is the gain of path j, d_j is the distance between the transmitter antenna and the receiver antenna j and λ is the wavelength. The vector $\mathbf{h}$ whose elements are h_{j1} is called the *spatial signature* of the transmitted signal on the receiver antenna array.

If the distance between the arrays, d, is much larger than the antenna spacing D_r, the paths can be assumed to be parallel. As a consequence, the gains of the paths a_j are all the same and the only difference between the signals received at different antennas is the phase, which depends on the different lengths of the paths to each antenna. Following Figure 11.12, and considering the propagation paths parallel ($d_j >> D_r$), the distances to each antenna will be

$$
\begin{aligned}
d_1 &\approx d \\
d_2 &\approx d + D_r \cos\phi \\
&\vdots \\
d_{n_r} &\approx d + (n_r - 1)D_r \cos\phi
\end{aligned}
$$

The angle ϕ_r is called the *angle of arrival* (AOA) and its cosine $\Omega = \cos\phi$ the *directional cosine* of the wave arriving at the receiver array. According to the notation introduced so far, the channel model in this case will be the vector $\mathbf{h}$:

$$
\mathbf{h} = a \exp\left(-\frac{j2\pi}{\lambda}\right) \begin{bmatrix} d \\ d + D_r \cos\phi \\ \vdots \\ d + (n_r - 1)D_r \cos\phi \end{bmatrix} = a \exp\left(-\frac{j2\pi d}{\lambda}\right) \mathbf{e}(\Omega)
$$

(11.30)

where $\mathbf{e}(\Omega)$ is the unitary spatial signature of the incident wave on the receiver array[6]:

$$
\mathbf{e}(\Omega) = \frac{1}{\sqrt{n_r}} \begin{bmatrix} 1 \\ \exp\left(-\frac{j2\pi}{\lambda}D_r\Omega\right) \\ \vdots \\ \exp\left(-\frac{j2\pi}{\lambda}(n_r - 1)D_r\Omega\right) \end{bmatrix}
$$

(11.31)

To optimally combine the signals received on the different antennas, receiver beamforming, the receiver should delay the signals from the different antennas according to the values in this vector. When there are n_t transmitter antennas and line of sight between transmitter and receiver, the expressions above can be generalized, and the channel model becomes the matrix $\mathbf{H}$ in Equation 11.28, built by the spatial signatures of the different transmitter antennas on the receiver array

$$
\mathbf{H} = a\,\mathbf{e_r}(\Omega_r)\,\mathbf{e_t}(\Omega_t)^*,
$$

(11.32)

---

[6] Note that the factor $\frac{1}{\sqrt{n_r}}$ only serves the normalization of the vector $\mathbf{e}(\Omega)$ to 1.

The *Angle of Departure* (AOD), or ϕ_t, is the equivalent for the transmitter antenna array of the AOA, or ϕ_r, for the receiver, and $\Omega_t = \cos\phi_t$. Similarly to receiver beamforming, transmitter beamforming should be performed according to the unitary spatial signature of the transmitter array $\mathbf{e}(\Omega_t)$.

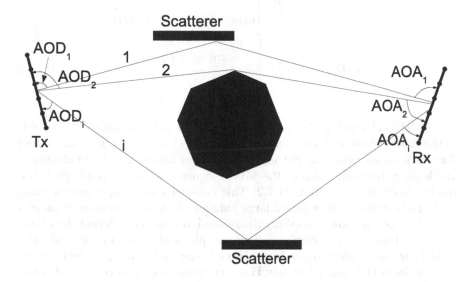

Fig. 11.13: MIMO wireless channel.

In an environment with obstacles and scatterers as shown in Figure 11.13, the previous model can be generalized to a multipath MIMO channel. Assuming that the distance between transmitter and receiver arrays and the scatterers is much larger than the dimensions of the arrays, the propagation paths can be assumed to be parallel, as above. The radio waves generated by the transmitter antenna array will travel parallel to each other and suffer similar propagation phenomena (reflection, diffraction, etc) along each path i between transmitter and receiver arrays. For a time invariant channel, the channel matrix $\mathbf{H}$ can be written as the sum of the gains of the n paths between transmitter and receiver antenna arrays.

$$\mathbf{H} = \sum_i a_i\, \mathbf{e_r}(\Omega_{ri})\, \mathbf{e_t}(\Omega_{ti})^*, \qquad (11.33)$$

where a_n is the gain of the i-th path, $\mathbf{e_r}(\Omega_{ri})$ and $\mathbf{e_t}(\Omega_{ti})$ are the transmitted and received unit spatial signatures of the i-th path along the direction Ω, respectively The factors in the sum follow the expressions below.

$$a_n = \sqrt{n_t n_r} \exp\left(-\frac{j2\pi d_n}{\lambda}\right) \tag{11.34}$$

$$\mathbf{e_r}(\Omega) = \frac{1}{\sqrt{n_r}} \begin{bmatrix} 1 \\ \exp(-j2\pi D_r \Omega) \\ \vdots \\ \exp(-j2\pi (n_r - 1) D_r \Omega) \end{bmatrix} \tag{11.35}$$

$$\mathbf{e_t}(\Omega) = \frac{1}{\sqrt{n_t}} \begin{bmatrix} 1 \\ \exp(-j2\pi D_t \Omega) \\ \vdots \\ \exp(-j2\pi (n_t - 1) D_t \Omega) \end{bmatrix} \tag{11.36}$$

A MIMO channel model that is often used due to its analytical tractability is the independent and identically distributed (i.i.d.) Rayleigh fading model, for which the entries of the channel matrix $\mathbf{H}$ are uncorrelated and identically Rayleigh distributed. This is the MIMO equivalent of the Rayleigh fading model described in Section 11.7.2. This channel model represents a richly scattered environment, where a large number of paths is received from each direction and the power is evenly distributed among the different directions.

Often this does not correspond to real physical environments and other models are used which differ from the i.i.d. Rayleigh fading models, in that the entries of the channel matrix $\mathbf{H}$ are spatially and time correlated. Thus, a MIMO channel simulator has to generate correlated entries of the channel matrix, which is achieved by using non-uniform distributions of the angles of departure (AOD) and arrival (AOA) (or directional cosines) in the previously mentioned models. A plethora of models have been recently developed, accounting for different scattering environments and modeling philosophies, and a thorough overview can be found in [33]. The most commonly used are finite scatterers models, like the *one-ring* [421, 24, 349] or *two-ring* [420] models which are used for scatterers located close to the receiver. The one ring model fits a scenario of communication between a base station and mobile station while the two-ring model fits a scenario of communication between two mobile stations. For details on how to implement/generate finite scatterer channel models for MIMO wireless channels refer to the work by Paetzold [349, 348, 515] or the specification of spatial channel models for MIMO simulations from the 3GPP initiative [18].

11.9   Hybrid Approaches

Hybrid propagation models are models that have complementary deterministic (mostly ray-tracing) and stochastic parts. Hybrid models are often used to speed up calculations of deterministic ray-tracing models, as is the case of the dominant path prediction model, or for actually improving the accuracy of ray-tracing models, as is the case of the second example below. Although this sounds counter-intuitive because one expects deterministic wireless channel models to be more accurate than stochastic ones, one should not forget that deterministic models base their calculations on models of the real world and can only be as accurate as the latter, and that often the deterministic models make assumptions that are not fully valid in the real world.

11.9.1   The Dominant Path Prediction Model

This model combines both ray-tracing and empirical models by use of a trained neural network. The method is able to find the most dominant propagation paths to minimize the computation time spent on ray-tracing. The method can be used in modified forms for either indoor or outdoor urban scenarios [492].

The advantage of this method is it's speed. On the downside, it depends on the quality of the neural network to choose the correct dominant propagation paths. Compared to the other deterministic approaches, it is not as intuitive, introducing some kind of oracle to pick propagation paths. However, Wölfe et al. have shown to produce good results with this method, if the neural network is trained correctly.

11.9.2   Hybrid Ray-Tracing Models for Indoor and Outdoor Propagation

As was mentioned in Section 11.4.2, ray-tracing models are computationally very expensive and thus inappropriate for large scale simulations, as are usually used for calculating the coverage of a base station in a cellular network and use mainly empirical models calibrated for a specific country and area (see, for example, Chapter 11 of Parson's book [353] for details). However, cellular networks also have small cells, for specific areas of a town or malls, stadiums and other indoor areas with large concentration of users. In these cases, common model for cellular network are of little help and ray-tracing models are often used to calculate the received signal for a transmitting base station. Another application is the planning of WiFi coverage.

The ray-tracing models used in these cases often use empirical data to improve the accuracy of the model [353]. The derivation of the mathematical expressions that are used to model the effects of propagation phenomena on electromagnetic waves are full of assumptions that are often only partially valid for the real world. As a consequence, empirical correction factors are introduced in the models to calibrate them and improve their accuracy [353], one of the best examples of this being the correction of the prediction by the Uniform Theory of Diffraction (UTD) [117] for multiple edges.

11.10   Noise and Interference

Two major sources of *additive effects* are considered in general which potentially distort the signal. The first one is *noise*. Noise is always of stochastic nature and varies with time. It is denoted by $n(t)$.

The second effect corrupting the received signal is *interference*. Interference is caused by other RF transmitting electronic devices. As with the noise, interference has a stochastic nature and varies with time. It is denoted by $\sum_{\forall j} P_j^I(t) \cdot h_j^2(t)$ which indicates that interference is a sum of single sources of interference and is subject to channel effects much like the signal of interest itself (therefore, each interfering source is attenuated by a time-varying channel gain $h_j^2(t)$). Interference is either caused by other systems operating in the same frequency band in the case of unlicensed bands or caused by co- and adjacent-channel interference in licensed bands. *Co-channel interference* happens due to frequency re-utilization, for example in a cellular environment. *Adjacent channel interference* is due to bandpass filters which produce a small power interference in neighboring bands.

11.10.1   Noise

Noise is always present and comes from several sources, for example atmospheric disturbances, electronic circuitry, human-made machinery etc. The first two belong to the group of thermal noise sources, described in depth below. Noise produced by human-made sources is described in more detail in [60].

Thermal noise is due to the movement of charged particles inside electronic components existent in every receiver system and is therefore unavoidable. The characteristics of thermal noise were firstly studied for a resistor. It may be modeled as a zero-mean, wide sense stationary Gaussian stochastic process. The power spectral density of thermal noise can be obtained using the maximum power transfer theorem (Equation 11.37).

$$S = n_0/2 = k \cdot \mathcal{T} [\text{W/Hz}] \tag{11.37}$$

Here, $k = 1.37 \cdot 10^{-23} J/deg$ is the Boltzman constant and $\mathcal{T}$ refers to the temperature.

This kind of process is called white, i.e. thermal noise sources are modeled as having a flat power spectral density. It contains all frequencies, in analogy to white light, which contains all light frequencies. Accordingly, white noise is uncorrelated. However, in practical systems of limited bandwidth, the noise is filtered and is at the output no longer white, taking the shape of the filter's transfer function. This means that the noise becomes correlated when it is low-pass filtered. The noise power at the output of the filter depends on the filter's bandwidth (B). This average noise power at the output of the filter can be expressed as given in Equation 11.38.

$$\sigma^2 = g \cdot n_0 \cdot B \,, \tag{11.38}$$

where g is the power gain of the filter at the center frequency.

11.10.2   Interference

In general, the source of noise is a source which primarily does not intend to produce electromagnetic disturbance patterns, for example microwaves ovens or other electrical or electronic equipment. Another source of noise is given by the thermal effects existing, for example, in any electric circuit as in amplifiers.

Apart from these sources of signal distortion, other communication systems might be active in the environment. Such sources, which have the primary goal to produce electromagnetic radiation for communication purposes, are not represented by noise, instead they are represented by interference. Like noise, interference has an additive distorting impact on the signal. For example, interference occurs in cellular systems, due to the fact that bandwidth is limited and system operators have to reuse certain spectra of the overall bandwidth. Frequency planning is a traditional method to control interference in cellular systems. In unlicensed bands, interference may stem from local wireless networks, which just happen to be deployed quite close to each other. In general, there are different kinds of interference with a different impact on the received signal.

First there is *co-channel interference* [93]. Co-channel interference occurs if two trans- mission devices operating within the same radio frequency band are active and a receiver, originally trying to receive the signal from one transmitter also receives a significant signal from the second transmitter. In cellular systems co-channel interference is an important factor limiting the systems performance – more important than noise [93]. Determining the power level of the interfering signal can basically be done in the same manner as for the signal of interest. The interfering signal is subject to path loss, shadowing and fading. Hence, for modeling the interfering signal as much detail can be applied as for the signal of interest. As mentioned in Section 9.4, problems arise if the interference level varies for example during the transmission of a single packet. In this case, an *equivalent SINR* needs to be determined. This basically also applies to interference signals that overlap partially in frequency. If several interference sources contribute significantly to the SINR, one might assume for simplicity that the resulting overall interference power equals a constant average value.

Apart from co-channel interference there is also the possibility that transmissions conveyed on different but closely neighboring frequency bands cause significant interference in a receiver. This is mainly due to imperfect filters in the analog front-end (see Section 9.2) and it is called *adjacent channel interference* [383]. Adjacent channel interference is encountered in cellular systems as well as in unlicensed bands. In network simulation it is best accounted for via an equivalent SINR model, see Section 9.4. Therefore its impact is considered to be of constant power and its variable behavior over frequency and also over time is not taken into consideration.

11.11   Modeling the Antenna Impact

The *antenna* of a device transmits or receives the electromagnetic waves that carry the information to be exchanged between two or more devices. The (theoretically) simplest antenna, the so-called isotropic antenna, radiates the radio waves uniformly in each direction. It has no preferred direction of radiation. An isotropic antenna can be modeled by an additional gain at the transmitter and receiver (if both use such an antenna). Thus the RX power $P_{rx,A,B}$ of a transmission from station A to station B can be described as follows (in decibel):

$$P_{rx,A,B}[dB] = P_{tx,A} + h^2(t) + G_{Ant,A} + G_{Ant,B} \qquad (11.39)$$

where $P_{tx,A}$ is the transmit power of station A, $h^2(t)$ is the channel gain between A and B at time t, and $G_{Ant,A}$ and $G_{Ant,B}$ are the gains of the antennas at station A and B, respectively.

For the above case of two isotropic antennas the gain is negative or (theoretically) 0 dB at its best. The practical relevance however is very limited: Such a radiator exists only in theory as an ideal point source.

If an antenna does not radiate the radio waves uniformly it must have a preferred direction of radiation. Towards this preferred direction the antenna shows a positive gain. Consequently, towards other directions a negative gain or loss is unavoidable. The term "omni-directional antenna" is not to be confused with isotropic antenna. An omni-directional antenna radiates the radio waves equally within one plane (e.g. x-y-plane). In another plane (e.g. x-z-plane) however it has a preferred direction. The *gain of an antenna* towards a certain direction is specified as:

$$G(\theta, \phi) = \frac{I(\theta, \phi)}{P_{in}/4\pi} \qquad (11.40)$$

where θ and ϕ are the angles as specified in the spherical coordinate system, P_{in} is the total power at antenna input and $I(\theta, \phi)$ is the radiant intensity in this direction.

Typically an antenna does not radiate the total fed power P_{in}. The directivity is defined as

$$D(\theta, \phi) = \frac{I(\theta, \phi)}{P_{rad}/4\pi} \tag{11.41}$$

where P_{rad} is the total radiated power. Thus the antenna's directivity is always higher than its gain.

The antenna gain in equation 11.39 needs to be extended by an angle for azimuth and elevation:

$$P_{rx,A,B}[dB] = P_{tx,A} + h^2(t) + G_{Ant,A}(\theta, \phi) + G_{Ant,B}(\theta, \phi) \tag{11.42}$$

The gain or directivity that is used to characterize an antenna is the *maximum* gain or directivity the antenna provides in its preferred direction. The gain or directivity is given in dBi or dBd. dBi refers to the gain as compared to an isotropic antenna, where dBd refers to the gain as compared to a $\lambda/2$-dipole. The gain of an isotropic antenna is 0 dB in each direction. A $\lambda/2$-dipole is the simplest practical antenna. It provides a gain of 2.14 dBi in its preferred direction. Thus, an antenna can either be characterized to have x dBi gain or (x-2.14) dBd gain (e.g. either 5 dBi or 2.86 dBd) in its preferred direction.

Figure 11.14 shows the antenna pattern of a $\lambda/2$-dipole. The preferred direction of this antenna is along the z-axis. There it provides a maximum gain of 2.14 dBi. The gain degrades towards the xy-plane.

From the diagram in Figure 11.14 a 2-dimensional antenna model can be created. Such a model describes the antenna characteristic within the x-y-plane (which is most important). Thus it does not take the elevation θ into account.

3-dimensional antenna models are closer to reality than 2-dimensional models, although 2-dimensional models may be sufficient for certain investigations. Figure 11.15 depicts the antenna gain versus azimuth and elevation. Note that the diagram has been normalized to the antenna's directivity of 18 dBi.

To demonstrate the advantages of a 3-dimensional antenna model, a simulation with a receiver moving away from a sender along the main lobe has been performed. The sender uses a transmission power of 33 dBm. The antenna characteristic from Figure 11.15 was used. We only consider a path loss model between sender and receiver employing a modified Okumura-Hata-Model as available from UMTS 30.03:

$$h_{pl}^2[dB] = 40 \left(1 - 4 \cdot 10^{-3} \Delta h_b\right) \log(R) - 18 \log(\Delta h_b) + 21 \log(f) + 80\, dB \tag{11.43}$$

where

- R is the distance between mobile and base station in kilometers
- f is the carrier frequency of 2000 MHz

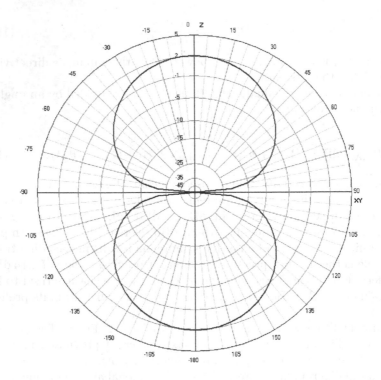

Fig. 11.14: Radiation pattern of $\lambda/2$-dipole

– Δh_b, the base station antenna height, in meters, measured from the average rooftop level, is assumed to be 15 m

Figure 11.16 shows the reception level at the moving station. The dashed curve is plotted for comparison with an isotropic antenna. The deep fades from 0 to 100 m result from the antenna characteristic. Remember that the station moves along the main lobe. Hence, the fades result only from taking the elevation into account. The expected gain of 18 dB is reached after 200 m.

Taking the antenna pattern into consideration in simulations of the wireless channel has the additional cost of the memory needed to store the antenna pattern and the computational effort necessary to lookup the desired value to use in the computation. The memory consumption of a 2-dimensional pattern with a resolution of 1 degree is

$$M_{2D} = 360 * 8\,\text{Byte} = 2880\,\text{Byte} \qquad (11.44)$$

assuming each value is stored as double with 8 Byte.

The memory consumption of a 3-dimensional pattern with the same resolution is then

$$M_{3D} = 180 * M_{2D} = 518400\,\text{Byte} \qquad (11.45)$$

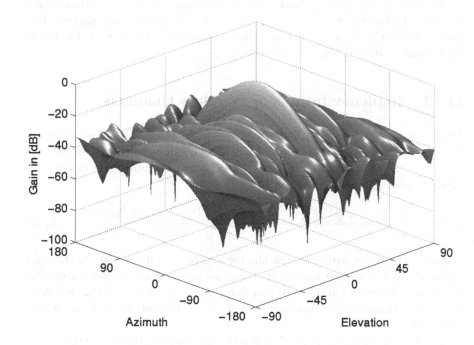

Fig. 11.15: 3-dimensional antenna characteristic

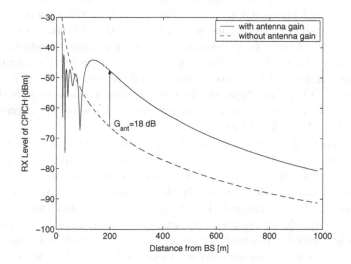

Fig. 11.16: RX level at receiver

approximately 0.5 MByte. Note that a 10 times higher resolution means 10 times higher memory consumption for the 2-dimensional pattern (approx. 0.028 MByte), but 100 times higher memory consumption for the 3-dimensional pattern (approx. 50 MByte).

11.12   Implementations of Wireless Channels

After having discussed the various ways of modeling the behavior of the wireless channel, we present in this section an implementation method for the simulation of the wireless channel. The presented approach considers the SNR as defined below in Equation 11.46.

$$\gamma = \frac{P_0(t)}{n^2(t)} = \frac{h^2(t) \cdot P_{\text{tx}}(t)}{n^2(t)} = \frac{h_{\text{pl}}^2(t) \cdot h_{\text{sh}}^2(t) \cdot h_{\text{fad}}^2(t) \cdot P_{\text{tx}}(t)}{n^{(t)}} \tag{11.46}$$

Hence, we take the path loss, the shadowing, the fading as well as the noise into account. Let us first assume that we consider a single-carrier system (i.e. we are only interested in the SNR of a single wireless channel). In the following we step through each component and discuss different ways of generating these values.

Let us start with the noise. Noise is often simulated by just considering a fixed power threshold which is constant over time. In reality it varies strongly over time. However, these variations are very fast and the simulation of these variations is only required if a system behavior on this small time scale is considered (typically in the range of μs for bit-true simulation models of the PHY layer, see Sections 9.3 and 9.4). For example, if the gain and transmit power stay constant over a time span of 1 ms, the difference between the bit error rate obtained from assuming a constant noise threshold and the bit error rate obtained from modeling a varying noise level is negligible, if the constant impact of the noise is determined correctly (taking the average noise power). Therefore, typically in network simulations we substitute in Equation 11.46 the instantaneous noise power $n^2(t)$ with the average noise power σ^2 from Equation 11.38

The impact due to the gain can be decomposed into three different elements, as described by Equation 11.2, which can be added after being independently generated according to the model chosen for each of them. For the impact of the path loss, primarily the distance between transmitter and receiver has to be determined. This is done by a mobility model (see Section 14) if terminals are assumed to roam. Otherwise, a static distance value has to be generated. Once each terminal is associated with a certain distance to the transmitter, a homogeneous path loss model according to Section 11.5 can be assumed, yielding the path loss for each terminal. As the terminals do not roam, the path loss is constant. In order to generate such a value, the parameterized path loss model must be implemented which is usually straightforward.

The impact due to shadowing is stochastic, in contrast to the impact due to path loss. Shadowing varies as objects within the propagation environment move and circumstances change. Hence, in order to determine a value for the shadowing a certain distribution has to be assumed and then values have to be drawn from it, as was seen in Section 11.6. Notice that these values can be required to be correlated in time or in space. If they are required to be correlated in space, the sample at distance r (calculated according to the mobility model $r = v \cdot t$) should have a shadowing gain calculated according to Equation 11.23.

Instead of assuming a separate model for path loss and shadowing, ray-tracing approaches allow a deterministic calculation of the combined impact of path loss and shadowing on the gain. A further advantage is that they compute these values from a map or a somewhat realistic characterization of the environment. On the other hand, this requires the mobility model to take the area description into account. Furthermore, ray-tracing approaches are computationally more expensive than the combination of a empirical path loss model plus a stochastic shadowing model.

The last factor regarding the gain is the fading. Fading is a stochastic element of the gain and varies on rather short time scales. Apart from being time selective, it is also frequency selective (depending on the considered bandwidth). This is in contrast to path loss and shadowing, which are both not frequency selective (unless rather large bandwidths > 100 MHz are considered). In order to model fading, one first has to decide on the scale of variability that should be taken into account. For example, for the time dimension one can model the fading statically, i.e. a single fading coefficient is generated and kept constant during the entire simulated time. This corresponds to a *static channel model*. In contrast, one can consider a variable fading coefficient, drawing one coefficient per transmitted packet. This model is termed a *block fading model* in contrast. In both cases, a common model for the first-order statistics of the envelope of the received signal is the Rayleigh distribution (as the SNR is of interest, the square of the envelope has a χ^2 distribution). Hence, in order to determine the fading component one can simply draw a random variate from the exponential distribution each time a new SNR value is required (either for the static or for the block-fading model). However, this leads to a quite strong variation of the fading component over short periods of time for the block-fading model as the fading samples are assumed to be uncorrelated (depending of course on the implementation of the random number generator for the exponential distribution function considered). In reality, fading can change its state quite rapidly but there is some correlation in time that governs the behavior. In order to take this into account for the block-fading model, a second-order statistical model must be implemented. A common model for this is a Jakes-distributed power spectrum to characterize the correlation in time. A common implementation for such correlated fading processes in time is the method of Rice [347]. This method employs the sum of sinusoids which are parameterized properly to achieve the statistical characteristics of interest. While these methods can be used to generate fading processes that are correlated in time [351] as well as processes that are correlated in time and frequency [485], it has to be mentioned that these methods require a very careful parameterization in order to achieve the desired characteristics especially regarding the correlation (in time or frequency).

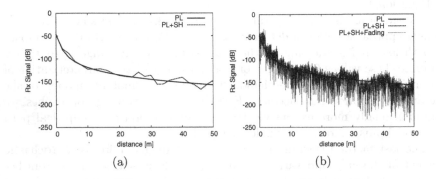

(a)   (b)

Fig. 11.17: Example of modeled received signal subject to the different components of channel gain: path loss (PL), shadowing (SH) and multipath fading.

Figure 11.12 shows the superposition of pathloss gain h_{pl}^2, shadowing gain h_{sh}^2 and fast fading h_{fad}^2, generated according to the free-space path loss, space-correlated shadowing and Rice method for fast fading, respectively, for a receiver moving away from the transmitter along a radial trajectory.

Some of the above mentioned models and their implementations for path loss, shadowing and fading are available in the simulation tool ChSim for Omnet++ maintained by the University of Paderborn.

In the following, we also present briefly some channel models that are used in standardization. These models mainly provide parameters for the previously mentioned models for path loss, shadowing and fading. In detail, we present models and parameters for IEEE 802.11, IEEE 802.16 and 3GPP LTE.

11.12.1   Channel Parameters used in Standardization - IEEE 802.11

In the following we discuss channel models used in the standardization process of IEEE 802.11n. They are split into SISO and MIMO types. All of them specify the behavior with respect to path loss, shadowing and fading. The SISO models are first mentioned in the work of Medbo [231] and are divided into five different models (A to E), while the MIMO ones extend previous work and consider six different models (A to F). In this case, the new set of models were introduced due to its enhanced accuracy to represent smaller environments, such as homes and small offices. Their classification is shown in Table 11.2.

The MIMO channel model employed in order to characterize the fading is based on the cluster modeling approach introduced by Saleh and Valenzuela [398]. This method basically groups the scatterers into different clusters, whose number depends on the considered scenario's type. While in the SISO channel model a clustering in time is performed, in a MIMO channel model the clustering considers time and angle properties of the incoming signals. In indoor environments the number of clusters typically varies between one and seven [137]. The signal copies coming from each cluster are called *taps*. These taps are assumed to follow an exponential decaying power delay profile and to be time-equidistant within a certain cluster. Furthermore the taps of a cluster share the same *angle of arrival* (AoA), *angle of departure* (AoD) and *angular spread* (AS) (variance of the power angular spectrum). The detailed methodology used to convert the reference SISO channel model [231] into a valid MIMO channel model can be found in [137]. This work also provides the chosen values for the tabs' power and delay, AoA, AoD and AS for the MIMO A to F channel models.

Model	Environment	Line of Sight
A	Flat Fading	LOS / NLOS
B	Residential	LOS ($K = 0$) / NLOS
C	Small Office	LOS ($K = 0$) / NLOS
D	Office	LOS ($K = 3$) / NLOS
E	Large Open Space / Office	LOS ($K = 6$) / NLOS
F	Large Open Space	LOS ($K = 6$) / NLOS

Table 11.2: MIMO Channel Models Classification

The model details regarding path loss, shadowing and fading are presented as follows.

Path Loss. For path loss a so-called break point is introduced. For distances lower than the break point distance d_{BP} a different model is used than for distances that are larger. Precisely, for any distance below the break point the path loss due to free space propagation models is assumed with a path loss exponent of 2. For distances larger than the break point, the following formula is used:

$$h_{\mathrm{PL}}^2[\mathrm{dB}] = 10 \cdot \log_{10} \left(\frac{\lambda}{4\pi d_{\mathrm{BP}}} \right)^2 + 35 \cdot \log_{10}(d/d_{\mathrm{BP}}) \qquad (11.47)$$

Hence, after the break point a path loss exponent of 3.5 is used. The values for the break points are given below in Table 11.3.

Shadowing. As with the path loss, different models are assumed for the shadowing depending on the considered distance in comparison to the break point. In general, the shadowing is assumed to be log-normal distributed without spatial correlation. Up to the break point distance the log-normal distribution is assumed to have a standard deviation of 3. For larger distances, the shadowing standard deviation takes on different values according to the considered model (A-F). Table 11.3 specifies the exact values.

Fading. In the MIMO channel models, fading is divided into LOS (Rician-distributed signal envelopes) and NLOS (Rayleigh-distributed signal envelopes) model, depending on whether the distance between transmitter and receiver is below the break point distance or above, respectively. The corresponding Rician k-factor for the LOS model is shown in Table 11.2. Different values are assumed for the root-mean square of the delay spread (assuming an exponentially distributed power delay profile). Table 11.3 holds the corresponding values for the different channel models. For the fading characterization in time a bell-shaped power spectrum density is assumed (in contrast to a Jakes power spectrum). For channel models A-E a maximum Doppler shift of approximately 3 Hz at 2.4 GHz is assumed while the value doubles for the 5 GHz band. Channel model F assumes in addition a power spike resulting from a car driving with 40 km/h which yields a modified bell-shape power spectrum. Further information about the channel models used in IEEE 802.11n can be found in [137].

Model	$d_{\mathrm{BP}}[m]$	Shadowing STD after d_{BP}	RMS Delay Spread [ns]
A	5	4	0
B	5	4	15
C	5	5	30
D	10	5	50
E	20	6	100
F	30	6	150

Table 11.3: Parameters for channel models of IEEE 802.11n

11.12.2   Channel Parameters used in Standardization – 3GPP Long Term Evolution

The channel model used in LTE simulations is based on the 3GPP guidelines found in [332, 331]. More precisely, the 6-ray Typical Urban channel model is assumed [332, p. 123] for non-MIMO simulations for all bandwidth modes.

Path Loss. In case of LTE, two different cell types are regarded, macro-cells and micro-cells. The distance dependent path loss d meters away from the base station can be computed by choosing the appropriate formula from Table 11.4. It consists of a path loss component and a penetration loss component. Macro-cells can be characterized by a cell diameter of more than 500 m, whereas micro-cells have a diameter of less than approximately 150 m. For a more detailed list refer to [332, p. 120ff].

Environment	Modeling approach	
Macro-cell	Application:	Urban / suburban macro-cells
	Setting:	$h2_{\text{pen}} = 20$ dB, $v_{\text{max}} < 350\frac{\text{km}}{\text{h}}$
	Basic model:	
	Formula: $h2_{\text{PL}}[\text{dB}] = 15.3 + h2_{\text{pen}} + 37.6\log(d)$	
Micro-cell	Application:	Urban micro-cell
	Setting:	$v_{\text{max}} < 30\frac{\text{km}}{\text{h}}$
	Basic model:	Outdoor to indoor
	Formula: $h2_{\text{PL}}[\text{dB}] = 7 + 56\log(d)$	
	Basic model:	Outdoor to outdoor
	Formula: $h2_{\text{PL}}[\text{dB}] = 39 + 20\log(d)$ for $10 < d \le 45$m	
	$-39 + 67\log(d)$ for $d > 45$m	

Table 11.4: Parameters for 3GPP LTE channel path loss models

Shadowing. In case of the macro-cell scenario, shadowing is assumed to follow a log-normal distribution with a standard deviation of 8 dB, and to possess a correlation distance of 50 m. Furthermore, a shadowing correlation between cells (factor of 0.5) and sectors (factor of 1.0) is modeled. In case of micro-cells, the standard deviation is set to 10 dB with a correlation distance of 10 m for outdoor to indoor and 25 m for outdoor to outdoor, while the correlation between adjacent cells and sectors is neglected.

Fading. According to the 3GPP Typical Urban channel model, the received signal is assumed to be made up of a multitude of single signal components traveling along different paths. None of these components is dominant leading to Rayleigh-distributed envelopes. The channel is modeled based on a WSSUS approach. Thus, the Doppler spectrum and the average delay profile (median root-mean-square delay spread of 0.5μs) needs to be determined. The model provides a certain, discrete number of taps for each of which an average delay and an average power is provided. The set of proposed parameters is given in Table 11.5.

Moreover, the Rayleigh-distributed envelope is modified with respect to the Doppler spectrum. In the context of LTE, the classical Doppler power spectrum density (also known as Jakes' spectrum) is commonly used:

Tap number	Average delay [ns]	Average relative power [dB]
1	0 m	−3.0
2	200 m	0.0
3	500 m	−2.0
4	1600 m	−6.0
5	2300 m	−8.0
6	5000 m	−10.0

Table 11.5: Parameters for 3GPP LTE channel fading model

$$S(f) = \frac{1}{\pi f_d \sqrt{1 - \left(\frac{f}{f_d}\right)2}} \quad \text{with} \quad f \in \,]-f_d, f_d[\qquad (11.48)$$

where $f_d = \frac{v}{\lambda}$ is the maximum Doppler shift for a receiver traveling at a fixed speed v and a signal of wavelength λ.

11.12.3   Channel Parameters used in Standardization – IEEE 802.16a/e

The channel modeling in case of a IEEE 802.16a/e based system resorts to the consideration of different cell sizes – namely macro-cell ($r > 1000$ m), micro-cell (100 m $< r < 1000$ m), pico-cell ($r < 100$ m) – and different mobility scenarios [180]. The mobility scenarios encompass two recommended ITU-T models, namely the Pedestrian-B and Vehicular-A model [211]. Also the ITU-T Pedestrian-A model could be used, offering a smaller frequency selectivity due to a smaller number of paths.

Path Loss. The path loss models depend on the considered environment. The respective information is provided in Table 11.6. In case of the formulas, d corresponds to the distance between the BS and the MS in meter, f_c to the carrier frequency in MHz, h_b and h_m to the antenna heights (in meter) of the BS and the MS, respectively, h_s to the height of the surrounding buildings in meter, and n is an environment-dependent parameter.

Shadowing. Shadowing is modeled via a log-normal distribution. The proposed parameters depend on the considered environment and are listed in Table 11.7. Furthermore, the IEEE 802.16 working group also proposes one alternative, common modeling approach for shadowing encompassing a standard deviation of 8 dB, a spatial correlation of 50 m and a correlation of 0.5 between sectors of different cells and 1.0 between sectors of the same cell.

Fading. The expected mobility determines the fading model parameters which is based on the ITU-T recommendations. One possible set of parameters is given in Table 11.8, where A.r.p. means average relative power in [dB], and A.d. means average delay in [ns]. For a more comprehensive set refer

Environment	Modeling approach	
Macro-cell	Application:	Urban macro-cells
		Suburban macro-cells
		($n \mathrel{\hat{=}}$ correction term for type of city)
	Setting:	150 MHz $\leq f_c \leq$ 1500 MHz,
		1000 m $\leq d \leq$ 20000 m,
		1 m $\leq h_m \leq$ 10 m, 30m $\leq h_b \leq$ 200m
	Basic model:	Okumura-Hata
	Formula: $h2_{\mathrm{PL}}[\mathrm{dB}] = (44.9 - 6.55\log(h_b)) \cdot \log\left(\frac{d}{1000}\right) - n$ $+ 26.16\log(f_c) - 13.82\log(h_b) + 69.55$	
Micro-cell	Application:	Urban micro-cell
	Setting:	800 MHz $\leq f_c \leq$ 2000 MHz,
		20 m $\leq d \leq$ 5000 m,
		1 m $\leq h_m \leq$ 3 m, 4m $\leq h_b \leq$ 50m
	Basic model:	Walfish-Ikegami NLOS
	Formula: $h2_{\mathrm{PL}}[\mathrm{dB}]$:	Equation 11.19
	Basic model:	Walfish-Ikegami LOS
	Formula: $h2_{\mathrm{PL}}[\mathrm{dB}] = 20\log(f_c) + 26\log(d) - 35.4$	
Pico-cell	Application:	Indoor pico-cell
		($n \mathrel{\hat{=}}$ number of penetrated floors)
	Basic model:	COST231 based Indoor model
	Formula: $h2_{\mathrm{PL}}[\mathrm{dB}] = 37 + 30\log(d) + 18.3 \cdot n^{\left(\frac{n+2}{n+1} - 0.46\right)}$	

Table 11.6: Parameters for IEEE 802.16e channel path loss models

Environment	Shadowing	
Macro-cell	*Basic model*:	Outdoor
	Standard Deviation:	10 dB
Micro-cell	*Basic model*:	Outdoor
	Standard Deviation:	10 dB
	Basic model:	Indoor
	Standard Deviation:	10 dB
Pico-cell	*Basic model*:	Indoor
	Standard Deviation:	12 dB

Table 11.7: Parameters for IEEE 802.16e channel shadowing models

to [211]. Basically, it is assumed that the signal envelope is Rayleigh and/or Rician-distributed for lower velocities. Equivalently, the Doppler spectrum is defined as in Equation 11.48.

Tap number	Pedestrian - B		Vehicular - A	
	6 paths, $\leq 3\frac{km}{h}$		6 paths, $30\frac{km}{h}$	
	A.r.p.	A.d.	A.r.p.	A.d.
1	0	0	0	0
2	−1	300	−1	200
3	−9	700	−5	800
4	−10	1100	−8	1200
5	−15	1700	−7.8	2300
6	−20	2500	−24	3700

Table 11.8: Power delay profiles for IEEE 802.16e systems

12. Selected System Models

F. Schmidt-Eisenlohr (Karlsruhe Institute of Technology (KIT))
O. Puñal, K. Klagges (RWTH Aachen University)
M. Kirsche (Brandenburg University of Technology Cottbus (BTU))

Apart from the general issue of modeling the channel, the PHY and the MAC of wireless networks, there are specific modeling assumptions that are considered for different systems. In this chapter we consider three specific wireless standards and highlight modeling options for them. These are IEEE 802.11 (as example for wireless local area networks), IEEE 802.16 (as example for wireless metropolitan networks) and IEEE 802.15 (as example for body area networks). Each section on these three systems discusses also at the end a set of model implementations that are available today.

12.1 IEEE 802.11 (WLAN)

The popularization of Internet during the 90's and the establishment in the market of notebook computers were responsible for the growing interest in mobile computing and mobile Internet access. These services could not be offered by means of a cable-based connection. Therefore, several companies that had identified there a market niche, started to offer wireless solutions. However, since there had been no agreement on how to design those solutions, most of them were incompatible with each other. A unified criterion was required and IEEE took the responsibility of setting up a *wireless LAN standard* from scratch. That standard had to provide the same set of services provided by wired systems (reliable data delivery, high transmission rates and continuous connection). The major challenge, though, was that it had to succeed in a wireless manner. The standard they came up with was named *IEEE 802.11* and first released in 1997. It specified the MAC and three different *PHYs*, namely Infrared (IR), Frequency Hopping Spread Spectrum and Direct Sequence Spread Spectrum. Operating in the 2.4 GHz frequency band, all three PHYs supported both 1 Mbps and 2 Mbps transmission rates.

As a reaction to the growing throughput demands, the standard was extended in 1999. The main improvements took place at the PHY, where two new PHYs were standardized. In the 2.4 GHz band, *IEEE 802.11b* extended the Direct Sequence Spread Spectrum (DSSS) PHY, by means of the Complementary Code Keying (CCK) modulation, to provide data rates up to 11 Mbps. *IEEE 802.11a*, which was defined in the 5 GHz band offers transmission rates up to 54 Mbps by employing *OFDM* and highly efficient modulation types. In 2003, *IEEE 802.11g* was released maintaining backward compatibility with IEEE 802.11b in the 2.4 GHz band, while at the same time using the IEEE 802.11a OFDM PHY to reach the throughput offered by the latter. Over the years new standard amendments have been developed to provide extra services and functionalities that were lacking in the first versions. Some examples are *IEEE 802.11e* offering Quality-of-Service, IEEE 802.11i offering extra security enhancements and IEEE 802.11h featuring dynamic frequency selection and transmit power control. Upcoming standards, whose progress can be followed at the official IEEE 802.11 working group's project website [208], aim at extending features and especially at providing larger throughput. Currently in finalization, *IEEE 802.11n* is expected to deliver a MAC throughput of 100 Mbps, corresponding to PHY rates of about 600 Mbps by means of Multiple-Input-Multiple-Output (MIMO) transmission techniques, channel bonding, and extended MAC protocol functionalities, among others. Currently at their initial phase, IEEE 802.11ac and IEEE 802.11ad strive for the goal of even higher throughput (1 Gbps) at the bands below 6 GHz and at 60 GHz, respectively. In the following the reference model that underlies all IEEE 802.11 amendments will be presented in more detail. The current version of the standard is [15] and a more detailed description of the standard can be found, e.g. in [174], [339].

12.1.1   System Reference Model

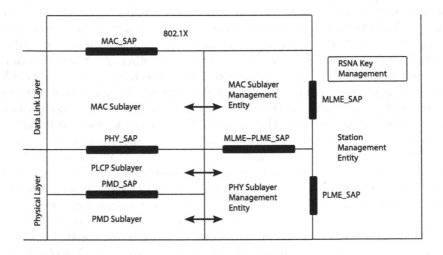

Fig. 12.1: IEEE 802.11 reference model [15]

Figure 12.1 shows the IEEE 802.11 reference model. Since the standard defines only physical and MAC layers, these are the *protocol stack* levels represented in the model. It is important to note that the reference model has mainly illustration purposes for a proper understanding of the inner structure and the requirements when developing or discussing the standard.

The functional blocks of the model are interconnected over a set of Service Access Points (SAPs), each defining several service primitives. The stack is separated into different functional layers and each layer is again separated into functional and management entities. Wireless communication is done throughout the blocks shown in the left column of the figure. The MAC sublayer includes all the functionalities to access the medium in a coordinated way while the two underlying PHY sub-layers, Physical Layer Convergence Procedure (PLCP) and Physical Medium Dependent (PMD), provide the functionality to transmit and receive the frames generated by the MAC over the wireless medium. Specifically, the PLCP sublayer enables the interaction and compatibility between MAC and the corresponding PHY. On the other hand, the PMD sublayer enables wireless transmission and reception of data and specifies which of the different available PHY s are being used. The management architecture of 802.11 consists of three different management entities as shown in Figure 12.1, namely the *MAC Layer Management Entity* (MLME), the *Physical Layer Management Entity* (PLME) and the *Station Management Entity* (SME). The latter is intentionally not defined in depth in the standard, since it is an implementation dependent structure and there is no need to have a unified definition. The first two entities contain the *Management Information Bases* (MIBs), which have all the necessary information to manage the functionality of a wireless station.

12.1.2 Physical Layer

The Physical Layer is the first layer of the OSI stack model. As stated previously, the current version of the IEEE 802.11 standard defines several PHYs. All specified PHYs are divided into two sub-layers, namely the *Physical Layer Convergence Procedure* and the *Physical Medium Dependent* sub-layers. The PLCP sublayer deals with all media-independent elements (like frame structure including preamble, header and trailer) and any processing steps during transmission (like scrambling, encoding, interleaving, modulation). It is also responsible for the frame exchange between the MAC layer (second layer of the OSI) and the PHY. On the other hand, the PMD sublayer is responsible for actually transmitting the data symbols over the wireless medium, respecting the frequency specific regulations like transmit power, spectrum mask and acceptable tolerances. On receiver side PMD forwards the symbols up to the PLCP sublayer, and provides CCA notification, i.e. the indication of transmission activity on the wireless medium. The most relevant PHY implementations are briefly described below. Special emphasis is placed on the *OFDM PHY* implementation.

Frequency Hopping Physical Layer

Frequency Hopping Spread Spectrum (FHSS) is one of the physical layers that was already defined in the original IEEE 802.11 standard. The available bandwidth is mapped into several frequency slots and one of the specified hopping sequences is selected for frame transmission, i.e. during the transmission, the frequency on which frames are coded switches after the duration of a defined time slot. Several hopping sequences can be combined to a set of orthogonal hopping sequences that can be used in parallel. The use of frequency hopping mitigates interference effects that may occur on only one of the frequency slots, i.e. the influence of frequency selective fading should be reduced. FHSS in IEEE 802.11 allows a data rate of 1 or 2 Mbps.

Direct Sequence Physical Layer

In *DSSS* a single frequency is used for data transmission. Again in order to overcome frequency selective fading, any data symbol is spread over a chipping sequence of 11 bits, i.e. a '0' is transmitted as a fixed combination of chips, while a '1' is transmitted as the reverse sequence. To encode these symbols Differential Phase Shift Keying (DPSK) is used, i.e. phase shifts define whether the next symbol is a '0' or a '1'. in the most simple case, if the next symbol is a '0' there is no phase shift, and if the next symbol is a '1' there is a 180° phase shift. 1 or 2 Mbps are reached with this technique in IEEE 802.11. Higher data rates up to 11 Mbps can be reached when using the PHY extension defined in IEEE 802.11b.

OFDM Physical Layer

The concept behind OFDM is already known for more than 40 years [94]. However, it was not until the mid 90's that OFDM started to be implemented in practice, e.g. in *Digital Audio Broadcasting* (DAB), *Digital Video Broadcasting Terrestrial* (DVB-T) and *Asymmetric Digital Subscriber Line* (ADSL), among others. OFDM is a transmission and modulation technique, although it can also be considered as a multiplexing technique. It extends the concept of single carrier modulation by splitting the total system's bandwidth into multiple sub-channels also known as *sub-carriers*, on which information is transmitted at the same time in a parallel manner. These sub-carriers are designed to be orthogonal to each other, i.e. at the center frequency of each sub-carrier the transmissions of all other sub-carriers do not contribute to its waveform, which frees the system from *Inter-carrier Interference (ICI)*.

The orthogonality is achieved by using a rectangular pulse of symbol time T for the transmission of each sub-carrier. By means of an Inverse Fast Fourier Transform (IFFT) the rectangular pulse is transformed into a *sinc* function in the frequency domain. This function has the characteristic of presenting zero amplitude at all frequencies, which are integer multiples of $1/T$. Choosing the carrier frequencies to be separated from the adjacent ones exactly by $1/T$ guarantees orthogonality in the system. In addition, since every single sub-carrier uses a narrow bandwidth compared to the total system's bandwidth, the sub-carrier symbol time becomes larger. This reduces the vulnerability of the system against far-echoed copies of the transmitted signals inherent to multi-path propagation environments. This robustness against the so-called *ISI* is one of the main benefits of OFDM. However, ISI may still appear and degrade the performance. For further mitigating these effects, redundancy is added at the beginning of each symbol in form of a *Cyclic Prefix*.

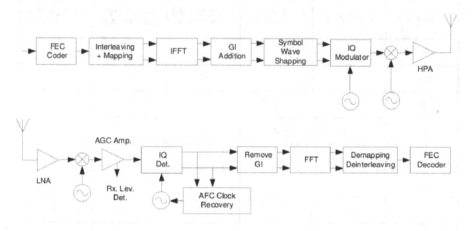

Fig. 12.2: OFDM transmitter and receiver chain [15]

The OFDM PHY is currently used in the IEEE 802.11a and IEEE 802.11g amendments and will further be used in the upcoming IEEE 802.11n. The first two split their 20 MHz wide channel into 52 sub-carriers (4 pilot and 48 payload sub-carriers). Then, data bits are scrambled, redundantly encoded by means of *convolutional coding*, interleaved and then spread over 48 of the sub-carriers so that the probability of error bursts is reduced and hence, the probability of a successful frame reception increases. Please refer to Figure 12.2 for a schematic representation of the OFDM transceiver chain. Each sub-carrier transmits at a fixed baud rate of $2.5 \cdot 10^5$ symbols per second (with a symbol time of $4\mu s$). On each symbol a certain number of bits is transmitted using different modulation schemes, such as BPSK, QPSK, 16-QAM and 64-QAM. The resulting transmission rates are shown in Figure 12.3. The complex symbols of all sub-carriers are converted into time

domain using an IFFT. After the addition of the cyclic prefix and the IQ
modulation, the resulting signal is transmitted over the air. At the receiver
side the complex symbols of the sub-carriers are recovered by applying a Fast
Fourier Transform (FFT).

The PHY Protocol Data Unit, whose structure is depicted in Figure 12.4,
is the frame format at the PLCP sublayer. This frame consists of a PLCP
preamble, control information fields and a Data field. The PLCP preamble
($16\mu s$ long), consisting of long and short training sequences, is used by the
receiver to obtain a channel estimate, necessary to recover the transmitted
symbols. In addition, it is used by the receiver to acquire the signal and
to synchronize the demodulator. The control fields ($4\mu s$ long) are transmitted at the base rate (BPSK with convolutional rate $R = 1/2$) and deliver
information about the rate and the length of the payload data.

MODULATION	CODING RATE	CODED BITS PER SUBCARRIER	CODED BITS PER OFDM SYMBOL	DATA BITS PER OFDM SYMBOL	DATA RATE (Mbps) (20 MHz bandwidth)
BPSK	1/2	1	48	24	6
BPSK	3/4	1	48	36	9
QPSK	1/2	2	96	48	12
QPSK	3/4	2	96	72	18
16-QAM	1/2	4	192	96	24
16-QAM	3/4	4	192	144	36
64-QAM	2/3	6	288	192	48
64-QAM	3/4	6	288	216	54

Fig. 12.3: IEEE 802.11 a/g PHY modes [15]

Channelization in OFDM Based WLANs. The frequency band, the
number of *available channels* and bandwidth of those channels depend on
various aspects. IEEE 802.11a operates in the 5 GHz band. Within this band
there are four different sub-bands intended for WLAN transmission, which
are placed within 5.150 GHz and 5.825 GHz where 23 different channels each
being 20 MHz wide are supported. The usage of these frequencies varies depending on the country, e.g. the *U-NII upper* band, ranging from 5.725 GHz
to 5.825 GHz, is a sub-band exclusively used in the United States. The carrier
frequencies of adjacent channels are separated by 20 MHz and the specifications of the standard indicate that in order to minimize adjacent channel

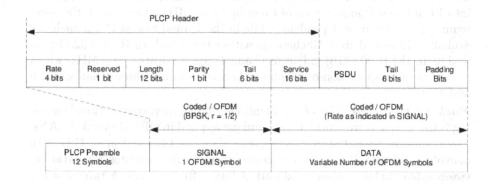

Fig. 12.4: OFDM PPDU frame format [15]

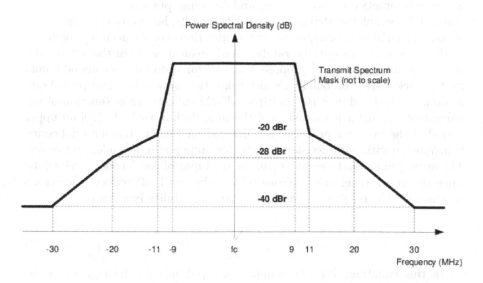

Fig. 12.5: IEEE 802.11a/g spectral mask [15]

interference, the power of a channel detected at the carrier frequency of an adjacent one should be attenuated at least by 28 dB as depicted by Figure 12.5. IEEE 802.11g operates in the 2.4 GHz band, which is broken down into 14 different channels each of them being 22 MHz wide. Again, the spectrum usage is country dependent, while in the United States 11 channels are available, Europe defines 13 channels within this band. In IEEE 802.11g (as well as in IEEE 802.11b), adjacent channels are separated by 5 MHz, which limits the number of non-overlapping channels to only three (channels 1, 6 and 11).

Packet Error Rate Model. As mentioned previously, convolutional encoding is the forward error correction technique applied in OFDM based WLANs. The coding is generated by the polynomials $g_0 = 133_8$ and $g_1 = 171_8$ with convolutional rate $R = 1/2$. The convolutional rate indicates the ratio between input (before coding) and output bits (after coding). A rate $R = 1/2$ means that for every information bit entering the encoder, two bits are present at its output. This effectively reduces the throughput efficiency, since half of the payload bits transmitted are redundant. On the other hand, it increases the robustness of the system. Higher rates, thus more efficient and less robust, are achieved by means of puncturing. This mechanism consists of removing some of the parity bits after encoding. The punctured convolutional rates used in the current WLAN standard are $R = 2/3$ and $R = 3/4$, although IEEE 802.11n will allow a higher one, namely $R = 5/6$. Viterbi algorithms are used in practice for both coding and decoding purposes.

Any WLAN simulator, that aims at realistic results, has to consider the effects of convolutional (de)coding on the error rate. However, an accurate modeling of the error rate can only be rarely found, even in state-of-the art simulators. The authors in [179] propose a *model* for obtaining an upper bound for the packet error probability, which takes the average bit error probability as input (calculated over the multiple OFDM subcarriers as function of the individual channel attenuations and the modulation used). In [70] an upper bound of the bit error probability is derived for binary convolutional coded transmission with hard-decision Viterbi decoding and independent bit errors. The assumption of independent errors at the input of the decoder can be done since the interleaving block (please refer to Figure 12.2) reduces the error's correlation. The resulting (coded) bit-error probability is given by:

$$P_{bit} \leq \frac{1}{k} \cdot \sum_{d=d_{free}}^{\infty} c_d \cdot P_d \qquad (12.1)$$

In this equation, k is the number of input bits to the register of the convolutional encoder, d_{free} is the free distance of the convolutional code, P_d is the probability that an incorrect path of distance d is chosen and c_d is the number of bits in error. The values for c_d can be obtained from diverse publications, such as [159] for the rate $R = 1/2$ and [190] for the punctured rates $R = 2/3$ and $R = 3/4$. Then, P_d can be upper bounded as given by:

$$P_d \leq (2 \cdot \sqrt{\beta \cdot (1 - \beta)})^d, \tag{12.2}$$

where β corresponds to the averaged uncoded bit error probability. In order to obtain this error probability per sub-carrier, the formulas in [100] for the BPSK, QPSK, 16-QAM and 64-QAM modulations under additive white Gaussian noise can be used. Given the bound on the resulting bit error probability P_b, we can obtain the Packet Error Rate for a packet of size ς bits by:

$$PER \leq 1 - (1 - P_{bit})^\varsigma \tag{12.3}$$

The upper bound given by Equation 12.3 is accurate and considerably tight for low input bit error rate (uncoded β), however it loses its precision under higher values (0.001 and higher). This divergence supposes an overestimation of the coded bit error probability (P_{bit}) and, consequently, of the packet error rate. We propose a correction of the bound by introducing a scaling factor to the coded bit error probability, which is obtained by Lagrange interpolation of the factors obtained from (exact) simulated values for selected uncoded bit error probability. For the purpose of simulating exact coded bit error probability given a certain convolutional code, MATLAB's Communication Toolbox can be used.

12.1.3   LLC/MAC

The LLC and MAC layer is commonly defined for all variants of IEEE 802.11, and different options are provided. The LLC functionality of IEEE 802.11 includes packet segmentation and reassembly (by packet fragmentation) and backward error correction (by acknowledgment and retransmissions). Concerning MAC three variants are currently defined: Point Coordination Function (PCF), DCF and Hybrid Coordination Function (HCF).

Frames and Frame Exchange

All IEEE 802.11 MAC *frames* have a unified principal structure that is shown in Figure 12.6, from which individual frame types are derived. Each frame starts with a header sequence that contains all important information on the frame. The first two bytes contain the frame control field (see Figure 12.7), in which are included the information on the type and subtype of the frame and several status and control bits related to the frame. The header further includes a field indicating the full duration of the frame exchange, the *Network Allocation Vector (NAV)*. The field explicitly reserves the channel for the complete frame exchange sequence and thus influences the MAC mechanism. The following address fields vary in number and meaning depending on the frame type, but typically represent transmitter, receiver, and the Basic Service Set, an identifier that groups together a set of wireless stations associated to the same network. Quality of service information is included in the header as well. The header is followed by the actual payload that is transmitted. The frame is finalized by a trailer that contains a Frame Control Sequence (FCS), i.e. a CRC checksum to identify errors in the frame that occurred during the transmission.

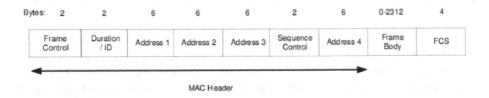

Bytes: 2   2   6   6   6   2   6   0-2312   4

| Frame Control | Duration / ID | Address 1 | Address 2 | Address 3 | Sequence Control | Address 4 | Frame Body | FCS |

MAC Header

Fig. 12.6: IEEE 802.11 MAC frame structure [15]

Bits: 2   2   4   1   1   1   1   1   1   1   1

| Protocol Version | Type | Subtype | To DS | From DS | More Fragments | Retry | Power Mgmt | More Data | Protected Frame | Order |

Fig. 12.7: IEEE 802.11 MAC frame control field [15]

Frames are exchanged with Layer 2 acknowledgments, i.e. the receiver of a unicast data frame sends back an acknowledgment frame after a defined duration, called SIFS. If a transmitter cannot successfully receive the ACK within this time, it reschedules the transmission until a defined maximum number of retransmissions is reached, afterwards the frame transmission is considered unsuccessful. For broadcast transmissions, in contrast, there is no acknowledgment scheme.

In order to reduce interferences and packet collisions caused by the *hidden terminal* problem, an additional *RTS/CTS* exchange preceding the transmission of the data frame is a possible option. The transmitter of a message first sends a short RTS control frame, the receiver replies with a CTS frame. Ideally, after this exchange of control packets all nodes that may possibly interfere the data transmission are informed and are not allowed to transmit for the duration of the data exchange that is encoded in the NAV field of the RTS and CTS frame. Yet, frames from different nodes can still be transmitted in parallel such that collisions still cannot be completely avoided. This may be the case when nodes move fast and miss the RTS/CTS exchange or when both the RTS and CTS frame is not received correctly by a node, e.g. due to channel fluctuations. The reduced probability of packet collisions and consequently the improved possibility of a successful frame exchange trades off with the additional overhead introduced by the RTS/CTS frame exchange.

The typical frame exchange thus consists of the frame sequence RTS - CTS - DATA - ACK, where the RTS and CTS frame can be omitted, and the ACK frame is not transmitted in case of a broadcast transmission. A successful exchange of frames depends on the transmission quality provided by the physical layer. In case any of the exchanged frames contains errors, the complete sequence has to be retransmitted, reducing the effective payload that the wireless channel can transport. Problems with transmission quality in particular occur when adverse channel conditions exist, e.g. due to high mobility or strong multi-path fading, or if too many nodes share the same wireless channel and medium access coordination fails (also see the next paragraphs).

MAC Schemes

IEEE 802.11 defines several MAC schemes to access the medium in a coordinated way. In the following the most important ones will be described. The DCF medium access scheme is most often used, while HCF is a further development based on DCF principles, but including different quality of service classes. The PCF scheme can only be used in infrastructure networks, i.e. with central coordinating access points.

DCF Medium Access. Distributed Coordination Function enables the coordinated usage of the medium following a *CSMA* access strategy. It bases on the principle that the status of the medium has to be detected before a transmission is actually performed. Consequently, a procedure is needed to detect the current status of the wireless medium as either being idle or being busy. Two mechanisms, a physical and a virtual one are provided, and the medium is considered as busy if at least one of them does so. The physical status indication is provided by the PHY and is called *CCA*. The medium is detected as busy if either a valid frame reception is currently detected or if the energy measured on the medium exceeds a specific threshold. The virtual mechanism is provided by the NAV described before: all frames contain a duration field, which indicates how long the related frame exchange sequence lasts. Nodes that are not part of the data exchange have to keep the medium virtually busy for that duration.

The distributed medium access is coordinated with the help of two concepts: defined time durations of different length (Inter Frame Spaces (IFSs)) and randomized waiting times prior to the medium access (random backoff). IFSs are time intervals during which a node has to detect the medium idle in order to proceed with a next step. The different lengths of IFS prioritize specific procedures; the SIFS interval is the shortest IFS and gives highest priority to the related tasks, followed by the Point Coordination Inter Frame Space (PIFS) and the Distributed Inter Frame Space (DIFS) interval.

If a node has data frames to be transmitted and if the medium is considered idle for the duration of DIFS, the frame can be directly transmitted. If, instead, the medium is considered busy, a backoff procedure has to be followed: a number of backoff slots (also having a defined duration) is chosen randomly within a specific interval, the contention window, and the frame may not be transmitted before the number of remaining slots reaches 0. The number of remaining slots is reduced whenever the medium is detected idle for the duration of DIFS. If the medium becomes busy again, the reduction of slots is paused and may not be resumed before the next idle period takes place.

The selection of random *backoff* slots is performed in order to reduce the probability that different nodes start to transmit frames at the same point in time what might lead to frame collisions. The number of selectable waiting times depends on the size of the contention window. As the number of contending nodes may be unknown the size of the contention window is adapted dynamically: in case a transmission fails, i.e. an acknowledgment cannot be successfully received, the frame is *retransmitted*. A backoff period has to precede the retransmission and the contention window (and with it the possible maximum length of the backoff period) is (nearly) doubled (more precisely, the contention window size always is represented by the term $2^i - 1$, with an i increasing by one with each retransmission, up to a maximum value). Consequently, if a frame is lost due to a collision with another frame, the probability of colliding again is reduced by the increased number of backoff slots for the retransmission, but with the trade-off of a possibly longer waiting time.

The number of retransmissions is restricted to a defined number, afterwards feedback is given to higher layers, that the frame failed to be transmitted. After every failed or successful transmission, the contention window is reset to its original value and a backoff algorithm is started, independently whether another frame to be transmitted is waiting. This way, other nodes have the possibility to access the channel before the node that just transmitted.

PCF Medium Access. The *Point Coordination Function* is an access scheme, where the access point controls the medium access in a centralized way. Two phases are defined: one is the distributed access as described for the DCF and the other is the Contention Free period in which the access point polls all nodes that have announced that they want to participate in the Contention Free (CF) period. This guarantees that nodes gain access to the medium. However, there is no product known in the market where PCF is actually implemented.

HCF Medium Access. *Hybrid Coordination Functions* are defined in the IEEE 802.11e amendment of the standard and introduce QoS functionality. Every data packet is assigned a certain access category and is thus handled prioritized, or not. Several types of HCF are defined, the most known and used being *Enhanced Distributed Channel Access (EDCA)*. Four access categories are defined, for each of them exists an own waiting queue and individual values for the contention window size and the IFS that has to be idle before medium access or further backoff is allowed. EDCA does not guarantee any maximum waiting times or strict prioritization; it only increases the possibility that packets with higher priority access the medium earlier.

12.1.4   Introduction of Available Models

In the previous chapters the general model of IEEE 802.11 was introduced. In the following are presented simulation models for IEEE 802.11.

NS-2 Wireless Extensions

⋆ **Intent:**

– The wireless extensions of the Network Simulator 2 (NS-2) allows the performance analysis and evaluation of IEEE 802.11 networks, especially when using the DCF on the MAC layer. Network Simulator 2 (NS-2) also includes models for the simulation of different wireless routing protocols like Ad-hoc On-demand Distance Vector (AODV) or Dynamic Source Routing (DSR).

⋆ **Authors / Contributors:**

– NS-2 originated as a variant of the REAL simulator in 1989 and was continuously improved and extended in the following years until today. The support of wireless networks and mobility was introduced from 1998 onwards by the CMU Monarch project at Carnegie Mellon University (CMU) where was established the basic layout for wireless nodes and radio channels. Contributions were made from various projects and many research institutions.

⋆ **Model Characteristics:**

– The model for wireless networks was first described in [2]. It includes the major pieces of the IEEE 802.11 reference model, i.e. the communication on the MAC and PHY layer. Node mobility is supported by the NS-2 framework. Improved MAC schemes, QoS functionality and station management functionality was not supported originally but there exist several extensions that extend the model in various ways. Among them is an implementation for infrastructure support [377], the support of IEEE 802.11e (QoS) [496], and the support of the dynamic selection of multiple transmission rates [5].

⋆ **Accuracy / Complexity:**

- On the MAC layer the model covers main functionality of IEEE 802.11. The DCF is covered by the model such that distributed coordinated access to the medium is modeled, including the backoff behavior due to physical and virtual medium status notification. The model does not cover PCF functionality. The PHY model is simplified and leads to low accuracy. The successful reception of a packet depends on a per-packet reception power that has to exceed a reception threshold to be configured. The arrival of another frame during an ongoing reception is handled such that the reception powers of both frames are compared and only if the ratio of the first and the second frame exceeds a specific threshold the reception is continued, otherwise the two frames collide and cannot be received successfully.
- The MAC model contains several inaccuracies and restrictions with respect to wrong collision handling, no preamble and PLCP header modeling, no cumulative SINR implementation, wrong backoff handling, the mis-usage of the NAV for Extended Inter Frame Space (EIFS), and incomplete capture capabilities.
- The default configuration parameters model a non-standard wireless interface. In order to represent IEEE 802.11 the parameters have to be adapted.
- The wireless extensions provide a simulated wireless channel that interconnects the wireless nodes and allows the exchange of frames between the nodes. Each transmitted frame is copied for each possible receiver and a propagation delay is applied with respect to the distance between nodes. Every possible receiving node uses a definable radio propagation model to determine signal reception strength on a per-packet basis. Radio propagation models can be either deterministic or probabilistic, and may model path loss, shadowing and fading effects.
- Higher protocol layers are connected via a callback interface to the LLC. A packet to be transmitted is either given to the MAC directly if it is idle, or enqueued in the interface queue otherwise. A received packet is given to the LLC layer after being handled in the MAC.

⋆ **Model Context:**

- In order to run simulations of wireless networks, NS-2 as a basic framework is required. It implements the discrete event simulator, defines packet formats and the composition of nodes, and interlinks the programmatic C++ implementation with the `Tcl` configuration part of NS-2. The wireless modules are included in the NS-2 distribution.
- A scenario is described via the script language `Tcl`, where the network scenario, the configuration and the parametrization is defined by scripts. Simulations can be run without adapting the C++ source code. The C++ sources are open such that individual adaptations and extensions can be included.

⋆ Inputs:

– The scenarios, models and nodes can be configured via the `Tcl` scripting files. A general setup for the scenario can be configured, and individulal configurations for each node extended. The files are simple text files and are interpreted on simulation runtime.

⋆ Outputs:

– NS-2 provides the output in the form of trace files. The files contain one line for each relevant event. The level of detail, models / layers of interest can be configured in order to reduce the size of the files. Two formats can be chosen , an old one that is more human-readable, and a new trace file format, that allows better support for trace file parsing.
– Additional output can be configured by callbacks to methods in the `Tcl` script where individual message handling and/or statistics can be performed.
– NS-2 does not include tools for direct statistical evaluation. The tool *nam* allows the visualization of scenarios and communication for simple scenarios.

⋆ Structure:

– No UML description is available.

⋆ Implementations:

– All functional components are based on a `C/C++` implementation and are available as source code. Each node consists of two parts, the `C/C++` implementation and a `Tcl` description that interconnects the different modules and allows their configuration. The implementation is available online and included in all versions of NS-2 since `ns-2.21` (1999) such that the current version as well as the development over time can always be reviewed.

⋆ Availability:

– The documentation and source code is available online. The PHY/MAC components of IEEE 802.11 can be found in the folder `ns-x.xx/mac/`.

⋆ Author of Model Description:

– Felix Schmidt-Eisenlohr (Karlsruhe Institute of Technology (KIT))

802.11Ext: Overhaul of NS-2 Wireless Extensions

⋆ Intent:

– See previous Section 12.1.4

⋆ Authors / Contributors:

- Qi Chen, Daniel Jiang, Luca Delgrossi (Mercedes-Benz Research & Development North America)
- Felix Schmidt-Eisenlohr, Marc Torrent-Moreno, Hannes Hartenstein (Karlsruhe Institute of Technology (KIT))

⋆ Model Characteristics:

- The model was first described in 2007 in [97]. It includes main pieces of the IEEE 802.11 reference model, i.e. of the MAC and PHY layer. The MAC layer includes the DCF structured and detailed. Other MAC schemes, QoS functionality and station management functionality is not supported originally, but can be extended. The PHY layer models reception behavior on a per-packet basis and decides on the successful reception with respect to the SINR, including noise and all other packets that are present in parallel. It handles packets transmitted with different rates and supports capturing technologies. The implementation provides a modular, clear and extensible design.

⋆ Evolution:

- The model is continuously improved and refined. Documentation, bug fixes, extensions and scripts are provided on the website [7].

⋆ Accuracy / Complexity:

- With respect to the MAC, the model provides the full functionality of the DCF mechanism in a modular and structured way. The behavior described in the standard documents is completely modeled and allows the simulation of decentralized medium access.
- With respect to the PHY the reception process is modeled as follows. Each frame that arrives at a node is modeled to be received with a specific reception power that is determined with the help of radio propagation models. The node inherits a transmission and reception state machine, and depending on the state and the reception power the start of a reception is either successful or not. In case the beginning of a frame can be received successfully, i.e. decoding the preamble as well as the header, the state machine enters payload reception phase of a packet. The reception is successful if the SINR of the packet remains above a certain threshold all time, otherwise the reception fails. If the beginning of a frame cannot be successfully decoded, the packet only contributes to the interference and noise power that a node obtains. During a reception, another incoming packet with strong reception power, i.e. an SINR above a certain threshold may be captured. Capture means that the receiver chipset stops decoding the bit sequence of

the current frame and switches to decoding the newly arriving one. Capture can be activated and deactivated individually for preamble/header reception phase and payload reception phase.

- The PHY model supports handling different modulation schemes and coding rates by providing different necessary SINR thresholds for each configuration. Preamble and header are always treated independently as the header is always encoded with the most simple modulation scheme.
- The model includes configuration parameters that represent IEEE 802.11a networks. The combination of the detailed PHY/MAC models with probabilistic radio propagation allows the detailed simulation of IEEE 802.11a and p networks.
- The model handles packets on packet-level accuracy, i.e. variation of reception power during one frame is not modeled. Further, the reception decision is based on the lowest achieved SINR during reception. The model may be extended with a decision based on a derived BER and PER but according models have to be developed and integrated.

⋆ **Model Context:**

- See previous Section 12.1.4
- Existing scripts for the standard NS-2 models can be easily adapted to work with the overhauled version. In principle, the classes for MAC and PHY defined in the script files only have to be replaced.
- A seamless integration into the existing NS-2 is possible, as the same interfaces are used.

⋆ **Inputs:**

- See previous Section 12.1.4

⋆ **Outputs:**

- See previous Section 12.1.4
- The model allows detailed tracing of PHY and MAC and provides additional output for detailed analysis.

⋆ **Structure:**

- In [97], SDL diagrams are included that allow detailed understanding of the PHY and MAC function.

⋆ **Implementations:**

- The implementation is available online and is included in all versions of NS-2 since **ns-2.33** (2008).

– The source code is written in C++ and freely available. Configuration parameters are provided as Tcl scripts.

⋆ Availability:

– The source code is included in NS-2 releases starting from version ns-2.33 under the folder ns-x.xx/mac/. The file names of the extended modules end with *Ext*.

⋆ Related Models:

– The new models are related to original implementation in the sense that they provide the same interfaces but replace the complete functional implementation. In comparison, a clear structure and a much more detailed behavior is modeled.

⋆ Author of Model Description:

– Felix Schmidt-Eisenlohr (Karlsruhe Institute of Technology (KIT))

OPNET Modeler WLAN Module

OPNET Modeler is a state-of-the-art network modeling and simulating tool. It delivers a huge set of functionalities combined with an intuitive and straightforward user interface. Despite of being a commercial product, a large number of Universities work with OPNET Modeler under the OPNET University Program. The Wireless LAN Module is available within the latter and offers a solid design, simulation and analysis tool for IEEE 802.11 wireless LAN networks. OPNET Modeler is in a continuous development state with new functionalities being released several times a year.

⋆ Intent:

– Design and performance evaluation of IEEE 802.11 networks.

⋆ Authors / Contributors:

– OPNET Modeler is a commercial simulation tool which falls within the Research and Development area of OPNET Technologies, Inc.
– Default models can be extended and improved by individual users, which may upload their work to the on-line section of contributed models.

⋆ Model Characteristics:

– The implementation is based on a hierarchical modeling concept, where three levels can be distinguished. The *Network Editor*, the *Node Editor* and the *Process Editor*. The first serves as graphical representation of the modeled network, where devices and linking mediums can be intuitively combined. The second displays the internal architecture of single objects and graphically describes the data flow between functional elements, including protocol layers, radio links and buffers, among others. These functional elements get process models assigned, consisting of finite state machines and transitions that can be accessed and modified (in C/C++ language) at the *Process Editor*. The WLAN MAC layer is a process, modeled as a finite state machine consisting of about 10000 lines of code. On the other hand, the radio link (physical layer) is modeled by the *Radio Transceiver Pipeline*. It is basically a concatenation of fully customizable C/C++ programmed stages, with a large set of specifically defined functions for a comfortable PHY design. At every of the fourteen different stages different effects dealing with transmission, reception and environment are considered. Based on certain inputs, each stage performs computations to obtain valuable metrics including received power, signal-to-noise ratio, interference level and bit and packet error rate, among others. The OPNET Modeler WLAN PHY implementation consists of about 2000 lines of code.

– It offers full support for IEEE 802.11a, b, g in both distributed (DCF) and centralized (PCF) medium access modalities.
– It offer partial support for IEEE 802.11e.
– Support for IEEE 802.11n is available through the on-line OPNET Contributed Model Library.
– It implements full protocol stack including PHY, MAC, IP, Transport and Application Layers.
– Mobility is available by means of customizable or random trajectories. In the context of mobility roaming is also supported.
– The supported wireless network configurations range from infrastructure (Access Point based) and Ad-hoc to extended service set and wireless backbone.
– It offers a huge number of *drag and drop* nodes covering all functionalities: router, bridge, mobile and fixed stations. Hundreds of protocol and vendor device models together with their source code are also available.
– It offers an integrated debugging environment that allows the setting of breakpoints for specific events, to trace simulation execution as well as memory usage. Furthermore, it offers an animated simulation progress display (packet transmission, mobility, etc.).
– The WLAN model contains a very solid and fully standard-conform MAC implementation. Furthermore, OPNET Modeler has been the simulator selected for the IEEE *Task Group E and N* for developing the IEEE 802.11e/n standards.

★ **Evolution:**

– Simulation engine and protocol functionalities are being regularly further developed. Different versions of OPNET Modeler are distinguished by their release numbering. The current available release (while this book is being written) is *OPNET Modeler 15.0 PL1* (February 2009).

★ **Applicability:**

– OPNET Modeler WLAN model provides support for design and performance evaluation of IEEE 802.11 networks, including 802.11a/b/g/e and both DCF and PCF configurations.

★ **Accuracy / Complexity:**

– The model supports the whole set of DCF functionalities of IEEE 802.11 a/b/g as specified in the standards. CSMA/CA medium access with exponential back-off procedure, RTS/CTS frame exchange, packet fragmentation and reassembly, backward compatibility between IEEE 802.11b and 802.11g together with mobility and roaming, are the most relevant protocol characteristics available with the model.
– The PCF configuration is supported as well, however, the model does not present a correct behavior when noisy links are considered or when the communication with the access point is lost.
– In a similar way, there are some functionalities of IEEE 802.11e that are not modeled at all. In the context of this standard amendment only the Enhanced Distributed Channel Access is supported, including Block Acknowledgment, transmission opportunity frame burst, four different traffic categories linked to different flow priority levels and different protocol behaviors, as well as interoperability between IEEE 802.11 b/g and IEEE 802.11e.
– The physical layers included in the model are Direct Sequence Spread Spectrum and Orthogonal Frequency Division Multiplex. Other PHY approaches defined in the IEEE 802.11 standard such as Frequency Hopping Spread Spectrum and *Infrared* (IR) are not modeled. Correspondingly, only the modulations employed by DSSS and OFDM are supported, including DPSK, BPSK, QPSK, CCK, 16-QAM and 64-QAM.
– The Physical Layer is implemented as a set of pipelined stages, which model the basic requirement of this layer, namely the data transmission and reception over the wireless medium. For that purpose a propagation model, a method for accounting for interferences, as well as a packet error model, among others, are delivered with the model.
– The accuracy and flexibility of the propagation depends on whether the OPNET Modeler user has access to the *Terrain Modeling Module (TMM) Package*, which requires extra licenses not included in the free-of-charge University Program. This package supports the inclusion of terrain effects

in the signal propagation (path loss calculations) and the selection of built-in propagation models and environmental effects. On the other hand, the default model includes only the free-space propagation, which is a significant shortcoming, since it does not suit well in indoor scenarios.

– *Frequency selective fading* is not modeled in the default libraries. Again, this is an significant limitation, as it is well known [42] how important this effect is when close-to-reality simulations are aimed.

– The Clear Channel Assessment threshold, which indicates the level of energy that has to be sensed by a node for it to declare the wireless channel to be busy is treated and modeled in the same way as the receiver sensitivity. The latter stands for the minimum energy level needed to differentiate low level signals from noise. These two effects are different and should correspondingly be modeled separately. Nevertheless, multiple contributions argue that the optimal CCA threshold corresponds to the receiver sensitivity, which in turn would mean that this model limitation may have a reduced impact on the system performance.

– Regardless of the channel conditions, which in the default model may change only due to the terminals mobility, the transmission rate is fixed over the whole simulation run. In other words, there is no link adaptation mechanism to select the most adequate transmission rate at any time.

– The whole set of PHY limitations are somehow balanced by the customization flexibility of the transceiver pipeline stages and extra built-in tools like the *Modulation Editor* or the *Antenna pattern Editor*.

⋆ Model Context:

– The Wireless LAN module is part of OPNET Modeler and requires the latter to work, since it is not an independent module.

⋆ Inputs:

– Any OPNET Modeler WLAN terminal consists of a large set of parameters that have to be set prior to the starting of a simulation.

– The most important medium access related parameters are the following: *Access point functionality*, since every station can act as an access point. *Rts Threshold* indicates the data frame length from which the RTS/CTS handshake is activated before payload transmission. Similarly, *Fragmentation Threshold* stands for the data frame length from which fragmentation of the packet (and reassembly of the fragments at the receiver) will be activated. *Short and Long Retry Limits* which specify the maximum number of transmission attempts for the frames whose size is less than or equal to the above mentioned *Rts Threshold*. The *Beacon Interval* is another customizable parameter indicating the frequency at which Beacon management frames are transmitted by access points.

– Nodes in a PCF or HCF configuration have additional parameters specific for these configurations.

– Before starting a simulation, traffic has to be added to the network. OP-NET Modeler offers three distinct ways of generating traffic. First, raw packet generation can be used. In this case, the user can manually set the statistical behavior of the traffic in each node (inter-arrival time and packet size) as well as the destination address (fixed, random, broadcast). In the second method, the user can employ already built-in applications like Email, web browsing, FTP, Video Conference and VoIP, among others. Furthermore, these applications consist of a considerable number of parameters modeling internal characteristics of the different traffic choices, e.g. the type of voice encoder that should be used for the VoIP application. In the third, method the user can define so-called *traffic demand flows* to specifically set a load level at any point in time between a transmitter and receiver pair.

⋆ **Outputs:**

– OPNET Modeler offers three different types of simulation's outputs: *Output Vectors*, *Output Scalars* and *Animations*.

– An output vector is basically a file containing the value of a system variable (or multiple variables) as a function of the simulation time. Built-in functions and tools help the user to manage these especial files and to extract data from them. Only one output vector is generated per simulation and both the variables' values and the time information are stored as C doubles.

– An output scalar is nothing more than the value of a system's variable that does not vary as function of the simulation time. Every single value is stored only once per simulation.

– A graphical representation of the system's behavior can be viewed during the simulation run or once it is finished. There are three types of animations available: *Statistic Animation*, which plots the value of a selected statistic in a graph as function of the simulation time. *Packet Flow Animation*, which depicts ongoing transmissions as packets traveling over the wireless medium from senders to receivers. The last modality corresponds to the *Node Mobility Animation*, which is active only if mobility also is and basically shows the mobile terminals moving through the considered scenario.

– The WLAN model contains a considerable amount of predefined statistics that can be selected to be stored as output vectors, output scalars or be graphically displayed as animations. One can differentiate between *Global Statistics* (at the network level considering the whole protocol stack but the PHY), *Node Statistics* (at the terminal level considering the whole protocol stack but the PHY) and *Module Statistics* (at the terminal level considering in addition transmitter and receiver radio interfaces). Available statistics are, e.g. total network load, node throughput, medium access delay, packet queue size, bit-error-rate, etc.

– Furthermore, the user can customize these outputs adding personalized statistics.

⋆ **Dependencies:**

– The Wireless LAN model is an extension of the OPNET Modeler simulator and is only operative in combination with the latter.

⋆ **Structure:**

– No UML or SDL descriptions are available.

⋆ **Implementations:**

– All functional elements of WLAN terminals (queues, processors, radio interfaces, traffic sources, etc.) are based on a C/C++ implementation.

⋆ **Availability:**

– OPNET Modeler downloads are available at the official OPNET Technologies Inc. website (www.opnet.com). For educational and research activities without commercial goals, University members can obtain free-of-charge licenses for OPNET Modeler Wireless LAN Module.

– OPNET Modeler is available for Windows, Linux and Solaris environments as well as for 32-bit and 64-bit architectures.

⋆ **Related Models:**

– Apart from the IEEE 802.11 model, there are other OPNET Modeler based wireless models available. Some of the most relevant are IEEE 802.15.1 (Blue-tooth), IEEE 802.16 (WiMAX), UMTS and the upcoming cellular standard LTE. Some of them are available under OPNETs University Program.

⋆ **Author of Model Description:**

– Oscar Puñal (RWTH Aachen University)

OMNeT++ / MiXiM framework

OMNeT++ [474] is a message passing based discrete event simulator. It is highly modular and scalable and can be used for generic protocol modeling, queueing networks modeling, multiprocessors modeling and basically for the modeling of any system that can be represented via a sequence of discrete events. Specific functionalities are provided by different independent frameworks. The MiXiM framework [319] combines several other existing frameworks to forge a powerful simulation tool focusing on wireless and mobile communications. For academic usage OMNeT++ and its associated frameworks are open source and free of charge. In the commercial area, there exists another edition of OMNeT++ called OMNEST [213].

★ **Intent:**

– Design and performance evaluation of wireless communication networks.

★ **Authors / Contributors:**

– OMNeT++ is a simulation tool mainly developed and maintained by Andras Varga. It is free for academic purposes only. Special functionalities are offered by frameworks provided by individual contributors.
– MiXiM is a combined framework for OMNeT++, which is mainly developed and maintained by the University of Paderborn, Technische Universiteit Delft and Technische Universität Berlin (Telecommunication Networks Group). This framework is under the GNU General Public License.

★ **Model Characteristics:**

– OMNeT++/MiXiM is a highly modular simulation tool. All components of a simulation network, such as a WLAN host or the MAC layer of a host are modules. Modules which contain other modules are called component modules. The basic or non-concatenated modules are also called simple modules.
– The Network Description Language (NED) language is used to describe the structure of the modules, consisting basically in module parameters, gates and channels. This description is usually the first step of any implementation and results in a NED file for each module. How the single modules behave is specified via C++ functions in CPP files.
– OMNeT++ is a message passing based discrete event simulator. Modules pass messages to each other through gates, which act as connection points between the modules and are defined in NED files. Message files can contain special data fields that can be customized.
– A WLAN node in MiXiM is implemented as a compound module. It contains a set of modules that provide the required functionalities and also the corresponding gates inter-connecting the modules. Application layer, network layer and the network interface card (NIC) conform the protocol stack of a basic node. The NIC is a compound module enclosing the MAC and PHY layers. Furthermore, nodes may be suited with a mobility module, an Address Resolution Protocol (ARP) module (translation between

network IP address and MAC address), a battery module (modeling of battery consumption) and a utility module (statistics gathering).
- The initialization of the module's parameters is performed in the so-called INI files. Some specific parameters can also be defined in XML files.
- The simulator supports both command line and graphical interface with animated simulation progress display.
- OMNeT++/MiXiM provides solely support for IEEE 802.11b with DCF medium access policy. However, due to its modular nature and clear structure, further extensions can easily be implemented.
- In MiXiM mobility is treated as a discrete time process. It provides various parameters like speed, direction and distance of the movement, the ending position of the host or the amount of time a movement should last. By combining these parameters, a rich palette of movements can be easily configured.

⋆ **Evolution:**

- OMNeT++ was first released in 2001 and the MiXiM framework in June 2009. Both are in continuous development with several releases each year.
- The current available release for OMNeT++ (while this book is being written) is OMNeT++ 4.0p1 for Linux (December 2009) and OMNeT++ 4.0 win32 for Windows (February 2009).
- The current available release for MiXiM (while this book is being written) is MiXiM 1.1 for all supported platforms (September 2009).

⋆ **Applicability:**

- OMNeT++/MiXiM supports the detailed modeling of wireless channels and of any communication protocol at the MAC layer.
- An IEEE 802.11b network with DCF configuration is already implemented. With extra changes other amendments of the 802.11 family could be easily added (IEEE 802.11g/a/e/n, among others), providing a tool for the performance evaluation of WLAN networks.
- The newest release of MiXiM has added an energy framework [141], which can model the battery consumption of wireless devices.

⋆ **Accuracy / Complexity:**

- The model supports the whole set of DCF functionalities of IEEE 802.11b as specified in the standard, such as CSMA/CA medium access with exponential back-off. The RTS/CTS frame exchange is also fully supported.
- Other 802.11 amendments, like the well known IEEE 802.11e/a/g/n are not implemented in MiXiM.
- Packet fragmentation and reassembly is not supported.
- PCF configuration is not supported.

- A simple signal-to-noise-ratio based rate adaptation scheme is available for IEEE 802.11b networks.
- MiXiM does not have an accurate implementation of the higher layers of the Open Systems Interconnection (OSI) protocol stack. Application and network layers are implemented in a very simple way, providing a reduced set of capabilities. For instance, instead of Internet Protocol (IP) MiXiM performs a simple address mapping method between the module's ID of a host and a IP address. The IP header encapsulation and decapsulation is also provided. The transport layer is not implemented at all.
- MiXiM provides full support in 3D for modeling walls and obstacles within the network scenario. Such modeling improves the accuracy of simulations, since they have an impact on signal attenuation and may influence the trajectory of moving nodes.
- MiXiM provides multi-channel support in space and frequency, which enables the modeling of the OFDM and MIMO techniques.
- The wireless channel is based on the implementation of the ChSim [338] framework for OMNeT, which has been merged in MiXiM. The channel model includes state-of-the-art models for path-loss, shadowing, large and small-scale fading. The small-scale fading is based on a Rayleigh distribution for the signal amplitudes, assuming non-line-of-sight conditions between transmitter and receiver (typical large office environment).
- The effects of the FEC are translated into a coding gain, which in turn is used as a gain factor enhancing the SNR. The resulting (effective) SNR is compared to a pre-defined SNR threshold value to decide if the frame transmission can be considered as signal, thus if it can be separated from the noise. In order to obtain the PER of the transmission, the effective SNR is used as input parameter of well known close-form formulae for the BER of the corresponding modulation employed. In the case of the IEEE 802.11b the modulations used are the BPSK, QPSK and CCK.
- In MiXiM the physical layer is implemented as a module (*Base PHY Layer*) and a set of classes, the *Analogue Model*, the *Radio*, the *Channel Info* and the *Decider*. The *Base PHY Layer* is responsible for the transmission and reception of PHY frames, also called *Air-frames* and the interaction of the different parts of the PHY. The *Analogue Model* performs the calculation of the effects associated with the wireless channel (path-loss, shadowing, large and small-scale fading). The *Radio* simulates some of the physical characteristics of the radio hardware, namely the radio switching times (e.g. from sleep state to receive state) and the simplex or duplex capability of the radio device. The *Channel Info* maintains a list of ongoing transmissions in the vicinity of a receiving node at a certain point in time. Hence, a node that is receiving a packet is able to track the total level of interference due to transmissions overlapping in time. Finally, the *Decider* is responsible for the classification of the air-frame into the category of signal or noise, depending on the detected SINR. In addition, this module takes

care of the air-frame demodulation and the error rate calculation. It also provides the means to perform channel sensing, an information which is then forwarded to the MAC. While more than one Analogue Model can be used simultaneously, only one Decider can be plugged into the Base PHY Layer.

- Channel capture is also supported, since the *Decider* can determine at which point in time a packet should be treated as noise or as an information signal. Hence, if while receiving a packet another one arrives with a much higher signal strength, the receiver may lock onto the decoding of the latest packet, thus dropping the first frame.

⋆ Model Context:

- MiXiM is a framework for OMNeT++. It is not independent and needs OMNeT++ to work.

⋆ Inputs:

- The initialization of application layer parameters and MAC parameters (e.g. RTS/CTS threshold, frame retransmission limits, beacon interval, etc.) is done via INI and XMl files.
- The mobility of the nodes and the PHY parameters (e.g. wireless channel type, center frequency, transmit power, receiver sensitivity, ...) are initialized via XML files.
- The traffic for the simulation is added by means of specific functions in the related node's application module. The only traffic model provided by MiXiM is a simple broadcast application. The user has to implement the traffic model himself if different traffic types are required.

⋆ Outputs:

- OMNeT++/MiXiM offers two types of simulation's outputs: output vectors and output scalars.
- The vector output consists of a file containing the values of a pre-selected system variable as function of the simulation time. The results are written always onto the same common file.
- The scalar output records only the value of a variable in the simulation. Simple statistical results of variables, such as the standard deviation, can also be recorded in the same file.
- Graphical representation of the outputs can only be done by means of external applications. There is no built-in tool for statistics representation provided.

⋆ **Dependencies:**

– MiXiM is a framework for the OMNeT++ simulator and works only in combination of the latter.

⋆ **Structure:**

– No SDL descriptions are available. UML descriptions are available for the classes in the OMNeT++ and MiXiM API.

⋆ **Implementations:**

– All functional elements are based on C++ implementations. Individual modules in the network, such as hosts or a wireless interface card, even the network itself are implemented using the NED language. In some specific situations, XML implementations are also needed.

⋆ **Availability:**

– OMNeT++ downloads are available at the official website [474]. It is free for academic use.
– MiXiM downloads are available at its official website [319]. It is also free of charge for non-commercial use.
– OMNeT++ and MiXiM are available for Windows and Linux/Mac OS platforms. Under Linux/Mac OS for 32-bit and 64-bit architectures. Under windows only for 32-bit architecture.

⋆ **Related Models:**

– The INET framework for OMNeT++ supports simulation for fixed networks. OverSim is a specific framework for peer-to-peer simulations. These frameworks and other specific ones can all be found under the OMNeT++ project.

⋆ **Author of Model Description:**

– Wei Hong (RWTH Aachen University)

ns-3

The discrete-event simulator *ns-3* was and is being developed as an eventual replacement for the aging ns-2 simulator, with a strong emphasis on models that closely resemble their real-world counterparts, and validation of simulator models. ns-3 is an open-source project under constant development, with releases several times a year, and free access to the constantly-updated repositories. It is increasingly being used in research, especially for its ease of use for scenarios that involve network emulation. The WLAN modules are part of the ns-3 core, as opposed to being a framework add-on.

⋆ **Intent:**

– Design and evaluation of networks, such as IEEE 802.11

⋆ **Authors / Contributors:**

– ns-3 is being developed by a large group of contributors. The core of the group is formed by George Riley (Georgia Tech), Tom Henderson (Boeing Research Seattle), Mathieu Lacage (INRIA), and several other researchers in the field of networking.

⋆ **Model Characteristics:**

– While ns-3 was developed with modularity in mind, the main wireless model at this point in time is taken from the yans network simulator [271], which was developed by two of the main contributors to ns-3 before they started their work on it. The model is split into a MAC and a PHY part.
– The MAC layer itself is split into several parts, each encapsulated as a C++ class. The WifiMac class allows the use of QoS and non-QoS setups for ad-hoc or AP/station networks. It handles tasks such as association and disassociation as well as beacon management. The MacRxMiddle and DcaTxOp handles sequence numbering of frames, retransmissions, and filtering of duplicate reception. It is also in charge of fragmenting and reassembling packets if necessary. Finally, the MacLow class handles RTS/CTS (also dynamically based on frame size) and interframe space timings.
– The PHY implements the sender and receiver, and determines, based on potential interference from other frames and an ErrorModel that takes into account modulation and coding rate, whether reception was errorless or not.
– The channel provides the medium and determines propagation delay and loss depending on factors such as position and the chosen loss model.

⋆ **Evolution:**

– New releases of ns-3 are published several times a year. At the time of writing, the current release was version 3.6, with 3.7 already in feature freeze period. A public mercurial server is available to follow the ongoing development.

⋆ **Applicability:**

– Being part of a large network simulation environment, it is possible to model IEEE 802.11 networks in a detailed fashion, while at the same time having a full network stack and applications to use the modeled network.

* **Accuracy / Complexity:**

- The channel model supports different propagation loss and delay models. Standard loss models include Nakagami, Friis and Jakes models.
- At the receiver's end, the PHY layer takes into account the received signal, receiver gain, modulation, and potential interference from other frames, and infers the error probability. ns-3 supports DPSK, BPSK, QPSK, 16-QAM and 64-QAM, as well as OFDM and DSSS.
- The MAC layer supports 802.11a/b/e, with 802.11n under development, with full DCF support and accurate simulation of interframe space timings. Also, Ad-hoc network modeling is supported, as well as APs and stations with beaconing, association, and handover. The MAC layer optionally allows the use of RTS/CTS, also dynamically depending on frame size.
- Not implemented as of yet are PCF in the MAC layer, as well as several more advanced features regarding the PHY and channel, such as frequency-selective fading, inter-channel interference, and a mobility model that allows the placement of radio obstacles to model shadowing.

* **Model Context:**

- As an integral part of ns-3, the IEEE 802.11 model is distributed with the simulator, and no further dependencies exist.

* **Inputs:**

- The ns-3 attribute system allows the user to set certain behavior values for each modeled entity, or standard values for all at the same time. For IEEE 802.11, attributes include among others SSID, number of missed beacons before reassociation attempt, and transmission and reception gain.
- Traffic is generally generated by application which are an object aggregated to a simulation node. These work very similarly to real-world applications, communication with the node's network stack via a socket, and the stack then hands over the packets to the IEEE 802.11 subsystem. It is also possible to use the advanced network emulation capabilities of ns-3, to create traffic via a real application that is attached to the simulator.

* **Outputs:**

- For every node in the simulation, it is possible to create a trace of all sent and received data in the form of a standard packet capture (pcap) file, like it is used by many network analysis tools. This will show every frame with all encapsulated protocols and payload data the way it is sent or received over the device. Radiotap headers that contain additional information such as reception signal strength can be added by the simulation for in-depth analysis.
- Internal variables of the simulation, such as the state of a node or retransmission counters, which are not obvious from the pcap files, can be collected

via traced variables and callbacks. In this case, the creator of a simulation setup can attach himself to variable changes or other events that happen during the runtime of the simulation, and have a custom C++ function called to aggregate data. This is a very flexible, but sometimes cumbersome way of data aggregation, because it requires a basic understanding of the internals of the simulator.

⋆ **Dependencies:**

– As an integral part of the ns-3 simulator, the IEEE 802.11 subsystem has no dependencies other than the simulator itself, that is, a C++ compiler and standard C++ libraries.

⋆ **Structure:**

– A strong inheritance hierarchy exists, with many parts of the simulation providing abstract framework classes from which to inherit when creating new models.
– No UML or SDL descriptions are available.

⋆ **Implementations:**

– ns-3 is fully written in C++. This includes the simulation setups, which are written as C++ programs that include the simulator itself as a library.

⋆ **Availability:**

– New versions are released on a regular basis at http://www.nsnam.org
– At the same site, a public mercurial repository is available to follow the constantly updated development branch.

⋆ **Related Models:**

– An IEEE 802.16 (WiMAX) model is currently being merged into the main ns-3 development tree and slated for release with the next version.

⋆ **Author of Model Description:**

– Florian Schmidt (RWTH Aachen University)

12.2   IEEE 802.16 (WMAN)

Both, the European Telecommunications Standards Institute and the IEEE Standardization Association identified the metropolitan area wireless broadband access technology as a key driver for future mobile Internet and voice applications. In 1999 both associations started the standardization of broadband wireless access technologies. The IEEE established the *802.16* working group which published the first draft in 2002 as IEEE 802.16-2001. European Telecommunications Standards Institute (ETSI) Broadband Radio Access Network (BRAN) published the High Performance Radio Access Network (HiperACCESS), which was based on the same single carrier physical layer.

12.2.1   System Reference Model

The IEEE reference model follows general IEEE 802 guidelines similar to other working groups of 802 and specifies the MAC and the PHY layer. Higher layer protocols as well as the management plane are outside the scope of the standard. *Figure 12.8* shows that the MAC comprises three sublayers. The service specific Convergence Sublayer (CS) provides interfaces for higher layers. It classifies external Service Data Units (SDUs) and associates them to the proper MAC connection. The CS may also process SDUs, e.g., to reduce overhead by performing Payload Header Suppression (PHS). Two CSs specifications are provided for interfacing Asynchronous Transfer Mode (ATM) as well as IP, Point-to-Point Protocol (PPP), or IEEE 802.3 (Ethernet).

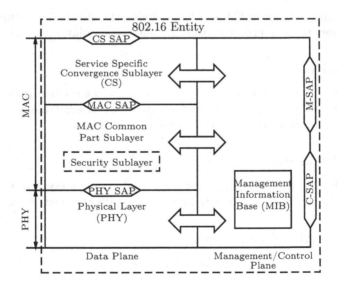

Fig. 12.8: IEEE 802.16 Reference Model

The MAC common part sublayer carries key functions such as system and channel access, connection management, and the application of QoS. Section details the common part sublayer. Below the MAC common part sublayer resides the security sublayer that provides authentication procedures, a secure key exchange, and encryption functions. The IEEE 802.16 PHY specification defines multiple PHYs, each appropriate to a particular frequency range and application. Thus, it is left unspecified how to develop, implement and deploy optimized systems with respect to available frequency bands, cell planning, equipment cost, and targeted services. Another reason for having several PHY specifications was the lack of support for a single common PHY during standardization. The PHY specifications supported by 802.16 are discussed in Section 12.2.2.

12.2.2 Physical Layer

The initial version of the standard (IEEE 802.16-2001) specified only one Single-carrier PHY. It targets frequency bands between 10 and 66 GHz, in which LOS communication is mandatory. The standard IEEE 802.16-2004 supersedes all previous versions and specifies three additional PHY techniques. They were designed for frequency bands below 11 GHz that allow for NLOS links. The new modes include a single-carrier, an OFDM and OFDMA based mode. The OFDM based transmission mode has been standardized in close cooperation with the ETSI standard HiperMAN. Both OFDM based protocols shall comply with each other in order to form the basis for the WiMAX certified technology. In the following, the OFDMA based PHY layer of 802.16 is presented in detail in Section 12.2.4.

12.2.3 Medium Access Control

The scope of the IEEE 802.16 standard comprises the data and control plane of the *MAC* and the PHY as illustrated in *Figure 12.8*. The MAC includes a service-specific convergence sublayer that interfaces higher layers. The MAC common part sublayer realizes key functions and the security sublayer is located below the MAC common part sublayer. The management plane is specified in three IEEE network management standard amendments (IEEE 802.16f/g/i) for the fixed as well as the mobile Management Information Base (MIB) and for procedures and services.

Service Specific Convergence Sublayer

The service specific CS provides any transformation or mapping of external network data, received through the CS SAP. This includes the classification

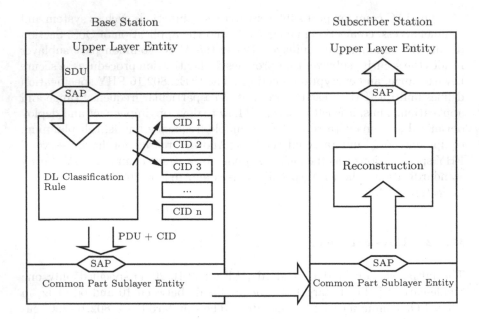

Fig. 12.9: Classification and ID mapping of packets at the BS

of external network SDUs and (if required) the processing of SDUs. Classi-fying incoming SDUs means to associate them with the proper connection identified by the connection identifier which is shown in Figure 12.9. Since a connection identifier is associated with a certain level of QoS, the association of an SDU to a connection facilitates the delivery with the corresponding QoS constraints. The CS processes higher layer SDUs to suppress unused higher layer protocol information. After classification and payload header suppres-sion, the SDU is delivered to the corresponding MAC common part sublayer service access point. At the receiving CS entity, the suppressed header is re-constructed before it is handed over to the higher layer protocol via the service access point. Since PHS is an optional feature, incoming SDUs can also be delivered without any modifications. The standard provides two conversion sublayer specifications, an ATM and a packet CS.

Packet Convergence Sublayer

The packet *CS* is used for packet-based higher layer protocols such as IP, PPP and IEEE 802.3 (Ethernet). Classification of SDUs is based on classi-fiers that consist of a reference to a connection identifier, a classifier priority and a set of protocol-specific matching criteria. Characteristic protocol en-tries are used as matching criteria as for instance the IP or Ethernet source / destination address, protocol source / destination port range, IP type of service / differentiated services codepoint, or the IEEE 802.1D-1998 user priority. If several classifier rules match with an incoming SDU, the classifier priority specifies which rule is to be applied. Since the packet CS handles various higher layer protocols, various header entries might have to be suppressed and reconstructed. Therefore, the optional PHS functionality defines a mechanism to adaptively suppress specific bytes of an unspecified SDU. All bytes of a specific region (PHS field) will be suppressed by the sending entity unless they are masked by the PHS mask. Compressed packet CS SDUs are prefixed with an 8-bit PHS index. The receiving entity reassembles the original SDU by adding the bytes that are stored in the PHS field associated to the connection identifier.

MAC Common Part Sublayer

The MAC common part sublayer provides system access, bandwidth allocation, connection establishment, and connection maintenance. The MAC common part sublayer receives from the convergence sublayer data classified to particular connection identifiers. QoS is applied to the transmission and scheduling of data over the PHY. IEEE 802.16 is optimized for Point to Multi Point (PMP) configurations, where several SSs are associated with a central BS. As an optional feature, the standard allows for a flexible Mesh deployment where direct communication between stations is possible. Since the Mesh frame structure is not compatible with the PMP frame, the Mesh deployment is especially foreseen for wireless backhaul networks based on IEEE 802.16.

Additional to PMP, an amendment for multi-hop communication in tree-based deployments is specified in IEEE 802.16j. The introduction of relay stations, which decode and forward data, extends the coverage area of a BS or increases the achievable capacity within a given area. The multi hop amendment requires being PMP compliant so that legacy SS will be able to participate in relay enhanced networks.

Section 12.2.2 outlines the specification of four different IEEE 802.16 PHYs, while one single MAC is controlling the access to the medium. Hence, the MAC protocol is PHY independent in general, but some mechanisms are PHY specific. PHY specific parts mainly focus on the MAC frame structure and the corresponding signaling messages.

Duplex Modes

Two duplexing techniques are specified for 802.16, namely TDD and FDD which are both introduced in Section 12.2.2. In short, FDD operation implies paired frequency bands, which are typically allocated in licensed spectrum. Thus, DL and UL operate on separate frequency channels. The asymmetry between DL and UL is predefined by the spectrum allocation and is therefore static. Thus, capacity can not be shifted during operation between DL and UL. In full-duplex FDD, stations simultaneously receive and transmit on both channels. Consequently, two Radio Frequency (RF) filters, two oscillators and two synthesizers are required. On the one hand, the increased need for components makes FDD devices more power consuming and more expensive. On the other hand, the MAC software can be less complex since DL and UL are not strictly synchronized. In order to avoid expensive hardware a Half Frequency Division Duplex (HFDD) mode is supported. In HFDD, DL and UL are still operating on separate frequency channels, but stations do not simultaneously transmit and receive. The resulting radio complexity is comparable to the complexity of TDD devices. A desirable network deployment, in which the BSs operate in FDD and the SSs in HFDD, combines the possibility to utilize both channels simultaneously with competitive user devices.

TDD overcomes the static asymmetry of FDD by sharing a common frequency channel for DL and UL transmission in the time-domain. Hence, capacity can be dynamically shifted in adapting the switching point between DL and UL in time. Since stations do not receive and transmit at the same time, only a single RF filter, one oscillator and one synthesizer are required. This results in cost- and power efficient devices, but the MAC scheduler of the BS tends to be more complicated since it has to synchronize many stations time slots in both DL and UL direction . In order to switch between receive and transmit phases turnaround gaps, i.e., guard intervals, have to be introduced between both phases. Assuming low mobile SSs, the reciprocity of the radio channel can be exploited in TDD systems, because the transmitter can take advantage of the channel knowledge available at the receiver. In license-exempt spectrum, the IEEE 802.16 TDD mode is mandatory.

12.2.4   OFDMA Frame Structure

IEEE 802.16 provides a frame based medium access. The frame duration is within the range of 2 ms to 20 ms according to Table 12.1.

The OFDMA frame may include multiple *zones* (such as Partial Usage of Subchannels (PUSC), Full Usage of Subchannels (FUSC), PUSC with all subchannels, optional FUSC, Adaptive Modulation and Coding (AMC), Tile Usage of Subchannels (TUSC), and TUSC, the transition between zones is indicated in the DL-MAP by the STC DL Zone Information Element (IE) or AAS DL IE . No DL-MAP or UL-MAP allocations can span over multiple zones.

In PUSC only a subset of the available data subcarriers are used by the BS. The subcarriers are grouped into six segments. The assignment of subcarriers

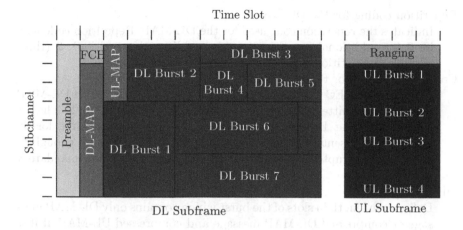

Fig. 12.10: Structure of the IEEE 802.16 OFDMA frame

Code	Frame duration [ms]	Frames per second
1	2	500
2	2.5	400
3	4	250
4	5	200
5	8	125
6	10	100
7	12.5	80
8	20	50

Table 12.1: Frame duration codes

to segments is done in a way that makes collision of subcarriers in adjacent segments unlikely.

As opposed in PUSC, the FUSC allocation schemes allows to allocate subcarriers in the whole bandwidth. Similar to PUSC, the subcarriers are grouped into segments that are used by the cells in a way to reduce collision probability.

The TUSC is similar to the PUSC scheme and allows the operation with adaptive antenna systems.

The DL Frame Prefix is a data structure transmitted at the beginning of each frame and contains information regarding the current frame and is mapped to the FCH.

Used subchannel bitmap

The bitmap is indicating which groups of subchannel are used on the first PUSC zone and on PUSC zones in which 'use all Subchannel (SC)' indicator is set to 0 in STC DL Zone IE. A value of 1 means used by this segment, and 0 means not used by this segment.

Repetition coding for the DL-MAP
    Indicates the repetition code used for the DL-MAP. Repetition code may
    be 0 (no additional repetition), 1 (one additional repetition), 2 (three
    additional repetitions) or 3 (five additional repetitions).

Coding indication for the DL-MAP
    Indicates the FEC encoding code used for the DL-MAP. The DL-MAP
    shall be transmitted with QPSK modulation at FEC rate 1/2. The BS
    shall ensure that DL-MAP (and other MAC messages required for SS
    operation) are sent with the mandatory coding scheme often enough to
    ensure uninterrupted operation of SS supporting only the mandatory
    coding scheme.

DL-MAP length
    Defines the length in slots of the burst which contains only DL-MAP mes-
    sage or compressed DL-MAP message and compressed UL-MAP, if it is
    appended, that follows immediately the DL frame prefix after repetition
    code is applied.

Figure 12.10 shows the *OFDMA frame structure* of the IEEE 802.16
system.

Despite the FCH the DL-MAP specifies the location of the following DL
bursts. The DL-MAP contains IE for each DL burst of the frame.

Downlink Interval Usage Code (DIUC)
    The code is identifying a specific burst profile that can be used for DL.

CID
    The connection identifiers represent the assignment of the IE to a broad-
    cast, multicast, or unicast address.

OFDMA symbol offset
    The offset of the OFDMA symbol in which the burst starts, measured in
    OFDMA symbols from the DL symbol in which the preamble is transmit-
    ted with the symbol immediately following the preamble being offset 1.
    The symbol offset shall follow the normal slot allocation within a zone so
    that the difference between OFDMA symbol offsets for all bursts within
    a zone is a multiple of the slot length in symbols.

Subchannel offset
    The lowest index OFDMA subchannel used for carrying the burst, start-
    ing from subchannel 0.

Boosting
    Power boost is applied to the allocation's data subcarriers.

12.2.5   Important Parameters

The IEEE 802.16 system defines a huge amount of system parameters. Only a few of them have a considerable impact on system capacity and performance.

System Bandwidth

The system bandwidth defines how many subcarriers can be used for data transmissions. Consequently, the system bandwidth limits the system capacity. In general the system capacity scales proportional to the system bandwidth.

Frame Duration

As shown in Figure 12.10 the frame is divided into uplink- and downlink subframe. As a result uplink packets can not be transmitted during the downlink subframe and downlink packets can not be transmitted in the uplink subframe. These packets need to be stored in buffers. Hence, the packet delay directly depends on the frame duration.

Scheduler and Resource Allocation Strategy

The IEEE 802.16 standard defines resource allocation formats with the help of DL- and UL-MAPs. The standard does not say anything about scheduling strategies or resource allocation rules. As a result, the implementation of the packet scheduling strategies is up to the manufacturer of 802.16 equipment. For evaluation of the IEEE 802.16 protocol the packet scheduler strategy is an important factor for QoS and system capacity.

12.2.6   Selected Models

WiMAX Medium Access Control Module of the openWNS - WiMAC

The *WiMAC* is the IEEE 802.16 protocol model of the openWNS simulator framework.

The module uses the Frame Configuration Framework (FCF), provided by the *libWNS* to create the periodic frame. The FCF has been developed to make frame based protocols easy to configure. For this, the frame is divided into several logical phases that do not overlap in time. For each of these phases a *Compound Collector* takes control of the frame phase. This FU completely describe the type of compounds that are created during the specific phase and when the compounds are transmitted. A set of compound collectors define the whole frame.

⋆ Intent:

- The open Wireless Network Simulator (openWNS) provides a model of the IEEE 802.16 protocol. The model implements the main protocol functions like radio resource management and packet scheduling.

⋆ Authors / Contributors:

- Karsten Klagges (ComNets, RWTH Aachen University, Germany)
- Christian Hoymann (Ericsson Eurolab, Aachen, Germany)
- Benedikt Wolz (ComNets, RWTH Aachen University, Germany)

⋆ Model Characteristics:

- Creation of MAC frames, including broadcast messages, DL and UL subframes and contention access period.
- Signaling of FCH, DL and UL - MAP
- Link Adaption with all available modulation and coding schemes specified by the standard
- Scheduling strategies
  - Round Robin
  - Exhaustive Round Robin
  - Proportional Fair
  - Maximum Throughput
- Support for adaptive antennas and SDMA
- Service flow and connection management
- Unsolicited grant service, bandwidth requests, persistent resource allocation

⋆ Evolution

- Since the IEEE 802.16 protocol has a lot of features in common with the ETSI HiperLAN/2 protocol, the WiMAC module has been built upon the HiperLAN/2 simulator sWARP, a simulator at ComNets.
- Major parts of the WiMAC are realized though the class library libWNS, which is a derived work of the SPEETCL class library.

⋆ Applicability

- System level simulation of multi cellular deployments.
- Investigation of radio resource management schemes.

* **Accuracy / Complexity**

− With the help of the openWNS simulation framework, the module provides detailed load generators, radio resource schedulers and interference simulation.

* **Known Use Cases**

− Scientific research at several Universities in the field of the IEEE 802.16 network.

WiMAX module of the NS-3

The WiMAX module provides the main functionality of the WiMAX standard. The core part of the MAC layer, which includes the generation of the MAC frames (in TDD mode), divided into downlink and uplink MAC subframes, and the construction and transmission of the key MAC management (control) messages (namely DL-MAP, UL-MAP, DCD, UCD, RNG-REQ and RNG-RSP). The first four management messages are the essential part of the WiMAX MAC as they are used to define the downlink and uplink channels and to allocate access to these channels. More specifically, the DL-MAP and UL-MAP are generated by the BS to allocate time-slots to the stations for the downlink and uplink transmissions. Furthermore this also includes the creation of the uplink and downlink burst profiles, the specific MAC layer data structures which define the PHY specific parameters to be used for receiving and transmitting in a particular downlink or uplink burst.

* **Intent:**

− NS-3 module of the IEEE 802.16 protocol.

* **Authors / Contributors:**

− Jahanzeb Farooq (INRIA, Sophia Antipolis, France)
− Thierry Turletti (INRIA, Sophia Antipolis, France)
− Mohamed Amine Ismail (INRIA, Sophia Antipolis, France)

* **Model Characteristics:**

− Model was first proposed and published in [517]
− The model implements the main components of the IEEE 802.16 2004 protocol.
− The module divides the protocol into Conversion Sublayer, Common Part Sublayer and Physical Layer.

⋆ **Evolution:**

– The INRIA ns-3 module has been completely written from scratch.

⋆ **Applicability:**

– Simulation of the PMP mode of the IEEE 802.16 protocol
– Support of two physical layers: trivial forwarding, OFDM physical layer
– QoS schemes according to IEEE 802.16
– Simulation of link and service flow management
– Basic packet scheduler
– Simulation of bandwidth management

⋆ **Accuracy / Complexity:**

– Due to the detailed implementation of many protocol features the model
  has a high complexity

⋆ **Known Use Cases:**

– Capacity analysis of IEEE 802.16.
– Protocol functions of the IEEE 802.16 system.

⋆ **Model Context:**

– The model requires network simulator NS-3 as ground laying framework
– The model needs further NS-3 components like network protocols and load
  generators

⋆ **Dependencies:**

– Model needs the NS-2 framework, depends on NS-2 components like energy
  and channel models and components for example

⋆ **Implementations:**

– The source code of the 802.16 module of the ns-3 simulator framework is
  available online: `http://code.nsnam.org/iamine/ns-3-wimax/`

12.3   IEEE 802.15.4

The *IEEE 802.15.4* standard focuses on *near-field* and *short-range communication*, suitable to cover the *Personal Operating Space (POS)* of a per-
son or device. A communication within a range of 1 to 25 meters is defined
as short-range or *personal area communication*. Consequently the so-called

Wireless Personal Area Networks (WPANs) are introduced by the standard. These networks are suited for low cost communication with little or no underlying infrastructure. Applications and technologies from this field have fundamentally different requirements compared to IEEE 802.11 WLANs or IEEE 802.16 (WiMAX). This section summarizes these differences and introduces different models for IEEE 802.15.4. Other technologies for personal area communication (e.g. Bluetooth, Z-Wave, IrDA) are not covered in this section.

12.3.1   Technical Introduction

The IEEE 802.15 working group consists of several task groups, all engaged in the area of personal area or short range communication. The IEEE 802.15.4 standard and its associated task groups are characterized by low data rates, very long battery lifetime (e.g. months or years), very low complexity and low hardware costs. IEEE 802.15.4 hardware is often used to provide low-power radios for small sensor nodes, long-running health care applications or transceivers for monitoring and sensing applications. The support for a high number of devices inside a single network is another feature of the standard. Other personal area technologies like high-rate *Ultra-Wideband (UWB)*, for example, are used in non-battery-powered scenarios with less participants and much higher data rates.

The standard was first published in [430], later revised by [429] and enhanced with amendments like [428] to support an UWB PHY. Several PHYs with different data rates and modulation schemes are specified in the standard, current standard conform devices operate on 868/915 MHz and 2.45 GHz. Apart from the PHY, a MAC is defined by the standard. The typical *protocol stack* of a compliant device is shown in Figure 12.11. The upper layers provide a network layer to support network configuration and message routing. It also provides an application layer, which defines the intended function of the sole device. The definition of these upper layers is outside the scope of the standard.

IEEE 802.15.4 supports features for *low-rate* and *low-power communication*. Important features are the support for real-time communication (via reservation of guaranteed time slots), the use of a collision avoidance mechanism (via CSMA-CA) and the support for secure communication (via AES encryption). The standard also defines power management functions like Link Quality Indication (LQI) and Energy Detection (ED). Different device types are specified: *Full-Function Devices (FFDs)* support the whole standard, while the *Reduced-Function Devices (RFDs)* support just a subset of the mandatory parts. RFDs, who are only able to communicate with FFDs, are used for simple operations like temperature or humidity sensing. FFDs support the whole standard and are used to build and set up networks. Two basic

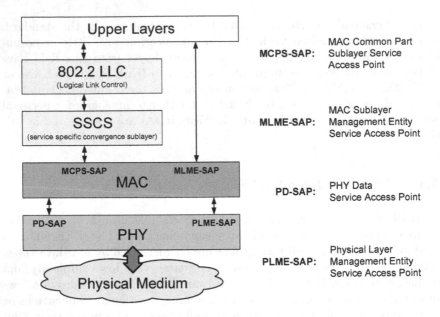

Fig. 12.11: IEEE 802.15.4 device architecture (based on [429])

topologies are defined in the standard: the *Peer-to-Peer (P2P) Topology* and the *Star Topology*. Both topologies and their specific communication flows are depicted in Figure 12.12.

The FFD that starts and builds up a new network, is usually selected as the *Personal Area Network (PAN) coordinator*, the central control and management entity inside a network. In a star topology, all messages are transfered over this PAN coordinator. In P2P topologies, the coordinator still provides important management functionalities, but normal communication takes place directly between entities, without the assistance of a PAN coordinator. Different usage scenarios are hence possible with the help of these two different network topologies.

Since the IEEE 802.15.4 standard does not specify the upper layers, additional frameworks or standards are required. *ZigBee*™ [32] is an example of an industry standard that incorporates IEEE 802.15.4 and defines the network layer and application framework on top of the standardized PHY and MAC. ZigBee provides additional security features and different application profiles. The *Cluster-Tree Topology* is defined in ZigBee as an enhancement to the two topologies provided by IEEE 802.15.4. In ZigBee, routing, network management, data transmissions between entities, and security functions are specified and standardized. For simplification reasons, researchers often use the sole IEEE 802.15.4 standard as the basic underlying framework for their own developed higher layer protocols. Modeling and simulation of ZigBee is

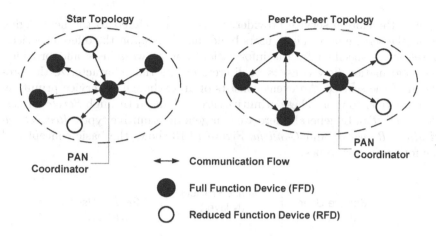

Fig. 12.12: IEEE 802.15.4 topologies (based on [429])

more interesting for industrial research. For academic research, though, the lower layers of IEEE 802.15.4 are often favored. Therefore, the focus of this section lies on IEEE 802.15.4 and its functionalities rather than on ZigBee.

12.3.2   IEEE 802.15.4 Reference Model

The subsequent paragraphs and subsections contain descriptions of the *modeling* of IEEE 802.15.4 WPANs. First, the *reference model* of IEEE 802.15.4 is analyzed. Subsequently, the consecutive subsections summarize descriptions for the modeling of the reference model components and layers. Descriptions for available models are presented in Subsection 12.3.6.

The area of WPAN modeling is quite complex. The important aspects in the modeling process are related to the structure, the setup and the protocol stack of IEEE 802.15.4 (refer to Figure 12.11). Many other details are also important in a simulation, for example the channel propagation system (refer to Chapter 11). Such components determine the modeling process of the IEEE 802.15.4 system itself. Descriptions of relevant surrounding components can be found in Chapter 9, Chapter 10 and Chapter 11 for example. Specifics and important characteristics will be outlined throughout this section.

Concept of Service Primitives

IEEE 802.15.4 uses the concept of *service primitives*, like many other ISO/IEC standards (for example the IEEE 802.11 standard - refer to Section 12.1.1). The following descriptions are only an introduction, for additional information see [518]. The capabilities of an specific layer are offered as services, the layer is therefore a service provider. Services are offered to the next higher layer, the service user. These users build functions upon the offered services. A service is specified by the information flow between user and provider. The information flow consists of discrete events that characterize the provision of the service. An event consists of an exchange of service primitives from provider to user. These primitives are exchanged through *Service Access Points (SAPs)*. In general, there are four generic primitive types: *Request, Indication, Response*, and *Confirm*. Figure 12.13 shows the basic concept and the four primitive types.

Fig. 12.13: Concept of service primitives (based on [429])

It is important to understand that this concept is the base for all operations inside a IEEE 802.15.4 entity. All functions provided by the different layers (e.g. changing the channel or sending an acknowledgment) are accessed and performed via service primitives. For a proper IEEE 802.15.4 protocol stack this concept has to be implemented for all components. Since most of the available models stick to this basic concept, a good understanding of service primitives is needed to work with the available models.

System Reference Model Overview

Protocol stack and architecture of IEEE 802.15.4 entities were introduced in Subsection 12.3.1 and illustrated in Fig. 12.11. The 802.2 LLC exists above the MAC. It can access the MAC sublayer through the Service Specific Convergence Sublayer (SSCS). Upper layer can send SDUs over the provided interface, the SDUs are then sent over the associated MAC connections. Refer to [429, Annex A] for information about the specific 802.2 LLC and SSCS.

The MAC sublayer provides two services: a MAC data and a MAC management service. The MAC data service enables the transmission and reception of MAC Protocol Data Units (MPDUs). It is accessed from upper layers via the MAC Common Part Sublayer SAP (MCPS-SAP). The particular PDUs are sent or received over the PHY data service and the appropriate SAP. The MAC management services are used to control the functions provided by the MAC through the associated MAC Sublayer Management Entity SAP (MLME-SAP). Functions of the MAC are: provision of channel access, beacon and Guaranteed Time Slot (GTS) management, frame validation and association and disassociation of network devices. It also provides functions and hooks for the implementation of application-appropriate security mechanisms. This is important when additional security functions are going to be implemented. Additional details about the MAC modeling are given in Subsection 12.3.4.

The PHY sublayer also provides a data service and a management service. The PHY data service enables the reception and transmission of PHY Protocol Data Units (PPDUs) across the physical radio channel. The PDUs are then sent from the PHY over the PHY Data Service SAP (PD-SAP) to the MAC. The management service provides different control functionalities that can be accessed through the PHY Management Entity SAP (PLME-SAP). Features of the PHY are the management of the radio transceiver, channel estimation and selection, CCA, and transmitting and receiving of packets across the physical medium. Refer to Subsection 12.3.3 for additional information on the PHY.

The IEEE 802.15.4 system reference model shares many similarities with the example packet domain PHY and DLL simulation model proposed in this book. For the PHY example part refer to Section 9.5 and Fig. 9.8, for the DLL part refer to Chapter 10 and Fig. 10.1. One can find all the functional blocks from the proposed example PHY model in the IEEE 802.15.4 reference model. Most functional blocks are either operations or services, like the carrier sensing and channel estimation block. These examples are represented in IEEE 802.15.4 as services provided by the PHY, accessible through the various SAPs of the PHY. A detailed description of the IEEE 802.15.4 PHY and DLL part follows in the next subsections.

12.3.3 Physical Layer

After the publication of the original standard in 2003, revisions and amendments added more features and specifications, especially for the *physical layer* (e.g. higher data rates and additional modulation schemes). Table 12.2 and Table 12.3 present important parameters for the PHYs specified in the 2006 revision [429]. UWB enhancements and the corresponding PHYs introduced through the 2007 amendment are not included in the tables (refer to [428] for more information on IEEE 802.15.4 UWB). While the first revision of the standard aimed at low-rate transceivers, the introduction of the UWB PHYs enabled the support for higher data rates like 851 kbit/s, 6.81 Mbit/s and 27.24 Mbit/s, and therewith new application fields.

The Direct Sequence Spread Spectrum (DSSS) modulation technique is used in combination with Binary Phase Shift Keying (BPSK) and

Channel parameters			Spreading parameters	
Frequency bands	Channel bandwidth	Channel distance	Chip modulation	Chip rate (kchip/s)
868 - 868.6 MHz	300 kHz	-	BPSK	300
902 - 928 MHz	600 kHz	2 MHz	BPSK	600
868 - 868.6 MHz	300 kHz	-	ASK	400
902 - 928 MHz	600 kHz	2 MHz	ASK	1600
868 - 868.6 MHz	300 kHz	-	O-QPSK	400
902 - 928 MHz	600 kHz	2 MHz	O-QPSK	1000
2400 - 2483.5 MHz	2 MHz	5 MHz	O-QPSK	1600

Table 12.2: IEEE 802.15.4-2006 PHYs with channel and spreading parameters

Data parameters			
Frequency bands	Symbol rate (ksymbol/s)	Bit rate (kbit/s)	Symbols
868 - 868.6 MHz	20	20	Binary
902 - 928 MHz	40	40	Binary
868 - 868.6 MHz	12.5	250	20-bit PSSS
902 - 928 MHz	50	250	5-bit PSSS
868 - 868.6 MHz	25	100	16-ary Orthogonal
902 - 928 MHz	62.5	250	16-ary Orthogonal
2400 - 2483.5 MHz	62.5	250	16-ary Orthogonal

Table 12.3: IEEE 802.15.4-2006 PHYs with data and transmission parameters

Offset Quadrature Phase Shift Keying (O-QPSK) in the 868/915 MHz and the 2.45 GHz frequency bands. Parallel Sequence Spread Spectrum (PSSS) is only used in combination with Amplitude Shift Keying (ASK) for the 868/915 MHz frequency bands. Another interesting parameter for the modeling of IEEE 802.15.4 is the *transmission output power*. It is fixed in the range of -25 to 0 dBm. A transmission power of 0 dBm equals 1 mW. The transmission output power is an important parameter for coexistence or interference evaluations.

Choosing an appropriate PHY is an important task in the WPAN modeling process. A decision should depend on local regulations, application types, requirements, and personal preferences. General advices for this decision are hard to give, however, one should keep the application type, needed data rates, and available energy amounts in mind. Since the different PHYs use different energy amounts for their operations, the total amount of energy available is especially important. The modeling of energy consumption should therefore be examined and considered before energy related choices can be made.

There is no standard *energy model* for IEEE 802.15.4. Different realizations exist in the research community today. A common approach for power and energy consumption modeling is the consideration of working states of the radio transceiver and the measurement of time spent in one of the working states. This method is of course not 100% accurate compared to real life experiments and testbeds. Depending on the provided simulation environment accuracy and the basic consumption values, the behavior and performance observed might be similar compared to real life experiments. Additional consumption aspects (e.g. CPU calculation time, energy spent through sensing, data processing) must also be considered if a more detailed and accurate energy consumption analysis is desired. Another interesting aspect in this case is the modeling of the energy source. Since certain sources (e.g. battery) have characteristics (e.g. recovery effect in batteries) that are important for the energy consumption, the modeling of energy sources should also be considered when accurate simulation results are needed. Further information on the topic of power modeling for IEEE 802.15.4 can be found in [327].

The general reference model for IEEE 802.15.4 was introduced in Subsection 12.3.2. Figure 12.14 shows an extract of this reference model: the PHY sublayer reference model. In addition to the already introduced SAPs, the PHY model contains the management entity of the physical layer and the PAN Information Base (PIB). The PIB comprises the different attributes required to manage the PHY of a device. The PHY Management Entity (PLME) manages and maintains the PIB. Examples of entries in this database are attributes for the current channel or the list of available channels, the CCA mode or other radio front-end constants. More information about these parameters and constants can be found in Subsection 12.3.5.

The connection to the MAC is provided by the two displayed SAPs: the PD-SAP and the PLME-SAP. Through the PD-SAP, *PD-DATA* primitives can be sent. General information about the concept of primitives were already presented in Subsection 12.3.2. There are three different *PD-DATA* primitives: *Request, Confirm* and *Indication*. The request primitive requests the transfer from a PDU from the MAC to the local PHY, while the confirm primitive confirms the end of the transmission. The indication primitive indicates the transfer of a PDU from the PHY to the MAC. This indication primitive contains a PDU length parameter and the Link Quality Indication (LQI) value measured during the receiving process.

Management commands between the MAC sublayer and the PHY sublayer are transfered over the PLME-SAP. The standard supports the following five primitives, each with a request and a confirm:

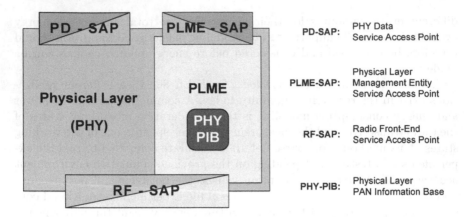

Fig. 12.14: IEEE 802.15.4 PHY sublayer reference model (based on [429])

- *PLME-SET-TRX-STATE:*

  The MAC can request an operating state change of the transceiver through this service primitive. Three main states are distinguished in the IEEE 802.15.4 standard: transmitter enabled (TX_ON), receiver enabled (RX_ON), and transceiver disabled (TRX_OFF). The associated confirm primitive enables a feedback about the change of state. An important parameter connected with this primitive is the *Transceiver-TurnaroundTime*, which describes the time that the hardware needs until the transceiver switched from receive into send state or back. Accurate modeling of IEEE 802.15.4 should consider this waiting period.

- *PLME-CCA:*

  When the PLME-CCA.request primitive is issued, a Clear Channel Assessment (CCA) is performed by the PHY. The PLME-CCA.confirm primitive reports the results (IDLE, BUSY, TRX_OFF) of the conducted CCA back to the MAC. An inquiry about the radio channel state can be made with these service primitives.

- *PLME-ED:*

  The PLME-ED.request primitive enables the MAC to request an Energy Detection (ED) operation. Depending on the transceiver state, either a SUCCESS, a TRX_OFF, or a TX_ON are reported back with the PLME-ED.confirm primitive. The confirm primitive also contains the ED result (energy level, a 8-bit integer value) in case of an enabled receiver and a successful energy detection operation.

- *PLME-SET:*

  The PLME-SET.request primitive enables the setting of PHY PIB attributes through the MAC. The attribute name and the according value are parameters of the request primitive. The confirm primitive reports back the results of the attempted setting operation.

- *PLME-GET:*
  With the PLME-GET.request primitive, a request about a given PHY PIB attribute can be made. If the requested PHY PIB is found in the database, the PLME-GET.confirm is issued with a SUCCESS status and the value of the given attribute.

Additional functional details of these service primitives depend on the actual hardware and the available firmware. In order to simulate the effects of these primitives it is necessary to implement them. In many existing models, these functions are only implemented in a simplified manner, which depends on the simulation environment functionalities. This depends on the functionality of the simulation environment. If a complex simulation environment with channel state information supply is available, then functions like energy detection and the according service primitives can be implemented. If the simulation environment or the simulator does not provide such a level of detail, then many of the introduced service primitives must be simplified. More information regarding the physical parameters, functionalities, modulation schemes, chipping sequences, and encoding and decoding functions are available in [429] and [428].

ED, CCA and LQI

Three PHY functions are important for the channel access management and should therefore be considered in the modeling process: *Energy Detection (ED), Clear Channel Assessment (CCA)*, and *Link Quality Indication (LQI)*. These three functions are used in the channel selection process, in the channel sampling of the CSMA CA algorithm and in the evaluation of the transmission quality.

Different approaches for the physical radio channel estimation were already presented in Subsection 9.2. The standard defines the ED functionality, which provides a measurement of the received signal power within the bandwidth of the selected channel. Possible signals on the channel are not identified or decoded here, just a power value is reported back to the MAC management entity. The standard proposes a certain mapping of received power values to integer values which are then reported back to the upper layers. This process is highly dependent on the receiver type and the hardware sensitivity. The user must be careful with the modulation and simulation process. The mapping of signal power and the accuracy always depends on the simulation environment and the channel simulation capabilities.

The PHY provides three different methods for the Clear Channel Assessment (CCA) (estimation of channel usage):

– CCA Mode 1 - Energy above threshold measurement
– CCA Mode 2 - Carrier sensing only
– CCA Mode 3 - Carrier sensing and energy above threshold measurement

In the first CCA Mode, the PHY measures the energy on the physical channel; if the detected energy level is above a certain threshold, the medium is reported back busy. In the second CCA mode, the PHY samples the channel and tries to detect a IEEE 802.15.4 compliant signal. The PHY checks the modulation and spreading characteristics; the energy level of the signal is not checked at this point. In the third CCA mode, the PHY tries to determine if a signal is being sent on the active channel and if the energy level of that signal is above a certain threshold. The threshold value should be set to a level where the receiver can still recover the signal at a certain quality. If the signal quality is too low, the receiver needs a higher sensitivity, the frame needs more redundancy data or the antenna gains needs to be increased. Parameters for the threshold value are again depending on the employed hardware or simulation environment.

The modeling of the different CCA modes is complex and difficult. In today's IEEE 802.15.4 simulation models, CCA is often reduced to the simple decision if either all devices in radio range are currently receiving, sleeping, or idling, or if at least one device in radio range is transmitting. The important aspect here is the radio range. For homogeneous network environments, path loss models are used to calculate the transmission and interference range and therewith the number of relevant devices for the CCA decision. Heterogeneous network environments represent challenging situations where different path loss or other more complex models need to be combined. More research in the area of interference in heterogeneous network scenarios (e.g. [286]) is needed.

Modulation and spreading characteristics, which are necessary for the second and third CCA mode, are not supported by most packet level simulation environments. Complex PHY models, which are necessary for the analysis and evaluation of energy measurements in heterogeneous and homogeneous network scenarios, are also not included in today's IEEE 802.15.4 simulation models. New simulation frameworks like MiXiM [262, 319] include a better support for complex and realistic PHY models, bit simulation capabilities and heterogeneous network environments. Future IEEE 802.15.4 models can hopefully use the abilities of new simulation frameworks like MiXiM and therewith model all CCA modes. For further information on CCA refer to [380], where an analysis of the different CCA modes is described. The paper illustrates the different modes, their metrics, and their impacts on MAC performance and power consumption.

The Link Quality Indication (LQI) is a PHY function, which provides the means for feeding back strength measurements of incoming packets. LQI can be realized in different ways: receiver ED or a signal-to-noise ratio estimation. Even combinations of different methods are possible. The standard does not specify how LQI is implemented, consequently different hardware vendors offer different solutions. In simulations, LQI is often reduced to a plain RSSI measurement, depending on the simulator's channel model type. Nowadays simple path loss models are often used in connection with IEEE 802.15.4 models to model the reduction of the signal power over the distance. The accuracy of LQI values in comparison to real life scenarios is therefore not guaranteed. Refer to Chapter 11 for more information on channel modeling.

12.3.4 Medium Access Control Layer

The *MAC* layer handles the access from the upper layers to the physical radio channel. Next to this basic function, it also provides the management and synchronization of beacon frames, the association of devices to networks, several security features, the handling of channel access, and the provision of a reliable link between the MAC entities of two peers/devices.

MAC and link layer are separated from each other in the standard [429]. In modeling and simulations, these two layers are usually modeled together. The MAC provides an interface between the SSCS and the PHY, as shown in Fig. 12.11. The necessary SAPs are shown in Fig. 12.15. They provide the interface connections to the management entity (MLME) and the common part. The MAC Sublayer Management Entity (MLME) is also responsible for the management and maintenance of the MAC sublayer PIB database with the important parameters and constants that are required for all MAC operations. Important MAC parameters are described in Subsection 12.3.5. The connections of the SAPs and the interfaces are shown in Fig. 12.15.

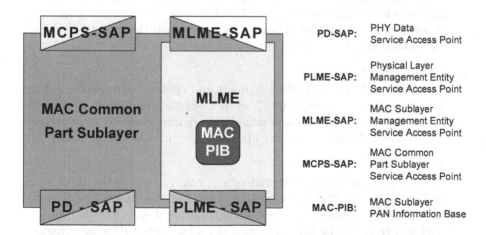

Fig. 12.15: IEEE 802.15.4 MAC sublayer reference model (based on [429])

The MAC data service, which runs through the MCPS-SAP, supports two different service primitives: *MCPS-DATA* and *MCPS-PURGE*. The data primitive is used for requesting, confirming, and indicating the transfer of SDUs from and to other entities. The purge primitive allows upper layers to delete a SDU from the transaction queue in the MAC layer. Refer to the standard [429] for more information on the ongoing processes, the exchanged data frames, and the primitive parameters. The following list describes all available service primitives:

- *MLME-ASSOCIATE:*
  The MLME-ASSOCIATE primitives (Request, Indication, Response, Confirm) enable the association of a device with a coordinator, and therewith with a PAN. The indication and response primitive are optional for RFDs. During the association process, information about the PAN associated 16-bit short address, about the security level and the device capabilities are exchanged. The message sequence chart for the exchange of service primitives is shown in [429, Figure 31].

- *MLME-DISASSOCIATE:*
  These primitives (request, indication, and confirm) are used by associated devices to announce their intent of leaving the PAN to the PAN coordinator. It can also be used by the coordinator to instruct an associated device to leave the PAN. The according message sequence charts are shown in [429, Figure 32, Figure 33].

- *MLME-BEACON-NOTIFY:*
  The MLME-BEACON-NOTIFY.indication primitive is used to send parameters from received beacon frames from the MAC layer to the next higher layer. The computed beacon LQI value and the reception time of the beacon are also provided by this service primitive.

- *MLME-GET/SET:*
  The GET and SET primitives (request and confirm) are used to get or set information from the PIB. They provide the connection of the PIB to the next higher layer. These primitives are important for management operations and should therefore always be included in the modeling.

- *MLME-GTS:*
  The GTS primitives (request, indication, confirm) are optional for both RFDs and FFDs. They are used to request and maintain GTSs. The usage of these primitives and the GTS is, in general, only possible when a device is tracking the beacon frames of its associated PAN coordinator. According message sequence charts are shown in [429, Figure 34, Figure 35]. GTS and superframes are described in detail in the successive subsection.

- *MLME-ORPHAN:*

  The MLME-ORPHAN primitives (indication and response only) are used by the coordinator to issue a notification of an orphaned device. Orphaned devices have lost the synchronization with their coordinator. If wanted, a coordinator realignment process can be started after the indication and response to re-synchronize the orphaned device with its PAN coordinator. These primitives are optional for RFDs.

- *MLME-RESET:*

  This self-explanatory primitive is used to reset the MAC sublayer to its initial conditions (including the MAC PIB, if enabled).

- *MLME-RX-ENABLE:*

  The MLME-RX-ENABLE primitives (request and confirm) allow a device to enable or disable its receiver. These receiver state primitives are optional for all devices. These primitives are always secondary to other responsibilities of the device. This must be considered during the modeling process. A message sequence chart for a change of the receiver state can be found in [429, Figure 37].

- *MLME-SCAN:*

  The SCAN primitives are used to initiate channel scan processes, energy measurements, search for associated coordinators, or searches for all beacon transmitting coordinators within the receiver range of the scanning device. These primitives are used by other operation and primitives (e.g. channel scan before a network is set-up). They are therefore crucial for the correct functionality of IEEE 802.15.4. The precise modeling of these primitives depends on the capabilities of the simulation environment and the level of detail that is required in the simulations.

- *MLME-COMM-STATUS:*

  The MLME-COMM-STATUS.indication primitive allows the MAC sublayer to indicate the status of communication (e.g. transmission status, channel access failures, security problems) to the next higher layer. It is again a crucial primitive as it enables a feedback about the current transmission status to higher layers.

- *MLME-START:*

  The MLME-START primitives (request and confirm) are mandatory for FFDs and optional for RFDs. A PAN coordinator can start a new PAN with the help of these primitives. Connected with these primitives are operations like starting or aborting beacon transmissions or the setup up of a new superframe configuration. If only static and pre-configured network scenarios are considered, these primitives can be simplified and reduced to ease the implementation.

- *MLME-SYNC:*

  This request primitive requests the synchronization, and if specified, the tracking of beacon frames of a PAN coordinator. By synchronizing with the beacons, a PAN coordinator can be enabled. The primitive is optional for both device types.

- *MLME-SYNC-LOSS:*

  This indication primitive reports the loss of synchronization with a PAN coordinator. If synchronization is lost, a coordinator realignment procedure is started to regain synchronization.

- *MLME-POLL:*

  The POLL primitives (request and confirm) are issued by higher layers to prompt the device to request data from the PAN coordinator. A data request command is sent from the device to the coordinator. An according message sequence chart is shown in [429, Figure 40].

Since many of these service primitives are optional for *RFDs* and some even for *FFDs*, one can simplify during the modeling process and reduce the number of primitives for modeling and implementation. PAN management functionalities, for example, could be left out of the modeling process if only performance aspects of plain data transmissions are of interest. Depending on the type of simulation and the required simulation aspects, a choice of necessary service primitives has to be made. A profound check of interconnections and interdependences between the different service primitives is important so that required primitives are not left out during the modeling process. Additional information on the service primitives can be found in [429, Table 46] and the referenced subclauses.

Superframes and Beacons

IEEE 802.15.4 introduces the so-called *superframe* structure. The PAN coordinator defines the format of the superframe by setting the necessary parameters. The superframe itself regulates the sending periods of all devices inside the local PAN. The superframe boundaries are *network beacons*, which are sent by the PAN coordinator (see Fig. 12.16). Format descriptions and parameters are included in these network beacons. As shown in Figure 12.16, the superframe can have an active and an inactive portion. The inactive periods can be used to put devices and transceivers to sleep, power management therefore goes hand in hand with the usage of superframe structures.

If a coordinator does not wish to use superframes, it simply turns off the transmission of beacons. The beacons are used to synchronize the associated devices inside the PAN. Devices inside the network listen for beacon transmissions and evaluate the parameters from received beacon frames. Depending

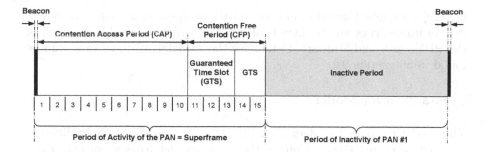

Fig. 12.16: IEEE 802.15.4 superframe structure (based on [429])

on the structure of the superframe, devices can use the contention period to content for channel access. Concurrent transmissions are avoided with the help of the CSMA-CA algorithm. The other option is the usage of *Guaranteed Time Slot (GTS)*, where devices can reserve time frames for undisturbed transmissions. Inside a GTS, devices transmit without using CSMA-CA. GTS are often used for time-critical or low-latency applications.

The modeling of beacons and superframes is often skipped in simulation models, when the creator is not interested in these features. The modeling is not very complex, however, the implementation is extensive, since superframes and beacons influence many other functions of IEEE 802.15.4.

Frame Structure

Frames are always a critical part of any standard. On the one hand, they should avoid complex structures and minimize overhead. On the other hand, they should be extensible and suited for various usage scenarios. The IEEE 802.15.4 standard tries to keep the complexity low while including some efforts to keep the frames robust enough for transmissions over noisy channels. Therefore, each frame type is equipped with a 16-bit frame check sequence where a CRC algorithm is used. There are four different frame types specified in the standard:

- MAC command frame
- DATA frame
- BEACON frame
- ACKNOWLEDGMENT frame

Each protocol layer adds to the structure of these frames layer-specific headers and footers. The MAC frame is used for the handling of control transmissions while the DATA frame is used for all data transmissions. ACKNOWLEDGMENT frames are used for the confirmation of successful reception processes and the BEACON frames are used by the PAN coordinator for beacon distribution. The structures of the different frame types are listed in [429], an explicit description is out of the scope of this book. The detection of frame types and borders is also not described here, this is a task of the PHY hard- and firmware. Details for the modeling of these tasks can be found in Subsection 9.2.

Data Transfer Model

The model for data transfers in IEEE 802.15.4 consists of three different transaction types. The first one is the data transfer from a normal device to the PAN coordinator. Acknowledgments are sent only if requested by the normal device. The second type is the data transfer from the PAN coordinator to the normal device. The normal device requests data from the coordinator, that sends the data afterwards. All transmissions are acknowledged in this case. The last transaction type specifies the data transfer between two normal peer devices. Star topology networks only support the first two transaction types, as shown in Figure 12.12. Devices can only send and receive data from and to a PAN coordinator. In P2P topologies, data can be exchanged between all devices freely, all transaction types can be used in this topology type.

CSMA-CA

General information about the functionality and the modeling of CSMA are described in Subsection 9.2. The IEEE 802.15.4 standard uses two types of CSMA-CA: a slotted and a unslotted version. PANs that do not use beacons (non-beacon-enabled PANs) use the unslotted CSMA-CA algorithm for the channel access management. Each time a device wants to transmit data, it waits for a random time period (backoff). The device samples the channel after this backoff period. If the channel is idle, the device accesses the channel and transmits its data. If the channel is found busy after the backoff period, the device refrains from accessing the channel and waits for another backoff interval. Acknowledgment frames are sent without using CSMA-CA in IEEE 802.15.4. Three parameters manage CSMA-CA: the Backoff Exponent (BE), the Contention Window Length (CW), and the Number of Backoffs (NB). NB specifies the number of times that CSMA-CA was required to perform a backoff while trying to access and transmit on the channel. CW (used for slotted CSMA-CA) specifies the length of the contention window, where no channel activity should occur prior to any transmission start. BE is used to calculate a random value of initial backoff periods before a device samples the radio channel.

Beacon-enabled PANs use the slotted version of CSMA-CA for channel access. The backoff periods are aligned with the start of beacon transmissions. If a device wants to access the channel during a contention period (active superframe portion) it waits for a random number of backoff slots. If the channel is busy, the device waits for another random number of backoff slots before trying to access the channel again. The contention period boundaries are transmitted in the beacon frame, the devices listen for this frame to align their backoff periods to the start of the beacon. In this operational mode, acknowledgments and beacon frames are sent without using CSMA-CA.

The different CSMA-CA parameters (BE, CW, NB) can be adjusted on the different layers. There are many research papers available where different parameter combinations for the optimization of the channel access are analyzed (e.g. [99, 263, 381, 382]). General guidelines are hard to give for the modeling of CSMA-CA and the parameter settings. For a start in this field refer to the standard and the proposed parameters ([429, Table 86]).

12.3.5 Important Parameters

The overall list of available PHY and MAC parameters for IEEE 802.15.4 is exhaustive. Starting points are the information about the attributes from the PHY and the MAC PAN Information Bases. These information can be found in [429, Table 23] for the PHY attributes and [429, Table 86] for the MAC attributes. Depending on the type of research or simulation, different parameters might be more or less useful. The following list is an example of adaptable parameters, which can be useful for IEEE 802.15.4 performance evaluations:

– Payload and/or packet size
– Addressing mode and address size (16-bit or 64-bit addresses supported)
– Packet overhead
– Type of node (PAN coordinator, RFD, FFD)
– Superframe parameters (Superframe Duration, Superframe Order)
– Beacon parameters (Beacon Interval, Beacon Order)
– CSMA-CA parameters
– CCA modes and characteristics
– GTS usage parameters

Several other parameters can not be influenced with GET or SET MAC management commands through the protocol stack in contrast to the listed parameters. The following incomplete listing presents several examples:

– Channel model parameters (values and influence depend on the simulation framework and the used channel model)
– Receivers sensitivity and transmitter power (either defined by the standard or taken from hardware data sheets)
– Antenna gain (taken from hardware data sheets)
– Interference type and interference characteristics (depend on simulation framework and used PHY models)
– Transmission or packet error model characteristics and parameters

These values also have a certain impact on the performance of WPANs and devices, but they are not alterable from the device itself (exceptions might be the delay values in case of mobile devices). Most of the time, these values and parameters are accessible through the simulation environment. Criteria for the selection of parameter values depend on the investigation scenario and the desired outcomes. Hardware-related parameters are usually taken directly from data sheets of real life hardware (e.g. Texas Instruments C2420 transceiver). Predetermined values for the other parameters are hard to predict since they depend on the chosen channel, error, or PHY model. Refer to the according sections in this book (e.g. Section 11.1 or Section 11.2) or example evaluations from the research community (e.g. [368, 423, 517]) for more information.

12.3.6   Introduction of Available Models

The previous subsections introduced the reference model for IEEE 802.15.4. The focus of this subsection lies on the description of existing models from the network simulation research community.

Models for WPANs and IEEE 802.15.4 are diverse. Some models are just used for the evaluation of single parameter alterations, while other models reproduce complex WPAN scenarios. Most of them are connected to a certain simulation software, like NS-2 [116] or OMNeT++ [474]. These connections and other important information, for example the abstraction level of the model, applied simplifications, and model characteristics, are presented for different models on the following pages. The described models are all available for free. Other existing models (e.g. OPNET 802.15.4 model) are not described here, since they are not published yet or not available for free.

NS-2 Simulator for IEEE 802.15.4

⋆ **Intent:**

– Comprehensive platform for simulations and performance analysis of IEEE 802.15.4, developed especially for NS-2 [116] on Linux (and Cygwin).

⋆ **Also Known As:**

– IEEE 802.15.4 Model of NS-2
– WPAN NS-2 Simulation Model

⋆ **Authors / Contributors:**

– Jianliang Zheng (Dept. of Electrical Engineering, City University of NY) (http://ees2cy.engr.ccny.cuny.edu/zheng/index.html)

- Myung J. Lee (Dept. of Electrical Engineering, City University of NY)
  (http://www-ee.ccny.cuny.edu/faculty/people/lee.html)

★ **Model Characteristics:**

- The model was first proposed and published in [517]
- The model implements the main layers of the IEEE 802.15.4 standard,
  most functionalities of the original reference model are also provided
- Special features of the model are the support for different routing protocols
  and the possibility to define wireless usage scenarios

★ **Evolution:**

- ZigBee routing is not included anymore starting from releases v1.1

★ **Applicability:**

- Simulation of routing protocols, e.g. AODV
- Simulation of beacon-enabled star and tree networks
- Simulation of P2P tree and cluster tree formations
- Performance evaluations of IEEE 802.15.4
- Direct and indirect data transmissions are supported
- Model does not support GTS, scenarios with GTS are not supported
- Contention Free Period (CFP) is not supported by the model
- This WPAN model does not define a specific energy model, it uses the one
  from the simulation platform NS-2 instead

★ **Accuracy / Complexity:**

- The model has a high complexity (many similarities to the reference model)
- Accuracy of the model depends on the usage and parameter setting in
  combination with the simulation platform (NS-2 for this model)
- Accuracy of energy usage and energy depletion is low, since the model does
  not implement its own energy sub-module, but uses the generic energy
  model of the NS-2 framework instead [376, Chapter 19]
- PHY and channel modeling (e.g. two-ray ground reflection model, omni-
  directional antenna model) is provided by NS-2, for more information on
  this topic refer to the NS-2 documentation [376, Chapter 18] and the source
  code [116], or the appropriate sections of this book

★ **Known Use Cases:**

- Performance analysis of IEEE 802.15.4
- Analysis of Superframe performance options
- Realization of ubiquitous networks with IEEE 802.15.4 nodes

– Performance studies of IEEE 802.15.4 slotted and unslotted CSMA-CA
– Formation of Star and P2P Tree networks and performance investigations of these networks

⋆ Model Context:

– Model requires network simulator NS-2 as ground laying framework
– Model needs description of network scenarios (via script language `Tcl`)
– Definition of deterministic error models for nodes and links needed, if wanted by user (samples are provided by simulation platform NS-2)
– Definition of traffic type (e.g. constant, random or Poisson distributed) needed (samples provided by simulation platform NS-2)

⋆ Inputs:

– Model supports two interfaces: the traditional link layer call-back (comparable to IEEE 802.11) and the IEEE 802.15.4 primitives
– The primitives are the main interface, the traditional link layer call-back is for users who are not familiar with IEEE 802.15.4 primitives

⋆ Outputs:

– Main output is a trace file, which can be visualized and analyzed with NAM (the Network ANimator of NS-2)
– Format of the trace file is the same as that of general NS-2 simulations, only new frame types for IEEE 802.15.4 were defined, more information can be found in the source code documentation of the trace format

⋆ Dependencies:

– Model needs the NS-2 framework, depends on NS-2 components, e.g. energy and channel models and components

⋆ Structure:

– No UML description available

⋆ Implementations:

– Implementation available online (refer to ⋆ **Availability**) and included in all versions of NS-2 since `ns-2.28`
– Source code written in `C++` (main components) and `Tcl` (simulation scripts)
– Implementation includes: IEEE 802.15.4 PHY and MAC, SSCS, routing layer, wireless scenario definition components, several demos and different routing algorithms for testing purposes

⋆ **General Issues:**

– GTS is not a part of the model
– Problem of *Task Overflow*:
  – IEEE 802.15.4 functions are primitives (described in Subsection 12.3.2)
  – When the upper layer sends down a request, it should wait for a confirmation, if it sends down another request before it receives the confirmation, a task overflow will happen
  – This overflow could be prevented with a task queue at the SSCS, but it is currently not implemented
– Sleep Mode of IEEE 802.15.4 is not supported:
  – The WPAN module does not implement its own energy model, it uses the generic one from NS-2
  – The NS-2 energy model does not distinguish between idle and sleep mode
  – Different energy consumptions for these two modes are therefore not supported at the moment, alterations of the source code for support of sleep mode are possible for everyone (might be fixed in future releases)

⋆ **Availability:**

– Source code included in NS-2 releases starting from version ns-2.28 under the folder ns-x.xx/wpan/
– Source code available online (http://ees2cy.engr.ccny.cuny.edu/zheng/pub/index.html)

⋆ **Related Models:**

– No related models

⋆ **Author of Model Description:**

– Michael Kirsche (BTU Cottbus)

IEEE 802.15.4 CAP Model for NS-2

⋆ **Intent:**

– Model developed for the analysis of the performance of the Contention Access Period (CAP) of IEEE 802.15.4 in star topologies and beacon-enabled modes, implemented for NS-2 [116] on Linux (and Cygwin).

⋆ **Also Known As:**

– IEEE 802.15.4 MAC Implementation in NS-2

⋆ Authors / Contributors:

- Iyappan Ramachandran (Fundamentals of Networking Laboratory (Funlab), University of Washington, Seattle)
- Arindam K. Das (Funlab, University of Washington)
- Sumit Roy (Funlab, University of Washington)

⋆ Model Characteristics:

- The model was first described and published in [381]
- The model provides several modifications of the previously described IEEE 802.15.4 model for NS-2
- The performance analysis of the CAP and the superframe structure of IEEE 802.15.4 are important parts of this model, therefore several simplifications are made in comparison to the reference model

⋆ Motivation and Simplifications:

- Since the model creators were just interested in the CAP, they proposed simplifications of the original reference model
- The model assumes that there is no Contention Free Period (CFP) in the superframe, the CAP contains the complete superframe period
- Only star topologies are supported by the model
- All packets are transfered over the PAN coordinator of the star topology
- No routing algorithm and no routing layer is supported by the model
- All nodes are assumed to be within the carrier sensing range of each other, no hidden nodes and no collisions from transmissions of hidden nodes are therefore possible or supported
- MAC level acknowledgments are not supported by the model
- The MAC layer does not have an interface queue (e.g. for message transfer)

⋆ Applicability:

- Simulation of beacon-enabled star topology networks
- Performance evaluations of IEEE 802.15.4 CAP

⋆ Accuracy / Complexity:

- Model has a lower complexity compared to the reference model
- Accuracy for certain scenarios (especially CAP scenarios) might be high, for all other scenarios the accuracy is supposed to be lower
- Since this model is an extension of the previously introduced NS-2 IEEE 802.15.4 model, stated comments about the accuracy and use of NS-2 PHY and channel models apply to this model too

⋆ Known Use Cases:

- Performance analysis of IEEE 802.15.4 CAP

⋆ Model Context:

– Model requires network simulator NS-2 as the basic framework

⋆ Inputs:

– The model supports the same interfaces like the previously described NS-2 Simulator for IEEE 802.15.4

⋆ Outputs:

– Main output is a trace file, which can be visualized and analyzed with NAM (the Network ANimator of NS-2)

⋆ Dependencies:

– Model needs components and other models from the NS-2 framework

⋆ Structure:

– No UML description available

⋆ Implementations:

– Implementation available online (refer to ⋆ **Availability**)
– Source code written in C++ (main components) and Tcl (simulation scripts)
– Most parts of the implementation were taken from the NS-2 Simulator for IEEE 802.15.4 from J. Zheng and M. J. Lee
– Modifications include the correction of certain NS-2 bugs, the incorporation of a new energy model that supports sleep modes, the incorporation of a shutdown command for nodes and more changes for the support of the proposed simplifications
– A description of code changes can be found on-line
(http://www.ee.washington.edu/research/funlab/802_15_4/)

⋆ General Issues:

– No known problems or general issues

⋆ Availability:

– Source code and modifications available online
(http://www.ee.washington.edu/research/funlab/802_15_4/)

⋆ Related Models:

– NS-2 Simulator for IEEE 802.15.4 (refer to page 294)

⋆ Author of Model Description:

– Michael Kirsche (BTU Cottbus)

IEEE 802.15.4 Model for OMNeT++/INET Framework

⋆ Intent:

– Simulation model of IEEE 802.15.4, developed especially for OMNeT++ [474] and the INET framework

⋆ Also Known As:

– IEEE 802.15.4 Model for INET

⋆ Authors / Contributors:

– M.Sc. Feng Chen (Dept. of CS 7, University of Erlangen-Nuremberg) (http://www7.informatik.uni-erlangen.de/~fengchen/)
– PD Dr.-Ing. habil. Falko Dressler (Dept. of CS 7, University of Erlangen-Nuremberg) (http://www7.informatik.uni-erlangen.de/~dressler/)

⋆ Model Characteristics:

– First description and publication in [95]
– The model was developed for performance evaluation
– The model was built to be conform with the standard's 2006 revision [429]
– The developed model consists of two sub-modules for PHY and MAC layers respectively, while supporting star and cluster tree topologies
– The model supports modifications of all important parameters of the IEEE 802.15.4 protocol stack (refer to Subsection 12.3.5)
– An energy model was developed to enable consumption measurements
– A configurable traffic generator is included in the model
– Different traffic schemes can be generated and used with the help of an incorporated traffic generator
– Through an XML-based parameter structure, several traffic types (e.g. Constant Bit Rate (CBR) traffic, ON-OFF-traffic, exponentially distributed traffic) can be generated and changed during simulation runtime

⋆ Motivation:

– Since performance evaluations were the main interest of the creators, the traffic generator and the energy consumption measurement are two of the most important components

– These features distinguish this model from other models where traffic patterns cannot be changed during runtime and where energy consumption (and the according measurements) are only supported in a rudimentary way

⋆ **Applicability:**

– Performance evaluations of IEEE 802.15.4
– Simulation of beacon-enabled star topology networks
– Evaluation of energy consumption of IEEE 802.15.4 nodes and networks under different traffic patterns
– Workload evaluation of IEEE 802.15.4 networks

⋆ **Accuracy / Complexity:**

– The model has a high complexity, comparable to the reference model itself
– Accuracy for many scenarios seems to be high, but it depends on the simulation platform and the settings
– This model builds upon OMNeT++ and INET framework PHY, propagation, channel, and error models
– For information on these models, refer to the OMNeT++ website [474] and the INET framework website (http://inet.omnetpp.org/)

⋆ **Known Use Cases:**

– Performance analysis of IEEE 802.15.4
– Analysis of IEEE 802.15.4 under QoS aspects
– Analysis of the superframe structure of IEEE 802.15.4

⋆ **Model Context:**

– The model requires simulation platform OMNeT++ and the INET framework

⋆ **Inputs:**

– Interface for traffic generation to describe traffic types

⋆ **Outputs:**

– Vector and scalar files (OMNeT++ file formats), which contain information about traffic, packet exchange, time usage, network and performance statistics, energy consumption, end-to-end delay, and other predefined performance metrics

⋆ **Dependencies:**

− Model needs OMNeT++ and the INET framework
− Requires traffic patterns, described within a XML file

⋆ **Structure:**

− No UML description available

⋆ **Implementations:**

− Implementation available online (refer to ⋆ **Availability**)
− Source code written in C++ (main components) and script language (NED files, OMNeT++ specific network descriptions)
− Implementation includes: the IEEE 802.15.4 PHY and MAC modules, an interface queue module, a routing and a traffic module and battery and mobility modules

⋆ **General Issues:**

− Pre-release of this model only supports beacon-enabled star networks

⋆ **Availability:**

− Source code available online
(http://www7.informatik.uni-erlangen.de/~fengchen/omnet/802154/)

⋆ **Related Models:**

− No related models

⋆ **Author of Model Description:**

− Michael Kirsche (BTU Cottbus)

This listing of IEEE 802.15.4 models is not complete. Because further information (and hands-on experience) on proprietary models (e.g. IEEE 802.15.4 OPNET model) could not be obtained, such models are not considered and described in this section. Refer to [246] for information on a IEEE 802.15.4 *simulation model for OPNET*. Current research work in this area is the development of standard-compliant implementations of the IEEE 802.15.4 MAC and the ZigBee protocol for the tinyOS 2 platform. Refer to the according working group websites [195] and [264] for more information.

A validation of simulation models against the standard or available hardware is often not made in research publications. This topic still needs more work and consideration, since only validated models will finally be accepted throughout the research community. Some researchers validate their own analytical models and simulations against the introduced NS-2 model from Zheng [517]. This model therefore seems to be the most distributed model in the community today. However, a complete and full validation of this or any other IEEE 802.15.4 model is still pending work.

12.3.7 Summary

The reference model of the IEEE 802.15.4 standard for WPANs and a technical introduction were presented in this section. The different layers of the standard were introduced along with specifics, parameters and important aspects of IEEE 802.15.4. Advices for simulations and investigations were given throughout this section. The section closed with an introduction and evaluation of available simulation models from the network research community. In Section 13.2, information regarding the use of available models in terms of simulation and evaluation of WPANs is given together with hints for practical usage in connection with a specific use case.

13. Wireless Networking Use Cases

M. Mühleisen, R. Jennen (RWTH Aachen University)
M. Kirsche (Brandenburg University of Technology Cottbus (BTU))

In this chapter two example use cases are presented on how a simulation study for a particular scenario is conducted and which modeling decisions are taken with respect to the goal of the study. These two sections are built on top of the previous chapters but focused on particular questions for investigation. Also they highlight important modeling options and their respective performance impact. In particular, we consider next the issue of coexistence for wireless local area networks as well as the issue of wireless personal area network performance.

13.1 Use Case - Coexistence

The term coexistence refers to multiple wireless systems operating on a shared resource. These systems usually operate on the same frequency channel. Figure 13.1 shows a common example of coexistence scenario. Here two households establish WLANs following the *IEEE 802.11* standard. The IEEE 802.11 standard is described in more detail in Section 12.1. The WLANs are established by Access Points (APs) providing Internet access through a router. Both follow the IEEE 802.11g standard operating in the Industrial, Scientific, and Medical (ISM) band and form two separate networks, since they have different Basic Service Set Identifiers (BSSIDs). However, they could be operating on the same frequency channel. In this case, they receive data from the other network enabling virtual carrier sensing using the Network Allocation Vector (NAV) as described in Section 12.1.3. They could also be operating on different, partly overlapping channels. Then frames from the other network cannot be decoded but the systems suffer from interference. Besides the APs, multiple other nodes can be present in the network. Most common application is Internet access for PCs and notebooks. New applications including Voice over IP (VoIP), IP-TV, and wireless access to hard-disks providing videos and music are currently emerging. It could be that all nodes are within mutual interference range and no hidden nodes are present. In general not all nodes interfere with each other. Nowadays it is very likely to have multiple systems operating in close proximity as more and more households deploy WLANs.

In the following we focus on inter-system interference emitted from nodes of one system to nodes from other systems. To narrow down the topic we

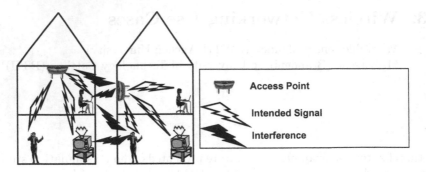

Fig. 13.1: Example scenario with two households each using a WLAN for various
applications

consider networks with a dedicated central node forming a star topology
(e.g. the AP in IEEE 802.11). Therefore, we do not consider Mesh or P2P
networks. We mainly discuss coexistence from a Data Link Layer (DLL)
point of view, so Transmission Control Protocol (TCP) (see Chapter 17) is
not considered. Layers between the application and the DLL do not delay the
PDUs. To further narrow down the topic we assume that networks cannot
directly communicate, but they can sense the emitted power of surrounding
nodes.

13.1.1   Regulatory Constraints

Previous section already introduced the *ISM* band, which can be used for
coexisting systems. The only regulatory constraint in this band is a limitation
on the total emitted power. Luckily the dominant system in the ISM band is
IEEE 802.11b/g, which uses Listen Before Talk (LBT) to assure every node
in any system gets a fair share of the channel. Other systems in the ISM
band are *IEEE 802.15.1* (Bluetooth) [12] and *IEEE 802.15.4* (ZigBee) (see
Section 12.3).

Other unlicensed spectrum is present at 5 GHz at most geographic locations. In the US this band is called *Unlicensed National Information
Infrastructure (U-NII)*. Besides limiting emitted power, many countries enforce Transmission Power Control (TPC) (see Section 10.1.5) in this band.
The dominant system in this band is IEEE 802.11a. The *IEEE 802.16h* [21]
standard draft currently develops protocol improvements allowing WiMAX
systems (see Section 12.2) to also operate in this unlicensed band.

New opportunities for unlicensed systems are currently established through
the so called *non-exclusive licensing*. If a license is not used at a certain time
and geographic location, other systems may use the spectrum. This is called
vertical coexistence. Systems operated by the license holder are called primary

systems, and the ones operating if the primary user is absent are called secondary systems. If multiple secondary systems operate in the spectrum, the same situation as in the ISM and U-NII band is created. In [14], non-exclusively licensed operations of systems in unused TV bands in the US is regulated by the Federal Communication Commission (FCC). Secondary systems must instantly stop transmitting if the primary system starts operating. Additionally, the FCC requires secondary systems to

"allow multiple users to share the same spectrum by defining the events that must occur when two or more devices attempt to simultaneously access the same channel and establishing rules by which each device is provided a reasonable opportunity to operate."

This is still not very specific but more restrictive than just limiting emitted power and enforcing TPC.

There are also unlicensed bands reserved to single technologies. Here "unlicensed" refers to the fact that the systems are set up by end-users and not operators. One example is the *Digital Enhanced Cordless Telephone (DECT)* system [215] operating at 1800 MHz - 1900 MHz in Europe. In such systems, the end-user buys and deploys the BSs creating a scenario similar to the example scenario in Figure 13.1. DECT systems in nearby households can interfere, but the protocol specifies rules on how to limit the impact. This kind of licensing enforces the most restrictive regulations, and only systems following defined media access rules may be deployed. Currently the ITU-T evaluates candidate systems within the *IMT-Advanced* process [16] for next generation mobile radio. Besides cellular scenarios, systems also have to prove their performance in a so called "Indoor hotspot" scenario at 3.4 GHz. Such a scenario may be formed of *Femto Cells*, where end-users deploy low power BSs to improve indoor coverage. It is therefore likely that the IMT-Advanced candidate systems *LTE* [19] and IEEE 802.16m [20] will also need the capabilities to deal with end-user deployed scenarios.

Finally the IEEE Standard Coordination Committee 41 [374] and the *DARPA XG* project [360] develop novel approaches for unlicensed operation. Here machine readable rules, so called policies, are downloaded by nodes operating in a given frequency band. In this way protocol behavior can dynamically be changed depending on frequency band, location, time, total load in the band etc. As new and more efficient systems are introduced to the market, authorities might change the policies for older and less efficient systems. Older systems which are not able to reach the state of the art efficiency might be banned from certain bands or forced to a subset of available resources.

This shows that multiple opportunities for unlicensed operation exist. Different bands have different restrictions. While the 2.4 GHz and 5 GHz bands are less regulated, they are already dominated by IEEE 802.11 systems. Any new technology operating in these bands must be able to coexist with IEEE 802.11. Other bands are currently becoming available with possibly higher restrictions. It is up to researchers in the field of coexistence to develop protocols outperforming IEEE 802.11 in terms of QoS support and spectral efficiency. In the following we present how system performance can be measured.

13.1.2 Performance Measures

As mentioned before, different applications for wireless communication exist. Each application has its specific demands. Real time services, like VoIP for example, require a low packet delay. Our focus lies on the impact of layer 2 to coexistence, including the MAC protocol and scheduling. Layer 2 does not have specific information to which application an IP-Protocol Data Unit (PDU) belongs. Many technology standards define *QoS classes* to map application demands to different priorities in layer 2. Each standard may have a different set of QoS classes and names them differently. The IEEE 802.16 standard for example defines the classes Unsolicited Grant Service (UGS), Extended Real-time Polling Service (ertPS), Real-time Polling Service (rtPS), Non-real-time Polling Service (nrtPS), and Best Effort (BE). When evaluating system performance with QoS classes, performance measures of the same class must be compared. In coexistence scenarios the same performance measures like in single system scenarios can be used. In both single system and coexistence scenarios, these measures can be evaluated separately by direction (uplink and downlink), QoS class and node. In addition, in a coexistence scenario, they can also be evaluated per system.

Utilization

The *utilization* describes the ratio between maximal possible data rate R and actual throughput T. It can also be defined by:

$$U = \frac{t_{transpMin}}{t_{total}}. \tag{13.1}$$

Assuming constant PDU length in bit L, $t_{transpMin} = L/R_{Max}$ is the time required to transmit a PDU at the highest possible data rate defined by the available MCSs. t_{total} accumulates all waiting times of the PDU from the point it is ready to be transmitted (head of queue) up to the point when it is successfully received. This includes some or all of the following:

- Propagation delay t_{prop}
- Transmission time $n \cdot t_{transp}$, with n retries if ARQ is used
- Channel idle time t_{idle} caused by backoff, turn-around times and inter frame spaces
- Time t_{col} the channel is occupied by unsuccessful transmissions (collisions)

– Additional overhead time t_{ctrl} introduced by the MAC or PHY protocol including for example beacons, RTS, CTS, ACK, pilot tones, preambles, Channel Quality Indicator (CQI) feedback, and all other control channel transmissions

An optimal ratio 1 is therefore reached if the system constantly transmits at maximal data rate. In general, some of the components of t_{total} are not constant. In this case the mean utilization can be measured.

Utilization can be measured per system, especially if the systems have different maximal transmission rates. Alternatively, the highest possible transmission rate of all systems can be used as a reference.

Delay and Jitter

Assuming single-hop communication and no delays in the layers above layer 2, the delay is the sum of previously described t_{total} together with the queuing delay in layer 2. Systems using scheduling, like LTE or IEEE 802.16, can introduce an additional delay caused by the offset in the frame where the PDU is scheduled as described in Section 10.1.2. The jitter is the standard deviation of the delay. Acceptable values for this indicators depend on the application. Since we map applications with different demands to different QoS classes, delay should be measured and compared per class. Depending on their position, nodes can experience different interference from a coexisting system. Delay should therefore be measured per node.

Loss

PDU losses occur if no ARQ is used, or if a maximum number of retries is reached with ARQ. Another possible reason for packet loss is drop tail queues. Since tolerable loss depends on the application it should be measured per QoS class and per node.

Throughput and Spectral Efficiency

The *throughput* describes how many bit were successfully received per unit time. Since different QoS classes have different throughput demands, it is measured per QoS class. If the distribution of the throughput is not of interest, its mean value can be derived as the ratio of all received bit over total simulation time, as long as the simulation has reached its stationary phase. In this way side effects from too short averaging windows are suppressed. Again results should be collected per node.

The *spectral efficiency* is the throughput normalized to frequency bandwidth and area and therefore measured in $Bit/(s \cdot Hz \cdot m^2)$. Since all systems use the same spectrum and are located in the same area, the spectral efficiency should be measured as a global performance indicator taking into account all successfully received bits in all systems. It may be collected separately for the uplink and downlink.

Fairness

A common index to measure *fairness* is *Jain's fairness index* [234] shown in Equation (13.2).

$$f = \frac{(\sum x_i)^2}{n \cdot \sum x_i^2} \qquad (13.2)$$

x_i can be any collected performance measure, e.g. delay. The index i stands for one of the n nodes of all systems. It makes no sense to compare measurements from different QoS classes. Previously collected performance measures, delay, jitter, and throughput can be evaluated for their fairness. There is usually a trade-off between maximizing throughput and maximizing fairness.

13.1.3   Simulation Setup

Simulations should be set up in a way that all factors influencing above performance measures are considered.

Deployment

Since we evaluate coexistence, the smallest number of systems is two. As described earlier in the example scenario, there can be more coexisting systems in general. Since node positions play an important role, a sufficient number of nodes with different distances to the own and the interfering systems should be deployed on the area covered by each system. It is possible to use multiple drops with random node positioning as described in [16]. In a cellular network the cell size limits the coverage area of a BS. Assuming no interference, a single end-user deployed system would be power limited, which for example allows IEEE 802.11 APs to cover areas up to $300m$. In coexistence scenarios interference is an important factor, so the assumption of a power limited system does not hold. One possible reference scenario is the IMT-Advanced Indoor hotspot scenario [16] mentioned before. Other scenarios could be based on our example scenario and include walls and different floors.

A simplified scenario can be created in a way where any simultaneous transmission causes data loss. Here no spatial reuse is possible. This can be seen as a two state or binary interference model.

Traffic

Suitable application models as described in Chapter 18 must be found and mapped to layer 2 QoS classes. The example scenario described above already gives some possible applications like IP-TV, video- and music streaming, and VoIP. Other traffic types like web browsing and file download using TCP can be modeled as full-buffer traffic using the QoS class with lowest priority.

Technology Standards

In Section 13.1.1 we give an overview of different bands where unlicensed operation and therefore coexistence is possible. Systems operating in such bands will likely have to coexist with other allowed systems. When evaluating performance, all possible other systems should be considered. On the other hand, it is not always required to include the most widely deployed standard, IEEE 802.11, in the scenario. The reason is that there can be bands in the future allowing unlicensed operation but not permitting operation of legacy IEEE 802.11 systems.

Multiple general methods exist to improve coexistence. Those methods can either be enforced by the technology standard, e.g. mandatory CSMA-CA in IEEE 802.11, or can be optionally applied such as TPC or Dynamic Frequency Selection (DFS). Further methods might be allowed within the parts of a standard left to the implementer. In a centrally controlled system with a scheduler this includes the scheduling algorithm. The GTS assignment for IEEE 802.15.4 described in Section 12.3 could for example be extended to allow multiple IEEE 802.15.4 systems to coexist. A general scenario might include systems extended by such coexistence improvements together with legacy systems.

13.1.4 Model

Besides simulation setup, the employed simulation model should also cover all factors influencing collected results.

From our DLL point of view the key factor for performance evaluation is what happens to user data PDUs as they pass through the protocol stack. We therefore track the journey of an application PDU from the traffic source to the sink and identify each component which influences our chosen performance indicators. Figure 13.2 shows the model created for our use case. Since we did not select a specific technology standard, some components remain generic.

We will now describe the components, their relation to our performance indicators and parameters of each component. We also have a look on information exchange between the components.

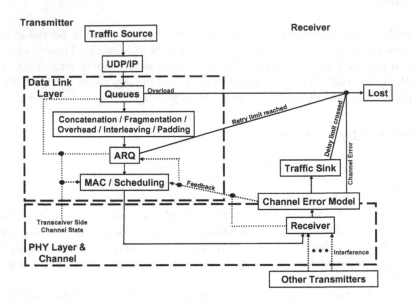

Fig. 13.2: Coexistence simulator model

Traffic Source

The traffic source generates application PDUs according to the traffic models for evaluated applications. Each application PDU has a size in bits. Information to map applications to DLL QoS classes is available.

UDP/IP

As explained in our assumptions in the beginning of this section, we do not consider TCP and assume *User Datagram Protocol (UDP)* and IP layers only add additional overhead and do not create any delays. The overhead size is 28 byte which is added to the size of the PDU. Total PDU length must be realistic since it is directly related to the transmission time t_{transp} influencing utilization, delay, and jitter. The layers might also perform segmentation. UDP PDUs have a maximum size of 65535 byte. IP PDU size is limited to the Maximum transmission unit (MTU) of used layer 2 technology. A typical value is 1500 byte which is the MTU for Ethernet.

Queues

As we use QoS classes, we assume there is one queue per class. Some systems might even implement a dedicated queue per receiving node. Overflowing drop tail queues are a possible reason for traffic loss, shown by the arrow to the right in Figure 13.2. The maximum queue length decides if arriving PDUs are accepted to the queue. It should, in general, provide enough space for queuing of PDUs waiting for channel access. Coexistence scenarios might require even larger buffers because channel access might be further delayed while waiting for other systems to stop transmitting. At least the *queue* with highest priority should not drop any PDUs as long as the channel is not in overload.

Concatenation, Fragmentation, Protocol Overhead, Interleaving, and Padding

This component is not specially related to coexistence scenarios. Still it has two important influences. First, it transforms the PDUs to the actual duration transmitted on the channel. Second it may be related to the channel error model since Packet Error Rate (PER) might depend on the PDU length and it might be that multiple fragments have to be received successfully to retrieve the original PDU. Fragmentation and interleaving can have considerable influence on the delay. Possible parameters can usually be found in the technology standard.

ARQ

The *ARQ* component is responsible to retransmit PDUs not received successfully. Some technology standards like LTE and IEEE 802.16 implement multiple ARQs. In LTE *Hybrid ARQ (HARQ)* is used in the PHY layer and another traditional ARQ in the upper part of the DLL. The use of ARQ might be optional depending on the QoS class, e.g. some applications such as VoIP might tolerate a certain loss. Additional delay caused by ARQ retransmissions might have a stronger negative impact on user experience than the loss. If ARQ is used, PDUs are usually dropped if not transmitted successfully up to a specified retry limit. Therefore the ARQ component can also be a source of loss. Section 10.2.2 gives multiple possibilities on how to model ARQ.

MAC / Scheduling

In this component, the actual decision is made when to transmit a PDU. As described in more detail in Section 10.1.5, possible input parameters can be the amount and size of queued PDUs per QoS class and receiver, information about the link to the receiver, transmission error probability, and the channel state at the transmitter. In this evaluation the *MAC / Scheduler* component plays the most important role. The decision in all nodes on when and how long to transmit forms the channel state at all receivers. This channel state is represented by the current SINR at the receiver and is used by the channel model to decide if a PDU was received successfully. Most possible protocol improvements for coexistence would be implemented in this component. It is therefore very important how the information, especially the one gained at the receiver, is modeled. Explicit signalling might be used providing channel state information from the receiver at defined intervals with defined quantization. Another approach allows to obtain the information from the simulation environment. In this case the information is available without delay and without transmission errors.

Receiver

The receiver has to take into account all simultaneous transmissions and calculate the SINR of a transmission before passing it to the channel error model component. Some requirements for the channel model used to derive the SINR are described below in Section 13.1.5.

Channel Error Model

Taking into account properties like PDU size, used MCS, and SINR the *channel error model* decides if a PDU was received successfully as described in Section 10.2.1. If not, it is considered as lost. If provided by the protocol, the transmitter might be immediately informed about the loss, for example by a Negative ACKs (NACKs) when using HARQ. The channel model might base its decision about transmission success on multiple PDUs and therefore depends on information from the concatenation, fragmentation, overhead, interleaving, and padding component to know which PDUs belong together.

Successfully received PDUs are transformed to their original state when leaving the traffic source. For that, all headers and padding bit are removed, and concatenations and fragmentations are undone. The PDUs are then passed to the traffic sink for final evaluation.

Traffic Sink

The traffic sink evaluates the received data. For some application classes maximum delays might be defined. Received PDUs which are not received within the maximal delay are then also considered as lost.

In this single-hop communication scenario PDUs are always delivered in order to the traffic sink. Sequence numbers can therefore be used to detect

PDU loss. Additionally the used layer 2 QoS class, source, delay, size, and arrival time of each PDU should be probed. In this way, all previously described performance indicators can be obtained.

13.1.5 Tips

In this section, a few tips on what should be considered when extending or creating a suitable simulator for coexistence evaluation are described. A special focus lies on what should be checked when using a simulator previously used for single system scenarios.

Control Traffic

Available simulators previously created to evaluate user data traffic performance might come with modeling assumptions not suitable in coexistence scenarios. In Section 10.1.1 possible modeling assumptions are described which control traffic does not have to be explicitly transmitted. The underlying assumption is that this traffic is transmitted with a very robust MCS. Coexistence scenarios can create interference levels high enough to cause a significant error probability for such traffic. In this case, it must be modeled. In a frame based scheduled WiMAX or LTE Femto Cell, nodes not being able to decode the preamble at the frame start or the *map* might not be able to communicate for a whole frame.

Also pilot channels, often not explicitly modeled, can influence performance. In [414] the authors show how a Bluetooth system transmitting at a pilot channel of a IEEE 802.11g system severely degrades the performance of the WLAN system. Also pilot channels often transmit at higher powers resulting in more interference.

Modeling of Resources

Channel and physical layer models of simulators designed for a specific technology standard often come with assumptions about channel bandwidth and center frequency. Technology standards usually provide a mapping of this parameters to integer channel-, *subchannel*, or *subcarrier* numbers (see Section 10.1.2). If systems following different technology standards coexist, transmission bandwidth can be partly overlapping. In this case the channel model needs to be adjusted to decrease the interference accordingly. Some systems, for example IEEE 802.11b, do not have an uniformly distributed *Power Spectral Density (PSD)*. Figure 13.3 shows the PSD of a coexisting IEEE 802.15.4 and IEEE 802.11b system approximated by an SI-function (see [209] for the exact shape). It is visible that spectral density, and therefore interference, decreases towards the edge of the transmission bandwidth. IEEE 802.15.4

operates on 2 MHz bandwidth, IEEE 802.11b on 22 MHz. Therefore a factor of 1/11 must be introduced for interference calculation. The PSD of IEEE 802.11b introduces another factor $c(f_{offset})$ depending on the center frequency offset f_{offset} of the systems. c can be calculated by integration over the normalized PSD of the IEEE 802.11b system within the limits of the 2 MHz used by the IEEE 802.15.4 system. Since only a finite set of frequency offsets is possible, correction factor c can be stored in a lookup table.

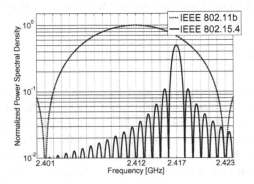

Fig. 13.3: Approximated Power Spectral Density of 802.11b and 802.15.4 with 5MHz Center Frequency Offset.

The same applies to possible modeling assumptions and optimization in the time domain. Simulators for cellular systems like *LTE* or *IEEE 802.16* might assume synchronized systems operating on defined time slots. The assumption made is that a station granted resources occupies a full time slot transmitting at equal power. This assumption does not hold for user-deployed coexisting systems. The channel model needs to be adjusted to support time weighted averaging as the model presented in Section 9.5 does.

Channel Sensing

In a simulator, very precise channel knowledge might be available at a receiver. It is possible to obtain the exact power of an intended signal together with the exact interference power. One could even implement receivers further distinguishing measured interference power by interference source. The information about the power is usually available as a high precision floating point value and can be obtained at arbitrary intervals. Alternatively an event-based approach measuring whenever power levels change is possible.

In reality this is not possible. The signal at the receiver is a superposition of all currently ongoing transmissions. Many systems have pilot channels and known preamble sequences which can be used to gain further knowledge about the current *channel state*. In this case the knowledge can only be refreshed when a new known sequence is received. In the case of OFDMA, this knowledge only applies to the subcarrier where the pilot symbol was received. The information about current power levels is usually passed to the DLL at a resolution of a few dB. Some technology standards can have the possibility to inform the DLL whenever a certain threshold is crossed or the channel has changed its power level by a certain magnitude since the last information. In other technology standards like IEEE 802.15.4 layer 2 has to explicitly request the PHY layer to perform channel measurement. The measurement duration then depends on the standard. The measuring result is therefore the average power over the measurement time.

Proposed coexistence algorithms relying on channel measurement must be applicable with channel state information available in the real system. It might be required to extend a simulator to model this aspect with more detail. Alternatively a random error on the measurement can be introduced to evaluate the sensitivity of a proposed algorithm. Finally it might be enough to have a close look at the proposed algorithm and establish an argumentation why it will work in the real system.

13.1.6 Conclusion

In this section we stressed the importance of the use case on the selection and development of an appropriate simulation model. We started by deciding which performance indicators we want to use and then inspected what influences them. If we cannot assure a sufficient modeling detail of this influences, we cannot draw general conclusions from our simulation results. Still it is not always required to evaluate the most generic and most realistic deployment with detailed modeling of all influences. Researchers are encouraged to isolate certain aspects influencing performance, while modeling other aspects less detailed or even neglecting them.

Above use-case description was kept general and should therefore be applicable to a variety of problems. The *openWNS* network simulator described in Section 5.1 is available for public download [6] and comes with an example scenario formed by a coexisting *IEEE 802.11* and *IEEE 802.16* system. The scenario and the simulation model were created considering the aspects described in this use-case.

13.2 IEEE 802.15.4 Performance Analysis

This section connects the introduction of *IEEE 802.15.4* from Section 12.3 with a practical *use case*. The range of possible use cases is rather large:

plain parameter measurements, complex performance evaluations, evaluation of network topologies, etc. *Performance evaluation* was chosen as an example. In this section a performance analysis use case of IEEE 802.15.4 under the viewpoint of achievable performance in coexistence scenarios is described. This use case is based on the introduction of the coexistence term and the connected problems for wireless communication systems from Section 13.1. The following subsections present the general goal of the analysis, the used metrics, parameters, characteristics, and the modeling process of the considered system. The section concludes with a brief examination of example simulation results and a short summary.

13.2.1   Goal of the Analysis

Important for an analysis is the definition of a goal. Without a defined goal, modeling and simulation would fail to produce proper outcomes. The goal of this use case is an analysis of the influence of coexisting IEEE 802.15.4 devices on the overall achievable performance of an examined IEEE 802.15.4 star topology network. The impact of packet buffer sizes on the MAC layer on this achievable performance is also studied. A single IEEE 802.15.4 network with one sink and a varying number of traffic sources with different traffic loads and buffer sizes is considered. By means of simulation it is expected to gain insight into the influence of IEEE 802.15.4 *intra-technology interference* in coexistence scenarios. The term *intra-technology interference* describes the interference caused by coexisting devices from the same technology class.

13.2.2   Metrics for the Analysis

Several metrics can be used to examine and analyze the performance of a IEEE 802.15.4 network. Usually, a subset of suitable metrics is selected from the range of available ones. This subset is then used to verify the achievement of the defined goal. An extensive list of commonly used performance metrics can be found in [235, pp. 37-40]. The following two metrics are defined and used for this example:

– *Application goodput* at the sink (throughput on the application layer)
– *Efficiency* (data sent by sources compared to data received at the sink)

Other typical metrics, which are not considered here, are the access delay, the plain throughput, and the packet loss ratio. For further usage the two mentioned metrics need to be specified. The application goodput stands for the total number of bits received at the application layer of the destination divided by the simulation time. The considered bits are just payload, since protocol overhead and packet headers are not included in the computation.

Application goodput can therefore be used to measure the performance of application layer traffic. The efficiency metric describes the ratio between the application traffic received at the sink and the application traffic sent by the sources. Mathematical definitions for both metrics are as follows:

$$\mathtt{Application\,Goodput} \; = \; \frac{\sum \mathtt{Bytes\,Received\,at\,Application\,Layer}}{(\mathtt{Simulation\,Time} \, - \, \mathtt{First\,Packet\,Time})}$$

$$\mathtt{Efficiency\,Ratio} \; = \; \frac{\sum \mathtt{Received\,Application\,Traffic}}{\sum \mathtt{Sent\,Application\,Traffic}} \times 100\,\%$$

Important for the measurement of these metrics are statistics, which are logged throughout a simulation run. The simulation model of the considered system should therefore include possibilities for statistical logging. If a pre-determined implemented simulation model is used, the choice of metrics can be limited depending on the model characteristics and its implementation.

13.2.3   Used Parameters

The next step in the performance evaluation of a given system is the definition of parameters, which are used as *adjustable screws* to analyze the performance of the system under changing conditions. Parameters have to be considered in the modeling process, so that the necessary parameters are already included in the system model. In the presented example, the following parameters are considered, due to their significant influence on the achievable performance of a IEEE 802.15.4 network:

- Superframe parameters BO and SO
- Number of traffic sources
- Packet buffer size on the MAC layer
- Application traffic load (e.g. packets/second) and related parameters:
  - Traffic scheme (e.g. on-off or interval traffic)
  - Inter-arrival-time of data from application layer
  - Payload size

This is an example listing. Depending on the examination goal, other parameters might be considered. It is important to consider all parameters which might have a relevant influence on the evaluation objective; in this case the network performance.

13.2.4   Modeling the System

After defining metrics and parameters, the system under investigation can be modeled. First, it has to be decided which components and characteristics of

the system should be included in the *modeling process* and which ones should
not be considered at all. A good model should be as simple as possible,
without missing any parts that may have an influence on the objective of
the examination. Therefore, the system modeling has to consider the goal of
the study and the necessary level of detail in order to achieve that goal in
a qualitative and quantitative sufficient way. The following list summarizes
important characteristics and components of the modeling process of the
investigated system:

- IEEE 802.15.4 superframe structure with according parameters
- Distribution of superframe parameters through network beacons
- Packet buffer on the MAC layer
- IEEE 802.15.4 medium access protocol CSMA-CA
- IEEE 802.15.4 frame structures
- IEEE 802.15.4 PHY functions like channel sensing, CCA, ED
- Necessary IEEE 802.15.4 service primitives for data transmissions
- Star topology and its requirements
- IEEE 802.15.4 node roles (e.g. PAN coordinator, FFD)
- PHY parameters, such as propagation and radio models
- Transmission failure and packet error aspects

Depending on the goal, further aspects have to be included, e.g. node
mobility models in case of mobile scenarios. All the listed components and
aspects have a significant influence on the overall performance of a IEEE
802.15.4 network and need to be modeled. Information about the modeling
of these various components and aspects can be found, e.g. in Section 12.3
and other related parts of this book.

The *level of detail* required for the modeling of the system characteristics
depends on the influence they may have on the goal of the study. If, for example, the radio propagation model has a significant influence on the achievable
application goodput, a more detailed radio propagation model should be used
to get more accurate results. If, on the other hand, the frame structure (headers, payload, footers) have only a small influence on the achievable goodput,
the level of detail of the frame structure modeling can be lowered down to a
grade where the influence is still accurate enough but the model is simplified.

While many aspects must be included in the modeling process, some parts
can also be left out to simplify the model and its creation process. Since
this example use case only considers star topology networks, the model does
not need to include other network topologies. Additional simplifications can
be introduced for the PAN management procedures, the PAN coordinator
selection and other management issues. For a simple performance evaluation,
it could be assumed that the investigation starts with the network already
set-up by a predetermined PAN coordinator. The procedure of nodes joining
or leaving the network could also be left out to further simplify the model.

During this modeling process it can be determined if a suitable model
already exists in the community or if an adequate model has to be created.

Usually, existing models need to be extended, because relevant parts are missing or have not been implemented with the necessary level of detail. For this example case, the existing IEEE 802.15.4 model for the OMNeT++/INET Framework (refer to Subsection 12.3.6) can be used, since it is an extendable model that provides support for all the required model characteristics.

13.2.5 Reference Scenarios

The reference scenario is the parameterization of the created model. It combines the chosen parameters with the newly created or extended existing system model. The reference scenario defines the boundaries in which simulations and evaluations take place. Within a reference scenario, important parameters (e.g. node count, traffic load, transmission range) and interactions between all relevant actors (sources and sink in the example use case) have to be declared before the simulation starts.

Three example reference scenarios with one, three, and ten data sources are displayed in Figure 13.4. These three scenarios are exemplifications of a generic reference scenario with different numbers of nodes (data traffic sources) inside the *WPAN*. The carrier sensing and the transmission range of the data sources and the data sink is set, so that all devices inside the WPAN can reach and overhear each other. The playground size for the reference scenario is limited so that all devices are in the same interference range. The interference range is an interesting parameter in scenarios where a larger playground size with hidden nodes is considered.

The different specified parameters (e.g. number of nodes, traffic load, payload size, MAC packet buffer size) from Subsection 13.2.3 are varied throughout various simulation runs to enable an evaluation of the influence of those parameters on the overall system performance. An outcome of the different simulation runs are statistics, which are then used for the analysis of the metrics of interest. These metrics are intended to provide a better understanding of the influence of the studied parameters on the achievable performance in this coexistence scenario. Examples for parameter values are given along with comments for the simulation and evaluation in the next subsection.

13.2.6 Simulation and Evaluation

After the specification of metrics and parameters and the creation of a model or the extension of an existing one, simulations can be started on the defined reference scenarios. The simulation process itself depends again on the goal of the study, the research type (e.g. performance evaluation or proof-of-concept) and the desired outcomes. For the considered use case, various simulation runs

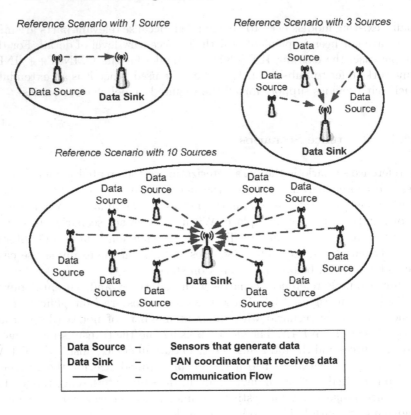

Fig. 13.4: Reference scenarios with one, three, and ten IEEE 802.15.4 data sources

with varying parameters are conducted to gain information on the influence of such parameters on the overall achievable system performance.

The described reference scenario from Figure 13.4 is transferred to a simulation environment (for this use case *OMNeT++*). The influence of the defined parameters is analyzed through various simulation runs. To exemplify this, simulations with the following parameter values are conducted:

- Payload size = 100 Byte
- Superframe parameters:
  - Beacon Order (BO) = 5; Superframe Order (SO) = 4
  - Duty cycle = 50%
- MAC packet buffer size = 1 and 10
- Traffic load:
  - Packets per second = 1; 4; 10; 20; 40; 100
  - Byte / s = 100; 400; 1000; 2000; 4000; 10000
- Number of data sources = 1; 3; 5; 10
- Other PHY and MAC parameters are set to standard values [429]

The payload size and the superframe parameters BO and SO are kept constant during all simulation runs. The number of data sources, the MAC packet buffer size and the traffic load are varied to determine their influence on the system performance. Statistical data is recorded during the simulation to compute the *application goodput* and *efficiency ratio* (according to the formulas presented in Subsection 13.2.2). With the calculated metric values, the outcome charts displayed in Figure 13.5 are generated after post-processing with a spreadsheet tool.

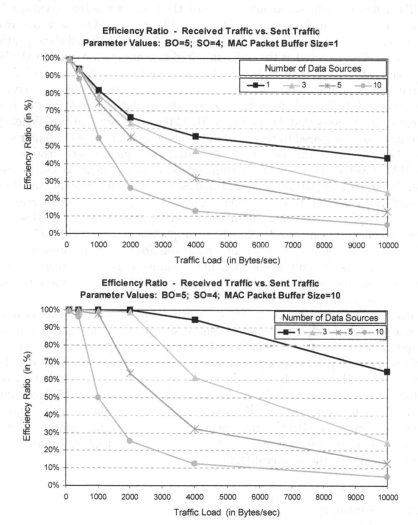

Fig. 13.5: Efficiency ratio with various *number of sources* and *traffic loads*

The application goodput metric is used to calculate the efficiency ratio (sent traffic compared to received traffic), shown in the two charts in Figure 13.5. All packets sent and received during the simulation time are added up to get the application goodput values. An initial transient phase can be ignored for this example case, since the overall simulation time period is considered. For other evaluations (e.g. channel access delay, routing delays), a transient recovery time has to be considered explicitly, because it may have significant influence on the metrics.

The efficiency ratio values are plotted on the y-axis while the varied traffic loads are plotted on the x-axis, as shown in Figure 13.5. This way, one can easily deduct how higher or lower traffic loads influence the efficiency ratio (amount of data received at the sink compared to sent data). As expected, the efficiency ratio drops with higher traffic loads and a larger number of data sources, since collisions on the radio channel, blocks radio channel access, and network interference rise with more coexisting data sources. The second outcome chart shows that with a larger MAC packet buffer size the efficiency ratio increases compared to the other outcome chart with a packet buffer size of 1. The reason for this lies on the fact that data packets get dropped at the MAC layer if they cannot be transmitted until the next packet arrives from the upper application layer. If statistics are only logged or measured on higher layers, such effects are often not easily visible. This is one of the reasons why it is important to think about the exact layer on which statistics and data are collected and recorded (in the example use case on the MAC or the PHY layer for example). Another important remark is that the lines between the plotted dots are only connection lines. Values were only calculated for the given parameters. There might be significant deviations in the intervals between the measured parameters.

Performance evaluations are always a crucial part. More information on typical problems and approaches for successful performance evaluations of computer networks and systems can be found in [235]. To enable a comparison of simulation results, the used system parameters should always be presented together with the simulation results. Many parameters have a direct or indirect influence on the performance; for the IEEE 802.15.4 example use case, such parameters could be the backoff and channel access times, scanning intervals, or PHY turnaround times. It is therefore always a good idea to give a list of set parameters, especially if the settings differ from the values specified in the standard [429].

13.2.7   Summary

This section presented a practical use case for the modeling of a performance evaluation of IEEE 802.15.4 WPANs. A typical approach for the modeling, simulation, and evaluation was described along with comments for the system modeling, the choice of metrics and parameters, and the creation of reference scenarios. Example outcome charts were presented and evaluated and general hints for practical appliance were also given.

14. Modeling Mobility

Andras Berl (University of Passau)

14.1 Introduction

In wireless networks, communication can take place based on an infrastructure (e.g. WLAN access point or GPRS base station) or it can take place in ad-hoc mode, where mobile devices are connected directly to each other and care for the routing by themselves (mobile ad-hoc networks). When such wireless networks are investigated and simulations are performed, it is often necessary to consider the movement of entities within the simulated environment. There are several common examples of scenarios that involve a movement of entities:

- A number of WLAN access points are installed in a building and config- ured in infrastructure mode. Users are moving within the building and are roaming between the different access points without loosing connectivity.
- Users with cell phones are walking in a city. While moving, the cell phone changes the base stations it is connected to (handover, see Chapter 15). The user is able to continue a telephone call without interruption.
- Cars (e.g. driving on a highway) use car-to-car communication to pass each other information about congestion or an accident. To do so, a mobile ad-hoc network is set up between cars that are near to each other. Such networks are often called vehicular networks.
- In an emergency situation (e.g. an earthquake or a fire in a big building) the fire brigade, ambulance, and police are setting up a mobile ad-hoc network to clarify further proceedings.

In such scenarios (and many others) the mobility of entities in the network plays an important role when communication has to be established. Protocols (e.g. routing or handover algorithms) need to be optimized with respect to the experienced mobility. Actually, the results of network simulations that include mobility of entities can vary significantly when the mobility patterns of moving entities are changed (see Section 14.4).

Often, it is difficult to gather real movement data (also known as traces, see Section 14.2) of a sufficient number of entities for simulations. To over- come this problem, synthetic *mobility models* have been developed that are generating simplified virtual movement data for a number of entities. There are several mobility models with different properties. Section 14.2 catego- rizes mobility model approaches. Section 14.3 presents several approaches of mobility models in detail. Section 14.4 discusses the appropriate selection of mobility models for certain simulation scenarios and gives hints for the selection. Section 14.5 concludes this chapter.

14.2   Categorization of Mobility Models

This section describes different categories of synthetic mobility models. Due to the vast amount of available models and scenarios, the categorization presented in this Section is not exhaustive, there are further categories of mobility models which are not discussed in this section. Furthermore, the categories are not disjunctive to each other. A single mobility model may fit in several of the presented categories. In spite of this incompleteness, the presented categorization helps to get an overview of mobility models and to get an impression of the diversity of available models and simulation scenarios.

14.2.1   Traces and Synthetic Mobility Models

Traces are mobility patterns that are logged from real life situations. Tuduce et al. [469] give an example for the logging of traces. The study monitored 350 WLAN access points spread over 32 buildings for three months. The access points were configured to run in infrastructure mode. MAC addresses of network interface cards identified the users. The access points were polled every minute for user association information. This way, the location of WLAN users was gathered (as long as the users were online) and implicitly also an estimation of the users movements. In another example, Tang et al. [453] traced the mobility of 74 users in a campus network for 12 weeks. Additionally, operators of mobile cellular networks might provide interesting traces of users that are using cell phones.

Synthetic mobility models, which are the main focus of this chapter, are not directly based on the logging of users' movement behavior. Instead, mobility patterns are generated by algorithms that specify virtual behavior of users and predict their movements. These movements of virtual users are usually constrained to a simulation area with limited border lengths. On one hand, synthetic mobility models can be inspired by traces, attempting to model the users' behavior in realistic situations. On the other hand, traces can be used to verify synthetic mobility models by comparison.

14.2.2   Entity and Group Mobility Models

Mobility models can be categorized by the number of entities that are described by a single mobility model.

Entity mobility models consider the movement of a single individual entity, e.g., a human being or an animal. If there are several entities, they are typically considered independently from each other and their movements are predicted independent from each other. Also the number of entities that are existing in the simulation area is not considered in the algorithm that predicts a single entity's movement. Examples of entity mobility models are the Random Walk Model, the Random Waypoint Model, the Random Direction Model, the Gauss-Markov Model, or the Manhattan Model (see Section 14.3).

Group mobility models in contrast, consider a set of individual entities as a group, which is moving as a whole. The movement of entities is related to each other. Usually, there is a group leader or another moving point of orientation. The group entities gather around this orientation point and follow its movements with specified deviations. Group models are often said to be more realistic than entity mobility models. In reality, the movement of human beings is usually not independent from each other. People are walking around in groups or have similar directions (e.g. towards a shopping center). Animals are often moving in herds or swarms. Examples of group mobility models are the Pursue Model, the Column Model, the Nomadic Community Model (see Section 14.3), or the Reference Point Group Model [44].

14.2.3 Human, Animal, and Vehicle Mobility Models

Another categorization of mobility models is based on the nature of the entity that causes the movement. The criteria of this categorization is not the amount of entities, but the behavior of the entities.

Human mobility models are describing the movements of human beings in certain scenarios. Examples for such scenarios are pedestrians in inner cities or employees during work in a building. Examples of human mobility models are the Random Walk Model, or the Random Waypoint Model.

Animal mobility models are analogously based the movement of animals, e.g. in herds or swarms. Examples of animal mobility models are the Random Walk Model, the Pursue Model, or the Nomadic Community Model.

Vehicle mobility models are predicting the movement of vehicles (e.g. cars or tanks). Often the mobility of vehicles is restricted to streets and traffic rules, which imposes particular restrictions on their mobility patterns. Examples of vehicle mobility models are the Freeway Model [44], or the Manhattan Model.

14.2.4 Normal Situation and Special Situation Mobility Models

Mobility models can also be categorized by looking at the character of the situations which they are describing.

Normal situation mobility models are assuming ordinary scenarios without special influences. People are walking in a pedestrian area, working in a building, or driving on streets, for instance. Examples of human mobility models are the Random Walk Model, the Random Waypoint Model, or the Manhattan Model.

Special situation mobility models are modeling unusual situations in which entities show specialized movement behavior. Emergency situations are examples of such special situations, e.g. a fire in a building or an earthquake. Examples of Special Situation Mobility Models are the Pursue Model or the Column Model.

14.2.5   Other Mobility Models

Apart from the presented categorization of mobility models there are further mobility models that are specialized to certain scenarios. These kinds of mobility models can often be found in special literature or they can be derived from available mobility models, if needed.

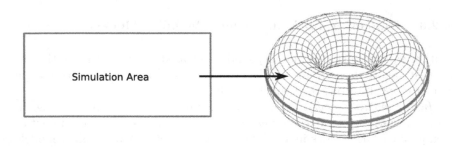

Fig. 14.1: Boundless simulation area

An example of such a special problem is the railway problem where trains run on rails without collisions. Another example is the correlation of movement to technical aspects (feedback). If a cell phone user looses contact to the base station, for instance, he might change his current movement in order to get a better quality of service. In some cases collisions of users are influencing the movement, e.g., avatars of computer games. *Social mobility models* [203], for instance, consider the interactions and relationships between mobile users. Mobility models can also be derived from natural or physical phenomena, e.g. the movement of molecules or fluids.

Sometimes specialized simulation areas are needed in mobility models. The question has to be answered, what happens to the mobile entity, when it reaches the boundary of the simulated area. Possible solutions are, for instance, slowing down, changing direction, or bouncing back. One example for such a special simulation area is the *Boundless Simulation Area* [87]. If a moving entity reaches the border of the simulation area, it appears at the opposite side. Therefore, entities can never reach the boundary of the simulation area. By applying the Boundless Simulation Area algorithm, the simulation area is mapped to a torus. This mapping is illustrated in Figure 14.1. When a Boundless Simulation Area is used, it is important to see that the metric of the mobility model has to be adapted to it.

Another problem related to simulation areas is the appearance of obstacles within the area. The *Obstacle Mobility Model* [44] provides an example for such a specialized simulation area. It allows to define obstacles that directly influence the movement of the entities.

14.3   Mobility Models

This section discusses several examples of widely used mobility models in detail. A more detailed description of the presented mobility models can be found in Camp et al. [87], Bai et al. [44], and Sanchez et al. [399].

The most important properties of the presented models are described and illustrated in figures that show possible movement patterns of the models.

14.3.1   Random Walk Model

The Random Walk Mobility Model is a widely used model that is based on the idea that entities in nature move in unpredictable ways. In this mobility model an entity moves from its current location to a following location by choosing randomly a new direction and speed. Direction and speed are limited to predefined ranges, i.e. they are chosen from [speedmin; speedmax] and [0;2π]. Every movement is limited to a constant time interval. After a movement, the direction and speed for the next movement is calculated. When the entity reaches the boundary of the simulation area, it bounces off the boundary with an angle that depends on the incoming direction and continues its path. Sometimes the movement is not limited to a constant time interval but to a constant distance.

In Figure 14.2 the Random Walk Mobility Model is illustrated. The square illustrates the simulation area, with the 0/0 coordinate as origin and the relative distance on the X and Y axis to the origin. The walk begins in the center of a simulation area. It can be seen, that this model utilizes especially the area around the starting point. It can also be seen that the algorithm generates movements with sharp turns and stops, which might be unrealistic

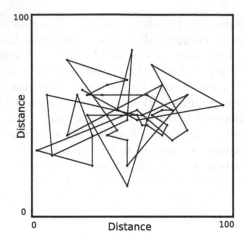

Fig. 14.2: Random Walk Mobility Model with constant time interval

for certain scenarios. This is caused by the fact that the Random Walk Mobility Model is a memoryless mobility pattern. In the calculation of the next movement, no knowledge of previous movements is used. The current speed and direction of a movement is completely independent of its past speed and direction.

14.3.2   Random Waypoint Model

The Random Waypoint Mobility Model is also a widely used model and is very similar to the Random Walk Mobility Model. In this mobility model, an entity chooses a random destination coordinate (within the simulation area) and a random speed (from [speedmin; speedmax]). Then it moves from its current location to the destination location. Additionally, the Random Waypoint Mobility Model defines pause times between two movements. After a pause, the new movement is calculated. If pause times are set to zero and the speed ranges are chosen to be similar, the Random Waypoint Mobility Model is identical to the Random Walk Mobility Model

Figure 14.3 illustrates a traveling pattern of an entity that uses the Random Waypoint Mobility Model. It starts in the center of the simulation area. Again, the algorithm generates movements with sharp turns and stops.

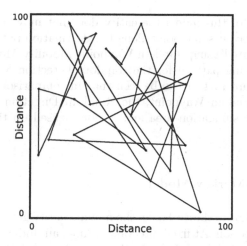

Fig. 14.3: Random Way Point Mobility Model

14.3.3 Random Direction Model

In the Random Direction Mobility Model, an entity chooses a random direction (in the range $[0;\pi]$) and a random speed (in the range [speedmin; speedmax]), similar to the Random Walk Mobility Model. The entity moves with the chosen direction and speed towards the boundary of the simulation area until reaching it. There it pauses for a predefined time, before choosing the next direction and speed, to move again.

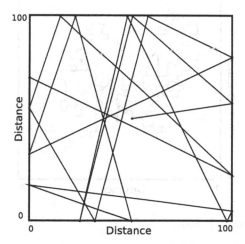

Fig. 14.4: Random Direction Mobility Model

In a variation of this model the entity does not move to the boundary, but stops on its way at some point along the destination path. This behavior can be also simulated using Random Waypoint Mobility Model.

A sample moving pattern for the Random Direction Mobility Model is illustrated in Figure 14.4. It can be seen that in comparison to the Random Walk and the Random Waypoint, the Random Direction Mobility Model utilizes the whole simulation area and is not focused on the center of the area.

14.3.4   Gauss-Markov Model

In the Gauss-Markov Mobility Model the moving entity gets initially assigned a speed and a direction. At fixed intervals of time, an update of direction and speed is applied to the entity. In contradiction to the models described before, the Gauss-Markov Mobility Model enables movements that are depending on previous movements. The degree of dependence on previous movements is adapted by a parameter α ($\alpha = [0,1]$).

$-\ \alpha = 0$: The new movement does not depend on previous movement and results similar to the random walk are achieved
$-\ 0 < \alpha < 1$: Intermediate levels of randomness are obtained
$-\ \alpha = 1$: The entity moves in a linear manner

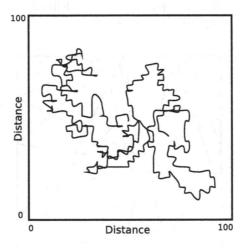

Fig. 14.5: Gauss-Markov Model

Additionally an average speed can be specified for an entity. To avoid collisions with the boundary of the simulation area, the direction of the entity is adapted when it approaches the boundary. When a certain distance to the boundary is met, the entity is forced away from the boundary. The current direction is adapted to directly move away from the boarder as a basis for the calculations of the next step. This avoids, that an entity remains near a boundary for a long period of time.

When the predefined time interval expires, a new direction and speed is calculated, based on the current location, speed and direction. Other implementations of this model with different properties exist.

Figure 14.5 illustrates an example traveling pattern of an entity using the Gauss-Markov Mobility Model, beginning in the center of the simulation area. By adapting the direction and speed updates based on the current direction and speed, the Gauss-Markov Mobility Model does not show the same sharp stops and turns than the mobility models described before.

14.3.5   Manhattan Model

The Manhattan Mobility Model is a widely used model which is based on the idea that the movement of entities is often bound to streets or highways.

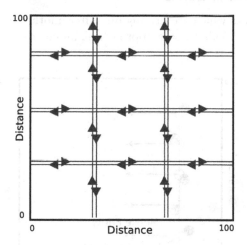

Fig. 14.6: Manhattan Model

A map is specified with streets (both directions) and crossings on which the entities move. A realistic acceleration can be defined (e.g. for cars) and also an average velocity. Additionally a safety distance between two entities is set.

Entities are moving on predefined streets and are changing the street at a crossing with a certain probability. An example configuration is:

− P(onwards) = 0.5
− P(left) = 0.25
− P(right) = 0.25

Figure 14.6 illustrates an example of a map with streets for the Manhattan Mobility Model. A moving entity will move on the predefined streets and change to another street at a crossing with the given probability.

14.3.6   Column Model

The Column Mobility Model is a group mobility model in which each mobile entity follows a *reference point*. Reference points are arranged in a line. The line itself is moving, following an entity mobility model. The angle of the line may be fixed or the line may be rotating. The mobile nodes are not directly approaching the reference points. Instead they are are moving towards a coordinate that is chosen randomly nearby their reference point. Examples for this group mobility model are

− a convoy of trucks which are driving one after another in a row
− or tanks which are side by side approaching an enemy.

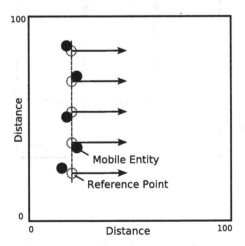

Fig. 14.7: Column Model

Figure 14.8 illustrates the group movement of the Column Mobility Model. It is shown that a group of mobile entities is following reference points on a vertical line. Every mobile node is approaching an own reference point, having small deviations in its direction. The line is moving as a whole, depicted by the direction vectors.

14.3.7   Pursue Model

The Pursue Mobility Model is a group mobility model in which a group of mobile entities is pursuing a single *reference entity*. The reference entity is using an entity mobility model, e.g. the Random Walk Mobility Model. The other entities are pursuing the reference entity, however, small deviations are added to their direction. Additionally, acceleration is simulated in this model. An example of this scenario is a group of tourists which are following a guide in a museum.

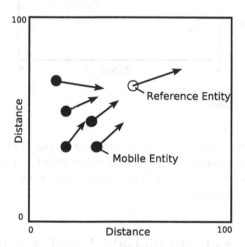

Fig. 14.8: Pursue Model

Figure 14.8 illustrates the group movement of the Pursue Mobility Model. A reference entity is illustrated which is moving in a certain direction (depicted by a vector). The other entities are approaching the reference entity with slightly varying directions (also depicted by vectors).

14.3.8   Nomadic Community Model

In the Nomadic Community Mobility Model the mobile entities are following a single *reference point*. All nodes are sharing the same reference point and are randomly moving around it. The reference point itself is moving, following an an entity mobility model (e.g. Random Walk Mobility Model). When the reference point stops its movement, the mobile nodes are continuing to move around the reference point. Examples for this group mobility model are nomads which are moving from one place to another.

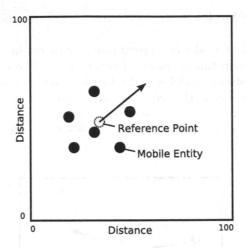

Fig. 14.9: Nomadic Model

Figure 14.9 illustrates the group movement of the Nomadic Community Mobility Model. A reference entity is illustrated which is moving in a certain direction (depicted by a vector). The other entities are randomly moving around the reference entity.

14.4   Selection of Appropriate Mobility Models

Similar to the use of other simulation models, a trade-off has to be made between the accuracy of a mobility model and its costs. The more accurate a mobility model is and the more it fits to the real-life scenario which is modeled, the more realistic results will be produced. However such realistic mobility models usually impose high complexity. This increases the costs in terms of implementation efforts and also in terms of slow performance in simulations which might be a serious problem. If the mobility model is kept simple on the other hand, its implementation is easy and the algorithms will allow for a good simulation performance. However, the results of the model will be also simplified.

Although the simple models are often used in simulations (e.g. in ad-hoc network research), it is reasonable to adapt the mobility model to the actual problem space. In [87] Camp et al. illustrated that mobility models are significantly influencing the results of simulations. The paper concludes, that the performance of ad-hoc protocols varies significantly under the influence of different mobility models. This implies that it is important to chose a mobility model which actually fits to the described problem. Also in [187] the appropriate selection of well known models for mobility and radio propagation is discussed with respect to the simulation of mobile ad-hoc networks.

Usually it is not a good idea to just take a simple model like the Random Walk without verifying that it fits to the problem. However the simple models can provide a good starting point for simulations. They can also be used as an alternative for more complex models. Results received with complex models can be compared to the results received with simplified models to validate that the behavior of mobile entities actually has impact on the results. However, even the use of a simple model (as described in Section 14.3, needs some thought. Each of the simple models shows different special movement patters that might be more realistic to special scenarios, than others. The Random Direction Model, for instance, utilizes the whole simulation area and is not focused on the center of the area as the Random Walk and the Random Waypoint model.

To find a suitable mobility model for a certain scenario, it is a good idea to review mobility models that solve comparable problems in other scenarios. Either the models can be used directly as they are or they can be adapted to the new problem space. Another approach is to simply use the same mobility models that other researchers use in the same research field (e.g. to investigate mobile ad-hoc network protocols), if possible. This approach provides at least comparability between different solutions for a problem.

14.5   Conclusions

There is a high number of mobility models that are used for simulations in wireless networks. This chapter has presented several categories of mobility models and has described a number of mobility models in detail.

It has been shown that it is important to find the appropriate mobility model for a certain research scenario, because mobility models usually have significant impact on simulation results. The model has to be complex enough to provide representative results and it has to be simple enough to be easily implemented and to provide fast simulation performance.

The most accurate entity movement patterns are, of course, achieved by gathering traces from real moving entities. If available, such traces can also be used to verify the mobility approximation of synthetic mobility models against real user behavior.

15. Modeling Handover from the Access Networks' Perspective

Sven Wiethoelter (Technische Universität Berlin)
Marc Emmelmann (Technische Universität Berlin)

15.1 Introduction

Simulation of handover processes is a complex methodological approach to performance evaluation as it involves modeling user mobility as well as technical details of the underlying communication system. On the one hand, depending on the degree of detail considered for both aspects, corresponding simulation models may become highly complex in terms of reflecting characteristics of the system under investigation. On the other hand, a thorough understanding and analysis of the research question to be elaborated, as well as considering handover-specific aspects of the analyzed technology can very well lead to a simple, compact, and satisfactory simulation model. This chapter provides a consistent methodology for modeling handover from the access networks' perspective. By following the presented approach, the reader may acquire the knowledge on how to gauge simulation models' required level of detail against employed simplifications and underlying assumptions yielding to well proportioned model designs and implementations.

The chapter is divided into three parts presenting the employed modeling methodology (c.f. Section 15.2), application examples (c.f. Section 15.3), and a general guide for modeling handovers (c.f. Section 15.4).

Part one starts with a taxonomy for modeling handovers (Section 15.2.1). Herein, the reader acquires an understanding on how different levels of detail may be applicable for the modeling process as well as on which different taxonomic groups affect the handover. Section 15.2.2 complements the taxonomy by presenting the wireless system view of the modeling process. It therefore classifies the different handover types and presents a choice of specific handover scenarios finally yielding to different model categories applicable in the modeling process.

Part two applies the presented methodology to two application examples:

- a handover scenario in a homogeneous 802.11-based wireless network studying the effect of a particular handover phase on the experienced service interruption time (Section 15.3.1) and
- a heterogeneous 802.11a/g system (c.f. Section 15.3.2) identifying the influence of each traffic flow on the wireless cells and performing handover decisions based on this assessment.

These two examples correspondingly illustrate the decision process yielding to a multi-cell model with a high to moderate level of detail of the underlying technology, and an abstract model allowing isolated studies in radio cells being involved in the handover process.

Finally, Part three provides the reader with a guide for modeling handover approaches and hereby summarizes the presented methodology.

15.2   Methodology

15.2.1   Taxonomy for Modeling Handovers

Modeling Aspects

For *modeling handovers*, two major aspects have to be considered: the level of detail describing the functional components of the handover process itself, and the amount of information that the model shall provide regarding the impact of a handover occurrence on a single user within the communication system respectively the system in its whole.

A typical application of the latter case is a model revealing the effects of arriving and departing users (as the result of handover) on the experienced quality of service within a radio cell or a particular user itself. Hereby, the handover process can most likely be modeled by a concatenation of all involved handover steps condensed in a single departure and arrival process which can include knowledge on the costs associated with each user in order to decide on the latter's departure, i.e., the disappearance due to a handover to another access network. Whereas the handover process can be modeled in a rather abstract way, the model of the radio access system itself might require a higher level of detail to accurately reveal the effects of the resource consumption by new mobile users respectively the benefits from their departure. Such a model of the access technology is comparable with those used to consider network behavior for systems supporting (mobile) users but not experiencing handover; aspects might include a granulated representation of the medium access and modulation and coding schemes, radio propagation models, as well as the user's mobility pattern within a cell affecting the overall system performance. Such models are not primarily driven by modeling handover itself and are hence not further elaborated.[1]

In contrast, a study may focus on the effects of a particular aspect of a handover–e.g., the time required to detect alternative access networks as potential handover candidates–on a single user or the overall system performance. Application examples include an evaluation of the experienced service interruption due to various handover schemes or an assessment of the

---

[1] Applicable models and modeling techniques are discussed in Chapters 9, 10, 12, 11, and 14.

influence of handover related signaling load on guaranteed QoS levels within a radio cell. In such a case, a subset of, or even all conceptual aspects of the handover process have to be modeled in detail. The following section discusses facets of the handover process which might be subject to such a thorough modulation.

Taxonomic Groups Affecting the Handover Process

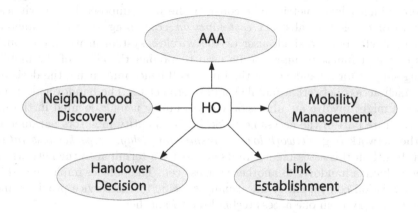

Fig. 15.1: Mechanisms affecting the handover process

Several mechanisms influence the handover process and, therefore, have to be considered in the process of modeling handover. Figure 15.1 depicts these *generic mobility functions* including mainly *neighborhood discovery, handover decision, link (re-) establishment, mobility management*, as well as *AAA (authentication, authorization, and accounting)*. Also referred to as handover phases, they may occur sequentially, in parallel, or may be skipped depending on the modeled technology or the required abstraction level of the model itself [131].

Within the *cell / neighborhood exploration* phase, the mobile becomes aware of available radio cells serving as a potential handover target. To obtain such information, mechanisms characterized by the underlying technologies as well as technology independent methods are applicable. The former typically involve scanning procedures in which the mobile either passively listens on the wireless channel for possible communication partners or actively probes potential interlocutors. The latter may involve an (external) information service which can be queried for neighborhood information depending on the mobile's current position. The hereby involved signaling may be specific to the underlying wireless technology (e.g., IEEE 802.11k MAC level neighborhood reports) or technology independent (c.f. IEEE 802.21's media independent information service) [133].

The main goal of the handover decision and criteria is to determine *when* to conduct a handover of *which mobile user* to *which target radio cell*. The inceptive choice, i.e., the decision which mobile has to conduct a handover, may be based on the station's mobility causing a degradation of the link eventually resulting in a connectivity loss, up to metrics representing the perceived quality of service at application level which a handover could improve. Typical *mobility-related metrics* are RSSI- or location-based triggers, whereas higher layer metrics may consider the jitter imposed by the wireless system or employ an abstract *cost function* combining several parameters and their effects on a single user or the wireless system in its whole. Such abstract cost functions may also be used to predict the effect of the mobile being subject for a handover on the target cell hence influencing the decision to which access network a mobile should connect to. The handover decision process might involve an admission control entity usually located in the infrastructure part of the access network. Such an entity monitors parameters of the network (e.g. *network load, transmission delay*, or *packet loss ratio*) and, based on this assessment, grants access for a terminal to the network or even induces a handover to another wireless cell. The policies implemented in the admission control entity are usually specific to the service provider and may even vary from one access technology to another.

In order to conduct a handover, the mobile has to set-up a layer-2 connection with the new access point referred to as *link establishment*. This can be either done *reactively* (*break-before-make handover*) or *proactively* (*make-before-break handover*). Whereas the former approach is most typical for *intra-technology handover*, the latter approach is more likely to be found for *heterogeneous handover* as they involve systems having multiple network interface cards hence being able to establish multiple layer-2 links in parallel. Another degree of freedom in classifying the handover is given by deciding which entity controls the handover process. For example, the latter may entirely be under the control of the mobile terminal or it may be controlled by a network entity in the backbone or base station. In addition to this distinction between *mobile* vs. *network controlled handover*, the mobile may also establish several link-layer connections in parallel during the handover process. Doing so, may result in receiving packets via several network connection points simultaneously which avoids packet loss and is hence denoted soft handover. In contrast, hard handover only have one simultaneous link layer connection at a time. Typical examples for mobile-controlled, hard handover are IEEE 802.11 WLAN systems whereas 3G UMTS enables network-controlled, soft handover. In either way, regardless of the classification, link establishment involves signaling between the mobile terminal and the access point which can, depending on the system model and underlying wireless technologies, even extend beyond the mere wireless link into the wired backbone.

A handover results in a change of the network topology as the mobile accesses the network via a different wireless attachment point. Mobility management schemes cope with the effects of this alteration and generally result in the delivery of traffic destined for the mobile via the new attachment point. Possible schemes range from layer-2 based mechanisms, over transport layer solutions, up to approaches on application level. Hence, the creation of a model for the handover under investigation has to account for the involved signaling cost, consider resulting delays (and delay jitter) of arriving packets at the mobile, or decide if the influence of the mobility management can be neglected under given modeling assumptions.

In addition to previously discussed, access-technology-related aspects, handover may also require a (re-) authentication of the mobile and the target access network, authorization for the usage, and accounting for costs. Included functions may be specific of the access technology, such as the key exchange of IEEE 802.11 to authenticate the mobile or to establish a wired equivalent privacy, or include signaling above layer-2.[2]

In order to model the handover process, a detailed understanding of each taxonomic group is necessary for every considered technology. This knowledge in combination with the considered system model and assumptions yields to the option of either modeling each aspect in detail, approximating its behavior by an abstract cost function, or discarding it entirely.

15.2.2   Wireless System View

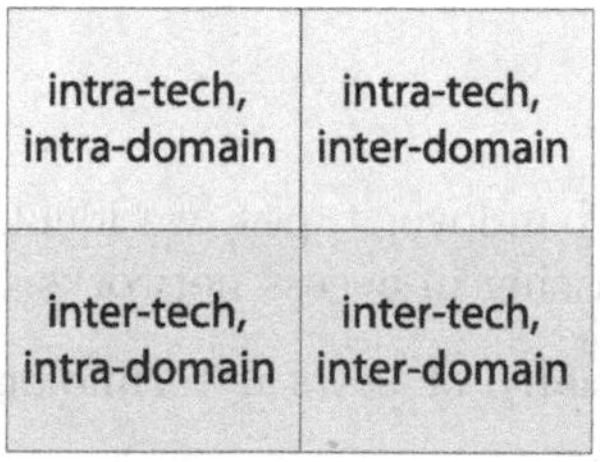

intra-tech, intra-domain	intra-tech, inter-domain
inter-tech, intra-domain	inter-tech, inter-domain

Fig. 15.2: Handover Taxonomy

This section firstly introduces a *classification of different handover types*. From this, we derive a set of specific handover scenarios. Finally, an abstraction of these scenarios leads to three distinct model approaches. They comprise of all aspects required to focus a simulation study on the important parts in wireless access networks.

---

[2] Please refer to Chapter 21 on Security and Privacy for some further aspects to consider.

Classification of Handover Types

The four general types of handovers are shown in Figure 15.2. Similar to [129] we classify handovers regarding the four properties of intra-/inter-technology and intra-/inter-domain approaches.

In an *intra-technology handover* (aka *horizontal handover*), a mobile just moves between cells of the same radio access technology. These kind of handovers are usually performed with one network interface card (NIC). In the following we refer to this as a homogeneous handover.

In case that a mobile has several NICs of different access technologies (ATs), e.g., WLAN and UMTS, it can perform an *inter-technology handover* (aka *vertical handover*) by switching from one to another technology. This type is denoted as *heterogeneous handover*.

A mobile may stay within the same administrative domain or move between several domains—the latter is denoted as inter-domain handover. As a domain, we understand here the network that is under control of one administrative instance such as a provider or a company. Since an *inter-domain handover* implies also a change of the IP subnet, it requires not only mobility management schemes at Layer 3 or above, but also appropriate procedures for *authentication, authorization, and accounting*.[3]

Further degrees of freedom for this handover taxonomy are achieved when including specifics on how the link-layer connections are established during the handover process. As mentioned before, the system under consideration may conduct a *mobile vs. network controlled handover*. Also, the mobile may establish several layer-2 links in parallel to conduct a soft handover or only uphold one physical connection at a time (*hard handover*).

Specific Scenarios

From the classification of handover types, we identify five specific scenarios when focusing on issues arising in access networks:

1. multiple cells (potentially of several technologies) with no overlap in space,
2. multiple homogeneous, overlapping cells,
3. heterogeneous cells, single cell of each access technology AT_1 and AT_2,
4. heterogeneous cells, single cell AT_1, more than one cell AT_2 (and vice versa),
5. heterogeneous cells, multiple cells of each technology.

The first case is a representative of the situation where the mobile is just associated with one cell having no overlap in space with other cells. Therefore,

---

[3] For an investigation regarding handover interruption times of different mobility management schemes, the reader is referred to [506].

the mobile can perform a handover only with interruptions, i.e., sooner or later, movements will bring the mobile in the coverage of another cell again.

The cases two to five represent the typical multi-cell scenarios that appear in today's wireless networks. Note that the focus is solely on the access networks themselves. Thus there's conceptually no difference whether cells are within one or several administrative domains.

Model Categories

Full-blown simulation models with lots of cells belonging to different technologies generate a high degree of complexity. Firstly, it requires an appropriate coupling of (heterogeneous) cells within the model. Secondly, a mobility management scheme is indispensable to conduct a handover. Thirdly, the behavior of the MAC scheme needs to represent a sufficient level of detail for modeling handovers. All three issues may increase the complexity of a complete model and make a validation as well as a verification extremely difficult due to the increase in functionality.

The time-consuming development process of a full-blown model gives reason to think about alternative time-saving simplifications to the modeling process first. This section presents a proposal for three conceptual model categories of increasing complexity that are suitable for handover investigations of increasing detail.

Single-Cell Model. The single-cell model comprises two conceptual parts: the originator and the recipient cell. The originator cell is the one with which the handover candidate was associated before actually executing the handover. In contrast, the recipient cell is the one which is supposed to accommodate the handover candidate afterwards. Following the conceptual view, a handover is nothing else than an arrival (or departure) process from the view of the recipient (or originator) cell. Assuming that originator and recipient cell do not influence each other, e.g. due to non-interfering channels, this approach allows for an isolated evaluation of both cells.

Note, that this approach is only feasible if one is interested in studying the impact of a handover on the originator (or recipient) cell and their associated terminals. It is not suitable for studies on the effect of a handover on the candidate itself, e.g, investigations of the interruption duration and QoS degradation during the handover.

The single-cell model may be applicable for multiple cells having no overlap in space (Scenario 1), for multiple homogeneous, overlapping cells having no interfering channels (Scenario 2), and for heterogeneous cells with a single cell of each access technology (Scenario 3).

Multi-Cell Model. Contrary to the single-cell model, the multi-cell approach covers studies which cannot neglect either the coupling of cells, the impact of the handover on the candidate, or interactions between originator and recipient cells. These cases require the simultaneous investigation of multiple cells. Here, modeling of the handover includes a chain of all important steps. Note, that this does not necessarily mean that really *all* steps have to be included in the model. If one decides to go for a multi-cell model, it will really simplify the modeling process by firstly identifying relevant steps discussed in Section 15.2.1. Note that the multi-cell model may be applicable for all Scenarios described in Section 15.2.2.

Cost-function Model.   The cost function model basically extends the single-cell approach. The design rationale for this concept is the idea to represent each single cell by its own cost function. Such a cost function is nothing else than a collection of (system) parameters reflecting effort and revenue to serve a specific user in the corresponding cell. The advantages of such an approach are twofold. Firstly, it allows studies for optimal access selection and handover candidate selection regarding specific criteria being represented by the cost functions. Secondly, it is beneficial especially for simulation studies of handovers in heterogeneous networks. The reason lies in the fact that appropriate cost functions allow a technology-independent comparison regarding the suitability of handover candidates for a specific access network. This allows fine-grained handover decisions.

This approach is beneficial if one is interested in studying the impact of a handover on the originator (or recipient) cell and its associated terminals. The cost-function approach allows for separate studies of each cell regarding arrival and departure process of mobile terminals. Extending this idea, even distinct methodological means (e.g., analysis, simulations, and measurements) are applicable for originator and recipient cell, i.e., while conducting simulations for one cell, analysis may be applied for the other.

Similar to the single-cell model, the cost-function approach may be applicable for multiple cells having no overlap in space (Scenario 1), for multiple homogeneous, overlapping cells having no interfering channels (Scenario 2), and for heterogeneous cells with a single cell of each access technology (Scenario 3).

15.3   Application Examples

15.3.1   Handover in an IEEE 802.11 Multi-cell Environment

IEEE 802.11 is today's most predominant WLAN technology and has become further a standard component of mobile devices such as cellular phones or Portable Digital Assistants (PDAs). As these devices do not only offer nomadic mobility but also allow their users to communicate while moving from one radio cell to another, the question comes up how well the IEEE 802.11 handover performs in terms of service interruption times.

More specifically, we focus on the handover decision phase. There, the longer it takes to decide for a handover, e.g. due to a bad channel, the longer the service of an application may be interrupted. We consider two approaches for deciding on a handover: a simple RSSI-based decision and a scheme triggering a handover if no beacon is received within three target beacon transmission times. As shown later, these two approaches can be modeled at a different level of detail and hereby illustrate how different abstraction levels may have significant impact on the required simulation time. Please note that the choice of the presented algorithms is not dominated by the most novel approaches reducing the handover delay, but rather by didactical reasons as it allows to model different mechanisms affecting the handover at different abstraction levels.

System Model

As the comparison of different mechanisms for the handover decision phase is subject of the investigation, the (homogeneous) multi-cell model as described in Section 15.2.2 is chosen. Depending on the model's level of detail regarding the underlying technology, it allows to specifically identify the effects of a particular handover phase on the experienced handover delay. Without loss of generality of this application example, only two overlapping IEEE 802.11 radio cells are considered and a single mobile terminal moves on a straight line from one AP to the other.[4]

The IEEE 802.11 working group has also conducted work on a common metric set to evaluate the performance of WLAN equipment [17]. The defined access point transition time *(APTT)* [47] metric is the most appropriate to describe the duration of the handover including all its sub-phases such as handover decision, neighborhood discovery, and link re-establishment. This metric classifies the times between the last successful reception of a user datagram via the originating AP and the first successful reception of a user datagram via the destination AP. Obviously, the resolution of the corresponding measurement depends on the packet inter-arrival time (IAT) of the user datagrams. If they derive from a point-to-point connection even possibly established on top of IP, the APTT would also include any time needed to move the connection within the backbone / distribution system from the originating AP to the new AP hence reflecting all possible effects of higher layer protocols (dealing with routing, spanning tree algorithms, etc.). In order to only focus on the pure handover phases using the APTT metric, we rather transmit broadcast user data frames via both APs. As a result, the mobile

---

[4] Please note, that other, more complex deployments of APs as well as other mobility models do not result in any change regarding the *methodology* for modeling the handover in this particular example and are hence not considered for the sake of simplicity.

STA immediately receives user datagrams after link re-establishment without depending on any higher layer protocols.

Regarding the radio channel, we simply assume distance-based path loss. In order to evaluate effects of short term fading as well as other mobility patterns for the mobile, the reader is kindly asked to decide on modeling alternatives as described in Chapter 11.

Modeling of the Handover Phases

IEEE 802.11 [15] as well as the by now withdrawn recommended practice 802.11.1 [13] discuss various mechanisms affecting the handover process. For the sake of simplicity, only neighborhood discovery (aka network discovery), handover decision, and link reestablishment are discussed. For the remaining aspects, the reader is referred to [132, 133] as well as to Section 12.1 and Chapter 21. Assuming an open system authentication and the given APTT metric, this abstraction from AAA and higher layer handover mechanisms is reasonable and can be, e.g., accounted for by a constant additional delay added to the measurements.[5]

The goal of the following paragraphs is to demonstrate to the reader three different abstraction levels in modeling handover phases. Two abstraction levels are applied when modeling the handover decision phase: a very detailed model capturing most of the actual 802.11 specific exchange of signaling messages, and a simplification eliminating such a detailed modeling. For the latter simplification, explicit knowledge on the system model (such as channel model and load of the network imposed during the simulation) is used. A third abstraction level found within the modeling process is applied to the neighborhood discovery & link-layer re-establishment phase. Again, explicitly applying knowledge on the system (model) results in simply representing this phase by a constant delay without any further modeling of the actually involved signaling messages.

Handover Decision. The IEEE 802.11 standard does not specify any decision schemes when to switch from one AP to another. Accordingly, one has to choose how to model the handover decision phase. Existing devices commonly implement either an approach based on the reception of beacons, or simply decide to conduct a handover if the RSSI value drops below a given threshold.

For the first approach, a STA should decide to start the neighborhood discovery phase (scanning) if a beacon is not received within three target beacon transmission times. Obviously, evaluating this approach requires a more detailed modeling of 802.11 itself: the model of the AP has to regularly transmit beacons. Also those beacons have to be recognized by the model at the receiving STA which has to remember when the last beacon was received

---

[5] The reader is kindly asked to study the corresponding sections of the IEEE 802.11 standard [15] when deciding on his/her own modeling abstractions as it is out of scope of this chapter to introduce the IEEE 802.11 technology itself.

in order to decide on starting neighborhood discovery after three target beacon transmission times. This very detailed model would give a rather precise description of the WLAN behavior and would even reveal effects of short term fading (which could theoretically cause the loss of beacons close to the AP and hence a handover to be triggered even though the STA is very well within the coverage of the AP). But this accurate model comes at the cost of simulation time.

Having knowledge on the overall system model, as described in Section 15.3.1, a more simulation-time-saving model could be implemented. As the system model only considers simply path loss, short-term fading cannot occur. Additionally, we assume only a low channel load and non-interfering STAs. As a result, for this specific simulation model beacons can only be lost if a STA's distance to the AP exceeds a given distance. Based on the parameters of the channel model, this distance can be pre-computed if an RSSI based handover decision is analyzed. Accordingly, beacons no longer need to be transmitted but the handover decision can be condensed to a simple query if the STA is farther away from the AP than a given cut-off distance. Such a modeling approach could significantly increase simulation speed.

Neighborhood Discovery and Link Reestablishment. The IEEE 802.11 standard defines two mechanisms to actively discover the neighborhood of a station (STA), namely active and passive scanning [15]. For the former, a STA merely listens on a channel for a beacon transmitted by APs in its surrounding whereas for the latter, a STA may actively probe for existing APs. As the standard does only apply the sequence and format of the employed protocol messages but not the algorithm behind them, e.g. if a STA should scan all available channels or merely a subset of them, we herein model the neighborhood discovery phase according to the following algorithm: *A station scans for all available channels and listens on each channel for three target beacon transmission times.*

Assuming open authentication, the link reestablishment consists of a simple four-way handshake which we herein assume to occur at the cell's border hence being transmitted at the most robust modulation and coding scheme.

Based on these two mechanisms, it is valid to model the neighborhood discovery (scanning) and link reestablishment phase with a constant delay and allow the mobile STA to immediately exchange user data at the MAC level after the handover decision scheme.

Conclusion

This application example showed how a very simplified and yet, considering the scenario constraints and underlying assumptions, valid simulation model for IEEE 802.11 clients can be built. On the other hand, the reader will most likely encounter an existing simulation environment with existing models for both, the underlying technology and the handover process. As these models are complex and in themselves based on simplifying assumptions, it is more than essential to analyze the employed models and understand how they abstract from the real world and how these abstractions could affect the topic under consideration.

15.3.2   Cost Function for an IEEE 802.11a/g System

This part presents an example for the *cost function model* described in Section 15.2.2. The example is based on a system with two heterogeneous IEEE 802.11 cells, namely one *IEEE 802.11g* and one *IEEE 802.11a* cell. All mobile terminals are equipped with separate network interface cards for each IEEE 802.11 flavor, such that a handover can be performed by switching from one to the other interface. For this simple example, we assume that all mobile terminals are in the coverage of both cells. This approach is applicable if one is interested in studying the impact of a handover on the originator (or recipient) cell and their associated terminals as well as for investigations of optimal allocation of users to cells regarding specific criteria as performed in [495].

The following section gives an example for the construction of cost functions. It is followed by an illustration how handover decisions can be based upon these cost functions.

Construction of Cost Functions

Regarding the cost function, we follow the common approach to combine costs and revenues for serving a specific user. Both aspects reflect the provider as well as the user perspective. The revenue could be represented by monetary incomes for the provider and resulting QoS level for the specific user. Contrary, costs may consider the load level in the network, signaling overhead, or effort for prioritized medium access for high-priority traffic.

For the sake of simplicity, this example focuses on one representative for each part. For the revenue, we select the QoS level of a specific user i. Costs are represented by the load level evoked by the transportation of user's traffic flow. Here, we consider a cost function that linearly combines weighted and scaled parameters for both parts:

$$c_{WLAN}(i) = \omega_1 \frac{t_a(i)}{\Delta t} + \omega_2 QoS(i)$$

$$\text{with } \omega_1 + \omega_2 = 1$$

(15.1)

The *QoS* parameter separates into several parts dependent on the requested service. Here, we distinct dependent on different QoS classes. For VoIP, it would consist of the end-to-end delay, jitter, and packet loss (normalized by their maximum tolerable values).

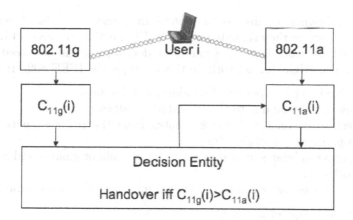

Fig. 15.3: Handover Decision Process

The load evoked for the transportation of user i's traffic is reflected by the airtime metric t_a measured over a certain interval Δt.[6] Basically the airtime is nothing else than the duration for which the wireless channel is occupied for a transmission. It is similar to the airtime link metric of the amendment IEEE 802.11s, which however uses link probe packets instead of measuring the actual traffic. The airtime is calculated as

$$\Delta t_{a_i} = t_{IFS} + t_d(Rate_j) + t_{ack} \tag{15.2}$$

Δt_{a_i} represents the amount of time that the wireless medium is occupied (or reserved, in case of inter-frame spaces and NAV settings[7]):This includes the whole transmission sequence consisting of the inter-frame spaces DIFS or AIFS and SIFS (t_{IFS}), the duration t_d of the complete data frame "on air", where the data part is encoded with a certain modulation scheme $Rate_j$ and the acknowledgment t_{ack}.

Handover Decisions on the Basis of Cost Functions

For the handover decision process, the involved access networks are divided into the two conceptual parts described in Section 15.2.2—the originator and the recipient cell. In principal, there exist three general concepts regarding the placement of the handover decision. This can be realized within the originator network, the recipient network, or by a separate arbitration entity.

---

[6] For a discussion about the choice of the interval, the reader is referred to [494].
[7] The backoff duration does not apply here, since only the occupation of the channel is of interest.

In the following, we discuss the outstanding tasks for a handover if the decision is made in the originator network. Figure 15.3 displays all involved entities and the work-flow for a handover decision that is discussed in the following. The originator network, in this example the IEEE 802.11g cell,

1. identifies user(s) as potential handover candidate(s),
2. estimates the gain due to the potential handovers,
3. requests cost function value estimates from the recipient network via appropriate means of signaling,
4. compares candidates' cost function values within originator and recipient network, and
5. finally decides for or against a vertical handover for each candidate.

Contrary, the recipient network

1. estimates the cost function value for each potential handover candidate currently served by the originator network, and
2. assesses the impact of a handover on other users.

A handover for user i from the 11g to the 11a cell takes place, if

$$c_{11g}(i) > c_{11g}(j) \ \forall \text{ users } j \neq i \tag{15.3}$$

$$c_{11g}(i) > c_{11a}(i) \tag{15.4}$$

Eq. (15.3) represents the identification of potential handover candidates within the IEEE 802.11g cell, i.e., the selection of the user with the highest cost function value. Eq. (15.4) describes the comparison of candidate's cost function value in IEEE 802.11g and IEEE 802.11a. Only in case that his value is significantly better in the IEEE 802.11a cell, a handover will be triggered. This part is indispensable, since serving the user with the highest costs in IEEE 802.11g may still be cheaper than putting him into IEEE 802.11a.

15.4   A Guide for Modeling Handover Approaches

The following guideline summarizes all methodological parts discussed in Section 15.2 and may hence be used by the reader during the initial planning phase of the simulation to carefully consider all relevant aspects of modeling handovers. In summary, stressing the importance to firstly decide on which modeling approach may be conceptually feasible, which models may be useful, and which level of detail is required in the modeling process are a major concern of this section. Figure 15.4 presents such a guide whose four main parts are shortly discussed in the following subsections.

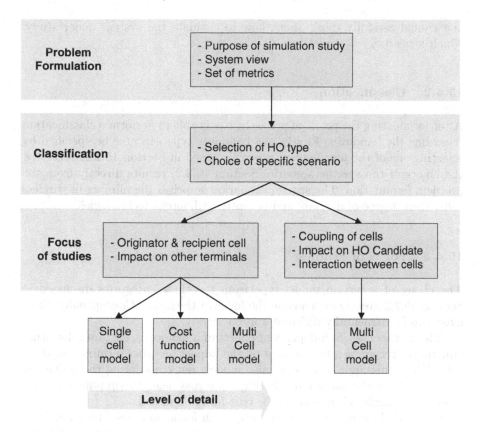

Fig. 15.4: Guide for modeling handovers

15.4.1 Problem Formulation

The first step of a simulative investigation is nothing else than asking yourself "What do I really want to investigate?" Without clarifying the goal of the simulations, one will likely have difficulties later on during the choice of simulation models and considerations regarding the level of detail. In a worst case this may lead to a waste of time not only for modeling but also regarding the computational effort—obviously, the more detailed a simulation model is, the longer will a simulation last.

A precise formulation of a problem being studied should consist of three main parts. First of all, the purpose of the simulation study must be very clear. This allows in a second step to define a detailed system view ("the big picture") including the choice of specific systems, traffic and user type selection, as well as the definition of requirements and assumptions. Finally, one should carefully think about how to evaluate the system under study, which leads to a set of metrics.

15.4.2   Classification

After formulating the problem precisely, one is able to perform a classification regarding the handover. Firstly, the handover type can now be specified by selecting one of the four general types discussed in Section 15.2.2. Secondly, the choice of the specific scenario (Section 15.2.2) results directly from the problem formulation. The specific scenario comprises the number of wireless cells, their degree of overlap, and potentially different technologies.

15.4.3   Focus of Studies

The choice of a certain model type from the three categories discussed in Section 15.2.2 greatly depends on the focus of the study. Conceptually, there exist two fundamentally different approaches.

The first focuses on independent effects of a handover, e.g., on cells either emitting or receiving a terminal, or on the impact on other terminals in these cells. Thus, this approach covers also models not considering the impact of a handover on the candidate himself. This may lead to simplified models namely the single-cell as well as the cost-function model.

Studies belonging to the second approach focus on cases which require a simultaneous investigation of multiple cells. This includes studies considering the signaling in the backplane, the impact on the handover candidate himself, or interactions between cells.

15.4.4   Level of Detail

Finally, determining the required level of detail leads to the selection of a certain model type. For this, one should carefully revise the taxonomic groups affecting the handover process (Section 15.2.1). Here, it is important to decide how detailed each handover phase must be modeled such that the overall complexity remains as low as possible but still meets the purpose of the simulation study.

Together with the requirements, the specified level of details further helps later on for the selection of external (already existing) simulation model implementations.

Part III

Higher Layer Modeling

16. Modeling the Network Layer and Routing Protocols

Pengfei Di (Universität Karlsruhe (TH) & TU München)
Matthias Wählisch (Freie Universität Berlin & HAW Hamburg)
Georg Wittenburg (Freie Universität Berlin)

16.1 Introduction

The network layer is in charge of ensuring end-to-end connectivity among the nodes of a network. This goal comprises the subtasks of providing a way of addressing all participating nodes, setting up a forwarding mechanism for packets on the nodes, and establishing paths along which packets are to be routed. The major challenge in achieving this goal is the scalability of the routing algorithms with regard to data structures and signaling overhead, especially in the light of a changing network topology.

In this chapter, we first cover the basics of routing protocols (Section 16.2) and then proceed to describe the impact of node mobility on routing (Section 16.3). For brevity, we limit our discussion on connectionless, i.e. packet-switched, networks as opposed to connection-oriented networks. The concepts presented here are thus mostly applicable to traditional Internet-style networks as well as all kinds of wireless ad hoc networks.

Models for the network layer are closely related to the data link layer as introduced in Section 10.1 and the network topology as discussed in Chapter 22. For most simulations, it is quite common that the simulated routing protocol consists of a slimmed-down implementation of the real protocol with special attention paid to the distinguishing features of the protocol. In such cases, one may also consider integrating a real-world implementation of the protocol as described in Chapter 6.

16.2 Routing

In the first part of this chapter, we discuss basic routing in wired and wireless networks. We start with a classification of routing protocols with examples for quick reference (Section 16.2.1), and then proceed to review the components of a routing protocol (Section 16.2.2), introduce the theoretical background (Section 16.2.3), describe commonly used metrics (Section 16.2.4), briefly cover issues related to virtual or overlay routing (Section 16.2.5), and conclude with some issues to keep in mind when

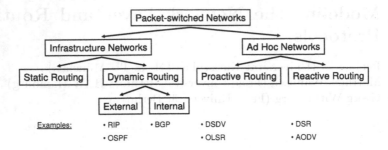

Fig. 16.1: Classification of Routing Protocols by Network Organization

simulating routing protocols (Section 16.2.6). For more in-depth information we suggest the discussions in [452, 367, 401].

16.2.1   Classification and Examples

Multiple *taxonomies for routing protocols* have been proposed in the literature, most of them focussing on specific types of networks ranging from the Internet backbone [452, Chapter 5] to sensor networks [29]. These classifications schemes emphasize different properties of the routing protocol, e.g. network organization, algorithmic concepts or delivery semantics, and we follow these approaches in our overview.

Routing protocols may be classified depending on the organizational structure of the network they are operating on (see Figure 16.1). Networks generally fall into two categories in that they are either infrastructure-based or of ad hoc nature, but the network may also follow a virtual higher-level structure in case of overlay networks which we cover separately in Section 16.2.5. For *infrastructure-based networks*, routing mechanisms can be subdivided into static mechanisms and dynamic routing protocols. Static mechanisms usually require a human administrator to setup the routes and thus emphasize predictability over scalability, while the opposite is true for dynamic protocols. Dynamic protocols are further subdivided into internal and external protocols based on whether the routers are part of the same administrative domain or not. Popular examples for internal, dynamic routing protocols in infrastructure-based networks are *RIP* [304] and *OSPF* [324], an example for an external routing protocol for the same type of network is *BGP* [386].

In *ad hoc networks*, routing protocols are commonly divided into proactive (or table-driven) protocols and reactive (or on-demand) protocols. The key difference between these two approaches is that proactive protocols periodically exchange neighborhood information to keep a global routing table on each node up to date, while reactive protocols only start the route discovery process when packets to specific nodes are handed down from the transport

	|| Distance Vector	Link State
Infrastructure	RIP [304]	OSPF [324]
	BGP [386]	
Ad hoc	DSDV [362]	OLSR [233]
	AODV [363]	

Table 16.1: Exemplary Routing Protocols by Network Organization and Algorithm

layer. As the data transfer can only be initiated once the route is in place, reactive routing protocols require appropriate models for the delays on the lower layers for an accurate simulation. Widely used reactive protocols include *DSR* [244] and *AODV* [363], while *DSDV* [362] and *OLSR* [233] are typical representatives for proactive protocols. Hybrid approaches, such as *ZRP* [189], combine the advantages of both proactive and reactive schemes.

Looking at the *algorithmic aspects of routing protocols*, they are commonly divided into two main categories: *Distance vector protocols* base their routing decision on destination-specific next-hop information which is disseminated hop by hop throughout the networks. *Link state protocols* construct a graph of the network on all participating nodes by flooding information about connectivity in their respective one-hop neighborhood. Each node can then locally extract routing information from this graph by running one of the shortest-path algorithms presented in Section 16.2.3. Of the routing protocols mentioned above, RIP, AODV, DSDV and at its core also BGP are distance vector protocols, while OSPF and OLSR are link state protocols. The relation between organizational and algorithmic concepts of these protocols is illustrated in Table 16.1.

For different delivery semantics, the routing schemes can be further classified into unicast, broadcast, multicast, concast and anycast. In *unicast*, the destination of a packet is a dedicated node; in *broadcast*, all nodes within the same logical network (referred to as broadcast domain) are the destination; in *multicast*, nodes are grouped and the group members should receive the packets destined to the group; in *concast* data will be sent by several sources to a single receiver, thus, being the counterpart of multicast; in *anycast*, nodes are also grouped, but only the closest group member should receive the packet. Most aforementioned routing protocols are unicast protocols with partial support for broadcast operation.

For a quick reference, Table 16.2 illustrates the available implementations of the routing protocols mentioned above in various simulators. Ns2 is one of the most widely used simulators in academic area. The routing models in OMNeT++ are integrated within its frameworks INET and INETMANET respectively. OPNET is a commercial simulator, but it provides free license for academic research and teaching. SWANS is a wireless network simulator and thus includes only ad-hoc routing protocols.

routing protocols/simulators	OMNeT[474]	ns2[116]	OPNET[212]	SWANS[9]
RIP	+	+	+	−
BGP	−	−	+	−
OSPF	+	+	+	−
AODV	+	+	+	+
DSR	+	+	+	+
OLSR	+	−	+	−
DSDV	−	+	+	−
ZRP	−	−	−	+

Table 16.2: Implemented Routing Protocols in Common Simulators

16.2.2   Components of a Routing Protocol

A routing protocol contains the following *components*: node addressing, topology maintenance, path selection and cross-layer operation.

Node Addressing

As a prerequisite for routing packets, each node in the network needs an address to identify itself. Addresses are normally unique in a network domain; however, in some cases duplicated addresses are also permitted, e.g., in networks supporting anycast.

Addressing schemes can be split into two groups: *structured addressing* and *unstructured addressing*. Unstructured addressing usually means a random ID allocation in a flat numerical space. An unstructured addressing scheme can be easily implemented in a distributed manner, since every node can assign itself an address locally and randomly. This addressing scheme is often used in ad hoc networks and overlay networks, while the traditional IP networks (like the Internet) rely on external administration, e.g., by using DHCP [125] or stateless address auto-configuration in IPv6 [464].

Many routing protocols assume a unique address assignment and do not have a mechanism to check for duplicate addresses. When modeling these kinds of protocols, the address length should be taken into consideration in order to reduce the probability of address duplication.

Assume that a uniform distribution is used to allocate m addresses to n nodes, the probability without address duplication is:

$$p(m,n) = 1 \times (1 - \frac{1}{m}) \times (1 - \frac{2}{m}) \cdots (1 - \frac{n-1}{m}) = \prod_{i=1}^{n-1}(1 - \frac{i}{m})$$

For a large m and n, the computational cost of the function above will be enormous. In this case, the Taylor series expansion can be used to calculate the approximation result. For a small x:

$$e^x = 1 + x + \frac{x^2}{2!} + \cdots \approx 1 + x$$

we get then

$$p(m, n) \approx 1 \times e^{-\frac{1}{m}} \times e^{-\frac{2}{m}} \cdots e^{-\frac{n-1}{m}} = e^{\frac{-n(n-1)}{2 \cdot m}}$$

For example, if assigning 32-bit addresses randomly to an ad hoc network with 50,000 nodes, the probability of address duplication will be approximately 25%. Obviously, this 32-bit random address assignment is not suitable for large networks.

Structured addressing subdivides the addresses into two or more parts in order to structure the network into static subnetworks or dynamic clusters. Such an addressing scheme is commonly used in infrastructure-based networks. For example, the IPv4 addresses in the Internet should follow the addressing guideline [164]. As a consequence of structured addressing, routing path information to all hosts in these subnetworks can be stored in the routing tables using one or a few prefixes [314] or address intervals [281]. It is important to note that the current Internet does not possess a fully summable address space mainly due to provider independent addresses.

Although structured addressing scheme is usually applied in infra-structure-based networks, there are some efforts [136] trying to apply this scheme to ad-hoc networks, where node movement can exist. Nodes using this addressing scheme have to update their addresses when they change their position, and that in turn introduces the overhead because some lookup service is now needed.

It is worth noting that some current *topology generators*, like Georgia Tech Internetwork Topology Model (GT-ITM) [511] and Boston University Representative Internet Topology Generator (BRITE) [312], generate only pure topologies without assigning any address to the nodes. However, some address assignment schemes [127] can utilize the topology information and increase the degree of address aggregation, thus reducing the average routing table size per node and making the simulation more similar and realistic to real networks.

Note that one node can also have multiple addresses. For example, a node having multiple network interface cards usually has one address for each card. Obviously, this is beneficial for the connectivity of such *multi-homed* nodes (cf. Section 16.3).

Finally, for networks in which the physical location of a host is central to the application, an addressing scheme based on the geographical coordinates of the hosts may be used, e.g., Greedy Perimeter Stateless Routing (GPSR) [248].

Topology Maintenance

The knowledge of a partial or complete *network topology* is fundamental to run any routing protocol. In a medium or large-scale network, it is impossible to manually configure the nodes with topology information due to cost and potential errors. Consequently, the routing protocol must be designed to detect the topology. Link-state routing protocols require complete topology knowledge, while distance-vector protocols need only to know neighborhood information and aggregate topology information from it, e.g., the distance from the neighbors to every other node.

When and how frequently the topology information should be obtained and refreshed depend mostly on the stability of the network topology. In proactive routing protocols, the topology information is exchanged regularly, thus resulting in a relatively constant signaling overhead. For example, *RIP* topology information is exchanged between neighbors about every 30 seconds. In reactive routing protocols, the topology information is exchanged only when a node needs to establish a path to unknown destinations. This may lead to signaling bursts. Note that in reactive routing protocols only the topology information related to the destination is exchanged.

For unstable network topologies, in which mobility and link failures are common, the topology information is just valid temporarily. Therefore, proactive routing protocols have to exchange the topology information to keep the route information up-to-date. For networks, in which node mobility and node failure rates are very high, the maintenance overhead would be enormous. This is the reason why proactive routing protocols are not feasible in these kinds of networks. In contrast, reactive routing protocols have to timeout the topology information frequently in order to avoid using paths based on obsolete information. However, this may cause signaling bursts due to the frequent new route establishments. Hence, routing protocol design for large and unstable networks is still a challenging topic in current research.

Path Selection

The core task of a routing protocol is to *find a path* to any destination node. After the node has obtained the necessary topology information either by proactive manner or reactive manner and has chosen a routing metric, it can run some routing algorithm (cf. Section 16.2.1) to select the path for any destination.

In classic routing protocols for wired networks, the number of forwarding hops is widely used as a metric, thus selecting the path with the least hops to a destination. In wireless ad hoc networks, a shortest path measured in hops is not always the optimal solution. Transmission time, radio interference, load balancing, etc. are also important metrics. For example, in link-state routing protocols, the link weight could be the transmission time rather than the hop count, and the resulted path will be the "fastest" instead of the topologically "shortest" one. Generally speaking, the shortest path denotes a least-cost path with respect to a specific metric. Each routing protocol has a path selection metric, which comprises one or more aspects mentioned above. Common metrics will be covered in Section 16.2.4.

Some routing protocols, e.g., GPSR [248], Virtual Ring Routing (VRR) [84] and Scalable Source Routing (SSR) [160] maintain only limited topology information. The path to some destinations cannot be selected directly, and the packet has to be delivered to another node, called intermediator, to whom the path is already known. The intermediator has to accept this packet and continue the routing process. This is not to be confused with reactive routing protocols, in which a node generates a signal burst to collect enough information and establish the path to an unknown destination. In these routing protocols, some metrics have to be introduced to select the intermediator node. The metrics employed in the intermediator selection process will be discussed in Section 16.2.4.

Cross-Layer Operation

Additional to the operations described above, a network-layer routing protocol should also interact with the layers above and below it. At the sender, the routing layer should receive messages from the upper layer, encapsulate them and deliver them to the lower layer. At the receiver, the routing layer receives packets from the lower layer and hands the decapsulated message to the higher layer. If more than one module exist above the routing layer, multiplexing is also one task of the implementation of the network-layer protocol. Cross-layering neglects or weakens this basic interaction between neighboring layers: It intends to communicate between non-adjacent tiers.

Generally, a router only inspects the packet header and does not deliver the packet to the upper layer until the destination has been reached. However, some routing protocols enable intermediate nodes to intercept the packet. For example, Resource Reservation Protocol (RSVP) [76] with the Router Alert Option in the IP header [250] lets the routers examine the contents of the IP packet more closely. Some applications can benefit from such interceptions, in particular in wireless networks [415, 436]. Note that such layer violation may only optimize or add new features to the routing process, and must not hurt the end-to-end service semantic.

The network layer routing protocol cannot only provide its routing information to the upper layers, but it can also utilize the under-lay information to improve the network performance. For example, energy efficient routing protocols for wireless sensor networks [412, 520] are developed with the consideration of limited energy supply on the nodes.

Service Mode

While path discovery and packet delivery are the basic services offered by a routing protocol, there are optional services that a routing protocol can provide additionally, e.g., bandwidth guarantee, no-loss guarantee and ordering. Although these services are not widely supported in the Internet, they are important for certain networks with more specific requirement, e.g., 3G telephone networks.

ATM [341] has several service modes in its network layer: Constant Bit Rate (CBR), Variable Bit Rate (VBR), Available Bit Rate (ABR) and Unspecified Bit Rate (UBR). For different applications, various service modes are applied, e.g., CBR for video conferencing. In contrast, the Internet operates on the basic service mode: best effort.

16.2.3   Theoretical Background

Computer networks are commonly modeled as a *graph* $G = (V, E)$ with the vertices V representing the nodes in the network and the edges E the links between them. The graph may be directed or undirected depending on whether it models a network with unidirectional or bidirectional links. Weights may be assigned to the edges of the graph to specify some property of the link, e.g. bandwidth, delay, reliability or combinations thereof. Chapter 22 discusses procedures and alternatives for modeling the topology of a network in more detail.

Shortest Path Algorithms

With the graph abstraction in place, routing problems in the network translate into finding paths in the graph that satisfy certain constraints, e.g. being the shortest path between two nodes. The fundamental shortest path algorithms are due to Dijkstra [118], Bellman and Ford [55, 154] and Floyd and Warshall [145, 487]. For brevity, we omit a detailed presentation of these algorithms, but merely point out their key ideas. A more in-depth discussion of these algorithms is available in [105].

Dijkstra's algorithm is a single-source shortest path algorithm, i.e. for a given vertex it finds the shortest paths to all other vertices. The algorithmic idea is to iterate over the vertices sorted by their shortest currently known distance to the source and set their respective distance to the smallest sum of the distance of any neighbor and the weight of the edge connecting to that neighbor. The shortest paths are then formed by storing for each vertex the information about which vertex was used in the above assignment. The runtime of the algorithm is quadratic in the number of vertices of the graph

Algorithm	Applicability	Complexity	Comments
Dijkstra	single-source shortest path	$O(|V|\log|V| + |E|)$	Edge weights must be non-negative.
Bellman-Ford	single-source shortest path	$O(|V| \times |E|)$	Edge weights may be negative.
Floyd-Warshall	all-pairs shortest paths	$O(|V|^3)$	Edge weights may be negative.

Table 16.3: Comparison of Graph Algorithms

and can even be further reduced if the graph is sparse. However, the algorithm is only applicable to graphs whose edges have non-negative weights.

The *Bellman-Ford algorithm* is another single-source shortest path algorithm with its main difference to Dijkstra's algorithm being that it relaxes the requirement that all edges in the graph must have a positive weight. This is achieved by processing all the edges in the graph in each iteration as opposed to Dijkstra's algorithm which only processes the edges of the currently selected vertex with the shortest known distance to the source. The runtime of the algorithm is thus increased and is linear in the product of the number of vertices and the number of edges. The algorithm also works correctly on graphs with negative edge weights, as long as the edges do not form a cycle of negative weight.

The *Floyd-Warshall algorithm* solves the all-pairs shortest paths problem, i.e. for a given graph it finds the shortest paths between all pairs of vertices. The key idea to this algorithm is to iteratively allow for an increasing subset of the vertices to be considered as intermediate vertices on a path. It starts with no vertices being allowed as intermediates – thus only considering vertices directly connected by an edge – and than iteratively checks whether the addition of a vertex to the set of allowed intermediates makes a shorter path available. The algorithm can deal with negative weights on edges, but not with negative circles in the graph. The runtime of the algorithm is cubic in the number of vertices.

The key properties of these three algorithms are summarized in Table 16.3. It is important to note, that the original versions of these algorithms require complete and global knowledge of the entire network graph, which is generally not available in real networks or changes over time. However, distributed versions of the algorithm exists and are used as building blocks for some of the routing algorithms presented in Section 16.2.1. Furthermore, in the context of simulation, the optimal paths found by these algorithms may be used to evaluate the quality of the routes discovered by simulated routing protocols.

Queuing Theory

Additionally to the path selection algorithms discussed above, one can extend the model by considering traffic patterns (see Chapter 18) and available resources on each node, in particular memory used as part of the store-and-forward procedure. With these additions, the routing problem effectively becomes a problem that can – at least in part – be described using *queueing theory*.

Queueing theory [254] applies probability theory to systems described by their storage capacity, number of service stations, queueing discipline (potentially considering priorities) and availability. Given probability distributions for the interarrival time of entities (e.g. tasks or packets) and their service time, it is possible to derive system properties such as waiting time, number of entities present in the system, length of busy and idle periods and backlog. Multiple queues may be interconnected by moving entities from one queue to another. The resulting queueing networks [66, Chapter 7] can be used to model packet-switched computer networks, with the entities mapped to packets, waiting time mapped to delay, and storage capacity mapped to memory allocated for packet queues.

Specific optimization problems that can be addressed using these tools are the capacity assignment (CA) problem, the flow assignment (FA) problem, the capacity and flow assignment (CFA) problem, and the topology, capacity, and flow assignment (TCFA) problem [255, Chapter 5]. In this context, *capacity* corresponds to the maximal data transfer rate of physical links and *flows* describe the utilization of each channel. All of the aforementioned problems try to minimize the average message delay under the constraint of a given total network cost, or, if stated in their dual form, minimize the total cost under the constraint of a given maximal tolerable delay. The CA problem does so by considering which capacities to procure for each channel given a set of flows and a topology, and the FA problem deals with assigning flows to channels given their capacity and the topology. The CFA problem considers both capacities and flows simultaneously for a given network topology, while for the TCFA problem neither capacities, flows, nor topology are given. Analytical solutions exist for the CA (using simple models for the cost function) and FA problems. The CFA problem is solved by iteratively applying the solutions to the CA and FA problems, which has the drawback that it may not find the global optimum. Finally, in order to solve the TCFA problem heuristics employing multiple iterations of the CFA solution with different initial topologies are used.

For an in-depth discussion how queueing theory is applied to a specific computer network, namely the ARPANET in the mid-1970s, the interested reader is referred to [255, Chapter 6].

16.2.4 Metrics

When the node has enough topology information, either obtained by regular signaling or collected on demand, to establish one or more path to the destination, the least-cost path with respect to a specific metric will be preferred. Thus, a *path selection metric* is required. If there is not enough information to obtain the path to the destination, an *intermediator selection metric* is needed to choose the proper intermediator node, which will route the packet to its destination.

The path selection metric depends on the network properties. For example, in wired networks, hop count is usually chosen as the metric. The packet loss rate and interference from neighboring nodes are typically ignored. However, in wireless network, they can impact the route performance heavily, thus should be considered into the metric.

Intermediator selection metrics vary between routing protocols. For example, in geographic routing, the intermediator node is the neighbor node with shortest physical distance to the destination.

Requirements for Metrics

In wired networks, the hop count is the commonly used as the routing metric, while in wireless networks, a lot of path selection metrics have been proposed, taking different network characteristics into account. These metrics have to obey the following requirements [505]: route stability, efficient algorithm and loop-free routing.

- *Route stability* means a stable route metric, in which the link weight varies rarely. For example, hop count and transmission time are stable, thus they are preferred for static and mesh networks. On the contrary, link traffic load, delay, etc. are not proper routing metrics, because they may change frequently and can result in route oscillations and even routing loops.
- *Algorithmic efficiency* indicates a low complexity of route calculations. Although the route calculation is not a critical issue for regular Internet routers, it plays important role in the networks with power-restricted nodes, e.g., Wireless Sensor Network (WSN).
- *Loop-free routing* means that no endless routing loop can be formed in a stable network. When the network is instable, loops can be formed, but they should be detected and solved by the routing protocol. Note that temporary routing loops are allowed even in stable networks in some routing protocols, e.g., hot-potato routing [142].

Proposed Metrics

In practice, quite a few path selection metrics have been proposed, such as hop count, bandwidth, Expected Transmission Count (ETX) [112], Expected Transmission Time (ETT) [123], Weighted Cumulative Expected Transmission Time (WCETT) [503], Metric of Interference and Channel-switching (MIC) [503], Exclusive Expected Transmission Time (EETT) [243], Interference Aware Routing Metric (iAWARE) [449], WCETT-Load Balancing (WCETT-LB) [298]. As listed in the following sequence, each routing metric was proposed as an improvement over the previous one. (Since the link loss rate in wired network is very low and can be ignored in most cases, only the first two metrics are usually applied in wired networks.)

- *Hop count* is the count of the intermediate nodes which a packet traverse from the source to the destination. Hop count is the most commonly used metric of routing protocols in both wired networks and wireless networks, e.g., AODV and RIP. The routing protocols using hop count as metric assume that all links have similar properties across the network. If a link property, e.g., capacity, varies largely, this metric does not result in good performance [113].
- *Bandwidth* assigns smaller weights to the high-capacity links, thus making them more likely to be selected.
- *Expected Transmission Count (ETX)* is the expected total transmission count along the path. Since some links may be lossy, and it cannot be indicated by hop count, ETX is used to capture this characteristic of wireless links.
- *Expected Transmission Time (ETT)* is proposed to improve ETX metric with the consideration of the different data rates on each link. ETT is the expected total transmission time along the selected path.
- *Weighted Cumulative ETT (WCETT)* was proposed for wireless networks, in which nodes support multiple physical channels. This metric is actually the ETT added by the maximal channel repeat times along the path. If only one channel is used in the network, it is equal to ETT.
- *Metric of Interference and Channel-switching (MIC)* considers the intra-flow interference as well as the inter-flow interference in a wireless network. Inter-flow interference means the interference to the packets in one traffic flow from the same source and destination; intra-flow interference means the interference to the packets from different traffic flows. MIC contains two parts: Interference-aware Resource Usage (IRU) and Channel Switching Cost (CSC). IRU is defined as ETT weighted by its physical neighbor number; CSC describes how diversified the channels are assigned.
- *Exclusive Expected Transmission Time (EETT)* improves MIC by taking the fact into account that interference range is always much larger than the transmission range. EETT groups the links into interference sets and sums

the ETT for each set. This metric considers just the intra-flow interference rather than inter-flow interference.

- *Interference Aware Routing Metric (iAWARE)* is also an improvement of MIC. MIC considers the inter-flow interference to be merely dependent on the physical neighbor number, while iWARE also takes the Signal to Interference-plus-Noise Ratio (SINR) from each neighbor into account.
- *WCETT-Load Balancing (WCETT-LB)* is another enhancement of WCETT. It introduces the congestion state of node into the routing metric. The congestion state is in turn represented by the node's relative queue length.

From the examples, we can see that the more characteristics a network has, the larger its metric design space is. Note that the metrics mentioned above are only for path selection, not for intermediator selection.

In some hybrid routing protocols, like VRR [84], the topology information at the node is not complete and nodes will always forward the packet to some intermediator node, which is "closer" to the destination, until the packet reaches its destination. The metric used to choose an intermediator node is the space distance to the destination with respect to the overlay structure used.

Using *virtual distance* as metric guarantees the success of the routing process, but it does not considered the *physical distance* it may introduce. *Proximity Neighbor Selection* (PNS) [184] selects the physically closest node in its routing table as the intermediator node, which has also a closer virtual distance to the destination at the same time. Methods for measuring the physical distance are covered in Chapter 20.2. The virtual distance is also used in overlay routing protocols covered in Section 16.2.5.

An intermediator node is also used in geographic routing protocols, in which the metric is the *physical distance*. That means the physical neighbor who is closest to the destination should forward the packet for the local node. Here, the measurement of the physical distance can be achieved by GPS receivers or other location devices.

It is worth noting that in theory the link weights are used as an input for the calculation of the optimal path. However, in practice, the order may be reversed. The network operator could configure the link weight in order to achieve certain traffic goals, e.g., distribute the traffic over more links, limit the link load, or limit the use of some special links.

16.2.5   Virtual Routing on Overlays

Overlay networks represent interconnections on top of an existing logical network. Data forwarding is based on a separate routing schema and carried by the underlay. In this section, we focus on overlay networks located at the application layer. Such overlays are typically constructed by P2P-technologies.[1] In the following, we give a short overview about general modeling aspects of overlay routing.

Overlay routing should be analyzed under two perspectives: (a) the inherent structural properties of the overlay routing mechanism and (b) its interaction with the underlay. It may be sufficient to neglect network layer properties (e.g. topology or link delays) in the modeling process if pure overlay characteristics are under observation.

P2P protocols can be classified in structured and unstructured approaches. The first distributes routing information among all peers. The latter establishes neighborship relations and distributes data using flooding or random walks. The decision for a next (overlay) hop or an adjacent peer can be completely agnostic of the underlay routing structure, or incorporate information of the network layer to reduce underlay load. There are commonly two metrics to measure the performance penalty caused by overlay routing:

Delay Stretch quantifies the ratio of the underlay path length (induced by the overlay routing) and the native path length.
Link Stress counts the number of identical copies of a packet traversing the same physical link.

The analysis of these metrics requires a careful modeling of the native network in terms of the underlay topology and link delay (cf. Chapter 20.2) respectively. It is worth noting that the calculation of the link stress assumes an identification of each intermediate underlay link.

Depending on the class of overlay protocols approaches may scale up to a very large number of nodes. Performance properties, e.g., routing table size or path length, may be logarithmically bounded, which is typically for structured P2P routing. Protocol effects, thus, will only be visible if the overlay dimension varies by several orders of magnitude. Although simulating such large networks can be very time-consuming it is inappropriate to consider only some thousands nodes in this case.

Application layer-based overlay networks are usually maintained at end devices. The P2P paradigm reflects the assumption that peers have equal functionality. Each peer, for example, should be capable to forward data. End devices of the current Internet, however, form per se a heterogeneous group of nodes. In contrast to traditional Internet routing or even ad hoc networks, overlay peers may be quite different, e.g., in processing capacity or provided bandwidth.[2] More importantly, peers are typically volatile, which results in higher fluctuations of routers in the (overlay) network. Joining and leaving of overlay nodes is mentioned as *churn*. The modeling of this process is described in Chapter 20.

---

[1] For a comprehensive introduction of P2P networks we refer to [379].
[2] The heterogeneity of P2P nodes has been in studied in [440] with a special focus on server-like capabilities.

16.2.6   Influence from Other Models

As stated in Section 16.2.2, routing model must interact with the surrounding models and the characteristics of these models should be taken into account when designing a routing metric and a routing algorithm.

Most of the network characteristics relevant to the path selection metric (cf. Section 16.2.4, except the hop count) are from the underlay, like link capacity and interference. Additionally to the aforementioned characteristics, there are some other important aspects: unidirectional links, shared-medium link, link detection time and others.

Quite a few routing protocols assume a *bidirectional link*. However, this assumption is wrong for wireless networks. Some routing protocols just ignore this problem, some exclude the usage of these *unidirectional links*, and just a few use these asymmetric links to optimize the network performance. While it is not required to use the existing unidirectional links, the routing protocol must detect them and distinguish them from bidirectional links.

Shared-medium links can exist in both wired network and wireless network. In graph theory, these links are typically replaced by several point-to-point links. Such a representation is not wrong, but eliminates the characteristic of the shared-medium, according to which the link cost cannot be just split up or duplicated to each point-to-point link.

Although the layer on top of the network layer is the transport layer, the network layer can be used directly by higher-layer components. Especially in sensor networks there are also cross-layer approaches. For different application scenarios, different routing models are required. In some sensor networks, the application traffic is always directed from a sensor node to the fixed sink node. Hence, the routing algorithm only has to calculate the optimal path for one node. As another example in sensor networks, the traffic may also be highly related, i.e., two traffic flows from adjacent nodes contain similar information. These flows can be aggregated along the path to the sink. Therefore, the network performance can be improved by aggregating the paths from the sensors to the sink. With different traffic patterns, the performance of a routing model will be affected. Hence, the traffic pattern from the application should also be considered when modeling a routing protocol.

The routing model interacts not only with the models above and below, but also with other models, e.g., energy consumption model and positioning model.

More and more work focus on wireless networks, in which many devices are battery-equipped. Energy efficiency is thus an emerging challenge in developing routing protocols. Since the transmission mode as well as receiving mode of the hardware have large impact on the energy consumption, they should be taken into consideration in the design process of a routing protocol.

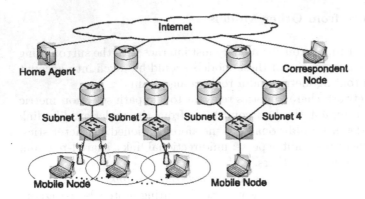

Fig. 16.2: Network layer mobility scenarios including typical Mobile IP
components

Not all the models limit the design space of a routing protocol. Instead,
the positioning model provides the physical positional information of the
node, from which the design of routing protocols can benefit. For instance,
geographic routing utilizes the positional information and greedily forwards
the packet towards the destination.

16.3   Internet Mobility

Mobility on the network layer describes the layer three address change of a
continuously operating node. This change may result from physical movement
in mobile regimes, but can likewise be initiated in wired networks. The first
case occurs, if logical domains are bound to geographical space. The latter
can be caused by network failures, reconfiguration (renumbering) or similar.
Thus, not every physical movement necessarily leads to network layer mobility, and network layer mobility is also possible without physical movement
(cf. Figure 16.2).

In general, an address change raises two issues: On the one hand, new
communciation parties require up-to-date contact information or application
layer address mapping has to be refreshed. On the other hand, established
transport connections break, as socket identifiers invalidate. It is worth noting
that applications on top of connection-oriented and connection-less transport
protocols are likewise affected. Current UDP applications, e.g., RTP-based
tools, use source addresses to identify communication end points.

In this section, we focus on the modeling of protocols which support network layer mobility.[3] There are several attempts to cope with mobility on the network layer. The most fundamental approach to obtain mobility is the Mobile IP (MIP) protocol [361, 245]. MIP transparently operates address changes on the IP layer as a device moves from one network to the other by sustaining original IP addresses. In this way, hosts are enabled to maintain transport and higher layer connections when they change locations. An additional component, the MIP Home Agent (HA), preserves global addressability, while the mobile node is away from home.

An inventive idea to obtain mobility on the IP layer is built on the location independence of multicast addresses [200]: If each mobile node is equipped with an individual multicast address, a correspondent node can send packets without knowing the current location of the mobile. To preserve connection oriented transport ability, an additional header is used. Handoff speed is supported by a vicinity argument of geographical close movement, which may reduce reconstruction complexity of multicast branches. Besides security issues, the major drawback of the multicast based mobility is due to the asymmetry of multicast routing: Correspondent nodes cannot be mobile, themselves. Further on, multicast routing is not globally deployed at present.

A transport layer approach to application persistence mobility is grounded on the Stream Control Transmission Protocol (SCTP) [444]. Initially designed for network redundancy, SCTP allows for multihoming of a single socket. The "Add IP" option [445] of extending this functionality to adding and deleting IP addresses gives rise to an address handover on the transport layer. Mobile SCTP (MSCTP) [391] carries the justification of performing a rapid handover on the client side, only, without any dedicated assistance of the infrastructure. MSCTP, though, conflicts with single bound layer 2 protocols such as 802.11, connectionless flows and multicast traffic.

As an application layer protocol, the Session Initiation Protocol (SIP) [396] provides some mobility management to session-based services. Employing the SIP server as an application specific anchor, handoff notifications are traded via regular SIP messages to the home server via *register* and the correspondent node via *reinvite*. As SIP mobility operates above the transport layer, it inherits all underlying delays in addition to its own signaling efforts. In many situations SIP mobility thus comprises a latency problem.

This section is exemplarily concerned with mobility based on Mobile IP, as it naturally extends the network layer with a mobility-transparent protocol. MIP, on the one hand, conducts changes of networks instantaneously and independent of the subnetwork layer technology. Mobile IP handovers, on the other hand, currently may cause an inaccessibility of nodes up to seconds on top of layer 2 delays.

---

[3] We limit our discussion to client-based mobility protocols. There are also approaches for network-based mobility management, e.g., PMIP [186].

In the following section, we will elaborate aspects of Mobile IP and generalize approaches to extend the MIP protocol. We will discuss common performance metrics to evaluate protocols coping with network layer mobility. Based on our abstraction, we will introduce a simulation model.

16.3.1   Aspects of Mobile IP & Protocol Enhancements

Mobile IP [361, 245] is standardized for IPv4 and IPv6[4]. It considers the scenario, where a Mobile Node (MN) moves between IP networks while continuously communicating with a Correspondent Node (CN). The IP interface of the MN keeps a permanent address derived from its home network, the Home Address (HoA), while it simultaneously configures changing addresses of visited networks, the Care-of Addresses (CoAs). The core objective of MIP lies in transport layer transparency, i.e., the persistent presentation of HoA to the socket layer, while performing local routing using the topological correct CoA on the network layer. An additional component, the MIP Home Agent, preserves global addressability, while the mobile node is away from home.

While at home, the MN uses its permanent HoA and communicates like a stationary IP device, but has a (pre-)configured Home Agent. When moving to a new IP network, i.e., after the discovery of a network change, the MN will use stateless (IPv6) or stateful (IPv4 and IPv6) automatic configuration to apply an IP address valid in the visited network. Having acquired a topological correct Care-of Address (CoA), the MN immediately submits an (acknowledged) binding update to its HA. A binding denotes the association of a HoA with the correspondent CoA for a MN. At this stage, it regained the ability to send and receive packets using its permanent HoA and IP tunneling mechanisms.

Depending on the Internet Protocol in use, MIP differs in detail. As an automatic address configuration and IP encapsulation support is not mandatory in IPv4, Mobile IPv4 (MIPv4) introduces the so called Foreign Agent (FA). This infrastructure component residing in the foreign network provides an address for each MN and may additionally serve as tunnel endpoint towards the HA. The FA can be omitted by the setup of DHCP servers in external networks and the implementation of a tunnel protocol on the MN, which removes a single point of failure. Thus, MIPv4 scenarios need not include a FA, even though it may be the more realistic deployment assumption.

In MIPv4, the MN communicates directly with its CN without any MIP specific binding by sending packets using its HoA as source address. This procedure is motivated with simplicity in mind, however, routing strategies do not commonly tolerate topologically incorrect source addresses. It is common practice to protect networks with ingress filters admitting only topological

---

[4] A very good presentation and detailed discussion for newcomers about Mobile IPv6 and beyond is given in [431] and in [261] for advanced learners.

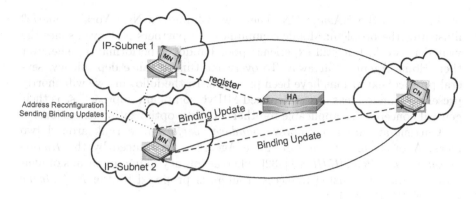

Fig. 16.3: Principle mobility management signaling (dashed lines) and data flow (solid lines) before and after a subnet change

correct addresses. For this reason, MIPv4 provides an optional reverse tunneling mechanism [322], which allows the MN to send packets back to the CN via the HA.

The Correspondent Node is not equipped with any MIPv4 protocol specific extension. For this entity, only the Mobile Node's HoA is visible. Consequently, packets sent from the CN to the MN are forwarded to the home network and tunneled by the Home Agent to the current CoA.

Mobile communication bears a phenomenon known as address duality: The technical address, which is used to identify and locate a stationary device, in the mobility case splits up into a permanent *logical identifier* (HoA) and a transient *topological locator* (CoA). In contrast to IPv4, IPv6 has been designed with respect to a flexible header architecture which eases protocol extensions. To achieve a direct, unencapsulated packet exchange with its correspondents Mobile IPv6 (MIPv6)[5] establishes a HoA-CoA binding between MN and MIP-aware CN on the one hand, and records the Home Address within a separate header on the other hand. Using such a route optimization, the MN needs to inform also its communication partners (CNs) about its new location. It does so by sending an additional binding update. HA and CN keep these binding update information within their binding caches. It is worth noting that a MIPv6 Mobile Node may fall back to a reverse tunneling if the CN does not support IP mobility. A model should consider the extended interaction between MN and CN, and tunnel mechanisms cannot generally be avoided for CNs.

After a subnet change, the MN has to update its current Mobile IP bindings before packets can be delivered with the correct Care-of Address (cf. Figure 16.3). The time to be IP connected again depends on the distances

---

[5] In the following, we only mention MIPv6 as this is based on the upcoming Internet Protocol.

of the MN to the HA and CN. The "Two Chinese in New York" scenario[6] illustrates the problem: Mobile communication partners may even share the visited network, but still experience poor handover performance, whenever their Home Agent is far away. To overcome this distance dependency, several protocol extensions have been proposed. In the following we will shortly present the main ideas of standardized MIPv6 compliant approaches, as their general concepts are applicable to other mobility optimization extensions.

Current attempts to improve *handover performance* rank around two ideas: A proxy architecture of Home Agents is introduced by the *Hierarchical Mobile IPv6 (HMIPv6)* [432], whereas latency hiding by means of handover prediction assisted by access routers is proposed by the *Fast Mobile IPv6 (FMIPv6)* [260].

Handover Acceleration by Proxy

A concept for representing Home Agents in a distributed fashion by proxies has been developed within the HMIPv6 [432]. While away from home, the MN registers with a nearby Mobility Anchor Point (MAP) and passes all its traffic through it. The vision of HMIPv6 presents MAPs as part of the regular routing infrastructure. The MN in the concept of HMIPv6 is equipped with a Regional Care-of Address (RCoA) local to the MAP in addition to its On-link Care-of-Address (LCoA). When corresponding to hosts on other links, the RCoA is used as MN's source address, thereby hiding micro-mobility, i.e., local movements within a MAP-domain. HMIPv6 reduces the number of 'visible' handover instances, but – once a MAP domain change occurs – binding update procedures need to be performed with the original HA and the CN.

Handover Acceleration by Delay Hiding

An alternate approach is introduced in the FMIPv6 scheme [260]. FMIPv6 attempts to anticipate layer 3 handovers and to redirect traffic to the new location, where the MN is about to move. The MN, thereby combines to receive data packets via its previous designated router up until the binding update is completed. A severe functional risk arises from a conceptual uncertainty: As the exact moment of layer 2 handover generally cannot be foreseen, and even flickering may occur, a traffic anticipating redirect may lead to data disturbances largely exceeding a regular MIPv6 handover without any optimization [407].

FMIPv6 extensively relies on layer 2 information and a layer 2 to 3 topology map, which is not present in current networks. Consequently, this

---

[6] This scenario assumes that the MN and CN are currently located in New York, but the HA is located in China.

approach requests for layer 2 specific extensions. FMIPv6 aims at hiding the entire handover delay to communicating end nodes at the price of placing heavy burdens onto layer 2 intelligence.

16.3.2   Performance Metrics

A layer 3 mobility protocol performs a transparent handover on the network layer. With respect to the objectives of such protocol the procedures should remain unnoticeable to applications and their users. The quality of the protocol can be measured on two general metric classes: protocol overhead and performance degradation at the end device.

In the event of a Mobile Node switching between access networks, a complex reconfiguration chain is initiated. At first, the mobile device may completely disconnect from the link layer, demanding layer 2-specific reassociation times (cf. Chapter 15). Thereafter it needs to perform a local IP reconfiguration and Binding Updates to its HA and CNs. Until completion of all these operations, the Mobile Node is likely to experience disruptions or disturbances of service, as are the result of *packet loss*, *delay* and *jitter* increases.

In synchronous *real-time* regimes, such as in voice and video scenarios, packet loss, delay and jitter need careful simultaneous control. A spoken syllable is about the payload of $100\,ms$ continuous voice traffic. Each individual occurrence of packet loss above 1%, latencies over $100 - 150\,ms$ or jitter exceeding $50\,ms$ will clearly alienate or even distract the user [229]. Delay and jitter are added by the handover procedure, if packets are buffered or transmitted via indirect paths.

These metrics can be measured by transmitting a Constant Bit Rate (CBR) stream of probe packets. For ease of use in multi-receiver scenarios, measurements should be done on the MN. This can be implemented by sending ICMP echo packets from the Mobile Node and awaiting replies, e.g., using *ping*. The resolution of gauging depends on the transmission interval. With respect to the values described above, transmission intervals starts at one packet per $10\,ms$. Real-world experiments can be complicated as operating systems may be specifically configured to allow corresponding rates.

The measurement of the *handover performance* may include impacts from different layers. A typical example are large layer 2 handover times. Interruption times range from 0 to several hundred milliseconds, the latter for poorly optimized 802.11b equipment [316]. This significantly increases packet loss independent of the mobility protocol in use. Thus, a performance analysis should clearly identify the causes of handover effects, as well as the layer they originated from.

Movement of the Mobile Node also affects the underlying network performance. Binding Updates will be sent by the MN to update contact information on the one hand. Agent assisted handover schemes like FMIPv6 may initiate signaling between infrastructure componentes on the other hand. This additional packet load can be summarized as network costs.

16.3.3   Evaluation Model

The simplest Mobile IP scenario consists of one Mobile Node sending data to a (MIP-aware or -unaware) Correspondent Node. Along the way, the MN moves between two subnets assisted by its agents. During the handover process, several layers will be crossed and influence performance results. Complex and sophisticated simulations need to be carefully conducted, as submodules may disturb the experiment, e.g., an incorrect layer 2 buffering. That complicates comparability. A full layer stack behavior is even more difficult to incorporate in analytical evaluation.

In this section, we try to reduce the complexity and focus on the main parts of MIP modeling.

Simple Topology Model

The plain Mobile IP *handover process* decomposes into the steps:

1. *Link layer handoff* which may be instantaneous or connection oriented, single- or multi-homed, depending on the technologies in use.
2. *Layer 3 movement detection* can be achieved in a passive or active manner. It will result in configuration of a new IP address and initiate update procedures of the mobility protocol. A MN may learn about a subnet change by regular router advertisements. In the presence of link-layer triggers [462], it may actively solicit a new IP address subsequent to layer 2 handoff to verify if the subnet changed as well.
3. *Care-of Address configuration* will follow without delay, after a valid address has been learned. This can be realized by stateful (e.g. DHCP) or stateless (e.g. autoconfiguration in IPv6) address setup.
   Dynamic address assignment includes a Duplicate Address Detection (DAD) scheme, which guides the MN into a timeout, in case a unique address has been configured that is already in use. To overcome this delay, asynchronous DAD processing has been suggested and widely implemented [323, 155].
4. *Binding Update* will be performed at least between MN and HA. Depending on the protocol in use, the MN also informs the CN about the address change. Typically, Binding Update (BU) requires binding acknowledgement from the HA and thus will take a round-trip time between MN and HA. Corresponding signalling to the CN is usually accompanied by authentication mechanisms, which may produce additional delay.

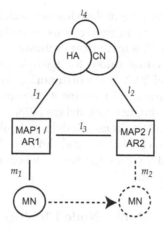

Fig. 16.4: A simple topological model for Mobile IP

Let t_{L2} denote the Layer 2 *handoff duration*, $t_{local-IP}$ the time for local IP reconfiguration including movement detection, and t_{BU} the Binding Update time. Then the following temporal decomposition for handovers holds:

$$t_{handoff} = t_{L2} + t_{local-IP} + t_{BU}.$$

While the first two summands represent local, topology-independent operations, Binding Updates depend on the sum of roundtrip times between nodes. Binding update times are defined by the topological set-up *beyond* the control of MIP and router stacks. Similar holds for inter-agent signaling to bridge the disconnection time. One crucial ingredients in performance modeling of a mobility protocol, thus, is the network topology.

The simplest topology model, which includes all MIP entities and the distances among each other, is displayed in Figure 16.4. Let t_l denote the transmission time of a packet along link l. A MN moves from access router 1 (AR1) to access router 2 (AR2) with intermediate link l_3. For simplification, the wireless link dimensions m_1 and m_2 to the MN can be assumed small. Distances l_1 and l_2 to HA or CN must be viewed as possibly large and represent the strongest topological dependence within the model. The distance between the access routers should be viewed as a variable, but characteristic geometric entity. As the MN moves between routers, their separation represents the gap to be bridged by forwarding, somewhat the "mobility step size", i.e., l_3.

Based on this model, for an unoptimized Mobile IP scenario the packet loss can be estimated, which is proportional ($\propto$) to the packet injection rate:

$$\text{Packet loss} \propto t_{L2} + t_{local-IP} + t_{m_2} + t_{l_2}.$$

The simple model covers the underlying network topology, while focusing only on distances – measured in router hops or milliseconds – between MIP components. It thus simplifies analytical evaluations and avoids side effects[7] in simulations. Corresponding values for path lengths can be modeled according to Chapter 22 and 20.2. It is worth noting, that there is a correlation between logical and geographical movement. Geographical vicinity will also be reflected in corresponding network delays [408].

Depending on the topology in use modeling should account for the placement of the point of attachment for end-devices. Typically, inter-provider networks associate the MN with edge nodes, whereas intra-provider topologies should consider all nodes.

Advanced Modeling: Mobile Node Mobility

A further ingredients in the Mobile IP modeling is the subnet change. Focusing on a physically moving Mobile Node two items are of interest: The expected number of handovers and the accuracy of handover predictions. Incorrect predictions may impose packet loss and additional signaling overhead. Physical movement can be modeled based on traces or analytical approaches, e.g., random waypoint model (cf. Chapter 14). To observe a subnet change, we suppose that a radio cell is directly connected to an access router.

In Mobile IP performance modeling, it is a common assumption that *cell geometry* is of honeycomb type, i.e., abutting hexagons completely fill the $2d$-plane.[8] The ranges of radio transmission are modeled as (minimal) circles enclosing the combs. Thus, regions of prediction are the overlapping circle edges. One may argue, that such modeling is insufficient. However, with respect to lightweight, universal mobility stacks this restriction is indeed appropriate.

The *handoff frequency* clearly depends on the Mobile Node's motion within cell geometry. Two measures for quantizing mobility have been established in the literature: The cell residence time and the call holding time [140]. Both quantities fluctuate according to the overall scenery and the actual mobility event. Let us make the common assumption that the cell residence time is exponentially distributed with parameter η and that the call holding time is exponentially distributed, as well, but with parameter α. Then the probability for the occurrence of a handover from MNs residence cell into some neighboring can be calculated analytically to

$$\mathcal{P_{HO}} = \frac{1}{1+\rho}, \text{ where } \rho = \frac{\alpha}{\eta}$$

is known as the call–to–mobility *factor* [140]. For an extension to proxy schemes compare [407]. It can be observed that the handoff probability

---

[7] For example, incorrectly modeled behaviour of re-used components.

[8] Note, this is usually the case in general wireless network simulation, as well.

increases as ρ decreases. Note that all probability distributions are homogeneous in space, e.g., $\mathcal{P}_{\mathcal{HO}}$ is independent of the current cell or the number of previously occurred handovers. Spatial scaling can be applied, accordingly.

Additional complexity arises in the case of proxy and delay hiding schemes. Delay hiding schemes like FMIPv6 predict the handover and react in advance to reduce packet loss (cf. Section 16.3.1). Mobility modeling thus should account for crossing overlapping transmission ranges without changing radio cells. Further on, configuration of the anticipation time, defining the period prior to handover, influences results significantly. A predictive handover is optimal, iff anticipation time matches á priori router negotiation. This parameter should be varied on the scale of access router distances, but chosen with large perturbations with respect to large uncertainty.

Proxy-based approaches show their advantages when a MN moves between Access Routers (ARs) covered by the same Mobility Anchor Point. Looking on the extrema, a single MAP – responsible for the whole Internet – is equivalent to a MIPv4 scenario with reverse tunneling. In contrast, a MAP directly linked with the MN's access point complies with a traditional MIPv6 handover. The AR-to-MAP ratio is not predefined in any standard and depends on the operators design choice. In general, a placement will be guided by an appropriate delay for the MN (distance MAP to ARs) and the maximum traffic caused by MNs. An evaluation should include different AR-to-MAP ratios.

16.4 Conclusion

The network layer bridges the logical gap between direct host-to-host and network-wide multi-hop communication. Hence, any model for the network layer builds upon several other models that describe link-level characteristics or per-node processing and routing issues. Both of these models are in turn closely related to the underlying network topology model. The key challenge is to derive metrics of global significance from the descriptions of local phenomena.

In this chapter, we introduced and classified a set of representative routing protocols and dissected them into their key components. With these examples in mind, we turned to the theoretical basics and discussed how graph and queuing theory may be utilized to model certain aspects of a routing protocol. We then elaborated on several metrics used in conjunction with path selection and the influence of models from the surrounding protocol layers. We then proceeded to motivate the problems specifically related to node mobility in an IP-based network, introduced potential solutions and discussed modeling alternatives.

For a bottom-up approach to network simulation modeling, the next logical step is to consider modeling the transport layer and application traffic as introduced in Chapters 17 and 18 respectively. Alternatively, as far as simulation methodology is concerned, Chapter 6 discusses how software components, such as a routing protocol, may be efficiently implemented to run on a simulator as well as on real systems.

17. Modeling Transport Layer Protocols

Raimondas Sasnauskas (RWTH Aachen University)
Elias Weingaertner (RWTH Aachen University)

17.1 Introduction

In a layered communication architecture, transport layer protocols handle the data exchange between processes on different hosts over potentially lossy communication channels. Typically, transport layer protocols are either connection-oriented or are based on the transmission of individual datagrams. Well known transport protocols are the connection-oriented Transmission Control Protocol (TCP) [372] and the User Datagram Protocol (UDP) [370] as well as the Stream Control Transmission Protocol (SCTP) [340] and DCCP, the Datagram Congestion Control Protocol [259]. In this chapter, we focus on the modeling process of the transport layer. While we mostly use TCP and UDP as a base of comparison from this point, we emphasize that the methodologies discussed further on are conferrable to virtually any transport layer in any layered communication architecture.

There are two different general approaches concerning transport layer models. *Direct transport layer models* implement the actual protocol using event-based network simulators (see Section 17.2). This way, the actual protocol interactions are recreated within a network simulator. Such an approach is important especially in the case if someone is interested in studying properties of the transport layer protocol itself, or if the investigation of an application layer protocol that uses the transport layer as base technology is desired. Another method following this goal is to integrate existing code, for example complete network stacks, into the simulation framework. This approach is discussed in Section 17.3.

Later in this chapter (Section 17.4ff.), we will discuss *indirect modeling techniques* not attempting to recreate the protocol behavior directly. Instead, they aim at the recreation of the footprint of a transport protocol on the network. This may be required if one needs to model background traffic or needs to obtain traffic patterns which resemble those produced by common transport layer protocols. The first obvious approach is to use actual network traffic that has been captured in a real computer network. We discuss this approach and its limitations in Section 17.4. Another option is to model certain performance metrics explicitly, e.g. throughput or delay. Such models are called *performance models* and are usually expressed using analytic expressions. We will further discuss performance modeling in Section 17.5. In Section 17.6, we conclude this chapter with an approach that integrates a special type of performance models, so called *fluid models*, with network simulations.

17.2   Existing Simulation Models

Existing transport layer simulation models offer the standardized protocol algorithmics on different levels of abstraction. They all provide a coherent end-to-end transport service between processes of a communication system. The details (e.g. technology, topology, addressing) of the underlying network are by definition abstracted. Both connection-oriented and connection-less transport layer protocols offer the service of transparent data exchange. In addition, the connection-oriented service implements connection establishment and termination.

Most transport layer simulation models are tightly integrated into larger network simulation frameworks such as INET in OMNeT++ [475]. Internet transport protocols (e.g. TCP, UDP) are built on top of the unreliable IP network layer, thus their implementations are bounded. Nevertheless, in particular cases the accuracy of the protocols below the transport layer should be sufficiently high. For example, the Fast Retransmit algorithm in TCP is a congestion control [491] strategy to reduce the time before retransmitting a lost data segment. It heavily relies on the simulation accuracy of IP and the protocol layers below. In Section 17.6.2, we will discuss in detail the combination of network fluid models and packet-level simulation which address this issue. Furthermore, when simulating wireless networks one may observe performance degradation since wireless connections show different characteristics [328]. Transmission errors on lossy links, frequent handoffs, and latencies due to error correction mechanisms on medium access layer are incorrectly interpreted as congestion.

In general, the abstraction level found in different transport protocol models provides the basic protocol functionality. However, the implementation details of the same protocol slightly differ. Furthermore, not all models are equipped with full-featured extensions which are found in real-world operating systems code. Table 17.1 provides an overview of network simulators and their support for the features of widely known connection-oriented transport protocols TCP and SCTP. Because of its simplicity, the connection-less protocol UDP is very easy to implement and it is supported by all known network simulators.

Although all prevalent simulators offer the basic transport layer functionality, the implementations still lack subtle protocol details. For example not modeling the receiver buffer size or absence of standard-conform handling of PSH ("push") and URG ("urgent") bits in TCP may impact the correctness of simulation results.

Features	OMNeT++	ns2	ns3	SWANS	GTNetS
TCP					
RFC793	+	+	+	+	+
TCP Tahoe	+	+	+	+	+
TCP Reno	+	+	−	−	+
TCP NewReno	−	+	−	−	+
TCP Vegas	−	+	−	−	−
Finite receive buffer	−	−	−	+	−
TCP header options	−	+	−	−	−
Timer granularity	−	+	−	−	+
UDP	+	+	+	+	+
STCP					
Basic operation	+	+	−	−	−
Experimental ext.	−	+	−	−	−

Table 17.1: Comparison of simulator support for TCP, UDP and SCTP protocols.

Moreover, the question arises how the given simulation models facilitate the study of certain performance metrics, for example throughput or the end-to-end delay between different hosts in a network. The core idea here is that the models reflect the behavior of the real world, and hence that the phenomena regarding those metrics are constituted by the model itself. This is achieved by the implementation of the protocol within the simulation. In the following, we describe the methodology behind the observation of such metrics.

One important measure in a network is the **throughput** of a transmission between two hosts, which is given by the ratio of sent bytes to the duration of the transmission. First of all, it is noteworthy that most models of transport protocols do not contain any actual payload in related message structures or objects. Instead, most transport models include only the number of payload bytes in the transmission segments. In order to compute the throughput, these payload bytes are simply added if a message is received. Once the transmission has ended, the throughput is retrieved by dividing the counted bytes by the time of the transmission.

While the **end-to-end delay** can be observed on the transport layer, it is mostly influenced by the underlying network, where the end-to-end delay is constituted by individual channel delays of the network links. Hence, these phenomena are in fact mostly covered by the models discussed in chapter 16. However, as processing of transport layer protocols may add additional delays, such a behavior can be reflected in a corresponding model as well. For example, if it is known that the verification of a checksum of a network packet takes $50\mu s$, this delay can be easily incorporated in the protocol model, if one is interested in obtaining more precise results in this regard. However, it is up to the modeler to decide which accuracy according to timing is needed to obtain meaningful results, as such processing times and hence the influence on the delay is very dependent on the actual system. As one is usually interested in more general results, processing delays at the transport layer are mostly neglected.

All modeling aspects of the end-to-end delay on the transport layer are essentially the same for the **packet delay variation**, often referred to as **jitter**. Here, the delay variation is directly dependent on the delay variation on deeper layers. Of course, the delay variation can be increased or also decreased at the transport layer models, as additional delays may occur or mechanisms such as token-buckets may homogenize the delay.

17.3   Using Real Implementations in Simulators

As previously mentioned, the simulation models of transport layer protocols are not complete and differ in the level of detail of their abstraction. To overcome this issue and model the system behavior more accurately one can use real-world implementations found in operating systems. Such software integration frameworks provide wrappers where OS protocol stacks can run and interact with the simulator without any further modifications. Please refer to chapter 6 where three exemplary frameworks are described in detail.

Although running real transport protocol code gives necessary implementation accuracy, this approach has several limitations compared to real protocol execution. First, the code execution within a simulator has no processing delays which is not the case in real network code. Second, the OS side effects are not modeled at all having impact on simulation result exactness. And third, real-world OS network stacks (e.g. Linux TCP/IP stack) are highly optimized and thus lack fine-grained modularity. Consequently, this might increase simulation performance overhead.

17.4   Transport Layer Traces

Network traces are probably the easiest method one can think of for the purpose of indirectly modeling the behavior of the transport layer: Traffic is captured on an actual networked system using a network traffic analyzer like Wireshark [104]. All recorded network packets are stored in so-called *trace files*. In order to feed those traces into the network simulation, the trace files are usually pre-processed. Network traces may contain packets of any protocol being used in the network in which the trace was recorded. Hence, the first step is to filter out unwanted packets from the trace. In the case of transport protocols, typically only the corresponding packets remain in the trace, e.g., TCP segments or UDP datagrams. In fact, it may eventually make sense to strip out the payload of the transport protocol during the pre-processing step in order to retrieve a file which exclusively contains descriptive information of the transport flow. Such an approach is discussed in [344].

Once the condensed trace file is available, the trace is usually fed into the network simulation through a trace replaying node which simply creates simulation messages from the information available in the trace file. In this step, the derived simulation messages may contain information from other layers as well. As the simulations' protocol implementation are usually abstracted from the real world, much of the information prevalent in the trace file is usually not needed for this step: For example, most implementations of transport protocols within network simulators usually do not use actual payloads. Hence, the payload information present in the trace is simply disregarded by the trace replaying node.

While trace files are easy to utilize and to implement into event-based network simulations, the accuracy of such an approach is generally limited. Many transport protocols, like TCP and SCTP, implement flow control and congestion avoidance mechanisms, which interactively adjust protocol parameters according to network effects, such as packet loss or end-to-end delay. However, as trace files consist of static, pre-recorded packets, trace files cannot be used for the reproduction of any interactive protocol behavior. For example, the Slow-start algorithm used for congestion control in TCP directly affects the throughput of the protocol. However, in order to adjust the window size, it requires feedback information from the receiver. If trace files are used, the packet data fed to the network is static. It can not incorporate the feedback information from the receiver. Hence, if a receiver in a TCP simulation reports congestion, the window size in the pre-recorded TCP segments will not be diminished, thus leading to potentially wrong performance results. Therefore, any protocol behavior which relies on feedback information is not modeled by trace files consisting of transport protocol segments.

Although trace files are not capable of modeling any interactive protocol behavior, they still may serve to model background traffic in a network simulation. However, in such a case, it is important to assure that the mutual influence of the investigated protocol's traffic and the background traffic is negligible, as otherwise this so-called open-loop behavior of trace files may corrupt the obtained results.

17.5 Analytical Performance Modeling

Direct simulation models as discussed in Section 17.2 employ packet processing and simple algorithmic calculations. Furthermore, the simulation itself can be combined with actual inputs and real hardware revealing further performance details or long-term behavior of the simulated system.

On the contrary, the analytical modeling attempts to predict a specific performance metric using a set of parametrized functions and initial conditions. Such mathematical models concentrate only on the essential properties of a certain phenomenon. The view of the hardware and software is abstracted. This leads to modeling results for large network setups much faster than simulation. Nonetheless, one needs to find and set up the correct model assumptions to simplify the equations without loosing the accuracy of the results. Such models are often based on stochastic techniques (for example [34], [318]).

Currently, almost all reliable connections in the Internet are based on TCP. Hence, the main focus in the research community has been drawn on TCP congestion control mechanisms and their impact on throughput behavior. In the following, we briefly present two analytical performance models for the derivation of the throughput and discuss the results.

17.5.1   Inverse Square-root Law for TCP Throughput

The basic idea how Internet congestion control can be modeled analytically is presented in [306]. The authors propose a simple TCP Reno [320] throughput model of a single, steady-state connection over a link with moderate packet loss. The model assumes sufficient bandwidth and no competing data flows inside the network. The impact of the underlying network topology and router queueing disciplines is neglected as well. Under these very simplifying assumptions the round trip time (RTT) of data packets is constant and hence no transmission timeouts due to packet drops may occur.

The packet loss probability is the only parameter considered to derive the throughput. The authors suppose packet loss which occurs after $1/p$ packets are successfully delivered, where p is constant and describes the ratio of dropped packets. Once a packet is dropped, TCP sender detects the loss through three duplicate ACKs from the receiver. Then it enters the congestion avoidance phase with the half of the congestion window ($W/2$) and continues data transmission until the next packet loss is detected. In this way the details of TCP data retransmission are neglected and the loss recovery completes in one round trip time. The resulting periodic TCP window size evolution is depicted in Figure 17.1.

During the congestion avoidance phase each acknowledged packet increases the congestion window size W: $W_{new} = W_{old} + 1/W_{old}$. TCP Reno adopts additionally the delayed ACK option where two consecutive data packets are acknowledged with a single cumulative ACK. Thus, the duration of a transmission cycle is $bW/2 \cdot RTT$, where b is the number of delayed ACKs [443]. The throughput has been already defined in Section 17.2 as

$$Throughput = \frac{Number\ of\ bytes\ sent}{Duration\ of\ the\ transmission}.$$

In this model, the number of sent bytes is the number of acknowledged packets per cycle. This corresponds to the area under the sawtooth in Figure 17.1, which equals $b\frac{3W^2}{8}$.

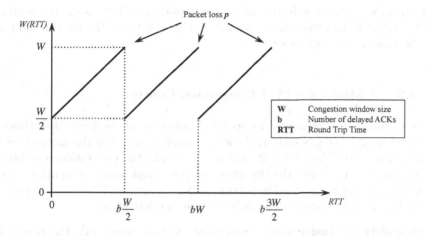

Fig. 17.1: TCP window size behavior (modified version from [306])

Solving the packet delivery rate $1/p$ for W per cycle, this leads to

$$W = \sqrt{\frac{8}{3pb}}.$$

Taking the transmission cycle duration

$$b\frac{W}{2} \cdot RTT$$

and the maximum segment size (MSS) we get the mean throughput

$$Throughput = \frac{b\frac{3W^2}{8} \cdot MSS}{b\frac{W}{2} \cdot RTT} - \sqrt{\frac{3}{2bp}} \cdot \frac{MSS}{RTT}.$$

As a result, the throughput is proportional to the maximum packet size and inversely proportional to the square root of loss probability and the round trip time. Consequently, large RTTs and high packet loss ratio result in poor TCP throughput. Furthermore, the constant $\sqrt{\frac{3}{2b}}$ can be seen an indicator for different loss and ACK strategy assumptions [306]. The authors show that the model can predict the bandwidth under many loss conditions with congestion avoidance-based TCP implementations. However, this model still remains very optimistic. First, it does not capture the timeout driven behavior of wide-spread TCP implementations occurring at high packet loss rates. With multiple packet losses within one transmission cycle the timeout expires before the sender can recover (Fast Recovery) and the congestion window W is reduced to 1 MSS. In this case the actual throughput can be much lower than predicted by the model. Second, the losses in the Internet are not random, mostly due to the existence of drop-tail queues in the routers [138, 147]. It follows that the model may not be able to predict the throughput in the Internet scenario accurately.

17.5.2   A Model for TCP Congestion Control

In addition to the observations so far, Padhye et al. propose also a more detailed model [346], which analytically characterizes the throughput as a function of packet loss rate. It captures not only the congestion avoidance phase, but also considers the timeouts and their impact on throughput. Contrary to the model described in Section 17.5.1, several confirmed assumptions [138, 147, 306, 343] have been made to ease the derivation:

− Slow-start and Fast Recovery phases of TCP are neglected. The reason is their minimal appearance in the measured traces.
− Packet losses within one round are correlated due to drop-tail queueing behavior in the Internet routers.
− Packet losses in one round are independent of losses in other rounds. Different TCP rounds are separated by one or more RTTs, hence, very likely resulting in independent router buffer states.
− The RTT is independent of the window size W.

A concise mathematical derivation of the throughput can be found in [346] which results in a well known TCP bandwidth equation

$$Throughput = \frac{1}{RTT \cdot \sqrt{\frac{2bp}{3}} + T_0 \cdot \min(1, \ 3\sqrt{\frac{3bp}{8}}) \cdot p \cdot (1 + 32p^2)}$$

where T_0 denotes the period of time the sender waits before he starts to retransmit the non-acknowledged packets.

In summary, live experiments have validated the model for a wide range of loss rates and indirectly validate the assumptions as well. Another important finding captured by the model is that timeouts have a significant impact on the overall TCP performance. Real measured traces showed that the majority of packet loss indications in a bottleneck bandwidth scenario occurred due to timeouts, rather than fast retransmits. Nonetheless, this model reflects long-term and bulky transmissions only. At the present time, short-lived TCP flows dominate the Internet [188] and, hence, further effects of TCP (Slow-start, Fast Retransmit, Fast Recovery) should be considered in more detail.

Both presented models have one major drawback: they do not consider data flows of the underlying network and their correlation with packet loss. In next Section, fluid models are introduced which are aiming to capture the complete behavior of the system. In addition, Section 17.6.2 presents the idea of integrating fluid models into packet-level simulations.

17.6   Fluid Models and Integration with Packet-level Simulation

Fluid models are a special type of performance models which describe the behavior of a network as a set of fluids that are modeled using arithmetic expressions. In the first part of this Section, we will briefly survey the notion of those models. In the following, we introduce an approach by Gu, Liu and Towsley [182], which allows the integration of fluid models with discrete event-based simulations operating on the packet level. The mathematical details are omitted for the matter of concision. The original publications [182, 292, 294] provide additional insight in this respect. The authors of these publications emphasize that the major advantage of fluid based models is their scalability; as the representation of the entire network is given by equations and as the evaluation is not based on individual packets, much larger topologies may be investigated.

17.6.1   TCP Fluid Models

Fluid models describe the transport of data within a network as a set of fluids. Following the notation in [182], a fluid model consists of a directed graph, consisting of a set of routers and a set of links. A set of differential equations is used to describe the information flows in the network and the behavior of its elements over time. More specifically, those equations model e.g. TCP window sizes, queue lengths as well as departure and arrival rates. Further on, the performance evaluation of a network is carried out by first applying a set of parameters to the network which is done by simply putting them into the equations. In the next step, the main performance evaluation is achieved by solving the set of equations.

17.6.2   Integration with Packet-level Simulations

In recent years, the demand of modeling large computer networks has grown steadily. Network simulations, however, are usually carried out only for scenarios with up to a couple of thousand nodes. For this purpose, different optimization approaches, such as the parallelization of network simulations (discussed in chapter 8), have been proposed and implemented to address such scalability concerns.

On the contrary, many analytical models scale to a much higher degree than network simulations. In this case, the integration of such into an event-based simulations enables the investigation of larger networks, using a hybrid methodology that combines analytical models with event-based simulations. One example of such an approach is the incorporation of fluid models with packet-level simulations, as proposed by Lu, Yong and Towsley [292]. The

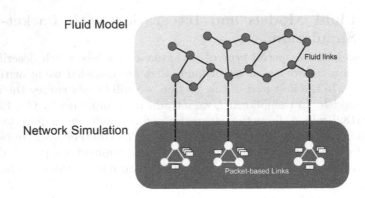

Fig. 17.2: Architecture for the integration of fluid models with packet-based simulation (cf. Towsley, 2004)

concept is outlined in Figure 17.2. The core idea behind this hybrid simulation methodology is to model the transport layer traffic of large background networks using a fluid model. Smaller networks, which operate on the packet level, interact with the fluid model, which is responsible to reproduce the background network's effect on inter-network traffic.

The challenge in combining fluid models with event-based simulation is given by the fact that both employ totally different modeling paradigms. As discussed earlier, packet-based network simulations usually utilize discrete events which are triggered, for example, when a packet is sent from one host to another. The simulation is constituted by serially processing all scheduled events. The fluid model, on the other hand, merely consists of a set of differential equations, which needs to be solved in order to investigate the TCP characteristics it models. While the equations conceptually can be solved for any point in time, the solving is usually carried out in an incremental fashion. So how does the interaction between the fluid model and the packet-level simulation take place? In their original publication, Lu, Yong et al. distinguish between two integrational modes for traffic interaction between those two worlds: a *one-pass traffic interaction model* and a *two-pass traffic interaction model*.

In the one pass traffic model, it is assumed that the influence of the packet-based traffic on the fluid network is insignificant. Thus, the fluid model is solved synchronously as the event-based simulation proceeds. At any point of the simulation time, the fluid model provides measures e.g. for the delay between two nodes in the fluid network. Hence, if a packet is about to travel through the fluid network, the end-to-end delay is obtained from the fluid model and the receiving events are scheduled using this delay.

The underlying assumption of the two-pass traffic interaction model is different. Here the packets originating at the event-based simulation influence the fluid model's outcome. This is achieved by twice passing through the simulation time. In the first pass, the packets created by the network simulations are converted into a so called "forward flow". This forward flow is then incorporated into the fluid model over the simulation time. In the second phase, the simulation is driven synchronously through the time, while the data is obtained from the altered flow model. This way, the reciprocal influence between the flow model and the packet level simulation is covered. Yong et al. have implemented the presented approach for ns-2. The evaluation of this approach presented in the original publication shows that it is a viable approach for a scalable simulation of transport layer protocols.

17.7   Conclusion

In this chapter, we have surveyed different approaches and techniques to model transport layer protocols, with an emphasis on event-based network simulations. Directly modeling the transport layer behavior is straightforward, as it is carried out by implementing the protocol semantics and their functional behavior in a network simulator. The accuracy of the results, however, requires a proper modeling of the lower layers. This is clearly demonstrated by TCP/IP, whose overall performance is the result of a complex interplay of the transport layer as well as the link and network layers. Besides the description of pure simulation models, we provided a brief overview of performance models which abstract from individual network packets and communication layers. Instead, these models describe the exchange of information as a set of flows using differential equations. Especially the incorporation of the latter concept with event-based network simulations operating on the packet-level is a promising concept for the analysis of transport protocols in large network topologies. However, this modeling approach requires a analytical performance model of the respective protocol. Obtaining a performance model for a transport protocol is not trivial. Moreover, one must prove the accuracy of the mathematical abstraction, for example by comparing the model output with real-world measurements. While this makes such an approach difficult to use for the development of new transport protocols, accurate analytical models exist for well-established network protocols. The integration of such performance models with network simulations is worth considering for very large networks that cannot be analyzed using a simulation alone.

18. Modeling Application Traffic

Ismet Aktas (RWTH Aachen University)
Thomas King (Universität Mannheim)
Cem Mengi (RWTH Aachen University)

18.1 Introduction

Communication networks require a deep understanding of the source of generated traffic, i.e., the application. A multitude number of applications exist that generate different types of traffic, for example web, peer-to-peer, voice, and video traffic. Within the scope of performance analysis of protocols for communication networks, modeling and generating of such traffic is essential to achieve *accurate* and *credible* results. This requires that the most relevant aspects are *captured* by analyzing the traffic and subsequently properly *represented* in the *application model*.

But to determine the relevant aspects is a challenging task due to the heterogeneity of applications which require specific considerations. For example, the used codec in a video stream is an important aspect for modeling video traffic, while this aspect is not important for *File Transfer Protocol (FTP)* models. Additionally, heterogeneity within one application hinders the selection of relevant modeling aspects. For example, the number of users in a voice conversation influences the design of the *voice model* (two vs. multi user conversation).

If the relevant aspects are somehow pointed out, measuring is required in order to find the suitable parameterization. Different approaches exist to collect data from traffic, e.g., *client logs*, *server logs*, or *packet traces*.

The next step after measuring is to represent the characteristics of the aspects in the application model. For example, some aspects such as the inter-arrival time do not require a specific data model, but other aspects such as a video sequence can be modeled with a more sophisticated data model, e.g., a markov chain.

This chapter gives the reader an understanding in building application models which generate traffic with accurate and credible results. For this purpose, we have chosen four applications: *web browsing, bulk file transfer, voice*, and *video*. We explain the relevant aspects for these applications and how to determine them in general. Furthermore, we explain in detail how to measure the relevant aspects. Finally, we give an idea about how to represent these aspects in the application model.

18.2   Modeling HTTP Traffic

World Wide Web (WWW) traffic is a substantial part in the Internet. If we want to simulate and subsequently evaluate a system that uses WWW traffic, we need accurate models. But modeling WWW traffic is a difficult task due to several reasons. Firstly, a lot of system components like Web browsers and servers coexist and interact with each other in a complex way. Particularly, each of these components has their proprietary version and probably behaves slightly different, e.g., a browser that allows multiple downloads in parallel generates different traffic compared to a browser that only allows to download sequentially. Besides that heterogeneity, the immense size and the permanent changing property of the Internet, i.e., topology or used protocols, make the modeling challenging. A further varying aspect that also should be taken into account is the *user behavior*, which has been varied over time based on the functionality that the browsers has been offered. As a result, the aforementioned diversity lead to various modeling approaches for *Web traffic modeling*. But nevertheless, the unit or rather the terminology Web page has been commonly used in most publications as a central building block for Web traffic modeling [91, 101, 467, 302, 50, 387, 296].

The basic structure of a Web page is explained next in order to give an understanding of a Web page transmission. A Web page primarily consists of Hypertext Markup Language (HTML) code described in ASCII. The content of the *HTML* code defines the structure and the interconnections of a Web page. In the remainder of this chapter this part of a Web page will be referred to as the *main object*. In the main object usually HTML code is embedded that has references to files on the same or other servers. For example, the main object may have references to images or further Web objects created with scripting languages. These embedded objects are referred to as *inline objects* in the remainder of this chapter.

The downloading procedure of the Web page starts commonly with a link that has a reference to this page or alternatively a precise Universal Resource Locator (URL) of the Web page is inquired (clicked). In that case, immediately a *Hypertext Transfer Protocol (HTTP) GetRequest* message is sent to the appropriate server. In order to transmit the web page between the client and the server, a Transmission Control Protocol (TCP) connection is established. After receiving the GetRequest message, the server sends the main object to the client. Subsequently, the HTML code is parsed and if necessary further inline objects are requested from the adequate server.

The way of downloading the inline objects heavily depends on the used HTTP version. In HTTP 1.0 [57] for each object (i.e., main and inline) a TCP connection is opened and immediately closed after the download of the object. The establishment of a new TCP connection requires a 3-way handshake. The opening of a TCP connection for each inline object implicates an increase of user-perceived latency. In order to handle this additional processing overload caused by the 3-way handshake, the HTTP version 1.1

[143] introduced persistent connections: Once an object is delivered from the server to the client, a persistent connection remains open until a time-out at the server expires. As a result, the client is able to send several objects via the persistent connection, which leads to shorter user-perceived latency compared to the early HTTP 1.0 version. But, in the later version of HTTP 1.0, the idea of persistent connections is imitated by the utilization of the so-called '"keep-alive'"' messages. A keep-alive message is send periodically by the client if the connection should stay open. Therefore, according to [91] there is no significant difference between HTTP 1.1 (*persistent connections*) and the later HTTP 1.0 version (keep-alive). As a consequence of the results (similarity of HTTP 1.0 and 1.1) shown in [91], the authors in [296] ignore in their HTTP traffic modeling for example any detail about the TCP connections.

Although it seems to be that there is no significant difference between the modeling of HTTP 1.0 and 1.1, the reason why the two schemes are introduced in this section has two reasons. The first intention is to show that there was a difference in the past and it was accordingly regarded when models for HTTP traffic are designed. Second, to give an understanding that the connection establishment scheme has a heavy correlation between the user behavior and the generated traffic at TCP level. In the following section, we give an overview about proposed and approved models for web traffic modeling.

18.2.1   Survey of HTTP Traffic Models

Several approaches to model *Web traffic* has been proposed in the past. But before creating such models, most of the authors at first tried to collect important data in order to have a credible basis for their models. In this context, there are three ways of gathering data for web traffic modeling. The first approach is called *server logs*. At this, the server is able to keep track of the files it serves. With the gathered information a workload model from the server perspective can be created. An important but neglected aspect here is that the user behavior is not considered and therefore not modeled.

A second approach is to do the same on the client side. But in this case, the used browser needs to be modified in order to enable data gathering. In the past, the mosaic browser was modified to enable the collection of data [92, 109]. But the studies with this browser are not up to date anymore since today's browsers offer a lot more functionality and techniques for downloading objects (e.g., HTTP 1.0 vs 1.1). The question arises why we are not able to modify today's browsers. A simple answer is that some are unfortunately not open source and some require too much effort and time to understand all the internals.

The third and most popular approach is the gathering of so-called *packet traces* [467]. In this case, the measurements gathered from *packet traces* are taken from a distinct network. A typical network could be Campus or Local Area Network (LAN) in own administration where traces can be collected from own routers. Today a lot of tools exists like Wireshark [500] or TCP-Dump [459] to collect packet traces. While observing passing packets, headers are logged that can be analyzed later on. Considering Web traffic, typically the transport layer (TCP) is a point of interest, although there also exists studies like [101] which inspects HTTP headers in the application layer. In a next step, based on the analysis taken from the collected traces a so-called synthetic model is designed. The *synthetic model* consists of events that are important from the model designer's point of view. After figuring out the important events, appropriate distributions and their parametrization are selected until the outcomes of the synthetic model matches the real measured values or rather the traces. The third approach suppresses the drawbacks of the two previous approaches and nevertheless enables the aspect of user behavior modeling. A deeper discussion about these three approaches are given in [467, 302].

Some well-known models derived from *packet traces* and *client logs* will be presented in the following section. These models can be classified into the categories "*page-oriented*" and "*ON/OFF*" models. First, we discuss the page-oriented modeling and review existing approaches like Reyes [387, 91, 89] and Luo [296]. In the later part of this section, the ON/OFF modeling of Mah [302] and Choi [101] will be covered. Finally, a model proposed by Tran-Gia in [467] will be presented that puts all aspects of both categories and their details together into one common model.

Page-oriented Modeling

The *page-oriented model* has been first presented in [387] where a hierarchical model of three levels, namely the session level, page level, and packet level has been introduced. In [91, 89] the model has been extended by the insertion of the connection level in-between the page and packet level. The description of each level taken from [91] is given in the following.

Session level: Describes the user behavior in terms of the number of Web sessions per period (day, week, month, or year) and the distribution of the session along this period.

Page level: Focuses on determining the number of web pages per session and the distribution of the time between web pages.

Connection level: A web page in turn consists of a bunch of objects (text, images, sound files, etc.), which are conveyed through one ore more TCP connections. Therefore, for this level it is necessary to model the number

of connections for each page, the time between two consecutive connections as well as the distribution of the connection sizes.
Packet level: Allows a low granularity of modeling. Thus, the total amount
of bytes for each connection has to be split in TCP/IP packets. For this
purpose, this level must characterize the distribution of the packet sizes
and their inter-arrival times.

In the following we will present two page-oriented models suggested by
Reys [387] and Luo [296]. In *Reyes'* model [387] the first step of constructing
was the way of how a user generates traffic by browsing the web. According
to their definition, in the session level a user begins a new session if the time
between two consecutive packets exceeds a certain threshold (30 minutes).
During the session the user browses several web pages and take up time for
reading the web page. Thus, a session is a set of pages that are separated by
a viewing time. The important parameters are time between starting points
of two consecutive sessions (session inter-arrival time) and the number of
web pages that the user visits within a session. Note, that in this modeling
approach pages do not overlap, i.e., if a subsequent page is requested while
the previous page is not completely downloaded is not considered. The authors argument that the amount of packets from a previous page is less than
1% of total number of received packets and therefore can be neglected. As
a result, at the session level it is important to know what time between the
end of one page and the beginning of the next page (within the same session) is. Another interesting parameter is the total amount of information
transferred per page. Reyes et al. distinguish between uplink and downlink
information. In [91] the connection level models a web page by distinguishing
it into main and inline objects which may conveyed through one ore multiple
(depending on the HTTP version) TCP connections. Two TCP connections
that began less than 30s apart were considered as belonging to the same page.
Thus, in this level the inter-arrival time, number and size of connections are
relevant parameters. At the *packet level* a connection is split into multiple
(IP) packets. Important parameters at the packet level are the inter-arrival
time (distinguished by uplink and downlink traffic) and the packet sizes. Besides, the end of a page is determined by the last packet received before the
beginning of the next page. Remark, for web traffic modeling typically the
granularity of packet level modeling is not considered since the packet level
is more shaped by the conditions in the network while higher levels like the
page level are independent from network influences.
Luo et al. have slightly modified this approach in [296] where they on
the one hand neglect the *packet level* and on the other hand use a different
definition for the beginning of a session and a page. In their definition a new
session starts if consecutive packets exceeds 30 minutes (remember in case of
Reyes' model the same threshold indicates a new page). Another difference is
the starting points of two consecutive TCP connections, which should indicate
the time of two mouse clicks (i.e., the request for two successive web pages

by a user). Remember, in Reyes' model the threshold of 30 seconds has been used. In contrary, in Luo's model this threshold is much lower namely one second. The reason for the shorter period is that they conducted experiments in wired networks that show that one second is more appropriate for such a scenario. In contrary, in Reyes' work the focus is rather on wireless networks. In the following a slightly different methodology of web traffic modeling is presented.

ON/OFF Modeling

A slightly different web traffic modeling approach is given in [302] and [101] where they used a two phase model. The first phase is the ON phase that indicates the page download period. The adjacent phase, which we refer to as the OFF phase, is the duration between the end of a download process of one page and the beginning of the download process of another page. Note that the term ON/OFF model is our classification, particularly we are inspired from [467]. The authors of the introduced models use a different nomenclature for their approach.

In *Mah's* model [302] central entities for modeling are the ON phase length (that is comparable with the page length) and the OFF phase length (viewing time in Reyes' model). For determining the length of the ON phase, two simple heuristics are used. First, the page request has to be originating from the same client. Second, if too much time (determined by a threshold of 30 seconds) lies between two HTTP connections this indicates the start of a new page. In case of a *HTTP* connection, the client sends a HTTP request message to the server. The server replies with one or more reply messages. The number of reply messages depends on the number of inline objects. Mah used their measured Cumulative Distribution Functions (CDFs) (heavy-tailed) for modeling the size of a whole page as well as for the size of the main and inline objects. Unfortunately, a distribution or rather measurements for the number of inline objects are not specified. Only measured mean values for the number of downloaded web pages (four pages per server) are given. For describing the HTTP request size a binomial distribution has been suggested. For the OFF phase (Mah called it user thinking time) no distribution is suggested. Again, measured CDFs are used that have a mean of about 15 seconds. All in all, in Mah's work no distribution are suggested, instead measured CDFs are presented and utilized for their simulation. Furthermore, an interruption of downloads which can be caused for example by a user (who sends a new HTTP request before the previous request gets a reply) is not considered. In contrary, Choi does not only considers these aspects but also provides more details for the coherences.

Choi's model is the most famous for web traffic modeling. It is also known as the behavioral model which consists of hierarchical layers as shown in Figure 18.1. The ON phase describes the page loading duration and the OFF phase describes the viewing time respectively. So far, the modeling does not differ from Mah's modeling. But if we look into the details, in Choi's model the ON phase as well as the OFF phase is described in more detail. The ON phase (called HTTP-ON) describes the downloading and the viewing in parallel which starts after a web-request of a user. A web-request is defined as page or a set of pages that result from an action of a user. If a single user request (click) on a link generates multiple pages than all of these pages belong to the same web-request. Therefore, it is possible to view a page without downloading it completely, i.e., a user can view a page while downloading the remaining parts of a web-request. Moreover, a user can decide to request further web pages by clicking on already available links while downloading, which starts another web-request. The OFF phase (called HTTP-OFF) is a period between two web-requests where the browser is inactive. This time also indicates the viewing time of a user. The structure of a web page is also taken into account in Choi's as well as in Mah's model but again with much more details. When a user generates a web-request a HTTP request is generated. Choi's models the *HTTP* request with a Lognormal distribution. Remember, Mah used a binomial distribution. Choi distinguishes explicitly between main and inline objects. In contrary to Mah, Choi gives a distribution for the number of inline objects. A further parameter that Choi considers in its model is the parsing time of the main object. The parsing time is the time that is spent for fetching the main object in order to download necessary inline objects. For the parsing time a Gamma distribution is used. An interesting point in Choi's model is that he also considers the local caching mechanism, i.e., before an HTTP request is sent, the browser checks its local cache for availability of the web page. If the web page is available in the cache, the validity time is checked. If the page is up-to-date, the server does not need to be contacted for requesting the web page. This fact influences obviously the generated network traffic. Choi also differentiates in its model between the different HTTP versions for its TCP modeling level.

Tran-Gia et al. give a good overview about the presented modeling approaches. Furthermore, Tran-Gia combines some of these models with their respective details in one comprehensive model. In particular, the page-oriented and the *ON/OFF models* are merged as shown in Figure 18.2. We don't discuss all shown aspects as it is a conflation and we already described the basic issues in the previous models.

Almost all above mentioned parameters or rather entities are taken into account. Therefore, the parameters that are explained above will not be discussed here again. Note, that most modeling aspects are taken from Choi. In the next section, an overview about the most important entities that are introduced above are given.

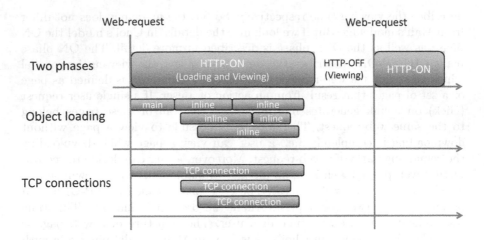

Fig. 18.1: Choi's "behavioral" model: HTTP-ON describes the downloading and the viewing in parallel, whereas HTTP-OFF indicates the period between two web-requests.

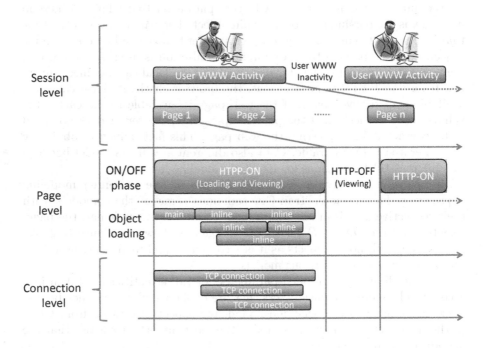

Fig. 18.2: Tran-Gia's comprehensive model: Utilizes Choi's model but also considers user activity. For this, the page-oriented modeling is used. A page is similar to Choi's HTTP-ON phase.

18.2.2   Parametrization

So far, we have described several web traffic modeling approaches. In the following, we give an overview about the main important entities regarding web traffic modeling and their parametrization. This overview can be used for simulation or for comparison reasons. The available entities are sorted in levels as in the page oriented design. Characterizations regarding the packet level are not given since almost all web traffic models do not consider this level of granularity. For clearness reasons, we utilize the following mathematical symbols within the presented parameterization tables: μ refers to the mean value, σ refers to the standard deviation and $\tilde{x}$ refers to the median.

Session Level

Regarding the *session level*, important parameters are the session inter-arrival time (Table 18.1), the viewing time (Table 18.2), and the number of pages or rather web-requests per session (Table 18.3).

Reference	Proposed Distribution	Proposed Parametrization
Choi [101]	Exponential	μ depend on desired traffic load
Tran [467]		
CDMA2000 [181]		
UMTS [321]		
Barford [50]	Pareto	α: 1.5, k: 1

Table 18.1: Session inter-arrival time.

Reference	Proposed Distribution	Proposed Paramterization
Choi [101]	Weibull	μ: 39.5s, $\tilde{x}$: 11s, σ: 92.6s
Barford [50]	Weibull	α: 1.46, β: 0.38
Reyes [387]	Gamma	μ: 25-35s, σ: 133s-147s
CDMA2000 [181]	Geometric	μ: 120s
UMTS [321]	Geometric	μ: 412s
Tran [467]	Weibull	μ: 39.5s, $\tilde{x}$: 11s, σ: 92.6s

Table 18.2: Viewing time.

Page Level

At the *page level*, important parameters are the time between two consecutive pages within the same session (Table 18.4), main or rather inline

Reference	Proposed Distribution	Proposed Parametrization
Choi [101]	Weibull	μ: 39.5s, $\tilde{x}$: 11s, σ: 92.6s
Barford [50]	Not modeled	-
Reyes [387]	Lognormal	μ: 22-25, σ: 78-166
CDMA2000 [181]	Geometric	μ: 5
UMTS [321]	Geometric	μ: 5
Tran [467]	Lognormal	$\alpha = 1.8$, $\beta = 1.68$, μ: 25, σ: 100
Vicari [479]	Not modeled	μ: 40.8

Table 18.3: Number of pages (web-requests) per session.

object relevant characterizations (Table 18.5) and the parsing time of the main object (Table 18.6).

Reference	Proposed Distribution	Proposed Parametrization
Choi i[101]	Weibull	μ: 39.5
Tran [467]	Weibull	μ: 39.5
Reyes [387]	Gamma	μ: 25-35
Vicari [479]	Pareto	μ: 43.5
Barford [50]	Pareto	μ: 3
UMTS [321]	Geometrical	μ: 12
Khaunte [253]	Weibull	μ: 21

Table 18.4: Time between two consecutive pages within the same session.

Connection Level

At the *connection level* important parameters are the number of connections per page (Table 18.7), the time between two consecutive connections within the same page (Table 18.8), and the connection size (Table 18.9).

18.3   Modeling FTP Traffic

Nowadays, *File Transfer Protocol (FTP)* [373] traffic is only responsible for 0.5 percent of the total traffic that flows through the Internet [219]. However, FTP is still important to transfer huge amounts of data between computers, because it is efficient and reliable.

The FTP protocol is a typical client-server application: The FTP *client* initiates a *session* with the FTP *server* and issues *requests* that are handled by the server. Typical requests are to list the files that are stored on the server and a file copy command to transfer files from the server to the client or the other way round. A FTP client is often operated by a user and sometimes controlled by an automatic script or an application. Depending on who is

Reference	Proposed Distribution	Proposed Parametrization
Choi [101]	Lognormal - main obj. size	μ: 10KB, $\widetilde{x}$: 6KB, σ: 25KB
	Lognormal - inline obj. size	μ: 7.7KB, $\widetilde{x}$: 2KB, σ: 126KB
	Gamma - no. of inline obj.	μ: 5.55, $\widetilde{x}$: 2, σ: 11.4KB
Tran [467]	Lognormal - main obj. size	μ: 10KB, $\widetilde{x}$: 6KB, σ: 25KB
	Lognormal - inline obj. size	μ: 7.7KB, $\widetilde{x}$: 2KB, σ: 126KB
	Gamma - no. of inline obj.	μ: 5.55, $\widetilde{x}$: 2, σ: 11.4KB
Mah [302]	Pareto - main obj. size	α: 0.85 - 0.97, $\widetilde{x}$: 2 - 2.4KB
	Pareto - inline obj. size	α: 1.12 - 1.39, $\widetilde{x}$: 1.2 - 2KB
	CDFs - no. of inline obj.	μ: 2.8 - 3.2, $\widetilde{x}$: 1
Reyes [387]	Pareto - main and inline	α: 1.5 - 1.7, β: 30000 - 31000
Barford [50]	Pareto - main and inline	α: 1, k: 1000
	Pareto - no. of inline obj.	α: 2.43, k: 1

Table 18.5: Main and inline object size and the corresponding distribution for the number of inline objects.

Reference	Proposed Distribution	Proposed Parametrization
Choi [101]	Weibull	μ: 39.5
Tran [467]	Weibull	μ: 39.5
UMTS [321]	Exponential	μ: 0.13

Table 18.6: Parsing time of the main object.

Reference	Proposed Distribution	Proposed Parametrization
Choi [101]	Gamma	μ: 5.5 (for inline objects)
Mah [302]	Measured CDFs	μ: 2.8 - 3.2
Vicari [479]	Measured	μ: 3.5
Barford [50]	Pareto	μ: 2.7
Khaunte [253]	Gamma	μ: 1.9

Table 18.7: Number of connections per page.

Reference	Proposed Distribution	Proposed Parametrization
Choi [101]	Gamma	μ: 0.860s (between inline objects)
Khaunte [253]	Gamma	μ: 0.148s (between the first connection of the page and the rest)
	Deterministic	μ: 0s (between the second and consecutive connections)

Table 18.8: Time between two consecutive connections within the same page.

Reference	Proposed Distribution	Proposed Parametrization
Barford [50]	Lognormal & Pareto	μ: 7.2-14.8KB
Khaunte [253]	Lognormal	μ: 8.3KB
Reyes [387]	Lognormal	μ: 7.7-10.7KB
Mah [302]	Heavy-tailed	μ: 8-10KB

Table 18.9: Connection sizes.

operating the client, a time span between the response of the server and the next request issued by the client can be seen. This time span is typically called viewing time. This layer is often called user level.

If we dig a bit deeper and leave the user level to descend to what is often called the object level we have to distinguish between so-called *control connections* and *data connections*. The control connection is initiated once at the beginning of a FTP session and alive as long as the session is alive. The FTP client initiates the control connection by connecting to the server. The control connection is used to transfer requests from the client to the server. It is also used to transfer answers containing status messages from the server back to the client. To transfer bulk data between the client and the server or the other way round a data connection is initiated. Such a data connection is only used for one request and closed after the single request is completed. For instance, if a client wants to see which files are stored in the current directory of the server it sends a "list" request to the server. To handle the data that has to be transferred in order to complete the request a data connection is established. Over this data connection the list of files that are stored on the current directory of the server is transferred. After the list of files is transferred, the data connection is shut down. Afterwards, the server replies with an answer over the control connection that tells the client that the "list" request is executed successfully. Originally, the data connection was initiated by the server by connecting to a port that has been announced by the client. This procedure is often called active FTP. However, due to firewalls and Internet connectivity issues (e.g., Network Address Translation (NAT)) [204]), it is often not possible for a server to connect to a client that is behind a firewall or behind a NAT. To resolve this problem a technique called passive FTP has been invented. With passive FTP the client initiates both connections to the server, solving the problem of firewalls filtering incoming connections requests. For this, the client issues a "PASV" command to tell the server that it is requesting passive FTP. The server answers with the port that it reserves for data connections that are associated with this session.

There is a close connection between the object level and the user level: The term control connection as coined in the object level means exactly the same thing as the term FTP session used in the *user level*. The only difference is the abstraction level.

If we split up each connection into the packets that convey the actual information we have reached what is often called the packet level. FTP is a TCP-only service which means no User Datagram Protocol (UDP)-based or any other transport layer based specification exists. So, all packets that are generated throughout a FTP session are TCP packets.

The different abstraction levels, as described in the previous section, are depicted in Figure 18.3.

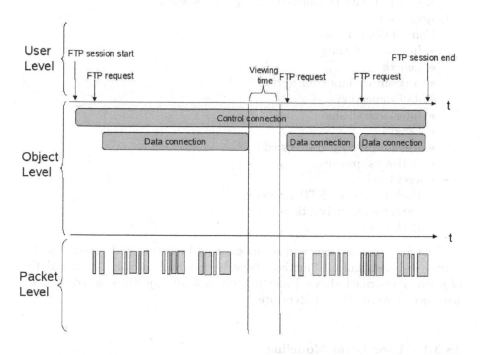

Fig. 18.3: Different abstraction levels of FTP traffic.

Based on the previous description how FTP works and depending on the abstraction level that should be modeled the following objectives are of interest:

- User level
  - FTP session inter-arrival time
  - FTP session duration
  - FTP request inter-arrival time
  - Number of FTP requests per FTP session
  - Viewing time duration
  - Amount of data transferred during FTP session
- Object level
  - Control Connection
    - Inter-arrival time
    - Length
    - Amount of data transferred
  - Data Connection
    - Inter-arrival time
    - Length
    - Amount of data transferred
    - Active vs. passive
  - Packet level
    - Packet calls per FTP session
    - Packet inter-arrival time
    - Packet size

The following sections review the existing literature and describe which values and distribution functions have been found in order to model the objectives described above. Unfortunately, not all objectives as listed above have been covered by the literature.

18.3.1   User Level Modeling

Paxson and Floyd showed in [358] that the inter arrival times of FTP sessions are well-modeled as homogeneous Poisson processes with fixed hourly rates. They also showed that the arrivals are dominated by a 24-hour pattern. During night time less FTP sessions are initiated than during day time.

18.3.2   Object Level Modeling

Paxson and Floyd state that data connection inter-arrival times within a FTP session are bursty and difficult to model [358]. The reason for this is that during file transfers many data connections are typically established at the same time. The authors investigated the amount of data that is transported during data connections. They found that a quite heavy-tailed distribution fits best. Half of the total FTP traffic comes from the largest 0.5 % of data connections. This finding means that modeling small FTP sessions or data collections is irrelevant. These results are backed up by Luo and Marin in [296], Jena et al. [242], and by the 3GPP2 project [23].

According to Paxson and Floyd, the number of connections per burst can be well-modeled as a Pareto distribution. In [242], the authors state that they observed many control connections without any data connection associated. The reason for this might be that applications automatically without doing any action. However, they also confirm that a Pareto distribution fits well.

18.3.3 Packet Level Modeling

Paxson and Floyd state that it is difficult to find a pattern that describes the inter-arrival times of packet during a FTP session, because the inter-arrival times are largely determined by network factors such as available bandwidth, congestion, and details of the congestion control algorithm of TCP [358]. However, they state that the inter-arrivals times are far from exponential.

18.3.4 Discussion

The previous sections reviewed the existing literature about the modeling of popular applications that rely mainly on TCP. If we compare the list of objectives that are of interest for FTP modeling (as listed above) with the objectives covered by the literature, we see a huge research gap. For instance, the packet sizes and viewing time duration are not studied for FTP so far. The question that arises is why are these uncovered objectives still unstudied? Especially, if you have in mind how long FTP and the Internet are around, it is questionable whether these uncovered objectives have any merit for modeling FTP. On a certain detail level it might be of interest to answer this questions. However, on a more abstract view, it looks like this questions are not of any importance.

18.4 Modeling Voice Traffic

Today there are many applications to realize the transmission of voice over digital networks for conversations between two or multi users. Examples are Skype, Google Talk or Windows Live Messenger. One reason for this variety is that a user requires low-cost services and a trend is observable that more applications of this kind are introduced to the market. Obviously, the impact of *voice traffic* in digital communication networks will therefore increase. Therefore, it is essential to include accurate models for voice traffic, when evaluating protocols of communication networks. The models should be able to initiate a session, simulate the speaker behaviors, and transmit coded voice packets. The goal of this section is to give the reader an idea about voice traffic modeling. Particularly, we give an overview of the entities, which are involved in a model for voice transmission and describe their most important attributes. Thereby, we also give hints about which of the entities have to be taken into consideration and which of the entities could be neglected in certain scenarios.

18.4.1   Entities of an Application for Voice Transmission

Figure 18.4 gives an overview of entities which should be considered to model voice conversations over digital networks. We have divided the model elements in two levels, user level and packet level.

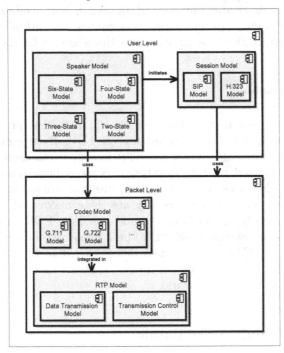

Fig. 18.4: Overview of involved entities in an application for voice transmission.

The user level includes all entities, that contribute to or interact with the user or the user behavior. Here, we have two main parts, the speaker model and the session model.

The speaker model comprises the user behavior in a voice conversation. Note that we regard only the modeling of conversations between two speakers in this section. There exists different models for two way conversations. Figure 18.4 shows four possible models, namely the six-state model, four-state model, three-state model, and two-state model. These models are mainly developed by *Brady* [77, 78, 79]. Depending on the accuracy requirement for a voice model one of these speaker models could be chosen.

Before starting a conversation between two users, a session should be initiated, i.e., one user initiate the session by involving the *session model*. The session model includes for example the *SIP model* or the *H.323 model*.

SIP was developed by the Internet Engineering Task Force (IETF) and published for the first time in 1999. In 2002 an enhanced version of the specification was published under RFC 3261 [396]. SIP is a transaction-based service, where sessions could be initiated, modified, and terminated. Furthermore, users could be integrated in running sessions. This is an important feature for multicast conferences. Therefore, UDP should be preferred as transport protocol.

In the same way, *H.323* fulfills the same tasks as SIP with the difference that it was published by the International Telecommunication Union (ITU) in 2003 [226]. Depending on the accuracy requirements, one of the models could be integrated to the voice model. It is also possible to neglect a session model completely, if this would not violate the requirements for the scenario.

In the packet level, we prepare the data, or rather the information, that comes from the user level and packetize them. The information from the speaker models uses the codec model which is integrated in the *Real-Time Transport Protocol (RTP) model*. The information from the session model is not further regarded here. For example, a UDP model could be used for session information.

The transmission of voice over digital networks is feasible only via compression methods, which are integrated in the codec. This means, that an analog signal, such as voice, has to be digitalized and compressed to send them over small bandwidth networks. Table 18.10 presents some examples for voice codecs which are widely used [220, 221, 222]. For example, the codec G.711 samples an analog signal 8000 times per second and each sample is quantized with 8 bits, which results in a bit rate of 64 kbit/s. Since a codec influences the transmission of voice data essentially, a codec model should be integrated in the overall voice model.

As voice, but also video transmissions, are multimedia applications, which have real-time requirements, appropriate transport protocols have to be considered. For this purpose, the IETF has developed *RTP* and published it under RFC 1889. In the meantime, a revised version of the standard was

Voice Codec	bits/sample	sample rate	bit rate
G.711	8	8000/s	64 kbit/s
G.722	8	16000/s	64 kbit/s
G.726	5	8000/s	40 kbit/s
	4	8000/s	32 kbit/s
	3	8000/s	24 kbit/s
	2	8000/s	16 kbit/s

Table 18.10: Examples for voice codecs.

published under RFC 3550. RTP enables the transmission of data with real-time requirements. The protocol has two parts [410, 364]:

1. **RTP Data Transfer Protocol:** This part of the protocol controls the data transmission. Packet losses are not addressed. It is also not ensured, that packets will be received in the correct order. It depends rather on the underlying transport protocol. RTP is often used in connection with UDP, but it can also used with TCP.

2. **RTP Control Protocol:** RTP Control Protocol (RTCP) records the quality-of-service and informs the user about the participants of the current session (the number of participants could be changed during one session, e.g., in an audiovisual conference). Even RTCP measures Quality of Service (QoS), there are no mechanisms to guarantee them.

As depicted in Figure 18.4 we have introduced an RTP model, which includes both the transmission protocol and the control protocol. Depending on the accuracy requirements, an RTP model has to be integrated in the overall voice model. Since the model characteristics belongs more to the modeling of transport protocols, we will not look into details in this section.

18.4.2   Speaker Models

In this section we describe the speaker models of two users in a voice conversation. Before we can design a speaker model, we have to think about which *speech events* we want to capture in our model. When we have defined the speech events we have to measure them, in order to rebuild their statistical characteristics in our model. There are mainly two attributes, that have to be regarded in a speaker model:

– **Session duration:** This attribute models the duration of one session between two users in a voice conversation. There are basically two ways to realize this attribute. Firstly, it could be projected to the target CDF, that is achieved from the measured data. Secondly, a standard CDF, e.g., a normal distribution, could be used to fit the statistical characteristics of a session duration in voice conversations.

– **Duration of speech events:** These attributes model the duration of the defined speech events. As for the session duration, these events could also be realized by first projecting the target CDF or second by using a standard CDF.

In the following, we will give a list of speech events, that should be analyzed when designing a speaker model.

Speech Events

In the literature their are ten events defined [77]. We will present these events with an example. Note that these events regard two speakers, A and B, in a conversation.

1. *Talkspurt:* A continuous sequence of speech.

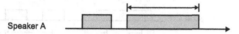

2. **Pause:** A continuous sequence without speech.

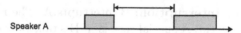

3. **Doubletalk:** A time period within A and B are talking simultaneously.

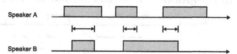

4. **Mutual-Silence:** A time period within A and B are not talking.

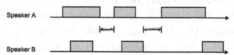

5. **Alternation-Silence:** The talkspurt of A ends. Then a time period begins, within A and B are not talking. Afterward, B's talkspurt begins. The time period within both speakers are not talking describes the alternation-silence event.

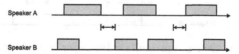

6. **Pause-in-Isolation:** The talkspurt of A ends. Then a time period begins, within A and B are not talking. Afterward, once again A's talkspurt begins. The time period, within both speakers are not talking describes the pause-in-isolation event.

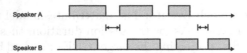

7. **Solitary-Talkspurt:** The talkspurt of A, that completely lies in the pause of B.

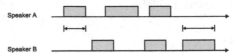

8. **Interruption:** B interrupts A. The time, when B's talkspurt begins, illustrates the time of the interruption. The interruption ends, when B's talkspurt ends, except for the case, when A's talkspurt ends and this time A interrupts the talkspurt of B. In this case, the interruption of B ends at the time, when A has interrupted.

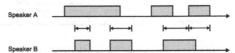

9. **Speech-after-Interruption:** B interrupts A. The rest of A's talkspurt describes this event. A special case is, if B's talkspurt ends and a renewed interruption inside the same talkspurt of A takes place. In that case the speech-after-interruption ends at the second interruption of B.

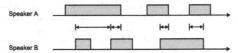

10. *Speech-before-Interruption:* B interrupts A. The time from begin of A's talkspurt until the time of the interruption describes this event. If B's interruption (B's talkspurt) ends in time t_1 and B begins a new interruption inside the same talkspurt of A in time t_2, the time $(t_2 - t_1)$ is regarded as the speech-before-interruption. If B's talkspurt hold up and A's talkspurt ends and this time A interrupts the talkspurt of B, then the pause time of A is measured as the speech-before-interruption.

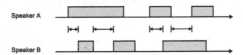

The described ten events represents a basis for modeling the speech behavior of two speakers. Depending on the accuracy requirements of the model, all or some of these events have to be rebuild in the model. There exists different suggestions to model the behavior. In the following, we present these possibilities.

State Models

After defining the speech events, we can now define the models themselves. In this section we describe four models, which should model the above mentioned speech events more or less.

Six-State Model. Figure 18.5(a) illustrates the *six-state model*. It describes the speech behavior of two speakers A and B. Speaker A is active in states 1, 2, and 3, while Speaker B is active in states 6, 2, and 3. The states 2 and 3 describe events, where both speakers are talking (doubletalk), while the states 4 and 5 describes events, where both speakers are silent (mutual-silence). Both doubletalk states, i.e., states 2 and 3, are distinguished by the additional information, which of the speakers is interrupted. In the same way the mutual-silence states, i.e., states 4 and 5, are differentiated by the additional information, which speaker has spoken last.

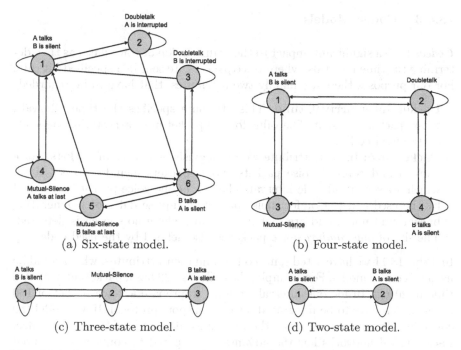

(a) Six-state model.   (b) Four-state model.

(c) Three-state model.   (d) Two-state model.

Fig. 18.5: State models for modeling the behavior of two speakers in a converstaion.

Four-State Model. Figure 18.5(b) illustrates the *four-state model*. In this model states 2, 3, and 4, 5 respectively of the six-state model are integrated into one state. Speaker A is now active in states 1 and 2, while speaker B is active in states 2 and 4. The state 3 describes the event, where both speakers are silent. With the four-state model we loose the additional information, that could be modeled with the six-state model, i.e., which speaker has interrupted and which speaker has spoken last respectively, but the model is capable to rebuild enough events.

Three-State Model. Figure 18.5(c) shows the *three-state model.* In that model state 2 of the four-state model is deleted, so that the doubletalk state can not be modeled yet. Speaker A is now only in state 1 active, while Speaker B is active in state 3. State 2 represents the mutual-silence event, i.e., both speakers are not talking.

Two-State Model. Figure 18.5(d) depicts the *two-state model.* This model is a simplification of the three-state model by deleting the state 2 of the three-state model. Now there exists only the possibility, that only speaker A is active, i.e., state 1, or only speaker B, i.e., state 2.

18.4.3   Codec Models

Codecs have a significant impact to the transmission of voice data, as they determine the time intervals, where voice packets are sent in a specified bit rate. For our purposes there are mainly two attributes, that have to be regarded:

- **Packet inter-arrival time:** This attribute specifies the time intervals, where packets are sent. The value for the packet inter-arrival time depends on the used codec.
- **Packet size:** In this attribute we distinguish two types of packets, voice packets and comfort-noise packets. Voice packets includes speech data, which are sent inside one interval. The size of one voice packet is specified by the used codec. Comfort-noise packets comprise data for regenerating background noise, and are sent in intervals, where no speech is detected. The size of one *comfort-noise* packet is also defined by the used codec.

In Table 18.11 we have listed some codecs and their attributes, which could be used in a codec model. For example, the codec G.722 has a packet inter-arrival time of 20 ms. Inside one interval we have to prepare a voice packet of 160 bytes, which have to be integrated into a transport protocol. If we model the codec in this way, we can reach the predefined 64 kbit/s of the G.722 codec. Packet-based networks has the advantage compared to connection-oriented networks, such as the telecommunication network, that in speechless intervals either no packets or comfort-noise packets are sent, so that bandwidth could be saved. In the example of the G.722 codec a comfort-noise packet of one byte could be sent in intervals where no speech is detected.

		G.723	G.728	G.729	G.722
packet inter-arrival time	[ms]	30	20	20	20
voice packet size	[Byte]	24	40	20	160
comfort-noise packet size	[Byte]	4	1	2	1
bit rate	[kbit/s]	6.3	16	8	64

Table 18.11: Examples for some codecs with their attributes.

18.5 Modeling Video Traffic

Regarding the traffic in digital communication networks we can observe that the transmission of video data requires most of the capabilities. This is not surprising, when we see services such as video-on-demand, live-streaming, but also websites with integrated video services such as Youtube. For the evaluation of current and future communication networks we need therefore accurate video models, which is the topic of this section. As for a voice model, a *video model* should also be able to initiate a session, simulate the user behavior, and transmit coded video packets.

18.5.1 Entities of an Application for Video Transmission

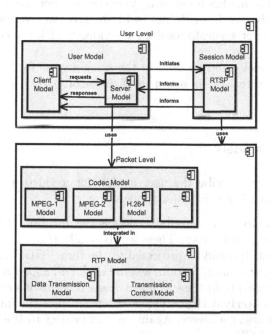

Fig. 18.6: Overview of involved entities in an application for video transmission.

Figure 18.6 illustrates the entities, which are involved in an application for video transmission. Similar to the overview diagram for voice transmission (see Figure 18.4), it is divided in two levels, user level and packet level.

The user level consists of a user model and a session model. In contrast to the speaker models in the voice model, where the two speakers are participated in a peer-to-peer manner, the user model in the video model comprises of a *client model* which requests to the *server model*, which responses with a service.

The client model initiates the *session model*, which is responsible for session establishment. For example, a Real-Time Streaming Protocol (RTSP) *model* should be used for this purpose. RTSP was published by the IETF in 1998 under RFC 2326 [411]. RTSP enables the transmission of streaming information and the control of them. However, the protocol does not send the streaming data. For this purpose, the use of RTP is possible. In RTSP there is no explicit session initiation. Control information could be sent both over TCP and UDP. If an RTSP model is involved into a video model, the tasks are to inform both the client model and server model about the ongoing session. As the RTSP model does not transmit video data it is also possible to neglect this model, if it does not violate the accuracy requirements for the scenario under investigation. In this section we will not further consider the design of an RTSP model.

The packet level comprises a codec model and an RTP model. The codec model includes the models for existing video codecs. For example, an *MPEG-2 model* could be used. In Table 18.12 we give an overview of existing video codecs. To get accurate results for a video model, the codec should be integrated.

The RTP model could be used in the same way as for the voice model. Since it has characteristics of a transport protocol we do not further look on it in detail.

18.5.2 User Models

In this section we describe the user models for a video model. The most important two attributes for these models are:

- **Session duration:** This attribute models the duration of one session between the client and server. There are basically two ways to realize this attribute. First, it could be projected to the target CDF, that is achieved from the measured data. Second, a standard CDF, e.g., a normal distribution, could be used to fit the statistical characteristics of a session duration.
- **Session inter-arrival time:** This attribute models the inter-arrival time of video requests at a server. Again, we can project to the target CDF or use a standard CDF.

Year	Name of the standards
1990	ITU-T Recommendation H.261 [223], *"Video Codec for Audiovisual Services at p × 64 kbit/s"*
1993	ISO/IEC 11172-2 [150], *"Information Technology - Coding of Moving Pictures and Associated Audio for Digital Storage Media at up to about 1.5 Mbit/s: Video"* (MPEG-1)
1995	ITU-T Recommendation H.262 [224], *"Information Technology - Generic coding of moving pictures and associated audio information: Video"*
	ISO/IEC 13818-2 [151], *"Information Technology - Generic coding of moving pictures and associated audio information: Video"* (MPEG-2)
1996	ITU-T Recommendation H.263 [225], *"Video Coding for Low Bit Rate Communication"* (1998 → H.263+, 2000 → H.263++)
2003	ITU-T Recommendation H.264 [227], *"Advanced Video Coding for Generic Audiovisual Services"*
	ISO/IEC 14496-2 [152], *"Coding of Audiovisual Objects: Visual"* (MPEG-4/ASP)
	ISO/IEC 14496-10 [153], *"Advanced Video Coding"* (MPEG-4/AVC)

Table 18.12: Activity of the development of video codecs over time.

The session duration could be managed in the client model and sent with the first request for a session initiation to the server model. Note, that this information could also be handled in a session model, if one would be integrated. The session inter-arrival time resembles the time of incoming video requests at a server. This information could also managed in the client model. The server model responses to the incoming requests by sending the video data to the client. Therefore, it uses the codec model that prepare the compressed video data, which is explained in the following section.

18.5.3 Codec Models

As video is coded before it will be sent over the network, it is important to build the attributes of a codec model correctly. The following attributes should be regarded, when a codec model is considered:

– **Packet inter-arrival time:** This attribute specifies the time intervals, where packets are sent. It is influenced by the settings of the used codec, e.g., quality of a video sequence.

- **Packet size:** This attribute reflects the size of one video frame, which are sent inside one interval. Typically a codec has different frame types with different characteristics, which would result in different packet types. There exists different methods to generate a frame size. We will look on this beneath.

A coded video sequence exhibit characteristics, that are reflected in the frame sizes. These characteristics have to be rebuild for the video model. We will now investigate this in more detail.

A typical frame consists of complex objects, e.g., an explosion in an action movie. Furthermore, the filmed objects are not always fixed in a place, but rather are moving, e.g., a car on a street. Besides, the camera is also moving, so that even for fixed objects the position in a frame sequence could change. When a codec is applied to this kind of frame sequence, we would get variable bit rates as an output. To determine the packet size for the transmission of video data, we have to consider this characteristic. Usually, this property could be determined through analyzing the CDF (alternatively the PDF) of such a sequence.

Normally, a movie consists of scenes. Inside a scene there are not so much changes, because the filmed objects persist equal. This means that the frames in a sequence inside a scene are correlated to each other. This is a characteristic that have to be considered when a sequence of packet sizes are generated for a scene. This characteristic could be investigated by analyzing the autocorrelation function of the frame sequence. The effect is reflected through high values in the first lags of the autocorrelation coefficient and is denoted as Short Range Dependency (SRD).

Beside of correlation inside one scene, there exists also similarities between different scenes, i.e., frames, which do not belong to the same scene or are temporarily away from each other, could also have correlations. The reason for this characteristic is, that frames of different scenes could exhibit the same complexity and movement intensity. In the same way as for the SRD, this characteristic could also be investigated by analyzing the autocorrelation function of the frame sequence. The effect is reflected with a low decay of the autocorrelation function and positive autocorrelation coefficients and is denoted as Long Range Dependency (LRD).

In the following, we look on how we could model the above mentioned characteristics, that is:

1. The CDF of frame sizes,
2. the SRD, and
3. the LRD.

In the literature there are different modeling strategies published to rebuild these statistical characteristics. Figure 18.7 illustrates a classification based on [90].

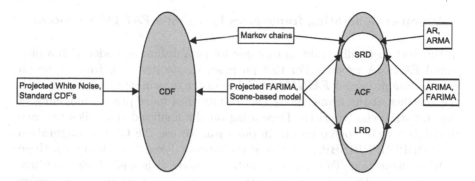

Fig. 18.7: Classification of different modeling strategies for capturing the statistical characteristics of a sequence of video frame sizes.

The statistical characteristics are illustrated in ellipsoidal circles, while the modeling strategies are visualized with rectangles. The arrows denote, which strategy could model which statistical characteristic.

Projected White Noise model the CDF by generating a white noise process which then is projected to the target CDF. Another alternative for modeling is to use standard CDFs. For example, a lognormal or a gamma distribution are standard CDFs, which could be used to rebuild the frame size statistics. These strategies have the disadvantage, that they could not model the SRD and LRD.

To model the SRD their exists models, such as the *Autoregressive (AR)* or *Autoregressive Moving Average (ARMA)* processes [74]. However with these processes we are neither able to model the LRD nor the CDF. This means that we have to combine this process with other strategies.

Autoregressive Integrated Moving Average (ARIMA) and *Fractional Autoregressive Integrated Moving Average (FARIMA)* processes are able to model SRD as well as LRD. However the CDF could not be modeled with these processes, so that further strategies have to be considered.

Markov chains could be used during modeling in a flexible manner. For example a markov chain could model the Group of Picture (GOP) configuration of an MPEG codec video sequence. Furthermore, scene changes could also be modeled. With this modeling strategy we are able to model both the SRD and CDF.

Scene-based models are able to model all three statistical characteristics by introducing scenes to model the SRD. Inside one scene the frame sizes are modeled with an appropriate CDF. The division into scenes effect that also LRD could be modeled. Another modeling strategy, which can rebuild all three statistical characteristics is the projection of the FARIMA process to a CDF.

Example: Generating frame sizes by using a FARIMA process

In this section we illustrate an example for establishing a model with a projected FARIMA process. For this purpose, we use for each frame type an appropriate projected *FARIMA* model in order to generate frame sizes with the specifics of the frame type. This results in a more precise modeling of the statistical characteristic. Depending on the analyzed trace files we have to define a GOP configuration. In our case, we use the GOP configuration IBBPBBPBBPBBIBBP..., because we have analyzed trace files with these GOP configuration. To get a representative model it is a good way to introduce a classification scheme, where the most important attributes of a video model are captured. The genre, quality, format, and used codec are examples for attributes in such a classification.

In the following, the process of generating the frame sizes are explained in detail. At first the required parameters are described. Then the generation of the FARIMA process are explained and subsequent to this the projection to a lognormal CDF is shown. Note that these steps have to be done for all frame types.

Parameter. The required parameters for generating a projected FARIMA process are the following ones:

– Autoregressive parameter $\phi_1, \phi_2, \ldots, \phi_p$
– Moving average parameter $\theta_1, \theta_2, \ldots, \theta_q$
– Fractional differencing level d
– Mean value μ and standard deviation σ of the lognormal distribution, which is used for the projection

Before the autoregressive and moving average parameter could be determined, we have to define first the order of the process. In the literature this order was never larger than two [74]. In our scenario we use $p = 1$ and $q = 1$.

The parameters ϕ and θ are determined through the *Yule-Walker equations* [74]. Parameter d is defined by the equation $d = H - 0.5$, where H denotes the *Hurst parameter* [207]. Therefore we have to define first the Hurst parameter to determine d. There exists basically three methods to calculate the Hurst parameter:

– *Rescaled Adjusted Range Analysis* (R/S Analysis)
– *Variance-Time Analysis*
– *Periodogram Analysis*

Cano and Manzoni compare in their paper [88] these three methods. The results of this investigation are, that the periodogram analysis was the easiest one to implement, but the R/S analysis the most robust one, while the variance-time analysis seems to be very unstable. Therefore, it should be appropriate to use the R/S analysis to determine the Hurst parameter.

FARIMA process. After the parameters are calculated, we have to generate a FARIMA(p, d, q) process (see [74] for more information). A FARIMA process of order (p, d, q) is defined as

$$\phi(B)\,\Delta^d z_n \;=\; \theta(B)\,a_n.$$

This equation could be transformed into an ARIMA(p, q) process of the following form:

$$z_n \;=\; \phi^{-1}(B)\,\theta(B)\,x_n, \tag{18.1}$$

where

$$x_n \;=\; \Delta^{-d} a_n. \tag{18.2}$$

The series x_n is a FARIMA(0, d, 0) process, also denoted as *Fractional Differencing Noise (FDN)*, and could be calculated through the *Hosking algorithm* [205]. Therefore there are basically two steps for generating a FARIMA(p, d, q) process required:

1. Generate an FDN process x_n with equation (18.2)
2. Generate a FARIMA(p, d, q) process z_n by using the equation (18.1)

Step 1 is calculated with the Hoskings algorithm as follows (see [205]):

– Calculate the autocorrelation function by the equation

$$\rho_k \;=\; \frac{d(1+d)\cdots(k-1+d)}{(1-d)(2-d)\cdots(k-d)}.$$

– Draw a random number for x_0 from a normal distribution $N(0, v_0)$. Set $N_0 = 0$ and $D_0 = 1$.
– Generate n values through iteration of the following steps ($k = 1, 2, \ldots, n$):

– $N_k = \rho_k - \sum_{j=1}^{k-1} \phi_{k-1,j} \cdot \rho_{k-j}$,

– $D_k = D_{k-1} - N_{k-1}^2 / D_{k-1}$,

– $\phi_{k,k} = N_k / D_k$,

– $\phi_{k,j} = \phi_{k-1,j} - \phi_{k,k} \cdot \phi_{k-1,k-j}, \quad j = 1, \ldots, k-1$,

– $m_k = \sum_{j=1}^{k} \phi_{k,j} \cdot x_{k-j}$,

– $v_k = (1 - \phi_{k,k}^2) v_{k-1}$

– Draw x_k from $N(m_k, v_k)$

In step 2 we have to generate an ARMA process. Instead using a white noise process, we use here the equation (18.1) of the FDN process x_n, so that we could generate a FARIMA(p, d, q) process.

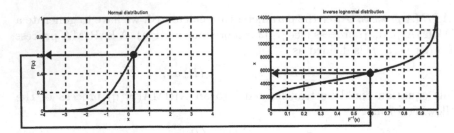

Fig. 18.8: An example projection of normal distributed random numbers to an inverse lognormal distribution.

Projection. After a FARIMA(p, d, q) process is generated, each generated value of the process must be projected to a lognormal distribution. The projection is illustrated in Figure 18.8. The generated series of the FARIMA process is a normal distribution with mean value μ_N and variance σ_N^2. Each value is first projected on its own CDF, so that we get a sequence of random numbers between [0, 1]:

$$F_{N(\mu_N,\sigma_N^2)}(z_n) \in [0,1]$$

Each random number is then delivered to the inverse lognormal distribution, which generates a value with the calculated lognormal parameters mean value μ_L and variance σ_L^2:

$$F_{LogN(\mu_L,\sigma_L^2)}^{-1}\big(F_{N(\mu_N,\sigma_N^2)}(z_n)\big)$$

18.6   Conclusion

Designing and evaluating a system without the proper understanding of the traffic can lead to unexpected performance behavior. Therefore, it is important to have a deep understanding about the source of generated traffic, i.e., the application traffic. In this chapter, we have shown four classic examples for application traffic and their modeling approaches. First, in Section 18.2 a survey about most popular HTTP traffic models are presented and a parameterization overview for the most relevant entities are given. Second, modeling approaches for FTP traffic and the research gap for such traffics are discussed in Section 18.3. Third, in Section 18.4 models regarding voice traffic are illustrated. For this case, the most relevant entities, i.e., speaker and codec models, and their interaction are presented in detail. Finally, in Section 18.5 modeling of video traffic has been described. Again, the most relevant entities, i.e., the user and codec models, are identified and subsequently described.

19. Modeling the Internet Delay Space and its Application in Large Scale P2P Simulations

Sebastian Kaune (Technische Universität Darmstadt)
Matthias Wählisch (Freie Universität Berlin & HAW Hamburg)
Konstantin Pussep (Technische Universität Darmstadt)

19.1 Introduction

The peer-to-peer (P2P) paradigm has greatly influenced the design of Internet applications nowadays. It gained both user popularity and significant attention from the research community, aiming to address various issues arising from the decentralized, autonomous, and the self-organizing nature of P2P systems [379]. In this regard, quantitative and qualitative analysis at large scale is a crucial part of that research. When evaluating widely deployed peer-to-peer systems an analytical approach becomes, however, ineffective due to the large number of simplifications required. Therefore, conclusions about the real-world performance of P2P systems can only be drawn by either launching an Internet-based prototype or by creating a simulation environment that accurately captures the major characteristics of the heterogeneous Internet, e.g. round-trip times, packet loss, and jitter. Running large scale experiments with prototypes is a very challenging task due to the lack of sufficiently sized testbeds. While PlanetLab [36] consists of about 800 nodes, it is still too small and not diverse enough [434] to provide a precise snapshot for a qualitative and quantitative analysis of a P2P system. For that reason, simulation is often the most appropriate evaluation method.

Internet properties, and especially their *delay* characteristics, often directly influence the performance of protocols and systems. In delay-optimized overlays, for instance, *proximity neighbor selection* (PNS) algorithms select the closest node in the underlying network from among those that are considered equivalent by the routing table. The definition of closeness is typically based on round-trip time (RTT). In addition, many real time streaming systems (audio and video) have inherent delay constraints. Consequently, the Internet *end-to-end delay* is a significant parameter affecting the user's satisfaction with the service. Therefore, in order to obtain accurate results, simulations must include an adequate model of the Internet delay space.

We begin by discussing the factors that may affect the Internet end-to-end delay in Section 19.2. Section 19.3 gives an overview on state-of-the art Internet delay models. In Section 19.4 and 19.5, we present background information and details on a novel delay model, which we evaluate in Section 19.6. Concluding remarks are given in Section 19.7.

19.2   End-to-end Delay and Its Phenomena

In order to accurately model the Internet delay characteristics, the influencing entities and their inherent phenomena must be identified. We define the term *Internet end-to-end delay* as the length of time it takes for a packet to travel from the source host to its destination host. In more detail, this packet is routed to the destination host via a sequence of intermediate nodes. The Internet end-to-end delay is therefore the sum of the delays experienced at each hop on the way to the destination. Each such delay in turn consists of two components, a fixed and a variable component [68]. The *fixed* component includes the transmission delay at a node and the propagation delay on the link to the next node. The *variable* component, on the other side, includes the processing and queuing delays at the node.

Normally, end-to-end delays vary over time[410]. We denote this *delay variation* as *end-to-end delay jitter*. According to [126], there are three major factors that may affect the end-to-end delay variation: queueing delay variations at each hop along the Internet path; intra-domain multi-path routing, and inter-domain route alterations.

Thus, the main challenges in creating a Internet delay space model can be summarized as follows:

– The model must be able to predict lifelike delays and jitter between a given pair of end-hosts.
– The computation of delays must scale with respect to time.
– The model must have a compact representation.

We argue that the first requirement is subject to the geographical position of the sender and the receiver. First, the minimal end-to-end delay between two hosts is limited by the propagation speed of signals in the involved links which increases proportionally with the link length. Second, the state of the Internet infrastructure varies significantly in different countries. As long-term measurement studies reveal (cf. Sec. 19.4), jitter and packet loss rates are heavily influenced by the location of participating nodes. For example, the routers in a developing country are more likely to suffer from overload than those in a more economically advanced country.

Asymmetric Delays

The Internet end-to-end delay refers to the packet travel time from a source to its receiver. This one-way delay (OWD) will typically be calculated by halving the measured RTT between two hosts, which consists of the forward and reverse portion. Such an estimation most likely holds true, if the path is symmetric. Symmetric paths, however, are not an obvious case. Radio devices, for instance, may experience inhomogeneous connectivity depending on coverage and interferences. Home users attached via ADSL possess inherently different up- and downstream rates. Independent of the access technology in use, Internet routing is generally *not symmetric*, i.e., intermediate nodes traversed from the source to the receiver may differ from the reverse direction. In the mid of 1996, Paxson revealed that 50 % of the virtual Internet paths are asymmetric [357]. Nevertheless, implications for the corresponding delays are not evident. Although router-level paths may vary, the forward and reverse OWD can be almost equal due to similar path lengths, router load etc.

Internet delay asymmetry has been studied in [354]. The authors show that an asymmetric OWD implies different forward and reverse paths. However, unequal router-level paths do not necessarily imply asymmetric delays [354]. An asymmetric OWD could be mainly identified for commercial networks compared to research and education backbones. It is worth noting that the end-to-end delay between two hosts within different autonomous systems (ASes) is significantly determined by the intra-AS packet travel time [512]. Combining the observations in [354] and [512] thus suggest that in particular delays between hosts located in different provider domains are poorly estimated by the half of RTT.

The approximation of the OWD by RTT/2 may over- or underestimate the delay between two hosts. In contrast to the RTT, measuring the OWD is a more complex and intrinsic task as it requires the dedicated cooperation of the source as well as its receiver [416], [480]. Consequently, hosts cannot instantaneously discover the OWD. Protocols and applications therefore use the RTT, e.g., P2P applications while applying this metric for proximity neighbor selection. The modeling process of network structures which include end-to-end delays should be aware of the asymmetric delay phenomena. Neglecting this Internet property seems reasonable when deployment issues allow for the simplification, or it is common practice in the specific context. Otherwise, the approximation is unreasonable.

In the following sections of this chapter, we will focus on geometric schemes to model the delay space. These approaches calculate the packet travel time based on the Euclidean distance of artificial network coordinates. Obviously, such models cannot account for delay asymmetry as the Euclidean distance between two points is symmetric per definition. Further, we often use the term delay as synonym for end-to-end or *one-way delay*.

19.3   Existing Models in Literature

Currently, there are four different approaches to obtaining an Internet delay model: analytical functions, the king method, topology generators, and Euclidean embedding. In this section, we will briefly discuss each of those approaches.

Analytical *function.* The simplest approach to predict delay is to randomly place hosts into an two-dimensional Euclidean space. The delay is then computed by an analytical function that uses as an input the distance between any two hosts, for example, the Euclidean distance. While this approach requires only simple run-time computations and does not introduce any memory overhead, it has one major drawback: it neglects the geographical distribution and locations of hosts on earth, which are needed for both the realistic modeling of lifelike delays (i) and jitter (ii).

King method. The second approach uses the King tool [247] to compute the all-pair end-to-end delays among a large number (typically dozens of thousands) of globally distributed DNS servers. In more detail, each server is located in a distinct domain, and the measured delays therefore represent the Internet delay space among the edge networks [513]. Due to the quadratic time requirement for collecting this data, the amount of measured data is often limited. For example, [247] provides a delay matrix with 1740 rows/columns. This is a non-trivial amount of measurement data to obtain, but might be too less for huge P2P systems consisting over several thousands of nodes. To tackle this issue, a delay synthesizer may be used that uses the measured statistical data as an input in order to produce Internet delay spaces at a large scale [513]. Nevertheless, this synthesizer only produces static delays and neglect the delay variation.

Topology generators. The third approach is based on using artificial link delays assigned by topology generators such as Inet [232] or GT-ITM [511]. This scheme initially generates a topology file for a predefined number of nodes n. A strategy for the final computation of the end-to-end delay depends on the specific scenario and should consider two issues: (a) on-demand vs. precomputation and (b) the single-source path (SSP) vs. all-pair shortest path (ASP) problem[1]. In contrast to an on-demand calculation, a pre-calculation may reduce the overall computational costs if delays are required several times, but increases the memory overhead. The ASP problem, which causes high computational power and squares the memory overhead to $O(n^2)$, should be solved in the case that delays between almost all nodes are needed. It is sufficient to separately calculate the SSP, if only a small subset of nodes will be analyzed.

---

[1] We refer to the SSP and ASP problem as example for solving a routing decision for some or all nodes.

Model	Computation cost	Memory overhead	Comment
Analytical function	low	$O(1)$	static delays neglects geographical pos.
King method	low	$O(n^2)$	static delays very high precision complicated data acquisition
Topology generators (pre-computation)	low	$O(n^2)$	static delays neglects geographical pos.
Topology generators (on-demand)	very high (Dijkstra's SSP)	low	static delays neglects geographical pos.
Euclidean embedding	low	$O(n)$	data freely available

Table 19.1: Different approaches for modeling the Internet delay space. The number of end-hosts is denoted by n.

Euclidean embedding. The fourth approach is based on the data of Internet measurement projects, e.g. Surveyor [450], CAIDA [85], and AMP [25], which are freely available. These projects typically perform active probing up to a million destination hosts, derived from a small number of globally distributed monitor hosts. This data is used as an input to generate realistic delay by embedding hosts into a multi-dimensional Euclidean space [167].

Table 19.1 gives an overview about the properties of the aforementioned approaches. Unfortunately, none of them considers realistic delay and jitter based on the geographical position of hosts. That is, these approaches aim to predict static delays, either the average or minimum delay between two hosts. Furthermore, most of them do not accurately reflect delay characteristics caused by different geographical regions of the world. This issue can, however, highly influence the performance of P2P systems, as we will see in Section 19.5.3. Only the Euclidean embedding seems to be an optimal tradeoff between computational costs and memory overhead.

In the remainder of this chapter, we therefore present an alternative approach of obtaining end-to-end delays that fulfills the requirements stated in the previous section. It exploits the compact and scalable representation of hosts in an Euclidean embedding, whilst considering the geographical position of hosts to calculate delays and lifelike jitter. This approach is based on rich data from two measurement projects as input.

19.4 Data from two Internet Measurement Projects

This section provides background information on the measured Internet delay data we use in our model. Firstly, we use the measurement data of the CAIDA's macroscopic topology probing project [85]. This data contains a large volume of RTT measurements taken between 20 globally distributed

monitor hosts[2] and nearly 400,000 destination hosts. Within this project, each
monitor actively probes every host stored in the so-called destination list by
sending ICMP [371] echo-requests. This lists account for 313,471 hosts covering the routable IPv4 space, alongside 58,312 DNS clients. Each monitor-
to-destination link is measured 5-10 times a month, resulting in an overall
amount of 40 GB of measurement data. As an example, Fig. 19.1 plots the
data of August 2007 in relation to the geographical distance between each
monitor host and its destinations. Both, the *geographical locations* of the
monitors and the destination hosts are determined by *MaxMind* GeoIP service[3] [309]. It can be observed that there is a proportionality of the RTT to
the length of the transmission medium. The 'islands' at 8000 - 12000 km and
300 - 400 ms RTT arises from countries in Africa and South Asia.

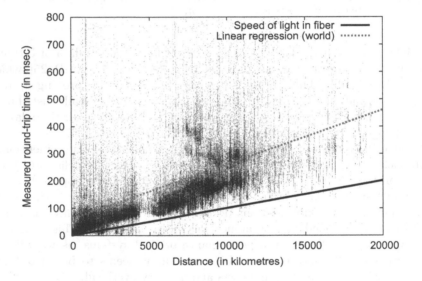

Fig. 19.1: The measured *round-trip* times in relation to the geographical distance
in August 2007

To study the changes of delay over time, we additionally incorporate the
data of the PingER project [463]. This project currently has more than 40
monitoring sites in 20 countries and about 670 destination sites in 150 countries. This number of monitor hosts is double than that of the CAIDA project,
whereas the amount of remote sites is by order of magnitudes smaller. Nevertheless, the RTT for one monitor-to-destination link is measured up to 960
times a day, in contrast to 5-10 times per month by the CAIDA project.

---

[2] For more information about the monitor hosts, see
http://www.caida.org/projects/ark/statistics/index.xml

[3] The obviously impossible RTT values below the propagation time of the speed
of light in fiber can be explained by a false positioning through MaxMind.

As seen later on, this allows us to accurately predict the inter-packet delay variation between any two hosts located in different countries or continents.

19.5 Model

This section details our model that aims to realistically predict end-to-end delays between two arbitrary hosts chosen from a predefined host set. This model approximates the OWD between two hosts by halving the measured RTTs as obtained from the above mentioned measurement projects. However, we are aware that this approach may over- or underestimate the actual OWD in reality (cf. Sec 19.2). Nevertheless, the obtained delays are non-static, and consider the geographical location of both the source and destination host. Further, the model properties in terms of computation and memory overhead are given.

19.5.1 Overview

We split up the modelling of delay into a two-part architecture. The first part computes the *minimum* one-way delay between two distinct hosts based on the measured round-trip time samples of CAIDA, and is therefore static. The second part, on the other hand, is variable and determines the jitter.

Thus, the *OWD* between two hosts $\mathcal{H}_1$ and $\mathcal{H}_2$ is given by

$$delay(\mathcal{H}_1, \mathcal{H}_2) = \frac{RTT_{min}}{2} + jitter. \qquad (19.1)$$

Fig. 19.2 gives an overview of our model. The *static part* (top left) generates a set of hosts from which the simulation framework can choose a subset from. More precisely, this set is composed of the destination list of the CAIDA measurement project. Using the MaxMind GeoIP database, we are able to look up the IP addresses of these hosts and find out their geographic position, i.e., continent, country, region, and ISP. In order to calculate the minimum delay between any two hosts, the Internet is modelled as a multidimensional Euclidean space $\mathcal{S}$. Each host is then mapped to a point in this space so that the minimum round-trip time between any two nodes can be predicted by their Euclidean distance.

The *random part* (top right), on the other hand, determines the inter-packet delay variation of this minimum delay; it uses the rich data of the PingER project to reproduce end-to-end link jitter distributions. These distributions can then be used to calculate random jitter values at simulation runtime.

Basically, both parts of our architecture require an offline computation phase to prepare the data needed for the simulation framework. Our overall

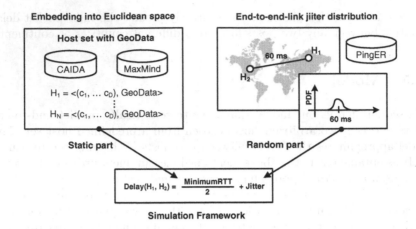

Fig. 19.2: Overview of our delay space modeling techniques

goal is then to have a very compact and scalable presentation of the underlay at simulation runtime without introducing a significant computational overhead. In the following, we describe each part of the architecture in detail.

19.5.2   Part I: Embedding CAIDA Hosts into the Euclidean Space

The main challenge of the first part is to position the set of destination hosts into a multidimensional Euclidean space, so that the computed minimum round-trip times approximate the measured distance as accurately as possible. To do so, we follow the approach of [335] and apply the technique of global network positioning. This results in an optimization problem of minimizing the sum of the error between the measured RTT and the calculated distances.

In the following, we denote the coordinate of a host $\mathcal{H}$ in a D-dimensional coordinate space $\mathcal{S}$ as $c_{\mathcal{H}} = (c_{\mathcal{H},1}, ..., c_{\mathcal{H},D})$. The measured round-trip time between the hosts $\mathcal{H}_1$ and $\mathcal{H}_2$ is given by $d_{\mathcal{H}_1 \mathcal{H}_2}$ whilst the computed distance $\hat{d}_{\mathcal{H}_1 \mathcal{H}_2}$ is defined by a distance function that operates on those coordinates:

$$\hat{d}_{\mathcal{H}_1 \mathcal{H}_2} = \sqrt{(c_{\mathcal{H}_1,1} - c_{\mathcal{H}_2,1})^2 + ... + (c_{\mathcal{H}_1,D} - c_{\mathcal{H}_2,D})^2}. \qquad (19.2)$$

As needed for the minimization problems described below, we introduce a weighted error function $\varepsilon(\cdot)$ to measure the quality of each performed embedding:

$$\varepsilon(d_{\mathcal{H}_1 \mathcal{H}_2}, \hat{d}_{\mathcal{H}_1 \mathcal{H}_2}) = \left(\frac{d_{\mathcal{H}_1 \mathcal{H}_2} - \hat{d}_{\mathcal{H}_1 \mathcal{H}_2}}{d_{\mathcal{H}_1 \mathcal{H}_2}} \right)^2. \qquad (19.3)$$

Basically, this function calculates the squared error between the predicted and measured RTT in a weighted fashion and has been shown to produce accurate coordinates, compared to other error measures [335].

At first, we calculate the coordinates of a small sample of N hosts, also known as *landmarks* $\mathcal{L}_1$ to $\mathcal{L}_N$. A precondition for the selected landmarks is the existence of measured round-trip times to each other. In our approach, these landmarks are chosen from the set of measurement monitors from the CAIDA project, since these monitors fulfill this precondition. In order to achieve a good quality of embedding, the subset of N monitors must, however, be selected with care.

Formally, the goal is to obtain a set of coordinates $c_{\mathcal{L}_1}, ..., c_{\mathcal{L}_N}$ for the selected N monitors. These coordinates then serve as reference points with which the position of any destination host can be oriented in $\mathcal{S}$. To do so, we seek to minimize the following objective function f_{obj1}:

$$f_{obj1}(c_{\mathcal{L}_1}, ..., c_{\mathcal{L}_N}) = \sum_{i=1|i>j}^{N} \varepsilon(d_{\mathcal{L}_i \mathcal{L}_j}, \hat{d}_{\mathcal{L}_i \mathcal{L}_j}). \tag{19.4}$$

There are many approaches with different computational costs that can be applied [295], [335]. Recent studies have shown that a five dimensional Euclidean embedding approximates the Internet delay space very well [397]. Therefore, we select $N(=6)$ nodes out of all available monitors using the maximum separation method[4] [167]. For this method, we consider, however, only the minimum value across the samples of inter-monitor RTT measurements.

In the second step, each destination host is iteratively embedded into the Euclidean space. To do this, round-trip time measurements to all N monitor hosts must be available. Similarly to the previous step, we take the minimum value across the monitor-to-host RTT samples. While positioning the destination hosts coordinate into $\mathcal{S}$, we aim to minimize the overall error between the predicted and measured monitor-to-host RTT by solving the following minimization problem f_{obj2}:

$$f_{obj2}(c_{\mathcal{H}}) = \sum_{i=1}^{N} \varepsilon(d_{\mathcal{H}\mathcal{L}_i}, \hat{d}_{\mathcal{H}\mathcal{L}_i}). \tag{19.5}$$

Because an exact solution of this non-linear optimization problem is very complex and computationally intensive, an approximative solution can be found by applying the generic *downhill simplex algorithm* of Nelder and Mead [230].

---

[4] This method determines the subset of N monitors out of all available monitors which produces the maximum sum for all inter-monitor round-trip times.

19.5.3   Part II: Calculation of Jitter

Since the jitter constitutes the variable part of the delay, a distribution function is needed that covers its lifelike characteristics. Inspection of the measurement data from the PingER project shows that this deviation clearly depends on the geographical region of both end-hosts. Table 19.2 depicts an excerpt of the two way-jitter variations of end-to-end links between hosts located in different places in the world. These variations can be monthly accessed on a regional-, country-, and continental level [463]. We note that these values specify the *interquartile range* (iqr) of the jitter for each end-to-end link constellation. This range is defined by the difference between the upper (or third) quartile Q_3 and the lower (or first) quartile Q_1 of all measured samples within one month. The remarkably high iqr-values between Africa and the rest of the world are explained by the insufficient stage of development of the public infrastructure.

To obtain random jitter values based on the geographical position of hosts, for each end-to-end link constellation we generate a log-normal distribution[5] with the following probability distribution function:

$$f(x; \mu, \sigma) = \begin{cases} \frac{1}{\sqrt{2\pi}\sigma x} \exp\left(-\frac{1}{2}\left(\frac{\ln x - \mu}{\sigma}\right)^2\right) & \text{if } x > 0 \\ 0 & \text{otherwise.} \end{cases} \tag{19.6}$$

The main challenge is then to identify the parameters μ (mean) and σ (standard deviation) by incorporating the measurement data mentioned above. Unfortunately, both values cannot be obtained directly from PingER. That is, we are in fact able to determine the expectation value of each constellation, which is given by the difference between the average RTT and the minimum RTT. Both values are also measured by the PingER project, and are available in the monthly summary reports, too. The variance or standard deviation is, however, missing.

For this reason, we formulate an optimization problem that seeks to find a parameter configuration for μ and σ having two different goals in mind. First, the chosen configuration should minimize the error between the measured inter quartile range iqr_m and $\text{iqr}(X)$ which is generated by the log-normal distribution. Second, it should also minimize the measured and generated expectation, E_m and $\text{E}(X)$ respectively. Formally, this optimization problem is given by

$$f_{error} = \left(\frac{\text{E}(X) - \text{E}_\text{m}}{\text{E}_\text{m}}\right)^2 + \left(\frac{\text{iqr}(X) - \text{iqr}_\text{m}}{\text{iqr}_\text{m}}\right)^2. \tag{19.7}$$

---

[5] In [167], it is shown based on real measurements that jitter values can be approximated by a log-normal distribution.

	Europe	Africa	S. America	N. America	Asia
Europe	1.53	137.14	3.07	1.29	1.19
Africa	26.91	78.17	3.69	31.79	1.11
S. America	14.17	69.66	13.14	10.78	14.16
N. America	2.02	73.95	3.63	0.96	1.33
Oceania	4.91	86.28	4.19	1.31	2.03
Balkans	1.83	158.89	3.89	1.43	1.25
E. Asia	1.84	114.55	3.02	1.38	0.87
Russia	2.29	161.34	4.79	2.53	1.59
S. Asia	7.96	99.36	8.99	16.48	7.46
S.E. Asia	0.86	83.34	4.43	13.36	1.27
Middle East	9.04	120.23	11.39	10.87	10.20

Table 19.2: End-to-end link inter-packet delay variation in msec (January 2008).

where $E(X) = e^{\mu + \sigma^2/2}$ and $iqr(X) = Q_3 - Q_1$ as described above. To solve this, we apply the downhill simplex algorithm [230]. Observation of measurement data shows that the iqr-values are usually in the range of 0 to 20 milliseconds[6]. With respect to this, the three initial solutions are set to $(\mu = 0.1, \sigma = 0.1)$, $(\mu = 0.1, \sigma = 5)$, and $(\mu = 5, \sigma = 0.1)$, because these parameters generate random jitter values fitting this range exactly. The minimization procedure iterates then only 100 times to obtain accurate results.

We note that the obtained values for μ and σ describe the distribution of the two-way jitter for a specific end-to-end link constellation. The one-way jitter is then obtained by dividing the randomly generated values by two. Further, each end-to-end link constellation is *directed* from a geographical region. For example, the delay variation of a packet that travels from Europe to Africa is significantly higher than the one from Africa to Europe (cf. Tab. 19.2). By using two directed end-to-end link constellations, one starting from Europe and the other one starting from Africa, we are able to reflect this asymmetry.

19.5.4   Algorithm and Memory Overhead

In this section, we briefly describe the properties of our model in terms of computational costs and storage overhead. These properties are of major importance since they significantly influence the applicability of the model in large scale simulations.

First of all, the embedding of all hosts n into a D-dimensional Euclidean space has a scalable representation of $O(n)$ while it adequately preserves the properties of the data measured by the CAIDA project. Since the process

---

[6] Africa constitutes a special case. For this, we use another initial configuration as input for the downhill simplex algorithm.

involved in obtaining this representation is complex and computationally expensive, it is typically done once. The resulting data can be reused for each simulation run, e.g., in terms of an XML file. In order to obtain the minimum delay between any two hosts in this embedding, the evaluation of the distance function takes then $O(D)$ time which is negligible.

The calculation of the jitter parameters of μ and σ for each possible end-to-end link constellation is also done once, either before the simulation starts or offline. Thus, similar to the pre-computation of the host coordinates, this process does not introduce any computational overhead into the actual simulation process. Nevertheless, the storage of the both parameters μ and σ takes at first sight a quadratic overhead of $O(n^2)$. Due to the fact that the amount of regions, countries and continents is limited, the required amount of memory is, however, negligible. For example, the processing of the data provided in the PingER summary report of January 2008 result in 1525 distinct link constellations. For each of them, the two parameters μ and σ must be precomputed and stored resulting in a overall storage overhead of $(1525 \times 2) \times 4\,\text{bytes} \approx 12\text{kB}$.

19.6   Evaluation

This section describes the setup of our experiments, and any metrics we think significantly influence the performance of P2P systems. We perform a comparative study against three existing approaches for obtaining end-to-end delays: (i) the King method, (ii) topology generators and (iii) analytical function. Our aim is to show that our model realistically reflects the properties of the Internet delay space. To this end, we show that the calculated delay between non-measured end-to-end links is also a suitable presumption compared to the delays that occur in the Internet.

19.6.1   Experimental Setup

The King method serves as a reference point in our analysis because it provides measured Internet delay data among a large number of globally distributed DNS servers. We use the measurement data of [513] collected in October 2005. This matrix contains 3997 rows/columns representing the all-pair delays between IP hosts located in North America, Europe and Asia.

With regard to the topology generators, we are especially interested in the GT-ITM and Inet generators because they are often used in P2P simulations. For GT-ITM, we create a 9090 node transit-stub topology. For Inet, we create a topology for a network size of 10000 nodes. We use the default settings of placing nodes on a 10000 by 10000 plane with 30% of total nodes as degree-one nodes.

As seen in Section 19.4, there is a correlation between the measured RTTs and the geographical distance of peers. In order to obtain an analytical function that reflects this correlation, we perform a least squares analysis so that the sum of the squared differences between the calculated and the measured RTT is minimized. Applying linear regression with this least squares method on the measurement data of 40 GB is, however, hardly possible. Therefore, we classify this data into equidistant intervals of 200 km (e.g. $(0\text{km}, 200\text{km}], (200\text{km}, 400\text{km}]\ldots$), and calculate the median round-trip time of each interval. Finally, linear regression gives us the following estimation for the RTT in milliseconds:

$$f_{world}(d_{a,b}) = 62 + 0.02 * d_{a,b} \qquad (19.8)$$

whereas $d_{a,b}$ is the distance between two hosts in kilometers. The delay is then given by $f(d_{a,b})$ divided by two. Fig. 19.3 illustrates this function and the calculated median RTT times of each interval.

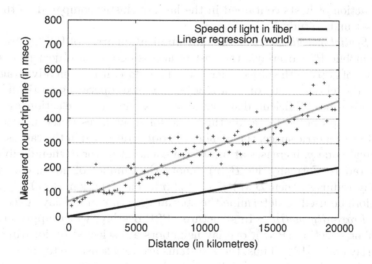

Fig. 19.3: Results of linear regression with least square analysis on CAIDA measurement data.

19.6.2   Metrics

To benchmark the different approaches on their ability to realistically reflect Internet delay characteristics, we apply a set of metrics that are known to significantly influence the performance of P2P systems [513]:

- *Cutoff delay clustering* – In the area of P2P content distribution networks, topologically aware clustering is a very important issue. Nodes are often grouped into clusters based on their delay characteristics, in order to provide higher bandwidth and to speed up access [168]. The underlying delay model must therefore accurately reflect the Internet's clustering properties. Otherwise, analysis of system performance might lead to wrong conclusions.

  To quantify this, we use a clustering algorithm which iteratively merges two distinct clusters into a larger one until a cutoff delay value is reached. In more detail, at first each host is treated as a singleton cluster. The algorithm then determines the two closest clusters to merge. The notion of closeness between two clusters is defined as the average delay between all nodes contained in both cluster. The merging process stops if the delay of the two closest clusters exceeds the predefined cutoff value. Afterwards, we calculate the fraction of hosts contained in the largest cluster compared to the entire host set under study.

- *Spatial growth metric* – In many application areas of P2P systems, such as in mobile P2P overlays, the cost of accessing a data object grows as the number of hops to the object increases. Therefore, it is often advantageous to locate the 'closest' copy of a data object to lower operating costs and reduce response times. Efficient distributed nearest neighbor selection algorithms have been proposed to tackle this issue for growth-restricted metric spaces [22]. In this metric space, the number of nodes contained in the radius of delay r around node p, increases at most by a constant factor c when doubling this delay radius. Formally, let $B_p(r)$ denote the number of nodes contained in a delay radius r, then $B_p(r) \leq c \cdot B_p(2r)$. The function $B_p(r)/B_p(2r)$ can therefore be used to determine the spatial growth c of a delay space.

- *Proximity metric* – In structured P2P overlays which apply proximity neighbor selection (PNS), overlay neighbors are selected by locating nearby underlay nodes [184]. Thus, these systems are very sensitive to the underlying network topology, and especially to its delay characteristics. An insufficient model of the Internet delay space would result in routing table entries that do not occur in reality. This would in turn directly influence the routing performance and conclusions might then be misleading. To reflect the neighborhood from the point of view of each host, we use the $\mathcal{D}(k)$-metric. This metric is defined by $\mathcal{D}(k) = \frac{1}{|N|} \sum_{p \in N} d(p, k)$, whereas $d(p, k)$ is the average delay from node p to its k-closest neighbors in the underlying network [297].

19.6.3   Analysis with Measured CAIDA Data

Before we compare our system against existing approaches, we briefly show that our delay model produces lifelike delays even though their calculation is divided into two distinct parts.

As an illustration of our results, Fig. 19.4 depicts the measured RTT distribution for the Internet as seen from CAIDA monitors in three different geographical locations, as well as the RTTs predicted by our model. We note that these distributions now contain all available samples to each distinct host, as opposed to the previous section where we only considered the minimum RTT.

First, we observe that our predicted RTT distribution accurately matches the measured distribution of each monitor host. Second, the RTT distribution varies substantially in different locations of the world. For example, the measured path latencies from China to end-hosts spread across the world have a median RTT more than double that of the median RTT measured in Europe, and even triple that of the median RTT measured in the US. Additionally, there is a noticeable commonality between all these monitors regarding to the fact that the curves rise sharply in a certain RTT interval, before they abruptly flatten out. The former fact indicates a very high latency distribution within these intervals, whereas the latter shows that a significant fraction of the real-world RTTs are in the order of 200 ms and above.

In contrast to this, Fig. 19.5 shows the RTT distribution as seen from a typical node of the network when using the topologies generated by Inet and GT-ITM as stated before. When comparing Fig. 19.4 and Fig. 19.5, it can be observed that the real-world RTT distributions significantly differ from the RTT distributions created by the topology generators. In particular, around 10-20% of the real-world latencies are more than double than their median RTT. This holds especially true for the monitor hosts located in Europe and in the US (see Fig. 19.4). Topology generators do not reflect this characteristic. Additionally, our experiments showed that in the generated topologies, the RTT distribution seen by different nodes does not significantly vary, even though they are placed in different autonomous subsystems and/or router levels. Thus, current topology generators do not accurately reflect the geographical position of peers, something which heavily influences the node's latency distribution for the Internet.

19.6.4   Comparison to Existing Models

We compare our model (coordinate-based) against existing approaches for obtaining end-to-end delays using the metrics presented before. The reference point for each metric is the all-pair delay matrix received by the King method. We use this because the data is directly derived from the Internet. However, we are aware that this data only represents the delay space among

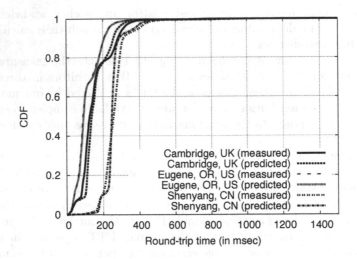

Fig. 19.4: The measured and predicted round-trip time distribution as seen from different locations in the world.

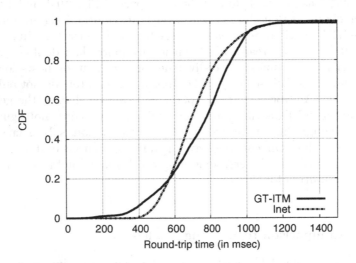

Fig. 19.5: The round-trip time distribution as seen from a typical node generated by topology generators.

the edge networks. To enable a fair comparison, we select, from our final host set, all hosts that are marked as DNS servers in CAIDA's destination list. We only utilize those that are located in Europe, Northern America or Asia. These nodes form the host pool for our coordinate-based model, and the analytical function, from which we chose random sub-samples later on. For the generated GT-ITM topology, we select only stub routers for our experiments to obtain the delays among the edge networks. For the Inet topology, we repeat this procedure for all degree-1 nodes. To this end, we scale the delays derived from both topologies such that their average delays matches the average delay of our reference model. While this process does not affect delay distribution's properties, it alleviates the direct comparison of results.

The results presented in the following are the averages over 10 random sub-samples of each host pool whereas the sample size for each run amounts to 3000 nodes[7].

We begin to analyse the cluster properties of the delay spaces produced by each individual approach. Fig. 19.6 illustrates our results after applying the clustering algorithm with varying cutoff values. It can be observed that for the reference model, our approach , and the distance function, the curves rise sharply at three different cutoff values. This indicates the existence of three major clusters. By inspecting the geographical origin of the cluster members of the latter two models, we find that these clusters exactly constitute the following three regions: Europe, Asia and North America. Further, the three cutoff values of the analytical function are highly shifted to the left, compared to the values of the reference model. Nevertheless, the basic cluster properties are preserved. The curve of our delay model most accurately follows the one of the reference model, but it is still shifted by 10-20 ms to the left. Finally, both topology generated delays do not feature any clear clustering property. This confirms the findings that have already been observed in [513].

To analyse the growth properties of each delay space, we performed several experiments each time incrementing the radius r by one millisecond. Fig. 19.7 depicts our results. The x-axis illustrates the variation of the delay radius r whereas the y-axis shows the median of all obtained $B_p(2r) / B_p(r)$ samples for each specific value of r. Regarding the reference model, it can be seen that the curves oscillates two times having a peak at delay radius values 20 ms and 102 ms. Also, our coordinate-based approach and the analytical function produces these two characteristic peaks at 26 ms and 80 ms, and 31 ms and 76 ms respectively[8].

In all of the three mentioned delay spaces, the increase of the delay radius firstly covers most of the nodes located in each of the three major clusters. Afterwards, the spatial growth decreases as long as r is high enough to cover

---

[7] It is shown in [513] that the properties we are going to ascertain by our metrics are independent of the sample size. Thus, it does not matter if we set it to 500 or 3000 nodes.

[8] The minimum delay produced by the analytical function is 31 ms, no matter the distance. This is why there are no values for the first 30 ms of r.

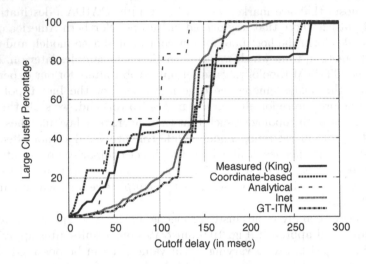

Fig. 19.6: Simulation results for cutoff delay clustering.

nodes located in another major cluster. Lastly, it increases again until all nodes are covered, and the curves flatten out. The derived growth constant for this first peak of the analytical function is, however, an order of magnitude higher than the constants of the others. This is clearly a consequence of our approximation through linear regression. Since this function only represents an average view on the global RTTs, it cannot predict lifelike delays with regard to the geographical location of peers. Nevertheless, this function performs better than both topology generated delay spaces. More precisely, none of both reflect the growth properties observed by our reference delay space.

The experiments with the $D(k)$-metric confirm the trend of our previous findings. The predicted delays of our coordinate-based model accurately matches the measured delays of the reference model. Fig. 19.8 illustrates the simulation results. While varying the number of k (x-axis), we plot the delay derived by the $D(k)$-function over the average to all-node delay. Whilst especially the measured delays and the one predicted by our model show the noticeable characteristic that there are a few nodes whose delay are significantly smaller than the overall average, the topology generated delays do not resemble this. As a consequence, it is likely that the application of PNS mechanisms in reality will lead to highly different results when compared to the ones forecasted with GT-ITM or Inet topologies. The analytical function, on the other hand, performs significantly better than the topology generators,

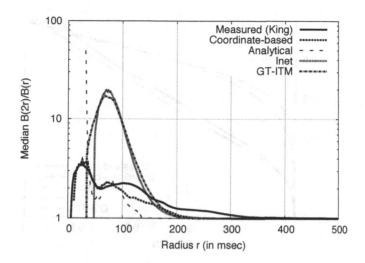

Fig. 19.7: Simulation results for spatial growth of the modelled delay spaces.

even though there is also a noticeable difference in the results obtained by former two delay spaces.

19.7 Summary

Simulation is probably the most important tool for the validation and performance evaluation of P2P systems. However, the obtained simulation results may strongly depend on a realistic Internet model. Several different models for the simulation of link delays have been proposed in the past. Most approaches do not incorporate the properties of the geographic region of the host. Hosts in a generated topology thus have overly uniform delay properties. The analytical approach, on the other hand, does not provide a jitter model that reflects the different regions and the absolute delays differ from more realistic approaches. Both the King model and our proposed coordinate-based system incorporating data from real-world measurements yield similar results. The only major drawback of King is its limited scalability. It requires memory proportional to n^2 and available datasets are currently limited to 3997 measured hosts. Statistical scaling of this data allows to preserve delay properties, but produces solely static delay values [513].

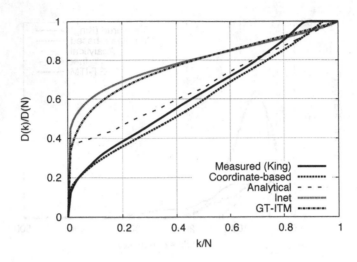

Fig. 19.8: Simulation results for the $D(k)$-function as proximity metric.

The model presented in this chapter has only linear memory costs and provides a much larger dataset of several hundred thousand hosts. Compared to topology generators the delay computation time is low. In summary, coordinate-based delay models seem to be an optimal tradeoff between many conflicting properties.

20. Modeling User Behavior in P2P Systems

Konstantin Pussep (Technische Universität Darmstadt)
Christof Leng (Technische Universität Darmstadt)
Sebastian Kaune (Technische Universität Darmstadt)

20.1 Introduction

The evaluation of *peer-to-peer (P2P)* systems is crucial for understanding their performance and therefore their feasibility in the real world. Different techniques, such as testbeds, analytical analysis, and simulations, can be used to evaluate system performance. For peer-to-peer systems, simulations are often the most reasonable approach, simply because P2P systems are both inherently large-scale and complex.

While simulations are a popular technique for estimating the performance of large scale P2P systems with an acceptable level of detail, the modeling of the system is crucial to obtain realistic results. Aside from a proper model of the underlying network, a proper evaluation has to take user behavior into account, since it is a critical factor of the system dynamics. The modeling of user behavior is already important in traditional client/server environments, because it heavily influences the workload. In addition to their role as consumers, users become providers in P2P systems which aggravates their importance to system performance.

In general, a good model of *user behavior* for P2P systems has to capture both the consumer and provider nature of the participating peers. For example, churn, which describes peers connecting to and disconnecting from the system, has a severe impact on data availability and consistency, while resource distribution and popularity have a significant impact on load balancing. Therefore, a user behavior model must be abstract enough to allow efficient implementations but at the same time capture the most relevant components.

In this chapter we describe a general user behavior model for the simulation of P2P systems, and show how it can be applied to Distributed Hash Tables (DHTs), using Kademlia [310] as an example. We discuss a general model and the alternative approaches for individual components and present their impact on evaluation results.

20.2   System Model

The behavior of P2P users is rather complex. We aim to break it down into understandable and independent components. The main categories shown in Figure 20.1 are *churn*, workload, and user properties.

Churn describes the participation dynamics of P2P nodes. Users join the network, leave, and come back several times. Sometimes they even leave forever because they do not use the system anymore. For example, in systems such as BitTorrent [103] the user is interested in exactly one download per torrent and will normally not join a distribution overlay in which he already completed downloading.

Churn consists of the *lifetime* of a node which starts with its initial creation and ends with its permanent departure. During its lifetime, a node goes through several online and offline cycles (see Figure 20.2). The time span a node is online is called a *session*. The time between sessions is accordingly called *intersession*.

Joining and *leaving* are system-specific operations. In most overlays joining includes finding neighbors, initializing routing tables, replicating data, and other setup operations. Leaving cleans up the session state. A regular leave normally includes the notification of neighbors to help them reorganizing their state. Not all nodes leave the network orderly, some simply *crash*, i.e., they disappear from the overlay without any notification. This can be caused by software crashes, hardware crashes, or loss of connectivity.

A node in a P2P system is both a server and a client. As such it provides *resources* and executes *requests* for available resources. The provision and consumption of resources specifies the *workload* of the system. A realistic workload model is crucial for sensible performance evaluation. For example, if resources are shared files in filesharing systems, a request would stand for downloading a file. As previous studies [185] have shown, the workload is not uniform over all resources. Some resources are abundant, many are scarce. The same is true for requests, some resources are far more *popular* than the others.

Both churn and workload operate directly on the simulated system which itself relies on an underlay model of the Internet in the simulator framework (see Figure 20.1). The *use properties* (especially his strategy) interact with churn and workload. The properties also include the goals and interests of a user. Similar to the global popularity of resources in the workload, a user has no uniform interest in all resources, but consumes only certain types or even very specific resources. This interest clustering is especially important for reputation systems, but has also been used to build specialized content-clustered overlays [107]. Also part of the strategy is the user's willingness to cooperate. Some users try to maximize their benefit, e.g., by not uploading at all or tricking a reputation system. On the other hand, many users do not leave the network immediately after a completed download [279]. Thus, the user strategy does influence both workload and churn.

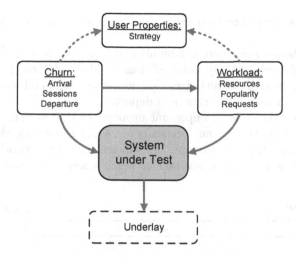

Fig. 20.1: P2P system under test. The *system* is controlled by the *workload* and *churn* components. Different users are modeled by *user properties*. Finally, the *underlay* decides about the transmission delays.

The *underlay*, the network infrastructure the overlay operates on, is important for a reasonable performance evaluation as well. Bandwidth, latency, message loss and other properties of the underlay links have to reflect the conditions of the target real-world environment. However, the modeling of underlays is out of scope for this chapter as it is mostly orthogonal to the user behavior (See Chapter for underlay modeling).

In the next three sections we discuss the components in more detail.

20.3   Modeling Churn

One of the most well-studied and analyzed components of user behavior in P2P systems is *churn*, i.e., the property of peers in the system to leave it and come again at will. Studies such as [448] by Stutzbach et al. measured and analyzed the churn behavior in different P2P systems, focusing on session and intersession times. They found churn characteristics being significantly different across systems.

A churn model can capture the change of online and offline events by considering the total lifetime of a peer and online sessions. Typically, a user participates in the system over a certain time, the *user lifetime* in the system. During this time a user may connect and disconnect from the system many times, therefore creating *online sessions*. Figure 20.2 shows an example lifetime of a peer with three sessions.

We divide the modeling of churn into *lifetime* and *session* models. The first model describes when a peer appears in the system for the first and the last time. The latter covers peer's online sessions during its lifetime in the system.

In a simulation run, there is a number of N peers instantiated and available for simulations. At any point of time a subset of these peers is online resulting in the actual network size. This network size depends on four factors: arrival rate, join rate, leave rate, and departure rate.

Because scalability is an important property of P2P systems, simulations have to show how the system performs for a given network size. Here the number of *online* hosts is relevant. We will see how the network size can be predicted and how long it might take to reach a steady network state.

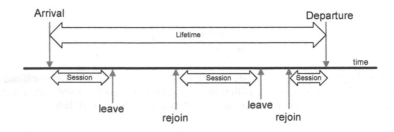

Fig. 20.2: Peer's lifetime can consist of several online sessions with different durations.

20.3.1   Lifetime Models

The lifetime of a peer is determined by two events: *arrival* and *departure*. The peers' arrivals in a system can be influenced by many factors, such as the application deployment process or the dynamics of social networks where people start using the system recommended by their friends. These factors are difficult to capture exactly and therefore a stochastic model appears reasonable to describe this behavior.

Similar arguments apply to peer departures, because users might stop using an obsolete system and switch to a new one. However, this process is typically of less interest for a simulation scenario.

Moreover, in real systems the lifetime of a peer in the system is much longer than the session time. The lifetime can be several days or even months long while the sessions are few hours long on average [59]. As the simulated time often ranges in the order of hours only, the rate of departures is so low that they can be ignored.

However, this is different for systems such as BitTorrent where peers are only interested in downloading one single file and depart from the system permanently afterwards. This applies because for each file a distinct short-living overlay is created.

In the following we consider two possibilities of modeling the *arrival process*:

Deterministic Arrival Process

Here all peers arrive with a constant inter-arrival interval τ. The complete network of N peers is built up after the fixed time $N \cdot \tau$.

A possible downside of this approach is the lack of randomness, often observed in real system. Furthermore, the fixed inter-arrival intervals can cause a synchronization of periodic events. For example, consider a network with 1000 peers that arrive with the interval of 1 minute. Upon arrival each peer starts some periodic maintenance operation each 10 minutes after the bootstrap process. In this case each minute 100 concurrent maintenance operations can occur.

Poisson Arrival Process

If peers are assumed to arrive independently from each other a Poisson arrival process can be applied [196]. Given a peer arrival rate λ, peer arrivals are distributed exponentially with the same rate λ resulting in the mean inter-arrival interval $\tau = \frac{1}{\lambda}$. For each arrival event an absent peer is selected and connected to the system. Therefore, for N peers the network will be completely built up after (roughly) the time $\frac{N}{\lambda}$.

This is a more realistic model because arrival events happen with different intervals.

20.3.2 Session Models

An online session model describes peers going online and offline after they joined the system for the first time. This model contains two events: *join* and *leave*. The reason why it can be important to distinguish *join* and *arrival* events in a system is that peers coming back to the system can reuse contact information of other peers and the data items stored locally.

The modeling of online sessions can be done either *globally* or *per peer*. In the first case, there is a global rate of join and leave events. Here, when a global join event occurs an offline peer is selected to join the network. The same can apply to leave events. In a simulation environment this method requires only one periodic join and leave event to be scheduled.

The second method schedules one session join/leave event per peer. Once a peer has arrived to the system, its session length is computed and the respective *leave event* is scheduled. After this time is reached and the event is fired, the intersession length is computed and the *join event* is scheduled. While this method has a larger memory footprint due to the number of scheduled events, it offers high flexibility. The session and intersession durations can follow any desired distribution: exponential, Weibull etc. Furthermore, the peers can be divided into groups, where some peers are long-lasting while others connect and disconnect frequently.

In the following we consider examples for each of both methods.

Exponential Session and Inter-Session Durations

In this model both the session and intersession time of peers follow an exponential distribution with the (possibly different) rates λ_s and λ_i respectively. The mean session duration of a single peer is $mean_s = \frac{1}{\lambda_s}$ and the mean intersession duration is $mean_i = \frac{1}{\lambda_i}$. Then the expected probability of a peer being online at a given time is the *connectivity factor* $c = \frac{mean_s}{mean_s + mean_i}$. Therefore, for N available peers only approximately $c \cdot N$ peers will be online for any given time.

This rises an interesting trade-off: If we want to simulate with a fixed number of *online* peers and have realistic session and intersession times, then we might end up with a much larger number of peers that must be *available* for the algorithm. This can be a problem if memory is the limiting resource in the simulation environment.

Global Leave Rate with Peer Replacement

In order to reduce the global number of join and leave events a *global leave rate* can be applied, as used e.g., in [388]. Here we can use only one periodic event that dictates when a peer will leave the network. Each time the event is triggered one randomly selected online peer leaves the system.

For the join process no additional events are used. Instead an offline peer is randomly selected and joins the network to replace the peer going offline. Therefore, the network size is constant.

In more detail, when the churn process starts, there is a Poisson process deciding when the next *leave* event should occur. If the leave process is timed by an exponential distribution with the rate of λ_{leave}, then the expected inter-event interval is $1/\lambda_{leave}$ and the corresponding session time is expected to be $t_{mean} = \frac{N_0}{\lambda_{leave}}$ where N_0 is the desired network size.

A benefit of this model is that the memory consumption can be easily limited, e.g we can keep 10,000 peers online from the set of 11,000 available peers, while still keeping the desired mean session duration. For example, if the desired session duration is 50 minutes than the global leave rate is set to $10,000/50 = 200$ events per minute.

20.4   Workload Model

This model comprises two parts: the resource distribution that describes the resources offered and used in the system and the user requests specifying how these resources are requested and consumed.

Since in a P2P application the users are accessing resources residing on other peers, the question arises how the information is distributed among the users. The content items are spread in the system according to some distribution and again depending on the application type and the user structure.

The resource distribution defines how many resources are present in the system. The replication distribution specifies how many replicas of each file are present in the system. Finally, the popularity specifies how often single resources are requested by users.

Several works consider the specifics of P2P file sharing systems regarding the user request patterns, e.g., [185] and [400]. One interesting result is that systems where users consume multimedia content (so most file sharing systems, too) show a download-once behavior, e.g., the user almost never request the same content twice. This leads to a different popularity distribution compared to classical client-server systems, such as web servers.

The actual requests to the system are issued depending on offered resources, resource popularity and user's interests. In a simple model a user issues requests on a regular basis, e.g., each m time units. In a more realistic approach the users issue queries following a distribution, e.g., an exponential distribution.

For systems dealing with content (file sharing, video streaming) the skewed popularity of content can be expressed by heavy-tailed distributions of content replicas and queries. In real P2P systems Zipf or Zipf-Mandelbrot were found to fit the content and query distributions well [185].

20.5   User Properties Model

This section briefly captures user specific properties, e.g., interests, strategy. The interests define which resources the user is interested in, this can be captured by a resource category the user is interested in and results in different request rates and targets per peer. Therefore, for user u it defines the interesting content as a subset of all available resources.

The strategy typically describes the cooperativeness of the peer, as some users are willing to contribute more resources than others. For this reason, *altruistic users* will stay online longer and offer more resources, e.g., files, to the network, while other *strategic users* will try to minimize their contribution. A model can further include *malicious users* who try to break the systems specification. There are many works dealing with the strategies of the users, such as [251].

User properties are very specific to the used application, which makes it difficult to discuss them in a general way. Nonetheless, in most cases user properties simply influence other aspects of the user's behavior, e.g., online time, resources, and requests. Thus, it is generally a good idea to model user properties on top of the churn and workload models.

20.6   Use Case: Kademlia

In this subsection we analyze how to model realistic user behavior for distributed hash tables in order to evaluate the performance of the Kademlia overlay routing protocol. Kademlia is probably the most popular DHT routing overlay, used in large-scale file sharing applications such as the different BitTorrent clients or the eMule client. It differs from other DHTs in two aspects: its large routing table that makes it more resilient to churn and the usage of the symmetric XOR metric, that creates a local tree view of the overlay for each peer.

As a generic DHT Kademlia has many use cases. We consider a file-sharing application in which the DHT is used to locate files offered by peers using a file ID. That results in rare lookup and store requests because users only use the DHT while searching for file sources but not within the actual file transfer. For example, in eMule KAD [447], a variant of Kademlia protocol is used.

In the BitTorrent [103] derivative Azureus[1], Kademlia is used as a decentralized alternative to a centralized tracker. Here the peers can obtain the addresses of other peers downloading the same file and publish their own addresses.

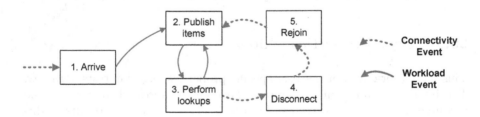

Fig. 20.3: User activities in a DHT. The events that cause the change the current activities are differentiated by the responsible component.

The general activity diagram of a Kademlia user is shown in Figure 20.3. At peer's arrival the Kademlia join procedure takes place. In the two following

---

[1] www.azureus.com

Component	Model
resources model	Zipf distributed popularity
request model	Zipf distributed popularity
lifetime model	constant arrival intervals
	exponential arrival intervals
session model	exponentially distributed sessions and intersessions
	Weibull distributed sessions/intersessions based
	Global (Poisson) leave rate with peer replacement
	no churn (for comparison)
departure rate	no permanent departure
user type model	simple user model
lookup rate (per peer)	1 lookup each 10 minutes

Table 20.1: Kademlia modeling parameters

phases, lookups and store operations are executed. Here especially the lookup rate and distribution are timed by the applied workload.

The arrival, leave and join events are timed by the churn component. If a peer goes offline then it cancels all running queries. Upon a peer's return to the system the workload component takes over the control of the peer and issues new publish and lookup operations. It further specifies the objects (representing any kind of resources to be published and looked up) available in the system together with their popularity and replication.

The following most useful characteristics for modeling user behavior in DHTs:

– Peer arrival rate: this one is important from two points of view: the initial creation of the network and the avoidance of event synchronization across peers. The latter might happen because of periodic maintenance operations running in the background (see Section 20.3.1) .
– Join and leave events: Performance of a DHT depends on the quality of the routing tables. Stale contacts in the table might cause expensive lookup timeouts and even the lookup success rate can degrade.
– Lookup/store activity: Bulk requests can overload peers responsible for popular content. Furthermore, Kademlia tries to minimize the maintenance overhead by refreshing routing tables during regular lookup operations. If there are no user requests over certain time intervals, active probing is done that increases maintenance overhead.
– Resources distribution, replication and popularity: Different popularity of content will distribute the load in the system unevenly. Also, resources with a low replication factor might become unavailable under churn and result in failed lookups.

20.7   Evaluation

In this section we analyze the impact of user behavior on the performance of the Kademlia protocol. Table 20.1 lists the different components of user behavior under consideration. We focus on the impact of churn being the main issue for the performance of search overlays. In detail, we compare the impact of varying churn setups: different churn models as introduced in Section 20.3 and the impact of single parameters: network size, session and intersession durations.

20.7.1   Methodology

Our simulation platform for the experiments is the discrete event-based simulator PeerfactSim.KOM[2]. The simulator offers a generic framework for different overlays and network models. We use the implementation of the Kademlia routing protocol with the basic setup as shown in Table 20.2.

Parameter	Value	Description
ID-Length	80	length of Kademlia id space
b	2	order of the routing tree
k	10	number of contacts per bucket
refresh-interval	1 hour	routing table refresh interval
α	3	number of concurrent messages
republish-interval	1 hour	how often the items are republished

Table 20.2: Kademlia setup

In order to estimate the impact of user behavior on overlay routing the following metrics are used:

- **Routing table quality** measured as the ratio of fresh contacts, i.e., contacts that are online at the given time. This metric is measured globally for all peers in periodic intervals of 5 minutes.
- **Success rate** determines the ratio of lookups being able to find the desired objects. The success rate is aggregated over intervals of 5 minutes. A lookup can fail either if the object is not available at online peers or the peers holding the object are not found by the routing protocol due to the inconsistency of routing tables.
- **Dropped messages per peer** reflects the impact of stale (offline) contacts in the routing tables. Overlay messages in Kademlia are sent via UDP and, hence, get dropped if the destination peer is offline.

---

[2] www.peerfactsim.org

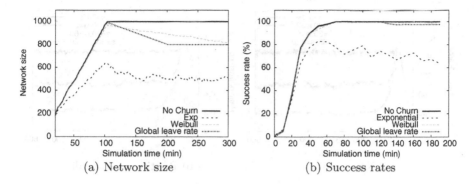

(a) Network size   (b) Success rates

Fig. 20.4: Impact of churn model on performance.

20.7.2   Setup 1: Fixed Network Size, Variable Session Models

At first we evaluate the impact of the session model used on the system performance. The following models are considered:

- Exponentially distributed session and intersession durations (see Section 20.3.2). Both the session and intersession rates are set to 0.05 events per minute (accordingly the means are 20 minutes each).
- Weibull distributed session and intersession durations (following the measurements of Steiner et al. in [441]). The Weibull distribution parameters scale and shape are set to 169.5385 and 0.61511 for session durations. The parameters for the intersession durations are set to 413.6765 and 0.47648 respectively.
- Global leave rate with peer replacement (see Section 20.3.2). Here the rate of leave events is set to 10 events per minute and the target network size to 800 peers.
- No churn for comparison. Here all peers are online once they arrived in the system.

The network sizes of each model during the simulation run are shown in Figure 20.4(a). As we can see here, depending on the distribution size the actual number of online peers is different. Most of them are similar, ranging between 800 and 1000 peers once the network is built up. Only the exponential churn model has different network sizes. For the exponential model with short session durations (both session and intersession means are set to 20 minutes) the network size oscillates around the expected mean of $\frac{N \cdot mean_s}{mean_s + mean_i} = \frac{1000 \cdot 20}{20 + 20} = 500$ peers.

For the model with a global leave rate the network size reaches the target size of 800 peers after 200 minutes. Here 100 minutes are required for all 1000 peers to arrive at the system and 100 more minutes to reach the desired

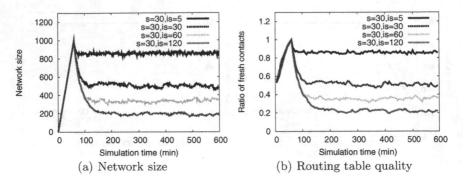

(a) Network size   (b) Routing table quality

Fig. 20.5: Impact of varying intersession durations (**is** = {5, 30, 60, 120} minutes)
with the fixed session duration (**s** = 30 minutes).

network size of 800 peers. Later the network size stays unchanged, because
each leaving peer is immediately replaced by an offline peer.

Figure 20.4(b) presents the impact of the churn model used on the success
rate. For most of the models no significant difference is visible except the
exponential session model, where the success rate degrades dramatically. The
explanation is that because of the high churn rate, some objects become
unavailable and therefore the lookups for these objects fail. We conclude
that the impact of the network size is more relevant than the actual model
being used.

20.7.3   Setup 2: Fixed Session Duration, Variable Intersession Duration

In order to evaluate the impact of intersession duration times on the overlay
performance we fix the model to the exponential session model and vary
the intersession durations. Four different values are used: 5, 30, 60, and 120
minutes. Figure 20.5(a) shows the network sizes for each of them. We can
see that after the arrival process is finished the system reaches the expected
size and the curve oscillates slightly. The quality of routing tables (shown in
Figure 20.5(b)) reflects the network size. For example, the network size of 500
peers out of 1000 available (curve **s=30, is=30**) results in the fresh contact
ratio of roughly 50%.

20.7.4   Setup 3: Fixed Network Size, Variable Event Rate

Furthermore, we analyzed the impact of varying online and offline event
rates for the constant connectivity factor. Because the equation for connec-
tivity $c = \frac{mean_s}{mean_s + mean_{is}}$ applies we obtain $mean_s = \frac{mean_{is}}{1-c}$. We fix the

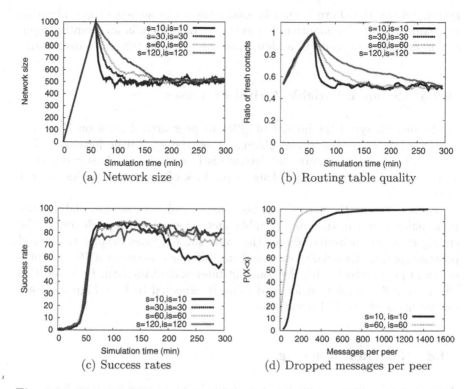

Fig. 20.6: Impact of varying intersession (**is**) and session duration (**s**) with the fixed network size of 500 peers.

connectivity factor to 0.5 and therefore obtain equal durations for the session and intersession intervals.

The experiments conducted have expected interval durations of 10, 30, 60, and 120 minutes for both sessions and intersessions. Hence, the expected network size is $0.5 \cdot 1000 = 500$ peers.

As shown in Figure 20.6(a) the network sizes are very similar. Similarly, the quality of routing tables is around 50%. (see Figure 20.6(b)). However, the success rate is very differently as shown in Figure 20.6(c). It drops significantly if the intersession durations are cut to 10 minutes. Here the global leave rate is $500 \cdot \frac{1}{5} = 100$ events per minute and reduces the success rate from 80 to 60%. We further observe that session times of 10 minutes result in an unstable success rate.

Additionally, 20.6(d) presents the distribution of dropped messages in the network per peer for the two extreme setups. We observe that this metric also suffer under high churn rates.

The direct implication of these results is that the replication rate has to be adjusted to the churn rate in order to assure successful lookups. In a real system where, the churn cannot be easily known in advance the replication mechanism has to be adaptive. For example, in Kademlia an adaptive replication factor k can result in a high recall rate without too much overhead.

20.7.5   Setup 4: Variable Arrival Processes

We further analyzed the impact of different peer arrival rates on Kademlia but found them having a negligible effect on the system performance. The alternatives compared were the deterministic and the stochastic processes as described in Section 20.3.1. Due to the lack of space the graphs are not shown.

Even if during the arrival process a part of objects is unavailable, once their holders arrive, the routing tables get repaired quickly. Hence, in the steady state we measured almost the same success rates despite the arrival process applied. Especially, we found no difference between a Poisson process and peer arrivals with the constant inter-arrival interval. However, this effect, even if not relevant for Kademlia, is expected to have higher impact on systems such as BitTorrent [103].

20.8   Further Reading

A substantial number of work exists on modeling of user behavior for single P2P overlays, such as Gnutella and DHTs. Herrera et al. proposed a group-based model [202] to model churn in a P2P system, where peers are divided into three groups, benefactors, peers and peepers, showing different characteristics regarding their session and intersession lengths. The modeling is based on the *connectivity factor*, that specifies the fraction of all available peers being online at any given point of time. This value is probabilistic, because the session and intersession times of peers are probabilistic and therefore fluctuate around the desired network size defined by the connectivity factor. This connectivity factor is computed by $C_f = \frac{OS}{OS+IS}$ where OS is the average session length and IS is the average intersession length.

The performance of different Distributed Hash Tables (DHTs) under churn was analyzed by Rhea et al. [388]. Here additionally to the churn the arrival process, i.e., with which rate and distribution the peers connect to the system is considered. This model is suitable especially for search overlays and we use it for comparison. The interesting property of the churn model applied, is that it allows a stable size of the network, i.e., the number of peers being online is constant during the simulation time. This is achieved by replacing each peer going offline by another peer connecting to the network immediately. This is different to pure probabilistic models and allows more control of the simulation parameters.

A work on DHTs with mobile participants [519] distinguishes churn behavior for heterogeneous networks, including mobile peers. Such peers might use mobile phones for Internet access and therefore show much higher churn rates due to expensive online access and failure rate. The modeling here is based on peer classes with different mean online times, failure probabilities, number of shared objects and average query rate.

Specific models can be applied for applications such as Gnutella, where the query circle model was introduced by Schlosser et al. [405]. They focus mostly on the query inter-arrival times and content popularity. Another work on Gnutella from Aggarwal et al. [26] concentrates on the impact of realistic and extreme user behavior types on the system. In their model, content replication, session length and query strings are considered.

Andreolini et al. characterized the resources distributed in Gnutella network [37], especially the file types (video, audio, archives), their sizes and popularity distributions.

20.9   Conclusions

In this chapter, we have studied the modeling of user behavior when simulating P2P systems. We presented modeling alternatives to represent the user behavior in a P2P system. As an example, we showed how it can be applied to Distributed Hash Tables.

We studied and demonstrated the impact of different modeling approaches using Kademlia as use case. In particular, arrival rates and churn have significant impact on the system performance resulting in diverging drop and success rates.

21. Modeling Security Aspects of Networks

Elmar Schoch (Ulm University)

21.1 Introduction

With more and more widespread usage of computer systems and networks, dependability becomes a paramount requirement. Dependability typically denotes tolerance or protection against all kinds of failures, errors and faults. Sources of failures can basically be accidental, e.g., in case of hardware errors or software bugs, or intentional due to some kind of malicious behavior. These intentional, malicious actions are subject of *security*. A more complete overview on the relations between dependability and security can be found in [31]. In parallel to the increased use of technology, misuse also has grown significantly, requiring measures to deal with it.

Generally, security can be seen from different perspectives. For instance, looking from an attacker's perspective, one can investigate attack motivation, attack technique, attack target etc. From the opposite, it is important to know about potential threats, which security goals need to be fulfilled and how security measures can be implemented. Table 21.1 lists important security goals and corresponding threats.

At first glance, the link between simulation and security is difficult to see. Security work mostly consists of penetration testing, bug fixes and software updates, code reviews, policies, system hardening, monitoring etc. Hence, the question is how simulation can help research on security? The answer to this question is included in the basic motivation why we use simulation generally: whenever it is too costly, not repeatable, too dangerous or simply impossible to do the same in real world, simulation can be an alternative. A typical case is that a fully deployed system comprises so many active instances that it is very hard to create a reliable testbed. For example, consider a wireless ad hoc network with hundreds or thousands of nodes.

One field of application for security simulation is to get insight how attacks affect the overall system, such as a complex network [336]. This may comprise a detailed understanding of the attack in progress or an analysis of the *impact of an attack*. For instance, the impact of a denial of service attack on a load-balancing system could be simulated. This can help to estimate potential damage as well as the likelihood of an attack. If the simulation results show that only few stations are needed to bring down the load balancer, the attack is much more likely than an attack with thousands of hosts involved.

Another usage of simulation considers experimentation during the design of security measures. First, the effectiveness of a security mechanism against

Goal	Threat
Authenticity	Identity theft
Integrity	Manipulation
Availability	Denial of service
Privacy, Confidentiality	Eavesdropping
Access Control	Intrusion
Non-repudiation, Liability	Impersonation

Table 21.1: Security Goals and Threats

an attack can be tested, and second, one can get insight on the additional efforts it introduces.

21.2   Role of Modeling and Simulation in Security Research

Dealing with security is a very widespread and multi-faceted field of work. One of the first steps usually comprises an overview on the system to inspect and an assessment of goals and risks. This delivers a rough picture of elements to protect. Based on that, one typically has to consider practically all parts of a system regarding their strengths and weaknesses. Then, one also has to adopt the viewpoint of an attacker and elaborate on potential goals and subsequent attacks on the system. With all that knowledge, one can start to think about measures to be integrated into the system, which help to prevent attacks or to mitigate the effect of attacks. However, often attackers also adapt their behavior to new preconditions and thus, the circle has to go another round.

Figure 21.1 shows an overview on the described procedure, from the perspective of simulation. This section first gives an introduction, what elements of security research can be modeled and how this fits into the overall simulation world. Another relevant aspect are the different kinds of metrics that the models deliver during a simulation. Finally, the discussion also names elements of security work that simulation cannot be used for.

21.2.1   Security Models

The typical starting point for security research is a security problem — which is mostly part of an existing system or a system under development. Hence, the first step towards simulation is to model the system itself. Models that are used in simulation basically are a simplified imitation of the real behavior of a certain portion of the system to be simulated. A (partial) simulation of a system comprises many single models. For example, in case of wireless ad

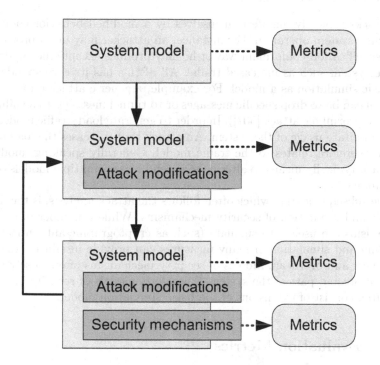

Fig. 21.1: Overview on process, involved models and metrics in simulation of
security

hoc networks, one has to model the environment (such as obstacles, signal propagation, etc.) and the network participants (movement, physical signal transmission, medium access, routing protocols, applications and so on).

As depicted in Figure 21.1, the next step towards simulation of security is to introduce attacks on the system. To thwart the attacks and their impact, security measures follow the attacks. Hence, simulation of security adds two additional model dimensions to the general system modeling:

− *Modeling of attacks*
− *Modeling of security measures*

Attacks typically manifest themselves by a modified behavior compared to normal system operation. For instance, an attacker may use a protocol in a not specification-conformant way or he may produce exceptional conditions for the system such as increased traffic. All of this has its correspondent in the basic simulation as a model. For example, a generic attack on a routing protocol can be to drop specific messages or to tunnel messages to a colluding attacker (wormhole attack [507]). In order to generate load, traffic models are used to imitate usage of the system. An attack that increases the load of the system therefore relates to the traffic model. Generally speaking, modeling an attack typically means to alter or to extend one or multiple models of the base simulation.

The subsequent step, which often follows the attack analysis, is the development and evaluation of security mechanisms. While a number of security mechanisms are useless to simulate (such as cryptographic authentication), modeling and simulation of many measures can provide insight on their effectiveness and overhead. Models of security mechanisms often closely relate to the protected part of the system. Therefore, models of security measures also often consist of extensions of the basic simulation model.

21.3   Evaluation Metrics

Evaluating the system from the security point of view can be a three-step approach, just like the development of models for attacks and countermeasures.

21.3.1   Normal System Operation

The first step is to simulate the system without attack. The models of the system deliver numerous metrics that subsequently serve as basis for comparison. For example, one can measure average delivery success, delay, throughput etc. in a wireless ad hoc network.

21.3.2   System under Attack

The simulation of a system under attack uses both, regular models and modified attacker models. From the usual metrics of the system, it is possible to draw conclusions on the impact of the attack on the overall system. As an output of two simulations, one normal and one including attack model(s), these metrics can be compared and thus, the influence of the attack can be estimated. In the example of the ad hoc network and an attack that disturbs correct routing, one probably observes reduced delivery success or longer delay. Moreover, more specific metrics can reveal the reason why an attack is successful or not and therefore deliver more insight on potential security measures.

21.3.3   System under Attack with Activated Security Measures

The outcome of such an attack analysis may subsequently be used during the design of security mechanisms to thwart attacks. Again, security mechanisms mostly modify or extend existing system models in order to secure the system against attacks. As a third step, one can conduct simulations of that including the attack model as well as the secured system component models.

One can distinguish the following metrics derived out of step three:

- Regular system performance metrics
- Explicit security mechanism metrics
  e.g., detection success of attacks, false positives of an intrusion detection system, metrics on achieved level of privacy/entropy
- Overhead of security mechanisms
  e.g., additional processing load, additional network load

Like before, system-immanent metrics deliver indications on the effectiveness of the introduced security mechanisms. In an ideal case, the attack has no impact on the system any more when security mechanisms are active, i.e., the normal system operation can be kept up. In addition, specifics metrics deliver information on the security mechanisms itself. For example, many security mechanisms also have their drawbacks such as false detections of attacks or additional overhead. If the system creates a "false alarm" (or false positive), the performance or the user experience can be affected. If messages are cryptographically authenticated, it may be required to compute, transport, and verify the signature of a message The computational overhead for asymmetric cryptographic operations can potentially exceed the capabilities of small devices.

In summary, the metrics delivered by the simulation can be used to optimize the security of the system.

21.4   Discussion

While many attacks and security measures can be simulated using modified or extended models, there are other issues of security which can hardly be addressed by simulation or which do not make sense to simulate.

The models hard to simulate are often related to specific real world phenomena. For example, when the user of a system is the initial target of an attack, like in social engineering attacks, a sophisticated model of the user would be required. In the simplest case, this is an empirical model where the user is tricked by an attack with a certain probability. However, in fact, so many real world factors influence the effectiveness of such an attack that it is hard to give an appropriate number for such a probability. Another example of such highly real world dependent attacks are exploits of implementation flaws such as buffer overflows. It would not make sense to model such an attack in detail, because one could simply assume success of such an attack in a certain percentage.

Like with attacks, some security measures that should be taken to secure a system can hardly be simulated. For example, the security of a server not only depends on the software that it is running, but also on the availability of a safe place. If the server can simply be shut down by a power outage or by physical destruction, the overall system is not secure. However, such security measures of course cannot be included in a simulation.

Besides these issues, there is often no need for accurate models of security measures. *Cryptographic functions* play a vital role in many security mechanisms, e.g., to encrypt data or to sign data. Their computational footprint is very expensive, i.e., they often require complex calculations. Simulating the complete calculation of the cryptographic operations is not needed, since simulation may simply assume a correct calculation of a cryptographic function.

Another issue for the simulation of security is the cyclic nature of attacks and corresponding countermeasures. Typically, security measures are introduced to cope with some specific attacks. Then, attackers may adapt their behavior and mount more sophisticated attacks. Based on these attacks, improved security measures are likely to be added and so on. Game theoretic models of attack and countermeasures investigate this cycle of adaption. Such an approach would require intelligent and self-adapting models of attackers and security measures, which is currently not feasible with simulation.

Beyond that, modeling security for simulation has the same typical problems of simulation in general. One of them is the credibility of a model, particularly regarding attacker models. Because there are so many different potential attacks and attack sequences, it is hard to set up an equally concise and wide-ranged attacker model.

21.5   Summary

Simulation can be very beneficial for security assessment and development. Particularly in very large and complex systems, other approaches (Markov models, Petri nets, etc.) come to their limits. Simulations can be used to quantify the impact of attacks. Based on the insight, specific security solutions can be developed and also verified against the attack models. Often, a three-step approach is useful, comparing normal system operation with the system behavior under attack, and with the results when security measures are applied.

Nevertheless, simulation of security struggles with the same issues that simulation has in general. Therefore, conclusions from simulation results must be drawn carefully as well.

22. Modeling the Network Topology

Matthias Wählisch (FU Berlin & HAW Hamburg)

22.1 Introduction

Network topologies are one major building block for data communication. They describe how network entities are directly interconnected with each other and thus define how information *may* flow. Such a structure of node relations can be built on different layers resulting in a physical or logical topology. The first will be constructed while connecting devices by a physical medium. On top of this structure, data exchange can be arranged via the network and application layer creating a logical or overlay topology.

Network communication depends on its underlying structure. This drives protocol performance, and has impact on routing behavior and complexity. Choosing an appropriate topology for simulations, analytical studies, or experiments is an important task. As a simple example consider Figure 22.1(a) and 22.1(b). Both scenarios represent a local area network that connects end devices via routers to the Internet, but differ in topological properties. Protocol evaluation thus may lead to completely different results. For instance, failover mechanisms of a routing protocol cannot be observed for a setting shown in Figure 22.1(a), as redundant paths are not available to bridge broken connections.

The network topology and its properties are important ingredients for protocol and system evaluation. They should be chosen characteristic of the problem under observation. Thus, the first step in selecting an appropriate topology is to clarify the scenario, in which the protocol will operate. In many cases, though, the characteristic properties of the underlying network are unknown or only vaguely specified. For this reason, there is a tendency to enrich topology modeling by network measurement. However, working with real data especially for large, evolving networks such as the Internet cause specific problems. First, it is an intricate task to retrieve real data for such structures. Second, every measurement represents only a snapshot, which may quickly obsolete. Moreover, sets of realistically large sizes may be difficult to process with currently available memory and CPU cycles. Thus, instead of applying the problem to a dedicated network topology, the corresponding topology space should be explored.

In this chapter, we will introduce some common topology models. The remainder is structured as follows: We present the basic abstraction principle for network topologies in Section 22.2, and explain how network models can

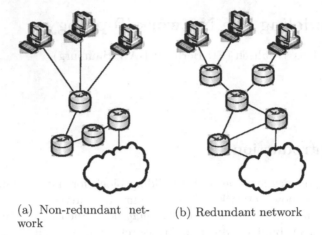

(a) Non-redundant net-   (b) Redundant network
work

Fig. 22.1: Different network topologies

be characterized in Section 22.3. Section 22.4 describes basic topology models. Finally, we discuss approaches to model the Internet in Section 22.5.

22.2   Abstraction of Network Topologies by Graphs

Physical and logical topologies consist of entities which are in a relationship with each other. In most networks, these entities represent different types. The topology of a computer network, for example, includes end hosts linked to switches (layer 2) connected via routers (layer 3), cf. Figure 22.2(a). In this chapter, we address the modeling of the resulting structures, i.e., the network.

The modeling process includes several levels of abstraction. A network topology model forms the structural properties of the network. Dedicated instances of network devices such as different types of routers, switches, or end system nodes are neglected based on unification (cf. Figure 22.2(a)). The second step 'eliminates' all entities that are transparent to the layer under observation and subsumes devices. In our example, we focus on the local routing structure. Thus, switches will be omitted and end devices can be merged to a domain represented by a single entity (cf. Figure 22.2(b)). At this stage, our network includes routers, end user domains, and an inter-network connection. From a structural point of view, the inter-network connection as illustrated does not include any further information. The last step transforms

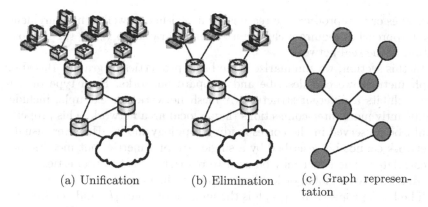

(a) Unification   (b) Elimination   (c) Graph represen-
                                          tation

Fig. 22.2: Abstraction process of network topologies

the concrete network in an abstract graph representation (cf. Figure 22.2(c)). Nodes and links equal *edges* and *vertices*, respectively.[1]

A graph G is a set of vertices connected via edges. The set of vertices is usually denoted by V, and the set of edges by E. Edges may be directed or undirected, and hence allow to model uni- and bidirectional, as well as symmetric and asymmetric links. Figure 22.2(c) shows an undirected graph. Vertices and edges can be extended by attributes, e.g., weighted edges, which represent link costs. Each vertex possesses an inherent structural property: its *degree*, usually denoted by k. The degree of a node is the number of its connections (which equal its number of nearest neighbors). In the case of directed edges, the degree can be split in in- and out-degree.

The degree property enables the indirect modeling of different node types. Considering the example in Figure 22.2, an end user domain has been merged to a single vertex. The inner structure of such domains is not under consideration, and they are connected to a single router. Consequently, the domains can be identified by vertices with a degree of 1. This simplification does not allow the modeling of multi-homed or redundant sites.

Typically, the characterization of a dedicated vertex is not very helpful and does not reflect the whole graph (or network). In the following, we describe properties of the complete graph.

22.3   Characterizing Graphs

The graph model can be based on two approaches: ad-hoc and measurement-based. An ad-hoc model is developed independently of real measurements. In contrast to this, a measurement-based model tries to reconstruct graph

---

[1] In the following, we will use both, the network engineering and graph term, interchangeably.

properties or to reproduce the reasons for it. Ad-hoc as well as measurement-based approaches require a characterization of graphs to verify the approximation of the real network.

In this section, we summarize some basic properties of graphs. Based on graph metrics, we can describe and compare networks. Each type of network exhibits a different structure. A mesh network, for example, includes significantly more inter-connections than a local area network. This property should be preserved in the corresponding topology model. However, usually a network cannot be described by a single (simple) metric, but metrics may be correlated. The latter may be used to restrict the set of properties.

Metrics have a global or local meaning for the graph.

The basic property of a graph is the number of edges $|E|$ and vertices $|V|$. For an undirected graph, it follows the average node degree $\langle k \rangle$ by $\langle k \rangle = 2|E|/|V|$. More significant (and often used) is the degree distribution $P(k)$, which calculates the probability that a randomly selected node has degree k. We denote the number of nodes with degree k by $n(k)$, then:

$$P(k) = \frac{n(k)}{|V|} \tag{22.1}$$

It is worth noting that based on this probability distribution the average value $\langle k \rangle$ can be evaluated. In this case, $\langle k \rangle = \sum_{k=0}^{k_{max}} k \cdot P(k)$.

Equation 22.1 calculates the degree distribution for a general instance of a network. Several realizations of networks may belong to the same (statistical) class of graphs that admit equal distributions. There are three common degree distributions [122]:[2]

Poisson distribution

$$P(k) = e^{-\langle k \rangle} \cdot \frac{\langle k \rangle^k}{k!}$$

Exponential distribution

$$P(k) \propto e^{-k/\langle k \rangle}$$

Power-law distribution

$$P(k) \propto k^{-\gamma}, k \neq 0, \gamma > 0$$

A closer insight into the interconnection properties of the graphs is given by the joint degree distribution. This correlation law defines the probability that a randomly selected edge connects nodes with degree k_1 and k_2. Let $m(k_1, k_2)$ denote the number of edges out of the total $|E|$ edges that connect two nodes of degrees k_1 and k_2 in an undirected graph. Then the correctly normalized joint degree distribution is calculated as

---

[2] The symbol $\propto$ means "proportional to".

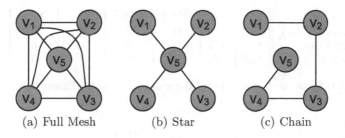

| (a) Full Mesh | (b) Star | (c) Chain |

Fig. 22.3: Three extreme graph topologies

$$P(k_1, k_2) = \frac{m(k_1, k_2)}{2|E|}$$

It does not only describe the one hop neighborhood structure of an average k-degree node, but can also be used to derive other well-known measures [333], [303]. Note that the single node degree distribution $P(k)$ does not directly follow from integration, but requires a bias correction factor, i.e., $P(k) \propto \sum_j P(k, j)/k$.

Delay sensitive applications or routing protocols are affected by the number of intermediate nodes between the source and destination. They adjust buffers or decide on a forwarding path based on the distance between nodes. The distance between two nodes is the length of the *shortest path* between them. In graph theory, this class of paths is also called geodesic. The distance distribution $d(x)$ measures the probability that two randomly selected nodes are connected via distance x, which typically is calculated in hops. The length of the longest shortest path taken over all pairs of nodes is called diameter of a graph, but in general the metric is not well-defined. In some publications, the diameter describes the average shortest path length [122], as well.

The average shortest path length $\langle d \rangle$ for an undirected graph is quantified as follows: Let $d(i, j)$ denote the distance of a shortest path between the two nodes i and j, then the normalized average path length is given by:

$$\langle d \rangle = \frac{2}{|V|(|V| - 1)} \cdot \sum_{i \neq j} d(i, j)$$

In any forwarding scenario, intermediate nodes between source and receiver attain a distinct role. The number of shortest paths passing through a node m (or link) is quantified by the metric betweenness $B(m)$. To calculate the relative amount, we count all shortest paths between any two nodes passing m, and divide this by the number of shortest paths of all node pairs excluding m. Thus, if the total number of shortest paths between two nodes i and j is $B(i, j)$, and the number of these paths going through m is $B(i, m, j)$, than the betweenness of m is defined as follows [122], [158]:

Figure	$\langle k \rangle$	$\langle d \rangle$	$B(v_1)$	$B(v_2)$	$B(v_3)$	$B(v_4)$	$B(v_5)$
Full Mesh 22.3(a)	4	1	0	0	0	0	0
Star 22.3(b)	8/5	8/5	0	0	0	0	6
Chain 22.3(c)	8/5	2	0	3	4	3	0

Table 22.1: Structural properties of the graphs shown in Figure 22.3

$$B(m) = \sum_{i \neq m \neq j, i \neq j} \frac{B(i, m, j)}{B(i, j)}$$

Betweenness is a common metric in the context of traffic engineering, or social networks. This measurement quantifies the importance of a node in information exchange, and the load on such intermediate vertex. Assuming uniformly distributed traffic that follows shortest paths, the traffic passing through a node coincides with its betweenness. For comparison of different sized, directed networks, the betweenness of nodes and edges can be normalized by $(|V| - 1)(|V| - 2)$ and $(|V|(|V| - 1))$, respectively [158].[3] Note that undirected graphs require an additional dividing factor of 2. The calculation of the betweenness in unweighted and weighted networks requires $O(|V||E|)$ and $O(|V||E| + |V|^2 \log(|V|))$ time, respectively, consuming $O(|V| + |E|)$ of memory [80].

Networks agreeing on one property may still differ in others. Table 22.1 presents the average node degree, the mean path length, and the betweenness for nodes of the graphs shown in Figure 22.3. For example, a star and a chain topology with the same number of nodes exhibit the same average node degree. Nevertheless, both topologies differ significantly in their robustness against attacks (average distance), and in their characteristic traffic flow per node (betweenness). In the case of a full mesh, the betweenness reveals that no vertex attains a dedicated role in the forwarding process. On the other hand, the central entity in the star topology can be identified easily.

22.4   Common Topology Models

In this section, we want to address the question of how to construct a graph that satisfy specific properties.

22.4.1   Random Graphs

The basic random graph model, and the corresponding theory have been derived by Erdős and Rényi [134, 135]. A random graph, which is also called

---

[3] The maximum value of betweenness is $|V|(|V| - 1)$. For simplification, some authors use this for normalization of node and link betweenness [303].

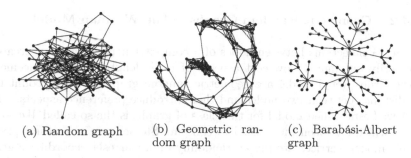

(a) Random graph   (b) Geometric ran-   (c) Barabási-Albert
dom graph   graph

Fig. 22.4: Visualization of differently generated topologies

Erdős-Rényi-graph, will be constructed as follows: Given a fixed number
of nodes and a probability p, then each edge between two vertices will be
constructed independently with probability p. The pseudocode is presented
in RANDOM GRAPH ALGORITHM:

RANDOM GRAPH ALGORITHM n, p
  ▷ A denotes the adjacency matrix of G with n vertices
  ▷ p denotes the probability that two arbitrary vertices are connected
  ▷ getRandom() returns uniformly distributed a number over $[0, 1]$
1 **for** all $0 \leq i, j \leq n - 1$
2   **do** $A_{i,j} \leftarrow 0$
3 **for** all $0 \leq i, j \leq n - 1$
4   **do if** $p \leq$ getRandom()
5   **then** $A_{i,j} \leftarrow 1$
6 **return** A

Another variant of the Erdős-Rényi-graph considers a fixed number of
edges: Given the set of all graphs that have n vertices and m edges, one is
uniformly selected. Both models generate a class of graphs with equal statistical degree properties. For large n, the random graph exhibits a Poisson
degree distribution. All connections are distributed with equal probability
over node pairs. Consequently, the classical random graph does not model
clustering properties, which makes it almost unsuitable for implementing realistic networks. However, there are contributions on generalizing the random
graph to correct these issues [334]. Detailed mathematical background in the
theory of random graphs is presented in [67].

It is worth noting that the following construction procedure does *not*
reflect the random graph model: Consider all graphs of a fixed number of
vertices. They differ in numbers and combinations of edges, and attain topologies of differing degree properties. Choosing random elements from this set
of graphs, will not lead to an unbiased sample of random graph. For example, the graph with no edges, or the full mesh topology represent a single
instance. The selection process is thus inherently biased preferring graphs
with the maximal number of link combinations.

22.4.2   Geometric Random Graphs – The Waxman Model

Physical connections between nodes of a computer network are not created arbitrarily but may follow cost aspects of cable lengths. An enhancement of the Erdős-Rényi-model are geometric random graphs. They account for the distance between two nodes and thus introduce preference aspects. The most well-established model for this class of graphs is the so called *Waxman graph*, which has been introduced to compare Steiner tree algorithms [489]. In this model, vertices are placed randomly on a Cartesian coordinate grid; the probability P that an edge connects two nodes u, v depends on their Euclidean distance $d(u,v)$:

$$P(u,v) = \beta \cdot e^{-d(u,v)/L\alpha}, \ 0 < \alpha, \beta \leq 1$$

L denotes the maximal distance of two vertices. An increasing β increases the edge density. A decreasing α reduces the ratio of long to short edges. Based on these parameters, we can also adjust the average node degree. The Waxman graph is an appropriate model for small networks that include locality aspects.

22.4.3   Hierarchical Topologies

Larger computer networks typically consist of several levels. Hierarchical models decompose the network into tiers, e.g., transit domains connect stub domains that connect local area networks (LANs) [86]. The general idea is that each tier is represented by multiple graphs with identical properties. For this purpose a $2d$–grid is divided into separate sub-regions with a scaling dependent on the network type. This approach allows for inherent support by Waxman graphs. LANs are modeled as star. Sub-regions are connected step by step following a top–down creation process. The properties of constructing a network rely on the (sub–)graph models in use.

There are two common, basic hierarchical models in the context of computer networks: The *Transit–Stub* [511] and *Tiers* [120] model. The transit–stub graph supports two tiers, and node labels contain hierarchical information. Edges are associated with policy weights. In contrast, the Tier model supports a three level hierarchy. All nodes in a single domain are connected by a minimum spanning tree algorithm. Inter-domain connections are based on the Waxman model.

22.4.4   Preferential Linking – The Barabási-Albert Model

A preferential linking model implements the key concept that highly connected vertices are likely to become even more connected. The first model combining network evolution and preferential linking is the Barabási-Albert model [49]. Motivated by their analysis of the web link structure, Barabási and Albert observed that complex networks evolve continuously by the emergence of additional vertices, and that new vertices prefer the establishment of links with already well-connected vertices. Let k_i denote the degree of node i, then the probability P that a new vertex attaches to i is:

$$P(k_i) = \frac{k_i}{\sum_j k_j}$$

The basic construction algorithm works as follows: Starting with m_0 connected vertices, and a predefined fixed degree k, at each time step a new k–degree vertex l is added and linked with probability $P(k_l)$ to j randomly selected, already existing different vertices. An extended version including a rewiring option has been presented in [30].

All new nodes follow the same weight in preferential attachment. To dynamically adjust the weight of the preference, the Generalized Linear Preference Model (GLP) has been introduced with a weighting parameter β [82]:

$$P(k_i) = \frac{k_i - \beta}{\sum_j (k_j - \beta)}, \text{ with } \beta \in (-\infty, 1)$$

This model addresses representative path length and clustering. Both, the Barabási-Albert model and the GLP model exhibit a power law degree distribution.

22.4.5 Intermediate Results

Based on the models presented so far, we can create random topologies without clustering, networks that reflect preferences in locality or popularity, and hierarchical structures. Hierarchical models typically inherit properties from sub-models. The random graph, the Waxman model, and Transit-Stub as well as Tiers model can be summarized as ad-hoc models, which are typically inappropriate for large-scale, evolving networks. The Barabási-Albert model is an example for measurement-driven approaches trying to reproduce empirically observed properties of real-world structures.

Figure 22.4 visualizes the (geometric) random graph as well as the Barabási-Albert model. This illustration tries to give some intuition behind these models. However, it is worth noting that the same instance of a graph may be drawn differently resulting in quite different pictures. A graph should not be identified based on its visual structure but on its measurable properties.

22.5   Modeling the Internet

In this section, we focus on the modeling of the Internet topology. The Internet is a multi-tier network, which involves communicating components of the applications down to the network, and even the physical layer. Referring to the Internet topology means looking at the structure that is responsible for packet forwarding. We thus exclude structures such as the World Wide Web graph [359, 149].

22.5.1   Background

The term Internet topology is not well-defined. The Internet consists of edge domains (or access networks) connected to at least one router, which may serve several IP networks. Such an access router is typically part of a larger domain, consolidating multiple IP prefixes. Routers administrated by a single authority are aggregated within an *Autonomous System* (AS). Border routers of ASes peer with each other. Routing within ASes may follow different protocols, routing between ASes is based on a single protocol, currently BGP [386]. In contrast to *intra-domain routing*, *inter-domain routing* need not follow shortest path selection, but economical or political rules, for example. Peering between ASes may be private, or publicly located at Internet Exchange Points (IXPs). An AS of an Internet Service Provider (*ISP*) that agrees to accept and forward traffic to other ISPs, but does not run own access networks, is called a transit domain.

Modeling the Internet topology implies the choice of granularity, i.e., the type of resolved entities (the AS-level, router-level or IP-level), or a combination. Augmenting an AS structure with access networks (router-level networks) is not trivial as autonomous systems are not homogeneous and the inner structures may differ. Autonomous systems can be classified by administrative categories or peering relationships (cf. [119] and related work therein).

22.5.2   Topology Inference & Data Sources

The accurate modeling and analysis of the Internet topology require the observation of its current state. Gathering the complete Internet structure is a complex challenge, which cannot be entirely successful as there is no global view on all connections, nor do we have a method to validate routes and guarantee global consistency. Nevertheless, several measurement studies have been pursued over the last decade to understand the Internet structure and to provide researchers with a realistic Internet topology. For a detailed overview about Internet topology inference and its problems, we refer to the surveys [191], [121].

Topology inference is done on different levels of the Internet. IP paths may be discovered by traceroute. Using *alias resolution* mechanisms [121], IP interface addresses can be summarized and mapped to a single router. Both steps, however, are not trivial: ISPs filter ICMP messages used by traceroute causing incomplete data sets. Additionally, VPNs, tunnels, or MPLS paths cannot be revealed by such technique. The aggregation of different IP hops to a single router usually follows heuristic approaches. Further on, routing paths need not be symmetric, and source routing is almost everywhere prohibited. This complicates traceroute measurement and require several vantage points to explore the diversity of the routing layer. There are studies around which evaluate the accuracy of traceroute-based data, e.g., [40].

The IP-level can be transformed into the AS-level based on an IP prefix to *AS number mapping.*[4] However, a prefix can be announced by multiple ASes, known as the multiple origin AS problem (*MOAS*) [516]. Inferring the AS-level Internet paths from router-level traces is a well-known issue, but still an unsolved problem. In contrast to active measurement, we can infer the AS-level topology by the usage of publicly available data. There are two sources: Internet registries, and BPG routing services. Routing registry information is based on data which is provided by the ISPs and may be incomplete or obsolete. Typically, this information is used to enhance other sources. AS topology information can also be derived from *BGP* routing table dumps and updates, route servers, and looking glasses. A *route server* is member of the BGP peering. It provides limited telnet-access to query BGP routing information. A *looking glass* is basically a web interface that acts as telnet-wrapper for route servers. An offline version of *BGP tables* provide BGP dumps. Projects such as RouteViews[5] globally distribute route collectors, which periodically store snapshots of the BGP table. To reconstruct routing changes, this is done in combination with a dump of all BGP updates obtained between current and preceding snapshot. BGP updates can also be used to include fluctuating, e.g., backup links [514]. It is worth noting that the peering with a route server is voluntary. There are several route servers, which may have different views on the *BGP topology*. BGP tables are location dependent. Consequently, the set of information will be merged.

There are two popular IP traceroute projects, *CAIDA*[6] and *DIMES* [419]. In contrast to CAIDA, DIMES establishes vantage points at end user systems, similar to SETI@home, and thus collects data from significantly more Internet perspectives (i.e., ASes). For a comparison of both data sets we refer to [481]. As mentioned before there are objections to derive the AS graph

---

[4] See http://www.team-cymru.org/Services/ip-to-asn.html, for example.

[5] http://www.routeviews.org/

[6] Actually, CAIDA is an organization that operates several measurement projects, e.g, Ark (formerly Skitter).

Data Source	Granularity	URL
DatCat	–	http://www.datcat.org
CAIDA	AS, IP(, Router)	http://www.caida.org/projects/ark
DIMES	AS, IP, Router	http://www.netdimes.org
RIPE RIS	AS	http://www.ripe.net/ris
RouteViews	AS	http://www.routeviews.org
UCLA	AS	http://irl.cs.ucla.edu/topology
NEC	AS	http://topology.neclab.eu

Table 22.2: Selection of sources for periodically updated measurement data

from traceroute. The *RouteViews* project as well as the *RIPE Routing Information Service (RIS)*, for example, provide *BGP* table dumps. The routing table dumps must be post-processed to generate AS relations. The Internet Topology Collection of the UCLA incorporates these both sources, and additional route servers and looking glasses to provide a merged data set on a daily base. Based on the processing of BGP updates, the created AS graph is particularly aware of backup links, which are not visible in the snapshots of BGP routing tables [514]. The project annotates the graph with AS relationships. A simplified AS graph based on RouteViews, RIPE RIS, and UCLA data, is calculated within the project of NEC [498]. It represents an unweighted and weighted next hop matrix, a shortest path calculation (using policy-free and weighted edges), and classifies the ASes in three tiers.

The Internet Measurement Data Catalog (*DatCat*) [418] indexes Internet measurements in a broader context. It does not only include Internet network topologies, but also DNS traces, P2P measurements, etc. It facilitates searching for and sharing of data among researchers. DatCat is a comprehensive database, which is freely accessible by the research community in the context of Internet measurement to allow for reproducible data.

All data sources are summarized in Table 22.2.

22.5.3   On Internet Topology Properties

Although the real Internet structure is unknown in absent of a complete Internet map, there has been various work on analyzing the measured portions. One of the most controversial assumptions of the Internet topology is the scaling relations of several properties according to *power laws*. In their seminal work, Faloutsos et al. [139] analyzed the Internet AS-level topology based on RouteViews BGP tables. They observed that the out-degree of a node, the degree distribution, and the Eigenvalue of a graph adjacency matrix follow power laws. The power law exponent has been related to basic graph characteristics (e.g., number of nodes and edges). The authors thus found a very elegant way to describe the evolving inter-domain Internet structure. Several researchers verified this work [424], [301], and tried to understand the origin of power laws [313]. A common model in this context is the Barabási-Albert model (cf., Section 22.4.4). Inspired by the work of Faloutsos et al., Bu and Townsley [82] empirically analyzed measured Internet topologies. They show that the AS-level topology is a small world graph [488].

Although the observations by Faloutsos et al. have been verified, there are indications contradicting power laws. Chen et al. [98] argue that the derived AS-level topology is not representative for the Internet connectivity as at least 20 − 50% of the physical links are missing. Using an extended data set they show that strict power law relationship does not hold for the node degree distribution. In a subsequent paper, Siganos, Faloutsos et al. [424] reanalyze their initial work [424] based on the extended AS map and reclaim power law observation using linear regression evaluation. A fundamental observation concerning power law relationship of the node degree distribution and sampling biases has been presented by Lakhina et al. [273]. The authors construct a subgraph which is based on a larger structure without any power-law characteristics (e.g., random graph). They show that this subgraph appears to have power-law degree distribution. Thus, an uneven sampling of a non-power law structure may lead to power law properties.

The inner structure of an AS domain with respect to its IP path diversity has been studied by Teixeira et al. [460]. Path diversity measures the number of available routes between two nodes. The analysis is based on real network information provided by the ISP Sprint, and inferred topologies. Teixeira et al. show that approximately 90% of pairs of Sprint's 17 Point-of-Presence (PoPs) in the US exhibit at least four link-disjoint paths, and that 40% of pairs are linked by eight or more routes. In contrast to this, the topologies derived from active measurements overestimate the number of disjoint paths.

The routing behaviour between two end hosts has been initially analyzed by Paxson [356]. Employing network probe daemons distributed over 37 Internet hosts located in 34 different stub networks, Paxson measured that about 30% of the site pairs cross at least one different AS in the forward or reverse path, and approximately 50% visited at least one different city. For further work on this topic see, for example, [197].

Routing on the AS-level structure depends on the Autonomous System relationships. They determine routing export and selection policies. Links between AS domains are classified in (1) provider-to-customer, (2) customer-to-provider, (3) peer-to-peer, and (4) sibling-to-sibling relationships [172]. No transit traffic is allowed along peer-to-peer-links, and ISPs typically prefer customer routes over peering or provider links. Following specific policies, which are bound to the relation type, realistically chosen AS paths (measured in router hops) are elongated in contrast to shortest path routing. Neglecting inter-ISP relationships and using a simplified shortest AS path policy model, Tangmunarunkit et al. [455] analyzed that 20% of Internet paths are inflated by more than 5 router-level hops. In their subsequent work, the authors extended the policy model but observed that 96% of paths still have the

Generator || AS-level	Router-level	Hierarchy	URL
GT-ITM || Yes	No	Yes	http://www.cc.gatech.edu/projects/gtitm
Inet || Yes	No	No	http://topology.eecs.umich.edu/inet
BRITE || Yes	Yes	Yes	http://www.cs.bu.edu/brite
IGen || No	Yes	Yes	http://www.info.ucl.ac.be/~bqu/igen

Table 22.3: Network topology generators

same length independently of the model in use [454]. Based on a routing policy model that reflects commercial relationships, Gao et al. [173] derive the path elongation in AS hops. More than 45% of all AS paths are inflated by at least one AS hop.

22.5.4   Topology Generation

A standardized Internet topology cannot be provided as long as the Internet structure is not completely understood. One may import real measurement data (cf. Section 22.5.2) into the simulator but the created topology remains incomplete (e.g., missing peering links at the AS-level [41], [198]). Additionally, for most simulators the inferred number of nodes and links is too large. Krishnamurthy et al. [267], for example, introduce a sampling method in order to reduce the graph size on the one hand, and preserve power law metrics and slope on the other hand. The created structure is an undirected graph at the AS level. To allow for realistic inter-domain routing, edges need to be annotated with AS relationships as included in some measurement data [514], [498].

There are several network generators available to create synthetic topologies (cf. Table 22.3). One of the first well-established generators was GT-ITM. It provides flat random graphs, and a hierarchical transit-stub model to reflect the AS structure. Inet-3.0 is also an Autonomous System level Internet topology generator. It creates a random network and tries to reproduce inter-domain properties based on the input parameters: number of nodes, and the fraction of degree-one nodes. The characteristics are similar to Internet observations between November 1997 and February 2002 [497]. The authors mention that the model does not represent the Internet well with respect to clique and clustering properties. A topology generator that reflects the Internet AS-level and router-level is BRITE. BRITE is suitable for large scale power law graphs. It uses the *Waxman*, two *Barabási-Albert models*, and the generalized preference model to create flat AS, flat Router, and hierarchical topologies. BRITE also implements several import and export schemes to transform graphs between different topology generators and simulators. BRITE, and GT-ITM are pure degree-based generators. More recently, the IGen generator has been introduced that attempts to create end-to-end paths. IGen follows a new generation approach, which includes network design heuristics and geographic restrictions.

22.6   Conclusion

The network topology represents the interconnection of communication entities. It describes the paths which information can flow, and may largely affect evaluation of communication protocols. Understanding existing structures, such as the Internet, is a prerequisite to model realistic topologies. The specification of a graph can be generally descriptive based on a sufficient set of properties, or constructive using generation rules. A constructive creation may again be distinguished in two different approaches: Pure algorithmic construction that defines the procedures to create a graph with specific properties independent of the actual reasons, derived from the network. In contrast, a causality inspired construction models the understanding of the graph evolution as synthesizing the underlying network building process. It is worth noting that the two construction mechanisms follow orthogonal perspectives and may lead to unwanted results when mixed without care.

In this chapter, we introduced basic background on topology modeling, in which we focused on fixed networks. We started with the first modeling step: the abstraction of the real network by a graph, which includes the elimination of unnecessary details. Subsequently, we discussed essential metrics to describe a graph, and to analyze existing structures. The presented examples are not complete, but should be considered as starting point. The selection of metrics and the understanding of their interplay with the subject of investigation are an important part in the modeling. After characterizing graphs, we introduced common topology models. All of them are not directly applicable to the Internet topology, as Internet connections are neither built by random, nor do they follow simple geometric or preferential attachment rules. We discussed Internet topology modeling in the last section.

The modeling of the Internet is an intricate task. First and foremost, we are not able to capture the complete Internet, and thus there is no complete understanding of its structure. There are measurement projects. Processing their output (e.g., merging different sources) can be part of the modeling. Presenting an Internet topology without mentioning its level of granularity (i.e., AS-, router-, or IP-level) is meaningless. Recent discussions [192] advise to enrich the topology generation by some level of randomness to reflect the various evolutionary aspects of the Internet.

Subsequent steps may include the modeling of the network layer (Chapter 16), augmenting connections by corresponding link delays (Chapter 19), and the evaluation of protocols based on realistic traffic patterns (Chapter 18). For an in-depth treatment of network topologies in the context of communication networks, we refer to the excellent books [69], [122], and [471].

List of Figures

List of Tables

List of Acronyms

ACK	Acknowledgment	**BRAN**	Broadband Radio Access Network
AES	Advanced Encryption Standard	**BRITE**	Boston University Representative Internet Topology Generator
AM	Amplitude Modulation		
AMC	Adaptive Modulation and Coding		
AODV	Ad-hoc On-demand Distance Vector	**BS**	Base Station
		BSS	Basic Service Set
AP	Access Point	**BSSID**	Basic Service Set Identifier
AR	Autoregressive		
ARMA	Autoregressive Moving Average	**BU**	Binding Update
		CAP	Contention Access Period
ARIMA	Autoregressive Integrated Moving Average	**CBR**	Constant Bit Rate
		CC	Chase Combining
ARP	Address Resolution Protocol	**CCA**	Clear Channel Assessment
ARQ	Automatic Repeat Request	**CCK**	Complementary Code Keying
ASCII	American Standard Code for Information Interchange	**CDF**	Cumulative Distribution Function
		CDMA	Code Division Multiple Access
ASK	Amplitude Shift Keying	**CF**	Contention Free
		CFP	Contention Free Period
ATM	Asynchronous Transfer Mode	**CN**	Correspondent Node
		CoA	Care-of Address
BI	Beacon Interval	**CPU**	Central Processing Unit
BE	Backoff Exponent		
BER	Bit-Error Rate	**CQI**	Channel Quality Indicator
BO	Beacon Order		
BPSK	Binary Phase Shift Keying	**CRC**	Cyclic Redundancy Check

CS	Convergence Sublayer	ED	Energy Detection
CSMA	Carrier Sense Multiple Access	EDC	Error Detection and Correction
CSMA-CA	Carrier Sense Multiple Access with Collision Avoidance	EDCA	Enhanced Distributed Channel Access
		EETT	Exclusive Expected Transmission Time
CTS	Clear to Send		
CW	Contention Window Length	EIFS	Extended Inter Frame Space
DAB	Digital Audio Broadcasting	EIT	Earliest Input Time
		EOT	Earliest Output Time
DAC	Digital-to-Analog Converter	ertPS	Extended Real-time Polling Service
DAD	Duplicate Address Detection	ETSI	European Telecommunications Standards Institute
DCF	Distributed Coordination Function	ETT	Expected Transmission Time
DECT	Digital Enhanced Cordless Telephone	ETX	Expected Transmission Count
DFS	Dynamic Frequency Selection		
DFT	Digital Fourier Transform	FA	Foreign Agent
		FARIMA	Fractional Autoregressive Integrated Moving Average
DHCP	Dynamic Host Configuration Protocol		
DIFS	Distributed Inter Frame Space	FCC	Federal Communication Commission
DIUC	Downlink Interval Usage Code	FCF	Frame Configuration Framework
DL	Down Link		
DLL	Data Link Layer	FCH	Frame Control Header
DNS	Domain Name System	FCS	Frame Control Sequence
DPSK	Differential Phase Shift Keying		
DQPSK	Differential Quadrature Phase Shift Keying	FDD	Frequency Division Duplex
		FDM	Frequency Division Multiplex
DSL	Digital Subscriber Line		
DSR	Dynamic Source Routing	FDN	Fractional Differencing Noise
DSSS	Direct Sequence Spread Spectrum	FEC	Forward Error Correction
DVB	Digital Video Broadcasting	FFD	Full-Function Device
		FFT	Fast Fourier Transform

FHSS	Frequency Hopping Spread Spectrum	**iAWARE**	Interference Aware Routing Metric
FM	Frequency Modulation	**ICMP**	Internet Control Message Protocol
FSK	Frequency Shift Keying	**IE**	Information Element
FU	Functional Unit	**IEEE**	Institute of Electrical and Electronics Engineers
FUN	Functional Unit Network		
FUSC	Full Usage of Subchannels	**IETF**	Internet Engineering Task Force
FMIPv6	Fast Mobile IPv6	**IFFT**	Inverse Fast Fourier Transform
FTP	File Transfer Protocol	**IFS**	Inter Frame Space
GMSK	Gaussian Minimum Shift Keying	**IP**	Internet Protocol
GOP	Group of Picture	**IR**	Incremental Redundancy
GPL	GNU General Public License	**IrDA**	Infrared Data Association
GPS	Global Positioning System	**ISM**	Industrial, Scientific, and Medical
GPSR	Greedy Perimeter Stateless Routing	**ISO**	International Standardization Organization
GSM	Global System for Mobile Communications	**ISP**	Ideal Simulation Protocol
GTS	Guaranteed Time Slot	**ITU**	International Telecommunication Union
GT-ITM	Georgia Tech Internetwork Topology Model		
HA	Home Agent	**LA**	Link Adaptation
HARQ	Hybrid Automatic Repeat Request (ARQ)	**LAN**	Local Area Network
		LBT	Listen Before Talk
		LCoA	On-link Care-of Address
HCF	Hybrid Coordination Function	**LDK**	Layer Development Kit
HMIPv6	Hierarchical Mobile IPv6	**LDPC**	Low-Density-Parity-Check
HoA	Home Address	**LGPL**	Lesser General Public License
HFDD	Half Frequency Division Duplex	**LLC**	Logical Link Control
		LOS	Line-of-Sight
HTML	Hypertext Markup Language	**LP**	Logical Process
		LRD	Long Range Dependency
HTTP	Hypertext Transfer Protocol	**LTE**	Long Term Evolution

LQI	Link Quality Indication	**OFDMA**	Orthogonal Frequency Division Multiple Access
MAC	Medium Access Control	**O-QPSK**	Offset Quadrature Phase Shift Keying
MAP	Mobility Anchor Point		
MCPS	MAC Common Part Sublayer	**openWNS**	open Wireless Network Simulator
MCS	Modulation- and Coding Scheme	**OSI**	Open Systems Interconnection
MI	Mutual Information	**P2P**	Peer-to-Peer
MIB	Management Information Base	**PAN**	Personal Area Network
		PASTA	Poisson Arrivals see Time Averages
MIC	Metric of Interference and Channel-switching	**pcap**	packet capture
MIMO	Multiple Input Multiple Output	**PCF**	Point Coordination Function
MIP	Mobile IP	**PD**	PHY Data Service
MIPv4	Mobile IPv4	**PDA**	Portable Digital Assistant
MIPv6	Mobile IPv6		
MLME	MAC Sublayer Management Entity	**PDES**	Parallel Discrete Event Simulation
MN	Mobile Node	**PDF**	Probability Density Function
MPDU	MAC Protocol Data Unit	**PDU**	Protocol Data Unit
MSCTP	Mobile SCTP	**PER**	Packet Error Rate
MSK	Minimum Shift Keying	**PHS**	Payload Header Suppression
MTU	Maximum transmission unit	**PHY**	Physical Layer
NACK	Negative Acknowledgment (ACK)	**PIB**	PAN Information Base
		PIFS	Point Coordination Inter Frame Space
NAT	Network Address Translation	**PLCP**	Physical Layer Convergence Procedure
NAV	Network Allocation Vector		
		PLL	Phase-Locked Loop
NB	Number of Backoffs	**PLME**	PHY Management Entity
NMA	Null-Message Algorithm		
		PMD	Physical Medium Dependent
NLOS	Non-Line-of-Sight		
nrtPS	Non-real-time Polling Service	**PMP**	Point to Multi Point
		POS	Personal Operating Space
NS-2	Network Simulator 2		
OFDM	Orthogonal Frequency Division Multiplex	**PPDU**	PHY Protocol Data Unit

PPP	Point-to-Point Protocol	**SAR**	Segmentation And Reassembly
PSD	Power Spectral Density	**SC**	Subchannel
		SCTP	Stream Control Transmission Protocol
PSK	Phase Shift Keying		
PSSS	Parallel Sequence Spread Spectrum	**SD**	Superframe Duration
		SDMA	Space Division Multiple Access
PUSC	Partial Usage of Subchannels		
		SDU	Service Data Unit
QAM	Quadrature Amplitude Modulation	**SIFS**	Short Inter Frame Space
QoS	Quality of Service	**SINR**	Signal-to-Interference-plus-Noise-Ratio
QPSK	Quadrature Phase Shift Keying		
		SIP	Session Initiation Protocol
ICI	Inter-carrier Interference		
		SNR	Signal-to-Noise-Ratio
ISI	Inter-symbol Interference	**SO**	Superframe Order
		SRD	Short Range Dependency
RCoA	Regional Care-of Address		
		SS	Subscriber Station
RF	Radio Frequency	**SSCS**	Service Specific Convergence Sublayer
RFD	Reduced-Function Device		
		SSID	Service Set Identifier
RNG	Random Number Generator	**STA**	station
		STC	Space Time Coding
RRM	Radio Resource Management	**TCP**	Transmission Control Protocol
RS	Reed-Solomon		
RSSI	Received Signal Strength Indication	**TDD**	Time Division Duplex
		TDMA	Time Division Multiple Access
RSVP	Resource Reservation Protocol		
		TPC	Transmission Power Control
RTCP	RTP Control Protocol		
RTG	Receive / transmit Transition Gap	**TTG**	Transmit / receive Transition Gap
		TTL	Time To Live
RTP	Real-Time Transport Protocol	**TUSC**	Tile Usage of Subchannels
rtPS	Real-time Polling Service		
		UDP	User Datagram Protocol
RTS	Ready to Send		
RTSP	Real-Time Streaming Protocol	**UGS**	Unsolicited Grant Service
SAP	Service Access Point	**UL**	Up Link

UMTS	Universal Mobile Telecommunications System	**WCETT**	Weighted Cumulative Expected Transmission Time
U-NII	Unlicensed National Information Infrastructure	**WCETT-LB**	WCETT-Load Balancing
		WiMAX	Worldwide Interoperability for Microwave Access
URL	Universal Resource Locator	**WLAN**	Wireless Local Area Network
UWB	Ultra-Wideband	**WPAN**	Wireless Personal Area Network
VoIP	Voice over IP		
VRR	Virtual Ring Routing	**WSN**	Wireless Sensor Network
SSR	Scalable Source Routing	**WWW**	World Wide Web

List of Authors

A. Aguiar, University of Porto

I. Aktas, RWTH Aachen University

M. H. Alizai, RWTH Aachen University

A. de Baynast, European Microsoft Innovation Center

A. Berl, University of Passau

M. Bohge, Technische Universität Berlin

D. Bültmann, RWTH Aachen University

P. Di, Universität Karlsruhe (TH) & TU München

M. Emmelmann, Technische Universität Berlin

L. Gao, RWTH Aachen University

J. Gross, RWTH Aachen University

M. Güneş, Freie Universität Berlin

T. R. Henderson, University of Washington, and Boeing Research & Technology

R. Jennen, RWTH Aachen University

S. Kaune, Technische Universität Darmstadt

T. Kempf, RWTH Aachen University

T. King, Universität Mannheim

M. Kirsche, Brandenburg University of Technology Cottbus (BTU)

K. Klagges, RWTH Aachen University

G. Kunz, RWTH Aachen University

O. Landsiedel, RWTH Aachen University

C. Leng, Technische Universität Darmstadt

S. Max, RWTH Aachen University

C. Mengi, RWTH Aachen University

M. Mühleisen, RWTH Aachen University

O. Puñal, RWTH Aachen University

K. Pussep, Technische Universität Darmstadt

G. F. Riley, Georgia Tech

R. Sasnauskas, RWTH Aachen University

J. Scharf, University of Stuttgart

M. Schinnenburg, RWTH Aachen University

F. Schmidt-Eisenlohr, Karlsruhe Institute of Technology (KIT)

A. Schmitz, RWTH Aachen University

E. Schoch, Ulm University

J. Sommer, University of Stuttgart

A. Varga, Opensim Ltd.

M. Wählisch, Freie Universität Berlin & HAW Hamburg

K. Wehrle, RWTH Aachen University

E. Weingaertner, RWTH Aachen University

S. Wiethoelter, Technische Universität Berlin

D. Willkomm, Technische Universität Berlin

G. Wittenburg, Freie Universität Berlin

References

[1]   Boost C++ Libraries. http://www.boost.org.

[2]   CMU Monarch Project. http://www.monarch.cs.rice.edu/.

[3]   The DWARF debugging standard. http://dwarfstd.org.

[4]   Microsoft portable executable and common object file format specification.

[5]   Ns-miracle: Multi-interface cross-layer extension library for the network simulator. http://www.dei.unipd.it/wdyn/?IDsezione=3966

[6]   openWNS - open Wireless Network Simulator. http://www.openwns.org.

[7]   Overhaul of IEEE 802.11 modeling and simulation in ns-2. http://dsn.tm.uni-karlsruhe.de/english/Overhaul_NS-2.php.

[8]   Ptolemy Project Home Page. http://ptolemy.eecs.berkeley.edu/.

[9]   Scalable wireless ad hoc network simulator. http://jist.ece.cornell.edu/people.html.

[10]   International Standards Organization: Technical Report on C++ Library Extensions. International Standard ISO/IEC TR 19768:2007.

[11]   Wireshark. http://www.wireshark.org/.

[12]   IEEE 802.15.1-2002 IEEE Standard for information technology - Telecommunication and information exchange between systems - LAN/MAN - Part 15.1: Wireless Medium Access Control (MAC) and Physical Layer (PHY) specications for Wireless Personal Area Networks(WPANs), 2002.

[13]   IEEE 802.11F – trial-use recommended practice for multi-vendor access point interoperability via an inter-access point protocol across distribution systems supporting IEEE 802.11, June 12 2003.

[14]   FCC Report and Order 05-56, Wireless Operation in the 3650-3700 MHz, Mar 2005.

[15]   IEEE 802.11-2007, Wireless LAN Medium Access Control (MAC) and Physical Layer (PHY) Specifications, June 2007.

[16]   Guidelines for Evaluation of Radio Interface Technologies for IMT-Advanced, November 2008.

[17]   IEEE 802.11.2 – recommended practice for the evaluation of 802.11 wireless performance, 2008.

[18] 3GPP TR 25.996 V9.0.0: Spatial channel model for Multiple Input Multiple Output (MIMO) simulations (Release 9). 3rd Generation Partnership Project; Technical Specification Group Radio Access Network, December 2009.

[19] Evolved Universal Terrestrial Radio Access (E-UTRA) and Evolved Universal Terrestrial Radio Access Network (E-UTRAN); Overall description , September 2009.

[20] IEEE 802.16m System Description Document, 2009.

[21] IEEE Std 802.16h/D13, IEEE Standard Draft for Local and Metropolitan Area Networks. Part 16: Air Interface for Fixed Broadband Wireless Access Systems. Improved Coexistence Mechanisms for License-Exempt Operation, November 2009.

[22] D. R. Karger and M. Ruhl. Finding nearest neighbors in growth restricted metrics. In *STOC '02: Proceedings of the thiry-fourth annual ACM symposium on Theory of computing*, pages 741–750. ACM, 2002.

[23] Third Generation Partnership Project Two (3GPP2). CDMA2000 Evaluation Methodology. Website: http://www.3gpp2.org/Public_html/specs/C.R1002-0_v1.0_041221.pdf, December 2004.

[24] A. Abdi and M. Kaveh. A space-time correlation model for multielement antenna systems in mobile fading channels. *IEEE Journal on Selected Areas in Communications*, 20(3), April 2002.

[25] Active measurement project. http://watt.nlanr.net.

[26] Vinay Aggarwal, Obi Akonjang, and Anja Feldmann. Improving user and isp experience through isp-aided p2p locality. In *Proceedings of 11th IEEE Global Internet Symposium 2008 (GI'08)*, Washington, DC, USA, April 2008. IEEE Computer Society.

[27] A. Aguiar and J. Gross. Wireless channel models. Technical Report TKN-03-007, Telecommunication Networks Group, Technische Universität Berlin, April 2003.

[28] Alfred V. Aho, Ravi Sethi, and Jeffrey D. Ullman. *Compilers: principles, techniques, and tools.* Addison-Wesley Longman Publishing Co., Inc., Boston, MA, USA, 1986.

[29] Kemal Akkaya and Mohamed Younis. A survey on routing protocols for wireless sensor networks. *Elsevier Ad Hoc Network Journal*, 3:325–349, 2005.

[30] Réka Albert and Albert-László Barabási. Topology of Evolving Networks: Local Events and Universality. *Physical Review Letters*, 85(24):5234–5237, 2000.

[31] Algirdas Avizienis, Jean-Claude Laprie, Brian Randell, and Carl E. Landwehr. Basic Concepts and Taxonomy of Dependable and Secure Computing. *IEEE Transactions on Dependable Secure Computing*, 1(1):11–33, 2004.

[32] Zigbee™Alliance. Zigbee-2006 specification - revision 13. Technical report, ZigBee Standards Organization, 2006.

[33] P. Almers, E. Bonek, and A. Burr et al. Survey of channel and radio propagation models for wireless mimo systems. *EURASIP Journal on Wireless Communications and Networking*, 2007, 2007. Article ID 19070, doi:10.1155/2007/19070.

[34] Eitan Altman, Konstantin Avrachenkov, and Chadi Barakat. A stochastic model of TCP/IP with stationary random losses. *IEEE/ACM Trans. Netw.*, 13(2):356–369, 2005.

[35] Mostafa Ammar. Why we still don't know how to simulate networks. In *MASCOTS '05: Proceedings of the 13th IEEE International Symposium on Modeling, Analysis, and Simulation of Computer and Telecommunication Systems*, 2005.

[36] An Open Platform for Developing, Deploying, and Accessing Planetary-Scale Services. http://www.planetlab.com.

[37] M. Andreolini, R. Lancellotti, and Philip S. Yu. Analysis of peer-to-peer systems: workload characterization and effects on traffic cacheability. In *Modeling, Analysis, and Simulation of Computer and Telecommunications Systems, 2004.(MASCOTS 2004)*, pages 95–104, 2004.

[38] Chi-chao Chao and Yuh-Lin Yao. Hidden Markov models for the burst error statistics of Viterbi decoding. *IEEE Transactions on Communications*, 44(12):1620 – 1622, Dec. 1996.

[39] Arm. Realview development suite.
http://www.arm.com/products/DevTools/.

[40] Brice Augustin, Xavier Cuvellier, Benjamin Orgogozo, Fabien Viger, Timur Friedman, Matthieu Latapy, Clémence Magnien, and Renata Teixeira. Avoiding Traceroute Anomalies with Paris Traceroute. In *Proceedings of the 6th ACM SIGCOMM conference on Internet measurement (IMC'06)*, pages 153–158, New York, NY, USA, 2006. ACM.

[41] Brice Augustin, Balachander Krishnamurthy, and Walter Willinger. IXPs: Mapped? In *Proceedings of the 9th ACM SIGCOMM conference on Internet measurement conference (IMC'09)*, pages 336 349, New York, NY, USA, 2009. ACM.

[42] O. Awoniyi and F. Tobagi. Packet Error Rate in OFDM-based Wireless LANs Operating in Frequency Selective Channels. In *Proc. IEEE INFOCOM*, April 2006.

[43] Rajive L. Bagrodia and Mineo Takai. Performance Evaluation of Conservative Algorithms in Parallel Simulation Languages. *IEEE Transactions on Parallel Distributed Systems*, 11(4):395–411, 2000.

[44] F. Bai and A. Helmy. A Survey of Mobility Models. *Wireless Ad Hoc and Sensor Networks, Kluwer Academic Publishers*, 2004.

[45] B. Bailey, G. Martin, and A. Piziali. *ESL Design and Verification*. Morgan Kaufmann, 1 edition, 2007.

[46] Constantine A. Balanis. *Antenna Theory: Analysis and Design*. John Wiley and Sons, 1997.

[47] S. Bangolae, C. Wright, C. Trecker, M. Emmelmann, and F. Mli-
      narsky. Test methodology proposal for measuring fast BSS/BSS tran-
      sition time. doc. 11-05/537, IEEE 802.11 TGt Wireless Performance
      Prediction Task Group, Vancouver, Canada, November, 14 – 18 2005.
      Substantive Standard Draft Text. Accepted into the IEEE P802.11.2
      Draft Reccomended Practice.

[48] Jerry Banks, John S. Carson II, Barry L. Nelson, and David M. Nicol.
      Discrete-Event System Simulation. Prentice Hall, fourth edition, 2005.

[49] Albert-László Barabási and Réka Albert. Emergence of Scaling in Ran-
      dom Networks. *Science*, 286(5439):509–512, 1999.

[50] P. Barford and M. Crovella. Generating representative work loads for
      network and server performance evaluation. *Proceedings of ACM SIG-
      MATRICS 98*, pages 151–160, June 1998.

[51] Rimon Barr, Zygmunt J. Haas, and Robbert van Renesse. JiST: An
      Efficient Approach to Simulation using Virtual Machines. *Software
      Practice & Experience*, 35(6):539–576, 2005.

[52] Rimon Barr, Haas J. Zygmunt, and Robbert van Renesse. JiST: Em-
      bedding Simulation Time into a Virtual Machine. In *Proceedings of
      EuroSim Congress on Modelling and Simulation*, 2004.

[53] K. L. Baum, T. A. Kostas, P. J. Sartori, and B. K. Classon. Perfor-
      mance characteristics of cellular systems with different link adaptation
      strategies. *IEEE Transactions on Vehicular Technology*, 52(6):1497–
      1507, 2003.

[54] I. Baumgart, B. Heep, and S. Krause. Oversim: A flexible overlay
      network simulation framework. In *IEEE Global Internet Symposium,
      2007*, pages 79–84, 2007.

[55] R. E. Bellman. On a routing problem. *Quarterly of Applied Mathemat-
      ics*, 16:87–90, 1958.

[56] Tore J Berg. oprobe - an OMNeT++ extension module. `http://
      sourceforge/projects/oprobe`, 2008.

[57] T. Berners-Lee, R. Fielding, and H. Frystyk. Hypertext transfer protocl
      - http/1.0. RFC145, May 1996.

[58] C. Berrou, A. Glavieux, and P. Thitimajshima. Near Shannon limit
      error-correcting coding and decoding: Turbo-codes (1). *IEEE Interna-
      tional Conference on Communications (ICC)*, 2, May 1993.

[59] Bhagwan, Savage, and Voelker. Understanding availability. In *Interna-
      tional Workshop on Peer-to-Peer Systems (IPTPS), LNCS*, volume 2,
      2003.

[60] K. Blackard, T. Rappaport, and C. Bostian. Measurements and models
      of radio frequency impulsive noise for indoor wireless communications.
      IEEE Journal on Selected Areas in Communications, 11(7):991–1001,
      1993.

[61] Roland Bless and Mark Doll. Integration of the FreeBSD TCP/IP-stack into the discrete event simulator OMNeT | |. In *Proc. of the 36th conference on Winter simulation (WSC)*, 2004.

[62] Stefan Bodamer, Klaus Dolzer, Christoph Gauger, Michael Kutter, Thomas Steinert, and Marc Barisch. IKR Utility Library 2.6 User Guide. Technical report, University of Stuttgart, IKR, December 2006.

[63] Stefan Bodamer, Klaus Dolzer, Christoph Gauger, Michael Kutter, Thomas Steinert, Marc Barisch, and Marc C. Necker. IKR Component Library 2.6 User Guide. Technical report, University of Stuttgart, IKR, December 2006.

[64] Stefan Bodamer, Martin Lorang, and Marc Barisch. IKR TCP Library 1.2 User Guide. Technical report, University of Stuttgart, IKR, June 2004.

[65] M. Bohge, J. Gross, M. Meyer, and A. Wolisz. A New Optimization Model for Dynamic Power and Sub-Carrier Allocations in Packet-Centric OFDMA Cells. *Frequenz*, 59:7–8, 2005.

[66] Gunter Bolch, Stefan Greiner, Hermann de Meer, and Kishor S. Trivedi. *Queueing Networks and Markov Chains: Modeling and Performance Evaluation with Computer Science Applications*. Wiley-Interscience, 2nd edition, April 2006.

[67] Béla Bollobás. *Random Graphs*, volume 73 of *Cambridge studies in advanced mathematics*. Cambridge University Press, New York, USA, 2nd edition, 2001.

[68] J. Bolot. Characterizing end-to-end packet delay and loss in the internet. *Journal of High Speed Networks*, 2:305–323, 1993.

[69] Stefan Bornholdt and Heinz Georg Schuster, editors. *Random graphs as models of networks*. Wiley–VCH, Berlin, 2003.

[70] M. Bossert. *Channel Coding for Telecommunications*. John Wiley & Sons, Inc., 2000.

[71] A. Bouchhima, I. Bacivarov, W. Youssef, M. Bonaciu, and A. A. Jerraya. Using abstract CPU subsystem simulation model for high level HW/SW architecture exploration. In *Proc. Asia and South Pacific Design Automation Conference the ASP-DAC 2005*, pages 969–972, 2005.

[72] Athanassios Boulis. Castalia: revealing pitfalls in designing distributed algorithms in wsn. In *SenSys '07: Proceedings of the 5th international conference on Embedded networked sensor systems*, pages 407–408, New York, NY, USA, 2007. ACM.

[73] Don Box. *Essential COM*. Addison-Wesley Longman Publishing Co., Inc., Boston, MA, USA, 1997. Foreword By-Booch, Grady and Foreword By-Kindel, Charlie.

[74] George Box, Gwilym M. Jenkins, and Gregory Reinsel. *Time Series Analysis: Forecasting & Control (3rd Edition)*. Prentice Hall, February 1994.

[75]   George E. P. Box and Norman R. Draper. *Empirical Model-Building and Response Surfaces*. Wiley, 1987.

[76]   R. Braden, L. Zhang, S. Berson, S. Herzog, and S. Jamin. Resource ReSerVation Protocol (RSVP) — Version 1 Functional Specification. RFC 2205, September 1997.

[77]   P. T. Brady. A Technique for Investigating On-Off Patterns of Speech. *The Bell System Technical Journal*, 44:1–22, 1965.

[78]   P. T. Brady. A Statistical Analysis of On-Off Patterns in 16 Conversations. *The Bell System Technical Journal*, 47:73–91, 1968.

[79]   P. T. Brady. A Model for Generating On-Off Speech Patterns in Two-Way Conversation. *The Bell System Technical Journal*, 48:2445–2472, 1969.

[80]   Ulrik Brandes. A Faster Algorithm for Betweenness Centrality. *Journal of Mathematical Sociology*, 25(2):163–177, 2001.

[81]   Lee Breslau, Deborah Estrin, Kevin Fall, Sally Floyd, John Heidemann, Ahmed Hemy, Polly Huang, Steven McCanne, Kannan Varadhan, Ya Xu, and Haobo You. Advances in Network Simulation. *Computer*, 33(5):59–67, May 2000.

[82]   Tian Bu and Don Towsley. On Distinguishing between Internet Power Law Topology Generators. In *Proceedings IEEE INFOCOM 2002*, volume 2, pages 638–647, New York, USA, 2002. IEEE Computer Society.

[83]   Frank Buschmann, Regine Meunier, Hans Rohnert, Peter Sommerlad, and Michael Stal. *Pattern-oriented Software Architecture Volume 1*. John Wiley & Sons, 1996.

[84]   Matthew Caesar, Miguel Castro, Edmund B. Nightingale, Greg O'Shea, and Antony Rowstron. Virtual Ring Routing: Network Routing Inspired by DHTs. In *Proc. ACM SIGCOMM '06*, Pisa, Italy, September 2006.

[85]   CAIDA. Macroscopic Topology Project. http://www.caida.org/analysis/topology/macroscopic/.

[86]   Kenneth L. Calvert, Matthew B. Doar, and Ellen W. Zegura. Modeling Internet Topology. *IEEE Communications Magazine*, 35(6):160–163, 1997.

[87]   T. Camp, J. Boleng, and V. Davies. A survey of mobility models for ad hoc network research. *Wireless Communications and Mobile Computing*, 2(5):483–502, 2002.

[88]   J. C. Cano and P. Manzoni. On the use and calculation of the Hurst parameter with MPEG videos data traffic. In *Euromicro Conference, 2000. Proceedings of the 26th*, volume 1, pages 448–455 vol.1, 2000.

[89]   E. Casilari, F.J. Gonzblez, and F. Sandoval. Modeling of http traffic. *Communications Letters, IEEE*, 5(6):272–274, Jun 2001.

[90]   E. Casilari, A. Reyes, A. Diaz-Estrella, and F. Sandoval. Classification and comparison of modelling strategies for VBR video traffic. *TELETRAFFIC ENGINEERING IN A COMPETITIVE WORLD*, 1999.

[91] E. Casilari, A. Reyes-Lecuona, F.J. Gonzalez, A. Diaz-Estrella, and
      F. Sandoval. Characterisation of web traffic. *Global Telecommunications
      Conference, 2001. GLOBECOM '01. IEEE*, 3:1862–1866 vol.3, 2001.

[92] L.D. Catledge and J.E. Pitkow. Characterizing browsing strategies
      in the World-Wide Web. *Computer Networks and ISDN systems*,
      27(6):1065–1073, 1995.

[93] J. Cavers. *Mobile Channel Characteristics.* Kluwer Academic, 2000.

[94] R. Chang. Synthesis of band limited orthogonal signals for multichannel
      data transmission. *Bell Systems Technical Journal*, 45:1775–1796, 1966.

[95] Feng Chen and Falko Dressler. A simulation model of IEEE 802.15.4 in
      OMNeT++. In *6. GI/ITG KuVS Fachgespräch Drahtlose Sensornetze,
      Poster Session*, pages 35–38, Aachen, Germany, 2007.

[96] Gilbert Chen and Boleslaw K. Szymanski. DSIM: Scaling Time Warp
      to 1,033 processors. In *Proceedings of the 37th Winter Simulation Con-
      ference*, pages 346–355, 2005.

[97] Qi Chen, Felix Schmidt-Eisenlohr, Daniel Jiang, Marc Torrent-Moreno,
      Luca Delgrossi, and Hannes Hartenstein. Overhaul of IEEE 802.11
      modeling and simulation in ns-2. In *MSWiM '07: Proceedings of the
      10th ACM Symposium on Modeling, analysis, and simulation of wireless
      and mobile systems*, pages 159–168, New York, NY, USA, 2007. ACM.

[98] Qian Chen, Hyunseok Chang, R. Govindan, and S. Jamin. The Ori-
      gin of Power Laws in Internet Topologies Revisited. In *Proc. of the
      21th IEEE INFOCOM*, volume 2, pages 608–617, Piscataway, NJ, USA,
      2002. IEEE Press.

[99] Zhijia Chen, Chuang Lin, Hao Wen, and Hao Yin. An analytical model
      for evaluating ieee 802.15.4 csma/ca protocol in low-rate wireless appli-
      cation. In *Advanced Information Networking and Applications Work-
      shops, 2007, AINAW '07. 21st International Conference on*, volume 2,
      pages 899–904, 2007.

[100] K. Cho and D. Yoon. On the general BER expressions of one-
      and two-dimensional amplitude modulations. *IEEE Trans. Commun.*,
      50(7):1074–1080, 2002.

[101] H. Choi and J. O. Limb. A behavioral model of web traffic. *Network
      Protocols, 1999. (ICNP '99) Proceedings. Seventh International Con-
      ference on*, pages 327–334, Oct.-3 Nov. 1999.

[102] L. Cimini. Analysis and Simulation of a Digital Mobile Channel using
      Orthogonal Frequency Division Multiplexing. *Communications, IEEE
      Transactions on [legacy, pre-1988]*, 33(7):665–675, 1985.

[103] B. Cohen. Incentives build robustness in bittorrent. In *Proceedings of
      the Workshop on Economics of Peer-to-Peer Systems*, Berkeley, CA,
      USA, 2003.

[104] Gerald Combs. *Wireshark Network Analyzer - User's Guide*, July 2008.

[105] Thomas H. Cormen, Charles E. Leiserson, Ronald L. Rivest, and Clif-
      ford Stein. *Introduction to Algorithms.* MIT Press, second edition,
      September 2001.

[106] T.M. Cover and J.A. Thomas. *Elements of Information Theory*. John Wiley & Sons, 1991.

[107] Crespo, A., Garcia-Molina, H.: Semantic overlay networks for P2P systems. In: Moro, G., Bergamaschi, S., Aberer, K. (eds.) AP2PC 2004. LNCS (LNAI), vol. 3601, pp. 1–13. Springer, Heidelberg (2005) http://www.springerlink.com/content/3u446458qk72504x/

[108] Ahmet Y. Şekercioğlu, András Varga, and Gregory K. Egan. Parallel Simulation made easy with OMNeT++. In *Proceedings of European Simulation Symposium*, Delft, The Netherlands, 2003.

[109] C.R. Cunha, A. Bestavros, and M.E. Crovella. Characteristics of WWW client-based traces. *Computer Science Department, Boston University*, 1995.

[110] E. Dahlman. *3G Evolution: HSPA and LTE for Mobile Broadband*. Elsevier Academic Press, 2007.

[111] Adnan Darwiche and Judea Pearl. On the logic of iterated belief revision. *Artificial intelligence*, 89:1–29, 1996.

[112] Douglas S. J. De Couto, Daniel Aguayo, John Bicket, and Robert Morris. A high-throughput path metric for multi-hop wireless routing. In *Proceedings of the 9th ACM International Conference on Mobile Computing and Networking (MobiCom '03)*, San Diego, California, 2003.

[113] Douglas S. J. De Couto, Daniel Aguayo, Benjamin A. Chambers, and Robert Morris. Performance of multihop wireless networks: shortest path is not enough. *SIGCOMM Comput. Commun. Rev.*, 33(1):83–88, 2003.

[114] M. Debbah, P. Loubaton, and M. de Courville. Asymptotic performance of successive interference cancellation in the context of linear precoded OFDM systems. *IEEE Transactions on Communications*, 52(9):1444–1448, Sep. 2004.

[115] M. Debbah and R.R. Muller. MIMO channel modeling and the principle of maximum entropy. *IEEE Transactions on Information Theory*, 51(5):1667–1690, May. 2005.

[116] Ns-2 Developers. The network simulator - ns-2. [online] http://www.isi.edu/nsnam/ns/.

[117] J. Deygout. Correction factor for multiple knife-edge diffraction. *IEEE Trans Antennas and Propagation*, 39, August 1991.

[118] E. Dijkstra. A note on two problems in connection with graphs. *Numerische Mathematik*, 1:269–271, 1959.

[119] Xenofontas Dimitropoulos, Dmitri Krioukov, George Riley, and kc claffy. Revealing the Autonomous System Taxonomy: The Machine Learning Approach. In Mark Allman and M. Roughan, editors, *Proceedings of the Passive and Active Measurement Conference. PAM2006*, pages 91–100, March 2006. http://www.pamconf.net/2006/papers/pam06-proceedings.pdf.

[120] Matthew B. Doar. A Better Model for Generating Test Networks. In *Proc. of the IEEE Global Telecommunications Conference (GLOBE-COM'96)*, pages 86–93, Piscataway, NJ, USA, 1996. IEEE Press.

[121] Benoit Donnet and Timur Friedman. Internet Topology Discovery: A Survey. *IEEE Communications Surveys and Tutorials*, 9(4):56–69, 2007.

[122] Sergei N. Dorogovtsev and Jose F. F. Mendes. *Evolution of Networks. From Biological Nets to the Internet and the WWW*. Oxford University Press, New York, 2003.

[123] Richard Draves, Jitendra Padhye, and Brian Zill. Routing in multi-radio, multi-hop wireless mesh networks. In *MobiCom '04: Proceedings of the 10th annual international conference on Mobile computing and networking*, pages 114–128, New York, NY, USA, 2004. ACM.

[124] Thomas Dreibholz, Xing Zhou, and Erwin Rathgeb. Simproctc – the design and realization of a powerful tool-chain for OMNeT++ simulations. In *OMNeT++ 2009: Proceedings of the 2nd International Workshop on OMNeT++ (hosted by SIMUTools 2009)*, ICST, Brussels, Belgium, Belgium, 2009. ICST (Institute for Computer Sciences, Social-Informatics and Telecommunications Engineering). poster.

[125] R. Droms. Dynamic Host Configuration Protocol. RFC 2131, March 1997.

[126] Z. Duan, K. Xu, and Z. Zhang. Understanding delay variations on the internet paths.

[127] Jonathon Duerig, Robert Ricci, John Byers, and Jay Lepreau. Automatic ip address assignment on network topologies. Technical report, University of Utah Flux Group, 2006.

[128] Philip Dutre, Philippe Bekaert, and Kavita Bala. *Advanced Global Illumination*. AK Peters, Ltd., July 2002.

[129] A. Dutta, Y. Ohba, H. Yokota, and H. Schulzrinne. Problem statement for heterogeneous handover. Internet-Draft, MOBOTS Research Group, draft-ohba-mobopts-heterogeneous-requirement-01, February 2006.

[130] Robert S. Elliot. *Antenna Theory and Design*. Prentice Hall International, 1981.

[131] Marc Emmelmann, Berthold Rathke, and Adam Wolisz. Mobility support for wireless PAN, LAN, and MAN. In Y. Zhang and H. Chen, editors, *Mobile WiMAX: Toward Broadband Wireless Metropolitan Area Networks*. Auerbach Publications, CRC Press, 2007. ISBN: 0849326249.

[132] Marc Emmelmann, Sven Wiethoelter, Andreas Koepsel, Cornelia Kappler, and Adam Wolisz. Moving towards seamless mobility: State of the art and emerging aspects in standardization bodies. In *WPMC 2006*, San Diego, CA, USA, September, 17 – 20 2006. Invited Paper.

510   References

[133] Marc Emmelmann, Sven Wiethoelter, Andreas Koepsel, Cornelia Kappler, and Adam Wolisz. Moving towards seamless mobility – state of the art and emerging aspects in standardization bodies. *Springer's International Journal on Wireless Personal Communication – Special Issue on Seamless Handover in Next Generation Wireless/Mobile Networks*, 2007.

[134] Paul Erdős and Alréd Rényi. On random graphs I. *Publicationes Mathematicae Debrecen*, 6:290–297, 1959.

[135] Paul Erdős and Alréd Rényi. On the evoluation of random graphs. *Publ. Math. Inst. Hung. Acad. Sci.*, 5:17–61, 1960.

[136] Jakob Eriksson, Michalis Faloutsos, and Srikanth Krishnamurty. PeerNet: Pushing Peer-to-Peer Down the Stack. In *Proceedings of IPTPS '03*, Claremont Hotel, Berkeley, CA, USA, February 2003. Springer Verlag.

[137] V. Erceg et al. TGn Channel Models. IEEE 802.11 document 11-03/0940r4, May 2004.

[138] Kevin Fall and Sally Floyd. Simulation-based comparisons of Tahoe, Reno and SACK TCP. *SIGCOMM Comput. Commun. Rev.*, 26(3):5–21, 1996.

[139] Michalis Faloutsos, Petros Faloutsos, and Christos Faloutsos. On Power-Law Relationships of the Internet Topology. In *SIGCOMM '99: Proceedings of the conference on Applications, technologies, architectures, and protocols for computer communication*, pages 251–262, New York, NY, USA, 1999. ACM Press.

[140] Yuguang Fang and Imrich Chlamtac. Analytical Generalized Results for Handoff Probability in Wireless Networks. *IEEE Transactions on Communications*, 50(3):396–399, March 2002.

[141] L. M. Feeney. Modeling battery consumption of wireless devices using omnet++.

[142] Uriel Feige and Prabhakar Raghavan. Exact analysis of hot-potato routing. In *SFCS '92: Proceedings of the 33rd Annual Symposium on Foundations of Computer Science*, pages 553–562, Washington, DC, USA, 1992. IEEE Computer Society.

[143] R. Fielding, J. Gettys, J. Mogul, H. Frystyk, L. Masinter an P. Leach, and T. Berners-Lee. Hypertext transfer protocl - http/1.1. RFC2616, June 1999.

[144] Daniel Fleisch. *A Student's Guide to Maxwell's Equations*. Cambridge University Press, 2008.

[145] Robert W. Floyd. Algorithm 97: Shortest path. *Communications of the ACM*, 5(6):345+, June 1962.

[146] Sally Floyd. Maintaining a critical attitude towards simulation results (invited talk). In *WNS2 '06: Proceeding from the 2006 workshop on ns-2: the IP network simulator*, October 2006.

[147] Sally Floyd and Van Jacobson. Random early detection gateways for congestion avoidance. *IEEE/ACM Trans. Netw.*, 1(4):397–413, 1993.

[148] Sally Floyd and Eddie Kohler. Internet research needs better models. *Computer Communication Review*, 33(1):29–34, 2003.

[149] Sally Floyd and Vern Paxson. Difficulties in simulating the internet. *IEEE/ACM Trans. Netw.*, 9(4):392–403, 2001.

[150] International Organization for Standardization (ISO). Information technology – Coding of moving pictures and associated audio for digital storage media at up to about 1,5 Mbit/s – Part 2: Video. *ISO/IEC 11172-2*, 1993.

[151] International Organization for Standardization (ISO). Information technology – Generic coding of moving pictures and associated audio information: Video. *ISO/IEC 13818-2*, 2000.

[152] International Organization for Standardization (ISO). Information technology – Coding of audio-visual objects – Part 2: Visual. *ISO/IEC 14496-2*, 2004.

[153] International Organization for Standardization (ISO). Information technology – Coding of audio-visual objects – Part 10: Advanced Video Coding. *ISO/IEC 14496-10*, 2005.

[154] Lestor R. Ford and D. R. Fulkerson. *Flows in Networks*. Princeton University Press, 1962.

[155] Andrea G. Forte, Sangho Shin, and Henning Schulzrinne. Passive Duplicate Address Detection for the Dynamic Host Configuration Protocol for IPv4 (DHCPv4). Internet Draft - work in progress (expired) 03, IETF, October 2006.

[156] G. Foschini and M. Gans. On limits of wireless communications in a fading environment when using multiple antennas. *Wireless Personal Communications*, 6(3):311–335, 1998.

[157] G.J. Foschini. Layered space-time architecture for wireless communication in fading environments when using multiple antennas. *Bell Labs. Tech. Journal*, 2, 1996.

[158] Linton C. Freeman. A Set of Measures of Centrality Based on Betweenness. *Sociometry*, 40(1):35–41, 1977.

[159] P. Frenger, P. Orten, and T. Ottoson. Convolutional codes with optimum distance spectrum. *IEEE Trans. Commun.*, 3(11):317–319, 1999.

[160] Thomas Fuhrmann. Scalable routing for networked sensors and actuators. In *Proc. 2nd Annual IEEE Communications Society Conference on Sensor and Ad Hoc Communications and Networks*, September 2005.

[161] Richard M. Fujimoto. Parallel Discrete Event Simulation. *Communications of the ACM*, 33(10):30–53, 1990.

[162] Richard M. Fujimoto. Performance of Time Warp under synthetic workloads. In *Proceedings of 22nd SCS Multiconference on Distributed Simulation*, 1990.

[163] Richard M. Fujimoto. Parallel and Distributed Simulation. In *Proceedings of the 31st Winter Simulation Conference*, New York, NY, USA, 1999. ACM Press.

[164] V. Fuller and T. Li. Classless inter-domain routing (cidr): The internet address assignment and aggregation plan. RFC 4632, August 2006.

[165] G. D. Forney, Jr. The viterbi algorithm. *Proceedings of the IEEE*, 61(3):268– 278, March 1973.

[166] K. Pawlikowski G. Ewing and D. McNickle. Akaroa2: Exploiting network computing by distributing stochastic simulation. In *ESM'900: Proc. European Simulation Multiconference*, pages 175–181. International Society for Computer Simulation, 1999.

[167] G. Kunzmann and R. Nagel and T. Hossfeld and A. Binzenhofer and K. Eger. Efficient simulation of large-Scale p2p networks: modeling network transmission times. In *MSOP2P '07*, 2007.

[168] G. Tyson and A. Mauthe. A topology aware clustering mechanism. In *In Proc. 8th EPSRC Annual Postgraduate Symposium on the Convergence of Telecommunications, Networking and Broadcasting*. ACM Press, 2007.

[169] R.G. Gallager. *Low Density Parity Check Codes (Monograph)*. M.I.T. Press, 1963.

[170] Lei Gao, Kingshuk Karuri, Stefan Kraemer, Rainer Leupers, Gerd Ascheid, and Heinrich Meyr. Multiprocessor performance estimation using hybrid simulation. In *DAC '08: Proceedings of the 45th annual conference on Design automation*, 2008.

[171] Lei Gao, Stefan Kraemer, Rainer Leupers, Gerd Ascheid, and Heinrich Meyr. A fast and generic hybrid simulation approach using C virtual machine. In *CASES '07: Proceedings of Compilers, architecture and synthesis for embedded systems*, 2007.

[172] Lixin Gao. On Inferring Autonomous System Relationships in the Internet. *IEEE/ACM Trans. Netw.*, 9(6):733–745, 2001.

[173] Lixin Gao and Feng Wang. The Extent of AS Path Inflation by Routing Policies. In *Proc. of the IEEE Global Telecommunications Conference (GLOBECOM'02)*, volume 3, pages 2180–2184, Piscataway, NJ, USA, 2002. IEEE Press.

[174] Matthew Gast. *802.11 Wireless Networks: The Definitive Guide, Second Edition*. O'Reilly Media, Inc., April 2005.

[175] A. Gerstlauer, Haobo Yu, and D. D. Gajski. RTOS modeling for system level design. In *Proc. Design, Automation and Test in Europe Conference and Exhibition*, pages 130–135, 2003.

[176] Walton C. Gibson. *The method of moments in electromagnetics*. CRC Press, 2008.

[177] L. C. Godara. Application of Antenna Arrays to Mobile Communications, Part II: Beam-Forming and Direction-of-Arrival Considerations. In *Proceedings of the IEEE*, volume 85, pages 1195–1245, 1997.

[178] J. Gross. Admission control based on OFDMA channel transformations. In *Proc. of 10th IEEE International Symposium on a World of Wireless, Mobile and Multimedia Networks (WoWMoM)*, June 2009.

[179] J. Gross, M. Emmelmann, O. Puñal, and A. Wolisz. Dynamic Single-User OFDM Adaptation for IEEE 802.11 Systems. In *Proc. ACM/IEEE International Symposium on Modeling, Analysis and Simulation of Wireless and Mobile Systems (MSWIM 2007)*, pages 124–132, Chania, Crete Island, October 2007.

[180] IEEE 802.16 Broadband Wireless Access Working Group. Channel models for fixed wireless applications. Technical Report Rev. of IEEE 802.16.3c-01/29r4, IEEE, 2003.

[181] Radio Communication Study Group. The radio cdma2000 rtt candidate submission. Technical report, ETSI, Tech. Rept. TR 101 112 v3.2.0, June 1998.

[182] Yu Gu, Yong Liu, and Don Towsley. On Integrating Fluid Models with Packet Simulation. In *In Proceedings of IEEE INFOCOM*, volume 2856, 2004.

[183] M. Gudmundson. Correlation model for shadow fading in mobile radio systems. *IEEE Electronics Letters*, 27(23):2145–2146, November 1991.

[184] K. Gummadi, R. Gummadi, S. Gribble, S. Ratnasamy, S. Shenker, and I. Stoica. The impact of dht routing geometry on resilience and proximity. In *SIGCOMM '03: Proceedings of the 2003 conference on Applications, technologies, architectures, and protocols for computer communications*, pages 381–394, New York, NY, USA, 2003. ACM.

[185] Krishna P. Gummadi, Richard J. Dunn, Stefan Saroiu, Steven D. Gribble, Henry M. Levy, and John Zahorjan. Measurement, modeling, and analysis of a peer-to-peer file-sharing workload. In *SOSP '03: Proceedings of the nineteenth ACM symposium on Operating systems principles*, pages 314–329, New York, NY, USA, 2003. ACM.

[186] S. Gundavelli, K. Leung, V. Devarapalli, K. Chowdhury, and B. Patil. Proxy Mobile IPv6. RFC 5213, IETF, August 2008.

[187] Mesut Günes and Martin Wenig. Models for realistic mobility and radiowave propagation for ad-hoc network simulations. In Sudip Misra, Isaac Woungang, and Subhas Chandra, editors, *Guide to Wireless Ad Hoc Networks*, chapter 11, pages 255–280. Springer, 2009.

[188] Liang Guo and Ibrahim Matta. The War Between Mice and Elephants, 2001.

[189] Zygmunt J. Haas, Marc R. Pearlman, and Prince Samar. The Zone Routing Protocol (ZRP) for Ad Hoc Networks. IETF Internet Draft, July 2002.

[190] D. Haccoun and G. Begin. High-rate punctured convolutional codes for viterbi and sequential decoding. *IEEE Trans. Commun.*, 37(11):1113–1125, 1989.

[191] Hamed Haddadi, Miguel Rio, Gianluca Iannaccone, Andrew W. Moore, and Richard Mortier. Network Topologies: Inference, Modeling, and Generation. *IEEE Communications Surveys and Tutorials*, 10(2):48–69, 2008.

514   References

[192] Hamed Haddadi, Steve Uhlig, Andrew Moore, Richard Mortier, and Miguel Rio. Modeling Internet Topology Dynamics. *SIGCOMM Comput. Commun. Rev.*, 38(2):65–68, 2008.

[193] J. Hagenauer. Rate-compatible punctured convolutional codes (RCPC codes) and their applications. *IEEE Transactions on Communications*, 36(4):389 – 400, April 1998.

[194] Roger F. Harrington. *Field Computation by Moment Methods*. Krieger Publishing Company, 1982.

[195] Jan-Hinrich Hauer. Tinyos IEEE 802.15.4 working group. [online] http://tinyos.stanford.edu:8000/15.4_WG, 2009.

[196] B.R. Haverkort. *Performance of Computer Communication Systems: A Model-Based Approach*. John Wiley & Sons, Inc. New York, NY, USA, 1998.

[197] Y. He, M. Faloutsos, S. Krishnamurthy, and B. Huffaker. On Routing Asymmetry in the Internet. In *Proceedings of the IEEE Global Telecommunications Conference (GLOBECOM'05)*, volume 2, Piscataway, NJ, USA, 2005. IEEE Press.

[198] Yihua He, Georgos Siganos, Michalis Faloutsos, and Srikanth Krishnamurthy. Lord of the Links: A Framework for Discovering Missing Links in the Internet Topology. *IEEE/ACM Trans. Netw.*, 17(2):391–404, 2009.

[199] Eugene Hecht. *Optics*. Addison-Wesley, 2002.

[200] A. Helmy. A Multicast–based Protocol for IP Mobility Support. In *Proc. of 2nd International Workshop of Networked Group Communication (NGC2000)*, pages 49–58, New York, 2000. ACM Press.

[201] John L. Hennessy and David A. Patterson. *Computer Architecture, Fourth Edition: A Quantitative Approach*. Morgan Kaufmann Publishers Inc., San Francisco, CA, USA, 2006.

[202] Octavio Herrera and Taieb Znati. Modeling churn in P2P networks. In *Annual Simulation Symposium*, pages 33–40. IEEE Computer Society, 2007.

[203] K. Herrmann. Modeling the sociological aspects of mobility in ad hoc networks. *Proceedings of the 6th international workshop on Modeling analysis and simulation of wireless and mobile systems*, pages 128–129, 2003.

[204] M. Holdrege and P. Srisuresh. Protocol Complications with the IP Network Address Translator. Website: http://tools.ietf.org/html/rfc3027, January 2001.

[205] J. R. M. Hosking. Fractional differencing. *Biometrika*, 68(1):165–176, April 1981.

[206] C. Hoymann. *IEEE 802.16 Metropolitan Area Network with SDMA Enhancement*. PhD thesis, Aachen University, Lehrstuhl für Kommunikationsnetze, Jul 2008.

[207] H. E. Hurst. Long-Term Storage Capacity of Reservoirs. *American Society of Civil Engineering*, 76, 1950.

[208] IEEE. Official IEEE 802.11 working group project timelines.
http://www.ieee802.org/11/Reports/802.11_Timelines.htm

[209] IEEE Computer Society. IEEE Std 802.11b-1999: Wireless LAN Medium Access Control (MAC) and Physical Layer (PHY) specifications: Higher-Speed Physical Layer Extension in the 2.4 GHz Band, 1999.

[210] F. Ikegami, S. Yoshida, T. Takeuchi, and M. Umehira. Propagation factors controlling mean field strength on urban streets. *IEEE Transactions on Antennas and Propagation*, 32(8):822–829, Aug 1984.

[211] ITU IMT-2000. Guidelines for evaluation of radio transmission technologies for imt-2000. Technical Report Recommendation ITU-R M.1225, ITU, 1997.

[212] OPNET Technologies Inc. OPNET Modeler.
http://opnet.com/solutions/network_rd/modeler.html.

[213] Simulcraft Inc. Omnet++ enterprise edition.
http://www.omnest.com/.

[214] Open S. Initiative. Systemc. http://www.systemc.org.

[215] European Telecommunications Standards Institute. "EN 300 175-3: Digital Enhanced Cordless Telecommunications (DECT); Common Interface (CI); Part 3: Medium Access Control (MAC) layer", September 1996.

[216] Institute of Communication Networks and Computer Engineering. IKR Simulation and Emulation Library, 2008. [Online]. Available: http://www.ikr.uni-stuttgart.de/IKRSimLib.

[217] Texas Instrument. *16-BIT, 1.0 GSPS 2x-4x INTERPOLATING DAC (Rev. D)*. Texas Instrument, 2009.

[218] International Standardisation Organisation. Open System Interconnection (OSI) - Basic Reference Model. Standard ISO/IEC 7489-1:1994(E), ISO, Nov 1994.

[219] Ipoque. www.ipoque.com/, August 2008.

[220] International Telecommunication Union (ITU). G.711: Pulse code modulation (PCM) of voice frequencies. *SERIES G: TRANSMISSION SYSTEMS AND MEDIA, DIGITAL SYSTEMS AND NETWORKS; General Aspects of Digital Transmission Systems: Terminal Equipments*, November 1988.

[221] International Telecommunication Union (ITU). G.722: 7 kHz audio-coding within 64 kbit/s. *SERIES G: TRANSMISSION SYSTEMS AND MEDIA, DIGITAL SYSTEMS AND NETWORKS; General Aspects of Digital Transmission Systems: Terminal Equipments*, November 1988.

[222] International Telecommunication Union (ITU). G.726: 40, 32, 24, 16 kbit/s Adaptive Differential Pulse Code Modulation (ADPCM). *SERIES G: TRANSMISSION SYSTEMS AND MEDIA, DIGITAL SYSTEMS AND NETWORKS; General Aspects of Digital Transmission Systems: Terminal Equipments*, December 1990.

[223] International Telecommunication Union (ITU). H.261: Video codec for audiovisual services at p x 64 kbit/s. *SERIES H: AUDIOVISUAL AND MULTIMEDIA SYSTEMS; Line Transmission of non-Telephone Signals*, March 1993.

[224] International Telecommunication Union (ITU). H.262: Information technology - Generic coding of moving pictures and associated audio information: Video. *SERIES H: AUDIOVISUAL AND MULTIMEDIA SYSTEMS; Infrastructure of audiovisual services - Coding of moving video*, February 2002.

[225] International Telecommunication Union (ITU). H.263: Video coding for low bit rate communication. *SERIES H: AUDIOVISUAL AND MULTIMEDIA SYSTEMS; Infrastructure of audiovisual services - Coding of moving video*, January 2005.

[226] International Telecommunication Union (ITU). H.323: Packet-based multimedia communications systems. *SERIES H: AUDIOVISUAL AND MULTIMEDIA SYSTEMS; Infrastructure of audiovisual services - Systems and terminal equipment for audiovisual services*, February 2006.

[227] International Telecommunication Union (ITU). H.264: Advanced video coding for generic audiovisual services. *SERIES H: AUDIOVISUAL AND MULTIMEDIA SYSTEMS; Infrastructure of audiovisual services - Coding of moving video*, November 2007.

[228] International Telecommunication Union (ITU). ITU-R M.2135 : Guidelines for evaluation of radio interface technologies for IMT-Advanced. Technical report, ITU, 2008.

[229] ITU-T Recommendation. G.114 - One-way transmission time. Technical report, Telecommunication Union Standardization Sector, May 2003.

[230] J. A. Nelder and R. Mead. A simplex method for function minimization. *Computer Journal*, 7:308–313, 1965.

[231] P. Schramm J. Medbo. Channel models for hiperlan/2, etsi/bran doc. no.3eri085b, 1998.

[232] J. Winick and S. Jamin. Inet-3.0: Internet topology generator. Technical report, University of Michigan, 2002.

[233] P. Jacquet, P. Mühlethaler, T. Clausen, A. Laouiti, A. Qayyum, and L. Viennot. Optimized Link State Routing Protocol for Ad Hoc Networks. In *Proceedings of the 2001 IEEE International Multi Topic Conference (IEEE INMIC)*, pages 62–68, Lahore, Pakistan, December 2001.

[234] R. Jain, D. Chiu, and W. Hawe. A Quantitative Measure of Fairness and Discrimination for Resource Allocation in Shared Computer Systems. *Arxiv preprint cs/9809099*, 1998.

[235] Raj Jain. *The Art of Computer Systems Performance Analysis: techniques for experimental design, measurement, simulation, and modeling.* Wiley, 1991.

[236] Raj Jain and Imrich Chlamtac. The p2 algorithm for dynamic calculation of quantiles and histograms without storing observations. *Commun. ACM*, 28(10):1076–1085, 1985.

[237] W. C. Jakes. *Microwave Mobile Communications.* IEEE Press, Wiley Interscience, 1994.

[238] William C. Jakes. *Microwave Mobile Communications.* Wiley & Sons, 1975.

[239] Sam Jansen and Anthony Mcgregor. Simulation with Real World Network Stacks. In *Proceedings of the 2005 Winter Simulation Conference,* December 2005.

[240] Sam Jansen and Anthony Mcgregor. Validation of Simulated Real World TCP Stacks. In *Proceedings of the 2007 Winter Simulation Conference,* 2007.

[241] D. R. Jefferson and H. A. Sowizral. Fast Concurrent Simulation Using the Time Warp Mechanism. In *Proceedings of SCS Distributed Simulation Conference,* 1985.

[242] Ajit K. Jena, Adrian Popescu, and Arne A. Nilsson. Modelling and Evaluation of Internet Applications. Research Report 2002:8, Blekinge Institute of Technology, Department of Telecommunications and Signal Processing, Dept. of Telecommunications and Signal Processing S-37225 Ronneby, 2002.

[243] Weirong Jiang, Shuping Liu, Yun Zhu, and Zhiming Zhang. Optimizing routing metrics for large-scale multi-radio mesh networks. In *Proceedings of the International Conference on Wireless Communications, Networking and Mobile Computing, 2007. WiCom 2007.,* Shanghai, China, 2007.

[244] David B. Johnson and David A. Maltz. Dynamic Source Routing in Ad Hoc Wireless Networks. *Mobile Computing,* 353:153–181, February 1996.

[245] David B. Johnson, Charles Perkins, and Jari Arkko. Mobility Support in IPv6. RFC 3775, IETF, June 2004.

[246] Petr Jurčík and Anis Koubâa. The IEEE 802.15.4 opnet simulation model: Reference guide v2.0. Technical report, IPP-HURRAY!, May 2007.

[247] K. P. Gummadi and S. Saroiu and S. D. Gribble. King: estimating latency between arbitrary internet end hosts. In *IMW '02: Proceedings of the 2nd ACM SIGCOMM Workshop on Internet measurment,* pages 5–18. ACM, 2002.

[248] Brad Karp and H. T. Kung. GPSR: Greedy perimeter stateless routing for wireless networks. In *Sixth Annual ACM/IEEE International Conference on Mobile Computing and Networking (Mobicom 2000),* pages 243–254, Boston, MA, August 2000.

[249] Karuri, K., Al Faruque, M.A., Kraemer, S., Leupers, R., Ascheid, G. and H. Meyr. Fine-grained Application Source Code Profiling for ASIP Design. In *42nd Design Automation Conference*, Anaheim, California, USA, June 2005.

[250] D. Katz. Ip router alert option. RFC 2113, February 1997.

[251] Sebastian Kaune, Konstantin Pussep, Gareth Tyson, Andreas Mauthe, and Ralf Steinmetz. Cooperation in p2p systems through sociological incentive patterns. In *Third International Workshop on Self-Organizing Systems (IWSOS '08)*. Springer LNCS, Dec 2008.

[252] Kempf, T., Dörper, M., Leupers, R., Ascheid, G. and H. Meyr (ISS Aachen, DE); Kogel, T. and B. Vanthournout (CoWare Inc., BE). A Modular Simulation Framework for Spatial and Temporal Task Mapping onto Multi-Processor SoC Platforms. In *Proceedings of the Conference on Design, Automation & Test in Europe (DATE)*, Munich, Germany, March 2005.

[253] Sunil U. Khaunte and John O. Limb. Statistical characterization of a world wide web browsing session. Technical Report CC Technical Report; GIT-CC-97-17, Georgia Institute of Technology, 1997.

[254] Leonard Kleinrock. *Queueing Systems, Volume I: Theory*. Wiley Interscience, New York, 1975.

[255] Leonard Kleinrock. *Queueing Systems, Volume II: Computer Applications*. Wiley Interscience, New York, 1976.

[256] Hartmut Kocher. *Entwurf und Implementierung einer Simulationsbibliothek unter Anwendung objektorientierter Methoden*. PhD thesis, University of Stuttgart, IKR, 1994.

[257] Hartmut Kocher and Martin Lang. An object-oriented library for simulation of complex hierarchical systems. In *Proceedings of the Object-Oriented Simulation Conference (OOS '94)*, pages 145–152, 1994.

[258] I. Koffman, V. Roman, and R. Technol. Broadband wireless access solutions based on OFDM access in IEEE 802.16. *Communications Magazine, IEEE*, 40(4):96–103, 2002.

[259] E. Kohler, M. Handley, and S. Floyd. Datagram Congestion Control Protocol (DCCP). RFC 4340 (Proposed Standard), March 2006.

[260] Rajeev Koodli. Fast Handovers for Mobile IPv6. RFC 5268, IETF, June 2008.

[261] Rajeev S. Koodli and Charles E. Perkins. *Mobile Inter–Networking with IPv6. Concepts, Principles and Practices*. John Wiley & Sons, Hoboken, New Jersey, 2007.

[262] Andreas Köpke, Michael Swigulski, Karl Wessel, Daniel Willkomm, Peterpaul, Tom E. V. Parker, Otto W. Visser, Hermann S. Lichte, and Stefan Valentin. Simulating wireless and mobile networks in OMNeT++ the MiXiM vision. In *Proceeding of the 1. International Workshop on OMNeT++*, March 2008.

[263] A. Koubaa, M. Alves, and E. Tovar. A comprehensive simulation study of slotted CSMA/CA for IEEE 802.15.4 wireless sensor networks. In *Factory Communication Systems, 2006 IEEE International Workshop on*, pages 183–192, 2006.

[264] Anis Koubâa.   Tinyos 2.0 zigbee working group.   [online] http://www.hurray.isep.ipp.pt/activities/ZigBee_WG/, 2009.

[265] Miklós Kozlovszky, Ákos Balaskó, and András Varga.   Enabling OMNeT++-based simulations on grid systems. In *OMNeT++ 2009: Proceedings of the 2nd International Workshop on OMNeT++ (hosted by SIMUTools 2009)*, ICST, Brussels, Belgium, Belgium, 2009. ICST (Institute for Computer Sciences, Social-Informatics and Telecommunications Engineering).

[266] Stefan Kraemer, Lei Gao, Jan Weinstock, Rainer Leupers, Gerd Ascheid, and Heinrich Meyr.   HySim: a fast simulation framework for embedded software development. In *CODES+ISSS '07: Proceedings of the 5th IEEE/ACM international conference on Hardware/software codesign and system synthesis*, 2007.

[267] Vaishnavi Krishnamurthy, Michalis Faloutsos, Marek Chrobak, Jun-Hong Cui, Li Lao, and Allon G. Percus.   Sampling Large Internet Topologies for Simulation Purposes. *Computer Networks*, 51(15):4284–4302, 2007.

[268] Frank R. Kschischang, Brendan J. Frey, and Hans-Andrea Loeliger. Factor graphs and the sum-product algorithm. *IEEE Transactions on Information Theory*, 47:498–519, 1998.

[269] K. Kumaran and S. Borst.   *Advances in Wireless Communications*, Chapter Statistical Model of Spatially Correlated Shadow-fading Patterns in Wireless Systems, pages 329–336. Springer US, 1998.

[270] Stuart Kurkowski, Tracy Camp, and Michael Colagrosso. Manet simulation studies: the incredibles. *Mobile Computing and Communications Review*, 9(4):50–61, 2005.

[271] Mathieu Lacage and Thomas R. Henderson. Yet another network simulator. In *Proceedings from the 2006 workshop on ns-2: the IP network simulator (WNS2 '06)*, Pisa, Italy, October 2006. ACM.

[272] Andreas Lagemann and Jörg Nolte.   Csharpsimplemodule – writing OMNeT++ modules with c# and mono. In *OMNeT++ Workshop*, March 2008.

[273] Anukool Lakhina, John W. Byers, Mark Crovella, and Peng Xie. Sampling Biases in IP Topology Measurements. In *Proc. of the 22nd IEEE INFOCOM*, Piscataway, NJ, USA, 2003. IEEE Press.

[274] O. Landsiedel, K. Wehrle, and S. Gotz. Accurate prediction of power consumption in sensor networks. In *EmNets '05: Proceedings of the 2nd IEEE workshop on Embedded Networked Sensors*, pages 37–44, Washington, DC, USA, 2005. IEEE Computer Society.

[275] Olaf Landsiedel, Hamad Alizai, and Klaus Wehrle. When timing matters: Enabling time accurate and scalable simulation of sensor network applications. In *IPSN '08: Proceedings of the 7th international conference on Information processing in sensor networks*, pages 344–355, Washington, DC, USA, 2008. IEEE Computer Society.

[276] A. M. Law and W. D. Kelton. *Simulation Modeling and Analysis*. McGraw-Hill Inc., December 1990.

[277] Averill M. Law. *Simulation Modeling and Analysis*. McGrawHill, fourth edition, 2007.

[278] Averill M. Law and David W. Kelton. *Simulation Modeling and Analysis*. McGraw Hill, third edition, 2000.

[279] Uichin Lee, Min Choi, Junghoo Cho, M. Y. Sanadidi, and Mario Gerla. Understanding pollution dynamics in p2p file sharing. In *5th International Workshop on Peer-toPeer Systems (IPTPS'06)*, 2006.

[280] W.C.Y. Lee. *Mobile Cellular Telecommunications*. McGraw-Hill International Editions, 1995.

[281] Jan Van Leeuwen and Richard B. Tan. Interval routing. *The Computer Journal*, 30:298–307, 1987.

[282] P. Lei, L. Ong, M. Tuexen, and T. Dreibholz. An Overview of Reliable Server Pooling Protocols. RFC 5351 (Informational), September 2008.

[283] K. K. Leung and L. C. Wang. Integrated link adaptation and power control for wireless IP networks. In *IEEE Vehicular Technology Conference*, volume 3, pages 2086–2092. IEEE; 1999, 2000.

[284] Philip Levis, Nelson Lee, Matt Welsh, and David Culler. TOSSIM: Accurate and Scalable Simulation of Entire TinyOS Applications. In *Proceedings of the First ACM Conference on Embedded Networked Sensor Systems (SenSys '03)*, 2003.

[285] Philip Levis, Sam Madden, David Gay, Joseph Polastre, Robert Szewczyk, Alec Woo, Eric Brewer, and David Culler. The emergence of networking abstractions and techniques in tinyos. In *NSDI'04: Proceedings of the 1st conference on Symposium on Networked Systems Design and Implementation*, 2004.

[286] Andreas Lewandowski, Volker Köster, and Christian Wietfeld. A new dynamic co-channel interference model for simulation of heterogeneous wireless networks. In Olivier Dalle, Gabriel A. Wainer, Felipe L. Perrone, and Giovanni Stea, editors, *SimuTools*, page 71. ICST, 2009.

[287] L. Li, A.M. Tulino, and S. Verdu. Design of reduced-rank MMSE multiuser detectors using random matrix methods. *IEEE Transactions on Information Theory*, 50(6):986 – 1008, June 2004.

[288] Michael Liljenstam and Rassul Ayani. Partitioning PCS for Parallel Simulation. In *Proceedings of the 5th International Workshop on Modeling, Analysis, and Simulation of Computer and Telecommunications Systems*, 1997.

[289] Shu Lin and Daniel J. Costello. *Error Control Coding, Second Edition*. Prentice-Hall, Inc., Upper Saddle River, NJ, USA, 2004.

[290] Yi B. Lin and Edward D. Lazowska. A Time-Division Algorithm for Parallel Simulation. *ACM Transactions on Modeling and Computer Simulation*, 1(1):73–83, 1991.

[291] J. Liu and D. M. Nicol. Lookahead revisited in wireless network simulations. In *Proceedings of 16th Workshop on Parallel and Distributed Simulation*, 2002.

[292] Jason Liu. Packet-level integration of fluid TCP models in real-time network simulation. In *WSC '06: Proceedings of the 38th Conference on Winter Simulation*, pages 2162–2169. Winter Simulation Conference, 2006.

[293] Jason Liu, Yougu Yuan, David M. Nicol, Robert S. Gray, Calvin C. Newport, David Kotz, and Luiz F. Perrone. Empirical Validation of Wireless Models in Simulations of Ad Hoc Routing Protocols. *Simulation: Transactions of The Society for Modeling and Simulation International*, 81(4):307–323, April 2005.

[294] Yong Liu, Francesco Lo Presti, Vishal Misra, Don Towsley, and Yu Gu. Fluid models and solutions for large-scale IP networks. In *In Proc. of ACM SIGMETRICS*, pages 91–101, 2003.

[295] L.Tang and M. Crovella. Geometric exploration of the landmark selection problem. In *Passive and Active Network Measurement, 5th International Workshop*, volume 3015, pages 63–72, 2004.

[296] Song Luo and G.A. Marin. Realistic internet traffic simulation through mixture modeling and a case study. *Simulation Conference, 2005 Proceedings of the Winter*, pages 9 pp.–, Dec. 2005.

[297] M. Castro and P. Druschel and Y. C. Hu and A. Rowstron. Proximity neighbor selection in tree-based structured p2p overlays. Technical report, Microsoft Research, 2003.

[298] Liang Ma and Mieso K. Denko. A routing metric for load-balancing in wireless mesh networks. In *AINAW '07: Proceedings of the 21st International Conference on Advanced Information Networking and Applications Workshops*, Washington, DC, USA, 2007.

[299] Maode Ma, editor. *Current Technology Developments of WiMax Systems*. Springer Publishing Company, Incorporated, 2009.

[300] David J.C. MacKay and Radford M. Neal. Near Shannon Limit Performance of Low Density Parity Check Codes. *Electronics Letters*, 32(18):1645, July 1996.

[301] Damien Magoni and Jean Jacques Pansiot. Analysis of the Autonomous System Network Topology. *SIGCOMM Computer Communication Review*, 31(3):26–37, 2001.

[302] Bruce A. Mah. An empirical model of http network traffic. In *IN-FOCOM '97: Proceedings of the INFOCOM '97. Sixteenth Annual Joint Conference of the IEEE Computer and Communications Societies. Driving the Information Revolution*, page 592, Washington, DC, USA, 1997. IEEE Computer Society.

[303] Priya Mahadevan, Dmitri Krioukov, Marina Fomenkov, Bradley Huffaker, Xenofontas Dimitropoulos, kc claffy, and Amin Vahdat. The Internet AS-Level Topology: Three Data Sources and One Definitive Metric. *ACM SIGCOMM Computer Communication Review*, 36(1):17–26, January 2006.

[304] G. Malkin. Rip version 2. RFC 2453, November 1998.

[305] R. Mathar, M. Reyer, and M. Schmeink. A cube oriented ray launching algorithm for 3d urban field strength prediction. *In IEEE International Conference on Communications (ICC '07)*, pages 5034–5039, June 2007.

[306] Matthew Mathis, Jeffrey Semke, Jamshid Mahdavi, and Teunis Ott. The Macroscopic Behavior of the TCP Congestion Avoidance Algorithm. *SIGCOMM Comput. Commun. Rev.*, 27(3):67–82, 1997.

[307] Norm Matloff. *Introduction to Discrete-Event Simulation and the SimPy Language*, February 2008.

[308] Makoto Matsumoto and Takuji Nishimura. Mersenne Twister: A 623-Dimensionally Equidistributed Uniform Pseudo-Random Number Generator. *ACM Trans. Model. Comput. Simul.*, 8(1):3–30, 1998.

[309] MaxMind Geolocation Technology. http://www.maxmind.com/.

[310] Petar Maymounkov and David Mazières. Kademlia: A peer-to-peer information system based on the XOR metric. In *International Workshop on Peer-to-Peer Systems, (IPTPS)*, 2002.

[311] D. A. McNamara, C. W. I. Pistotius, and J. A. G. Malherbe. *Introduction to the Uniform Geometrical Theory of Diffraction*. Artech House Inc, 1990.

[312] Alberto Medina, Anukool Lakhina, Ibrahim Matta, and John Byers. Brite: An approach to universal topology generation. In *MASCOTS '01: Proceedings of the Ninth International Symposium in Modeling, Analysis and Simulation*, page 346, Washington, DC, USA, 2001. IEEE Computer Society.

[313] Alberto Medina, Ibrahim Matta, and John Byers. On the Origin of Power Laws in Internet Topologies. *SIGCOMM Computer Communication Review*, 30(2):18–28, 2000.

[314] Xiaoqiao Meng, Zhiguo Xu, Beichuan Zhang, Geoff Huston, Songwu Lu, and Lixia Zhang. Ipv4 address allocation and the bgp routing table evolution. *SIGCOMM Comput. Commun. Rev.*, 35(1):71–80, 2005.

[315] Richard A. Meyer and Rajive L. Bargrodia. Path lookahead: A data flow view of pdes models. In *Proceedings of the 13th Workshop on Parallel and Distributed Simulation (PADS '99)*, pages 12–19, Washington, DC, USA, 1999. IEEE Computer Society.

[316] Arunesh Mishra, Minho Shin, and William Arbaugh. An Empirical Analysis of the IEEE 802.11 MAC Layer Handoff Process. *SIGCOMM Computer Communications Review*, 33(2):93–102, 2003.

[317] J. Misra and K. M. Chandy. Distributed Simulation: A Case Study in Design and Verification of Distributed Programs. *IEEE Transactions on Software Engineering*, SE-5(5):440–452, 1978.

[318] Vishal Misra, Wei-Bo Gong, and Don Towsley. Stochastic differential equation modeling and analysis of TCP-windowsize behavior, 1999.

[319] A. Köpke. Mixim simulator for wireless and mobile networks using OMNeT++. [online] http://mixim.sourceforge.net/.

[320] J. Mo, R. J. La, V. Anantharam, and J. Walrand. Analysis and comparison of TCP Reno and Vegas. In *INFOCOM '99. Eighteenth Annual Joint Conference of the IEEE Computer and Communications Societies. Proceedings. IEEE*, volume 3, 1999.

[321] ETSI: Universal mobile telecommunication system (UMTS). Selection procedures for chice of radio transmission technologies of the umts. Technical report, ETSI; Tech. Rept. TR 101 112 v3.2.0, April 1998.

[322] Gabriel E. Montenegro. Reverse Tunneling for Mobile IP, revised. RFC 3024, IETF, January 2001.

[323] Nick '. Moore. Optimistic Duplicate Address Detection (DAD) for IPv6. RFC 4429, IETF, April 2006.

[324] J. Moy. OSPF Version 2. RFC 2328, April 1998.

[325] Steven S. Muchnick. *Advanced compiler design and implementation*. Morgan Kaufmann Publishers Inc., San Francisco, CA, USA, 1997.

[326] K.K. Mukkavilli, A. Sabharwal, E. Erkip, and B. Aazhang. On beamforming with finite rate feedback in multiple-antenna systems. *IEEE Transactions on Information Theory*, 49(10):2562 – 2579, Oct. 2003.

[327] Marcello Mura, Marco Paolieri, Fabio Fabbri, Luca Negri, and Maria G. Sami. Power modeling and power analysis for ieee 802.15.4: a concurrent state machine approach. In *Consumer Communications and Networking Conference, 2007. CCNC 2007. 4th IEEE*, pages 660–664, 2007.

[328] Ashish Natani, Jagannadha Jakilnki, Mansoor Mohsin, and Vijay Sharma. TCP for Wireless Networks, 2001.

[329] M. C. Necker, C. M. Gauger, S. Kiesel, and U. Reiser. IKR EmuLib: A Library for Seamless Integration of Simulation and Emulation. In *Proceedings of the 13th GI/ITG Conference on Measurement, Modeling, and Evaluation of Computer and Communication Systems (MMB 2006)*, 2006.

[330] Marc C. Necker and Ulrich Reiser. IKR Emulation Library 1.0 User Guide. Technical report, University of Stuttgart, IKR, December 2006.

[331] Technical Specification Group GSM/EDGE Radio Access Network. Radio transmission and reception. Technical Report 3GPP TS 05.05, v8.20.0, 3rd Generation Partnership Project, 2005.

[332] Technical Specification Group Radio Access Network. Physical layer aspects for evolved universal terrestrial radio access (utra). Technical Report 3GPP TR 25.814, v7.1.0, 3rd Generation Partnership Project, 2006.

[333] Mark E. J. Newman. Assortative Mixing in Networks. *Physical Review Letters*, 89(20):208701, November 2002.

[334] Mark E. J. Newman. Random graphs as models of networks. In Stefan Bornholdt and Heinz Georg Schuster, editors, *Handbook of Graphs and Networks*, pages 35–68. Wiley–VCH, Berlin, 2003.

[335] E. Ng and H. Zhang. Towards global network positioning. In *Proceedings of the First ACM SIGCOMM Workshop on Internet Measurement*, pages 25–29. ACM, 2001.

[336] D. M. Nicol. Modeling and simulation in security evaluation. *IEEE Security and Privacy*, 3(5):71–74, September 2005.

[337] Nohl, A., Greive, V., Braun, G., Hoffmann, A., Leupers, R., Schliebusch, O. and H. Meyr. Instruction Encoding Synthesis for Architecture Exploration using Hierarchical Processor Models. In *40th Design Automation Conference (DAC)*, Anaheim (USA), June 2003.

[338] University of Paderborn. Chsim: Wireless channel simulator for omnet++. http://www.cs.uni-paderborn.de/en/fachgebiete/research-group-computer-networks/projects/chsim.html.

[339] B. O'Hara and A. Petrick. *IEEE802.11 Handbook: A Designer's Companion*. IEEE Press, 1999.

[340] L. Ong and J. Yoakum. An Introduction to the Stream Control Transmission Protocol (SCTP). RFC 3286 (Informational), May 2002.

[341] Raif O. Onvural. *Asynchronous Transfer Mode Networks: Performance Issues,Second Edition*. Artech House, Inc., Norwood, MA, USA, 1995.

[342] Fredrik Österlind, Adam Dunkels, Joakim Eriksson, Niclas Finne, and Thiemo Voigt. Cross-Level Sensor Network Simulation with COOJA. In *Proceedings of the First IEEE International Workshop on Practical Issues in Building Sensor Network Applications (SenseApp '06)*, Tampa, Florida, USA, November 2006.

[343] T. Ott, J. Kemperman, and M. Mathis. The stationary behavior of ideal TCP congestion avoidance.

[344] Philippe Owezarski and Nicolas Larrieu. A trace based method for realistic simulation. In *International Conference on Communication (ICC)*, Paris, France, june 2004.

[345] L.H. Ozarow, S. Shamai, and A.D. Wyner. Information theoretic considerations for cellular mobile radio. *IEEE Transactions on Vehicular Technology*, 43(2):359–378, May 1994.

[346] J. Padhye, V. Firoiu, D. Towsley, and J. Krusoe. Modeling TCP Throughput: A Simple Model and its Empirical Validation. *Proceedings of the ACM SIGCOMM '98 conference on Applications, technologies, architectures, and protocols for computer communication*, pages 303–314, 1998.

[347] M. Paetzold. *Mobile Fading Channels*, chapter 4.1. J. Wiley & Sons, Inc., 2002.

[348] M. Paetzold. Modeling, analysis, and simulation of mimo mobile-to-mobile fading channels. *IEEE Trans. on Wireless Communications*, 7, February 2008.

[349] M. Paetzold and B. O. Hogstad. A space-time channel simulator for mimo channels based on the geometrical one-ring scattering model. *Wireless Communications and Mobile Computing, Special Issue on Multiple-Input Multiple-Output (MIMO) Communications*, 4(7), November 2004.

[350] M. Paetzold and B. O. Hogstad. A wideband mimo channel model derived from the geometrical elliptical scattering model. *Wireless Communications and Mobile Computing*, 8, May 2007.

[351] M. Paetzold, U. Killat, F. Laue, and Y. Li. On the statistical properties of deterministic simulation models for mobile fading channels. *IEEE Transactions on Vehicular Technology*, 47(1):254 – 269, 1998.

[352] M. Park, K. Ko, H. Yoo, and D. Hong. Performance analysis of OFDMA uplink systems with symbol timing misalignment. *IEEE Communications letters*, 7(8):376–378, 2003.

[353] J. D. Parsons. *Mobile Radio Propagation Channel*. John Wiley and Sons, 2000.

[354] A. Pathak, H. Pucha, Y. Zhang, Y. C. Hu, and Z. M. Mao. A Measurement Study of Internet Delay Asymmetry. In Mark Claypool and Steve Uhlig, editors, *Passive and Active Network Measurement. 9th International Conference, PAM 2008. Proceedings*, pages 182–191, Berlin Heidelberg, 2009. Springer-Verlag.

[355] J. Pavon and S. Choi. Link adaptation strategy for ieee 802.11 wlan via received signal strength measurement. In *Prodeedings of the IEEE International Conference on Communications (ICC '03)*, volume 2, pages 1108–1113, 2003.

[356] Vern Paxson. End-to-End Routing Behavior in the Internet. In *Proc. of the ACM SIGCOMM Conference 1996*, pages 25–38, New York, NY, USA, 1996. ACM.

[357] Vern Paxson. End-to-End Routing Behavior in the Internet. *IEEE/ACM Transactions on Networking*, 5(5):601–615, 1997. An earlier version appeared in Proc. of ACM SIGCOMM'96.

[358] Vern Paxson and Sally Floyd. Wide area traffic: the failure of Poisson modeling. *IEEE/ACM Transactions on Networking*, 3(3):226–244, 1995.

[359] Vern Paxson and Sally Floyd. Why we don't know how to simulate the internet. In *WSC '97: Proceedings of the 29th conference on Winter simulation*, 1997.

[360] F. Perich. Policy-based network management for next generation spectrum access control. In *New Frontiers in Dynamic Spectrum Access Networks, 2007. (DySPAN) 2007. 2nd IEEE International Symposium on*, pages 496–506, April 2007.

[361] Charles Perkins. IP Mobility Support for IPv4. RFC 3344, IETF, August 2002.

[362] Charles E. Perkins and Pravin Bhagwat. Highly Dynamic Destination-Sequenced Distance-Vector Routing (DSDV) for Mobile Computers. In *Proceedings of the ACM SIGCOMM 1994 Conference*, pages 234–244, London, United Kingdom, 1994.

[363] Charles E. Perkins and Elizabeth M. Royer. Ad hoc On-Demand Distance Vector Routing. In *Proc. 2nd IEEE Workshop on Mobile Computing Systems and Applications*, pages 90–100, New Orleans, LA, USA, February 1999.

[364] Colin Perkins. *RTP: Audio and Video for the Internet*. Addison-Wesley Professional, June 2003.

[365] Kalyan S. Perumalla. Parallel and Distributed Simulation: Traditional Techniques and recent Advances. In *Proceedings of the 38th Winter Simulation Conference*. Winter Simulation Conference, 2006.

[366] Larry Peterson and Timothy Roscoe. The design principles of planetlab. *SIGOPS Oper. Syst. Rev.*, 40(1):11–16, 2006.

[367] Larry L. Peterson and Bruce S. Davie. *Computer Networks: A Systems Approach*. Morgan Kaufmann, third edition, May 2003.

[368] M. Petrova, J. Riihijarvi, P. Mahonen, and S. Labella. Performance study of ieee 802.15.4 using measurements and simulations. In *Wireless Communications and Networking Conference, 2006. WCNC 2006. IEEE*, volume 1, pages 487–492, 2006.

[369] Martin Plonus. *Applied Electromagnetics*. McGraw-Hill Internation Editions, 1978.

[370] J. Postel. User Datagram Protocol. RFC 768 (Standard), August 1980.

[371] J. Postel. Internet Control Message Protocol. RFC 792 (Standard), 1981. Updated by RFCs 950, 4884.

[372] J. Postel. Transmission Control Protocol. RFC 793 (Standard), September 1981.

[373] J. Postel and J. Reynolds. File Transfer Protocol (FTP). Website: http://tools.ietf.org/html/rfc959, October 1985.

[374] R. V. Prasad, P. Pawczak, J. A. Hoffmeyer, and H. S. Berger. Cognitive Functionality in Next Generation Wireless Networks: Standardization Efforts. *IEEE Communications Magazine*, 46(4):72, 2008.

[375] J. Proakis. *Digital Communications*. McGraw-Hill, 1995.

[376] Vint Project. *The NS Manual*. The VINT Project, August 2008.

[377] Ilango Purushothaman. IEEE 802.11 Infrastructure Extensions for NS-2.

[378] Alfonso Ariza Quintana, Eduardo Casilari, and Alicia Triviño. Implementation of manet routing protocols on OMNeT++. In *OMNeT++ 2008: Proceedings of the 1st International Workshop on OMNeT++ (hosted by SIMUTools 2008)*, ICST, Brussels, Belgium, Belgium, 2008. ICST (Institute for Computer Sciences, Social-Informatics and Telecommunications Engineering). poster.

[379] K. Wehrle R. Steinmetz. *Peer-to-Peer Systems and Applications (Lecture Notes in Computer Science)*. Springer-Verlag New York, Inc., 2005.

[380] I. Ramachandran and S. Roy. Clear channel assessment in energyconstrained wideband wireless networks. *Wireless Communications, IEEE [see also IEEE Personal Communications]*, 14(3):70–78, 2007.

[381] Iyappan Ramachandran, Arindam K. Das, and Sumit Roy. Analysis of the contention access period of IEEE 802.15.4 mac. *ACM Trans. Sen. Netw.*, 3(1), 2007.

[382] Vaddina Rao and Dimitri Marandin. Adaptive backoff exponent algorithm for zigbee (ieee 802.15.4). In *Next Generation Teletraffic and Wired/Wireless Advanced Networking*, pages 501–516. Springer, 2006.

[383] Theodore S. Rappaport. *Wireless Communications - Principles and Practice*. Prentice Hall, 1996.

[384] Theodore S. Rappaport. *Wireless Communications*. Prentice Hall, 1999.

[385] D. Raychaudhuri, I. Seskar, M. Ott, S. Ganu, K. Ramach, H. Kremo, R. Siracusa, H. Liu, and M. Singh. Overview of the orbit radio grid testbed for evaluation of next-generation wireless network protocols. In *in Proceedings of the IEEE Wireless Communications and Networking Conference (WCNC*, pages 1664–1669, 2005.

[386] Yakov Rekhter, Tony Li, and Susan Hares. A Border Gateway Protocol 4 (BGP-4). RFC 4271, IETF, January 2006.

[387] A. Reyes-Lecuona, E. GonzâÁ ales-Parada, E. Casilari, and A. DâĂŽaz-Estrella. A page-oriented www traffic model for wireless system simulations. *Proceedings of the 16th International Teletraffic Congress (ITC'16)*, pages pp. 275–287, 1999. Edinburgh, United Kingdom.

[388] Sean C. Rhea, Dennis Geels, Timothy Roscoe, and John Kubiatowicz. Handling churn in a DHT. In *USENIX Annual Technical Conference, General Track*, pages 127–140. USENIX, 2004.

[389] T. Richardson, M. Shokrollahi, and R. Urbanke. Design of capacityapproaching irregular low-density parity-check codes. *IEEE Transactions on Information Theory*, 47(2):619–637, 2001.

[390] I. Richer. A Simple Interleaver for Use with Viterbi Decoding. *IEEE Transactions on Communications*, 26(3):406 – 408, Mar 1978.

[391] Maximilian Riegel and Michael Tuexen. Mobile SCTP. Internet Draft - work in progress 09, IETF, November 2007.

[392] J. Riihijärvi, Mähönen P., and M. Rübsamen. Characterizing Wireless Networks by Spatial Correlations. *IEEE Comm Letters*, 11(1):37–39, 2007.

[393] George F. Riley. The Georgia Tech Network Simulator. In *Proceedings of the ACM SIGCOMM workshop on Models, methods and tools for reproducible network research*, pages 5–12. ACM Press, 2003.

[394] George F. Riley, Richard M. Fujimoto, and Mostafa H. Ammar. A Generic Framework for Parallelization of Network Simulations. In *Proceedings of the 7th International Symposium on Modeling, Analysis and Simulation of Computer and Telecommunication Systems*, 1999.

[395] H. Roder. Amplitude, Phase, and Frequency Modulation. *Proceedings of the IRE*, 19(12):2145 – 2176, 12 1931.

[396] J. Rosenberg, H. Schulzrinne, G. Camarillo, A. Johnston, J. Peterson, R. Sparks, M. Handley, and E. Schooler. SIP: Session Initiation Protocol. *Internet Engineering Task Force (IETF): RFC 3261*, 2002.

[397] S. Lee and Z. Zhang and S. Sahu and D. Saha. On suitability of euclidean embedding of internet hosts. In *SIGMETRICS '06: Proceedings of the joint international conference on Measurement and modeling of computer systems*, pages 157–168. ACM, 2006.

[398] A. Saleh and R. Valenzuela. A statistical model for indoor multipath propagation. *IEEE Journal on Selected Areas in Communications*, 5(2):128–137, Feb 1987.

[399] M. Sanchez and P. Manzoni. A java-based ad hoc networks simulator. *Proceedings of the SCS Western Multiconference Web-based Simulation Track*, 1999.

[400] Stefan Saroiu, P. Krishna Gummadi, Richard J. Dunn, Steven D. Gribble, and Henry M. Levy. An analysis of internet content delivery systems. In Proceedings of the 5th ACM Symposium on Operating System Design and Implementation (OSDI-02), 2002.

[401] Jochen Schiller. *Mobile Communications*. Addison Wesley, second edition, May 2003.

[402] M. Schinnenburg, F. Debus, A. Otyakmaz, L. Berlemann, and R. Pabst. A Framework for Reconfigurable Functions of a Multi-Mode Protocol Layer. In *Proceedings of SDR Forum 2005*, page 6, Los Angeles, U.S., Nov 2005.

[403] M. Schinnenburg, R. Pabst, K. Klagges, and B. Walke. A Software Architecture for Modular Implementation of Adaptive Protocol Stacks. In *MMBnet Workshop*, pages 94–103, Hamburg, Germany, Sep 2007.

[404] G. Schirner, A. Gerstlauer, and R. Domer. Abstract, Multifaceted Modeling of Embedded Processors for System Level Design. In *Proc. Asia and South Pacific Design Automation Conference ASP-DAC '07*, pages 384–389, 2007.

[405] M.T. Schlosser, T.E. Condie, and S.D. Kamvar. Simulating a file-sharing p2p network. In *Workshop on Semantics in Peer-to-Peer and Grid Computing*, 2003.

[406] T. Schmidl and D. Cox. Robust frequency and timing synchronization for ofdm. *IEEE Transactions on Communications*, 45(12):1613–1621, 1997.

[407] Thomas C. Schmidt and Matthias Wählisch. Predictive versus Reactive — Analysis of Handover Performance and Its Implications on IPv6 and Multicast Mobility. *Telecommunication Systems*, 30(1/2/3):123–142, November 2005.

[408] Thomas C. Schmidt, Matthias Wählisch, and Ying Zhang. On the Correlation of Geographic and Network Proximity at Internet Edges and its Implications for Mobile Unicast and Multicast Routing. In Cosmin Dini, Zdenek Smekal, Emanuel Lochin, and Pramode Verma, editors, *Proceedings of the IEEE ICN'07*, Washington, DC, USA, April 2007. IEEE Computer Society Press.

[409] Arne Schmitz and Leif Kobbelt. Wave propagation using the photon path map. In *PE-WASUN '06*, pages 158–161, New York, NY, USA, 2006.

[410] H. Schulzrinne, S. Casner, R. Frederick, and V. Jacobson. RTP: A Transport Protocol for Real-Time Applications. *Internet Engineering Task Force (IETF): RFC 3550*, 2003.

[411] H. Schulzrinne, A. Rao, and R. Lanphier. Real Time Streaming Protocol (RTSP). *Internet Engineering Task Force (IETF): RFC 2326*, 1998.

[412] Curt Schurgers and Mani B. Srivastava. Energy efficient routing in wireless sensor networks. In *Proceedings of MILCOM '01*, October 2001.

[413] Robin Seggelmann, Irene Rüngeler, Michael Tüxen, and Erwin P. Rathgeb. Parallelizing OMNeT++ simulations using xgrid. In *OMNeT++ 2009: Proceedings of the 2nd International Workshop on OMNeT++ (hosted by SIMUTools 2009)*, ICST, Brussels, Belgium, Belgium, 2009. ICST (Institute for Computer Sciences, Social-Informatics and Telecommunications Engineering).

[414] S. Selby, A. Amini, and C. Edelman. Simulating Interference Issues between Bluetooth PANs, and 802.11 b and 802.11 g WLANs.

[415] S. Shakkottai, T. S. Rappaport, and P. C. Karlsson. Cross–Layer Design for Wireless Networks. *IEEE Communications Magazine*, 41(10):74–80, October 2003.

[416] S. Shalunov, B. Teitelbaum, A. Karp, J. Boote, and M. Zekauskas. A One-way Active Measurement Protocol (OWAMP). RFC 4656, IETF, September 2006.

[417] C. Shannon. A mathematical theory of communication. *Bell Sys. Tech. Journal*, 1948.

[418] Colleen Shannon, David Moore, Ken Keys, Marina Fomenkov, Bradley Huffaker, and k claffy. The Internet Measurement Data Catalog. *SIGCOMM Compututer Communication Review*, 35(5):97–100, 2005.

[419] Yuval Shavitt and Eran Shir. DIMES: Let the Internet Measure Itself. *ACM SIGCOMM Computer Communication Review*, 35(5):71–74, 2005.

[420] D.S. Shiu. *Wireless Communication Using Dual Antenna Arrays.* Kluwer Academic Publishers, 1 edition, 2000.

[421] D.S. Shiu, G.R. Foschini, M.J. Gans, and J.M. Kahn. Fading correlation and its effect on the capacity of multielement antenna systems. *IEEE Transactions on Communications*, 48(3), March 2000.

[422] Victor Shnayder, Mark Hempstead, Bor R. Chen, Geoff W. Allen, and Matt Welsh. Simulating the power consumption of large-scale sensor network applications. In *SenSys '04: Proceedings of the 2nd international conference on Embedded networked sensor systems*, pages 188–200, 2004.

[423] Khaled Shuaib, Maryam Alnuaimi, Mohamed Boulmalf, Imad Jawhar, Farag Sallabi, and Abderrahmane Lakas. Performance evaluation of ieee 802.15.4: Experimental and simulation results. *Journal of Communications*, 2(4):29–37, 2007.

[424] Georgos Siganos, Michalis Faloutsos, Petros Faloutsos, and Christos Faloutsos. Power Laws and the AS-Level Internet Topology. *IEEE/ACM Trans. Netw.*, 11(4):514–524, 2003.

[425] B. Sklar. *Digital Communications: Fundamentals and Applications.* Prentice-Hall, Inc. Upper Saddle River, NJ, USA, 1988.

[426] B. Sklar. Rayleigh Fading Channels in Mobile Digital Communication Systems, Part I: Characterization. *IEEE Communications Magazine*, 35(9):136–146, Sept 1997.

[427] S.M. S.M. Alamouti. A simple transmit diversity technique for wireless communications. *IEEE Journal on Selected Areas in Communications*, 16(8):1451–1458, Oct. 1998.

[428] IEEE Computer Society. Part 15.4: Wireless Medium Access Control (MAC) and Physical Layer (PHY) Specifications for Low-Rate Wireless Personal Area Networks (WPANs) – Amendment 1: Add Alternate PHYs. The Institute of Electrical and Electronics Engineers, Inc., 2007.

[429] IEEE Computer Society. Part 15.4: Wireless Medium Access Control (MAC) and Physical Layer (PHY) Specifications for Low-Rate Wireless Personal Area Networks (WPANs). The Institute of Electrical and Electronics Engineers, Inc., 2006.

[430] IEEE Computer Society. Part 15.4: Wireless Medium Access Control (MAC) and Physical Layer (PHY) Specifications for Low-Rate Wireless Personal Area Networks (LR-WPANs). The Institute of Electrical and Electronics Engineers, Inc., 2003.

[431] Hesham Soliman. *Mobile IPv6. Mobility in a Wireless Internet.* Addison-Wesley, Boston, 2004.

[432] Hesham Soliman, Claude Castelluccia, Karim Elmalki, and Ludovic Bellier. Hierarchical Mobile IPv6 (HMIPv6) Mobility Management. RFC 5380, IETF, October 2008.

[433] M. Speth, H. Dawid, and F. Gersemsky. Design & Verification Challenges for 3G/3.5G/4G Wireless Baseband MPSoCs. In *MPSoC'08*, June 2008.

[434] N. Spring, L. Peterson, A. Bavier, and V. Pai. Using planetlab for network research: myths, realities, and best practices. *ACM SIGOPS Operating Systems Review*, 40(1):17–24, 2006.

[435] R. Srinivasan, J. Zhuang, L. Jalloul, R. Novak, and J. Park. Draft IEEE 802.16 m Evaluation Methodology Document. *IEEE C802. 16m-07/080r2*, 2007.

[436] V. Srivastava and M. Motani. Cross-Layer Design: A Survey and the Road Ahead. *IEEE Communications Magazine*, 43(12):112–119, December 2005.

[437] Steffen Sroka and Holger Karl. Using akaroa2 with OMNeT++, 2002.

[438] R. Steele. *Mobile Radio Communications*. Pentech Press, 1992.

[439] R. Steele and L. Hanzo, editors. *Mobile Radio Communications*. J. Wiley & Sons Ltd, 2000.

[440] P. Krishna Gummadi Stefan Saroiu and Steven D. Gribble. Measurement Study of Peer-to-Peer File Sharing Systems. In *Proceedings of Multimedia Computing and Networking 2002 (MMCN'02)*, volume 4673 of *Proc. of SPIE*, pages 156–170, Bellingham, WA, USA, 2001. SPIE.

[441] M. Steiner, T. En-Najjary, and E.W. Biersack. A global view of kad. In *Proceedings of the 7th ACM SIGCOMM conference on Internet measurement*, pages 117–122. ACM New York, NY, USA, 2007.

[442] J. Stevens. DSPs in communications. *IEEE Spectrum*, 35(9):39–46, Sep. 1998.

[443] W. Richard Stevens. *TCP/IP Illustrated, Volume I: The Protocols*. Addison-Wesley, Reading, MA, 1994.

[444] Randall R. Stewart. Stream Control Transmission Protocol. RFC 4960, IETF, September 2007.

[445] Randall R. Stewart, Qiaobing Xie, Michael Tuexen, Shin Maruyama, and Masahiro Kozuka. Stream Control Transmission Protocol (SCTP) Dynamic Address Reconfiguration. RFC 5061, IETF, September 2007.

[446] G.L. Stuber and C. Kchao. Analysis of a multiple-cell direct-sequence CDMA cellular mobile radio system. *IEEE Journal on Selected Areas in Communications*, 10(4):669 – 679, May 1992.

[447] D. Stutzbach and R. Rejaie. Improving lookup performance over a widely-deployed dht. In Proceedings of 25th IEEE International Conference on Computer Communications (INFOCOM 2006), volume 6, 2006.

[448] D. Stutzbach and R. Rejaie. Understanding churn in peer-to-peer networks. In *Proceedings of the 6th ACM SIGCOMM on Internet measurement*, pages 189–202. ACM Press New York, NY, USA, 2006.

[449] Anand Prabhu Subramanian, Milind M. Buddhikot, and Scott Miller. Interference aware routing in multi-radio wireless mesh networks. In *Proceedings of the 2nd IEEE Workshop on Wireless Mesh Networks*, Reston, VA, USA, 2006.

[450] Surveyor. http://www.advance.org/csg-ippm/.

[451] A. S. Tanenbaum. *Computer Networks*. Prentice Hall, 2002.

[452] Andrew S. Tanenbaum. *Computer Networks*. Prentice Hall PTR, 4th edition, August 2002.

[453] D. Tang and M. Baker. Analysis of a local-area wireless network. *Proceedings of the 6th annual international conference on Mobile computing and networking*, pages 1–10, 2000.

[454] Hongsuda Tangmunarunkit, Ramesh Govindan, Scott Shenker, and Deborah Estrin. Internet Path Inflation Due to Policy Routing. In *Proc. SPIE International Symposium on Convergence of IT and Communication (ITCom)*, 2001.

[455] Hongsuda Tangmunarunkit, Ramesh Govindan, Scott Shenker, and Deborah Estrin. The Impact of Routing Policy on Internet Paths. In *Proc. of the 20th IEEE INFOCOM*, volume 2, pages 736–742, Piscataway, NJ, USA, 2001. IEEE Press.

[456] V. Tarokh, H. Jafarkhani, and A.R. Calderbank. Space-time block codes from orthogonal designs. *IEEE Transactions on Information Theory*, 45(5):744–765, July 1999.

[457] V. Tarokh, N. Seshadri, and A. R. Calderbank. Space-time codes for high data rate wireless communication: Performance criterion and code construction. *IEEE Trans. Inform. Theory*, 44(2):774–765, 1998.

[458] V. Tarokh, N. Seshadri, and A.R. Calderbank. Space-time codes for high data rate wireless communication: Performance analysis and code construction. *IEEE Transactions on Information Theory*, 44(2):744–765, March 1998.

[459] TCPDump. www.tcpdump.org, August 2008.

[460] Renata Teixeira, Keith Marzullo, Stefan Savage, and Geoffrey M. Voelker. In Search of Path Diversity in ISP Networks. In *Proceedings of the 3rd ACM SIGCOMM conference on Internet measurement (IMC'03)*, pages 313–318, New York, NY, USA, 2003. ACM.

[461] S. ten Brink. Convergence behavior of iteratively decoded parallel concatenated codes. *IEEE Transactions on Communications*, 49(10):1727–1737, 2001.

[462] Fumio Teraoka, Kazutaka Gogo, Koshiro Mitsuya, Rie Shibui, and Koki Mitani. Unified Layer 2 (L2) Abstractions for Layer 3 (L3)-Driven Fast Handover. RFC 5184, IETF, May 2008.

[463] The PingER Project.
http://www-iepm.slac.stanford.edu/pinger/.

[464] S. Thomson, T. Narten, and T. Jinmei. IPv6 Stateless Address Autoconfiguration. RFC 4862, September 2007.

[465] Ben L. Titzer, Daniel K. Lee, and Jens Palsberg. Avrora: Scalable Sensor Network Simulation with Precise Timing. In *Proceedings of the Fourth International Conference on Information Processing in Sensor Networks (IPSN '05)*, pages 477–482, Los Angeles, USA, April 2005.

[466] Jim Tourley. Survey says: software tools more important than chips, April 2005.

[467] P. Tran-Gia, K. Leibnitz, and D. Staehle. Source traffic modelling of wireless applications. In P. Tran-Gia, D. Staehle, and K. Leibnitz, editors, *AEU - International Journal of Electronics and Communications*, volume 55, Issue 1, pages pp 27–36, 2000.

[468] David Tse and Pramod Viswanath. *Fundamentals of Wireless Communication*. Cambridge University Press, 2005.

[469] C. Tuduce and T. Gross. A mobility model based on WLAN traces and its validation. *INFOCOM 2005. 24th Annual Joint Conference of the IEEE Computer and Communications Societies. Proceedings IEEE*, 1, 2005.

[470] Michael Tüxen, Irene Rüngeler, and Erwin P. Rathgeb. Interface connecting the inet simulation framework with the real world. In *Simutools '08: Proceedings of the 1st international conference on Simulation tools and techniques for communications, networks and systems & workshops*, pages 1–6, ICST, Brussels, Belgium, Belgium, 2008. ICST (Institute for Computer Sciences, Social-Informatics and Telecommunications Engineering).

[471] Piet Van Mieghem. *Performance Analysis of Communications Networks and Systems*. Cambridge University Press, New York, USA, 2006.

[472] A. Varga and B. Fakhamzadeh. The k-split algorithm for the pdf approximation of multi-dimensional empirical distributions without storing observations. In *ESS'97: 9th European Simulation Symposium*, pages 94–98, 1997.

[473] András Varga. *JSimpleModule*.

[474] András Varga. OMNeT++ discrete event simulation system. [online] http://www.omnetpp.org/.

[475] András Varga. The OMNeT++ discrete event simulation system. *Proceedings of the European Simulation Multiconference (ESM'2001)*, 2001.

[476] András Varga, Ahmet Y. Şekercioğlu, and Gregory K. Egan. A Practical Efficiency Criterion for the Null-Message-Algorithm. In *Proceedings of European Simulation Symposium*, Delft, The Netherlands, 2003.

[477] B. D. V. Veen and K. M. Buckley. Beamforming: A versatile approach to spatial filtering. *IEEE ASSP Magazine*, pages 4 – 24, Apr. 1988.

[478] S. Verdu and S. Shamai. Spectral efficiency of CDMA with random spreading. *IEEE Transactions on Information Theory*, 45(2):622 – 640, March 1999.

[479] N. Vicari. Models of www traffic: A comparison of pareto and logarithmic histogram models. Technical Report Report No. 198, Research Report Series, Institute of Computer Science, University of Wurzburg (Germany), 1998.

[480] L. Vito, S. Rapuano, and L. Tomaciello. One-Way Delay Measurement: State of the Art. *IEEE Transactions on Instrumentation and Measurement*, 57(12):2742–2750, December 2008.

[481] Matthias Wählisch, Thomas C. Schmidt, and Waldemar Spät. What is Happening from Behind? - Making the Impact of Internet Topology Visible. *Campus–Wide Information Systems*, 25(5):392–406, November 2008.

[482] J. Walfisch and H.L. Bertoni. A theoretical model of UHF propagation in urban environments. *IEEE Transactions on Antennas and Propagation*, 36(12):1788–1796, December 1988.

[483] B. Walke, P. Seidenberg, and M. P. Althoff. *UMTS: The Fundamentals*. Wiley, 2003.

[484] B. H. Walke. *Mobile Radio Networks 2nd Edition*. John Wiley & Sons, 2002.

[485] C. Wang, M. Paetzold, and Q. Yao. Stochastic modeling and simulation of frequency-correlated wideband fading channels. *IEEE Transactions on Vehicular Technology*, 56(3):1050–1063254 – 269, 2007.

[486] Zhenyu Wang, E. K. Tameh, and A. R. Nix. Joint Shadowing Process in Urban Peer-to-Peer Radio Channels. *Vehicular Technology, IEEE Transactions on*, 57(1):52–64, Jan 2008.

[487] Stephen Warshall. A theorem on boolean matrices. *Journal of the ACM*, 9(1):11–12, January 1962.

[488] Duncan J. Watts and Steven H. Strogatz. Collective dynamics of 'small-world' networks. *Nature*, 393:440–442, June 1998.

[489] Bernard M. Waxman. Routing of Multipoint Connections. *IEEE Journal on Selected Areas in Comm.*, 6(9):1617–1622, 1988.

[490] J. Weitzen and T.J. Lowe. Measurement of angular and distance correlation properties of log-normal shadowing at 1900 mhz and its application to design of pcs systems. *IEEE Transations on Vehicular Technology*, 51(2), March 2002.

[491] Michael Welzl. *Network Congestion Control: Managing Internet Traffic (Wiley Series on Communications Networking & Distributed Systems)*. John Wiley & Sons, 2005.

[492] P. Wertz, R. Wahl, G. Wölfle, P. Wildbolz, and F. Landstorfer. Dominant path prediction model for indoor scenarios. *German Microwave Conference (GeMiC) 2005, University of Ulm*, 2005.

[493] Karl Wessel, Michael Swigulski, Andreas Köpke, and Daniel Willkomm. MiXiM - the physical layer: An architecture overview. In *Proceeding of the 2. International Workshop on OMNeT++*, pages 1–8, March 2009.

[494] Sven Wiethoelter. Virtual Utilization and VoIP Capacity of WLANs Supporting a Mix of Data Rates. Technical Report TKN-05-004, Telecommunication Networks Group, Technische Universität Berlin, 2005.

[495] Sven Wiethoelter and Adam Wolisz. Selecting vertical handover candidates in IEEE 802.11 mesh networks. In *Proc. of IEEE WoWMoM Workshop on Hot Topics in Mesh Networking*, Kos, Greece, June 2009.

[496] Sven Wiethoelter and Christian Hoene. IEEE 802.11e EDCA and CFB simulation model for ns-2.

[497] Jared Winick and Sugih Jamin. Inet-3.0: Internet Topology Generator. Technical Report CSE-TR-456-02, University of Michigan, 2002.

[498] Rolf Winter. Modeling the Internet Routing Topology – In Less than 24h. In *Proceedings of the 2009 ACM/IEEE/SCS 23rd Workshop on Principles of Advanced and Distributed Simulation (PADS '09)*, pages 72–79, Washington, DC, USA, 2009. IEEE Computer Society.

[499] T. Winter, U. Türke, E. Lamers, R. Perera, A. Serrador, and L. Correia. Advanced simulation approach for integrated static and short-term dynamic UMTS performance evaluation. Technical Report D2.7, IST-2000-28088 MOMENTUM, 2003.

[500] Wireshark. www.wireshark.org, August 2008.

[501] Georg Wittenburg and Jochen Schiller. A Quantitative Evaluation of the Simulation Accuracy of Wireless Sensor Networks. In *Proceedings of 6. Fachgespräch "Drahtlose Sensornetze" der GI/ITG-Fachgruppe "Kommunikation und Verteilte Systeme"*, pages 23–26, Aachen, Germany, July 2007.

[502] R. W. Wolff. Poisson Arrivals See Time Averages. *Operations Research*, pages 223–231, 1982.

[503] Jun Wang Yaling Yang and Robin Kravets. Interference-aware load balancing for multihop wireless networks. Technical report, Department of Computer Science, University of Illinois at Urbana-Champaign, 2005.

[504] S. C. Yang. *CDMA RF System Engineering*. Mobile Communications Series. Artech House Publishers, 1998.

[505] Yaling Yang, Jun Wang, and Robin Kravets. Designing routing metrics for mesh networks. In *Proceedings of the First IEEE Workshop on Wireless Mesh Networks*, Santa Clara, CA, September 2005.

[506] Svetoslav Yankov and Sven Wiethoelter. Handover blackout duration of layer 3 mobility management schemes. Technical Report TKN-06-002, Telecommunication Networks Group, Technische Universität Berlin, 2006.

[507] Yih-Chun Hu, Adrian Perrig, and David B. Johnson. Packet Leashes: A Defense Against Wormhole Attacks in Wireless Sensor Networks. In *The 22nd Annual Joint Conference of the IEEE Computer and Communications Societies (INFOCOM'03)*, San Francisco, CA, USA, March 2003.

[508] K. Yu and B. Ottersten. Models for mimo propagation channels: a review. *Wireless Communications and Mobile Computing*, February 2002.

[509] J. Zander and S.-L. Kim. *Radio Resource Managements for Wireless Networks*. Mobile Communications Series. Artech House Publishers, 2001.

[510] Ellen W. Zegura, Kenneth L. Calvert, and Michael J. Donahoo. A Quantitative Comparison of Graph-Based Models for Internet Topology. *IEEE/ACM Transactions on Networking*, 5(6):770–783, 1997.

[511] E.W. Zegura, K.L. Calvert, and S. Bhattacharjee. How to model an internetwork. In *INFOCOM '96. Fifteenth Annual Joint Conference of the IEEE Computer Societies. Networking the Next Generation. Proceedings IEEE*, volume 2, pages 594–602, 1996.

[512] Amgad Zeitoun, Chen-Nee Chuah, Supratik Bhattacharyya, and Christophe Diot. An AS-level Study of Internet Path Delay Characteristics. In *Proceedings of the IEEE Global Telecommunications Conference (GLOBECOM'04)*, volume 3, pages 1480–1484, Piscataway, NJ, USA, 2004. IEEE Press.

[513] B. Zhang, T. S. Eugene Ng, A. Nandi, R. Riedi, P. Druschel, and G. Wang. Measurement-based analysis, modeling, and synthesis of the internet delay space. In *IMC '06: Proceedings of the 6th ACM SIGCOMM conference on Internet measurement*, pages 85–98. ACM, 2006.

[514] Beichuan Zhang, Raymond Liu, Daniel Massey, and Lixia Zhang. Collecting the Internet AS-level Topology. *ACM SIGCOMM Computer Communication Review*, 35(1):53–61, 2005.

[515] H. Zhang, D. Yuan, M. Pätzold, Y. Wu, and V.D. Nguyen. A novel wideband space-time channel simulator based on the geometrical one-ring model with applications in mimo-ofdm systems. *Wireless Communications and Mobile Computing*, March 2009. Published online: 10.1002/wcm.787.

[516] Xiaoliang Zhao, Dan Pei, Lan Wang, Dan Massey, Allison Mankin, S. Felix Wu, and Lixia Zhang. An Analysis of BGP Multiple Origin AS (MOAS) Conflicts. In *Proceedings of the 1st ACM SIGCOMM Workshop on Internet Measurement (IMW'01)*, pages 31–35, New York, NY, USA, 2001. ACM.

[517] Jianliang Zheng and Myung J. Lee. A comprehensive performance study of ieee 802.15.4. *Sensor Network Operations*, pages 218–237, 2006.

[518] H. Zimmermann. OSI reference model–the ISO model of architecture for open systems interconnection. *IEEE Transactions on Communications*, 28(4):425–432, 1980.

[519] Stefan Zöls, Zoran Despotovic, and Wolfgang Kellerer. On hierarchical DHT systems - an analytical approach for optimal designs. *Computer Communications*, 31(3):576–590, 2008.

[520] Gil Zussman and Adrian Segall. Energy efficient routing in ad hoc disaster recovery networks. *Ad Hoc Networks*, 1:405–421, 2003.

Index

Printed in the United States
By Bookmasters